THE THREE ROOSEVELTS

THE THREE

ATLANTIC MONTHLY PRESS
New York

ROOSEVELTS

PATRICIAN LEADERS WHO TRANSFORMED AMERICA

James MacGregor Burns
& Susan Dunn

Published simultaneously in Canada
Printed in the United States of America

FIRST EDITION

Library of Congress Cataloging-in-Publication Data
Burns, James MacGregor
    The three Roosevelts : patrician leaders who transformed America / by James MacGregor Burns and Susan Dunn.
    p. cm.
    Includes bibliographical references and index.
    ISBN 0-87113-780-1
    1. Roosevelt, Theodore, 1858–1919—Influence. 2. Roosevelt, Franklin D. (Franklin Delano), 1882–1945—Influence. 3. Roosevelt, Eleanor, 1884–1962—Influence.
4. Presidents—United States—Biography. 5. Presidents' spouses—United States—Biography. 6. Social reformers—United States—Biography. 7. Upper class—United States—Biography. 8. United States—Politics and government—20th century. 9. United States—Social conditions—20th century. I. Dunn, Susan. II. Title.
E757 .B96 2001
973.91—dc21   00-060896

DESIGN BY LAURA HAMMOND HOUGH

Atlantic Monthly Press
841 Broadway
New York, NY 10003

01 02 03 04   10 9 8 7 6 5 4 3 2 1

To the memory of
Andrea Catania (1945–2000)
and Carl Burns (1921–1965)

CONTENTS

Prologue   I

Part I: Passion

Chapter One: *TR, Reformer or Regular?*   7
  1. In New York: The Happiest Year   14
  2. A Reformer from the "Governing Class"   24
  3. Pluck and Luck   50

Chapter Two: *Reform in a Silk Hat*   60
  1. New Doctrine, Big Stick   63
  2. In TR's Steps   78
  3. Power with a Purpose   91

Chapter Three: *Two Roosevelts Move to the Left*   112
  1. "He Seen His Opportunity"   115
  2. 1912: TR and FDR, Progressives   122
  3. The Unneutralist   142
  4. A Meeting of Minds   162
  5. Observing Leadership   165

Chapter Four: *Rehearsal for the Presidency*   169
  1. "The Most Trying Winter of My Entire Life"   175
  2. The Education of Eleanor Roosevelt   181
  3. Albany Again: The Testing Ground   193

Part II: Action

Chapter Five: *People: Pride and Fall*   207
  1. Fear and Want   209
  2. Shame and Despair   212
  3. Anger and Impotence   213

Chapter Six: *The Pragmatists: Making It Work*   218
  1. Ideologies and Practicalities   221
  2. The Deal and the Ideal   225
  3. A New Deal?   234

Chapter Seven: *The Policy Makers: Stormy Passage*   244
  1. Strange Interlude: Piloting Without Power   246
  2. The One Hundred Days: Uncharted Seas   252
  3. Eleanor: Sailing by the Stars   265
  4. The Explorer: Midcourse Corrections   276

Chapter Eight: *The Populace: Armageddon*   285
  1. Winter of Discontent   288
  2. Followers as Leaders   300
  3. They Hate Roosevelt   307
  4. "I Welcome Their Hatred"   324

Part III: Conflict

Chapter Nine: *Checkmate?*   333
  1. The Fall: A Drama in Five Acts   336
  2. Unneutral Neutrality   347
  3. Interventionist Nonintervention   353

Chapter Ten: *The Twilight of the New Deal*   360
  1. Cloudburst: The "Roosevelt Recession"   365
  2. The Disruption of the Democratic Party   374
  3. The New Deal Half Dealt   381
  4. Eleanor Roosevelt: The Other New Deal   388
  5. A Valley Transformed   399

Chapter Eleven: *The Nightmare Begins*   405
  1. The Living Nations Wait   407
  2. Illusions and Disillusions   419
  3. Leadership or Manipulation?   424
  4. A Christian and a Democrat   428

Chapter Twelve: *The Grand Strategists' War*   434
   1. Toward War: Leading and Misleading   437
   2. Europe First, Asia Second   442
   3. Command Leadership   444

Chapter Thirteen: *The People's War*   456
   1. A People Mobilized   461
   2. The Soldier and the Prince   468
   3. The Power of a President   474
   4. The Transformation of a President   483
   5. Triumph: FDR's Last Hundred Days   489

Part IV: Change

Chapter Fourteen: *The Entire World Her Family*   499
   1. United Nations   504
   2. Flight to Palestine   512
   3. Agenda: Human Rights   521

Chapter Fifteen: *Facing the Future*   533
   1. The Only Thing to Fear   538
   2. Civil Rights: 1956   541
   3. Eleanor, the Party Broker   556

Epilogue: *A Century of Reform*   567

Notes   579

Acknowledgments   645

Index   647

Philadelphia Record, November 9, 1932.
(*Courtesy FDR Library*)

PROLOGUE

Union Square, New York City, April 25, 1865:
Two young boys peer out from a second-floor window of the mansion
of the wealthy merchant Cornelius Van Schaack Roosevelt. They are watch-
ing the funeral procession of Abraham Lincoln as the mourners tread slowly
up the avenue under a drizzling rain. Everywhere the boys look seems bleak:
the lowering clouds, lampposts hooded in black shrouds, the facades of houses
draped in black, black umbrellas over dark-coated mourners, frock-coated
officials, the giant canopied hearse drawn by sixteen black horses. The
hubbub in Union Square quiets as an archbishop, a rabbi, and a minister
offer prayers.

. . .

The two boys, preserved in a photograph, are seven-year-old Theodore Roosevelt and his younger brother, Elliott, who came to this privileged observation post in their grandfather's brownstone from their home on nearby East 20th Street. News of the assassination had struck the Roosevelt family like a thunderclap. Their father, Theodore Sr., a fervent abolitionist, was a loyal member of Lincoln's Republican party in Manhattan. In Washington, as a civilian official during the war, Theodore Sr. had enjoyed cordial relations with President and Mrs. Lincoln, joining them on carriage drives and sharing their pew in church.

But their mother, Martha, having grown up on a Georgia plantation surrounded by her family's slaves, never forgave Lincoln, always remaining, according to her son TR, "entirely unreconstructed." Her brothers, James and Irvine Bulloch, were not included in the general amnesty after the war and found themselves forced to emigrate to England, because of the critical work they had performed as officers in the Confederate Navy. As for little "Teedie," he was aware that the family were not one in their views about the war. "Once, when I felt that I had been wronged by maternal discipline," he later wrote in his *Autobiography*, "I attempted a partial vengeance by praying with loud fervor for the success of the Union arms." According to family legend, when TR's mother overheard his prayer, he said, "But, mother, I thought I could tell the truth to God."

I

In Union Square the historian George Bancroft delivered a tribute, an ode by William Cullen Bryant was read, and Lincoln's second inaugural address was solemnly intoned:

"With malice toward none; with charity for all. . . ."

When the tributes ended, Theodore and Elliott watched the procession move north. At 34th Street it would turn west to the Hudson River Railroad Depot, where the waiting funeral train would steam alongside the Hudson, stopping at the old river towns before reaching Albany and then turning west to Chicago and finally to Springfield.

. . .

The boys would grow up in a home where the heritage of Lincoln was pervasive. Theodore would become the twenty-sixth president of the United States in 1901, after the assassination of William McKinley. Elliott's first-born, Eleanor, would marry a distant cousin, Franklin, who would die as another great war neared its end, in April 1945, eighty years almost to the day after Lincoln's death. Eleanor Roosevelt would pursue her own brilliant public career into the first two years of the presidency of John F. Kennedy; she would die in November 1962, just a year before his death—like Lincoln's—from an assassin's bullet.

These three New York patricians, Theodore, Franklin, and Eleanor Roosevelt, would resurrect and incarnate Lincoln's legacy, turning to it at critical moments in their lives as their pole star. But which Lincoln and which legacy? To some, Lincoln was but another politician: a compromiser, a power broker, a man who put the preservation of the Union above one of the great purposes of the Union, equality. These critics saw in Lincoln simply a skilled mediator, a masterful negotiator. But to many he was the great emancipator who had delayed taking the bold step of freeing the slaves until he knew that abolition would stick. In Lincoln they discerned a true leader, a captain of events, a shaper of his and his nation's destiny.

Which Lincoln would the Roosevelts choose? Why not both? As TR himself remarked, it is possible to combine the characteristics that historians put in antithesis: a great leader could be both conciliating and principled, compromising and strong, practical and idealistic, shrewd and heroic. On the one hand, Lincoln was a visionary. He was, TR wrote, "stirred to his depths by the sense of fealty to a lofty ideal." But on the other hand, Lincoln showed himself to be a pragmatic politician, who "worked with keen, practical good sense to achieve results with the instruments at hand."

Inspired by Lincoln's example, the Roosevelts would define a new brand of pragmatic yet courageous political and moral leadership that would set a standard for American leaders—on the right and on the left—that endures to this day.

Yet nothing could have been less obvious in the childhoods of the three patricians than the paths their lives would take, paths that led from the confined, insular community of their elite privileged class to a commitment to progressive change and to an identification with the aspirations of the working classes, immigrants, the disenfranchised, the victims of discrimination. Resolute believers in democracy and equality, they repudiated the world of inherited wealth into which they were born. In declaring war on the "beneficiaries of privilege" and America's "plutocrats," Theodore Roosevelt was convinced that he was merely applying "the principles of Lincoln to the issues of the present day" and advocating Lincoln's "sane and tempered radicalism." His cousin Franklin concurred. "Inherited economic power," FDR stated in 1935, "is as inconsistent with the ideals of this generation as inherited political power was inconsistent with the ideals of the generation which established our government." And TR's niece Eleanor also worked at creating what she called a "social revolution," the goal of which was to provide "all our people with an equal opportunity to enjoy the benefits that have been the privileges of a few." The commitment to social change and economic justice of Theodore, Franklin, and Eleanor Roosevelt still stands at the heart of all progressive agendas.

How did these patricians escape from the triple cocoon of a protected family life encased in a self-segregated social set securely ensconced at the top of a powerful class—if not caste—system? And once they broke free from the family and the social forces holding them tightly within their embrace and started to crack open a solidified social and economic structure, what changes to that structure did they seek to create? What inspired them all to explode the deeply entrenched American myth that associated wealth with virtue? What role models, what politicians, what events influenced them, helping them to focus their energy? How did they balance political compromise and deal-brokering with the bold, principled leadership and commitment to progressive change that they associated with Lincoln's presidency? And what were the reactions of their fellow patricians to these "class renegades"?

The answers lie in the intertwining lives, ideas, and deeds of the three Roosevelts as they led the nation through the crises of their times and forged the Roosevelt century.

PART I:
PASSION

Chapter One
TR, REFORMER OR REGULAR?

William Balfour Ker, 1906.

"I have become acquainted with a very nice fellow named Townsend, from Albany," young Theodore wrote home from Harvard. "He is a cousin of Mr. Thayers. It is really a relief to find someone whom I know something about as I have not the slightest idea about the families of most of my 'friends.'"

The Roosevelts had packed off their son to Harvard in September 1876. Harvard was in fact his first school; until then he had been educated entirely by private tutors. In his new environment in Cambridge, Theodore both protected and asserted himself by being aggressively conscious of class and status. "I most sincerely wish I knew something about the antecedents of my friends," he complained to his sister Corinne during his freshman year, confiding that "on this very account I have avoided being very intimate with the New York fellows." But when he did make the acquaintance of someone from New York who he felt could possibly become his friend, he would quickly write to his mother to ask if she knew anything about the young man's family.

Theodore applied rigorous standards of breeding to his classmates—and to the Bostonians who invited him to their homes. On occasion he bemoaned that some persons with whom he dined, acquaintances of his family, "did not seem very refined." His social circle, like that of his family, would have to belong to "polite" society. The Roosevelts—among the oldest families of New York—valued breeding and grace, not wealth and conspicuous display. Their world consisted of intermarried clans from the colonial aristocracy and the great pre–Civil War overseas merchants.

In Cambridge, Theodore quickly discovered that there were two Harvards. One encompassed the "Yard": the leafy, enclosed campus of stately buildings and gravel paths, where students of mildly diverse middle-class backgrounds lived in dormitories. The other comprised the "Gold Coast": the privately run, expensive halls and rooming houses along Mt. Auburn Street and especially the elite social and eating clubs, mysteriously called "final clubs" to this day.

Arriving in Cambridge, young Roosevelt found a soft coal fire burning in the grate in his new rooms in a private boardinghouse. His ever-protective sister Anna, whom he called Bamie and Bysie, had furnished and decorated the living room and bedroom for him with everything from pretty wallpaper to thick carpeting. It was all, he exclaimed, "just as cozy and comfortable as it could look." Surrounded by family photographs, his books and dictionaries, and his stuffed birds under glass domes, and aided by a woman to do his laundry and a manservant to black his boots and light the fire each morning, he pronounced himself quite satisfied to be in Cambridge. Decidedly discontented with the food at Commons, he preferred to join a private eating club, rejecting the democratic community of meals that most students shared.

Though Harvard, under the innovative leadership of its new president, Charles W. Eliot, had become more open and diverse than Princeton and Yale, there were no African-Americans, no Boston Irish, no Italians, and no Jews in the class of 1880. Despite this seeming homogeneity, for TR Harvard consisted of two distinct groups: a small population of upper-class "gentlemen" and everyone else. He wasted no time in finding his own "set," made up largely of men with upper-crust Boston names like Saltonstall and Weld, who stood out in their English-cut clothes, walking sticks, gold watch fobs, and hair parted in the middle. "I stand 19th in the class," TR later wrote to his sister, explaining that "only one gentleman stands ahead of me." The seventeen plebeian students evidently did not count. Still, one classmate later conceded that, although Theodore belonged to the "high set," he was "perfectly willing to talk to others if the occasion arose."

He cut a slightly outré figure among the Harvard "swells" (those of birth) and "nobs" (those of wealth). He dazzled passersby in his beaver hat, cutaway coat, and colorful cravats. He was five feet eight and around 125 pounds—bespectacled, with prominent teeth, a reedy voice, and a slight speech impediment perhaps caused by his asthma. None of this appeared to inhibit the torrent of words that poured from his lips on every subject of Harvard interest, from the aerodynamics of birds to medieval German literature, to the degree that his schoolmates were tempted to suspect him of the worst of vices, zeal. "He puzzled us by his effusive manner," one of his friends later wrote. "It must have been sheer good nature and vitality. But in college we were a cautious, critical crowd and in truth Roosevelt was the most un-Harvardlike man that ever came out of Harvard."

Yet they were somehow attracted to this curious New Yorker and accepted him, even conferring on him the highest social recognition at Harvard, membership in the Porcellian Club—despite the objection of one young patrician who felt that Roosevelt's "tenacity in argument was not altogether a clubable quality."

Theodore was "dee-lighted" to be accepted into Harvard's most elite private club. It was outfitted with a billiard table, a magnificent library, and a punch room for social affairs. It was "great fun," he told his sister, adding that "my best friends are in it." "Night before last Harry Shaw and I had a little supper up there, the chief items on the bill of fare being partridges and burgundy." On Sundays, the boys enjoyed champagne breakfasts.

Social life also consisted of football games at Yale, sleighing parties, theater evenings, dancing classes, teas and dinners, social calls, lawn tennis, whist, and Sunday drives with Dick Saltonstall, his sister Rose, Minot Weld, and Miss Alice Lee. By senior year, Theodore had his own horse and buggy. An average American family, the historian David McCullough noted, could have lived for years on what Harvard student Theodore Roosevelt spent on clothes, club dues, and stabling his horse.

This happy, carefree life fell under a dark cloud during his sophomore year, when his father died an excruciatingly painful death from colon cancer at the age of forty-six. A "stunned" Theodore endured the most "bitter agony," having lost the one he loved "dearest on earth." "I remember so well how, years ago, when I was a weak, asthmatic child, he used to walk up and down with me in his arms for hours together, night after night, and oh how my heart pains me when I think that I never was able to do anything for him in his last illness!" But after a few months of intense grief and disorientation, by summer Theodore had recovered, confiding to his diary that he was "astonished" to find himself going about his daily life "as if nothing had happened." He was now the male head of his little family. But he was still a college student, and in the fall he returned to Harvard to continue the agreeable life he had known.

"Take care of your morals first," Theodore's father had written to him, "your health next and finally your studies." There was nothing the young man wanted more than to live up to his father's expectations of ethical behavior and personal duty. He followed his father's example of public service by teaching Sunday school throughout his Harvard years, though instead of theology he preferred to teach his young pupils the virtues of "loyalty and manliness." "My Sunday School is getting along swimmingly," he reported in his diary. "It is very sweet to think how [Father] liked my taking a Sunday School class."

Theodore Sr. had also presented the boy with physical challenges. According to Martha, her husband had finally had enough of young Teedie's recurring illnesses. He may have suspected that the little boy's asthma attacks had a psychological as well as a physical source, since the attacks occurred mostly on weekends when father was home and available for cuddling and comfort. One day father stood son in front of him, declaring, "Theodore, you have the mind but you have not the body, and without the help of the body the mind cannot go as far as it should." It would be hard drudgery, he warned, but "you must *make* your body." So at eleven young TR had begun a regime of bodybuilding, lifting weights, punching bags, hefting dumbbells, and swinging along parallel bars.

He expanded his strenuous life by trying every sport he could handle: riding, rowing, tennis, running, leaping, boxing, polo, shooting. He did not become expert at any of these, partly because of his poor eyesight, but he won much notice for the intensity of his play. At Harvard, he hiked, played tennis, wrestled, rowed, skated, and boxed. "Isn't this bully?" he exclaimed, as he skated over the rough ice of nearby Fresh Pond with a friend whose toes, fingers, and ears nearly froze. Temperamentally bellicose, he boasted of "thrashing" his boxing foes and bloodying an occasional fellow student who annoyed him. Nor would he shrink from performing a "citizen's arrest" when confronted with a swindler, congratulating himself on having "quite a struggle with him" and then having him indicted and "put into the penitentiary for six months."

The cruel edge was there. As a boy he slaughtered many hundreds of birds and while riding once in Oyster Bay did not hesitate to shoot a neighbor's dog that was harassing his horse. He later justified his aggressiveness and his fixation on masculinity as shields for his own "decency" and idealism. "My ordinary companions in college would I think have had a tendency to look down upon me for doing Sunday school work if I had not also been a corking boxer," he later explained. "I intended to be a middling decent fellow, and I did not intend that anyone should laugh at me with impunity because I was decent." A man could be "as virtuous as he wished," he taught his sons, "*if only he was prepared to fight.*"

Theodore was also determined to follow his father's advice to devote himself to his studies. "For the next two years," he wrote in his diary after his father's death, "my duty is clear—to study well and live like a brave Christian gentleman."

Fortunately, he found most of his Harvard courses interesting and challenging. Classes in political economy, one friend commented, were very cold and uninteresting before Roosevelt came. But with his appearance and torrent of questions, "things livened up." Indeed, so persistent was Theodore in one course in natural history that the professor exploded, "Now look here, Roosevelt, let me talk! I'm running this course." "I wonder whether he is the real thing," a classmate mused, "or only the bundle of eccentricities he appears."

Exploring a wide variety of fields—classical literature, German, Italian, forensics, logic, metaphysics, philosophy, constitutional history, geology, zoology, and natural history—he won excellent grades in virtually all his courses. He possessed a gift for concentration along with his iron self-discipline. His friend Dick Saltonstall later recalled that Theodore could sit down in a noisy room and read, "oblivious to all that was going on around him." Unperturbed by friends roughhousing and bumping into his chair, he looked up from his book only when he smelled the soles of his boots burning in front of his fireplace. Thanks to his excellent tutoring at home he did not need to work very hard in Cambridge save for occasional periods of intense study, but he read omnivorously. He even had time to write a few chapters of his history of the naval war of 1812, published after he graduated from Harvard.

He had the good fortune to study his favorite subject, the anatomy and physiology of vertebrates, with the celebrated William James. By the end of the summer after his freshman year he had already published his first short work, *The Summer Birds of the Adirondacks,* and the serious young naturalist also presented papers to the Harvard Natural History Society on such subjects as the coloration of birds and the gills of crustaceans. Still, he cast a critical eye on the way science was taught, complaining that, instead of encouraging his interest in the natural world, his Harvard courses had reduced to a "fetish" the study of minutiae in a laboratory. "I had no more desire or ability to be a microscopist and section-cutter than to be a mathematician," he sniffed.

At the end of his junior year, looking back over the past nine months, he congratulated himself on leading a most enjoyable life. "I cannot possibly conceive of any fellow having a pleasanter time than I have had," he noted in his diary. "I have done well in my studies and I have had a most royally good time with the Club, my horse, and above all the sweet, pretty girls at Chestnut Hill."

One of his few regrets was not having taken elocution or practiced debating at Harvard. But perhaps this was not really a loss, he reflected. "I have not the slightest sympathy," he remarked years later, "with debating contests in which each side is arbitrarily assigned a given proposition and told to maintain it without the least reference to whether those maintaining it believe in it or not." The purpose of education, in his mind, was to "turn out of our colleges young men with ardent convictions on the side of the right; not young men who can make a good argument for either right or wrong as their interest bids them." As a student no less than as a president, he valued "sincerity and intensity of conviction."

Three decades later, looking back on his Harvard education, TR withheld his praise. Though he admitted having "thoroughly enjoyed" his years in Cambridge, at the core of his Harvard education, he diagnosed a gaping hole. Harvard's innovative president, Charles W. Eliot, had been determined to liberalize and expand the curriculum in order to transform Harvard into one of the great universities of the world, but, for the most part, during the 1870s, Harvard professors remained traditional and conservative in their outlook. They had cheerfully adopted and methodically transmitted the nineteenth century's unquestioned dogma of the self-sufficient individual—autonomous, striving, competitive, and successful. They rarely viewed individuals as interdependent citizens, members of a national community who were responsible not only for their own well-being but also for the common good of all.

Though "individual morality" had been drummed into his ears, Theodore bitterly complained decades later in his autobiography that there had been "almost no teaching of the need for collective action, and of the fact that in addition to, not as a substitute for, individual responsibility, there is a collective responsibility." All the messages he had absorbed at Harvard had stressed only that individuals must make the best of themselves. He regretted that books such as Herbert Croly's *The Promise of American Life* and Walter E. Weyl's *New Democracy* would have been treated either as unintelligible or else as "pure heresy." In economics, too, the mantra in Cambridge was laissez-faire. Harvard provided no education in citizenship, in how to "join with others in trying to make things better for the many by curbing the abnormal and excessive development of individualism in a few." It would take Theodore Roosevelt decades to realize—and to act forcefully on the realization—that government had a central role to play in creating equality and social justice for all, in fostering "real civilization" rather than merely permitting "lawless individualism."

Harvard, he concluded, had ultimately failed to teach him what he needed to learn to do his part in the work that lay ahead for his generation of Americans.

1
In New York: The Happiest Year

Duri ng his senior year at Harvard, Theodore had paid court to the young Alice Lee, daughter of the Boston Brahmin family that helped create Boston's Old Guard investment firm of Lee, Higginson & Co. With his new "cart and horse," he drove out to Chestnut Hill to see Alice and her family and friends. He plunged into this relationship with his usual intensity, finally overcoming the Lees' doubts about giving up their young daughter. "I have been in love with her for nearly two years now," he wrote a fellow Harvard science student, "and have made everything subordinate to winning her; so you can perhaps understand a change in my ideas as regards science, &c."

His mother had doubts too. "Really you mustn't feel melancholy, sweet Motherling," he consoled her. "I shall only love you all the more." He needed her help, too. "Please send my silk hat on *at once*," he asked, as engagement festivities neared.

Alice Lee and Theodore Roosevelt were married in late October 1880, on the groom's twenty-second birthday, in the Unitarian Church in Brookline. A few weeks earlier another Roosevelt, Theodore's fourth cousin once removed, James, had married Sara Delano, a friend of Theodore's sister Bamie, at James's estate on the Hudson. James, who had originally wished to marry Bamie, had met the beautiful Sara at a reception Theodore's mother, Martha, had given for Alice in the spring. Sara too descended from a distinguished family whose ancestry stretched back into colonial history. Twice Sara's age, James "never took his eyes off her at the reception," Martha remarked to Bamie afterward. When Sara bore a son named Franklin a year and a half later, Theodore's younger brother, the charming, irresistible, alcoholic Elliott, served as godfather.

The winter of 1880–81 was perhaps the most joyful—and one of the most determining—of Theodore Roosevelt's life. He was infatuated with Alice and marriage itself. He had graduated from Harvard and settled in New York with Alice in the Roosevelt family home, over which he now presided in place of his father.

Somehow Alice adjusted to sharing her husband with his mother and sisters, who also adored him. Theodore was starting a new career by attending Columbia Law School. Shortly before graduation from Harvard, he had mentioned his ambitions to a friend. "I am going to try to help the cause of better government in New York City," he said, adding, "I don't know exactly how." He decided that law school would open up a political career for him. Still, his studies at Columbia hardly interfered with the long hours he spent with Alice and his family. On snowy evenings he would whisk Alice away for a sleigh ride along the Hudson. On New Year's Eve 1880, he noted in his diary, "This ends by far the happiest year I have ever spent."

It was a winter of glittering social events, especially for the newlyweds. "Jolly little dinners" at the Iselins', the Delanos', the Stuyvesant Fishes' and the Leavitts', parties at Delmonico's, society balls, private dances, banquets, receptions, whist parties at the Beekmans', Mondays at the opera, concerts, theater outings—all followed one another in relentless succession. At a large dinner party, TR wrote in his diary in December 1880, "I sat between Mrs. Newbold and Mrs. Astor." A few days later he and Alice held a "great ball" at their home to which "every living individual" he knew came. Then followed a Mendelssohn concert, a "great afternoon reception" at the Iselins', another one at the Morans', several teas, and the Patriarch Ball.

Most of the social affairs were not brief events but endless rituals: the exhibiting of elaborate gowns created for the occasion, parading into dining rooms arm in arm, sitting down at tables twenty feet long to accommodate a multitude of forks and knives, a different type of china for every course, liveried footmen smoothly filling water and wine glasses, strict protocol requiring one to alternate speaking with the person on the right and left with every course. This was the New York leisure class in all its resplendent, self-admiring, stifling glory. Though their ancestors had been pioneers and revolutionaries, bursting with energy and ideas, courage and daring, by the late nineteenth century these men and women of leisure seemed "exhausted," commented the novelist Edith Wharton. They resembled "an old vintage," she wrote, "too rare to be savoured by a youthful palate."

The Roosevelts' set was, for the most part, made up of the elite old Dutch and English families of New York: the Fishes, the Brevoorts, the Rutherfurds, the Stuyvesants, the Hoffmans, the Schermerhorns—and Edith Wharton. They were known as the "Knickerbocker" families, named for the fictitious author, Dietrich Knickerbocker, of Washington Irving's comic *History of New York,* published in 1809. They valued inherited social status, a relatively modest and self-contained lifestyle, and, above all, the past. The men were gentlemen of the mercantile class, engaged in commercial activities, not industrialists or financiers. But now, after the Civil

War, American society was changing, becoming more dynamic and money-oriented. And there seemed to reign over "polite" society, Edith Wharton observed, a "strange apathy" that few were able to shake off. Were the Knickerbockers sinking into passivity? Irrelevance?

In her novels and memoirs, Wharton (the cousin of Theodore's second wife, Edith Carow) conveyed the essence of life behind the facades of the handsome brownstone town houses and grandiose marble mansions of New York. "Our society was a little 'set,'" she recalled, "with its private catch-words, observances and amusements, and its indifference to anything outside of its charmed circle." The talk was never intellectual and seldom brilliant, she noted, but it was always easy and sometimes witty. Serious subjects like art and music and literature were timorously avoided, displaced by bland observations about food, wine, horses, the laying out and planting of country seats, the selection of "specimen" copper beeches and fern-leaved maples, and European travel. One's principal activity consisted in paying social calls, "leaving one's card, the upper left-hand corner turned down, with the servants."

New York's oldest families, TR's niece Eleanor later remarked, formed a "compact" society, "chary of outsiders." Did they comprise a caste? Castes, as the great sociologist Max Weber pointed out, while being resolutely closed to outsiders, maintain their status through conventions, laws, and rituals, through distance and exclusiveness, avoiding contact with members of lower castes out of fear of "ritualistic impurity." Unlike economic classes, which Weber believed are defined by their relations to the production and acquisition of goods, an elite caste is determined by the goods it *consumes* and by its own special "style of life."

The sense of dignity of the members of this caste, Weber acutely remarked, is related to their own "beauty and excellence." Thus tied to the shallow world of appearances, "their kingdom," Weber continued, "is of this world." Whereas underprivileged strata of society religiously hope for a better future, the overprivileged, disavowing any idea of transcendence, "live for the present by exploiting their great past." Turning his attention to late-nineteenth-century America, Weber noted that Americans' traditional esteem for labor and entrepreneurial activity had become a "disqualification" of status in the privileged elite. Even artistic and literary activity, as soon as it was exploited for income, was considered no less degrading than physical exertion.

Still, the leisure class was not an idle class, as the economic theorist Thorstein Veblen noted. But though the leisure class kept busy, he remarked, its consumption of time was always "nonproductive." The lives of the members of this caste were focused on ceremonial observances of etiquette, and such ceremonies required a great expenditure of time and energy; vast amounts of money and effort were spent demonstrating good breeding and refined tastes. Indeed, the "conspicuous leisure" time necessary to cultivate such manners was the ultimate proof of one's status. "Society is an occupation in itself," pronounced one of its inside members. "Only a man who has a good deal of leisure and a taste for it," he explained, "can keep up with its demands and with what interests it."

High society in New York, the financial capital of the nation, was a more porous and less stable elite than that formed by upper-crust families in Boston—the Welds, Saltonstalls, Cabots, Lees, Lodges, and Higginsons—or in Philadelphia—the Cadwaladers, Ingersolls, Rushes, Whartons, and Peppers. Little by little, the small patrician world of graciousness, tradition, and modesty of Knickerbocker society was being displaced by the new fashionable set, the Four Hundred. "There are only about four hundred people in fashionable New York society," pronounced Ward McAllister, the arriviste credited with coining the term in 1888. The Knickerbocker elite of old New York families and old money was dismayed at the eclipse of their "polite" society by the new "fashionable" group, which flaunted wealth in extravagant, conspicuous consumption.

Indeed, Theodore Sr., clinging to his world of refinement and tradition, voiced disgust for the new fashionable set. "The Morrises go away tomorrow," he wrote from Newport, "and with them depart all whom I know well at all at Newport. . . . The rest seem to be rather disposed to be 'fast' and you know how utterly I despise a woman who forgets her true charater so entirely." He enjoyed socializing with a certain family in Roswell, he admitted, because they were "so much the most refined people in the place." But his Knickerbocker world was shrinking.

As TR's proximity to Mrs. Astor—the reigning doyenne of the Four Hundred—at a dinner party illustrates, by the 1880s "polite" society and the new "fashionable" society were beginning to overlap. But "overlap" did not mean "merge." They remained in separate social spheres, and yet the two elites had one thing in common: Virtually all their members lived essentially trivial, nonproductive lives.

They had achieved mastery over the ineffably useless. The principal accomplishments and contributions of members of the leisure class were their bearing and their decorum, along with their success in isolating themselves from the rest of society. In their eyes, manners had acquired, as

Veblen diagnosed, "a sacramental character." In their minds, they remained in a state of grace as long as their lives were uncontaminated by anything or anyone vulgar, by anyone tainted by labor, by the poor, and especially by the immigrants and the Jews who were rushing, in wave upon wave, to the American shores. One visitor from England, H. G. Wells, discerned "a sterile aristocracy" floating on top of a "vast torrent of strangers, speaking alien tongues."

Possessing status, prestige, and often notoriety, upper-crust New York society could boast of no real power. Whether its members were devoted to their world of tradition or their world of leisure and extravagance, they were determined to remain remote from the rest of American society, displaying no interest in acquiring political, moral, or intellectual authority. Ensconced in imitation Renaissance palaces and faux-French châteaus, with their priceless European antiques, roaming around their new Atlantic seaboard playgrounds on their oversized yachts, arranging their children's marriages with titled European aristocrats, their lack of accomplishments was stunning.

Elites in Boston and Philadelphia produced civic leaders: financier and philanthropist Henry Lee Higginson in Boston, lawyer and Republican senator George Wharton Pepper in Philadelphia. But among the New York Four Hundred only twenty-three men were listed in *Who's Who*, the catalog of the national "achievement elite." When someone of accomplishment appeared on the social scene—Theodore Roosevelt Sr. and his son, novelist Edith Wharton, astronomer Lewis Rutherfurd—they inevitably came from the Knickerbocker set. "The Four Hundred would have fled in a body from a poet, a painter, a musician or a clever Frenchman," pronounced one bored society hostess. But not everyone shared her opinion. There was no art, profession, or trade, there was no mental work so taxing, asserted Mrs. Vanderbilt, "as being a leader of Society."

Nor were the ladies' husbands interested in civic life or public welfare. Mrs. Astor's husband left one-third of 1 percent of his fortune to charity. William Vanderbilt left three-quarters of 1 percent of his fortune to charity. There was not yet any sense, as Arthur Schlesinger Sr. remarked, of *richesse oblige*.

The plutocrats on the other hand—those with economic power and the will to use it, the great industrialists and banking families of the Goulds, Harrimans, Seligmans, Morgans, Loebs, Rockefellers, and Andrew Carnegie—either shunned fashionable society or were shunned by it, although they were listed in the *Social Register*, which included virtually all of the city's millionaires. As a group, these millionaires were far more phil-anthropically inclined than the Four Hundred set. But as for the "social" elite, they lived in and for Society, not society.

. . .

Young Theodore possessed the family background and social status to be utterly secure in New York high society. The Roosevelts, who could trace their family's arrival in America back to the 1640s, counted them-selves among the country's most socially prominent families. When once asked his father's profession, Theodore instantly replied, "Gentleman."

He certainly had enough money to be a gentleman among gentlemen. His grandfather, Cornelius Van Schaack Roosevelt, though not as wealthy as John Jacob Astor, had been listed as one of Manhattan's ten millionaires. The family's wealth came primarily from real estate, though they had also gone into the business of importing plate glass for New York's builders. Theodore had inherited from his father $125,000 and an annual income of $8,000 and would inherit an additional $62,500 upon his mother's death in 1884. Although this was considerably more than the salary of the president of Harvard, he felt "comfortable," he told his friends, "though not rich." Curiously, some of TR's biographers have referred to his father as an upper-middle-class man of modest wealth, given that the money his father left him, like the money FDR's father would leave him, was a modest sum in comparison to the fortunes of the wealthiest men in the country. But such a comparative standard ignores the fact that TR had inherited enough wealth to live a materially comfortable life of leisure and, more important, the fact that social status was based not on wealth alone but also on birth and breeding—indeed, on the prestige of the intangible, as the etymological meaning of the word "prestige" (*proestigium,* Latin for "illusion") suggests.

The new Roosevelt mansion on West 57th Street epitomized their class status. The house of Teedie's childhood on East 20th Street, with its tasteful decoration and comfortable furniture, had been as unpretentious as it was gracious. But during the family's Grand Tour of Europe in 1873, Theodore Sr.—who had come into his inheritance in 1871 when his father died—commissioned a fashionable architect to build a new home for them amid the ducal edifices farther uptown, near Central Park. It turned out to be a Gothic showplace, staffed by an array of butlers, footmen, maids, and cooks and crammed with heavy brass-studded chairs, fancy urns, Persian rugs, tiger skins, tasseled chandeliers, tiled fireplaces, and huge mirrors. Theodore Sr. had loved every inch of it and delighted in throwing open the doors to his and his children's friends for Friday-evening dances. Theodore Jr., too, found the mansion ideal for dinners and receptions. He felt perfectly at home in it and in the social world it symbolized.

He rarely seemed bored by the conversation among essentially trivial people, perhaps because he did most of the talking. "What he could not and would not endure," commented his friend Edith Wharton, "was talking about things which did not interest him when there were so many that *did*." He did not protest against the lavish spending, the conspicuous consumption, the sharp class divisions that this extravagant way of life represented. Occasionally he attacked the "vulgar rich" but this was to cleanse the system, not abolish it. He led a secure, elegant, interesting life. New York was his.

Yet something else was tugging at him.

Perhaps he intuited the despair of the unproductive life. "Why is it," he wrote to his sister, "that even such of our friends as do things that sound interesting do them in a way that makes them very dull? The Beekmans are two fine-looking fellows of excellent family and faultless breeding . . . but, oh, the decorous hopelessness of their lives!"

"To be a man of the world," TR confessed after one winter of society dinners and balls, "is not my strong point." Seeing his brother Elliott engaged primarily in polo and hunting and in the vacuous world of horses and hounds, TR wrote to his sister Bye, another of Anna's nicknames, that Elliott's life was "certainly very unhealthy, and it leads to nothing." Elliott himself, in his rare moments of lucidity and self-restraint, realized its emptiness. In a short story he wrote, his high-society female protagonist, just before putting a pistol to her heart and pulling the trigger, confesses, "I lived for pleasure only." Looking at herself in the mirror, she utters her final words: "What a frivolous, useless thing you were."

And of course there was also the lofty example of moral virtue and public service set by his father, who was not only a "gentleman" but also a businessman, as well as the very model of the hands-on philanthropist. "I feel that as much as I enjoy loafing," Theodore Sr. had written his wife in 1873, "there is something higher for which to live." Young Theodore had admired his father for having been "the first American to drive four horses handsomely through New York—in style, in the good English style, with everything that belonged," but there was more to his father than that.

"My father was the best man I ever knew," wrote TR in his *Autobiography*. "He combined strength and courage with gentleness, tenderness, and great unselfishness." Philanthropic work was not uncommon for the

Roosevelts' class, but Theodore Sr. went about it to an extraordinary degree. He had been a key leader in creating the State Aid Society, the Orthopedic Hospital, the American Museum of Natural History, the Metropolitan Museum of Art, the Children's Aid Society, and the Newsboys' Lodging House, which provided overnight rooms for "street rats"— the city's stray boys, most of whom were newsboys. On Thanksgiving and Christmas he always went to dinner at the Newsboys' Lodging House, and every Sunday evening, after supper, he would dash out and talk to the newsboys about good citizenship and morality. Decades later, when TR was governor of New York, Governor Brady of Alaska introduced himself as one of his father's homeless newsboys. "I can never repay what he did for me," he told TR.

And perhaps tugging at him too was the sinking feeling that Knickerbocker society, for all its graciousness, code of honor, and belief in its members' superiority and entitlement, was a dying class, languishing at the margins of a dynamic country that, every day, was growing more prosperous and diverse. The patricians, as Edith Wharton had intuited, were becoming ever more remote, ever more ineffectual, ever more passive and irrelevant.

Confronted with a new, unrecognizable nation of plutocrats and immigrants, a number of New York Knickerbockers and Boston Brahmins chose to retreat into a backward-looking world of their own. The vulgar disorder of the new age appalled Harvard professor Charles Eliot Norton. "It has been a pathetic experience for me," he confessed, "to live all my life in one community and to find myself gradually become a stranger to it."

The fabulously wealthy industrialists and financiers, sneered Brahmin Charles Francis Adams, were "mere money-getters and traders," noting that "a less interesting crowd I do not care to encounter." Still, Adams would rise in their ranks to become president of the Union Pacific Railroad while his brothers, Brooks and Henry, preferred to withdraw from active lives into a consoling pessimism and contempt for the modern world.

"Fastidiousness" was Henry Adams's solution: a combination of aesthetics and etiquette that one historian calls "the last refuge of the aristocrat." To "fastidiousness" Adams added a heavy dose of anti-Semitism. "Infernal Jewry," he was convinced, had put him "more than ever at odds with [his] time." He would find a haven in the study of the Middle Ages.

Still, some patricians decided not to turn their backs on public life and civic responsibility. Disheartened that their elite society was faltering and that the world they had known was changing radically, a few upper-crust men turned to politics to reclaim the role that they and their class had played in American society before the Civil War. These patricians were known as the Mugwumps. Believing themselves to be the custodians of public morality, they felt it was their responsibility to condemn and oust the corrupt party machines. "Not all men of a certain class were Mugwumps," commented historian Gerald McFarland, "but nearly all the Mugwumps were members of one class."

It was another swing of the pendulum. In the mid-nineteenth century, American politics had moved toward more democratization. In 1845, New York, like many other states, had eliminated property qualifications and other restraints on office-holding. That 1845 amendment to the New York State Constitution had been designed, as historian Dixon Ryan Fox noted, to banish "the theory that any class of men was wiser, abler, or better than another in the public business." But now the patricians wanted back in. The Mugwump movement was an "aristocratic revolt against plutocracy." The Mugwumps were Republicans for the most part, but they claimed the right to bolt the party when necessary.

They possessed a sense of noblesse oblige, convinced that on the shoulders of the social elite fell the duty to lead society intellectually, culturally, and politically. Indeed, while the Civil War still raged, Henry Adams had written home from London, "We want a national set of young men like ourselves or better to start new influences not only in politics but in literature, in law, in society." The Mugwumps were determined to revive their moribund class and simultaneously to cleanse society by restoring the "best people" to leadership roles in government. They would follow the advice of George William Curtis in his *The Public Duty of Educated Men* and of Moorfield Storey's *Politics as a Duty, and as a Career* and inspire young educated men—the best men—to take on new civic responsibilties, to forge themselves into "an organized class." "We want a government," proclaimed liberal Republican Missouri senator Carl Schurz in 1872, "which the best people of this country will be proud of." Mugwumps like historian Francis Parkman were determined to take on two "enemies": "an ignorant proletariat and a half-taught plutocracy."

They conceded that political parties might be necessary, but along with "abuse" of party and party "machines" they rejected party loyalty. The Mugwumps led the reform movement in New York City. "Reform" meant clean government—government without fraud, corruption, waste, bossism, and party machines; government without Boss William Tweed systematically plundering city coffers, controlling patronage, contracts, and even justice; government without judges selling justice "as a grocer sold sugar." The Mugwumps were not impressed when people said that if Boss Tweed stole, at least he was "good to the poor."

Although the Mugwumps called themselves reformers, their agenda was a deeply conservative one. They had no interest in correcting the economic injustices that accompanied the Gilded Age. As Richard Hofstadter noted, they either resolutely ignored those injustices or accepted them complacently as an inevitable result of the struggle for existence or the improvidence and laziness of the masses. They yearned not for a more democratic and just society but for an impeccably clean government by the elite.

The Mugwumps' aim was to rid municipal politics of the corruption of party bosses who colluded with nouveau-riche plutocrats on the one hand and immigrant masses on the other. But how would they accomplish their goal of clean government? Why not just prevent immigrants from voting? Rolling back suffrage constituted one of the Mugwumps' top priorities. Universal male suffrage, wrote historian Francis Parkman in 1878, was a "questionable blessing." The tens of thousands of workers and foreigners who had entered the political system as voters, Parkman held, were unfit to be citizens. For the immigrants, "liberty means license and politics means plunder," and the public good means nothing. *The New York Times* concurred, editorializing in 1878 that people's rights to life, liberty, and the pursuit of happiness implied also a right to have good government—but *not* a "right to take part, either immediately or indirectly, in the management of the State."

With at least some portion of the teeming masses disenfranchised, power in New York, the Mugwumps believed, could be placed in the hands of a board of finance selected by taxpayers and certain rent payers. The administration of the city would be conducted according to "business practices" and business principles, not according to party politics. The city was not a government, the reformers argued, "but a corporative administration of property interests in which property should have the leading voice."

Theodore Roosevelt Sr., along with John Jacob Astor and other wealthy New Yorkers, publicly endorsed the recommendations for modified disenfranchisement made in 1877 by the Tilden Commission, convened by Governor Samuel J. Tilden in response to corruption scandals in the Tweed political machine. But Democrats were furious; the Tilden Commission, they objected, was trying to "set up an oligarchy of wealth." Though reformers ultimately gave up the struggle to limit suffrage, they were not without other resources: Also on their agenda were limitations on immigration, voter education, ballot reform (so that voters could split their vote among different parties), tariff reform, changes in the monetary system, and especially removal of patronage from the civil service.

But city governments easily resisted the Mugwumps' anticorruption efforts, and Mugwumps were reduced to igniting occasional rebellions from the marginal fringes of politics, the city park commissions and charitable institutions on which they served. Their work had produced no visible results, announced the *Brooklyn Daily Eagle* in 1877. "In conventions, to be beaten is to them just as much of a success as to win." So marginalized were the reformers that party regulars ridiculed them for lacking "political virility"; they were dismissed as "eunuchs" and "miss-Nancys." They had become critics, not actors.

When Mugwump E. L. Godkin, the editor of *The Nation,* retired in 1899, President Eliot of Harvard spoke insightfully about the futility of trying to reform a system from the outside. "I have sometimes been sorry for you and your immediate coadjutors," said Eliot to Godkin, "because you had no chance to work immediately and positively for the remedying of some of the evils you exposed. The habitual critic gets a darker or less cheerful view of the social and political state than one does who is actively engaged in efforts to improve that state." The reform movement had become, in the words of one historian, a vehicle for "disappointed" Americans.

"Almost immediately after leaving Harvard in 1880 I began to take an interest in politics," wrote Theodore Roosevelt. Would he take up the fight against corruption and patronage that his father, tempted by the political arena, had briefly fought? Would he join his fellow patricians in the Mugwump movement? Or would he join party regulars, dirty his hands, and enter the fray?

2
A Reformer from the "Governing Class"

"Every moment of my time is occupied," TR noted in his diary in January 1881. On a typical day, he would walk three miles downtown to Columbia Law School, study a bit, work in the Astor Library on the final chapters of his book on the naval war of 1812, meet some old Harvard friends, walk back uptown, and dine with the Astors or at the homes of other members of the upper class. But before dinner, already dressed in his evening clothes—and just as his father used to dash out to visit the Newsboys' Lodging House—Theodore would rush from the West 57th Street mansion, cross Fifth Avenue, run two blocks north to 59th Street, leap up a dreary flight of stairs, and enter Morton Hall.

His life was taking a sharp turn.

When TR's fashionable friends heard that he had been frequenting Morton Hall, the clubroom for the 21st District Republican organization, they laughed at him. Politics was "low," they sniffed, and the organizations were not controlled by gentlemen. These patricians deplored his association with Irish saloonkeepers and other brutes and rascals smoking their cigars among the spittoons and beer tables of the clubroom. But such an attitude, TR wrote in his autobiography, "merely meant that the people I knew did not belong to the governing class, and that the other people did— and that I intended to be one of the governing class; that if they proved too hard-bit for me I supposed I would have to quit."

TR did not regret abandoning the "men of cultivated taste and easy life" or their world of the "clubs of social pretension," the institution that, more than any other, defined upper-class existence. After visiting the United States, Max Weber had commented that "affiliation with a distinguished club was essential above all else. He who did not succeed in joining was no gentleman." Even the president of Princeton University, Woodrow Wilson, had remarked that the young gentleman scholars at Princeton needed to be "companionable and clubable." Whereas Wilson, the presidential candidate in 1912, would argue that in the United States there existed "no distinction of class, no distinction of blood, no distinction of social status," insisting that "men win or lose on their merits," as president of Princeton he was more candid. If his students' "qualities as gentlemen and as scholars conflict," he remarked, "the former will win them the place."

Few men had been more "companionable and clubable" than Theodore Roosevelt. But the life of a nonproductive patrician gentleman bored him to death. While club members were focused on their own status and prestige, TR was attracted by power and action. And he would enter that arena by frequenting not a club but a "party." Whereas a club feeds parasitically off its own prestige, a party, as Weber noted, is always oriented toward a goal or "cause" that its members will strive for in a planned manner. And a party, unlike a club, *had* to be inclusive.

Like the upper-class Mugwumps, Theodore believed that young men of breeding and wealth had an obligation to play leadership roles in soci-

ety. The "lack of interest in the political questions of the day among respectable, well-educated men, young men especially," he confessed, remained
unfathomable to him. He considered his fellow patricians' unwillingness
to assume their civic responsibilities nothing less than a severe moral failing. "People of means in all great cities have shamefully neglected their
personal duties," he judged, adding that "they have been contemptuously
disregarded by the professional politicians in consequence." It came down
to a question of character. The upper-class young men who lived "petty"
lives of leisure amid luxurious surroundings did so, TR judged, "at the cost
of degeneration in character."

TR would consistently criticize men of great wealth for "associating
only with the people of [their] own caste," urging them to repudiate lives
of leisure and refinement. Only work, public service, and contact "with the
rough people who do the world's work" could save them and their class.
If they refused, he wrote in the *Atlantic Monthly* in 1894, the country would
be the poorer, "but the loss to the class itself is immeasurable." The educated elite would degenerate into cultivated, ineffective parasites, he
warned, "with a taste for 'bric-a-brac.'" But the man who devotes himself
to a life of public service "can do a measure of good such as is never possible for the refined, cultivated, intellectual men who shrink aside from
the actual fray."

Like the Mugwumps, Theodore hoped that upper-class men like himself would participate in the political arena. And like them he hoped that
honest and capable men, without regard to party, would enter municipal
government and "administer their offices on business principles as opposed
to party methods." But despite his ambivalence about the party system,
TR would not reject party politics as did the Mugwumps. A life on the
fringes held no appeal for him. Some "instinct of political realism" kept
TR—like his Brahmin friend Henry Cabot Lodge—out of the Mugwump
movement. Indeed, in the late 1880s, TR would congratulate some patricians for playing a more dominant role in "machine" party politics. "In good
city districts," he commented, "the 'machine' is also generally good. Thus
in our three New York districts, the 'brownstone front' ones, we have good
machines." In those districts, he pointed out, "the assemblymen and aldermen are all gentlemen—club men, of 'Knickerbocker' ancestry, including
a Hamilton, a Van Rensselaer, etc. etc. In none of these districts is there
the least difficulty, now, in a decent man's getting into the machine."

. . .

So TR wanted to be where the action was, and that meant joining a political party. To fight corruption, he realized, he would have to work with men "who are sometimes rough and coarse, who sometimes have lower ideals than they should, but who are capable, masterful, and efficient." To succeed in politics, he knew that he would have to mingle "on equal terms with such men" and prove to them "that one is able to give and to receive heavy punishment without flinching, and that one can master the details of political management as well as they can."

What did TR want to accomplish in politics? "When I went into politics," he would later recall, "I was not conscious of going in with the purpose to benefit other people but of getting for myself a privilege to which I was entitled in common with other people." The "privilege" he sought meant being part of the politically "in" group, not the socially "in" group.

Unlike the Mugwump gentry, the "miss-Nancys," TR insisted on being active, relevant, opinionated, tenacious, loud, and conspicuously, histrionically masculine. The "strenuous" life—physical, aggressive, and also Spartan and self-sacrificing—that he would advocate in 1899 as an antidote to a "gold-ridden" emasculated society was the life he desired for himself and acted out in politics no less than he would in the Badlands and in Cuba.

He aspired to be a hero in an age without heroes.

"Such words as national honor and glory, as courage and daring, and loyalty and unselfishness," TR mused, had become "meaningless," superseded by a "mean and sordid" commercial ideal. "Thrift and industry" had displaced all the old heroic virtues. The attorneys and the bankers of the Gilded Age had ousted the warriors and the knights. In this climate, Theodore Roosevelt cast himself as a knight politician, restoring potency to an enfeebled patriciate, bringing honor and mastery to the sphere of the party hacks. His goal was to synthesize the virtues of the politician, the statesman, and the soldier. By so doing, TR would incarnate, as political scientist Bruce Miroff remarked, a new breed of leader—the opposite of the demagogue, the party boss, and the doctrinaire reformer. TR was ready to fight.

. . .

It was not immediately quite so heroic. First came routine meetings in Morton Hall, above a saloon on East 59th Street, amid the usual cigar smoke, with a dais at one end from which Jake Hess, the district leader, ran things. Hess, a German Jew who was also a City Commissioner of

Charities and Corrections, knew of Teddy's father's charitable work as well
as of the political value of his name. Second in command was a burly red-
faced Irishman, Joe Murray, who had fought his way up the party hierarchy with brains and brawn. After the meetings, Teddy would sometimes
linger, showing himself to be a man of the people.

Morton Hall was the "social rallying point" for a certain type of man,
TR explained. Men would congregate there to smoke, drink beer, and play
cards "precisely as the wealthier men gather in the clubs whose purpose is
avowedly social and not political—such as the Union, University, and
Knickerbocker." The local party, like the private club, had an "esprit de
corps," he noted; party members, like the members of a club, stood by one
another. But there was one crucial difference. The party was a group with
a *purpose*, while "the great and rich society clubs are composed of men who
are not apt to take much interest in politics anyhow, and never act as a
body"—that is, except when they "devote their time and money to advancing the interests of a yacht club or racing stable."

During that busy 1880–81 social season, Teddy had found time, while
studying law at Columbia, to join some friends in backing a "nonpartisan"
street-cleaning bill. While not identifying with the Mugwump movement,
he shared the Mugwumps' desire for nonpartisan municipal government.
They approached Morton Hall, but the regulars there could hardly understand why organization leaders would want to cut off party control of street-
cleaning jobs. Morton Hall's man in the State Assembly, William Trimble,
who had duly opposed the bill, was coming up for annual renomination
and reelection in the fall of 1881. The stage seemed set for Theodore to
challenge Trimble for renomination, which in that heavily Republican
district was tantamount to reelection.

But Roosevelt hesitated, for good reason. First of all, Jake Hess, like
all bosses, knew how to control nominations, and Theodore was not about
to commit political suicide in his first try for office by bucking Hess's
authority. Then a stroke of luck: Joe Murray was busy organizing a club-
house revolt against Hess and looking for a man to unseat Trimble. He
sounded out the young swell from 57th Street. Theodore was still reluctant, calculating the odds. But Murray convinced him that he could produce the votes, and he did, late in the evening of October 28, 1881, at
Morton Hall, 16 to 9.

His State Assembly platform would be Republican but, TR insisted,
he would be independent in municipal matters. Still torn between party
loyalty and the "purity" of nonpartisanship, in 1884 he would make Mug-

wump noises: "We have been under the rule of an aristocracy," he wrote, "composed of the worst instead of the best element."

Were there issues other than clean government that Theodore cared about? In later years he would take himself to task for his focus on municipal reform at the expense of social justice for the city's masses. "Neither Joe Murray nor I nor any of our associates at that time were alive to social and industrial needs which we now all of us recognize," he admitted. "But we then had very clearly before our minds the need of practically applying certain elemental virtues, the virtues of honesty and efficiency in politics."

. . .

The reactions of family members and friends to his candidacy for the Assembly were mixed. Mother and siblings proudly saw him carrying on their father's interest in public life, while his uncles and his first cousin Emlen remained "bitterly opposed" to his entering politics, even though Emlen had often accompanied him to Morton Hall. As for his friends, even those who had laughed at his political ambitions supported him. "Most of my friends are standing by me like trumps," Theodore wrote in his diary. "Have a good chance of being elected if I am not sold out."

Influential family friends, including notable clubmen J. P. Morgan, Joseph H. Choate, and Elihu Root, enthusiastically cheered him on, praising his "high character" and integrity. They were delighted that a "reformer" and a gentleman would speak for the district. "Mr. Roosevelt needs no introduction to his constituency," proclaimed *The New York Times.* "His family has been long and honorably known as one of the foremost in this city."

Theodore Roosevelt, twenty-three years old and a Republican, went on to win the election and become the new representative to the New York State Assembly from the 21st District. Always a good party man, Hess accepted the verdict; soon he and Murray were taking TR around to the shops and bars. "Too true! Too true!" Theodore wrote ambiguously to a friend. "I have become a 'political hack'!"

"We hailed him as the dawn of a new era," one friend recalled, "the man of good family once more in the political arena." At a celebration dinner at the chic Delmonico's, Theodore thanked his supporters for their help. Republican newspapers were pleased that a "substantial property owner" and able spokesman for the taxpayers of New York would join the Assembly. Joe Murray was most pleased of all. He had fashioned an alliance between his ward heelers at Morton Hall and the wealthy businessmen over toward Central Park. Money from the rich, votes from the poor—that was always a magical combination in the American democracy.

Stories quickly spread about the "dude"—the new term for a wealthy playboy—on his arrival in Albany to assume his assembly seat the day after New Year's, 1882. TR acted like a wide-eyed tourist; in all his travels he somehow had never laid eyes on the huge Romanesque-Renaissance-Arabesque pile that was the new capitol and legislative home on the Hudson. Making his way to the Republican caucus room, he burst through the door and stood while eyes turned to him. "His hair was parted in the center, and he had sideburns," an observer wrote later. "He wore a single eye-glass, with a gold chain over his ear. He had on a cutaway coat with one button at the top, and the ends of its tails almost reached the tops of his shoes. He carried a gold-headed cane in one hand, a silk hat in the other, and he walked in the bent-over fashion that was the style with the young men of the day."

Republican ridicule was benign compared to the open hostility of the Democratic majority when the young dandy strode into the assembly chamber. Doubtless they sensed TR's contempt for them. "There are some twenty-five Irish Democrats in the house, all either immigrants or the sons of emigrants, and coming almost entirely from the great cities—New York, Brooklyn, Albany, Buffalo," he wrote in his diary. "They are a stupid, sodden, vicious lot, most of them being equally deficient in brains and virtue." There were a few good Democrats, to be sure, but "the average Catholic Irishman of the first generation, as represented in this Assembly, is a low, venal, corrupt, and unintelligent brute." He noted the occupational differences between the two parties: the Democrats mainly liquor sellers, bricklayers, plus a pawnbroker and a tobacconist; the Republicans mainly farmers and lawyers. Still, bipartisan in his personal dislikes, he made scathing remarks about some of his fellow Republicans too; one was corrupt, another "smooth, oily, plausible, and tricky," yet another "entirely unprincipled." But he liked most of his "fellow members as a whole."

Mornings in Albany, TR would take a three-mile "constitutional spin" across the Hudson River to Troy, New York, have a sandwich and a beer in Troy, and then sprint back to the legislature. One day, as he stood at a bar in Troy, a young tough recognized him and remarked, "There's that ——— dude!" Roosevelt, according to the *Chicago Press* report, calmly set down his glass, asked, "Who called me that name?" and seconds later had the offender sprawled on the floor. "Now, boys," Roosevelt said to the crowd, "step up and all take a drink with me." He had begun to create his own myth.

In the Assembly, TR became an instant, impulsive, and bumptious reformer. Even his reform allies complained that they had to "sit on his coattails" to prevent him from popping up in continuous indignation. "What do you want to do that for, you damn fool?" one cried. "You will ruin yourself and everybody else!" The trouble was that every wrong caught his censorious eye: Republicans trafficking with Tammany over patronage, machine control of the election of aldermen in New York City, irregularities in the city's sinking fund.

He was eclectic in his approach to reform. One of his bills would purify New York's water supply, another its election of aldermen, another sought an end to patronage in the Civil Service, another would impose corporal punishment on wife beaters. In his most conspicuous crusade he pressed for an investigation of reports that a Republican-appointed member of the state's Supreme Court had colluded with millionaire Jay Gould and other financiers in a "stock-jobbing" raid for control of Manhattan's elevated railroad. His speech, branding Gould and his associates "sharks" and "swindlers," denouncing "that most dangerous of all dangerous classes, the wealthy criminal class," and demanding an investigation of Judge T. R. Westbrook—who would shortly thereafter die in a hotel room in Troy, a probable suicide—was "the hit of the season so far," TR immodestly reported to Alice. His "boldness," noted the *New York Sun,* was "almost scathing." *Harper's Weekly* praised his indifference to party bullies.

Another bill that caught TR's attention was one introduced by the Cigarmakers' Union to prohibit the manufacture of cigars in tenement houses. To eke out their meager living, poor immigrants, who were denied proper and safe workplaces, agreed to do cigar-manufacturing "piecework" in their cubbyhole apartments.

At the onset, TR thought he would oppose the legislation. "It was contrary to the principles of political economy of the laissez-faire kind," he later wrote, recalling that "the businessmen who spoke to me about it shook their heads and said that it was designed to prevent a man doing as he wished." But TR energetically conducted his own investigation, traveling to the Lower East Side of Manhattan to see conditions for himself. What he saw in the tenement houses appalled him. "The work of manufacturing the tobacco by men, women, and children," he reported, "went on day and night in the eating, living, and sleeping rooms, sometimes in one room." In one tenement, he found two families—Bohemians, with no knowledge of English—living in abject squalor in one room; tobacco was everywhere, alongside the foul bedding, next to food.

TR championed the bill, and Governor Grover Cleveland signed it. But the Court of Appeals declared it invalid. TR deplored the judges' ruling; they knew "legalism, but not life." Their legal opinion refusing to outlaw the manufacturing of cigars in tenements contained words like "hallowed" and "home," TR remarked, as if such words applied to the "revolting conditions" he had witnessed. But the experience of seeing poverty firsthand sparked less a sentimental outpouring of compassion than cool insight into the negative relationship between poverty and citizenship. "These conditions," concluded TR, "rendered it impossible for the families of the tenement-house workers to live so that the children might grow up fitted for the exacting duties of American citizenship."

For the rest of his career, such antilabor decisions would disgust him, and he would mock the hollow judicial rationalizations that working people "must not be deprived of their liberty" to work under unhealthy conditions. In 1912, the memory of cases like the tenement cigar legislation spurred then former president Theodore Roosevelt to make the radical proposal that there should be plebiscites on judicial decisions.

Did any of TR's early reform efforts succeed? Was he able to bring about any real change? A number of his bills, designed to weaken Tammany control in New York City, contributed to more efficient city government. His Civil Service Reform Bill, with the support of Democratic governor Cleveland, passed in the House and in the state Senate. It had been TR's longstanding goal to distribute government jobs on the basis of merit instead of party favor. But on the whole, few of his attempts at reform met with success. Even so, they did project TR into the public eye, though he would have vigorously denied that this was his motive. He was indeed utterly sincere about reform. And somehow, despite his moralistic and impulsive behavior, he made an increasing number of friends in the legislature, easily held his seat in the elections of 1882 and 1883, became minority leader, and one of the top leaders of the reform Republicans in Albany by 1884.

While *The New York Times* lauded him for "calling men and things by their right names" and for courageously avoiding all subservience to the robber barons, while ex-senator Carl Schurz (now editor of the *New York Evening Post*) praised him for stemming "the tide of corruption," and while some of the city's leaders—J. P. Morgan, Joseph Choate, Jesse Seligman— again supported TR, not all of TR's father's wealthy friends agreed with the young man's positions. One family friend invited TR to lunch one day and warned him not to "overplay" his hand. TR had gone far enough, the

older man remarked, adding that it was now time to leave
return to "the right kind of people, the people who would
long run control others and obtain the real rewards which
having." There existed a true "inner circle," he went on to e
comprised big businessmen, politicians, lawyers, and judges, all in alliance.
This conversation, TR wrote years later in his autobiography, gave him
his first glimpse of the collusion between business and politics that, as
president, he would fiercely oppose.

His work in the New York State legislature undermined one of the
dominant myths he had grown up with. As a child, he had always looked
up to prominent businessmen and lawyers, but as a politician he saw them
acting in ways that "astounded him." He could no longer believe in the
myth of the successful businessman as *the* good citizen. Still, he admitted,
it would take more "to shake me out of the attitude in which I was brought
up." Indeed, though in the Albany legislature he had already denounced
the plutocrats who constituted "the wealthy criminal class," he had also
opposed increasing the minimum wage and raising salaries for firemen and
policemen.

All his work appeared to turn to ashes in February of that year when
he was suddenly summoned home from Albany to find both his wife and
his mother mortally ill. His mother died from typhoid fever, her four children at her bedside. Alice, her baby daughter just born, died in Theodore's
arms eleven hours later, of Bright's disease, a kind of kidney failure. The
day she died he marked a lone, dark **X** in his diary, writing below it, "The
light has gone out of my life."

He dealt with his grief by containing it. He never spoke about Alice,
he never mentioned her again in his letters, he remained tight-lipped when
friends pressed their condolences on him. Their baby, named for her
mother, was passed on to his sister Bamie. "She was beautiful in face and
form, and lovelier still in spirit," he wrote later in the year about his wife.
"As a flower she grew, and as a fair young flower she died." He found himself again mainly by throwing himself into his legislative work, reporting
out a flood of bills, laboring far into the night. That therapy worked. "I think
I should go mad," he wrote to Carl Schurz, "if I were not employed." By
April he not only attended the New York State Republican Convention
in full vigor, he became a hero in the press when he brought off a brilliant
coup against the Old Guard Republicans by winning the election of himself and three allies as "independent" delegates who would go to the 1884

national convention as foes of corruption and campaigners for reform. TR was back in the fight.

. . .

When twenty-five-year-old Theodore Roosevelt joined ten thousand delegates and votaries at the Republican National Convention in Chicago at the end of May 1884, he plunged into the heart and guts of the most potent political organization the nation had known since the first Republican party, that of the Jeffersonian Republicans, in the early decades of the Republic. It was already coming to be called the Grand Old Party. First through his father's eyes and then his own, Theodore had watched the Republicans try to carry on the heritage of the beloved Lincoln, then to fail to "reconstruct" the South for the protection of the recently freed slaves, then to fall into the pervasive corruption scandals of the Grant presidency, at the same time shifting its main concern from the protection of African-Americans to the protection of property.

Yet for both father and son the party appeared to be the only available political vehicle. Repelled by the scandals, liberal Republicans had split away from the party in 1872, joining with defecting Democrats to form a third party, only to see their candidate, Horace Greeley, lose to Grant as the Civil War hero won a second term. The respectable Rutherford B. Hayes, the well-meaning Republican reform governor of Ohio, had barely beaten the Democratic nominee, Samuel J. Tilden, in the disputed election of 1876, but he had been succeeded by James Garfield, a loyal Republican organization man. Garfield's assassination in 1881 brought to the White House another Republican, Chester A. Arthur, whose tepid reform efforts and frustrated presidency had left him with little hope to win reform support for nomination in 1884.

This was an old story in the history of American political parties: "Conscience Whigs" had fought "Cotton Whigs" over slavery; now it was "Reform Republicans," coming to be called "Mugwumps," versus "Regulars," often called "spoilsmen," machine politicians, or worse. The lesson seemed clear to reformers of the Roosevelt stripe. Reform from outside the party doesn't work. Single-issue third parties had isolated activists who might otherwise have agitated within the major parties and pushed them toward more programmatic politics. It seemed wiser to stick with the party and try to reform it from the inside.

But 1884 had brought the toughest crisis of confidence for reformers—indeed, for the whole party. Leading the pack for the presidential nomination was James G. Blaine, the idolized "Plumed Knight," but a man widely suspected of using political influence for personal gain, who represented the corrupt machine politician. TR helped lead the fight against Blaine, but Blaine won. Writing to his sister, TR called the reformers' defeat "an overwhelming rout."

So vociferous had TR been in opposition to the Plumed Knight that the burning question after the Chicago convention was: What would the young reformer do? Famous Mugwumps such as Carl Schurz and Charles F. Adams Jr. prepared to support the likely Democratic nominee, Governor Grover Cleveland of New York. TR had plausible reasons to support Cleveland. He had worked closely with the governor in Albany on "good government" measures, and he knew the Democrat's reputation for honest and decent government.

But TR would have none of it—or of the reformers.

"We can take part in no bolt," he wrote his good friend Henry Cabot Lodge. He was, he explained, a Republican by inheritance and education; he would remain a Republican and abide by the outcome of the convention. Maybe he would just sit out the presidential campaign, including election day. But soon he waxing furious at the Mugwumps because they were taking a clear stand against Blaine; he had only "scorn and contempt for them," he wrote Lodge.

By election time he was openly supporting Blaine, making speeches for the party, and indulging in public quarrels with the bolters. It did not help that Boston Mugwumps of high society were openly snubbing Lodge on the street because of his support of Blaine and that the Lees of Brookline, his late wife's parents, were making derogatory comments about the moral weakness of their onetime son-in-law whose political independence they had once admired. Nor did it help that Cleveland beat Blaine, after a contest in which Cleveland's fathering an illegitimate child was matched against further revelations about Blaine's corrupt dealings. Still, the young Roosevelt who had embraced party regularity back in his Morton Hall days once again demonstrated a party loyalty that would pave his way to political success within the decade—though one wonders what kind of a deal he made with his conscience by supporting the party's choice.

For the next two years he indulged his love for cattle ranching in the Badlands of South Dakota, but the pull of New York and politics was irresistible. Irresistible also was Edith Carow, three years younger than Theodore and an old family friend. She was immensely attractive and reflective in a way his first wife had not been. Only with their marriage in

1886 was he able, friends thought, really to begin to exorcise the memory of Alice; some also felt that his second wife was more appropriate for a man of TR's political intensity, intellectual habits, and peripatetic life than his first.

Party loyalty soon began to pay off for TR. Party loyalty meant that when GOP leaders met in their smoke-filled rooms to choose candidates, they would remember those who had stuck with the party during stormy times. It meant too that if an election contest required a Republican nominee who might appeal to reformers and independents, the party bosses could reach down into the ranks and pluck a blossoming young politico. Such was the opportunity offered to TR when party leaders turned to him to run in the New York City mayoralty race of 1886. After some initial reluctance, TR accepted, knowing that the odds were heavily against him, because of the strength of Tammany Democrats in New York City and the unpredictable effect of a third candidate. TR's nomination was ratified at a Republican gathering populated with Astors, Choates, Whitneys, Peabodys, and Rockefellers. It was, a reporter remarked, "a millionaires' meeting."

The third candidate was the famous Henry George, who had dramatized economic exploitation and injustice in his best-seller *Progress and Poverty,* a tract pointing to the paradox of increasing poverty in a country growing ever more prosperous. "The gulf between the employed and employer is becoming wider," George had written in 1879. "Social contrasts are becoming sharper; as liveried carriages appear, so do barefooted children." His solution to the problem: equal distribution of wealth and land. His call for a single tax on the value of land, which he believed to be the source of all privilege and wealth and therefore of all inequality, had brought him world attention. A plain-looking, almost runtlike man, George was everything Roosevelt loathed: a radical enemy of capital and private property, especially private ownership of land; a denouncer of the established parties; a preacher of class warfare; and a passionate defender of the laboring class. Worst of all, George posed a real political threat; he had gathered over thirty thousand pledges from workingmen to support him in his run on an independent Labor ticket. Making prospects even worse for TR was the Democratic party's decision to nominate no party hack but the highly regarded Abram S. Hewitt. Hewitt was a wealthy industrialist with a reputation as a benign employer.

TR calculated that the vote for George might well cut into Tammany's strength with the masses. He also calculated that, by taking on such a formidable race, he would win a stunning victory at the most or garner future credit with the GOP at the least. But it did not work out that way. George conducted a fiery campaign, calling for an end to "industrial slavery" and declaring that the job of government was "to prevent the strong from oppressing the weak and the unscrupulous from robbing the honest." For his part, TR, while claiming to be a "radical reformer" who stood above class, color, and party, fell back on the worn remedies of his social class. Problems of economic inequality and injustice would vanish, he suggested, if people rediscovered "that capacity for steady, individual self-help which is the glory of every true American." Stronger government, he insisted, was not the solution.

Years later, in his autobiography, Roosevelt would comment ruefully on his earlier repudiation and fear of the radical reformers, professional labor leaders, and demagogues, explaining that, had he been less indignant and less threatened by their demands, he might have perceived the justice of their claims. But their incendiary rhetoric of class warfare "prevented those of us whose instincts at bottom were sound from going as far as we ought to have gone along the lines of governmental control of corporations and governmental interference on behalf of labor." TR would deeply regret having written—and believed—that "the worst capitalist cannot harm laboring men as they are harmed by demagogues."

Moderate Republicans deserted Roosevelt to put down Henry George's radical threat by voting for kindhearted and fair-minded Hewitt. Democratic newspapers seized on this opportunity, warning, "A vote for Roosevelt is a vote for George." TR had assumed he would run second if not first; to his chagrin he finished last, after George, while Hewitt beat both his foes by decisive margins.

Bitterly disappointed, TR took his beating with his usual outward stoicism. And he had a fine distraction; a few days after the election he boarded a Cunard ship for London to meet his fiancée. He had agreed to run for mayor only after making long-range plans with Edith for a quiet wedding and then an extensive honeymoon abroad—which would have had to be cut short if he had won. And so, even for TR, a political setback could have its compensations. After a small family wedding in London, he and Edith had a fifteen-week honeymoon trip through England, France, and Italy, not returning to New York until the end of March 1887.

But his poor showing in the race for mayor rankled for years. TR disposed of the campaign in one sentence in his autobiography. Perhaps he should have reflected more on his experience than he appeared to. Sud-

denly the usual tame two-party combat, loud in oratory but trivial in substance, had burst open as a reform-minded labor candidate challenged
established leadership. This was a portent of times to come. But so angered
was TR by the desertion of his wealthy Republican friends in the brownstones—though he himself had always held that party counted on the
national level and not on the municipal level—that he hardly noted the
surge of support he had received from working-class voters and from
African-Americans.

TR feared he was through with politics. He contemplated withdrawing
from the active life and retreating to the aesthetic pursuits of backward-
turning, inward-looking patricians. "I would like above all things to go into
politics," he confessed to Lodge in 1889, "but in this part of the State that seems
impossible, especially with such a number of very wealthy competitors. So
I have made up my mind that I will go in especially for literature, simply
taking the part in politics that a decent man should." The informative biography of revolutionary politician and statesman Gouverneur Morris that TR
published in 1888, into which he sprinkled his insights into the Civil War
and Tammany Hall, reveals an author who was both a knowledgeable, farsighted historian and a backward-looking patrician preoccupied with gene-
alogy and class in colonial America.

. . .

Nationally, two-party combat followed its usual stately course. The
big, stout Grover Cleveland was narrowly defeated in 1888 by the small,
stocky Benjamin Harrison, who would yield the White House back to
Cleveland in 1892. There was hardly a dime's worth of difference in the
two candidates' positions, aside from the issue of the tariff. While Republicans supported high duties on imported goods in order to protect American industry and provide revenue for the federal government, Democrats
like Cleveland opposed the tariff. Labor and Socialist candidates won tiny
percentages of the presidential election vote. TR saw few political prospects in New York as a result of the Democratic party capture of state and
local offices.

But what of prospects in the nation's capital? Having duly campaigned
for Harrison in 1888, TR began to anticipate his party reward. His friend
Henry Cabot Lodge, who had been rising in the Republican firmament
since his election to Congress in 1886 and who continued to keep in close
touch with Theodore, prevailed on the new president to find a position
for his friend. Why not a place on the Civil Service Commission? Here

the young reformer could do his work without harm to anyone, since the commission had virtually no power. But would the ambitious TR accept such a boring sinecure, with low visibility and a small salary, a job that was also bound to entangle him in petty conflicts with Washington politicians? Without hesitation, Roosevelt said yes.

TR's tenure on the commission was marked by furious investigations of civil service irregularities: fraud in civil service examinations, incompetence and mismanagement in the bureaucracy, and corruption in the Post Office. Ironically he succeeded in making many of the reforms dear to the Mugwumps, but only because he had not followed their example of bolting the party in 1884, choosing instead to remain a party regular. In Washington an exuberant TR exulted in his public confrontations with Old Guard politicos and editors. "I have made this Commission a living force," he wrote, "and in consequence the outcry among the spoilsmen has become furious." But he would not retreat. "As long as I was responsible," he militantly informed Lodge, "the law should be enforced up to the handle *everywhere*, fearlessly and honestly."

Still, he had virtually no impact on the course of the slow-moving ship of state, and the job became stale. "Here I am back again at work," he grumbled to Henry Cabot Lodge, "and there is mighty little work to do." For TR the whole commission experience was a lesson far more in the limitations of government than in its power, as historian John Blum pointed out. But it was also a marvelous learning experience in the intricacies and idiosyncracies of the federal bureaucracy. TR came to know a wide range of officials and politicians and some of the Washington literati, including Henry Adams. After writing some books about famous Americans such as Thomas Hart Benton and Gouverneur Morris, TR had come out with the initial volumes of a scholarly work, *The Winning of the West*, a book about the sweep of the United States across the continent that won wide and deserved praise. He had a warm welcome in the more literary salons of the capital.

Some in Washington compared Roosevelt's career to an express locomotive rushing toward a set destination. In fact he was more like a loose cannon careening back and forth on a ship called "Ambition." He knew that his Washington job was no springboard to fame, but the alternatives were so sparse that he worked on the Civil Service Commission for four years under Harrison and then continued for another two years under Cleveland.

Behind his show of vigor and decision there was a growing sense of the futility of his work. "I do wish the President would give me a little active, even if only verbal encouragement," he wrote to Lodge, complaining about Harrison. "It is a dead weight to stagger under, without a particle of sympathy from any one of our leaders here." For the first time in his life, TR felt uncertain as to what to do next. "My career is over," he wrote forlornly to Lodge. "I have spent and exhausted my influence with the party and country. I am at the end of my career, such as it is." He regretted not having tried his luck in the 1894 mayoralty race in New York. The boy wonder seemed stalled in mid-career. Haunted by the idea of remaining idle, of not being a "useful citizen," he confessed to his sister that "the only thing I am afraid of is that by and by I will have nothing to do, and I should hate to have the children grow up and see me having nothing to do."

In his mid-thirties his political philosophy was as protean and unfocused as his career. Although he did not consider himself a compassionate person, he did have a concern for the poor, however paternalistic and intellectualized. Little by little he was coming to believe that the government must intervene to prevent extremes of poverty and wealth, though he admitted to being "still ignorant of the extent to which big men of great wealth played a mischievous part in our industrial and social life." The reach of his concerns was short, at this point in his career. He wanted more equality of opportunity, but men had to compete and fight their way to the top. And not all men had the potential for this: the "English-speaking race," in particular, struck him as superior to others and also the most capable of self-government. But he was adamant that there was no place for racial discrimination in the United States, and throughout his life he enjoyed meeting and mingling with people from a variety of ethnic backgrounds.

As a young naturalist, Roosevelt had been attracted to Darwinian views of the survival of the fittest. But he did not share the radical extension of this idea into economic life at the hands of "business" Darwinians, who used it to justify the most extreme forms of "rugged individualism" and limitations of government action. TR's paternalistic and philanthropic background—and his knowledge of science—would not allow that. Thus he was already parting company with those conservatives, mainly Republican but including "Cleveland" Democrats who preached and practiced laissez-faire, who venerated Spencerian "social Darwinism" that rationalized unprecedented wealth and power in the hands of a few and who lionized Herbert Spencer himself when the English philosopher spoke at Delmonico's and other fashionable venues.

Still, there was a strange side to TR's politics and personality, at least by today's standards—an appetite for cruelty and violence. Almost from early childhood he seemed to be enraptured by guns, shooting, killing. After slaughtering thousands of birds during his youth, he graduated to killing game of all varieties and sizes in the West. Many of these he had mounted, but his killings far exceeded his exhibits. He seemed to glory in gore, vividly describing just how much blood a boxing foe or a wounded grizzly had shed. A violence of language accompanied all this, as, reveling in his own moral absolutism, he attacked opponents in the most extreme language. His political adversaries were "hypocrites," "fossils," "plunderers," "hysterical and mendacious," and just plain "contemptible." Immigrants he branded "moral paupers and lunatics."

Why this twist toward violence? Because he suffered—and suppressed—devastating feelings of weakness and insecurity as a youngster, as some have said? Or because he felt humiliated that his father had not actually fought in the Civil War? Or because he grew up in a time of strong passions, vengeance, violence, and retribution after that war? Or because he saw life and politics as moral battles between good and evil, epic struggles that could be won only by a righteous warrior, a manly hero? Perhaps the answer lay in all these factors and in others. Whatever the causes, they must have been powerful, because TR's verbal rage against his adversaries persisted until the end of his days.

At least his preoccupation with order and disorder, with law abiders against criminals, and with reform stood him in good stead with his next two job opportunities. In April 1895 he was offered the presidency of the Board of Police Commissioners of New York City. "I think it a good thing to be definitely identified with my city once more," he wrote his sister. "I would like once more to have my voice in political matters."

TR swept into the job with his usual vigor, combativeness, and enthusiasm. He had not been in the police headquarters building on Mulberry Street an hour, reported *The Evening Sun*, "before he had made the personal acquaintance of every man in it, from the nursery up under the roof to Tim, the janitor, in the cellar." New appointments also made news. THE POLICE BOARD'S NEW PRESIDENT CREATES A SENSATION IN MULBERRY STREET —WOMAN SUCCEEDS MEN. "It quite took the breath out of the old stagers in the Mulberry Street barracks yesterday," commented the *World*, "when the news was passed around that President Roosevelt had installed a young lady to take the places of the two men employed by the former President." The young female secretary's appearance was duly sketched for the readers.

Theodore seemed to be single-handedly ushering in a new era in New York. Accompanied by reporters—Jacob Riis, the author of *How the Other Half Lives,* documenting ghetto poverty; Lincoln Steffens; and others—an incognito TR roamed the city streets at night, making sure that policemen were dutifully patrolling their beats. By morning they knew who the truants were and by 9:30 A.M. errant officers had already been summoned to appear before the commissioner; corrupt police officers were sacked or forced to resign.

Day after day, headlines dramatized TR's midnight prowls and accusations. TRIALS ARE TRIALS NOW: NAUGHTY POLICEMEN FIND A BIG DIFFERENCE IN THE NEW BOARD'S METHODS, trumpeted the *New York World.* SLY POLICE CAUGHT BY SLYER ROOSEVELT, blared the *Journal.* The front page of the *New York Advertiser* hollered TURN THEM OUT: POLICE BOARD WILL GIVE NO QUARTER TO TAMMANY RASCALS: "OLD SYSTEM" DOOMED.

Theodore was a one-man show. So great was his visibility that he was seen as *the* police commissioner, rather than as one of four. "We have had Napoleons of finance, Napoleons of the banana trade, and Napoleons of the pulpit," shouted the *New York Journal.* "Now we have a Napoleon of the Police!"

As an ex-officio member of the Health Board as well as police commissioner, TR insisted on learning firsthand about conditions in the tenements rather than listening perfunctorily to tales of misery. With Jacob Riis in tow, he would spend hot summer nights striding through the tenement-house districts and visiting police stations to see what was being done. The suffering, he discovered, was "heartbreaking."

TR's nocturnal excursions taught him a variety of lessons. One lesson was the "mischief" wreaked by the American system of division of powers. The abject conditions in the tenements called for effective remedies, but effective remedies called for strong, centralized leadership and the concentration of decision-making power in the hands of one man. The division of powers thwarted the politician's ability to make swift and substantive changes and reforms. A second lesson awakened him once again to the power of business interests—who owned the tenements and could hire the best and most expensive lawyers—to block social reform, fair play, and decency.

While New York provided Roosevelt with a training school in executive leadership as well as a political battleground, it also furnished him a stage. His every move was observed, commented on, and applauded; his caricature appeared in almost every political cartoon. He was playing the starring role in an exciting new drama, mesmerizing the city with his deeds while earning the reputation for being an honest, efficient, and dashing administrator—a new kind of urban hunter. "President Roosevelt, of the new Police Board, talks as straight as he shoots," reported the *World*. "There are no savage beasts in the Rocky Mountains which he has not encountered and slain," remarked another paper. "Worse, however, than the grizzly or the panther are the beasts of prey in the city which he will now have to face—the heelers, and bummers, and parasites, and suckers who have for years fattened upon public plunder."

TR's wealth and upper-class social status, far from detracting from his reputation, contributed to a George Washington–like myth of the disinterested, self-sacrificing public servant. Under the headline A REPRESENTATIVE AMERICAN, the *Outlook* called him "a specially notable figure because he represents the American citizen of position, culture, and means devoting himself to public affairs. In his position Mr. Roosevelt has developed an energy, an independence, and a zeal for reform which, in the light of recent years, seems almost incredible." Other papers concurred. "Whether judged from the standpoint of intelligence, social prestige, wealth, or personal force, Mr. Roosevelt is easily one of the first young men of the nation." The reporter congratulated him for attending to "the shifting masses of the people" rather than associating only with his own class.

In reality, TR's feelings toward his own class were still ambivalent. In February 1897, in the midst of a stinging economic depression, Mrs. Bradley Martin decided to hold an extravagant ball at the Waldorf to cheer up her wealthy friends. TR and Edith declined the invitation to the ball because, as he told his sister, "we have never liked the Bradley Martins." But then stories hit the newspapers about the ball's incendiary theme, "Versailles," and its cost, a quarter of a million dollars. "New York is now convulsed over the Bradley Martin ball," TR wrote. But enraged denunciations in newspapers and from pulpits of the corrupt wealthy elite seemed to make TR feel somewhat protective of his "own." "I was almost tempted to retract my refusal," he told his sister. TR did not attend the ball but, as police commissioner, sent his officers to the hotel on the evening of the affair. "I shall have to protect it by as many police as if it were a strike." After the event, ridicule and denunciation of the Bradley Martins continued, and the couple sought permanent refuge in England.

During his brief term as a member of the Police Board, TR made some sweeping and lasting reforms. He centralized executive control to reduce political influence on police matters; fought crime more effectively through extensive use of special squads; increased employment opportunities for women and appointed the first woman to hold an executive position in the Police Department; appointed Jews to the police force; set new standards—from literacy to height requirements—for policemen; created the School of Pistol Practice, which would later become the Police Academy; and introduced several new technologies, such as the telephone, the Bertillon system of identification through body measurements and photographs, and more efficient horse-drawn patrol wagons.

"Are you working to become president of the United States?" TR's friends Jacob Riis and Lincoln Steffens abruptly asked him one day in his Mulberry Street office. "Don't you dare ask me that!" TR roared, explaining that if a man working on a political job thinks that he might be president, "he loses his nerve, he can't do his work." Then, in a lowered voice, he added, "I must be wanting to be President. Every young man does. But I won't let myself think of it."

With great success, TR had dramatized the need for reform and presented himself as head reformer. But the tide eventually turned against him.

TR had decided to fight the saloons because he felt that the core of the problem of police and political corruption lay in violations of a state law prohibiting the selling of liquor and drinks on Sunday. That law enabled the "machines" to raise enormous sums by winking selectively at violations in return for bribes. TR's arrests of saloonkeepers and closings of bars provoked more outrage and protest than admiration, but he stuck to his guns. Politicians knew full well, he insisted, that the law would be used as a weapon in keeping the saloons subservient to their interests. Enforced only against the poor, it had been, TR declared, "violated with impunity by every rich scoundrel and every corrupt politician."

But during a sweltering New York summer, while TR's police were enforcing the liquor laws, tired New Yorkers were fleeing the city. As they flocked to Long Island and New Jersey for their Sunday relaxation and drinks, the city's newspapers denounced the reformer gone amok. TR's popularity dwindled. "The outcry against me at the moment is tremendous," he wrote to his friend Henry Cabot Lodge. "The *World, Herald, Sun, Journal,* and *Advertiser* are shrieking with rage." In the end his campaign failed when German-Americans, who loved their beer, Sunday or no Sunday, deserted the GOP in the next city election. As a reformer, TR had won many skirmishes, but he lost the battle.

On the evening the grim returns came in marking the Republican defeat, Roosevelt betrayed his rage when he wrote a military friend, "If I were asked what the greatest boon I could confer upon this nation was, I should answer, an immediate war with Great Britain for the conquest of Canada," and he added that he wanted to drive the Spaniards out of Cuba too.

This aggressiveness was neither unlikely nor untimely. For years he had been picking quarrels with Germany, Spain, and Britain over the small issues that disturbed international peace during the late 1880s and 1890s. He had his own personal foreign policy—bellicose, vocal, volatile, intensely nationalistic. "A dangerous and ominous jingo," Henry James called him. Even President Eliot of Harvard expressed concern about his former student's bellicosity, though TR himself admitted being a "ferocious jingo." "Life is strife," he had shrieked to a Chicago crowd, bemoaning the decline of "the great manly virtues, the power to strive and fight and conquer." He scorned people whose "cult is nonvirility," along with those who were "servile in their dread of war" and those, like President Eliot of Harvard, who were "flabby" and "timid."

He had every reason now to desert the sinking reform effort in New York. The work was souring, becoming "grimy," "harassing," "stormy." Already in 1896 politicians were choosing sides for the presidential nominations and elections ahead. The GOP leadership was moving toward William McKinley—but not yet TR. He feared that the Ohioan, a Civil War combat veteran and the latest in an eminent line of midwestern GOP leaders, might fail in a crisis, he confided to his sister, whether a gigantic labor riot or foreign conflict. McKinley and most of the GOP Old Guard had reciprocal fears of TR's bellicosity, impulsiveness, and flair for grabbing the headlines. But a danger was rising in the West that would unite the Republican party: the crusading figure of William Jennings Bryan, Boy Orator of the Platte.

Bryan, a populist Democrat, was seeking to rout the conservative Cleveland Democrats. He was preaching in favor of the new doctrine of bimetalism and against the gold standard, advocating the unlimited coinage of silver as the best means for relieving the debt burdens of people living in rural areas as well as for stabilizing farm prices and industrial wages. "You shall not crucify mankind upon a cross of gold!" he thundered, using his favorite metaphor. He was appealing to people for whom TR had little sympathy—populists, free silverites, the jobless, the rural poor. Bryan won the Democratic nomination for president, and an alarmed Roosevelt confessed that he feared Bryan's "semianarchistic, political revolutionary movement."

By election time Roosevelt was lambasting Bryanites, comparing them to "the leaders of the Terror of France in mental and moral attitude." Indeed, Bryan reminded TR of the American founder who most admired the French Revolution. "Bryan closely resembles Thomas Jefferson," TR wrote a friend, adding that the accession to the presidency of Jefferson, who not only insisted on majority rule but, like Bryan, favored small landowners, was a "terrible blow to this nation." Bryan's "genuine fanaticism" worried TR, for among Bryan's followers he perceived above all a wish for class warfare, for striking down the more fortunate and prosperous. The election, he told his sister, represented the "greatest crisis" in American history, with the exception of the Civil War. His relief was immense when McKinley won.

TR had his eye on more than a Republican victory; he had targeted the exact position he wanted in a new Republican administration: assistant secretary of the navy. The author of *The Naval War of 1812* deeply admired the work of another naval historian, Alfred Thayer Mahan, who published *The Influence of Sea Power upon History* in 1890. Mahan's compelling advocacy of a larger and more powerful American navy made TR "intensely interested" in the idea of a first-class navy. Roosevelt mused about adding "perhaps half a dozen battleships"; he wondered why the navy was putting 4- and 5-inch quick-firers on its new battleships, instead of 6-inch, and railed against "futile sentimentalists" who preferred international arbitration to building up strong naval defenses.

Once again TR had to depend on his party connections to win a job he prized. A small phalanx of influential friends and party leaders—Mrs. Bellamy Storer, John Hay, Speaker Reed of the House of Representatives, the young judge William Howard Taft of Ohio—helped make his case. Hardest of all for the part-time reformer, he had to go hat in hand to the most powerful party boss, McKinley's close ally, businessman-turned-senator Mark Hanna, and to the top GOP leader in New York State, Tom Platt. Warned by Lodge that the party leadership feared TR would "want to fight somebody at once," TR offered assurances of his reliability.

Installed in the navy job, TR lived up to all the worst fears of his sponsors. Almost from the first he began to make department-wide decisions, especially in the absence of his superior, Navy Secretary John D. Long, to the point where he became the dominant leader in the department. He called for navy expansion beyond the wishes of the administration; he criticized McKinley and expressed "disgust" for the "deep and damnable alliance between business and politics" that Mark Hanna was forming. He became the chief navy contact with Congress and the press, garnering much personal publicity in the process.

How did he get away with this "insurgency," especially in a department that stressed discipline and teamwork? It was mainly because he was beguilingly honest and open about his views, cloaked his decisions in a broad concept of a stronger defense, and based that concept on a powerful nationalistic philosophy. Privately and publicly he contended that, although a strong defense was the best way of preserving peace, a nation's glory came from war. He was convinced that "all the great masterful races have been fighting races." "Cowardice in a race, as in an individual, is the unpardonable sin," he exclaimed, adding that "no triumph of peace is quite so great as the supreme triumphs of war." And he spouted these ideas with an intensity and a publicity skill that won press headlines across the country.

Too, he possessed an almost mysterious magnetism that could disarm even a staid superior whose authority TR was undermining, could bewitch even so astute an observer of leaders as Kansas newspaper editor William Allen White. White and Roosevelt first met in 1897 when TR was assistant secretary of the navy. On a Washington summer day, the two men lunched at the Army and Navy Club and then walked along together, under the elms on F Street. TR "poured into my heart," White later wrote, "such visions, such ideals, such hopes, such a new attitude toward life and patriotism and the meaning of things, as I never dreamed men had." The encounter changed White's life: "So completely did the personality of this man overcome me that I made no protest and accepted his dictum as my creed."

What was the magic? White wondered later. "It was youth and the new order calling youth away from the old order. It was the inexorable coming of change into life, the passing of the old into the new."

And yet the man White was idolizing held some extremely nationalistic and bellicose views, most of which White himself disdained.

. . .

It was this extraordinary combination of imagination, intensity, and magnetism that drew followers to this rising leader; it was also his jingoism, which perfectly fit his navy rostrum and the times of escalating tensions. Relations with Spain were deteriorating. In 1895, Cubans had revolted against Spanish rule, razing sugar plantations and mills and demanding independence. The Spanish government assigned General Valeriano "Butcher" Weyler to the task of suppressing the revolt, and concentration camps were consequently established in which prisoners, harshly treated, lived in deplorable conditions. The Cuban rebels rapidly gained the support of the American public, thanks especially to the interventionist goading of the "yellow press," such as William Randolph Hearst's *New York Journal.* By the end of 1897, American "patriots" were attacking Spanish presence and pretensions in the Caribbean, and American humanitarians were deploring the horrifying conditions of life for most of the Cuban peasantry.

The tinder of war awaited only a spark, which was struck by the sinking of the U.S. battleship *Maine* in Havana Harbor in February 1898. While the Hearst press and other jingoistic newspapers erupted in war cries, McKinley and Long remained calm, awaiting official findings as to the cause of the disaster. Sensing the temper of the country, Roosevelt busied himself with war strategy. Ten days after the sinking, after Long went home leaving instructions not to take any policy action without consulting the president and himself, Roosevelt promptly cabled Commodore George Dewey, head of the Asiatic Squadron, in Hong Kong:

ORDER THE SQUADRON, EXCEPT THE *MONOCACY,* TO HONG KONG. KEEP FULL OF COAL. IN THE EVENT OF DECLARATION OF WAR SPAIN, YOUR DUTY WILL BE TO SEE THAT THE SPANISH SQUADRON DOES NOT LEAVE THE ASIATIC COAST, AND THEN OFFENSIVE OPERATIONS IN PHILIPPINE ISLANDS. KEEP *OLYMPIA* UNTIL FURTHER ORDERS.

Furious though he was at this "bull in a china closet," Long neither countermanded the order nor sacked his assistant secretary. But while TR waited with feverish impatience for war, the administration dithered. "McKinley has no more backbone than a chocolate éclair," the assistant secretary complained. Finally, McKinley followed press and people into war.

At last TR was in his element; the young scholar of ships and sea power could now help plan strategy for real ships. His insubordinate cable to Dewey was vindicated when the commodore crushed the Spanish squadron at Manila Bay. Two months later, five U.S. battleships off Santiago destroyed another Spanish fleet. The assistant secretary could claim some credit for the victories because of the administrative and operational reforms he had been pushing in the navy for months. But Roosevelt's true element was not sea war but land war. He of course wanted to get directly into the fight, and, on the pretext that "I shall be useless on a ship," he pestered the War Department for an army combat command.

His friends were astonished. "What on earth is this report of Roosevelt's resignation?" Henry Adams demanded. Had Roosevelt "quarreled with everybody? Is he quite mad?" TR knew just what he was doing. He wanted to raise and command his own regiment, manned by the kind of men he had known in the Badlands out west. He wanted to fight the enemy on land, to come to close grips with him, to shoot and kill and perhaps be killed. He wanted to prove himself under close-in fire.

Few who dream of glory on the battlefield have lived their dream as fully as TR did. The army gave him his unit, the First Volunteer Cavalry Regiment. Over twenty thousand men of all types and occupations, including Indians, cowboys, New York policemen, and Ivy League athletes, mailed in applications. In a remarkable display of self-effacement, Roosevelt granted that, although he had had enough foresight to become a captain in the New York National Guard, he lacked hard military experience and would be pleased if the army chose his friend Colonel Leonard Wood to serve as the commanding officer. The army obliged him on this too.

Then the dream came true. Soon the Rough Riders were in training, with their slouch hats, emblematic neckerchiefs, flannel shirts, and "leggins." Somehow Wood and Roosevelt got their men trained in Texas, transported to Tampa, and shipped to Cuba, all amid indescribable mixups, delays, and confusion. To his men's anguish their horses were left behind. With Wood promoted to brigade commander, TR was now a colonel and in full command of the Rough Riders.

After initial skirmishes came the glorious day of battle. Fortune favored the brave. Leading and rallying his men from horseback, Roosevelt seemed to have a charmed life, while his men struggled up Kettle Hill and San Juan Hill on foot. "Are you afraid to stand up when I am on horseback?" he demanded of a cowering soldier. He got the perfect wound for a fighter, a nick in his elbow from a bullet. A final charge brought his regiment triumphantly to the top of San Juan Hill, joining regulars who had made the main assault.

Later it was called the "splendid little war," and for TR it surely was. "I rose over those regular army officers like a balloon," he told a biographer years later. Somehow he escaped the malaria and dysentery that felled hundreds of his men. He returned home to find himself "the most famous man in America." It was not of course a splendid war for the five thousand or more Americans who died in all the operations, probably 90 percent from disease. TR noted proudly that the Rough Riders suffered the heaviest loss of any regiment in the cavalry division. The final Paris peace treaty of 1898 provided that Spain would surrender to the United States all claims to Cuba and Puerto Rico, as well as to the Philippines and Guam. TR pronounced himself "overjoyed."

3
Pluck and Luck

"The most famous man in America": Roosevelt basked in the adulation but understood the volatility of public opinion. "The good people in New York at present seem to be crazy over me," he grumbled to Lodge. "It is not very long since on the whole they felt I compared unfavorably with Caligula." And he knew they might change back by election time. But for Roosevelt's voracious need for the admiration of others—and hence for his own self-worth—it was not enough to be a war hero and to hear calls across New York State that he run for governor in the fall. He wanted something more: the Congressional Medal of Honor. He collected affidavits about his heroism, solicited eyewitness accounts, piled up testimonials; he wrote friends and allies. The War Department, unhappy with TR's grabbing the Cuba spotlight, said no.

Still, TR had to admit to himself that he had had great luck—an easy Assembly nomination in a Republican district, job openings in Washington and New York City at just the right time, crucial help from that same War Department in gaining his own regiment in Cuba. But he had been daring, too, in provoking the reformers' wrath by endorsing Blaine, confronting thugs and corrupt police officials in New York, taking on a regimental command while lacking military experience, and charging up Cuban hills under fire. And now he faced another opportunity that called for pluck and luck: running for governor of New York.

There were problems. The office was already occupied—inconveniently—by a Republican, Frank Black. Tom Platt's GOP "machine," as Roosevelt called it, which essentially controlled nominations, had views of TR that were as mixed as the War Department's and for the same reasons: He was impulsive, unpredictable, a publicity hound, and no team player. But Roosevelt had luck on his side again. Platt had lost confidence in Governor Black and feared he was not reelectable because of "improper expenditures" on an Erie Canal "improvement" project. He needed a winner, and the hero of San Juan Hill looked like one. TR could expect the backing of many reform Republicans and independents as well.

Delicate party and factional forces were cantilevered against one another. Although called a "boss," Platt was far more a negotiator than a dictator, and his vaunted "machine" was as creaky as an old stagecoach. Some of his "lieutenants" had ambitions of their own, including his dethronement, and the Republican umbrella covered disparate economic and ethnic groups, including a Jewish Republican club on the East Side, that during Roosevelt's term as police commissioner had given him warm support. If he rejected Roosevelt, one of his rivals could ride to power by backing the hero of the day.

That hero had his own coalition problems. Welcoming support from his old reform allies, he had seemed to agree to run on a separate "Independent" ticket as well as on the regular Republican slate. Some Independent leaders suspected that Roosevelt would welsh on the deal as soon as he won the GOP nomination.

They were right. After parleying with Platt, TR stated that he had agreed not to "make war on Mr. Platt or anybody else" and would go along with the Republican party, except that on ethical questions he would follow his own conscience. The "boss" wrote later that Roosevelt had agreed to "consult with me and other party leaders about appointments and legislation." TR wrote to one of the Independent leaders and an old friend: "It seems to me that I would not be acting in good faith toward my fellow candidates" on the GOP ticket "if I permitted my name to head a ticket designed for their overthrow." Furious, reform leaders now dubbed him the "dough-faced" puppet of Boss Platt.

The party wheels were now greased for the smooth nomination of Theodore Roosevelt as governor over Black at the GOP state convention. Platt delivered. At first, party leaders tried to manage TR's election campaign, but they began so ineptly that the candidate resolved to run his own fight. Seizing on the latest corruption issue, and with only three weeks before election day, he recruited a squad of Rough Riders, including a flag waver and a bugler to summon crowds, and launched a statewide campaign that became an epic in Empire State annals.

Something quite remarkable was happening during those autumn weeks of the campaign of 1898. Huge crowds were flocking to TR's little train stops—20,000 people in one day, it was estimated. As his train rumbled off, men and women ran after it, cheering and waving hats and handkerchiefs. He had a shrill voice, he spoke in jerks, he squinted at audiences behind his spectacles, he spoke on routine corruption issues. What were his ideas for the state? Little more than good government and honest administration. But as a friendly observer wrote, "The speech was nothing, but the man's presence was everything. It was electrical, magnetic."

Roosevelt's intensity, his energy, his sheer passion were producing a phenomenon hardly known in the conventional politics of the 1890s: a charismatic hero. Still, charisma is noted for its emotional volatility more than its vote-gaining. Roosevelt won the governorship by fewer than 18,000 votes, a narrow victory in a big state. It was a triumph of sheer personality over discouraging obstacles, politicians noted.

TR recognized his good fortune. "I have played it with bull luck this summer," he wrote an English friend. "First, to get into the war; then to get out of it; then to get elected. I have worked hard all my life, and have never been particularly lucky, but this summer I *was* lucky, and I am enjoying it to the full. I know perfectly well that the luck will not continue."

The youthful new governor—he had turned forty during the campaign—did continue to have luck, however, but now he demonstrated the kind of skill that helps produce it. On the issue most crucial to Platt, patronage—or appointments and disappointments, as Jefferson had put it—he worked out a deal with the senator: Roosevelt would submit several names and let Platt take his pick. Differences were hashed out in face-to-face meetings. TR tried to remain friendly with the reformers who had stuck with him in the election but were now scrutinizing his every move as governor. He was unforgiving to the reformers who had deserted him, and especially to Carl Schurz, the former Republican Missouri senator who was now the chief editorial writer for *Harper's Weekly*. Schurz had opposed TR as a militaristic "imperialist" and had voted for the Democratic ticket. Refusing to join in giving a dinner to Schurz, the governor wrote loftily that "we could do no greater harm to the youth of America" than to honor a man who had voted for "Tammany" because he opposed "those who believe that the nation should face its responsibility abroad."

On another front, however, the governor took action that delighted those Mugwumps who believed in economic as well as political reform. This issue had long been debated among reformers, but seldom by Roosevelt. He knew that the two key party chieftains—Platt and national chairman Mark Hanna—not only practiced but preached and personified close cooperation between business and politics, especially between big corporations and the GOP. But now that he was safely ensconced as governor for at least two years, he began to sound out reporters during press conferences on his growing conviction that the party-business alliance was an unnatural one, morally dubious and politically dangerous.

Shortly he proposed setting stricter controls on gas and transportation companies and taxing their earnings. When a utility franchise is of great value, he argued, and when that value is based upon the franchise's use of a city's or a state's real estate—"whether this property consists of poles, pipes, or tracks"—the state should see substantial returns. Explaining that the existing tax structure put an unfair burden on farmers, mechanics, and tradesmen, TR called for a comprehensive study of the whole system, but he did not wait on the outcome of this investigation before demanding higher taxes on utility and transportation franchises. TR explicitly distanced himself from Chief Justice Marshall's opinion that "the power of taxation is the power of destruction." "The man of means and the great corporation," TR concluded in a speech he gave in 1899, setting a startling new tone for the century to come, "shall pay their full share of taxes and bear their full share of the public burdens."

Platt was not amused. "I had heard from a good many sources that you were a little loose on the relations of capital and labor, on trusts and combinations," he wrote the governor, and on many questions "affecting the security of earnings and the right of a man to run his business in his own way, with due respect, of course, to the Ten Commandments and the Penal Code." As the struggle intensified during spring 1899, Platt wrote further that in pressing for quick action, "to my very great surprise, you did a thing which has caused the business community of New York to wonder how far the notions of Populism, as laid down in Kansas and Nebraska, have taken hold upon the Republican party of the State of New York." Then he added the most cutting threat of all: If TR did not change his ways, the Democrats would capture control of the state in 1900.

In a surprisingly moderate answer, Roosevelt contended that the action was forced on him by reformers in the legislature, but that in any case the party should take a stand "as resolutely against improper corporate influence on the one hand as against demagogy and mob rule on the other."

Corporations, TR was coming to believe, had to be regulated by government, their earnings made public and taxed. But while newspapers were attacking Roosevelt's tax on gas and transportation companies as "communistic," asserting that he had come to resemble Bryan, the governor inflamed the conflict further by working more closely and conspicuously with union leaders than any of his Republican predecessors had done. After listening to labor men, he demanded the annulment of a law permitting private ownership of New York City's water supply. He signed a string of labor bills; he stepped up inspection and regulation of working conditions in tenements, he placed limitations on the hours of women and minors, and he defended the eight-hour day for state employees. He also fought to raise minimum pay for teachers, though he insisted on a "merit" clause. Teachers, he explained, were "responsible for the upbringing of the citizens of the next generation." And in his gubernatorial message in January 1900, he challenged big business by calling for inheritance taxes.

Despite his public posture of strong leadership, at the end of his first year of office the governor was admitting privately to be cautiously feeling his way. Many of the bills he supported favored labor, but some pro-labor bills he vetoed. "As for my impulsiveness and my alliance with labor agitators, social philosophers, taxation reformers" and the like, he wrote a Platt lieutenant, "I want to be perfectly sane in all these matters, but I do have a good deal of fellow feeling for our less fortunate brother, and I am a good deal puzzled over some of the inequalities in life, as life now exists." Still, he noted that he would rather have no change than change that would put a premium "upon idleness and folly."

Was he becoming a Progressive—concerned with labor and social welfare, urban problems, and the interests of the consumer? Or was he making significant concessions to labor out of fear of class warfare, out of a desire to head off and thwart radical movements? TR was indeed still feeling his way, on how much business should be regulated and taxed, on how much he should go beyond paternalistic protection of labor. While advocating reform, he simultaneously feared reform. Arguing that it was his duty to protect "the individual against wrong" and against exploitation by the wealthy, he also noted that "many of the worst and most dangerous laws which have been put upon the statute books have been put there by zealous reformers with excellent intentions." It was important, he felt, that the remedy not be more harmful than the disease; while recognizing that people feel "generous indignation" at the "callous disregard for the suffering of others," he also believed that one should not be blinded by "the emotional side of the question." He was walking a verbal—and political—tightrope.

But if he was uncertain of some of the continuing economic issues, he was confused about some of the newer moral ones. The fight for women's suffrage obviously perplexed him.

The average woman, he wrote to a female activist opposed 'suffrage, "has a harder time than the man, and must have, from the .. fact that she must bear, nurse, and largely rear her children." There was no use blinking at a simple fact: "The first duty of woman is the duty of motherhood, just as the first duty of man is breadwinning—homemaking." The normal healthy man should be ready at any time to go to war or into a hazardous job, and the normal healthy woman to be a mother. While TR seemed willing to fight the plutocrats of industry, the women themselves for the most part had to wage their battle against the "odious aristocracy" of men, the "oligarchy of sex."

"Work—fight—breed—a race may do all these things," he summed up, "and yet be worthless; but unless it does them, it certainly *must* be worthless." As for the vote, he was for it; it could be introduced "tentatively in new groups of either sex." In most countries, especially in Asia and Africa, the great majority of either sex were not fit to vote. "Only in the highest country, like our own, is it wise to try universal suffrage." If women were voters they would gain in self-respect.

Neither uncertainty nor confusion nor ambivalence marked the governor's feelings toward clean government. "You have evidently entirely failed to understand my desire," he lashed out at one of his Forest, Fish, and Game commissioners as he demanded his resignation, "that the Commission should be managed, not as a patronage machine but solely for the purposes for which it was created." He would not put up with the slightest taint of corruption or negligence, he angrily informed the head of the "Lunacy Commission" as he removed him, too, from office. Only citizens of the "highest type" were fit to serve in a Roosevelt administration.

· · ·

He never lost a chance to moralize. Teeth gleaming, pince-nez flashing, arms pumping, Theodore Roosevelt was performing the task that most delighted him: exhorting schoolboys to do their civic duty. On this occasion it was the boys of the Groton School in Massachusetts, where TR himself might have been a master if he had accepted the invitation of headmaster Endicott Peabody, a few years earlier, to join the school faculty. And he was exhorting them to become leaders in a talk enlivened by tales of his adventures as New York police commissioner.

"You are not entitled, either in college or after life, to an ounce of privilege because you have been to Groton," he told the graduating class.

Indeed, Groton boys would be held to special accountability. "Much has been given to you, therefore we have a right to expect much from you." He could not resist a parting shot: "Don't be snobs." There were "worse creatures than snobs, but none more contemptible."

No boy there watching TR's histrionics was more enthralled than his distant cousin, fifteen-year-old Franklin D. Roosevelt. "After supper to-night," young Franklin wrote to his parents, Cousin Theodore "kept the whole room in an uproar for over an hour, by telling us killing stories about policemen and their doings in New York." And when TR won the gover-norship of New York, Franklin and his parents were elated. Franklin wrote home that he and his classmates were "wild with excitement."

The TR electricity indeed had already helped spark a rare rebellion by Franklin against his parents. His mother, Sara, in her genteelly imperi-ous way, had declined an invitation sent to Franklin to spend the Fourth of July at Oyster Bay. When first Bamie and then TR at Groton urged Franklin to come, he defied his mother and accepted. "Please don't make any more arrangements for my future happiness," he wrote his mother. And to Oyster Bay he blithely went.

Did his mother grasp Franklin's near compulsion to join the "large party & lots of fun on the 4th," as the young Grotonian described it? For Franklin, Oyster Bay was everything that Hyde Park was not. An only child, he had spent countless solitary days on his parents' estate, Springwood, bird-watching, reading, ice skating, and riding, enjoying only fleeting afternoons with friends from similar Hudson Valley homes nearby. He had seen something of the different life at Oyster Bay: Theodore's six children playing with one another and with countless friends for hours on end. For Franklin, Oyster Bay had something else special—girls, including TR's niece Eleanor.

In earlier days, Theodore Sr. had set the pace and the tone in Oyster Bay. "There were lovely mornings on horseback," in David McCullough's evocative description, "with Father leading the cavalcade, long sparkling afternoons on the water. Everyone had his own horse or pony. There were rowboats, a sailboat, other large Roosevelt houses for children to charge in and out of, miles of shoreline to explore, woods and fields to tramp and shoot in." Father indeed was the central actor, leading the gang on horseback, su-pervising their theatrical productions, requiring young guests to give im-promptu talks at dinner and amid all of this naming his house "Tranquility."

Tranquil was hardly the name for the place when Theodore *Jr.* ar-rived in later years with *his* brood. He had purchased 155 acres on Cove

Neck, making plans with his first wife, Alice, to build a home overlooking Long Island Sound. But Alice died before the house, Sagamore Hill, was finished, and it was only in 1887 that Theodore moved in with his second wife, Edith. In addition to Theodore's daughter Alice from his first marriage, the family would comprise young Theodore, known as Ted, born in 1887; Kermit, 1889; Ethel, who would arrive in 1891; Archie, 1894; and Quentin, 1897; Sagamore Hill was a crowded home.

TR rode ahead of the youngsters at breakneck pace as he charged up hill and down dune. He appeared to love the place even more than his father and doubtless because of his father. During 1899, his first year as governor, he stayed there at least eighty days, despite the need to spend months in Albany and many days making speeches throughout the state. The family lived most of the year in the huge governor's mansion, the lower floor of which appeared to TR to bear a resemblance to the "meeting room of a board of directors of a wealthy railroad, or to a first-class Chicago hotel." Edith "likes being the Governor's wife," he wrote a friend, and the children have "great games there," but in fact they could hardly wait for Oyster Bay, where they would have husband and father to themselves.

TR watched his oldest son grow up with the same care and apprehension with which his father had watched his sickly older son. Young Ted also appeared to be ailing. The father worried that he had been too hard on him. "The fact is that the little fellow, who is peculiarly dear to me, has bidden fair to be all the things I would have liked to have been and wasn't, and it has been a great temptation to push him." A year later he was describing Ted as a "queer little fellow . . . a good little fellow." Clearly the father was reliving his own frailties and insecurities in the weaknesses of his son. Forty-five years later the "little fellow," General Theodore Roosevelt Jr., would die during the Normandy invasion, winning the Medal of Honor that had eluded his father.

. . .

The governor's second year in office, 1900, was in many respects a continuation and repetition of his first. "I want results!" he exclaimed, as he pressed for stronger employer's liability laws and for public disclosure of corporate earnings. It did not matter to the governor that Platt continued to oppose his "antibusiness" policies. A significant change in the second year was TR's increased dependence on academic experts as he grappled with highly complex issues of business and finance. But all TR's actions—and his opponents'—were dwarfed by the political calendar.

It was 1900, the first year of the new century, a presidential election year, a year in which Platt & Co. hoped that the obstreperous young governor might be kicked upstairs. But how? McKinley was due to be renominated as president, as was his venerable vice president, Garret Hobart. In timely fashion for ticket makers, the elderly and long-ailing Hobart died. All eyes turned to the White House. Whom would McKinley want as his running mate? Secretary of the Navy Long, TR's old boss, as kindly and laid back as ever? Or would the Republican convention demand the hero of San Juan?

Politicians quickly took their battle stations. Lodge and other influential friends of Roosevelt urged him to run. So did Platt, partly to get him out of his hair but also to keep New York represented in the national party and government. Flatly opposed was national chairman Mark Hanna, who did not want to inherit Platt's problem child in Washington. He shouted to party cronies, "Don't any of you realize that there's only one life between this madman and the Presidency?" But one fact few could ignore: the intense enthusiasm for TR among the party rank and file.

The most ambivalent among all these politicians was Roosevelt himself. Not that he was suffering a sudden lapse of ambition. But it had been widely assumed that he would succeed McKinley as the standard-bearer *after* the president's second term. Meantime he had no relish for the vice presidency; the job was deadly dull. Presiding over the Senate was hardly TR's forte. And he rightly feared Platt's motives. The "big-monied men with whom he is in close touch," he wrote Lodge, "and whose campaign contributions have certainly been no inconsiderable factor in his strength, have been pressing him very strongly to get me put in the Vice Presidency, so as to get me out of the State."

And yet—there was the siren call of the people, or at least the seductive voice of the party activists. TR made all the standard disclaimers, but he was just ambivalent or ambiguous enough for the convention rank and file to smell blood. His seconding speech of McKinley's renomination was broad enough to be presidential: "We stand on the threshold of a new century." But it was passionate enough to make a woman in the audience feel that he would "make a first-class lover" who would "bear her away despite herself."

Once again the foe would be William Jennings Bryan; TR wasted no time on his nominal opponent, Democratic vice-presidential nominee Adlai E. Stevenson, grandfather of the future presidential candidate. Once again Bryan campaigned on an enlightened social platform. It was a battle between the "corporate interests of the United States, the moneyed interests, aggregated wealth and capital, imperious, arrogant, compassionless" and the "unnumbered throng" who, "work-worn and dust-begrimed," make "their mute appeal."

In addition to proposing an inheritance tax and a graduated income tax, Bryan was adding something new to his repertoire—anti-imperialism—and thus became an even choicer target for Roosevelt. While McKinley stayed in Ohio conducting his famed "front-porch" campaign, his vice-presidential candidate carried the fight to the country. Appealing to honor, duty, and the flag, rejecting the notion that the Philippines or other parts of empire be abandoned, he called the conflict with Spain "the most righteous foreign war that has been waged within the memory of the present generation." "It is of vital importance," TR wrote to a friend, "to beat Bryan this year if we are to continue to hold up our heads with pride as Americans."

While TR's proposals for reform at home remained pathetically vague, it was the intensity of his campaign, rather than its content, and the extremism of his attacks on his opponents that were unforgettable. Crossing and recrossing the country, he traveled over 21,000 miles, making a total of 673 speeches in more than 500 towns in 24 states. Hostile cartoonists had a field day; one showed Hanna—the villain in the contest—urging votes for "McRoosey and Kinvelt!"

Bryan had little chance in a year when the "full dinner pail" really seemed full for most Americans. The Republicans increased their vote over 1896 in both the electoral and the popular count. After McKinley's second inauguration, on March 4, 1901, TR served exactly four working days as the new vice president before the Senate adjourned until December, under the archaic congressional calendar of the time. Facing eight months of official idleness, TR actually contemplated resuming his abandoned legal studies but preferred to spend his time at Oyster Bay, aside from occasional speaking duties. McKinley resumed his ordered life as president, while making arrangements for a long tour of the country.

The president had planned to visit the celebrated Pan-American Exposition at Buffalo during the spring of 1901, but his wife's illness delayed the trip. And so he came to the Exposition early in September. There amid the glistening domes and towers that foretold the new century, and amid the potted palms and screens and a huge pipe organ in the Temple of Music that bespoke the old, McKinley was shot and mortally wounded by a young anarchist who knew nothing about him except that he stood for evil government and coercive order.

Chapter Two
REFORM IN A SILK HAT

PRESIDENT ROOSEVELT: "During the next sixteen months of my term of office this policy shall be perserved in unswervingly."

AMERICAN EAGLE: "Je-hosaphat!"

"The Soap-and-Water Cure," Bernard Partridge, *Punch.*

A
t a political rally on an island in Lake Champlain, TR first heard
the news that McKinley had been shot. Reassured at first that the
president was out of danger, TR traveled with his family to the
Adirondacks for vacation. There, while picnicking beside a brook, TR saw
a runner dart toward him, out of the woods. "I instinctively knew," TR
said, "he had bad news, the worst news in the world." Shortly after, another message followed. McKinley had died.

On his way home from McKinley's funeral, Republican senator Mark
Hanna was in despair. "I told William McKinley it was a mistake to nominate that wild man at Philadelphia," he fumed. "Now look, that damned
cowboy is President of the United States!"

The new president was not yet forty-three, the youngest man ever to
fill that office. As the shock of the assassination reverberated across the land,
TR's first instinct was to calm the roiled waters and hold steady the ship
of state. He kept McKinley's cabinet intact—easy to do since Secretary of
State John Hay and Secretary of War Elihu Root were close friends, and
Secretary of the Navy Long appeared perfectly happy now to have his
former protégé as his new boss. Roosevelt also indicated that he would carry
on McKinley's policies—for a time. "It is a dreadful thing to come into
the Presidency this way," he wrote Lodge, "but it would be a far worse
thing to be morbid about it."

But TR's fiery temperament—and the course of events—would not
permit him to be nothing more than McKinley's fill-in. An exuberant,
ebullient, expansive force of nature had entered the White House, along
with his wife, six children and assorted pets, plus bicycles, tennis rackets,
and roller skates.

A few weeks after assuming office he took a step—perhaps ingenu-
ously, perhaps calculatingly, more likely both—that aroused a roar of indignation and controversy across the land. He invited the educator Booker
T. Washington, the leader of African-American Republicans in the South,
to dine at the White House. The president, some Southerners cried, was
encouraging dangerous ideas of racial and social equality, and hence unrest and disorder. Roosevelt's reaction to the reaction was revealing. He

found the burst of feeling in the South "literally inexplicable," he wrote a friend. It did not anger him, but he was "very melancholy that such feeling should exist" in any part of the country. A few days afterward he was blaming the "idiot or vicious Bourbon element of the South." Later he rationalized that, as things turned out, "I am very glad that I asked him, for the clamor aroused by the act makes me feel as if the act was necessary."

Warned that he might alienate southern delegates to the 1904 nominating convention, he stood his ground. "I would not lose my self-respect by fearing to have a man like Booker T. Washington to dinner if it cost me every political friend I have got," he wrote. But never again did he invite a black man to dine at the White House. Similarly, in 1902, TR decided that his nominee for ambassador to Germany, George von Lengerke Meyer, a Boston Brahmin who was the ambassador to Italy and later ambassador to Russia, would not receive "social recognition" in Germany because of the erroneous and "strange belief" that he was of Jewish origin, and so he nominated someone else.

Theodore Roosevelt was a political leader still in transition. In his first decade or two as a politician he had appeared to be a "good-government reformer," focusing largely on ways to purify politics through civil service reform: curbs on Tammany and other bosses, attacks on corruption, and cutting down patronage jobs. To some degree during his police commissionership, and to a much greater degree during his governorship, he had had to confront the needs for economic reforms, especially in the regulation of business. While flatly hostile to any kind of revolution or violence, he did welcome change and was becoming more and more open to the idea of government intervention to help labor and the poor and to regulate big business.

Some doubted the sincerity of his commitment to reform. They noted that he had sided with the "regulars" at every critical political junction, that he hobnobbed socially with the rich, that he still practiced the elitism of a "Porcellian man," that he favored only superficial reforms, that for all his sermonizing about democracy he was lukewarm on women's right to vote, and that he was more patronizing than helpful to the causes of African-Americans and certainly American Indians. He believed in doing things *for* people, it appeared, not *with* them, and for reasons of duty, not empathy.

The New York press establishment also doubted that TR would bring about real change. Roosevelt was in "perfect sympathy" with McKinley's "triumphant policies," commented the *New York Tribune*. The temper of his mind would hardly incline him to "more shining glory" than that of his predecessor, said the *Times*. The *Sun* had reasons why he would be as prudent and sagacious as McKinley, explaining that Roosevelt's "political future, his whole reputation, depend on his fidelity to the sentiment of his party." Fortunately, he was a "strict party man," and his policies would not "depend on the possible vagaries of an individual judgement."

They hardly knew their man.

1
New Doctrine, Big Stick

Just what causes political landscapes to change, old elites to fall and new leaders to rise, in a nation's capital and across the country? Superficially, the 1880s and 1890s might have seemed to be an era of relative political and ideological calm, as respectable Republicans—Chester A. Arthur, Benjamin Harrison, and William McKinley—alternated in national office with the respectable, conservative Democrat Grover Cleveland. And superficially it might have seemed that burgeoning middle class Americans, as they achieved social status and some economic independence, were increasingly complacent and conservative as they began to move out of the brawling cities into nearby suburban areas.

But beneath the surface, a middle-class revolt was germinating, one that would explode after the turn of the century. It was not a revolt of the masses—in America the masses were too suppressed and divided to rebel— though workers and immigrants, along with professional elites and church leaders, and middle-class Americans, helped energize the movement.

Was the uprising triggered by new political ideas? By the radical presidential campaign of William Jennings Bryan? By the emergence of the progressive Robert La Follette in Wisconsin?

Or was it ignited by the depression of 1893–97, years of hardship that dramatized some of the country's problems, making people more resentful of the conspicuous consumption of the wealthy, more irate about megacorporations and monopolies? Unemployment had reached 20 percent across the nation; in 1894 alone there were 1,394 strikes, including the famous Pullman strike that ended when President Cleveland sent in federal troops. In 1894, one Ohio businessman, Jacob Coxey, led a group of 500 unemployed men to Washington, demanding federal public works projects, only to be beaten and arrested on the steps of the Capitol. "Up those steps the lobbyists of trusts and corporations have passed unchallenged," fumed *Harper's Weekly,* furious that "the representatives of the toiling wealth-producers have been denied."

Was these Americans' sense of social justice awakened by the Social Gospel movement, which called on churches and church members to help the underprivileged of society, or by the proliferation of settlement houses that the Social Gospel movement inspired? By a new army of social workers, by calls for child labor laws, better schools, playgrounds, factory inspection, and regulation of working hours?

Was the sense of revolt galvanized by a meeting that took place in Buffalo in 1899? The National Social and Political Conference—attended by some reform mayors along with Samuel Gompers, head of the American Federation of Labor; Henry Demarest Lloyd; Eugene Debs, the socialist chief of the American Railway Union; and others—agreed on a program that called for more direct popular control over government, more equitable forms of taxation, public ownership of public utilities, and regulation of the trusts.

While the Buffalo meeting led to no lasting organization, other nationwide groups were emerging. Dotting the landscape were the National Consumers' League, the National Child Labor Committee, the National Housing Association, the American Association for Labor Legislation, the Committee of One Hundred on National Health, and many other organizations.

Was it a revolt partly encouraged by reform legislation passed by Congress—the Interstate Commerce Act of 1887 and the Sherman Antitrust Act of 1890—along with social legislation passed by states, setting housing standards and regulating workers' hours, child labor, factory safety, and working conditions? People were awakening to the realization that desperate poverty was not, as Mugwump Francis Parkman had asserted, a function of "an ignorant proletariat," but rather the inevitable result of a variety of social and economic conditions, ranging from gross inequities in the tax system and inadequate and unsafe public transportation to child labor.

Or was the revolt inspired by Theodore Roosevelt's ebullient leadership? Perhaps to some degree, but Henry George had already been writing about poverty, Edward Bellamy about an egalitarian utopian world, Charles Sheldon about the morality of business, and Henry Demarest Lloyd about the sins of the Rockefellers and other capitalists—while TR was still politicking in New York.

Perhaps the seeds of revolt were planted and nurtured by journalists and other writers, who often viewed themselves as members of an economic proletariat. Time was, the author Finley Peter Dunne's satirical character "Mr. Dooley" observed to his friend Mr. Hennessy, when magazines were calming to the mind. "But now whin I pick me fav'rite magazine off th' flure, what do I find? Ivrything has gone wrong. . . . Graft ivrywhere. 'Graft in th' Insurance Comp'nies,' 'Graft in Congress,' . . . 'Graft be an Old Grafter,' . . . 'Graft in Its Relations to th' Higher Life.'"

Far more than the subject of old-fashioned graft now took the place of entertaining travel stories and escapist romances in the nation's magazines and novels. Edward Bok denounced patent-medicine evils in the *Ladies' Home Journal,* Thomas W. Lawson crooked finance in *Everybody's,* David Graham Phillips "The Treason of the Senate" in *Cosmopolitan.* In *McClure's,* Lincoln Steffens dramatized the "Shamelessness of St. Louis," the "Defeated People" of Philadelphia, the "Hell with the Lid Lifted" of Pittsburgh. Ida Tarbell, whose father had been forced out of business by Rockefeller, wrote a blistering series of articles for *McClure's* on the corrupt business practices of Standard Oil. Stephen Crane depicted abject urban existence in his novel *Maggie: A Girl of the Streets,* while Frank Norris exposed exploitation in the railroad industry in *The Octopus.* W. T. Stead penned *If Christ Came to Chicago.* Most arresting of all was a novel, *The Jungle*—Upton Sinclair's horrifying portrait of conditions in the meatpacking industry. These works and a host of other exposés by America's first large stable of investigative reporters aroused middle-class anger to a peak.

These were the muckrakers—investigative reporters, journalists, novelists—who were shaping progressive opinion. Yet the term "progressive" is problematic, for the progressive movement was, in truth, protean, contradictory, and almost indefinable, and the word itself was not much used until 1909.

Still, between the 1890s and 1920, the United States was swept by powerful calls for progressive reform. Every level of government was involved, from local and state to national; every dimension of civic life was involved, from religion to women's rights to conservation. Progressive wings existed in both major parties. The movement was weakest in New England and in the South, strongest in the Midwest and West.

Unlike the Mugwump reformers of the 1880s, the new progressives desired popular government, not government by the elite—although, like their Mugwump forebears, the progressives too resented the swollen wealth of the plutocrats and the private unaccountable power of the trusts.

But progressives were divided as to the remedy. Some desired a return to the old laissez-faire competitive system; others favored government regulation of corporations. On foreign policy they were also divided. Those in favor of laissez-faire tended to advocate American isolationism; those pushing for government regulation also saw a strong role for government in international affairs. Progressives differed on policy toward immigrants and immigration, toward labor and unions, and toward Prohibition. Taking up the progressive banner were those who sought efficiency and clean government only to insulate government from more meaningful reform. And whereas a progressive like Robert La Follette, who became the Republican governor of Wisconsin in 1900 and helped make his state the "laboratory of democracy," was passionate about social justice, he could simultaneously be nostalgic for the nineteenth-century sense of community. The one thing that virtually all progressives agreed upon was race: racism and the suffering of black Americans were simply not on their agenda.

So divided were progressives that some historians suggest discarding the terms "progressive" and "progressive movement," while others discern, underlying all the divisions, a progressivism that was a real movement of modernization, bringing together a coalition that cut across class, economic, religious, and ethnic barriers and led to concrete results. Indeed, unifying progressives was a commonly held and galvanizing sense of moral responsibility for the public good. A new spirit of sacrifice, commented newspaper editor William Allen White, seemed to be overcoming the spirit of commercialism. Appearing on the scene was a nationwide army of young men, wrote White, whose "quickening sense of the inequities, injustices, and fundamental wrongs" in American society motivated them to join the progressive reform movement.

Theodore Roosevelt's voice and intensity, more than any concrete results he might have obtained, spoke to these people. At the turn of the century, Republican leaders acknowledged that TR, in the words of historian Lewis Gould, "possessed a hold on the public mind." Prizing social order above all, eager to avoid upheaval and class warfare, the unpredictable Roosevelt bent to the winds of progressive public opinion. To a progressive movement that was turbulent and unfocused, TR brought his sense of practicality, his respectability, his national authority. Little by little he would come to possess a "spiritual power," William Allen White remarked years later about his hero. "It is immaterial whether or not the Supreme Court sustains him in his position on the rate bill, the income tax, the license for corporations, or the inheritance tax." What seemed to matter to a generation of progressive reformers was that "by his life and his works he should bear witness unto the truth."

"Teddy was reform in a derby," said White, "the gayest, cockiest, most fashionable derby you ever saw." But some reformers saw it as more of a silk hat.

. . .

The burning issues were wealth and power. Who ran the United States? The federal government, in the name of the supposedly sovereign people, or the industrialists, bankers, and financiers? Was the government merely their "satellite"? Free enterprise and economic individualism were, for many, the American religion, not only economically correct but socially and morally valid. Millionaires were the product of natural selection, argued the expounders of laissez-faire capitalism. Furthermore, they held, neither the rich nor the poor should receive aid from government. "The Government must get out of the 'protective' business and the 'subsidy' business and the 'improvement' and the 'development' business," wrote the Mugwump E. L. Godkin. The government's job, insisted these laissez-faire Spencerians, was solely to maintain order and administer justice.

Justice for whom? In 1888, President Eliot of Harvard pointed out that while the Pennsylvania Railroad had receipts of $115 million and employed 100,000 people, the state of Massachusetts had receipts of $7 million while employing 6,000 people. In that same year, Edward Bellamy wrote the runaway best-seller *Looking Backward,* the story of a young Boston millionaire who falls asleep in 1887 and wakes up in the year 2000, in an orderly, affluent, egalitarian Boston bearing no resemblance to the cruel, class-ridden, and altogether bleak city of the late nineteenth century. Looking back on his earlier life, he recalls "living in luxury, and occupied only with the pursuit of the pleasures and refinements of life, [deriving] the means of my support from the labor of others, rendering no sort of service in return."

Like Bellamy, TR would also attack the idle rich, the "fashionable" society of nouveaux riches who had no interest in civic affairs, no sense of responsibility for the body politic, no philanthropic commitments. The nouveaux riches were displacing the "polite" society of old Dutch families like his own. Men of "mere wealth" were, he judged, both a "laughingstock and a menace to the community." Venting his "contempt and anger for our socially leading people" a month before McKinley's assassination, he confessed to a friend that he felt nothing but scorn for the "ineffective men who possess much refinement, culture, knowledge, and scholarship of a wholly unproductive type," for they "contribute nothing useful to our intellectual, civic or social life. At best, they stand aside." The spectacle of their lives at Newport varied only "from rotten frivolity to rotten vice." Indeed, TR would go so far as to prevent a British fleet in 1905 from making its usual stop in Newport, so contemptuous was he of "the antics of the Four Hundred when they get a chance to show social attentions to visiting foreigners of high official positions."

But there existed, for TR, two other categories of wealthy people. The first was the one in which he placed a few men like himself and his friend Henry Cabot Lodge, men in public service who were able to make a contribution to society thanks to their inherited wealth. "Each of us has been able to do what he has actually done because his father left him in such shape that he did not have to earn his own living. My own children," TR acknowledged, "will not be so left." The second class was that of powerful men, like J. P. Morgan, "who use their wealth to full advantage."

Though TR was disgusted by the idle rich, the kind of people with whom his brother had socialized and hunted on Long Island, they had become irrelevant. As he had noted, now they willingly stood aside, displaced by a new class of capitalists. Analyzing this displacement of one capitalist class by a newer, more dynamic one, the historian Henri Pirenne argued that when there is a change in economic organization, often the old capitalists cannot adapt to the new conditions. Instead, they withdraw from the struggle to become a passive aristocracy. In their place arise new men, courageous, innovative, and enterprising.

Repelled by the leisure class, TR breezily abandoned them with disgust and contempt. But it would be a more serious and complex challenge to take on the new aristocracy, that of coal barons, steel kings, railroad magnates, cattle kings, and Napoleons of finance. "It is useless for us to protest that we are democratic," Josiah Strong had written in 1885. "There is among us an aristocracy of recognized power, and that aristocracy is one of wealth." Indeed, in just one generation the new plutocrats had sprung into seats of power that even kings had not dreamt of. So wrote Henry Demarest Lloyd, author of *Wealth Against Commonwealth*. New conditions and altered circumstances of society had rendered possible the "creation of new privileges and pretensions for those who were energetic and alert."

As president, TR's goal would be to regulate and restrain this new capitalist caste, this new plutocracy. In his autobiography, he admitted that, as president, it took him a considerable amount of time before "going as far as we ought to have gone along the lines of governmental control of corporations and governmental interference on behalf of labor." But, little by little, TR would evolve from the mild regulator of megacorporatons and the neutral umpire in labor-management disputes that he was during his first term to—in the last year of his presidency and beyond—a militant foe of those he called "representatives of predatory wealth" and a committed supporter of the rights of labor.

President Roosevelt's first target was the trust—and what he called the "deep and damnable alliance between business and politics." Though the Sherman Antitrust Law had been passed in 1890 in reaction to the formation of the tobacco trust and the sugar trust, President Cleveland used the act to prosecute labor leader Eugene Debs on the grounds that union organizers were acting in restraint of trade. Although more trusts were formed during McKinley's presidency than ever before, McKinley had brought only three antitrust suits. And in the wake of the Knight case—the Supreme Court's decision in 1895 not to break up the sugar trust on the grounds that it was engaged in manufacturing and not in commerce—trusts were proliferating all over the American economic and industrial landscape. In addition to Andrew Carnegie's United States Steel Corporation and John D. Rockefeller's Standard Oil—which controlled iron as well as oil—there were also the National Biscuit Company's food trust, a leather trust, a life insurance trust, a beef trust, and a concrete trust. The Supreme Court, TR fumed, was upholding "property rights against human rights."

But now the business world was worried. What would be the policies, Wall Street fretted, of the "bucking bronco" in the White House? Even before TR had been sworn in as president, business leaders had pressured his brother-in-law, Douglas Robinson, to urge Roosevelt to toe a pro-business line. "I must frankly tell you," Robinson wrote to TR, "that there is a feeling in financial circles here that in case you become President you may change matters so as to upset the confidence . . . of the business world." Mark Hanna agreed. "Go slow," he cautioned.

Five weeks into Roosevelt's presidency, a huge trust was incorporated, J. P. Morgan's Northern Securities Company. Convinced that competition was wasteful, Morgan created this "holding company" type of trust, combining stock in three railroads, the Northern Pacific, Union Pacific, and Burlington, as well as shipping interests. TR feared that a small group of financiers had taken "the first step toward controlling the entire railway system of the country."

In TR's first message to Congress, in December 1901, he congratulated the titans of American business for their supremacy in the world, but he also warned of the "real and grave evils" that stemmed from "overcapitalization." As president, he proposed that the federal government exercise control of corporations and that, if necessary, a constitutional amendment enabling it to do so be passed. Corporations were necessary, he maintained, but they must be "beneficial to the community as a whole." In a speech in Providence, Rhode Island, TR declared that while the poor were not necessarily growing poorer, the rich were growing so much richer that the contrast struck one violently. Later he would criticize a "riot of individualistic materialism" accompanied by a complete "absence of governmental control."

Despite the warnings he had received, TR charged ahead. He first confronted the formidable J. Pierpont Morgan himself. Bypassing his cabinet, Roosevelt in great secrecy instructed his attorney general, Philander Knox, to move against Morgan and the Northern Securities Company on grounds of conspiracy in restraint of trade, in violation of antimonopoly laws.

A commanding personality with his huge flaming red nose, piercing eyes, and beetling brows, Morgan, having just bought out Carnegie and other steelmakers to put together the nation's first billion-dollar corporation, radiated economic power. He had, moreover, bailed out the Cleveland administration in 1894. During a rush on the U.S. treasury's gold supply, Morgan and August Belmont Jr. purchased 3.5 million ounces of gold. Afterward, Morgan considered himself the head of a "fourth branch" of government.

Now Morgan was indignant. Hadn't he given TR $10,000 when he ran for governor? Why, he had even supported TR for reelection to the New York Assembly back in 1882! As for TR, as vice president he had hosted a dinner for Morgan at the Union League Club. (The dinner, TR had confided—perhaps tongue-in-cheek—to Elihu Root, "represents an effort on my part to become a conservative man, in touch with the influential classes.") Thanks to the young president, Morgan had received, Henry Adams gleefully reported to a friend, a "tremendous whack square on the nose."

Morgan felt that the only way to resolve their differences was a friendly talk among gentlemen—after all, both he and TR belonged to the old gentry. Confronting the president in the White House, he offered an olive branch. "If we have done anything wrong, send your man"—Attorney General Knox—"to my man and they can fix it up."

"That can't be done," the president said. He would not attack any of Morgan's other interests—"unless . . . they have done something that we regard as wrong." Morgan viewed him, the president reflected later, as simply a big rival operator. But for TR it was a heroic joust, between the young president, champion of the people as well as of responsible wealth, and the the plutocrats, men of "swollen fortunes" whom he labeled "predatory capitalists." These reactionary "Bourbons," according to TR, "oppose and dread any attempt to place them under efficient governmental control."

TR really wanted government regulation of the trusts, not their dissolution, for he was convinced that dissolution would have meant a return to a nineteenth-century rural economy. What was called for was legislation to "protect labor, to subordinate the big corporation to the public welfare, and to shackle cunning and fraud." But a recalcitrant Congress was not about to pass regulatory measures that were opposed by intransigent business leaders, and so TR was thrown back on the Sherman Antitrust Act as his only alternative. In any case, he felt strongly that the core issue was not the method by which the government would control the trusts but, more fundamentally, whether the government had the power to control them at all.

Two years later, in March 1904, the Supreme Court upheld the government's action against Morgan's Northern Securities. TR considered this one of the great achievements of his administration, proud that the case demonstrated "the fact that the most powerful men in this country were held to accountability before the law." In the wake of his victory, he brought suits against the American Tobacco Company, Standard Oil, Du Pont, the New Haven Railroad, the beef trust, and forty other trusts, crediting his three attorneys general, Philander Knox, William Moody, and Charles Bonaparte, with fearless perseverence. Standard Oil and the tobacco trust were eventually ordered dissolved. Even so, TR, still preferring regulation to dismantlement, felt that the government had asserted its power to curb monopolies but had not yet devised the proper method of exercising that power.

. . .

Another test of TR's leadership loomed: the coal strike.

In the spring of 1902, 147,000 anthracite coal miners walked out in northeastern Pennsylvania, a bleak land reeking of the sooty smell of coal dust, crisscrossed by coal trains running through "on loud rails"—a land where, in the words of poet Jay Parini, miners chipped away in the "world's rock belly." In the mine shafts, explosions and cave-ins maimed hundreds, killing six men out of a thousand every year. Most miners were ravaged by asthma, bronchitis, chronic rheumatism, tuberculosis, or heart trouble. By the age of fifty, many were broken.

The major coal operators, who also owned six railroad corporations, were refusing to discuss a wage increase with John Mitchell, president of the United Mine Workers. Despite their own sizable annual income raises, the operators would not decrease working hours or make any other concessions to the miners' union. Coal was a business, reasoned George F. Baer, president of the Philadelphia and Reading Coal and Iron Company and the industry's spokesman, noting that if wages went up, prices would also have to go up. But even more important than controlling wages and prices, Baer wanted to break the back of the United Mine Workers and its young president. "There cannot be two masters in the management of business," he declared. The operators claimed that they would deal with their own workers but not with the union representatives, whom they denounced as criminals. Though some independent mine operators wanted to reach a settlement with the union, they were prevented from doing so by the six great railroads.

Coal was the major source of heating in the country, and, as the strike continued through the summer and the price of coal almost tripled, alarm was rising. In September, with schools in New York closing to conserve fuel, fear of a cold winter gripped the city. The patrician mayor of New York, Seth Low—the former president of Columbia University—wired President Roosevelt, urging that mining be resumed "in the name of the City of New York." In the face of growing public anxiety, the mine operators were giving the impression, at least to some people, of being recklessly indifferent to the welfare of the nation.

But the operators were acting on deeply held principles. In a letter to a citizen in Pennsylvania who had urged him to end the strike, Baer expressed his belief that workers did not need unions and that employers did not need to recognize them. Workers would be protected sufficiently by the "Christian men to whom God in His infinite wisdom has given the control of the property interests of the country." The letter was quickly leaked to the country's newspapers, which had a field day capitalizing on the arrogance of big business. The *New York American and Journal* attacked the "thieving trusts." The *New York Churchman*, an Episcopal paper, called Baer's letter "blasphemy." A Baptist paper in Boston, the *Watchman*, wrote that "the doctrine of the divine right of kings was bad enough, but not so intolerable as the doctrine of the divine right of plutocrats."

What would the president do? Would he send in federal troops to crush the strike and open the mines? Presidents before him would have done no less. Rutherford Hayes had intervened in the general railroad strikes in 1877, sending federal troops to restore order in Martinsburg, West Virginia, and in Pittsburgh. In 1894, when the American Railway Union, under the leadership of Eugene Debs, struck all Pullman cars, paralyzing the industry, President Cleveland sent federal troops to restore order; Debs was jailed, and the strike was smashed. "We have come out of the strike very well," TR had then written approvingly to his sister. "Cleveland did excellent." The president and attorney general had acted with "wisdom and courage," while the governor of Illinois, who had wavered, was a "Benedict Arnold."

There was little reason to imagine TR more sympathetic to strikers than Hayes and Cleveland. About fifteen years earlier, when news had reached TR of the Haymarket Massacre, in which seven policemen were killed and seventy others wounded following a labor meeting in Chicago, he had expressed no sympathy for the claims of labor. Writing to his sister from the Badlands, he had commented on the difference between the real American men out west and the anarchic strikers in Chicago. "My men here are hardworking, labouring men, who work longer hours for no greater wages than many of the strikers," he wrote, adding that "they are Americans through and through; I believe nothing would give them greater pleasure than a chance with their rifles at one of the mobs."

But now TR was faced with a strike of his own. Engineers, firemen, and pump men joined the coal miners in the largest national work stoppage up until then. The strike dragged on, week after week, punctuated by violent clashes between strikers and nonunion men who wanted to go down into the mines. The nation's newspapers—some attacking the coal operators, others whipping up antiunion feelings—were demanding an end to the work stoppage. Princeton University's new president, Woodrow Wilson, suggested that the real issue in the strike was the union's unhealthy drive "to win more power."

In August, TR briefly considered bringing antitrust proceedings against the coal operators under the Sherman Antitrust Act. "I am at my wits' end how to proceed," he wrote. But in October he called the miners and operators to a meeting, urging an immediate resumption of operations. John Mitchell stood up and, in the name of his workers, accepted the idea of an arbitration board to resolve the strike's issues. But Baer categorically rejected such a board, refusing to "waste time negotiating with the fomenters of this anarchy." On the contrary, he demanded that federal troops be sent in and that the union be prosecuted. Throughout the depressing day-long conference, TR noted, only one man had behaved like a gentleman "and that man was not I."

"I have tried and failed," the tired president sighed. But encouragement arrived from an unlikely source. Grover Cleveland, the former president, admitted that he was "disturbed by the tone and substance of the operators' deliverances." Now, with the support of this antilabor conservative, TR could look for another way out. One solution he did not entertain was calling in troops to quash the union. Although he wrote to a friend that "the preservation of law and order would have to be the first consideration," in truth, merely restoring order was not his top priority.

TR began to conceive of himself as a neutral umpire representing the public interest. The titans of business, he bristled, forget that they "have duties toward the public." A few days later he explained that the turbulence and violence that some people feared from the strike were "just as apt to come from an attitude of arrogance on the part of the owners of property and of unwillingness to recognize their duty to the public as from any improper encouragement of labor unions." His conclusion? The public did indeed have its own "rights in the matter."

Accordingly, TR no longer viewed the production and distribution of coal as a private business. "I feel most strongly," he wrote to Mark Hanna, "that the attitude of the operators is one which accentuates the need of the government having some power of supervision and regulation over such corporations." TR's plan was now to take over the mines and run them in a kind of receivership. He had decided to take strong action, rejecting out of hand the idea of looking for "some constitutional reason for inaction." When one congressman objected that the Constitution did not permit the government to seize private property without due process, TR snapped, "The Constitution was made for the people and not the people for the Constitution."

He chose Major General J. M. Schofield and asked him to be ready to follow orders to dispossess the operators and run the mines. Next he asked Senator Quay of Pennsylvania to inform the governor of that state that TR would like him to request that the president send in federal troops. TR wanted Quay to assume—as Quay did—that the troops would be used to keep order only. According to the plan, when he was ready, TR would give Quay the signal.

But in the meantime, Secretary of War Elihu Root paid a visit to J. P. Morgan in New York, informing him of the plan but hoping to enlist the great financier's intervention in setting up an arbitration commission. Root and Morgan, who had always favored negotiations, composed a memorandum urging Baer to accept arbitration with the anthracite miners. Hurrying to Washington, the next day Morgan himself presented TR with a document signed by the six operators accepting an arbitration commission.

But once again the operators proved recalcitrant, refusing to include a union representative on the commission and even refusing a spot for President Cleveland. TR exploded; the operators were stupid and obstinate, he sneered, mired in the "narrow, bourgeois commercial world." Suddenly TR devised a solution. On the commission there was a place for a "sociologist," and to that seat he appointed a union representative. The idea of labeling a labor leader an "eminent sociologist" was, TR scoffed, an "utter absurdity" but one that everyone received with delight. "I at last grasped the fact," he wrote, "that the mighty brains of these captains of industry had formulated the theory that they would rather have anarchy than tweedledum, but if I would use the word tweedledee they would hail it as meaning peace." To his friend Finley Peter Dunne, author of Mr. Dooley's political observations, TR confided that "nothing that you have ever written can begin to approach in screaming comedy the inside of the last few conferences."

"My dear Mr. Morgan," TR wrote, soon after the strike was ended, "let me thank you for the service you have rendered the whole people. If it had not been for your going into the matter I do not see how the strike could have been settled at this time. I thank you and congratulate you with all my heart."

In Cambridge, Massachusetts, a future president of the United States did not approve of the settlement. "Now that the strike is settled the coal has begun to come in small quantities," Harvard student Franklin Roosevelt wrote to his mother. "In spite of his success in settling the trouble, I think that the President made a serious mistake in interfering—politically, at least. His tendency to make the executive power stronger than the Houses of Congress is bound to be a bad thing, especially when a man of weaker personality succeeds him in office."

The miners had returned to work, and five months later an agreement was reached. Miners' wages went up 10 percent, the workday was reduced to nine hours, in some cases eight, and many of management's flagrant abuses were corrected. Finally, an anthracite board of conciliation was set up, though the operators had still not officially recognized the union.

In his confrontation with Northern Securities, as in his role in the coal strike, the president was challenging the private power of industry, making the government a third party in labor-management disputes and superior to the two other parties. Conservatives were horrified that the president had dared to interfere with the sacred ideology of free entreprise and laissez-faire capitalism. Though TR's wily stratagem for ending the coal strike fell short of John F. Kennedy's energetic mobilization of the whole executive branch to force the steel industry to roll back a price increase, in the context of his own times TR had struck a new note.

The government would play an active role, yet the role, as TR conceived it in the early years of his presidency, was "neutral," a mild one. The government would be umpire, defending the interests of the nation as a whole. "I am President of the United States," TR proclaimed, "and my business is to see fair play among all men, capitalists or wage workers." But such a neutral stance often favors the status quo. In 1903 TR sent federal troops to put down a strike in Arizona territory and, the following year, refused to send troops to protect mineworkers under attack in Colorado.

TR had not yet reached the point in his presidency and his moral development that would lead him to believe, as he later wrote in his autobiography, that government "must inevitably sympathize with the men who have nothing but their wages, with the men who are struggling for a decent life," as opposed to those who are "merely fighting for larger profits and an autocratic control of big business."

. . .

In his third year in the White House, Theodore Roosevelt took a step that would profoundly influence American foreign policy—and ultimately world history—during the twentieth century. In this case he did not grab some real estate or start a war but, instead, issued a statement, the Roosevelt Corollary to the Monroe Doctrine. That corollary, announced in reponse to the threat of German invasion of Venezuela and foreign creditors' intervention in the Dominican Republic, transformed the doctrine from a mere safeguard against intervention by European powers in Latin America to a presidential decree establishing the right of the United States to intervene. Like many presidential decrees in the following century, this doctrine was never formally ratified by the Senate, endorsed by the American people, or even cleared with foreign governments, friendly or hostile.

"If a nation shows that it knows how to act with decency in industrial and political matters, if it keeps order and pays its obligations, then it need fear no interference from the United States," Roosevelt stated, but "brutal wrongdoing, or an impotence which results in a general loosening of the ties of civilizing society, may finally require intervention by some civilized nation; and in the Western Hemisphere the United States cannot ignore this duty." These words bespoke TR's key ideas: his moralizing, his fear of weakness, his respect for "civilized" nations, and above all his insistence on law and order. The very elasticity and vagueness of these values would open door after door for United States interventions abroad.

Washington's practice of intervention was of course nothing new. For decades the "Yankees" had been preaching their values to Latin America and backing them up with threats, dollars, and gunboats. Roosevelt himself had fought in a war that not only drove Spain out of Cuba but also out of the Philippines and Puerto Rico, leaving the United States with responsibilities in those lands—especially the Philippines—that became difficult to fulfill. Washington's insistence on nonintervention by European nations was so strong and continuous that Britain abandoned its claim to a major role in Central America.

If the practice of Yankee intervention was not new, TR's explicit defense and promulgation of it was. Equally clear was his insistence that he was taking on this burden neither out of "land hunger" nor out of antagonism to the other powers. On the contrary, the corollary was for the benefit of the protected peoples, even at the expense of Americans at home.

What appeared to some—especially in London and Paris—like saber rattling actually was a doctrine rooted in TR's core beliefs: that peace was not the natural order of things, that Americans were not insulated against social upheavals and power politics in the rest of the world, that "spheres of interest" were not threats to peace but were rather an inevitable part of world order. Hence, great powers must police the world, assuming, of course, that they were doing so for moral purposes. These views were based on a concept of global—including military—strategy in turn founded on age-old balance-of-power theories. Roosevelt had adopted these theories during the 1890s. A century later Henry Kissinger, no neophyte in this area, would judge that TR "approached the global balance of power with a sophistication matched by no other American president and approached only by Richard Nixon."

. . .

Bashing meddling nations abroad and arrogant capitalists at home would be TR's election strategy in 1904. For the Democrats, 1904 was the year to "stop Roosevelt." Still switching back and forth between conservative Clevelandism and progressive Bryanism, the Democrats nominated conservative judge Alton B. Parker for president. His campaign was as colorless and cautious as TR's was dramatic and strident. Carrying every state in the North, Roosevelt won 7.6 million popular and 336 electoral votes to Parker's 5.1 million and 140 electoral votes, with socialist candidate Eugene Debs garnering 400,000 votes. Parker had not won a single state outside the South. As for Roosevelt, now he could say that he was no longer a political accident. The *New York Sun* called it the most "illustrious personal triumph in all political history."

In his euphoria on election night, the president revealed the qualms he had about holding personal power and his need to reject power, even as he clung to it, through some kind of Washingtonian abnegation. Evoking the two-term tradition, he said, "Under no circumstances will I be a candidate for or accept another term." Even so, TR was not prematurely opting out of the power game. After receiving the news of his victory, he was also reported to have said, "Tomorrow I shall come into my office in my own right. Then watch out for me." Would his rejection of office haunt his future wielding of power?

2
In TR's Steps

Few rejoiced more in Theodore Roosevelt's 1904 victory than twenty-two-year-old Franklin Roosevelt. FDR so adored and esteemed his distant cousin that four years earlier he—nominally a Democrat—had joined the Republican party in order to campaign for the McKinley-Roosevelt ticket. He wrote home then: "Last night there was a grand torchlight Republican Parade of Harvard and the Mass. Inst. of Technology. We wore red caps & gowns and marched by classes into Boston & thro' all the principal streets." Four years later, in 1904, he cast his first vote in a presidential election—of course for Cousin Theodore. "My father and grandfather were Democrats and I was born and brought up as a Democrat," Franklin later said, explaining that, in 1904, "I voted for the Republican candidate, Theodore Roosevelt, because I thought he was a better Democrat than the Democratic candidate."

Later that November of 1904 the engagement of Franklin Delano Roosevelt to marry Anna Eleanor Roosevelt, his fifth cousin, was formally announced. "We think the lover and the sweetheart are worthy of one another," a pleased Uncle Ted wrote to his niece. "Dear girl, I rejoice deeply in your happiness." The couple attended TR's inauguration the following March 4, lunched at the White House, and danced together at the Inaugural Ball.

Their wedding took place two weeks later in New York, on March 17, 1905—Saint Patrick's Day. "Only some utterly unforeseen public need will keep me away," the president had written to Eleanor. On the morning of the wedding, leading his Rough Riders, President Roosevelt exuberantly marched in the massive parade, 30,000 strong, as it surged up Fifth Avenue, surrounded by throngs of office workers, storekeepers, shopgirls, and cheering onlookers. Uptown, Roosevelt left the parade and its working-class commotion, making his way to the brownstone of Eleanor's aunt, Mrs. E. Livingston Ludlow, on East 76th Street, where the elegant wedding guests of the social elite—Livingstons, Ludlows, Jays, Astors, and the grande dame Mrs. Frederick Vanderbilt—were already assembled.

Franklin Delano Roosevelt stood in a small foyer, chatting about schooldays with his former headmaster, the Reverend Endicott Peabody, and his friend and best man Lathrop Brown. The bride, in her grandmother's lace and her mother-in-law's pearls, attended by her bridesmaids, nervously waited upstairs.

Shamrocks in his buttonhole, top hat in hand, President Roosevelt dashed in. The wedding could begin.

Concerned about Eleanor's welfare ever since the death of her father, his brother Elliott, ten years before, TR was mightily pleased to give the bride away. Taking his niece by the arm, the beaming uncle escorted her down the circular staircase. "Who giveth this woman in marriage?" the Rev. Mr. Peabody asked. "I do!" the president announced loudly, so as to be heard above the voices of the Ancient Order of Hibernians singing "The Wearing of the Green" in the street.

"Well, Franklin," the president barked at the end of the ceremony, "there's nothing like keeping the name in the family!" and promptly went off in search of refreshments. The guests followed, irresistibly drawn to his aura of energy and high spirits. Franklin and Eleanor trailed after everyone else into the library and together cut the wedding cake while Uncle Ted regaled the group with his stories.

The president and his wife then traveled downtown, escorted by the 69th Regiment, to the famous Delmonico's restaurant, where TR was the featured speaker at the annual dinner of the Friendly Sons of St. Patrick. Franklin and Eleanor left for their honeymoon, first in Hyde Park and then in Europe. Not only had Franklin "kept the name in the family" by marrying the president's niece, he had entered the ebullient Oyster Bay side of the family.

The startling similarities between Theodore's and Franklin's careers were no coincidence. Sons of socially established New York families, both attended Harvard, studied law and were bored by it, entered politics in their twenties, served in the New York State legislature, won appointments as assistant secretary of the navy, married well, fathered six children (one of FDR's and Eleanor's died), served as governor of New York, and ran for vice president of the United States. That the two patterns are identical is perhaps less extraordinary than one might think, for Franklin deeply admired TR and fervently wished to emulate him. And perhaps Theodore to a degree was encouraged by the support of young people like Franklin and wished to inspire and lead them.

The early years of the two men, on the other hand, were quite dissimilar. Theodore grew up among loving siblings; Franklin was an only child. He played with a niece and nephew who were actually older than he—Helen and James ("Taddy") Roosevelt, children of Franklin's half brother, "Rosy"—as well as with boys from neighboring estates along the Hudson. But mostly he was alone or in the company of adults. Thrown on his own resources, he started a lifelong interest and expertise in trees, birds, crops, boats, and, perhaps to a lesser extent, books.

Still, young Franklin was brought up, as one governess. said, "in a beautiful frame." On the Roosevelt side, he, like Theodore, descended from Claes Martensen Van Rosenvelt, who sailed to New Amsterdam from Holland in the 1640s. His mother's family, the Delanos, besides liking to trace their origins back to William the Conqueror, were proud to claim Philippe De La Noye, who arrived in Plymouth in 1621, as their ancestor.

The Roosevelts lived gracious lives on their secure Hudson estate. When they traveled—to Fairhaven, Massachusetts; to Campobello Island, in Canada, opposite Eastport, Maine; or to England and the Continent—they may have seen new places but they always surrounded themselves with the same kind of people. When they went by rail, they traveled in a private car. And aboard ship, as Franklin's mother, Sara, said, there were always "people one knows." Although Paris and London were familiar places, much of the world was invisible to them—the world of immigrants and grimy New York tenements, the world of strikers and farmers, the world of the squabbling Irish politicians in nearby Poughkeepsie. The Delanos, it was said, "carried their way of life around them like a transparent but impenetrable envelope wherever they went."

They particularly frowned upon the "new" millionaires—like the Vanderbilts—who had built pretentious, mausoleumlike palaces along the Hudson, so unlike the comfortable and relatively simple estates of the old aristocratic families who never "showed off." One day in 1890, Franklin's mother announced at breakfast that Mrs. Cornelius Vanderbilt had invited the Roosevelts to dinner. "Sally, we cannot accept," pronounced FDR's father. "But she's a lovely woman, and I thought you liked Mr. Vanderbilt too," objected Franklin's mother. His father conceded that he served on boards with Mr. Vanderbilt and liked him. "But," he added, "if we accept we shall have to have them at our house."

In the manner of the English upper-class families they knew, Sara and James Roosevelt sent their son off to private school when he turned fourteen. The school was Groton, which had already achieved standing among the social elite because of the leadership of its rector, Endicott Peabody, also a member of the elite. Here Franklin was not listened to, as he had been at home. Most of his classmates had arrived one or two years earlier than the fourteen-year-old from Hyde Park, and they "had already formed their friendships," he later told Eleanor; he had remained "always a little the outsider." The older boys, in typical prep school fashion, hazed him; his classmates were put off a bit by his slightly English accent, the perfect punctuality he achieved in order to win a school prize, his courtly deference to Rector Peabody. He conformed both to Peabody's rules and to peer pressure to survive, meanwhile writing letters home that chirped about his small successes and occasional failures, which he explained away with minor rationalizations and a fib or two.

He already displayed a desire to excel, an ambition to gain recognition and praise—an ambition probably fueled all the more by his failure to be more than a grade-C athlete and a grade-B scholar. Yet it was not Grotonian to expose this ambition to Peabody or the school, and he dared not share his feelings with his doting mother and his ailing father. Those feelings spilled over, though, when Peabody did not include him among the senior prefects he chose, while including the headmaster's own nephew.

"Everyone is wild at the Rector for his favoritism to his nephew," Franklin wrote home, "but the honor is no longer an honor & makes no difference to one's standing." But he seethed for weeks afterward.

Deepening the pain was his own ambivalence. He loved the school but had been thwarted by it; he liked many of his schoolmates but felt merely liked in return and not well liked; he both revered the Rector as something of a father substitute and feared him as well. He was caught between an ambition to achieve and a longing to be one of the boys. These ambivalences intensified at Harvard, which Franklin entered in the fall of 1900.

. . .

Anyone walking into Franklin's suite in Westmorly Court on Harvard's Gold Coast would have thought he had nothing but the happiest memories of Groton. School pennants festooned the walls; team photographs and school mementos lined the marble mantels. He and his roommate Lathrop Brown breakfasted, lunched, and dined with other Grotonians, and in the evening, becoming less exclusive, they congregated at Sanford's famed billiard parlor with Saint Paul's and Saint Mark's fellows.

Freed of Peabody's stern discipline, Franklin became a man about town, dropping in on Boston society parties, socializing with other private-school graduates in various Harvard clubs, and spending plenty of time cheering Harvard teams. He seemed destined to divide his life between being an amiable clubman and a Hyde Park squire and gentleman.

Yet within this apparently frivolous socialite there burned an ambition to be something much more. This ambition was first centered on *The Crimson,* Harvard's student newspaper. He missed selection for the initial freshman roster, tried again, won a post as editor, worked his way farther up the ladder, won the position of managing editor over a rival, and automatically succeeded to the editorship, grandly called "President," of *The Crimson.* The twenty-two-year old editor was hardly a crusader, though, except for wider boardwalks in the Yard, better fire protection in the dormitories, and more freshman enthusiasm for their football team.

His ambition burned for something still more prestigious than editing *The Crimson.* He was desperately eager to become a member of Porcellian. Sons customarily followed their fathers into this organization. Franklin's own father had been an honorary member, without making too much of it; far more important, Theodore Roosevelt had been a member and he *did* make much of it. It was a Roosevelt family tradition. But Franklin was rejected—literally blackballed by one or more of sixteen students who secretly deposited a black ball into a wooden ballot box that was passed around the table.

He was astonished, mortified, and angry, for he had considered acceptance into Porcellian the "highest honor." Many years later he said that his rejection had been the "greatest disappointment" of his life; Eleanor Roosevelt thought it gave him an inferiority complex, though perhaps it also helped him sympathize with life's outcasts. But disappointment merely goaded Franklin to more effort. In his senior year he ran for a single prized position, class marshal, and lost again. Once more deeply mortified but undaunted, he tried again, for head of the 1904 class committee. This time he won—by 168 out of 253 votes. Thus he learned a lesson from this, his first electoral victory: Sheer persistence paid off, even in the rarefied politics of Harvard.

What else did Franklin learn at Harvard? He was lucky to have a wide choice of courses as a result of President Charles W. Eliot's having broadened the curriculum and pioneered a freer choice of electives. After taking such required basic courses as English literature and European history in his freshman year, Franklin chose recent American history, English parliamentary history, and economics among other courses in his second year, and a somewhat similar set in his third, along with a scattering of "liberal arts" electives such as paleontology, public speaking, fine arts, and philosophy. His general grade average in these years was a gentleman's C+.

Grades aside, his educational experience was mixed at best. He had as teachers some of Harvard's "greats": Shakespearean scholar George Lyman Kittredge, political scientist and later Harvard president A. Lawrence Lowell, American historian Edward Channing, speech and drama teacher George Pierce Baker, and Frederick Jackson Turner, who taught Development of the West. How faithfully he attended such courses varied widely, depending on how "practical" he found them and on other pressures of time.

The problem was not the teachers or the courses, tedious though some of them were, but how slowly Franklin's mind was maturing. Despite later suppositions that Turner, who had written a famous essay on the influence of the Western frontier on American history, might have influenced FDR's later political views, he in fact missed half of Turner's course because he was on a Caribbean cruise. He complained later to a roommate that his courses had been "like an electric lamp that hasn't any wire. You need the lamp for light, but it's useless if you can't switch it on."

It was Franklin's job to switch it on, but his mind, according to historian Kenneth Davis, seemed to "have remained at eighteen and twenty-two essentially what it had been at age fourteen"—"a collector's mind almost exclusively, quick to grasp and classify bits and pieces of information, but unresponsive to the challenge of the abstract." He dropped a course given by the great philosopher Josiah Royce after three weeks; if his views were affected by even more eminent Harvard philosophers such as William James and George Santayana, there is no record in FDR's letters or anywhere else.

FDR's most striking quality during this stage of his life was his seeming ability to ingratiate himself with almost everyone he met. He "got along" not only with his student friends in several clubs but with many of his teachers, not only with his *Crimson* workers but with the two Scottish printers who had to cope with late copy, not only with Boston matrons but with old Groton friends at Sanford's. Above all, he got along with the most central and formidable person in his life—his mother.

He could not escape her. She dominated his life at Hyde Park, rented accommodations to be near him in Boston during many of his months at Harvard, managed his social life as far as she could. Franklin's father died in 1900, during his freshman year at Harvard, and that loss had more tightly bound mother and son. Franklin rarely faltered in his expressions of devotion and almost invariably let her have her way when differences loomed, reluctant to repeat that open rebellion at Groton when he wished to visit Oyster Bay.

"Dearest Mama," he wrote home from Harvard, "last week I dined at the Quincy's, the Armory's & the Thayer's, three as high-life places as are to be found in blue-blooded, blue stockinged, bean eating Boston!," admitting that it is "dreadfully hard to be a student a society whirler a 'prominent & democratic fellow' & a fiancé all at the same time."

It was this sociable, extroverted, accommodating facade of Franklin that most struck those who knew him. He always seemed smooth, too smooth. An admirer at *The Crimson* noted his "geniality," "a kind of frictionless command." Others found him superficial, lacking in conviction, overeager to please. Young women of his caste in particular found him smug, shallow, trivial, and always self-assured; at best Franklin Delano was, they joked, a "*f*eather *d*uster," at worst a prig.

Perhaps those who called this young man superficial, however, shared some of that quality themselves. For there was another, less obvious side to Franklin. If he tended to cater to persons he met, it was his way of accumulating a wide range of information, especially in his travels abroad. If he was more a book collector than a book reader, at least it was books he was collecting rather than big-game trophies or some of the other fashionable acquisitions of the time. And if he wrote a paper at Harvard (with research help from his mother) about "The Roosevelt Family in New Amsterdam Before the Revolution," he portrayed not only a great Dutch family in all its luster but one, he insisted, that had a "very democratic spirit" and that did "its duty by the community." Indeed, if most of the old Dutch families had nothing to boast about but their superannuated names, it was because "they lack progressiveness and a true democratic spirit."

To what extent Franklin deliberately modeled his Harvard career after Cousin Theodore's we do not know; but he did appear to follow almost literally in TR's steps. Inevitably Theodore remained far more Franklin's political hero than intellectual model; the younger man could not begin to compete in the world of scholarship and ideas with his cousin, who authored dozens of historical books and articles and would even become the president of the American Historical Association. When Franklin graduated with the class of '04—he had remained an extra year, purportedly to work on a master's degree but actually to continue editing the *Crimson*—he found the commencement anticlimactic. The real excitement was thirty miles north, where Cousin Theodore was Groton's Prize Day orator. Franklin hurried up to his old school. He heard familiar words. "Much has been given you," President Roosevelt told the boys, "therefore we have the right to expect much from you."

. . .

One Roosevelt who did not find Franklin superficial was his fifth cousin Eleanor. They had known each other since childhood, when Franklin as a little boy had let baby Eleanor ride on his back during a family visit. But it was only when Eleanor returned to New York from her English finishing school and they met in the Madison Square Garden box of Franklin's half brother, James "Rosy" Roosevelt, in November 1902 that their friendship quickly blossomed.

Although they inhabited the same stratum of high society, Eleanor and Franklin could not have had more contrasting upbringings. While Franklin had been the center of his parents' world, doted on by nurses, governesses, and tutors, Eleanor had been a gangly, self-conscious child who had lost both her parents by the age of nine. Her patrician mother, Anna Hall Roosevelt, circulated in the upper reaches of high society. Judging Mrs. Astor's Patriarchs' Balls insufficiently exclusive, she helped start a more closed series of dances at Sherry's restaurant.

Lovely and sociable as she was, Anna had maintained a distance from Eleanor, emotionally disowning her only daughter for her plainness. "You have no looks," she informed the little girl, "so see to it that you have manners." Taken to Europe by her parents, she was planted at one point in a convent that she hated, "to have me out of the way," she later noted. Affectionate toward her two sons, Anna was cold and critical toward Eleanor, nicknaming her "Granny" and telling visitors, "She is such a funny child, so old-fashioned." "I was always disgracing my mother," Eleanor recalled painfully. But Anna was suffering herself, in a profoundly troubled marriage.

Eleanor's father, Elliott, warm and expressive, clearly adored his daughter. Yet he was as volatile as he was exuberant, and Eleanor often feared she disappointed him by her timidity and her sensible and serious nature. But his problems ran far deeper; he was alcoholic, addicted to morphine, suicidal, violent, lurching from mistress to mistress, even sued by a servant for paternity. Theodore, convinced that his brother Elliott was "a maniac, morally no less than mentally," insisted that he enter a mental institution for treatment. The family's desperation became a public scandal when the *New York Herald* announced, ELLIOTT ROOSEVELT DEMENTED BY EXCESSES. WRECKED BY LIQUOR AND FOLLY, HE IS NOW CONFINED IN AN ASYLUM FOR THE INSANE NEAR PARIS.

Eleanor would later write that, as a child, she "acquired a strange and garbled idea of the troubles which were going on around me. Something was wrong with my father, and from my point of view nothing could be wrong with him." While her father languished in an asylum in France, Eleanor lived with her mother and brothers in New York. Her mother suffered from severe migraines, and little Eleanor sensed that she could be of some use. Gently massaging her mother's head, reveling in this newfound intimacy, Eleanor was thrilled just to watch her self-absorbed mother dress to go out in the evenings. "I was grateful to be allowed to touch her dress or her jewels." Still, her happiest moments were spent alone, at her Aunt Bye's house, in the maid's sewing room. "No one bothered me," she sighed in relief.

Elliott returned to the United States in 1892, but his wife, depleted by the ordeal of the marriage, refused to see him. That December, she died of diphtheria, and eight-year-old Eleanor was taken in by her maternal grandmother, Mrs. Mary Ludlow Hall. Little Eleanor moved into the stately brownstone on West 37th Street, peopled by a staff of servants as well as by her grandmother, her aunts and uncles, and their friends.

Whatever sense of loss Eleanor might have felt upon her mother's death was wiped out, she confessed, by one fact: "My father was back and I would see him very soon." Living for her father's letters and infrequent visits, Eleanor was shuttled, with her brother Hall, back and forth between the Hall family's Manhattan house and their estate along the Hudson River in Tivoli, New York. Time spent with her cherished father could be as traumatic as it was rare. One day, Elliott took Eleanor for a walk with his three terriers. Passing by the Knickerbocker Club, he stopped in for a drink, instucting Eleanor to wait outside with the dogs. When he emerged staggering, six hours later, Eleanor was still standing at the door. The doorman sent her home in a cab. Occasionally she glimpsed another world when she accompanied her father to serve Thanksgiving dinner at one of the newsboys' clubhouses or when she helped her uncle decorate a Christmas tree for children in Hell's Kitchen.

Her father's condition deteriorated after the death of his wife in 1892 and the death of his four-year-old son, Elliott, in May 1893. After a period of drunken, violent upheaval, he died in August 1894. Eleanor, not yet ten, was not permitted to attend her father's funeral. A few years after his death, Eleanor wrote in a school essay that her father was "the only person in the world she loved." Years later, in 1933, she would edit and publish her beloved father's letters, *Hunting Big Game in the Eighties.*

Bereaved, lonely, and painfully shy, Eleanor found solace in books, music, nature, and a rich fantasy world. Little by little, she came to feel at home on 37th Street and at Tivoli. She would later remember happy evenings when family members played with her and her brother, but she would also recall that her grandmother said no to her requests so often that she stopped asking her if she might do anything outside the daily routine. Grandmother Hall spent most of her time in her bedroom, and her four children, daughters Pussie and Maude and sons Vallie and Eddie, lived their mostly self-absorbed, increasingly erratic, upper-crust lives, her uncles principally engaged in drinking, gambling, and socializing with the high-living Diamond Jim Brady, her aunts engaged in "elegant leisure." Still, Pussie and Maude were Eleanor's "early loves."

While her aunts and uncles, Eleanor later admitted, could scarcely have been said to have contributed to "the greater social organization we call civilization," she did nevertheless feel that the elite milieu taught her "self-discipline." "Social life was very important in my grandmother's world," Eleanor would later write, "and her social code demanded a great deal of self-discipline—particularly of women. Social obligations were sacred—no matter how you felt, the show must go on." Eleanor would credit this stern code of behavior for getting her through myriad difficult occasions later in life. Her upbringing also provided her with a powerful conscience and sense of duty. Her grandmother made it clear that the "well-born" had obligations to those less well endowed. "I remember how, as a girl of five, I was taken to wait on the tables at the Thanksgiving dinner for the Newsboys' Club," she wrote. "My grandmother made me go to the Baby's Hospital [sic] one afternoon a week to play with the sick." As a young girl, Eleanor's "chief objective" was to do her duty, she admitted, adding, "not my duty as I saw it, but my duty as laid down for me by other people."

Once a year Eleanor was invited to her aunt and uncle's home in Oyster Bay. "Eleanor, my darling Eleanor," the ebullient TR would joyfully greet her, hugging her so tightly that, his wife Edith remarked, "he tore all the gathers out of Eleanor's frock and both buttonholes out of her petticoat." For Eleanor, visits to Sagamore Hill were "a great joy"; they swam, picnicked, camped, chased through haystacks in the barn, and climbed up to the gun room on the top floor where Uncle Ted would read poetry aloud. But neither the Hall family, wary of the boisterous Roosevelts, nor the Theodore Roosevelt family, fearful that Eleanor had inherited her father's "genes" and would be a bad influence on daughter Alice, who was Eleanor's age, were truly eager to mingle, and visits to Oyster Bay were rare.

Mrs. Hall's decision to send Eleanor to England in 1899 to attend Marie Souvestre's Allenswood School transformed the fifteen-year-old girl's life. As a child, education and learning had been far less important than the "social graces which made you attractive and charming in Society," Eleanor recalled. Now, at Allenswood, a school chosen for her by one of TR's sisters, her world would widen.

The young girl found a glowing inspiration and mentor in Mlle. Souvestre, a woman she considered "intellectually emancipated." Eleanor flourished under her care. Intellect, sensitivity, kindness, and nobility of soul: these were cherished at Allenswood. Because Mlle. Souvestre loved and esteemed Eleanor, more and more the other girls did too.

Like TR in the West, Eleanor was reborn at Allenswood. "I felt I was starting a new life," she later wrote. Eleanor studied French, Italian, English, German, Latin, history, and music. The Halls, Eleanor realized, had taken "very little interest in public affairs," but at Allenswood, Eleanor soon began to engage with the world, in heated discussions of politics, social issues, and art. She learned to speak French fluently, made close friends among students and teachers alike, and traveled throughout Europe with Mlle. Souvestre, gaining a new self-assurance. "Though I lost some of my self-confidence and ability to look after myself in the early days of my marriage," she later commented, "when it was needed again, later on, it came back to me more easily because of these trips with Mlle. Souvestre."

In the late spring of 1902, Eleanor left Allenswood for good: at eighteen, it was time, her grandmother insisted, for a young woman to "come out" in society, and "not to 'come out' was unthinkable." Eleanor was heartbroken to leave her studies and her dear teacher, who warned her not to get "carried away in a whirl of exciting social activities," urging her to defend herself against all the "temptations" of the frivolous upper-caste life. As long as she lived, Eleanor would cherish those letters, always keeping Marie Souvestre's portrait on her desk.

She returned to New York a poised, accomplished, and self-assured young woman. Her debut, for which she wore a becoming Paris gown, subjected her to "utter agony." She found the social whirl of the city—dances, cotillions, theater parties—intimidating and irrelevant, but it nevertheless sucked her in. "Haunted" by her upper-class upbringing, she admitted believing that "what was known as New York Society was really important."

Yet, that winter, with like-minded friends in the Junior League—"just a group of girls anxious to do something helpful in the city in which we lived"—she found stimulating volunteer work teaching children on the Lower East Side and investigating sweatshops and women's working conditions for the Consumers' League. Taking the elevated railroad downtown, she walked across the Bowery to the Rivington Street Settlement House, along streets she described as "filled with foreign-looking people, crowded and dirty." Though the "foreign-looking people" and filthy streets filled her with "terror," she learned not to fear contact with poverty. One day, one of her little pupils invited her to come home with her. "Needless to say," she remarked, "I did not go." Eleanor, after all, was still a debutante, the niece of the president of the United States.

Occasionally Franklin would come down to the settlement to escort Eleanor home. Was he her "feller"? the little girls asked, but Eleanor did not know what the word meant. One day, Franklin arrived at Rivington Street only to find that one of the little girls was ill and needed to be taken home. He and Eleanor carried the child through the noisy streets and up the grimy, smelly, unlit stairs to her parents' tenement apartment. "My God," an astonished Franklin blurted out after the experience, "I didn't know anyone lived like that."

In New York City high society, she later observed, "you were kind to the poor, you did not neglect your philanthropic duties." One accepted invitations to dine and to dance "with the right people only" and arranged one's life to live in their midst. "In short, you conformed to the conventional pattern." Oddly, that conventional pattern, of charitable works and settlement houses, enabled some of the ladies of Eleanor's social class not only to become social activists but even—as in the cases of Eleanor, Frances Perkins, and others—to enter the political arena.

The friendship between Franklin and Eleanor might have surprised some of their friends. The two seemed like polar opposites: he, the urbane, self-assured, handsome Harvard student and man about town; she, the shy, serious, plain young woman. Yet amid their differences each recognized an important complementary quality in the other. Franklin could make her feel lighthearted—something she had hardly known since her father's death. His presence was like a fresh current stirring the depths of her loneliness. She in turn aroused his deeper, more thoughtful self.

"Eleanor has a very good mind," he told his mother. They talked for hours, read poetry aloud, spent New Year's at the White House together. "Sat near Eleanor," Franklin penned in his diary. "Very interesting day."

Her name appeared with increasing frequency in his diary and letters, and finally he proposed during a visit to see her younger brother Hall at Groton. The following week the couple apprehensively told Franklin's mother of their plans. Sara, her own intimacy with her son threatened, persuaded them to wait a year before announcing their engagement, in order to make sure they had made the right decision. They reluctantly agreed.

During the following year, between Thanksgiving of 1903 and that of 1904, the couple was supposed to observe the strictest propriety. Until their engagement was announced, they were to go nowhere unattended by a chaperone. Trailed by a maid, Eleanor would travel to Cambridge for football weekends; in New York their time would be spent attending plays, luncheons, church, and other public affairs. Yet they found ways of slipping away. And Franklin increasingly came to see Eleanor in New York instead of his mother in Hyde Park.

Eleanor's biggest worry was the gracious but imperious mother. Franklin, after all, was the sun around whom Sara's world revolved. Eleanor learned to show remarkable tact and sensitivity toward her mother-in-law. Always highly attuned to people in need, she knew what it was to feel abandoned; she diligently strove to include Sara. After all, she herself wanted, if not a mother, then stability and security.

When the couple finally announced their engagement just after Thanksgiving, 1904, excited congratulatory messages streamed in from friends and family, among them a letter to each from Eleanor's Uncle Theodore.

"No other success in life," he wrote Franklin, "not the Presidency, or anything else—begins to compare with the joy and happiness that come in and from the love of the true man and the true woman, the love which never sinks lover and sweethearts in man and wife. You and Eleanor are true and brave, and I believe you love each other unselfishly; and golden years open before you. May all good fortune attend you both, ever."

Marrying into the president's family did not make TR any less of a hero—rather the opposite. "Everyone is talking about Cousin Theodore, saying that he is the most prominent figure of present-day history," Franklin wrote to his mother while on his European honeymoon. More and more, Cousin Theodore was Franklin's model. On occasion Franklin saw the president close up, in Washington or nearer home, but TR always loomed on the horizon, symbolizing moral leadership, political energy, Rooseveltian vigor. More than anyone else he helped Franklin to shape his own identity, sharpen his own ambition, point him toward a future of some kind of public service. For Franklin, Cousin Theodore had been more than a model. He had become his absentee mentor.

Franklin's hero worship made it all the more distressing to sense that the Oyster Bay Roosevelts held him in hardly veiled contempt. They joked about his overeagerness in games, his tall skinny frame, and—always—his superficiality. Much of this Franklin could ignore, or pretend to. But sometimes he could not, especially on the occasion when the president attended the wedding of his beloved daughter Alice, offspring of his first marriage to Alice Lee. After the wedding breakfast was served in the White House state dining room, the president slipped away with his new son-in-law, Nicholas Longworth, into a private dining room, followed by a small procession of exuberant men.

Franklin, standing aside, knew what was happening; Porcellians, whenever they congregated at a brother's wedding, met separately to toast the groom. Through the door Franklin could hear the merrymakers exchanging toasts and singing club songs. Once again he was left outside—a reminder of the most painful disappointment of his life.

3
Power with a Purpose

Those who expected the president to settle down and coast during his elective—and "last"—term underestimated the power of TR's ideas once harnessed to his moral imperatives. Buttressed by his big victory, buoyed by the strong winds of reform—middle-class Americans supporting reform governors, organized labor demanding improvements in working conditions, people all over clamoring for change—in his second term he veered tempestuously to the left. The Old Guard of his party was worried. "There is a craze on now," one Republican warned, "not at all unlike what preceded the Alliance and Populist movements." But opposition to TR from conservatives in his party only stimulated him.

During 1905 and 1906 he used all his powers of negotiation, compromise, threat, and maneuver to push railroad regulation through Congress. Railroads in the United States, all in private hands, now stretched to over 170,000 miles and were virtually the sole means of transport for all agricultural and industrial products. While farmers, small shippers, and professional men—as well as the muckrakers—were decrying abuses of the railroads and calling for regulation of rates, militant farmers were demanding government ownership of the rails.

"There must be lodged in some tribunal the power over rates," TR insisted. Viewing the issue once again in terms of economic justice, he declared, "We do not intend that this Republic shall ever fail as those republics of olden times failed, in which there finally came to be a government by classes, which resulted either in the poor plundering the rich or in the rich ... exploiting the poor." Republicans and Democrats finally rallied to the bill, which passed in the Senate with only three negative votes in 1906, testimony to TR's leadership skills. The Hepburn Act, reinforcing the Interstate Commerce Act, vested in the Interstate Commerce Commission (ICC) the authority to set "just and reasonable" railroad rates, among other reforms. The act broadened the commission's jurisdiction to cover sleeping-car and express companies, oil pipelines, ferries, and bridges. TR left the conservatives furious over this intrusion into private property, yet reformers were disappointed because the ICC could not initiate rate-making processes and its decisions could be challenged in the courts.

. . .

In 1905 and 1906, at the high point of the muckrakers' exposés of the nationwide "process" of corruption, a powerful issue exploded in the public consciousness: meat.

The revolting conditions in the slaughterhouses and meatpacking plants in Packington, outside of Chicago, suddenly came to light. Everyone—from housewives to journalists to the president of the United States—was repelled and outraged. "There was never the least attention paid to what was cut up for sausage," Upton Sinclair wrote in *The Jungle,* his incendiary novel about the meatpacking industry. "There were things that went into the sausage in comparison with which a poisoned rat was a tidbit."

Interestingly, Sinclair had not written *The Jungle* to frighten people about meat but rather to expose the brutalizing working conditions of thousands of men and women, many of whom were immigrants, exploited and living in abjection. In winter, when the slaughtered animals' blood would freeze, the workers would tie up their feet in newspapers and old sacks, which would become soaked in blood and frozen too. In summer, the factory was transformed into a purgatory, "the air motionless, the stench enough to knock a man over." Among the meatcutters there was scarcely a person who had the use of his thumb; "it was a mere lump of flesh." In the pickling division, the acid had eaten workers' fingers off. And to make matters worse, these crushed workers, eager for their pitiful pay, were often cheated out of their wages. When they dared to join a union, they were fired. *The Jungle* was essentially a socialist book and a union book, and Sinclair's message to workers was "Organize! Organize! Organize!"

But it was rotten meat, not rotten work, that galvanized American citizens, alarmed to have discovered that spoiled, adulterated meat had made its way to their kitchens and dining rooms. Sinclair's accusations were taken seriously and viewed in the context of the abuses of big business. Indeed, many of the individual butcher shops of time gone by had been replaced by mass-produced meat products from the packinghouses. Rotten meat seemed to be another symptom of big business and the profit motive gone amok.

Though President Roosevelt was preoccupied with the Hepburn bill and railroad rates, he fired off an order to his secretary of agriculture. "I would like a first-class man to be appointed to meet Sinclair," he commanded. "We cannot afford to have anything perfunctory done in this matter." TR appointed a commission to conduct an investigation, naming known reformers to the panel. One of them, James Reynolds, described the facts he had uncovered as indeed "hideous." The report was devastating, although TR released only the less inflammatory parts that described decaying meats, stinking offal and entrails, filthy floors, tubercular workers, and bits of garbage incorporated into the food products. In his message to Congress, TR branded the conditions in the Chicago stockyards "revolting," demanding that conditions be improved "in the interest of health and of decency" and that government inspectors supervise all stages in the production of meat.

But the packers were opposed to stricter regulations, and their friends in Congress fought to dilute legislation. The *New York Evening Post* editorialized with a poem:

Mary had a little lamb
And when she saw it sicken,
She shipped it off to Packingtown,
And now it's labeled chicken.

Only when the sale of meat products declined by 50 percent did the packers decide to accept government inspection. Still, the final legislation, the Pure Food and Drug Act and the Meat Inspection Bill of June 1906, represented a compromise measure, for there was great resistance to TR's forceful leadership. "It is better that Congress pass a bad law as the result of its own free and independent deliberation than enact a good law at the dictation of the Executive," judged the *Washington Post,* applauding the idea of a weak executive branch.

But TR prevailed. The Pure Food and Drug Act addressed more than meat. Coal tars, alum, acids, sulfites, and other chemicals were common adulterants in a variety of foods, from coffee to milk and butter. Medicines—from Lydia Pinkham's Vegetable Compound and Dr. Kline's Great Nerve Restorer to Mrs. Winslow's Soothing Syrup—contained opium (laudanum), morphine, cocaine, and always alcohol. TR had won. His administration had made a pivotal breakthrough in improving public health, in protecting consumers, and in regulating big business and interstate commerce, as well as in asserting executive leadership. A sea change had taken place. *The World's Week,* gratified that "a stimulating breeze was blowing over the national government," congratulated the president.

. . .

Indeed, for the Old Guard, much worse was soon to come. In 1907, TR urged the legislature to ban the use of court injunctions that gave unfair advantage to employers in labor disputes. He asked also for a workmen's compensation law for federal employees, with the suggestion that the same broad principle could be made to apply to employees of private corporations; and he twice, in 1906 and again in 1908, demanded an Employers' Liability Law, binding employers, including the federal government itself, to compensate workers injured in the course of interstate commerce. It was a "gross injustice" for helpless workers, victims of industrial accidents, to have no recourse. Ultimately this legislation led to workmen's compensation systems in many states. And he kept up his big-stick talk— if not big-stick action—against the trusts.

But even more traumatic for the Old Guard was TR's message to the 60th Congress on December 3, 1907, in which he repeated his 1906 calls for the two bills that his own caste most feared: federal income and inheritance taxes. His demand for an inheritance tax stood at the heart of his concept of citizenship and community.

One of TR's most knowledgeable biographers, William Harbaugh, criticized TR for his "rudimentary" knowledge of economics and for construing the inheritance tax as a vehicle for his "moralistic urge to strike at the malefactors of great wealth." But this was precisely TR's agenda.

The New York patrician, who had decided to use the fortune he inherited from his father to lead a life of public service rather than a life of leisure, felt nothing but contempt for his own class. Wealth, he declared in May 1907, should only be "the foundation on which to build the real life, the life of spiritual and moral effort and achievement." TR always remained convinced that the transmission of enormous wealth to young men "does not do them any real service and is of great and genuine detriment to the community at large." "I would not apply the Inheritance Tax to small inheritances," he explained, "but I would apply it progressively and with such heaviness to big inheritances as to completely block the transmission of enormous fortunes to the young Rockefellers, Vanderbilts, Astors, and Morgans."

Scorning inherited wealth and leisure-class society, TR was prescribing a formula for robust citizenship and a new nationalism based on a sense of moral purpose. "If ever our people become so sordid as to feel that all that counts is moneyed prosperity, ignoble well-being, effortless ease and comfort," he warned, "then this nation shall perish, as it will deserve to perish, from the earth." TR wanted citizens to believe in national ideals that were "worth sacrifice" and to be "splendidly eager" to do volunteer work and perform acts of public service. He even went so far as to advocate two years of obligatory hard manual industrial service for all men. TR's friend Herbert Croly agreed, writing in his book *The Promise of American Life* that the American credo of unbridled, chaotic individualism needed to be subordinated to a constructive national purpose. What really mattered was to have a national community based on citizens' political equality, relative economic equality, and interdependence.

TR sought to redefine virtue and especially to subvert the accepted equation of virtue and wealth, the assimilation of the successful businessman with *the* good citizen. Virtue and wealth were, he believed, as antithetical as money and spirituality. Indeed, the words IN GOD WE TRUST on American coins revolted Roosevelt, irate at the sacriligious cheapening of religious sentiment and the cynical attempt to elevate money to the level of the transcendent. But his arguments failed to convince Congress, which decided to make the contested slogan mandatory on American coins.

TR's tax proposals met with no immediate success. The Sixteenth Amendment, giving Congress the power to lay and collect taxes on incomes, was not ratified by the states until 1913, and it was only in 1916 that an inheritance tax was passed. But in hammering out his message in moralistic, sermonizing speech after speech, TR began to change people's perceptions of their society and provoked a national debate on the issue of inherited wealth and power in an egalitarian democracy, creating a climate in which reform would eventually become possible. TR fully realized that it might take decades before the country was ready for his radical proposals, for what he called his "campaign against privilege." "I well know that it must be a slow process of education through generations," he admitted to a friend. He considered himself the leader of "an ethical movement" that would take years before "it sinks deep into the heart and the conscience of the whole people."

In 1935, another patrician, Franklin Roosevelt, would take up the same crusade, striking out at great fortunes for moral and democratic reasons. "The transmission from generation to generation of vast fortunes by will, inheritance, or gift," declared FDR, "is not consistent with the ideals and sentiments of the American people," adding that "inherited economic power is as inconsistent with the ideals of this generation as inherited political power was inconsistent with the ideals of the generation which established our government."

TR was more aggressively personal than FDR would be in this crusade, openly attacking "wealthy men of enormous power, some of whom have shown themselves cynically and brutally indifferent to the interests of the people." Promising to "cut out rottenness from the body politic," he announced that his mission was to prevent "those rich men whose lives are corrupt and evil" from dominating the "destinies of this country."

Theodore Roosevelt liked to separate his business foes into good capitalists and bad capitalists. One man above all personified the latter, John D. Rockefeller. For one thing, he was not a "gentleman" of old family wealth, eastern high society, or college education. Even more, Rockefeller's Standard Oil, with its control of railroads, pipelines, and ships, was the biggest and strongest trust of them all. When TR suspected that Rockefeller and company were "buying" senators and congressmen, he ordered the return of campaign contributions made by the company.

Morgan, on the other hand, was a gentleman, whatever his financial manipulations. When the country experienced a deep economic slump in 1907, Morgan came to the administration's assistance, as a gentleman should. The Panic of 1907 began when the Knickerbocker Trust Company, in the heart of the New York financial district, was forced to close, unable to pay its frantic depositors. The stock market plummeted and other banks closed, the Westinghouse Company went into receivership, the Stock Exchange in Pittsburgh stopped trading, and the Trust Company of America came close to folding.

The House of Morgan made huge private deposits that helped rally the market and avert further panic. Newspaper headlines shouted that Morgan had single-handedly saved the nation's economy. In comparison, TR had been almost powerless to act, though he knew he would be "certainly held responsible" for the financial panic. Indeed, he could only publicly laud "those conservative and substantial businessmen" who had acted so wisely and responsibly as compared with those guilty of "dishonest dealing."

Still, Morgan wanted something in return: the merger of his United States Steel Corporation with the Tennessee Coal and Iron Company— if the president approved the purchase. TR accepted the buyout but at the cost of compromising antitrust regulation—and of making himself vulnerable to future accusations of collusion with big steel. Even more important for the future, as historian William Harbaugh points out, the Panic of 1907 sparked new banking legislation and ultimately the Federal Reserve Act of 1913. But in 1907, the health of the economy and the success of TR's presidency seemed to hinge on the vast economic resources of the gentleman financier, J. P. Morgan. TR's power to deal with a major economic crisis was limited, and he knew it. "The trouble is," he wrote, "that the minute I try to get action, all the financiers and businessmen differ so that nobody can advise me; nobody can give me any aid."

. . .

But while TR could maintain a relationship of mutual dependency with the patrician Morgan, virtually all conservative Republicans were as upset by the president's words attacking big business as by his actions. They clearly sensed that attitudes toward the privileges of the wealthy were changing. They had supported TR in his presidential campaign of 1904, making huge contributions to the war chest of the man who had confessed that he found it "far more satisfactory to work" with the conservative leaders of Congress like Nelson Aldrich of Rhode Island and Mark Hanna than with radical "reformers" like Littlefield. They had been lulled into complacency, into believing, along with Elihu Root, that TR was in reality "a great conservator of property and rights." Root himself was convinced that the purpose of TR's reforms was not social justice but rather social stability—so that the elite could enjoy their wealth and privileges in safety. "Never forget," Root had told the Wall Street titans at TR's behest, that "the continued opportunity for enterprise, for the enjoyment of wealth, for individual liberty, is possible only so long as the men who labor with their hands believe in American liberty and American laws." But now Republican party unity was fractured.

Already during his first presidential term, TR had voiced strong objections to men of great wealth. "I do not see very much of the big-moneyed men in New York," he acknowledged in 1900. "To spend the day with them at Newport, or on one of their yachts, or even to dine with them . . . fills me with frank horror." Such feelings, he realized, were entirely mutual. "I have not a doubt that they would mortally object to associating with me— but they could not possibly object one hundredth part as much as I should to associating with them."

One man was more blunt. "We bought the son of a bitch," railed the industrialist Henry Clay Frick, a large contributor to TR's presidential campaign of 1904, "and then he did not stay bought." TR was unmoved. He was no longer cowed by the specter of class warfare. "Our whole effort," he told Congress, "is to insist upon conduct, and neither wealth nor property nor any other class distinction, as being the proper standard by which to judge the actions of men." He attacked the plutocrats because he became convinced that the "worst revolutionaries," those who were propelling the country toward just such class warfare, were the reactionary businessmen who opposed basic forms of industrial justice.

In the world of the elite clubs and salons he used to frequent, TR had become persona non grata. His former friends now looked on him, he admitted, "as a violent and extreme radical." He had even appointed Oscar Straus as his secretary of commerce and labor in 1906, the first Jew to serve in a cabinet post, another affront to the anti-Semitic leisure class. While the old patrician Mugwumps and even many of the progressives took a dim view of the waves of new immigrants arriving in America, TR felt differently. "I grow extremely indignant," he wrote, "at the attitude of coarse hostility to the immigrant." Immigrants who agreed to become Americanized could "stand on exactly the same plane as the descendants of any Puritan, Cavalier, or Knickerbocker among us."

Two decades later, TR was still considered, at least according to one scholar, "a traitor to his caste" and a man who "should have been on the side of capital."

But in one domain, TR as president had remained loyal to the agenda of the Mugwumps of the 1880s. They had proposed a nonpolitical administration to manage municipal affairs. A board of finance would have governed New York, had they had their way. Similarly, TR had created a new administration of bureaucrats and specialists, experts in economics, social welfare, forestry, food, and drugs. Clean government and efficiency—the Mugwump goals—always remained among his top priorities. And he was still ambivalent about big labor. "It is very gratifying to have ridden iron-shod over Gompers and the labor agitators," TR gloated, after Republicans—despite losing twenty-eight seats in the House—held their majority in the 1906 midterm elections.

. . .

TR did not limit his attacks to men of wealth and power. The chief executive also attacked the other two branches of government, which often represented them, thus challenging in effect the sacred "checks and balances" that Harvard professors had taught Theodore to respect as constitutional holy writ. Even though Congress had finally come through in 1906 with laws he and other reformers had demanded, the president became more and more indignant over conservative influence on Capitol Hill. By the end of his term he was engaged in open warfare with the House czar, Speaker "Uncle Joe" Cannon, and he so infuriated Congress on a relatively minor matter of Secret Service investigation that each house in turn voted to eject his message at the door.

"Oh, if I could only be President and Congress too for just ten minutes!" TR bellowed in frustration, overheard by the visiting Franklin Roosevelt.

As for the most sacred of all the checks and balances, the judicial veto of congressional acts, TR did not genuflect before this altar either. He did not conceal his displeasure when the Supreme Court invalidated the Employers' Liability Act of 1906 and took other "anti-Administration" actions. Once again he clothed his criticism in the broadest moral terms; the Constitution should be interpreted, he said, "not as a straitjacket" but "as an instrument designed for the life and healthy growth of the nation."

But he used his moral absolutes as attack weapons by stigmatizing individuals. Having appointed his old Harvard friend Oliver Wendell Holmes Jr. to the Supreme Court, and having been reassured by Lodge that Holmes was "in entire sympathy with your views and mine," he could not refrain from criticizing the Bostonian when the new justice dissented from the administration's trust-busting. Typically, he overreacted, reportedly saying he "could carve out of a banana a judge with more backbone than that."

This was the famous "bully pulpit" in action—and not always "bully" in tone or intent. But the president did much more than talk; he built the White House into a powerhouse that could face down legislators, judges, businessmen, and reporters. Only such a powerhouse, he believed, could deal with the huge corporations, which he wanted to control rather than break down into smaller units through "trust-busting." He used all the arts of bargaining, rewarding, punishing, conniving, co-opting, persuading, threatening, manipulating, and cooperating, always expertly combining little carrots with the big stick. And he did all these in his usual style—with vigor, flamboyance, and passion. "While President I have *been* President, emphatically," wrote TR. "I have used every ounce of power there was in the office and I have not cared a rap for the criticism of those who spoke of my 'usurpation of power'; for I knew that the talk was all nonsense and that there was no usurpation." He had come a long way from the vice-presidential candidate in 1900 who had jeered at Democrats: "They have raved against trusts, they have foamed at the mouth, prating of impossible remedies they would like to adopt."

. . .

Were TR's crusades—his attacks on trusts and on wealth, his support for strengthening the attorney general's authority to prosecute trust cases under the Sherman Act, his call for tight regulation of securities, his regulation of the railroads, his creation of the Department of Commerce and Labor, his support for the Workmen's Compensation Act, his proposals for an eight-hour workday, his Pure Food and Drug Act, his Meat Inspection Act, his executive order broadening the pension base for veterans, his struggle against checks and balances, his rage at judges who acted on behalf of the "criminal rich"—were these part of his quest to empower the government to act on behalf of a democratic community? Or were they, as historian Richard Hofstadter suggested, so many "public-relations" ploys, a "charade," nothing more than conciliatory gestures to assuage public demands for reform and defuse class antagonisms?

For Hofstadter, Roosevelt was almost a schizophrenic politician, "the type of Progressive leader whose real impulses were deeply conservative, and who might not perhaps have been a Progressive at all if it were not for the necessity of fending off more radical threats to established ways of doing things." For historian Daniel Aaron, TR was nothing but a patrician "pseudo-progressive."

TR indeed gave mixed signals. In a speech in 1906, he seemed suddenly and inexplicably to turn on his journalistic reform friends and foes by branding them "muckrakers," "wild preachers," and "wild agitators" whose eyes were fixed only on what is "vile and debasing" in American society. A typical muckraker, TR went on, "becomes not a help to society, not an incitement to good, but one of the most potent forces for evil." Why? Because in hearing continuous, sweeping condemnations of society, citizens only become cynical and indifferent.

But a few seconds later, TR made a complete about-face. Though the hysterical excitement produced by the muckrakers was evil, he explained, "a sodden acquiescence in evil is even worse." Was he now approving the muckrakers' work? "So far as this movement of agitation throughout the country takes the form of a fierce discontent with evil, of a determination to punish the authors of evil, whether in industry or politics," he judged, "the feeling is to be heartily welcomed as a sign of healthy life." His speech ended with radical proposals demanding a progressive tax on all fortunes, government supervision over corporations engaged in interstate business, and government control over corporate wealth. Had TR meant to attack the muckrakers or only to demand from them responsible solutions equal to the enormousness of the corruption they had exposed? This was the same position he had taken in 1900, when he denounced socialists who raved against the existing order without lifting a hand "to make our social life a little better," and the position he had taken in 1894 when he wrote that people interested in politics should remember that they "must act, and not merely criticize the actions of others."

Who was the real TR? What did he have in mind when he entitled one of his essays "The Radical Movement Under Conservative Direction"?

Just four weeks before he made his famous muckraker speech, he had invited Upton Sinclair to Washington. In his letter to Sinclair, TR made two different points. On the one hand, he wrote that every individual must find within his heart and head the intelligence and character to "raise himself to a position where he [has] steady work and where he could save and lead a self-respecting life." But, on the other hand, he wrote that "in the long run radical action must be taken to do away with the effects of arrogant and selfish greed on the part of the capitalist."

Individualism and the old Mugwump cult of "character" or government intervention and regulation? Four days after giving his speech about the muckrakers, TR attempted to clarify his position. "I am no more to be frightened out of a sane and courageous radicalism by the creatures who yell that it is socialism," he wrote to his friend Jacob Riis, "than to be frightened out of a proper conservatism by the equally senseless yell that it represents reaction."

TR was distinguishing between means and ends, between strategy and goals. He was convinced that his great political and moral hero, Lincoln, was "a great radical" but he understood that Lincoln had to be "a wise and cautious radical—otherwise he could have done nothing for the forward movement." In other words, Lincoln's radicalism became "efficient" because of the kind of moderate leadership he provided. He practiced "a constructive, and not merely a destructive, radicalism." Similarly, TR aspired to be cautious in his strategy, daring in his goals; conservative in his means, radical in his ends. "I too am a dreamer of dreams," TR wrote a few years later. "I hold the man worthless who is not a dreamer, who does not see visions; but I also hold him worthless unless in practical fashion he endeavors to shape his actions so that these dreams and visions can be partially realized."

Had Lincoln been alive during TR's times, TR was sure that he would have "furnished a wisely conservative leadership; but he would have led in the radical direction." In 1912, George Roosevelt remarked to his uncle TR that while TR had earlier been the progressive leader of the conservatives, he had become the conservative leader of the Progressives. "Yes, that's it," concurred TR. "I have to hold them in check all the time. I have to restrain them."

Unlike conservative politicians, TR was "temperamentally disposed to act," in the words of William Harbaugh. Scorning the "well-meaning men" who had permitted themselves to "fossilize" no less than the young muckrakers who offered no effective solutions to the problems they uncovered, TR wanted "results." Intellectually engaged in the issues of the day, morally indignant at social and economic injustice, he was energized by the idea of change.

Passion, not compassion, fueled his commitment to justice and change. Anger and outrage—certainly not a penchant for "sharing people's pain"—fired him to act. He conceived of social justice in rational and practical, not emotional, terms.

TR loved wielding power to create change—more power than the system of checks and balances allowed. "I don't think that any harm comes from the concentration of power in one man's hands," he observed, "provided that the holder does not keep it for more than a certain, definite time, and then returns to the people from whom he sprang." Adamant about the need for a powerful presidency, TR disputed the view that the president could not act "unless he could find some specific authorization" to do so.

As for the muckrakers he criticized, Roosevelt himself would join their ranks in 1913, publishing "Sarah Knisley's Arm" in *Collier's* and detailing, through words and drawings, the hideous crushing of a woman's hand in the cogwheels of a machine in a hardware factory. TR was carrying on the crusade for safety standards in the workplace.

Continually seeking to make the political arena more inclusive and more representative of American diversity, TR ultimately advanced the interests of the most modern and progressive of the reformers, creating a climate, as Hofstadter himself conceded, that made meaningful reform legislation possible, a climate that itself constituted one of the resources on which American democracy has continued to draw.

TR also exerted a powerful personal influence on his followers. His "attachment to the principles of social justice has never been sufficiently developed by his biographers," judged Frances Perkins. Perkins, whom FDR would later appoint secretary of labor, belonged to a generation inspired to public service by TR. She recalled that TR had recommended that people read Riis's *How the Other Half Lives,* and that after having read it and also TR's inaugural address of 1905, her life was changed. She had "straitaway felt that the pursuit of social justice" would be her vocation.

A principled, feisty president using the bully pulpit to shape a national agenda for change; a bureaucracy of experts and specialists; a government mobilized to intervene on behalf of citizens, defending their interests, securing for them new rights, recognizing new claims—all these were the makings of the modern presidency that Theodore Roosevelt bequeathed to his country.

. . .

For TR, power had a purpose but, as purpose broadened, TR could sense power slipping away toward the end of his elective term. Early in 1908, he revealed a sense of desperation and frustration that overflowed in three scathing messages he sent to Congress on the same day, January 31, 1908. In the first message, he demanded that the Employers' Liability Law, passed in 1906 but declared unconstitutional by the Supreme Court, be passed again. In his second message of the day, he attacked the use of court injunctions to prevent peaceable action by labor organizations and then denounced the cynicism of "men of property" who either defend abuses committed by capital or pander to popular feeling, depending on where they perceive their interests to lie. But TR was just building up steam.

In his third message, he demanded sweeping powers for the ICC so that it could "pass on any rate or practice on its own initiative," he called for the federal government to assume a "certain measure of control over the physical operation of railways," and he urged legislation to give the government "effective and thoroughgoing supervision" over all the operations of big interstate business concerns. The three measures, he explained, were part of the "campaign against privilege," his crusade to make great property holders realize that they have "duties no less than rights." Here was his real target: the plutocrats, the elite, his "own kind."

He bitterly struck out at the "representatives of predatory wealth —of the wealth accumulated on a giant scale by all forms of iniquity" ranging from oppressing wage workers to crushing the competition to defrauding the public. The only way to counteract their "hideous" behavior and attempts to "overthrow and discredit" the honest people who administer the law was to make their corrupt practices clear to the public. There had to be, he insisted, control over "law-defying wealth" and over the men who were "cynically and brutally indifferent to the interests of the people." Indeed, the "extraordinary violence" of the plutocrats' attacks on him, made by their highly paid hired guns, TR contended, gave "a fairly accurate measure of the anger and terror which our public actions have caused the corrupt men of vast wealth to feel in the very marrow of their being." He blamed the previous year's financial panic on speculators, and he named names, including the heads of Standard Oil. Then he launched more missiles, against rich land thieves, rich contractors, Chicago bankers, corporation lawyers, and corrupt editors, finally attacking the "most baneful" of all alliances, that between corrupt politicians and corrupt businessmen. The torrential words came pouring out, now with a religious twist. He called for the "moral regeneration" of the business world, reminding people that the "Federal Government does scourge sin."

Was this moral crusade against wealth the ploy of a fundamentally conservative leader aiming to take the wind out of the sails of the left? Hardly. The fury, indignation, passion, frustration, and righteousness were genuine. Not for another quarter century would a president—another Roosevelt—speak out in such scathing terms.

. . .

Critics saw TR's outbursts not so much as the natural reaction of a leader who felt hopelessly frustrated by business, Congress, conservative state governors, and the Old Guard but rather as the kind of power madness that the framers had feared in setting up the executive under the Constitution. Some of TR's aberrations, to be sure, appeared more quixotic than dangerous. He campaigned for simplified spelling and even ordered the government printer to use "nite" and "thoro" until the House of Representatives said no to the printer. Interestingly, what TR admired in language was simplicity and grammaticality: anything else was fatuous and, far worse, "underbred."

But TR's eccentricity and impulsiveness could also take an ugly turn. A gang of black soldiers quartered near Brownsville, Texas, went on a wild midnight raid in which a white bartender was killed. When no one in the black regiment would confess or talk, the commander in chief ordered the whole complement "discharged without honor" and "forever barred from enlistment." This punishment of 160 black men, including six Medal of Honor winners, without a trial left a stain on the man who not only had had Booker Washington to dinner but had appointed qualified blacks to federal positions, over white opposition, and who had condemned "Lily White" movements in Alabama and South Carolina. All that was forgotten in the uproar over Brownsville. Although Brownsville for TR was not about race but rather about military conduct and discipline, many never forgave him.

In foreign-policy making Roosevelt appeared to be increasingly ambivalent if not schizophrenic during his elective term. On the one hand, he never put down the "big stick," at least in dealing with Latin Americans, but this jingoist became so much of a conciliator that he won the Nobel Peace Prize—the first American to be so honored—something his earlier critics would have found incomprehensible. They continued to see TR's Panama Canal project as sheer highway robbery, but he looked back on it as an act of courage. Later he immensely enjoyed visiting the canal in construction; while his white suit wilted he climbed aboard a huge steam shovel, dug a bit on his own, and asked about everything: equipment, engineers' salaries, the crews' kitchens.

But if one strand of Rooseveltian power diplomacy was made up of force and conflict, a contrasting strand was conciliatory. He was the moving force behind the Hague Conference of 1907, which outlawed the use of military force to collect foreign debts and tried to restrict uncivilized conduct in war. Watching the emergence of Roosevelt as a "diplomatist of high rank," the London *Morning Post* expressed surprise. He had displayed great tact, foresight, and finesse. "Alone" he had met every situation, and "shaped events to suit his purpose," showing "remarkable patience, caution, and moderation." Actually TR rarely governed alone, since he worked with the gifted and experienced John Hay; Hay died in 1905 and was succeeded by TR's trusted adviser and secretary of war, Elihu Root.

Roosevelt's crowning achievement as peacemaker was his mediation between Russia and Japan. It was another accident of timing, because the long-festering conflict between the two rivals over Manchuria and Korea erupted in war during TR's presidency. And he was hardly impartial between the two powers; he viewed the Russians as both incompetent and arrogant, while several Japanese diplomats in Washington had become so close to the White House that they were virtually members of his informal "kitchen cabinet." On the other hand, Japan's crushing defeat of the Russian naval force at Port Arthur and its other military successes had put TR on guard as to whether the Japanese might go on to menace Britain and even the United States in their possible design for more victories.

With both vigor and finesse the president sounded out St. Petersburg and Tokyo, meanwhile bringing London, Berlin, and Paris into the negotiations as needed. When convinced he would receive a favorable response, he formally invited Japan and Russia together for direct negotiations. The president designated the Portsmouth, New Hampshire, naval base as the conference site, thus dissipating any fears that he might choose Oyster Bay. He did not attend the Portsmouth meetings in August 1905, but from Sagamore Hill the president followed every nuance of the discussions and also met with both sides in Oyster Bay throughout the talks. Negotiations soon became deadlocked when the Russians refused to concede defeat or pay an indemnity, while the Japanese would give up none of their military gains. The Japanese "ask too much," TR fumed to his son Kermit, while the Russians were "stupid" and untruthful. "When I feel gloomy about democracy," he wrote to an English friend, "I am positively refreshed by considering the monstrous ineptitude" of Russian "absolutism."

At a critical point the president invited first the Japanese and then the Russians to Oyster Bay for private talks. From the Japanese he secured compromises on two of the four points still at issue. He then offered the Russians a change of wording that put a better face on their concessions.

Among the compromises was cutting the Russian island Sakhalin in half, ceding the southern part to Tokyo. The Treaty of Peace followed in September 1905, and he was awarded the Nobel Peace Prize in 1906.

There were smaller international interventions too, equally laudable if unsuccessful. In 1903 and 1906, TR had protested against Jewish pogroms in Russia. And in 1902, Secretary of State John Hay sent an official protest to Romania, condemning "the treatment to which the Jews of Romania are subjected," branding the actions of the Romanian government "repugnant to the moral sense of liberal modern peoples."

. . .

But the American landscape and its wildlife were always dearer to Theodore's heart than foreign lands. At the very outset of his administration, he had proclaimed that the conservation of water and forest resources was a vital national priority, halting the policy of private indiscriminate mining on government lands and the selling off of government land to private individuals. He then began educating the country about the need to develop resources in a planned manner. Almost 150 million acres were set aside as national forest lands, and more than 80 million acres of mineral lands and a million and a half acres of waterpower sites were withdrawn from public sale.

He created five national parks: Crater Lake in Oregon, Platt National Park in Oklahoma, Wind Cave in South Dakota, Sully Hill in North Dakota, and Mesa Verde in Colorado. Under the National Monuments Act, passed in 1906, eighteen national monuments were established, including Muir Woods in California and Mount Olympus in Washington. Four game preserves, including the National Bison Range in Montana, were set up. He convened the Inland Waterways Commission for the study of transportation routes as well as waterpower and flood control; fought for irrigation projects, dams, experimental tree-planting projects, and federal bird reserves; revitalized the Forest Service; held a White House conservation conference attended by thirty-four governors and other notables; and established the National Conservation Commission. All these steps aroused controversy.

It was TR's love of the outdoors and especially of hunting and killing animals, and the influence of his uncle Robert B. Roosevelt, that brought him to his pioneering environmental positions. Robert Roosevelt, the author of *Superior Fishing, The Game Birds of the Coasts and Lakes of the Northern States of America,* and other books on natural history, had helped found the

American conservation movement, pushing for legislation establishing the New York State Fisheries Commission in 1867, which he would head. It was wealthy sportsmen like Robert and Theodore Roosevelt, John Muir, and Gifford Pinchot who paved the way for the later environmental movement.

. . .

Roosevelt enjoyed power, for it permitted him to express his principles and his passion. He had long believed in a "Hamiltonian" presidency: strong executive leadership, central policy-making power with or without congressional participation, presidential political power based in his party but, where necessary, in his own personal constituencies. Hence he stood in opposition philosophically and politically to the checks and balances that the Framers had contrived so carefully to thwart one-man rule. And their fear of such power seemed justified when power appeared to go to TR's head. At a Gridiron dinner the president castigated senators to their faces for their lack of respect for the presidency; when the senators demanded respect for *their* branch, TR stalked out.

Well, at least the Framers had set the terms of office, and George Washington had set the precedent for only two. To the critics of his abuse of executive power, TR had a compelling answer: The president did not govern for life; he had only a few years to do his work. He had long since selected his secretary of war, William Howard Taft, as his successor as the GOP nominee. Although he experienced occasional pangs about leaving the White House, he stuck to his promise, despite his conviction—which he did not hide—that he could have the nomination by merely lifting his finger.

. . .

Cousin Theodore went to Columbia Law School after Harvard: ergo, Franklin went to Columbia Law School after Harvard. But it was not only that. Columbia was the nearest acceptable law school to Hyde Park; he and Eleanor could easily go home for weekends. He would presumably practice law in Manhattan, where he could simply remain after graduation. And he would be near his mother, who had her own house three blocks away, until Sara and they moved into adjoining brownstones on East 65th Street in 1908—houses that, years later following Sara's death, Franklin would sell for a moderate sum to the Hillel Foundation of Hunter College.

Certainly he did not go to Columbia for intellectual excitement, any more than Cousin Theodore had. TR indeed had been bored by the school, which in 1880 could boast of no more than a minuscule faculty and a seedy old building. By the time Franklin entered twenty-four years later, however, Columbia had moved uptown to 114th Street, and the law school had quarters in the splendid domed University Library that had been designed by the noted architect Charles F. McKim. While the energetic TR had hiked fifty blocks or so to Great Jones Street, FDR could take the new IRT subway uptown to the still unfinished Columbia campus.

Franklin was bored with law studies. His scores of absences from classes brought him a mortifying penalty: In his first year he failed two courses, the basic Pleading and Practice course and, even more important for a future Manhattan lawyer, Contracts. He finally got around to telling his mother, complaining about the "uncertainty of mark" but promising almost like a child to work harder. Since he usually learned more from people than from books, his social outlook might have been broadened by a student body at the law school that was far more diverse than Harvard, but Franklin had little contact with most of the class and continued to hobnob with family and upper-class friends. He appeared to have little aptitude for the law, one of his professors later recalled, and "made no effort to overcome that handicap by hard work." As Eleanor wrote perceptively to her aunt, "He will not find himself altogether happy with the law he is studying at Columbia unless he is able to get a broad human contact through it." By the end of his second year he had only a C average.

Unlike Theodore Roosevelt, who neither finished law school nor took the bar exam, Franklin had only one goal at law school: to learn enough to pass the bar. He did so in 1906 and saw no need to stay on at Columbia any longer, thereby abandoning an LLB degree. Now he could practice.

But where—with whom? And how to get a job? For one who moved in Franklin's circle, these were not difficult questions. He would work only with a prestigious law firm, and the prospering Wall Street law firm of Carter, Ledyard & Milburn met the test. Two partners were members of the New York Yacht Club, as was FDR. He hardly needed to put in applications; friends and probably his mother smoothed the way for him.

The terms were not flattering. The arrangement, he was told, would be the same one the firm usually made: The first year without salary, and after that, "if you remain, to pay you a salary which, however, at the outset would necessarily be rather small." In effect this meant that he would continue to be dependent financially on his mother.

Nor did he take his new duties all that seriously. With a wry understanding of his own underachievement, he put out a mock handwritten flyer
about himself as a counselor who specialized in "unpaid bills," the chloroforming of "small dogs" (especially his mother's), the preparation of "briefs
on the liquor question" for ladies, and the care of babies "under advice of
expert grandmother, etc., etc., etc." He was not above slipping away from
the office for some pastime, and he continued to be bored by much of his
work. What did interest him were the cases that brought him into contact
with the problems of a wide variety of clients: Harvard friends accused of
being drunk and disorderly in Times Square, a compositor charged with
second-degree assault against an elderly proofreader.

To some he appeared to be the same frivolous socialite they had known
at Harvard and Hyde Park, a young man who liked his golf, his private clubs,
his yachting, and his poker with the boys. "Everybody called him Franklin
and regarded him as a harmless bust," a friend said years later; his temperament was "almost adolescent in its buoyancy." One of his bosses, accosting
him when he came in late after taking in several innings of baseball at the
Polo Grounds plus a few beers, interrupted Franklin's long and hazy excuses.
"Roosevelt, you're drunk!" This same partner, the one whom Franklin's
mother had originally approached, now told her that her son could not concentrate on his work and would never be a successful lawyer.

Franklin had countless acquaintances—something he *was* good at—
and many later recalled their impressions of him. These were mixed at best.
The one person whose sense of him we know least about is Franklin himself. He rarely revealed to others such private feelings, especially if they
were negative; to Eleanor, Sara, his men friends, his fellow law clerks he
was invariably optimistic, breezily self-confident, and enthusiastic about
small matters, such as his latest suit from Brooks Brothers.

Yet he could only have felt twinges of mortification when he looked
beyond his law office and Manhattan to his mentor in Washington. There
stood Cousin Theodore, at the center of action, wielding his club against
the bad guys, a moral leader applying conscience to politics—and here in
New York was Franklin, occupied with petty legal disputes, occasionally
fighting for the good guy but more often representing a corporation such
as American Express. He must have wondered how Cousin Theodore felt
about his work when he read of the president's attack on "corporation lawyers" who sought to thwart administration efforts to enforce laws regulating rugged individualism. That was just what Franklin was—a corporation
lawyer—and not even a well-paid one.

One effect was to bind him more tightly to home, mother, and his growing family. Eleanor and he had their first baby, Anna, on May 2, 1906, at home in New York, followed in December 1907 by a son, James. Motherhood did not come naturally to Eleanor, not surprisingly, given her lack of a role model. She hired a trained nurse, at Sara's suggestion; and Sara was always there too, giving advice. Eleanor later fervently wished she had cared for her own children. She was becoming, she later confessed, "an entirely dependent person," supportive of others, self-deprecating, a "fairly conventional, quiet, young society matron."

Franklin, in contrast, was confident and relaxed like Eleanor's father, and led exuberant games and expeditions, especially at Hyde Park and Campobello. Eleanor was determined to quell her childhood fear of water and boats—and did so, over time, growing to love Campobello as a home.

On March 18, 1909, Franklin Jr. was born. Though a large baby like the others, at eleven pounds, he was a sickly child, diagnosed in October with heart trouble. On November 1 he died.

Chapter Three
TWO ROOSEVELTS MOVE TO THE LEFT

Robert Carter, 1912.
(Courtesy TR Collection, Harvard College Library)

In 1910, three years after beginning as a law clerk, Franklin was still a law clerk. In contrast, Cousin Theodore, even though no longer president, was winning a new kind of fame as an explorer and big-game hunter in Africa and as a hero and celebrity feted in the courts of Europe while he made his grand tour of the Continent. More than ever, ambition gnawed and chafed Franklin. Earlier, passing the time of day with his fellow law clerks, he had revealed the extent of that ambition.

He was tired of the law, he told them, and would seek political office the first chance he got. And he would follow precisely the path of Theodore Roosevelt: Run for a state assembly seat, win appointment as assistant secretary of the navy, gain election as governor of New York, and—"Once you're elected Governor of New York," he went on, "if you do well enough in that job, you have a good shot to be President." He made it all seem simple and natural, a fellow clerk remembered. Nobody laughed at him.

Well might they have laughed, for this was sheer daydreaming on Franklin's part. He was talking not only about a cousin who had hopelessly outdistanced him intellectually but about a political universe in which he played no part. In turning so strongly to the left during his final presidential years, Theodore Roosevelt had challenged the social world to which FDR and Eleanor still belonged. Franklin had kept his memberships in the highly exclusive New York Yacht Club and the Knickerbocker Club, he was still a Hudson River grandee and hobbyist, and he maintained social connections with his upper-class friends. Franklin and Eleanor moved, with the seasons, between their three different homes—in New York City, Hyde Park, and Campobello Island—never employing fewer than five servants.

But now there was the exciting spectacle of Cousin Theodore, who had defied the economic power and pretensions of key male members of high society. Even more, there was TR's moral leadership as he appeared to be applying conscience to politics. Franklin had given little hint of a strong social conscience during his school and college years. At Harvard, to be sure, he had engaged in genteel philanthropic activity such as helping out the St. Andrew's Boys Club in Boston. But he hardly appeared engagé, as tested by deep concern and commitment. Certainly he had few

connections with the muckrakers and reformers who supported Cousin
Theodore. Later, FDR would tell the unlikely story that his mother had
read Upton Sinclair's *The Jungle* to him at the breakfast table. More likely
Sara was reading Kipling's *Jungle Stories*. But buried deep in Franklin's
unconscious, Frances Perkins told an interviewer years later, was a "desire to outshine Ted," a desire moreover that "made him so active when
there was a great deal of indolence in his nature."

Politics was still an unusual career choice for a young man of Franklin's
class. Before 1929, commented Cornelius Vanderbilt, it was considered a sign
of "outright insanity" for a young man of wealth and position to run for
political office. On the contrary, such a young man was educated and socialized to understand the difference between "us" and "them." "We" stood
for members of his social set and the leaders of Wall Street, Vanderbilt explained. "They" stood for ninety-six men in the Senate and the rest of Washington. Had Franklin not gone into politics, mused his friend Cornelius, he
would have been "just another corporation lawyer, summering in Newport
and hibernating in Wall Street."

. . .

It was Theodore Roosevelt's passionate idealism and principled leadership of 1907–1908 that was crucial in turning Franklin away from high
society and toward grass-roots politics at a critical period of the young law
clerk's life. In the same spirit, two of Eleanor's relatives—Teddy Robinson
and Corinne's husband, Joe Alsop—were inspired to enter politics. TR "has
certainly infected you all with large ambitions as citizens," Eleanor's aunt
wrote, "and I am sure will be proud of you all."

But where to start? And in what party? Unlike TR a quarter century
earlier, Franklin could not run for the New York Assembly or Senate from
New York City. The mid-Manhattan area in which FDR lived had changed
politically. In the first decade of the new century, immigration from Europe had soared to record numbers: two million Italians, a million and a
half Russians, more millions from eastern Europe, including Jews escaping from oppression. Hundreds of thousands had settled in lower Manhattan, but the whole immigrant population was pushing steadily uptown.
Theodore Roosevelt's family had fled north to 57th Street before the newcomers moved into once-fashionable homes in the Union Square area.
Nothing in Franklin's background equipped him to appeal to this polyglot population, with its own cobblestone leadership. Rather, he looked
home, to Hyde Park, where his grass roots lay.

Run in what party? Biographers have long assumed that FDR naturally and inevitably turned to the Democrats. It was not that clear-cut. His father had been a long-time Democrat, to be sure, as had many members of his family. But the Hudson River Democrats were typically Cleveland-style Democrats, not ideologically much apart from the GOP right. Both Sara and Eleanor had been raised as Republicans. And two other young relatives who were also inspired by Uncle Ted, Teddy Robinson and Joe Alsop, both chose to get involved in Republican politics, to TR's delight. Young Franklin took after his father politically, but his Democratic loyalty was tenuous, having enthusiastically backed Cousin Theodore every time TR ran for office.

The implication is inescapable: Intentionally or not, Franklin was so positioned in 1910 that he could be a candidate in either party—and would run for the first slot that opened up.

1
"He Seen His Opportunity"

Prospects, alas, seemed bleak in both parties: A Democrat, Lewis Chanler, was ensconced in Franklin's assembly district; a Republican, John F. Schlosser, in the senate district, which reached out to envelop the more rural areas. Franklin's hopes rose on rumors that Chanler, an Astor, had grown bored with the job and might either quit or run for the Senate. Then Franklin encountered the vagaries of politics and politicians; Chanler decided to stay right where he was. Desperately Franklin turned to the party leaders, who, perhaps with tongue in cheek, suggested that he try for that senate seat against Schlosser. It had gone Democratic once in the past half century. At least, the party elders calculated, young Franklin could pay for his own campaign and, even better, help the whole Democratic party ticket financially.

In politics, Boss Plunkett said of himself, "he seen his opportunity and he took it." So did Franklin Roosevelt. He had grasped the first copybook maxim for the man of ambition: Try, and if at first you fail, try, try again. And he quickly showed his grasp of the second lesson: Size up your constituency, adapt yourself to it, move quickly, campaign indefatigably. Perhaps even more remarkable than his taking this political gamble was the brilliant campaign that this political neophyte waged.

He was innovative. At a time when campaigning by auto was almost unknown, he hired a red Maxwell touring car and decked it out with flags and banners. He was cautious. Knowing that farmers feared the steaming monsters would cause their horses to bolt, he halted his car well in front of an approaching wagon and thus had a chance to extend his hand and smile to the grateful farmer. He was "democratic," introducing himself as "Frank" to a Hyde Park citizen who had seen him only at a distance. He used time-tested methods, too, learning to work a crowd as smoothly as any Tammany pol, paying attention to the small details that often turn out to be pivotal factors.

He quickly learned the more aggressive tricks of the trade as he attacked Schlosser's rural bastions while relying on city Democrats to protect his urban bases. Charged by the leader of another great clan, Republican congressman Hamilton Fish (father of FDR's New Deal opponent of the same name), with being a carpetbagger who owned no property in Dutchess County, he first ignored it and then falsely denied it; in fact, his mother, not he, owned Springwood. He "coattailed" dexterously, tying in with other Democratic candidates in areas where they appeared popular, and even with Republican governor Charles Evans Hughes. Asked if he liked Hughes's reform policies, he shot back, "You bet I do." Above all he grabbed the coattails of Cousin Theodore, who had already helped by not endorsing Schlosser.

Nor would Franklin refrain from exploiting that still-Republican name. Introduced to a crowd as a Roosevelt, he protested with a smile, "I'm not Teddy." This always brought a chuckle from his audience. "A little shaver said to me the other day," he went on, "that he knew I wasn't Teddy—I asked him 'why' and he replied: 'Because you don't show your teeth.'"

And he learned to speak by speaking. Eleanor, who gave birth to Elliott in September, did not accompany her husband but was supportive. She heard him speak for the first time just before the election. He "spoke slowly," with long pauses, she remembered, and she "worried for fear he would never go on." To her he "looked thin then, tall, high-strung, and, at times, nervous." He spoke more smoothly, and even eloquently, when toasting the district itself before small audiences of dirt farmers.

"In the course of the last two weeks," he would say, "I have been traveling from town to town, from farmhouse to farmhouse, in these magnificent counties along our great river, and my heart has grown glad and I have thanked God that it fell to my lot to be born and to have lived as one of the people of this Hudson Valley. For with every new face that I have met it has been impressed upon me that here we have a population that is truly American in the best sense of the word; a people alive, a people desirous of progress." This was the most authentic, the most lasting, voice of the young FDR, who always would have a feeling for place, a sense of home.

. . .

Much mightier forces than even Franklin's skillful campaigning brought him his victory, the senator-elect had to grant, as he pondered the overall results of the 1910 election and the nationwide Democratic sweep. His congressional district had turned out of office the Republican who appeared to own this constituency like a fiefdom, Hamilton Fish himself. Miraculously, it seemed, Henry L. Stimson had lost his bid for the governorship to a lackluster Democrat. And in the gubernatorial race next door in New Jersey, a scholarly neophyte from Princeton, Woodrow Wilson, won the most notable among scores of Democratic victories across the nation.

Ideas were still dominating politics. After a decade of muckraking, reformism appeared stronger than ever. Popular journals read by middle-class voters kept up their barrages against trusts, economic and political bosses, corruption, profiteering, exploitation of women and children, slums, poverty; middle-class leaders and writers were now rallying to the reform banner on behalf of the underclass. The women's suffrage and settlement-house movements had grown; now Jane Addams and Florence Kelley invaded political battlefields to fight for measures protecting women and children.

The reform movement had gained power and focus toward the end of the decade by coming up against a most satisfactory villain, William Howard Taft, TR's handpicked successor in the White House. Taft, with his jovial countenance and enormous belly, hardly looked menacing, but he increasingly fell under the influence of the very men TR had fought during the climactic years of his presidency.

By 1910, Republican unity was crumbling as regulars jousted with reformers. The new state senator from Hyde Park might not have grasped some of the broader dimensions of the reform trend, but at least he recognized the still rising progressive spirit in the land and supported it. Not only did he inveigh against graft and corruption and bossism in the currently popular style, he supported in general Charles Evans Hughes's reform program, especially the adoption of the direct primary, aimed at weakening party machines in their power over nominations. During his campaign, FDR also endorsed some measures for the poor, such as untainted and inexpensive milk for slum children. In general, though, he

offered few specific promises or new remedies, relying instead on elec-
tioneering tactics that later would become his campaign hallmarks—fine
rhetoric, a sense of humor, moral appeals, and attacks on his Republican
opponent that were carefully honed not to antagonize potential Republican supporters.

The average citizen tends merely to note who wins and who loses in
elections; professional politicians analyze how much candidates win or lose
by, compared with the rest of the ticket and with past election results. On
all counts, FDR passed the professionals' tests. He had won in a traditionally Republican district; in his district he had run ahead of the whole state
Democratic slate of candidates, overcoming the Republican, Schlosser, by
15,708 to 14,568, a margin of 1,140, whereas the Democratic gubernatorial
victor had won in that district by only 663 votes.

Touring the district, pumping voters' hands, addressing small rallies,
debating in the newspapers, promising to represent his constituents "every
day of the 365, every hour of the 24"—aside from the big Maxwell, it had
been an old-fashioned campaign. The senator-elect celebrated in an old-
fashioned way too, awaiting the results at home with his family rather than
joining a noisy crowd at party headquarters. Sharing the excitement of the
evening was the proud mother, happily toting up election returns on a sheet
of her personal stationery. "Franklin carries Poughkeepsie by 927 . . . carries
Hudson by 499"—and, most satisfying of all, he won Hyde Park.

The senator-elect exuberantly passed out cigars to friends, as soon as
he felt home safe. Even more than his victory, he was excited by running
ahead of other Democrats. That was something that might impress the
hard-eyed politicians in Albany, who would be working with him and
against him when he entered the New York Senate two months later.

"Every one of our friends," recalled Franklin's mother about his senate win, "said that it was both shameful and ridiculous for as fine a young
man as my son to associate himself with dirty politicians. They hoped he
would be defeated." And when Franklin won, she continued, "our friends
came to console me. Yes, to console me!"

. . .

Early in 1911, Eleanor and Franklin, with a large staff of servants headed
by the customary formidable butler, settled into a large rented house on
Albany's Upper State Street. Later, with three children, three nurses, and
household staff, they moved to a still more prestigious home on Elk Street,
built by Martin Van Buren in the late 1820s. Whatever pleasure FDR took

from this connection with a man who had been governor and later president, he could well have contrasted Van Buren's Democratic party with the same party eighty years later. Van Buren had helped lead the Albany Regency, which with its disciplined party organization, collective leadership, party press, and party power, had set a standard for party responsibility and, indeed, party honesty. Already, in FDR's time, that party unity had begun a long process of disintegration into factions; the only discipline left lay in the hands of Tammany bosses.

It was those Tammany ranks that confronted Franklin as he strode into the Capitol in January 1911. He hardly achieved the dramatic pose struck by the newly elected assemblyman Theodore Roosevelt on sauntering into the Capitol three decades earlier. But Franklin did catch the eye of a woman reporting for the *New York Globe,* who gushed about his "tall well-set-up figure," Grecian nose, ruddy "glow of country health," and curly brown hair. He was "physically fit to command," she concluded. The reporter for *The New York Times* also noted that young Roosevelt had "the finely chiseled face of a Roman patrician."

"Are you an admirer of your uncle-in-law?" a reporter asked the young senator. "Why, who can help but admire him?" Franklin answered, praising Cousin Theodore. "It is only a question of time before people generally will appreciate what he has done in arousing the public conscience and in driving corruption out of politics."

The young senator caught the eyes of others. Tammanyites, with their memories of TR's crusades against corruption, watched sourly as another Roosevelt took his seat. Boss "Big Tim" Sullivan of the Bowery muttered to his cronies that the Roosevelts "run true to form" and this "kid is likely to do for us what the Colonel is going to do for the Republican Party, split it wide open." He had a simple solution for the new maverick: "Take him down and drop him off the dock."

While FDR confronted a disciplined band of glowering Tammanyites, the Tammany machine faced a smaller cohort of reformers itching for a fight. The triggering event was a big one: the upcoming election of a new United States senator (at a time when state legislatures still chose senators). The Tammany candidate was the barely respectable William F. "Blue-eyed Billy" Sheehan, while the reformers quickly banded behind a proper Cleveland Democrat, Edward Shepard. The "Democratic party is on trial," FDR wrote in a briefly kept diary. Having won the last election with their upstate votes, the party could not "afford to surrender its control" to the Tammany organization in New York City.

The fight got off to a glorious start as a crusade of good versus evil. While FDR had not initiated the reform effort, he soon became its leader, or at least spokesman, not only because his name was well known but also because his house was near enough to be handy and big enough to accommodate the reformers. There the party rebels met virtually every day to plot tactics and concert efforts, and—FDR admitted to reporters—to "swap stories like soldiers at the bivouac fire." Eleanor presided over the dinners and gatherings with warmth and grace; for her the conflict was an exhilarating education in practical politics. Anna Roosevelt, old enough at the age of five to note such matters, would never forget the hushed meetings, so drenched in cigar smoke that the younger children had to be moved to an upper floor. For some time the struggle was front-page news, with FDR often cast as its leader.

But as the fight settled into a stalemate, with each side methodically casting its vote for its man, the struggle suffered the worst setback for any crusade—it became boring. Both candidates, Shepherd and Sheehan, gave up the fight, deciding not to run. FDR indicated his willingness to deal and find a Democratic compromise candidate, proposing to the Republican boss, William Barnes Jr., that the insurgents and the Republicans agree on some Democrat who was "conservative in regard to business interests and yet a man whose position can never be questioned by the radical element of society." But Barnes would not deal.

In desperation FDR turned to the Tammany leader, Charles F. Murphy, who would deal with a fellow Democrat. They agreed finally on a compromise candidate, James A. O'Gorman, who had managed both to become a Tammany bigwig, a "Grand Sachem," and maintain his respectability. It was an inglorious ending. Newspaper editors were critical, as they recalled the insurgents' moralizing call to arms earlier and noted that O'Gorman would be at least as manipulable by Murphy and Tammany as Blue-eyed Billy Sheehan would have been. Franklin had to sit through an Albany correspondents' dinner and watch a reporter in Tammany Indian garb sing:

Franklin D., like Uncle "The,"
Can't compete with Tammany.

Was it such a defeat? For Roosevelt the outcome was a considerable personal victory. He had won a small national reputation as a reformer, he had demonstrated a flair for leadership; and a quick trip to his constituency convinced him that voters in both parties remembered him more for his weeks of insurgency than for the final compromise. Moreover, FDR converted the defeat into a victory simply by calling it a victory. The party had "taken an upward step," he proclaimed, and privately he boasted that at least they had stopped Tammany from choosing any man it wished. But like TR, FDR sermonized too much in public. "Murphy and his kind must, like the noxious weed, be plucked out, root and branch," he orated. "From the ruins of the political machines we will construct something more nearly conforming to a democratic conception of government." He castigated individual Democrats by name. A Tammany phrasemaker angrily attacked this speech as "bristling with the silly conceits of a political prig."

The ultimate test of FDR's success was what he learned from the whole mixed experience—especially what he learned about power and morality. How hard did he reflect on the complexity of power? He had grossly underestimated Boss Murphy's strength: the party discipline of the Tammanyites, Murphy's own flexibility and resourcefulness. Power was ephemeral, volatile; what appeared to be victory at one point could turn sour, most notably in the losses Democrats suffered to GOP candidates for the Assembly in the fall, losses blamed by some on the insurgency. Power often lay in appearances, a fact FDR evidently grasped when he claimed victory in the absence of real victory.

Morality? This was even more complicated. It was easy to sermonize against bossism, corruption, Murphy, and the whole Tammany organization. But bossism existed in both parties, in corporations, education, even in reform organizations. Corruption existed throughout society, most notably in the trusts that Theodore Roosevelt denounced. And Tammany was not a mere collection of faceless, mindless robots but an organization that represented the Irish and other upward-striving ethnic minorities in all their vigor and variety and talents, as well as their resentments and their parochialism. Tammany was at its best an incubator and recruiter of talent, most notably exemplified by state senate leader Robert Wagner and assembly leader Al Smith. FDR knew these men and had to respect at least their political skills and, increasingly, their values.

Perhaps FDR reflected on how he appeared in the eyes of his rivals. Most of them disliked him personally. Smith and Wagner found him insufferably unpleasant and self-serving. Woman suffragists found him, through 1911, cautious and limited in his thinking. For her part, Eleanor was even more conservative than Franklin on women's suffrage. She still saw women as supporters of the main action of politics, not as the actors themselves. She was "somewhat shocked," she admitted, when Franklin came out for women's right to vote, for she "took it for granted that men were superior creatures."

Franklin did not at that time have a wife with whom he could debate political issues, Eleanor herself later stated. When someone asked her what the relationship was between the federal government and the states, she was "terrified." "I could not say one word. I looked frantically at my husband and he came to my rescue." People assumed that the niece of President Roosevelt had lived in a political atmosphere, but, on the contrary, Eleanor confessed that politically she was "totally ignorant as a young girl and as a young woman." Her Uncle Ted had passed on to his niece and his children his love of the outdoors and of books and poetry, not his acumen in politics.

No one watched FDR more closely during these years as he made his political rounds than Frances Perkins, a young Mount Holyoke graduate and political activist who moved in similar upper-class circles. In 1911 she had been hired by state leaders Robert Wagner and Al Smith to help investigate the infamous Triangle Shirtwaist fire in which 148 sweatshop garment workers, mostly female, perished. The fire exits had been locked shut, and the trapped women either burned or jumped to their deaths. Roosevelt had not joined her as she took Smith and Wagner for a first-hand look at New York sweatshops, nor did he support the bill she was promoting in Albany to limit the workweek for women to fifty-four hours. "I believe that at that time," she later wrote, "Franklin Roosevelt had little, if any, concern about specific social reforms." The memory lingered of him moving around the floor of the state Senate, "rarely talking with the members, who more or less avoided him, not particularly charming (that came later), artificially serious of face, rarely smiling." He had a habit, she noted, of throwing his head up, which, "combined with his pince-nez and great height, gave him the appearance of looking down his nose at most people."

Frances Perkins could not tell whether FDR knew how he came across. Perhaps he did. He told Perkins—his future secretary of labor—later, "You know, I was an awfully mean cuss when I first went into politics."

2

1912: TR and FDR, Progressives

In June 1910, Theodore Roosevelt had returned from his long safari through Africa and a triumphant tour of Europe. At fifty-one he was jobless, restless, and powerless, an explosive combination in a Roosevelt.

Indeed, right after McKinley's funeral TR had already been worried about what he would do when he left the White House. "I don't want to be the old cannon loose on the deck in the storm," he confided to his friend William Allen White.

During his trip he had received reports that a listless and uninspiring President Taft was beginning to fall into the old GOP ways: courting the Old Guard on Capitol Hill, ignoring some of TR's progressive friends and the forces they spoke for, drifting back and forth between the two wings—conservative and progressive—of the party. Nor was TR interested, as Lodge had proposed, in campaigning for a Republican congressional victory in 1910. The Republican leaders of Congress, the former president bristled, had always "gone back on their promises and have put me in the position of having promised what there was no intention of performing."

The ex-president had resolved to keep his hands off politics, just to be a "regular with a conscience." But within a few minutes of setting foot on American soil he was telling a great welcoming throng that he was glad to be back among people he loved. "And I am ready and eager to do my part, as far as I am able, in helping solve problems which must be solved if we, of this the greatest democratic republic upon which the sun has ever shone, are to see its destinies rise to the high level of our hopes and its opportunities." Within a few weeks, he was off on a carefully planned speaking trip that reached five thousand miles through sixteen states, from Kansas to California.

Denver, Sioux Falls, Omaha.... Living on a train for almost three weeks, meeting with correspondents from the attached press car, receiving hosts of visitors who crowded into the smoke-filled cars, speaking to vast audiences who greeted him with jubilation, for TR it was a reenactment of his strenuous campaign trips of the past. His major addresses were long, forceful, packed with facts and ideas and ideals. They reached back to his later presidential years and reached forward to—what? He denied political plans and paid occasional tributes to Taft and some of his policies. But everything he said sounded "presidential" and almost everything he did reminded people of the strong moral leadership of the past. Thus in Chicago he refused to sit at dinner with a senator involved in an election scandal.

The main theme of his western talks was conservation, and here the ex-president could speak from a strong hand because of his pioneering leadership in the White House. Now, in his "precampaign" trip, TR toughened his stand on conservation. "We have passed the time," he told a meeting of livestock men in Denver, "when we will tolerate the man whose only idea is to skin the country and move on." As far as possible, "resources must be kept for the whole people and not handed over for exploitation to any single individual or group of individuals." It was really a question of the national community, trying to protect its natural environment, pitted against corporations and plutocrats intent on appropriating public lands.

Most compelling and controversial in his handling of this subject was TR's insistence that the states could not handle nationwide problems and that the judiciary should not protect established wealth. Thus he was questioning the whole system of government itself, especially federalism and judicial review.

In Columbus, Ohio, he took his strongest position to date for labor's right to organize. After lengthy moralizing against violence and "bad conduct," he said that while it would be "infamous" to sack a man because he asked for a wage hike, "it would be almost as bad to discharge a man because he belonged to, or was preparing to enter, or organize, a union." He was an "honorary member" of a union himself, he added. "If I were a wage worker, I should certainly join a union; but when I was in I would remember that I was first of all an American citizen. Uncle Sam comes on top in everything."

Years earlier TR would have preached property rights as well as labor rights. But now he deemed labor rights paramount—a milestone for the ex-president. He did go on, however, to some balancing. "Of course, it is outrageous to force a man to join a union," he said, "just as it is outrageous to take part in, or encourage, the so-called secondary boycott; but it is no less an outrage to discriminate against him because he wishes to have a union, or to refuse to deal with a union when organized."

It was in Osawatomie, Kansas, that TR set the stage for his own great progressive power move ahead. He did not miss the significance of the place. This was where John Brown had helped trigger the Civil War, and "Kansas was the theater" upon which one of "our great national life dramas was played." Here it was "determined that our country should be, in deed as well as in name, devoted to both union and freedom; that the great experiment of democratic government on a national scale should succeed and not fail. In name we had the Declaration of Independence in 1776; but we gave the lie by our acts to the words of the Declaration of Independence until 1865; and words count for nothing except insofar as they represent acts." He could not resist moralizing: "A broken promise is bad enough in private life. It is worse in the field of politics."

And the new promise? The rights of labor, the end of privilege, a graduated income tax, a steeply graduated inheritance tax, conservation, regulation of women's and children's labor, a workmen's compensation act, an energized federal government that sees itself as "the steward of the public welfare, and a judiciary that puts human welfare before property rights."

TR had outlined in Osawatomie what he and his friend, progressive writer Herbert Croly, called the New Nationalism. "I stand for the square deal," TR declared, explaining that he was not advocating mere fair play under the present rules but, rather, demanding the transformation of those very rules. "I stand for having those rules changed so as to work for a more substantial equality of opportunity and of reward for equally good service." Property itself would have to give way to a higher value, that of "human welfare," and would be "subject to the general right of the community to regulate its use to whatever degree the public welfare may require."

The New Nationalism, TR explained, meant putting "national need before sectional or personal advantage" and putting an end to "the impotence which springs from the overdivision of governmental powers." Offering an alternative to socialism, a rethinking of the nature of property rights and government-society relations, Roosevelt was speaking as a "left-wing statist," remarked business historian Martin Sklar. TR did "not care a rap," he said later, about the size of corporations. "What I am interested in is getting the hand of government on all of them—this is what I want." The alternative to his own progressive vision, TR believed, was a country that would "drift along, alternating between reaction on behalf of sordid money interests and violent and foolish radicalism."

TR had come "180 degrees from the standpat assumptions that had governed his party when he had been elected Vice President in 1900," commented historian Nell Painter. The Colonel no longer believed that government's prime responsibility was to aid big business and that what was good for business was good for the American people. On the contrary, the object of government, TR was now convinced, was the welfare of the people. He had also come 180 degrees from the positions of the Mugwumps—and from his patrician friends.

The reaction among members of TR's own upper class and among the plutocrats was swift, strong, and predictable. TR's use of the word "property" had "startled" people in the East, a perturbed Henry Cabot Lodge reported to his friend. TR now seemed to be "little short of a revolutionist." The *New York Herald* attacked TR for "waving the red flag," while the progressive *Denver Republican* happily announced that it "takes it for granted that Theodore Roosevelt will be the next Republican candidate for President."

Though TR had been determined to stay out of politics, especially until the election of 1916, seductive praise and pleas from the populace—along with his unquenchable ambition—propelled him forward. After fighting off temptation, he began to yield. The telltale sign was the "no—but" that began to creep into his letters. "I very emphatically feel that to me personally to be nominated in 1912 would be a calamity," he wrote a supporter. "Moreover, I am absolutely certain that it would be criminal folly under any circumstances to nominate me unless it could be made as clear as day that the nomination came not through intrigue or political work, not in the least to gratify any kind of wish or ambition on my part, but simply and solely because the bulk of the people wanted a given job done, and for their own sakes, and not for mine, wanted me to do that job."

In short, yes. Roosevelt was a "thirsty sinner," commented Elihu Root, TR's old friend and former secretary of war and state, who would also win the Nobel Peace Prize.

"My hat is in the ring and the fight is on," an elated TR announced early in 1912, determined to turn the Republican party around and recapture the White House. He lamented the "sordid baseness of most of the so-called Regulars" in the Republican party and lambasted Taft's inertia, despite the president's energetic prosecutions of a record number of trusts. TR saw his duty as restoring control of the party to "sensible and honorable men who were progressives and not of a bourbon reactionary type." The political landscape, moreover, was changing. Many conservative Republicans had lost their congressional seats in 1910, and Old Guard conservatives like Nelson Aldrich of Rhode Island had retired. The militant reformer Senator Robert "Battling Bob" La Follette of Wisconsin was challenging Taft from within the Republican party.

TR, of course, realized that many members of his own social class had repudiated him. "The great bulk of my wealthy and educated friends," he confided to an acquaintance, "regard me as a dangerous crank." His sister Corinne sadly agreed. Never before, she observed, had Theodore felt such a sense of loneliness, for many of his "nearest and dearest" friends had no sympathy for his radical beliefs. One of TR's fellow Harvard overseers also concurred in that judgment: People in TR's own elite social class indeed hated him ("their number is legion in our walk of life"). But many more people were demanding real reforms. It was Roosevelt, wrote that same Harvard overseer, who "has the reputation of being the most farsighted politician in the Country." In addition, some of the representatives of big business and high finance did indeed support Roosevelt, believing that, of all the progressive candidates, he was the safest. And, as historian George Mowry reported, 20 percent of the Republican members of the New York Stock Exchange selected TR as their choice for president.

More and more people were rallying to Roosevelt. Progressive Republicans like Hiram Johnson of California, who had already endorsed La Follette as an alternative to Taft, now left the Wisconsin progressive's camp and joined TR. Patrician Henry Adams's brother, the historian Brooks Adams, wrote to Roosevelt, "I am with you" after hearing TR's speech in the Boston Arena. Julius Caesar met the same kind of resistance that Roosevelt was now meeting in Wall Street, Adams told him, adding that just as Caesar "prevailed," so would Roosevelt. A few wealthy business tycoons, such as George Perkins, who believed that the interests of business and those of social justice were not necessarily antithetical, also offered support.

As for the Taft camp, they were outraged by their former leader's rebellion and efforts to split the party. "Friends" of both the president and the ex-president brought in reports of outrageous sayings and doings in the rival camps. Republican regulars urged TR to withdraw. "You could not advise me to do anything more utterly destructive of my good name," TR replied to one of them.

One of TR's most radical new stands, popular review of judicial decisions, was the final blow for Republican regulars who opposed his candidacy and for some conservative businessmen who, up until then, were still supporting him; Roosevelt had entered the ranks of revolutionaries. A variety of judicial decisions disgusted TR: the egregious Dred Scott decision of 1857; the more recent New York Court of Appeals decision declaring invalid legislation that TR had worked for in the New York Assembly to prohibit the manufacture of cigars in tenement apartments; the Bakeshop case, in which the Supreme Court again declared invalid legislation to safeguard and protect the health of workers.

Now, in a speech in Denver, Roosevelt turned his attention to the courts' pro-business decisions. The courts, he declared, had created "neutral ground in which neither the state nor the nation has power" and which served as a refuge for lawless men of great wealth. Because so many state judicial rulings obstructed justice and the desire of the majority of the people for reform, TR felt, the people should be able to vote in a referendum sustaining or rejecting the courts' decisions. "For the past thirty years," he wrote Herbert Croly, "there has been a riot of judicial action looking to the prevention of measures for social and industrial betterment which every other civilized nation takes as a matter of course, and in some way or other this riot must be stopped."

Indeed, already in 1884, when he was still an assemblyman in the New York legislature, TR had excoriated Chief Justice Taney for announcing "from the bench that a black man had no rights that a white man was bound to respect." By 1911, he was convinced that American judges were "absolutely reactionary" and that their decisions virtually barred the "path to industrial, economic, and social reform." Why, he himself, TR admitted, had named men to the bench who he had believed at the time were "excellent." Indeed, he thought he was making "unusually good appointments, and yet they turned out to be men who, if not dishonest, were at least without any conception of real social justice." Too many judges, he bitterly concluded, were acting "against the interests of the people." And now he would do no less than wage "war against these abuses." He was, he announced at a rally in Carnegie Hall, "for the rule of the many in the interest of all of us."

TR's proposal for review and recall of judicial decisions proved to be too much to swallow for his close friend Henry Cabot Lodge, who sadly informed him that he could not support his candidacy. Their friendship had always been based more on intellectual and class affinities than on political ones. "My dear fellow," TR reassured Lodge, "you could not do anything that would make me lose my warm personal affection for you. For a couple of years I have felt that you and I were heading opposite ways as regards internal politics," and he signed his letter, "Ever affectionately."

If conservatives had been wary of TR before his attack on the judiciary, now they feared him, accusing him of undermining constitutional government and advocating the rule of men, not the rule of law. But TR was convinced that popular review of judicial decisions would restore power to the people, taking it away from "corporation attorneys on the bench" who serve the "cause of special privilege." *The New York Times* was "appalled," judging the recall proposal a threat "to our institutions." But many thoughtful lawyers, William Harbaugh reported, began to reflect seriously on the issues that TR had raised. Indeed, the following year lawyer Felix Frankfurter criticized the American Bar Association for refusing to inquire into the cause of the ferment as it clung to a static view of the law. Franklin Roosevelt could not have known, in 1912, that TR's attempt to overcome pro-business court decisions foreshadowed his own famous attempt a quarter of a century later at "court packing" as a remedy against a reactionary Supreme Court.

TR was unstoppable. He saw himself as a righteous fighter for "honest and genuine democracy" and for the revolutionary goal of "ascertaining and putting into effect the will of the people." The longtime foe of checks and balances and a weak administration spoke out strongly for democratic, majoritarian government. "I have scant patience," he exclaimed, "with this talk of the tyranny of the majority. The only tyrannies from which men, women, and children are suffering are the tyrannies of minorities."

No longer motivated by a sense of paternalistic noblesse oblige or worried about social upheaval or about organized militancy from below, TR was now striving to empower the government and the people "so that the people may jointly do for themselves what no man can do so well for them." Recalling that his hero Lincoln had been similarly committed to a government "managed justly and honorably by these plain people for their own welfare," TR saw himself engaged in a contest about nothing less than "two radically different views of the function of politics in a great democracy."

"He had a feeling for social justice which was ahead of his time," his niece Eleanor Roosevelt later wrote. Deliberately avoiding the question of whether her uncle was a "traitor to his class," she proposed instead that he was "a pioneer, pointing the way that this country had to follow if it were going to be true to the ideas on which it was founded."

But TR refused to skirt the issue of class warfare. "We are fighting," he explained, "against entrenched privilege, both political privilege and financial privilege." The struggle for human liberty, he declared combatively, had always been and must always be "to take from some one man or class of men the right to enjoy power, or wealth, or position, or immunity, which has not been earned by service to his or their fellows." Even when the elite had earned some of its privileges, those distinctions were no longer seasonable in a democratic society. "We must not repeat, in the interests of a mere plutocracy," he confided to Arthur Hamilton Lee, "all the old-world injustices which were partially atoned for by the splendid services of the fighting and governing aristocracies on whose behalf they were perpetuated." Ending those "injustices" was the only way to avoid full-blown disastrous class war.

While no longer striving to steer a middle course between "sordid money interests and violent and foolish radicalism," TR nevertheless wanted to incarnate "wise, progressive leadership." He did not consider himself one of the "extremists of progress" but believed, he told a friend, "with all fervor and intensity in moderate progress." The Colonel who led the Rough Riders was defining himself as a moral leader, indeed, using the words "politics" and "applied ethics" interchangeably.

The campaign among TR, Taft, and La Follette for the Republican presidential nomination in 1912 became increasingly bitter and vituperative, Taft branding Roosevelt a "demagogue" and an "egotist," Roosevelt, shooting back, labeling Taft a "fool," a "blackguard," a "fathead," and a "puzzlewit" with an intellect slightly less advanced than that of a guinea pig. Taft was struggling to understand his old friend's betrayal of him while defending himself against TR's often unfair accusations of colluding with party bosses and big business. One day, a bone-tired, despairing Taft sighed, "Roosevelt was my closest friend," and then began to weep.

For his part, TR was determined to win. "He is essentially a fighter," commented Elihu Root. Root remarked that when Roosevelt gets into a fight, "he is completed dominated by the desire to destroy his adversary. He instinctively lays hold of every weapon which can be used for that end."

Though TR performed well both in the state primaries and in state party caucuses, even defeating Taft in Taft's home state of Ohio, he fell seventy delegates short of the majority needed for nomination. Disputes broke out about how fairly delegates were chosen, La Follette's *Weekly Magazine* asserting that TR was entitled to about fifty more delegates than he received, which would have given him control of the convention. Would Roosevelt go along with a compromise candidate? "I'll name the compromise candidate. He'll be me," snapped an unyielding TR. "I'll name the compromise platform. It will be our platform." La Follette was also unwilling to compromise, preferring to let Taft win than to throw his support and his forty-one delegates to his fellow progressive. On the uproarious convention floor in Chicago, delegates chanted, "We want Teddy!" Fistfights broke out. "We fight in honest fashion for the good of mankind," exclaimed an overwrought TR. "We stand at Armageddon, and we battle for the Lord."

Still, despite the fact that TR had won a popular vote of 1,157,397 to Taft's 761,716, the GOP political machines gave Taft the convention nod— and on the first ballot. TR's 344 delegates stormed out of the convention hall. "I regard Taft as the receiver of a swindled nomination," fumed an indignant Roosevelt. Newspapers agreed. THOU SHALT NOT STEAL blasted the *Chicago Tribune*.

TR, who had once promised to support Taft if he won the party's nomination, now bolted his party—just as the Mugwumps, to his consternation, had done in 1884. "My loyalty to the Republican party is naturally very great," he had written a friend in February 1912, explaining that "my aim is to make it and to keep it the Republican party that it was in the days of Lincoln." Taft, TR confided in his friend, might think that he "is loyal to Lincoln Republicanism, but in reality he is the spiritual heir of the cotton whigs of Lincoln's time." TR would bolt a party that betrayed Lincoln.

That Republican convention was a historical turning point, commented historian Arthur Schlesinger Jr. "By rejecting Roosevelt, the Republicans turned their backs on responsible conservatism." When TR and the Progressives bolted, the Old Guard was left in unchallenged control of the Republican party. Though some progressives remained—Borah, La Follette, Norris, and others—the loss of Roosevelt, who had championed an inclusive party and a program of reform and innovation, was a blow to the Grand Old Party. "By 1932," remarked historian Lewis Gould, "it had no answer to the political genius of another Roosevelt."

The "privileged classes seldom have the intelligence to protect themselves," concluded Brooks Adams, "by adaptation when nature turns against them."

. . .

TR had not even left Chicago before it was decided that he would run as a third-party candidate. In TR's hotel suite at the convention, two millionaires, Frank Munsey and George Perkins, told him, "Colonel, we will see you through." "At that precise moment," reported Amos Pinchot, "the Progressive Party was born."

Americans had never witnessed such a convention as the one that, seven weeks later, founded the National Progressive Party—nicknamed the "Bull Moose Party"—and nominated Roosevelt. It was a gathering of youthful idealists, political opportunists, social reformers, urban planners, job seekers, cranks, suffragists, muckrakers, academics, and seasoned progressive politicians who converted the convention hall into an evangelical camp meeting.

Greeted rapturously, TR strode to the podium to offer his "Confession of Faith." He stood in his old familiar style, his body rocking back and forth to the blasts of applause. Fifteen thousand people, wrote historian George Mowry, for "fifty-two minutes, wildly waving red bandannas," cheered him as they had never cheered anyone. They broke into song:

> *Thou wilt not cower in the dust,*
> *Roosevelt, O Roosevelt!*
> *Thy gleaming sword shall never rust,*
> *Roosevelt, O Roosevelt!*

TR's "Confession"—some twenty thousand words—was interrupted 145 times by applause. The old parties, the exuberant candidate declared as he raised the banner of class warfare, were "boss-ridden and privilege-controlled." "The real danger to privilege," he explained, "comes from the new party, and from the new party alone." The Progressives were offering a "contract with the people," he boasted, that would better "social and economic conditions throughout this land." Indeed, the first "essential" in the Progressive platform, he continued, "is the right of the people to rule." Not only did he call for women's suffrage and the direct election of senators, he demanded minimum wage legislation, factory and mine inspection standards, workmen's compensation laws, strengthening of the pure food law, social security insurance, business regulation, help for farmers, and conservation of natural resources. "We stand at Armageddon," he concluded once again, "and we battle for the Lord."

Thus spoke the authentic voice of the old Republican conscience, histrionics and all—the conscience of the abolitionists, of the crusaders against bossism and spoils, of the middle-class respectables who despised the vulgar new rich, of the urban reformers who glimpsed the problems and possibilities of the future. But the "old Colonel" now commanded a cavalry without foot soldiers, a movement made up of captains and sergeants. Indeed, the Progressive party was not a labor party, as historian Nell Painter remarked. "Progressives meant to help the workers, but from above, and without their participation."

Jane Addams, the founder of the settlement-house movement, seconded TR's nomination, the first woman ever to speak at a national political convention; California governor Hiram Johnson agreed to serve as his running mate; longtime progressive Senator George Norris of Nebraska backed him even while remaining nominally a Republican, as did many other influential businessmen, writers, and labor leaders.

Intently watching Roosevelt, a reporter at the convention noted that he appeared as much bewildered as pleased by the wild welcome. "They were crusaders; he was not." This was not quite true, for TR had become a crusader. But he was confronting men and women who had been fighting for progressive causes for years—even decades—while he had had to campaign and compromise, who were now pressing him to push ahead more strongly than ever, and with whom he had barely concealed differences. He "deeply prized" Jane Addams's support, he wrote a friend. Though he had complained that she was a pacificist and a "confused thinker," he felt that she had done "really practical work for the betterment of social conditions. La Follette would back no candidate in 1912, and Elihu Root, ailing and aging and sick at heart over the split, remained committed to Taft.

It had been a century and a half since Americans had beheld such a galaxy of leaders as those who fought one another on the hustings in 1912. Not since the battles over slavery had the nation produced leaders so passionately dedicated to their causes, so willing to risk the politician's ultimate gamble—defeat—in fighting for their goals. And not for many years later would voters—and hundreds of thousands turned out—forget their glimpses of the men on the stump: the socialist Eugene Debs, his thin body coiled like a spring; the Democratic candidate, Woodrow Wilson, vibrant, impassioned, but disdaining the demagogic or theatrical; Taft, outwardly calm and resolute but actually despairing of victory and hoping only to place ahead of the man he now hated; and TR himself, pulsating with energy, grimacing, gesturing, snapping his teeth, screeching out his denunciation of the two old parties.

The battle of 1912 was far more than a struggle among top national leaders; more than at any time since the slavery and reconstruction conflicts, it was a battle of ideas, reflecting the great chasm that had emerged in previous decades between rich and poor. With Debs pounding away on the left and Taft still finding time to play golf, Roosevelt and Wilson confronted each other on the most vital questions of liberty and democracy, Roosevelt speaking for the New Nationalism, Wilson for the New Freedom.

Trust-busting, Roosevelt declared, was "madness." It was nothing less than "preposterous" to return to the era of cutthroat competition. Large corporations were here to stay, he argued, and the government should regulate them, tax their excessive profits, and eventually move toward public ownership of natural monopolies. Pushing the New Freedom, Wilson retorted that huge trusts were neither inevitable nor desirable, that they should be broken up, and that competition should be returned to the economy. Debs's policy on trusts was simple: Take them over and nationalize them. Taft held to the conservative line—and awaited his defeat.

TR's position was as powerful as it was radical. During World War I, Wilson would be forced to suspend the antitrust act in order to increase war production in 1917. Roosevelt then observed that if the Sherman law hurt business during wartime, it also hurt business during peacetime. Wilson was intent upon helping the small entrepreneur and labor against megacorporations while Roosevelt was, in one historian's words, "laying the foundations for central economic planning and for the welfare state."

"Liberty has never come from the government," Wilson lectured the New York Press Club. "Liberty has always come from the subjects of government. The history of liberty is the history of the limitation of governmental power, not the increase of it." Did "these gentlemen" think 1912 was an exception?

One "gentleman" pounced on this remark when he read it in the *New York Tribune*. Calling it the key to Wilson's position (though taking it somewhat out of context, as John Wells Davidson has shown), TR labeled it "professorial rhetoric" without "a particle of foundation in facts." A statement of a decades-old English "laissez-faire" dogma, it meant that "every law for the promotion of social and industrial justice on the statute books ought to be repealed, and every law proposed should be abandoned." Would Professor Wilson raze the Interstate Commerce Commission? While TR attacked Wilson, Louis Brandeis (the self-styled "people's attorney" who defended public causes without a fee and whom Wilson would later appoint to the Supreme Court) seriously damaged TR's chances by writing anonymous editorials falsely claiming that Progressives did not uphold the right of labor to organize and by misrepresenting the Progressive position on trusts.

Women's rights too were part of the battle of 1912. TR had long supported women's suffrage and improved working conditions for women, though his approach to women tended to be paternalistic and proprietary. Still, the Progressive national convention was, as historian John Gable noted, the first convention of a major party to admit women delegates. Four women were to be members-at-large of the national committee, to ensure female representation, and there were at least eighteen women delegates on the floor.

Roosevelt had, even longer than he had supported women's suffrage, upheld the rights of African-Americans, which inspired black leaders to attend the Progressive convention. But he was unable in this case to carry out the transforming aspect of leadership; instead, he compromised with southern "progressives" and approved mixed black-white convention delegations from border states and all-white delegations from the South. Wilson, the native Virginian, now spokesman for a heavily southern-dominated Democratic party, would not touch the subject.

On issues affecting the great mass of the wanting and the needy, however, TR was bold and innovative. The Progressive party platform called for the "protection of home life against the hazards of sickness, irregular employment, and old age through the adoption of social insurance adapted to American use." In his address to the convention, TR was even more explicit: "The hazards of sickness, accident, invalidism, involuntary unemployment, and old age should be provided for through insurance." More than eighty years later, when Congress once again failed to face up to the nation's health needs, some Americans remembered TR's voice in the wilderness in 1912. As for Wilson, although claiming to agree with the broad social goals of the Progressive party, he would not endorse a minimum-wage law for women or support a national child-labor law.

TR favored another issue that would remain controversial into the next century: campaign finance reform. Strict limitations on campaign contributions was one of the planks of the Progressive platform. Despite the large sums he had received from a few millionaires and from his own cousins, TR insisted that he had "only a few supporters among the very rich." The Bull Moose campaign, he boasted, would be financed by average Americans. An Italian laborer, he noted, had sent him five dollars, the equivalent of two days' wages; a veteran in an old soldiers' home sent in a dollar, and the young Hermann Hagedorn, TR's future biographer, donated ten dollars from the sale of a poem.

A thousand delegates left the convention, carrying home little mementos, effigies of the Bull Moose, badges identifying themselves as delegates. They hoped, commented William Allen White, that these trinkets would some day become—as they did—family heirlooms. "The occasion had all of the psychological trapping and habiliments of a crusade."

TR had undergone a radical sea change. He had long been the ardent admirer of Alexander Hamilton and the opponent of Thomas Jefferson. "In my estimation," TR had written in 1896, "Jefferson's influence upon the United States as a whole was very distinctly evil." But now he saw Hamilton as a true Federalist, a believer in "privilege or vested rights against popular rights," and he viewed Jefferson as a great leader "because he was for the people," and, he added, because he was "for our Western expansion." Finally, in 1912, Theodore Roosevelt bowed to Jefferson.

. . .

By summer 1912, FDR was going through an extraordinary transformation that paralleled TR's. In the 1911 New York State Senate session he had acted essentially as a Cleveland Democrat like his father: anti-spoils, anti-bossism, and for such political reforms as the popular election of U.S. senators and the direct primary, two ideas scorned by "regulars" as being against the party machine. He was cool to bills limiting the workweek to fifty-four hours for boys and women. And even after the horrifying Triangle Shirtwaist fire in 1911, Roosevelt was slow to support legislative action, compared to the strong lead taken by Wagner and Smith and other "machine" Democrats.

In FDR's second year in the New York Senate, all this appeared to change. He supported the fifty-four-hour bill for women, a workmen's compensation measure, and a packet of reforms that came out of an investigation of the Triangle disaster. Noncommittal on women's suffrage in 1911, he flatly backed it the next year. And on matters closer to the heart of a Hudson River conservationist—public power and forestry conservation—he took much stronger positions than in the previous year. Following in Uncle Ted's path, Franklin chaired the committee on forest, fish, and game and tried, unsuccessfully, to pass legislation limiting tree cutting on privately owned land. He even became a bit of a socialist, backing a measure to authorize the state to build and run hydroelectric plants. By the end of the 1912 session, along with his support of agricultural bills, FDR was a "farm laborite."

Why such a quick and thorough flipflop? In part, perhaps, because 1912 was the culmination of one of the most intellectually challenging decades in American history: the decade of outspoken progressives, relentless woman suffragists, muckraking writers. But 1912 was also the year of the dramatic shift to the left of Theodore Roosevelt, his political mentor. Some of his new ideas appeared in an almost philosophical address that Franklin Roosevelt gave at a People's Forum in Troy, just north of his Hudson River district.

He had been thinking of a "new theory," he said, about liberty of the community as against liberty of the individual. "Every new star that people have hitched their wagon to for the past half century, whether it be anti-rebating, or anti-trusts, or new-fashioned education, or conservation of our natural resources, or state regulation of common carriers, or commission government" and many others, "almost without exception . . . are all steps in the evolution of the new theory of the liberty of the community." This was about as far as FDR went, except for some warnings about the dangers of undue conflict.

The young state senator was far more influenced by people than by abstract ideas, however, and the main source of his shift lay in the emergence of another leader in 1912. If, in 1911 and the beginning of 1912, FDR's hero and mentor still was Cousin Theodore, by the end of 1912, FDR was turning to another man who also would become his mentor and hero: Woodrow Wilson.

Franklin had watched admiringly as the scholar-politician from Princeton had gained the backing of a New Jersey kingpin and boss of the Essex County Democratic organization, James R. Smith Jr., to win the gubernatorial nomination in 1910 and then skillfully threaded his way between an indignant Smith and militant progressives in supporting adoption of the direct primary. He watched, too, as the newly elected governor took progressive stands on other issues, including workmen's compensation, though he was slower to embrace women's suffrage. A Virginian who had shown his liberal credentials in the North as a scholar and reform president of Princeton, Wilson soon loomed as a promising contender for the White House.

Franklin had lost no time in seeking Wilson out in Trenton. He was impressed with the governor's ability to confront and overcome the New Jersey bosses, but, even more, he wanted to open up the possibility of a key job in a Wilson administration. Embarrassingly, he had little to offer Wilson in return. As a result of his own insurgency and Boss Murphy's experience in such matters, he would be shut out from membership in the New York delegation to the Democratic national convention. All he could promise Wilson was to help mobilize progressive voters in the Empire State.

Unable to sit with the New Yorkers on the 1912 Democratic convention floor, FDR did not sulk in his gallery seat. He was all over the place, roaming the corridors, buttonholing delegates, working the lobbies, meeting—and favorably impressing—delegates from across the country. One of these was Josephus Daniels, longtime North Carolina politico, editor of the *Raleigh News and Observer,* and future secretary of the navy, who found Franklin "as handsome a figure of an attractive young man as I have ever seen." The nondelegate watched with rising excitement as Wilson first ran behind in the balloting to Beauchamp "Champ" Clark of Missouri, then grew stronger as state bosses maneuvered and traded through four hot and suspenseful days and nights. Even William Jennings Bryan, who had electrified the convention with a resolution that the delegates oppose the nomination of any candidate "under obligation to J. Pierpont Morgan . . . or any other member of the privilege-hunting and favor-seeking class," teetered back and forth as he tried to foil state bosses allied with "corrupt" corporations. When Wilson eked out his victory on the forty-sixth roll call, it was as much a result of the maneuvering of Wilson lieutenants in smoke-filled rooms as of the governor's standing as a reformer and progressive.

WILSON NOMINATED THIS AFTERNOON ALL MY PLANS VAGUE STOP SPLENDID TRIUMPH, Franklin wired Eleanor, who had left the convention for Campobello. In fact, his plans were not all that vague. He knew he must secure his state senator base even while jockeying for a position within a Wilson administration.

After a quick auto tour of his district and harmony meetings with local Democrats, FDR won renomination for his senate seat without opposition. He then joined the family in Campobello and prepared for a strenuous reelection fight. It was not to be. He and Eleanor both came down with severe cases of typhoid fever—evidently from contaminated water on the steamer from Campobello—and the candidate lay flat on his back for weeks in New York. Franklin sent out an emergency call to Louis Howe to take over the campaign. More than FDR's assistant and a former correspondent for the *New York Herald,* Howe was a visionary who, early in their acquaintance, declared that FDR would someday be president. Devoted to this goal, he had worked for FDR ever since, providing information, connections, and support of every kind, sharing with Franklin his intuitive grasp of politics, shaping him into a candidate with national appeal. Soon farmers along the Hudson spotted the big red Maxwell puttering along but were amazed to see in the back seat not the tall young senator they knew but a little man with a cigarette sticking out from a pockmarked face.

While Franklin endured the worst torture for him—inaction—he could at least follow the national campaigns.

. . .

At a campaign stop in Milwaukee, a man shouting "No third term!" pumped a bullet into Theodore Roosevelt's chest. TR's courage, combativeness, and defiance now converged. Mounting the campaign platform, he calmly announced to a horrified audience, "There is a bullet in my body" and proclaimed, "It takes more than that to kill a Bull Moose." And as if he had a premonition of political defeat and wished to die in the heat of battle, TR told the crowd, "The bullet is in me now. . . . And now, friends . . . I want you to understand that I am ahead of the game anyway. No man has had a happier life than I have led." TR continued to orate for more than an hour and a half as listeners begged him to quit.

At his next campaign rally in Madison Square Garden, a *Times* reporter noted; 16,000 people went "absolutely crazy for forty-one minutes." Respectable middle-aged people climbed on chairs, waved flags and handkerchiefs, and danced around the floor in a frenzy. And during the last days of the campaign, TR took a final shot at the courts. "We recognize in neither court, nor Congress, nor President," he declared, "any divine right to override the will of the people."

When the election returns came in, they were almost as dramatic as the shooting: 6.3 million votes for Wilson, 4.1 million for TR, 3.5 million for Taft, and a surprising 900,000 for Debs. Though Wilson did not garner a popular majority, he had won an electoral landslide. TR could brag that he won 27.4 percent of the total popular vote, a better showing than almost all other third-party candidates both before and after 1912. He had carried Michigan and California overwhemingly. Throughout the country he had performed best in urban and prosperous rural areas and among the most educated segments of the population, who understood a party platform drafted by intellectuals and social scientists. He fared poorly among the immigrant population, especially among immigrants from southern and eastern Europe who tended to vote with traditional party machines. Organized labor had supported Wilson. Significantly, 75 percent of the popular vote had gone to the three candidates—Roosevelt, Wilson, and Debs—perceived as being left of center. Many businessmen bemoaned "radical politics" running rampant in America.

In presidential elections, there are no second prizes. In his official concession statement, TR accepted "the result with entire good humor and contentment," proud that he had fought a hard fight for a high cause. But his wife confessed to a friend that Theodore was "rather blue." Should he have played it safe, he wondered, and not run at all? And while professing to some friends that he had no regrets, to others he admitted that, by cutting loose from the Republican party, his movement had dealt a disastrous blow to the Progressive cause at the grassroots level. He did not mention the blow that he himself had dealt to the Republicans.

As for Franklin, he naturally was following Howe's reports of his New York Senate reelection campaign even more eagerly than the presidential campaign. Howe, a canny newspaperman, was making full use of his press contacts and—much to the chagrin of Sara, who had taught her son that gentlemen keep their names out of the newspapers—was taking out full-page advertisements that reflected the 1912 progressive stands of his boss. Howe's election-night phone call reported that Roosevelt had won, and by a larger margin than two years earlier. While FDR benefited from the cut taken in the Republican vote by a Progressive candidate, he outran both Wilson and the Democratic gubernatorial candidate in his district.

Whatever his hopes of a Washington job, FDR carried on his senate role energetically. It was curious, but also impressive, that this politician looking toward Washington focused in late 1912 on comprehensive state aid measures for farmers. By far the most controversial of these was a bill for the licensing and inspection of commission merchants, long a target for their allegedly bloated profits from farm products. Roosevelt even committed a most unlikely act when he appeared at a New York City dock to watch the unloading of produce from Norfolk, Virginia, and then shadowed a crate of spinach as it passed through a series of middlemen and ended up costing consumers four times what the grower had received. He then introduced a controversial regulatory measure that was later passed in altered form.

Still, his ear was always tuned to any siren call from Washington. It came in a telegram from New Jersey, summoning him to a meeting with the president-elect. Possible appointments were discussed. FDR was already falling under the spell of this unusual president and politician. Rumors soon were flying that he would have a major appointment.

These rumors did not sit well in Oyster Bay. The Theodore Roosevelt clan felt wounded by FDR's failure to support Uncle Theodore in the presidential election. Only Eleanor had remained loyal. Like a good Oyster Bay Roosevelt, she had urged her husband—in vain—to join other Democrats who were deserting their own party to support the Bull Mooser.

. . .

TR's sense of isolation and rejection were becoming profound. At home in Oyster Bay, the radical politician was viewed as "wild" and "revolutionary." Casual encounters on the roads or in church with his neighbors were correct but cold. "All respectable society is now apoplectic with rage over me," TR remarked. He stood outside the pale, having done the unforgivable thing. "He had 'turned against his class,'" commented TR's biographer, Hermann Hagedorn.

"You don't know how lonely it is for a man to be rejected by his own kind," TR said to a guest at Sagamore Hill. "I have just come from Boston, where I attended a meeting of the Harvard overseers. They all bunched at one end of the room away from me, and I stood all alone there except for one man, nice General Hallowell, who acted like a perfect trump, standing by me through it all, gnashing his teeth in rage at those other fellows. By George! we were like a pair of Airedale pups in a convention of tomcats!"

For patricians like Harvard-educated Moorfield Storey, Theodore Roosevelt had presided over the Progressives like a radical out of the French Revolution, precipitating the dissolution of the patrician world. "The world you and I have loved," Storey wrote to a friend, "seems likely to be destroyed." Even Ted Jr. found himself occasionally thrown out of Wall Street offices for the offense of being his father's son. It was one thing for TR to have attacked the nouveaux riches and the plutocrats; another for him to have denounced wealth itself. At dinner parties in the closed New York community of Tuxedo Park, millionaires denounced "the iniquities of Theodore Roosevelt." Herbert Pell, the nephew of Tuxedo Park's developer, Pierre Lorillard IV, would later recall that his uncle's elite class "hated TR and raved against him far more than they ever did against Franklin. By the time Franklin came along there was no less hostility, but there was less surprise."

TR was paying a high price for class betrayal. And yet, although he denounced the elite world of privilege and inherited wealth in favor of the rights of the many, he still felt there was a role for the "best people" in government. "We stand equally against government by a plutocracy and government by a mob," he wrote in 1913. "There is something to be said for government by a great aristocracy which has furnished leaders to the nation in peace and war for generations; even a democrat like myself must admit this."

Despite TR's own hurt feelings, the election of 1912 demonstrated, according to editor William Allen White, that "the progressive or liberal movement was overwhelmingly in the majority in the United States." But, White sadly confessed, "I lost my first choice and my heart's political desire."

Still, TR's prescient moderate radicalism, synthesizing different strains in American political and economic thought, contributed mightily to pushing the country toward transformational change. The man whom Richard Hofstadter described as a conservative posing as a progressive was, in truth, the opposite: an upper-class progressive with radical tendencies posing occasionally as a conservative.

Decades after TR's defeat in 1912, William Allen White observed that much of TR's reformist agenda had ultimately been adopted and enacted. "When the New Deal came with its program," he remarked, "it went little further than Colonel Roosevelt's Progressive party had gone twenty years before." TR had suspected as much. "I firmly believe," he wrote after his defeat, "that we have put forward the cause of justice and humanity by many years."

As for the future author of the New Deal, he expressed amazement at his cousin's radicalism. After reading the handbook of the Socialist party in the early 1920s, FDR remarked to Frances Perkins, "You know, it's a funny thing—the Socialists have what they call their immediate and long-term programs. The immediate program, as you read it over, sounds almost exactly like the Bull Moose party of Ted's day."

But in 1912, FDR hardly felt a pang as he moved from the orbit of one mentor to another. More and more, his mind was set on the great adventure that awaited him in Washington.

3
The Unneutralist

At the age of thirty-one, Franklin Roosevelt became civilian boss of that part of the navy department which purchased large quantities of coal and steel, supervised shore installations, handled management-labor relationships, and spent a large portion of the department's almost $150 million budget, which in turn represented about 20 percent of total federal spending for 1913. He also helped handle emergencies, such as midwestern floods that suddenly required immense quantities of navy blankets and rations, and he had to deal with tough technical problems, most notably one arising from the collapse of a big drydock being built at Pearl Harbor.

How did FDR get this plum? He was, after all, only one state senator out of dozens in New York, a young man with no naval or military background who had never even managed a household—Sara and Eleanor had done that—much less a government department. Why did Wilson give him, a green unknown on the national scene, such a big job? Simply, the name Roosevelt was magic—and someone with that name had already held the same job. But it was also longtime acceptance of the idea of party patronage: To the victor belong the spoils. "It is interesting that you are in another place which I myself once held," TR wrote to Franklin, congratulating him. "I am sure you will enjoy yourself to the full as Ass't Secty of the Navy and that you will do capital work."

If FDR had the slightest feeling of inadequacy at the job, he never gave a hint of it. He took on his work with Rooseveltian gusto and brimming self-confidence. Attired in a blue naval cape, he welcomed the seventeen-gun salute that greeted him on inspection trips. He expected that his flag—which he had personally designed—would be flown on such occasions. When Secretary of the Navy Josephus Daniels left town for a couple of days, the newly appointed FDR cheerily informed reporters, "There's another Roosevelt on the job today." And in case the newspapermen did not get the point, that TR had taken advantage of *his* superior's absence in 1898 to order a bellicose fleet movement in the western Pacific, Franklin added, "You remember what happened the last time a Roosevelt occupied a similar position?" The reporters—and the public—did.

All this bordered on arrogance. He was sometimes contemptuous of Daniels, whose southern background, populist ways, and simple, unheroic demeanor he could neither understand nor appreciate.

In Washington he and Eleanor lived in Theodore Roosevelt's sister Anna's house, the same gloomy but genteel house on N Street in which Theodore had lived for a brief period after becoming president. Franklin and Eleanor continued to move in the same social circles they had occupied in New York and Boston. Patronizing to the Irish, he shared, with Eleanor, prevailing upper-class WASP attitudes toward Catholics and Jews and casually referred to African-Americans as "niggers" and "darkies." These conventional attitudes did not, however, make him more popular with Harvard classmates and other friends, many of whom merely disliked and distrusted him—and not simply because he was a Democrat.

Still, the test of an assistant secretary of the navy was less tolerance and hubris than quick intelligence, rapid learning ability, and willingness to dig into tough human and technical problems. The U.S. Navy faced formidable problems in trying to modernize its fleet in competition with other Great Power navies—the shift from coal to oil raised a whole set of difficulties—and FDR moved from complexity to complexity with skill. The toughest of all problems was the most human one: labor relations, which he and Howe also saw as offering possible political benefits and liabilities. Taylorism—a system of "scientific management" to increase workers' productivity, named for its inventor, engineer Frederick W.

Taylor—was coming into vogue about this time. FDR saw its efficiencies, but he also knew that union chiefs were suspicious that Taylorism was a device not only to speed workers up but to deprive them of control over their own work lives, so he delayed action until Congress could deal with this hot potato. It was much easier to listen to labor's day-to-day complaints and act on them.

"The laboring men all liked him," Secretary Daniels said later. "If there was any Groton complex (which there was in his social life), he did not show it in the Department."

Auntie Bye, as Bamie was also called, in whose house Eleanor and Franklin were living, was able to advise the young couple about Washington political and naval circles. Eleanor should call on naval officers' wives, and she faithfully did so, paying sixty calls in one week. At dinner parties Eleanor met and conversed with cabinet members, senators, justices, lobbyists. To help organize her busy social life, she hired a young woman named Lucy Mercer, of impeccable background but little means.

Amid this intense activity—and within a year of his taking on the job—FDR began maneuvering to run for statewide office in New York. How could it be, with all the satisfactions and gratifications of his Washington job, that he would seek another and wholly different political prize? The answer was sheer ambition, fired by earlier rebuffs, a burning desire to emulate Cousin Theodore, continuing opposition to Tammany, and a genuine devotion to public service. Believing Franklin had great promise, partly thanks to his name, others encouraged him—even, perhaps, his boss. "His distinguished cousin T.R. went from that place to the Presidency," wrote Daniels in his diary. "May history repeat itself." In late summer 1914, Franklin announced for the Democratic nomination for the U.S. Senate.

He lost ignominiously, the only defeat he would ever suffer on his own. Despite Howe's help, he did everything wrong. He announced late (partly because Franklin Roosevelt Jr. was born in mid-August at Campobello). He assumed that the Wilson administration would support him against a Tammany aspirant, while in fact the president was careful to keep out of a state contest at a time when he was seeking support from Tammany congressmen for his domestic program. And once again he underestimated the skill and resourcefulness of Boss Murphy, who maneuvered into the race not a Tammany hack but no less than James W. Gerard, Wilson's ambassador to Germany, who stayed at his Berlin post during the gathering European crisis and denied FDR a target even to shoot at. Gerard beat him by almost three to one.

. . .

The most bizarre aspect of this failed political venture was its timing. Through these weeks the war clouds thickened in Europe and then the storm broke. War abroad would enormously enhance the importance of FDR's navy post, but what was this seeker of glory and action doing? During the first days of August 1914, while Germany declared war on Russia and then on France and invaded Belgium, and while Britain declared war on Germany, he was planning his impending bid for the U.S. Senate seat. In mid-August he joined his family at Campobello, where he read news reports of Wilson's August 19 public appeal to Americans to be "impartial in thought as well as in action." On that same day Roosevelt wrote a friend that he longed "to go over into the thick of it & do something to help right the wrong." Instead, he got into the thick of his own primary fight, cast his ballot in Hyde Park at the end of September, received stoically the dismal election results, and then meandered to Washington.

Once back in his post, however, he appeared to forget his defeat, with his usual cheery aplomb, and plunged into the navy world as though he had never left it. And he soon made clear that he would be impartial in neither thought nor action.

From the start he was an activist. Even while concentrating on his coming primary campaign he had returned from a ceremony—the formal opening of the Cape Cod Canal—to find everyone else seemingly asleep at the navy department. Nobody "seemed the least bit excited about the European crisis!" he wrote "Dearest Babs" (Eleanor). So he "started in alone to get things ready and prepare plans for what *ought* to be done" by the navy. Daniels, he added, "totally" failed to "grasp the situation."

But of course *he* did; he had no doubt. From the start he was wholeheartedly, enthusiastically, on the side of Britain. "England's course has been magnificent," he burst out in a private letter. "Oh, if that German fleet would only come out and fight!" There was a limit, of course, to how much an assistant secretary could *do* unneutrally, as against *thinking* unneutrally, but FDR could at least boast he was running the war. "*I* am *running* the real work, although Josephus is here!" he wrote "Dearest E." early in August 1914. "He is bewildered by it all, very sweet but very sad!" It hardly occurred to the young assistant secretary that Daniels, seeking funds and support from Congress, might find it harder to deal with populist isolationists than with belligerent Germans.

Even during the early months of the war, FDR was at odds not only with Daniels but with much of the "neutral" administration about "preparedness" and strategy. Not only was he socializing regularly with his English and French friends—sometimes at their embassies—he was keeping company with some of Daniels's critics, especially in the Navy League.

Nor could he break away from the mesmerizing influence of Cousin Theodore, who moved erratically but passionately during 1914 toward an aggressive stance against Germany, or from the political embrace of such TR friends as Republican senator Henry Cabot Lodge of Massachusetts, who saw Franklin as an ally within the administration.

But in wartime, events above all are in the saddle, the rulers of people's attitudes and actions. The United States and its navy could not escape fallout from the teetering balances between the inhuman strategies of the belligerents, as London sought to starve Germany into submission and as Berlin sought to cut off Britain's lifelines to Canada and the United States. Events turned on the latest horrifying incident—and the most staggering of all came in May 1915 with a German U-boat's sinking of the British liner *Lusitania* and the drowning of almost twelve hundred persons, including 128 Americans. Wilson dispatched protests to Berlin strong enough to precipitate the resignation of his isolationist secretary of state, the venerable William Jennings Bryan, but not strong enough to defang the onetime Rough Rider.

TR lambasted Wilson's "supine inaction" over the sinkings as "milk and water" policy. Wilson, he sneered, spoke for the "solid flubdub and pacifist vote," for "every soft creature, every coward and weakling, every man who can't look more than six inches ahead." The president was an "abject creature," TR fumed to his son Archie.

Campaigning in New York for the Progressive candidate for governor in 1914 and simultaneously attacking Wilson, TR received an invitation from Sara Roosevelt to spend a night at Springwood. "If it were not for the campaign," he wrote her, "there is no place where I would rather go." But, he added, his appearance at Hyde Park would only harm Franklin's reputation within the Wilson administration. Franklin would soon return the thoughtful gesture of loyalty when he testified on TR's behalf in a libel trial. For in the midst of his attacks on Wilson, TR, speaking out for Progressives, had also attacked the Republican party boss, William Barnes Jr., accusing him of collusion with the Democratic boss, Charles Murphy.

When Barnes unsuccessfully sued TR for libel, Franklin was among the few people willing to testify on TR's behalf. "His hero actually needed him," remarked historian Geoffrey Ward, and Franklin did not disappoint. "Franklin Roosevelt was up here yesterday," a jubilant TR wrote to Edith, "and made the best witness we have had yet." The former president wrote his cousin that he would "never forget" the young man's "capital" action.

Nothing inflamed TR more than Wilson's speaking of Americans as "too proud to fight," a statement that represented "the nadir of cowardly infamy." "I am so sick at heart," he wrote his friend Arthur Lee, "over affairs in the world at large at this moment and particularly over the course of my own government and my own people." The "screaming and shrieking and bleating of the peace people," he lamented, had caused the country to follow a "course of national infamy." There was little the Nobel Peace Prize winner scorned more, he confessed, than "the pacifist frame of mind." As far as the Colonel was concerned, the conflict in Europe was terrible and evil but also "grand and noble." There was an element of "splendid heroism" in the war, he told his son Kermit in 1915. His personal loathing of Wilson, combined with his belief in military preparedness, his exaggerated sense of nationalism, his scorn for isolationism, his fear that a German victory might threaten American security, and his own cult of heroism and masculinity, all convinced TR that American participation in the war was as necessary as it was inevitable.

Perhaps recalling his own father, who had bought himself a "substitute" to fight in his stead in the Civil War, TR now called for universal military service. "I would have the son of the multimillionaire and the son of the immigrant who came in steerage . . . sleep under the same dog tent."

Though out of power, TR was singlehandedly provoking a national debate on preparedness and war. By 1916, commented historian William Harbaugh, the words "preparedness" and "Roosevelt" had become synonymous. Oddly, added Harbaugh, TR did nothing to counteract the belief held by socialists and antiwar progressives like La Follette that munitions makers and the House of Morgan were behind the preparedness movement.

FDR was solidly in TR's camp, ideologically and rhetorically. In the navy department, backed from outside by Lodge and Big Navy men, he pressed for preparedness to the point of insubordination to Daniels and Wilson. He had the good luck to have an especially tolerant boss, who also prized FDR's ability to handle problems quickly and effectively, and he had the skill to walk the tightrope between the contending political and military forces. "I just know I shall do some awful unneutral thing before

I get through," he had written Eleanor early in the war, but he stayed on the tightrope, in large part because he glimpsed the political abyss if he fell off.

. . .

Another presidential election was looming. "Lord, how I would like to be President!" TR had written a close friend in 1915. TR was at a low point. He had returned from his 1914 trip up the River of Doubt—now called Rio Roosevelt—in Brazil. The desire to wield power once again overtook him, like a revitalizing, rejuvenating drug. "Don't imagine that I wouldn't like to be at the White House this minute," he burst out during the winter before the election. Though TR was the candidate—who else was there?—of the still extant Progressive party, he held out little hope that the Progressives could survive. After the defeats of 1914, the party, he recognized, had become a "cropper." The winds had shifted, he explained to his friend William Allen White. People were feeling the pinch of poverty; they wanted prosperity and "did not care a rap for social justice." The identification of the Progressive party with prohibition had also hurt the reform movement.

Yearning to be back in the White House, TR was ready to make his peace with the Republican party. Indeed, he hoped that the breach between Progressives and Republicans—who were holding their conventions in Chicago at the same time—could perhaps be repaired and that the Progressives too could return to the Republican fold. TR hoped there would be a groundswell of support for him at the Republican convention, despite the opposition of the party bosses. Support among Republicans indeed seemed to be building: Thomas Edison, a Bull Mooser in 1912, wrote a public letter stating that TR was "absolutely the only man" who could handle the crisis.

But despite the usual jubilant floor demonstrations for him, Roosevelt was not even permitted to address the Republican convention. The political class he had betrayed would not forgive him. Conservatives were not disposed to forget that his defection in 1912 had made possible Wilson's victory. "The standpat Republicans," commented TR's sister Corinne, "were still smarting from what they considered, I think unjustly, his betrayal of them, and they were not ready to enroll themselves under his banner." Instead, Republicans nominated Charles Evans Hughes. "Well, the country wasn't in heroic mood!" TR sulked. "We are passing through a thick streak of yellow in our national life."

"Ah, Teddy dear, and did ye hear the news that's goin' round?" wrote the *Chicago Evening Post* right after TR's defeat at the Republican convention. "They say you're gone from off the stage." Passion, imagination, laughter, and friendship, the *Post* lamented, were doomed to disappear from the political scene along with him. "Gray is the prospect; dull is the outlook" in the post-Teddy world.

TR endorsed Hughes, accepting him as a unity candidate because he disliked—or rather, despised—Wilson far more. Many of the Progressive party leaders followed TR back into the Republican party, though a significant minority supported Wilson.

The Progressive party, knowing it could not survive as a party without Roosevelt, tailored a moderate platform to fit TR but containing virtually none of the reformist planks of 1912. And to make matters worse, even after Progressives had compromised their principles for TR, he urged them to choose Henry Cabot Lodge instead, praising him improbably as one of the "staunchest fighters for different measures of economic reform in the direction of justice." The Progressives, however, wanted nothing to do with the putative fighter for economic justice from Massachusetts who that very summer had refused to support a child-labor bill. Instead, they nominated TR anyway. When TR's telegram from Oyster Bay, declining the nomination, was read out loud to the convention, hundreds of angry heartbroken delegates roared their disapproval, tearing up Roosevelt's picture and ripping Roosevelt badges from their coats. "I had tears in my eyes," William Allen White wrote, as he looked back on that second and last Progressive convention. Deserted by Theodore Roosevelt, the Progressive party was now defunct.

His excuse? Foremost in his mind stood America's obligation to go to war, and thus it was imperative that people rally to Hughes as the interventionist candidate. "The essential thing," wrote TR's Progressive supporter Amos Pinchot the following year, "was to get rid of Wilson," and for TR to have run as a Progressive would "have meant to reelect Wilson." And indeed, in 1916 while Wilson campaigned with the slogan, "He kept us out of war," TR denounced the president's "incapable leadership," declaring that "if we elect Mr. Wilson it will be serving notice on the world" that Americans had turned their backs on the "courageous purposes of Washington and Lincoln" and had become "sordid, soft, and spineless." For his part, FDR campaigned for Wilson, but even more for preparedness and for a "Navy second to none."

Within three months of Wilson's reelection, events lurched toward a new crisis, as Germany announced resumption of unrestricted submarine warfare. During February 1917 sinkings mounted. Wilson ordered the arming of American merchantmen—a move FDR had long urged—and a wave of belligerent and nationalist feeling swept the country. On April 2, Wilson, standing before Congress, called for a war resolution. The whole assemblage, Eleanor and Franklin included, roared its approval, and the applause swelled as the president went on.

"The world must be made safe for democracy." They would never forget the tall, erect figure, his face pale and unsmiling, as he rose to his climax. "It is a fearful thing to lead this great peaceful people into war, into the most terrible and disastrous of all wars, civilization itself seeming to be in the balance. But the right is more precious than peace, and we shall fight for the things which we have always carried nearest our hearts—for democracy, for the rights of those who submit to authority to have a voice in their own Governments, for the rights and liberties of small nations, for a universal dominion of right by such a concert of free peoples as shall bring peace and safety to all nations and make the world itself at last free."

Those ideals would dominate the lives of Eleanor and Franklin Roosevelt to a far greater degree, and for a far longer time, than they could possibly have imagined that evening.

. . .

For Eleanor the war was a crucial time of self-discovery. In the early years of her marriage, her world had narrowed. "I had lost a good deal of my crusading spirit where the poor were concerned," she explained, "because I had been told I had no right to go into the slums or into the hospitals, for fear of bringing diseases home to my children." Now, in Washington, her awareness of others was broadening, igniting her sense of duty. When her grandmother proposed that Eleanor's brother Hall avoid serving in the army by buying himself a "substitute," as gentlemen like Eleanor's own grandfather had done during the Civil War, Eleanor hotly responded that a gentleman was no better than any other kind of citizen. This was, she later recalled, her first declaration against the accepted standards and class conventions of her childhood.

As society gossip yielded to talk of enormous world changes, as her dutiful social calls gave way on the calendar to visits with wounded sailors at naval hospitals, as society luncheons were replaced by trips to pour coffee for weary doughboys at Union Station, Eleanor found a new energy taking hold of her.

She rose at 5 A.M. to work at the Red Cross canteen at the station, providing soup, coffee, and sandwiches for soldiers on the troop trains that toiled through Washington. Tireless and efficient, she supervised more than forty units of knitters for the navy department. The urgency of the war gave her life purpose; she found that for once she was needed—even indispensable—and she thrived on the feeling. "I loved it," she said. "I simply ate it up." "The war was my emancipation and education," she later remarked.

Still, the transition from female society ornament to compassionate democrat and politically attuned operative was not altogether easy. When a reporter for *The New York Times* asked what contribution she and her family were making to the wartime challenge of food conservation, Eleanor patriotically replied, "Making the ten servants help me do my saving has not only been possible but highly profitable." The media-savvy FDR exploded when he read the interview, firing off a scornful message to his wife. "I am proud to be the husband of the Originator, Discoverer, and Inventor of the New Household Economy for Millionaires!" he wrote.

It would take decades for Eleanor to transcend the prejudices of her class. "The Jew party was appalling," she would groan a few years later in 1920, after attending a reception at which she met the financier Bernard Baruch, probably not realizing that Baruch's great-grandmother had danced with Lafayette when he visited America in 1824. Felix Frankfurter fared no better. The Harvard law professor was, she wrote her mother-in-law, "an interesting little man, but very Jew."

For Franklin Roosevelt the war was sheer relief and excitement. It removed the main roadblocks to preparedness. It opened up a world of new opportunities. Above all it was a tonic, a heady, bracing draught for this navy department activist. But all this was not enough. He wanted to become a naval officer, to *fight*.

. . .

"You must resign," Cousin Theodore told Franklin. "You must get into uniform at once." TR could speak feelingly. *He* wanted to fight—to raise a volunteer division of infantry, lead it to France and into action, and thus stiffen Allied morale. "I should of course ask no favors of any kind," TR wrote to the secretary of war, "except that the division be put in the fighting line at the earliest possible moment." He would raise the money, he promised the secretary, explaining that his division would comprise three brigades of infantry, cavalry, artillery, engineers, a motorcycle machine-gun regiment, an aero squadron, supply branches, and others! Tens of thousands of volunteers were already flocking to the Colonel.

"If I am allowed to go, I could not last," TR admitted to his sister and the French ambassador over a quiet cup of tea. "I should *crack* but I *could* arouse the belief that America was coming." He added, significantly, "What difference would it make if I cracked or not!" As if yearning for a heroic death, as he had when the bullet struck him in Milwaukee, TR wrote William Allen White, "I think I could do this country most good by dying in a reasonably honorable fashion at the head of my division in the European War." When the secretary of war declined his offer, he asked his friend Henry Cabot Lodge to try to intervene on his behalf.

Finally, swallowing his pride, he appealed in person to Commander in Chief Wilson. Franklin had arranged the appointment in the White House. Wilson pointed out that the grinding Western Front was no "Charge of the Light Brigade" but promised "careful consideration." "I was charmed by his personality," Wilson remarked after his meeting with the Colonel. "There is a sweetness about him that is very compelling. You can't resist the man."

Meanwhile the "Roosevelt Division" had become a cause célèbre. Even Marshal Joseph Joffre, visiting the United States from France, agreed that it would galvanize the world, though the State Department censored newspaper accounts of Joffre's remarks. And Georges Clemenceau, the soon-to-be prime minister of France whose main task would be to battle against French "defeatism," praised the Colonel's "simple vital idealism," imploring Wilson, in an open letter in his Paris newspaper, to accede to Roosevelt's request. "Believe me—send us Roosevelt!"

Nevertheless the president left it to General John J. Pershing and the rest of the army brass to squelch the idea. "I really think the best way to treat Mr. Roosevelt is to take no notice of him," said Wilson, adding that that strategy constituted "the best punishment that can be administered."

Wilson's refusal was a "bitter blow" from which TR never quite recovered, said his niece Eleanor. Excluded from the great conflict, he felt reduced, he sighed to his sister, to "utterly pointless and fussy activities." The only consolation for the old Colonel was that his sons were entering the battle. "They are keenly desirous to see service," TR had written to General Pershing, attempting to intervene on his sons' behalf. That same summer Ted and Archie landed in France, Kermit was offered a position on the staff of the British army in Mesopotamia, and Quentin had passed his exams for the flying corps. "You have the fighting tradition!" a proud TR wrote to Ted Jr. "I am overjoyed that you four have your chance, whatever the cost." To his son-in-law he admitted that "the pride and the anxiety go hand in hand."

Franklin had no better luck getting into uniform than TR, even with Daniels interceding for him. "Neither you nor I nor Franklin Roosevelt has the right to select the place of service," Wilson said with all his Presbyterian sternness. Later FDR appealed personally to the president, to no avail. Doubtless his superiors wondered how a man who boasted of running the naval war virtually singlehanded could argue that he would be indispensable in uniform.

TR at least could vent his spleen—and contribute to the war effort—by writing more than a hundred syndicated articles for the *Kansas City Star* between September 1917 and January 1919. The themes he stressed over and over—in increasingly shrill and intolerant essays—were complete, unwavering, undivided loyalty and duty to America, military preparedness, hostility to everything German (including the teaching of German in public schools), admiration for everything English, the demonic nature of anything and anyone associated with European Bolshevik radicalism, opposition to the idea of a League of Nations (though he himself had supported the league concept in 1914 and 1915), and scathing criticism of almost everything said and done by Woodrow Wilson. Even Wilson's prescient warning that there should be "peace without victory" outraged TR. The Colonel demanded "punishment" for the criminal nation.

So the three Roosevelts, from their civilian vantage points, could only watch—and criticize—their commander in chief in action. And what they saw was a Wilson almost totally transformed from the would-be mediator and peacemaker, the leader of a nation too proud to fight, into the warrior. "Once lead the people into war," he had told a journalist, "and they'll forget there ever was such a thing as tolerance." A year after America's entry, however, he noted that Germany had said that force, and force alone, should decide; hence there was "but one response possible from us: Force, Force to the utmost, Force without stint or limit."

FDR not only admired Wilson's Hamiltonian executive leadership, he gloried in it and imitated it. Years later, when a writer intimated that the war effort had been a vast people's movement that energized the administration, FDR denied it. The war organization, he said, had been "created *from the top down*, not *the bottom up*." In fact confusion, delays, bungling, along with amazing production feats, marked the 1917–18 mobilization. In his sector the assistant secretary overcame delays and "business as usual" through improvisation, cutting corners, pulling rank, and sheer energy.

Least troubling of all to FDR was the centralization of power and the near-dictatorship in Washington that enormously enhanced presidential power. Nor was he disturbed that the White House sponsored an Espionage Act, passed by Congress in June 1917, that imposed heavy penalties for persons aiding the enemy, obstructing recruiting, or causing disloyalty, or that President Wilson signed a May 1918 sedition amendment that banned "disloyal, profane, scurrilous, or abusive language" against the American form of government, the Constitution, the flag, the armed forces, and necessary war production.

"To fight you must be brutal and ruthless, and the spirit of ruthless brutality will enter into the very fiber of our national life," Wilson had told a journalist. It entered his administration as well. Wilson not only supported prosecutions—most notably of Eugene Debs, sentenced to ten years' imprisonment under the sedition law—but he was silent when, amid a wave of hate and hysteria, the teaching of German was banned in schools and celebrated musicians such as Fritz Kreisler were barred from concert stages.

Although TR had famously attacked the sedition bill for its clause prohibiting "contemptuous or slurring language about the President," lambasting it as unconstitutional and as an "American adaptation of the German doctrine of lese majesty," none of this bothered FDR. When several socialists were convicted of passing out antiwar publications, Franklin expressed his approval to the prosecuting attorney. As for "slackers," like people who failed to buy Liberty Bonds, they should be "taught" better.

But what if he were himself a slacker, remaining in mufti while thousands of young men went off to war—when all four of TR's sons were fighting? At least he could "inspect" the Western Front as a civilian, perhaps even in the thick of it. And so off he went to Europe—to London, where he carried out naval inspections and met with a "cordial" King George V, and on to France, where he toured the front, experiencing the stench and stillness of death, driving through villages littered with rubble and corpses, and seeing the most devastated area of all, Verdun. Along the way he called on Marshal Joffre and Premier Clemenceau and even picked up an invaluable lesson in executive leadership from General Foch. In the peaceful old château where the general had set up his headquarters, Roosevelt found Foch sitting in a comfortable chair reading a French novel, his entire staff consisting of half a dozen officers and a dozen enlisted men. "If I concerned myself with details, I could not win the war," explained Foch, observing

that "only major results and major strategy concern the m
of a commander in chief."

Exhausted by intensive days and long evenings, Fran͏
arriving in New York that he had to be carried down the gangp͏l͏a͏.͏.͏.
stretcher. He was taken to Sara's city home in an ambulance arranged by
his mother and by Eleanor.

. . .

While Franklin was convalescing—he had double pneumonia—Eleanor
took care of his mail, and there she discovered a packet of love letters to
her husband from her own social secretary, Lucy Mercer. Her life was
changed forever.

Apparently, the affair had been going on for several years. Lucy, with
her refined background and charming manner, was often invited to dinner parties when a young woman was required to fill out the table. When
Eleanor was in Campobello during the summer of 1916, Lucy was often
Franklin's partner, especially when the hostess was Alice Roosevelt Longworth, whose own marriage was disintegrating and whose venom toward
her cousin Eleanor had intensified when both women lived in Washington. During that summer Franklin and Lucy fell in love, finding time for
riding, driving, sailing, while Eleanor took care of the five children a thousand miles away.

By the following summer Eleanor may have suspected a romantic
involvement—judging by her reluctance to go to Campobello at all and
Franklin's insistence that she do. His letters were gay and lighthearted,
often mentioning Lucy, and Eleanor's replies were brittle or plaintive: "I
don't think you read my letters for you never answer a question and nothing I ask for appears!"

That winter Eleanor had written Franklin that Alice Longworth "inquired if you had told me and I said no and that I did not believe in knowing things which your husband did not wish you to know so I think I will
be spared any further mysterious secrets!"

Instead she had plunged into her own work, spending the summer of
1918 in Washington without the children, living in her Red Cross uniform,
working in the station canteen, and making the rounds of wounded and
shell-shocked men in the hospital. As Franklin sailed for Europe in early
July to inspect the fleet she was feeling more independence and self-
esteem, born from the confidence that she was doing good and useful work,
not from her marriage. Her instinct that something was wrong between

her and Franklin drew her closer to Sara in warm and effusive letters, but her new independence shows this to be a tactical move; she was strengthening her bond with a potential ally.

Eleanor was shattered when Franklin admitted the truth. It was the collapse of everything she had lived for. As in her childhood, she had been abandoned by the one she loved most, but now the pain was sharpened by the sense of betrayal—by Franklin, by Lucy, by a number of colluding Washington friends. She offered him his freedom, she later told Joseph Lash. Either they would divorce or they would stay together for the children, as long as he never saw Lucy again.

Franklin hesitated, according to family accounts, but Sara, horrified by the situation, laid down the law: She would not give him another penny if he left Eleanor and the children. Louis Howe, for his part, told Franklin that divorce would devastate his political career. And Lucy, a Catholic, evidently would not marry a divorced man—although nothing had prevented her from having an affair with him.

Franklin agreed to give Lucy up, but the marriage would never be the same. Like green life slowly returning to a landscape scorched by fire, mutual respect and even love would eventually revive, but the physical relationship was over. Eleanor would never again trust Franklin on a deeply intimate level, nor would she allow her identity and sense of worth to merge with his, but her respect for him as a political leader would grow for the rest of their life together. For his part, Franklin lost both Lucy (though, as Blanche Wiesen Cook points out, he arranged to have Lucy present at his first inaugural and also saw her, contrary to his promise, on occasion in Washington) and any chance of deep intimacy with Eleanor. His suffering over this double bereavement may have given him a deeper compassion for the weaknesses of other people or at least may have caused him to begin to shed his air of frivolity and superciliousness.

Eleanor, a thirty-four-year-old woman with five children ages two to twelve, plunged into a depression that would lift only as she began slowly to remake herself.

. . .

A different sort of scandal began to brew early in 1919, one that later would threaten to engulf Franklin. That winter the navy began receiving reports about drug use and homosexuality among sailors at the naval base in Newport, Rhode Island. To trap these men, the local commander sent new recruits to Newport bars expressly to meet and have sex with homosexual sailors. The device netted eighteen sailors within a month teen of whom would be court-martialed that summer and two dis ably discharged; two others would desert.

At some point the rumors reached Franklin, acting secretary of the navy while Daniels was traveling. He set up Section A, a secret investigation unit that continued to recruit enlisted men to make connections with homosexual sailors. In July they arrested sixteen Newport residents, one of them a military chaplain, Samuel N. Kent, charged with being a lewd and wanton person.

But when the policy of entrapment came out in open court during Chaplain Kent's trial, a public commotion followed. Franklin concealed his own involvement. An order came to close down Section A, and Franklin did so on September 4, 1919. Still, the Episcopal bishop of Rhode Island and twelve colleagues, outraged by the treatment of Kent, went to the top, demanding that President Wilson fire the officials responsible for the idea of entrapping the sailors.

In response, Daniels set up a naval court of inquiry and the Senate also began an investigation. The court was headed by a good friend of Franklin's, Admiral Herbert O. Dunn. Franklin denied all knowledge of the methods used by Section A. The court finally decided, in January 1921, that Franklin's actions were "unfortunate and ill-advised," a relatively mild rebuke. The Senate probe would continue.

The year and a half following the war's end was one of the unhappiest periods in Franklin Roosevelt's life. What might have been a period of rest and relief and self-congratulation for a job well done became a time of troubles. The Newport affair put him on the defensive. The Lucy Mercer mortification hung over his relationship with Eleanor and was not helped when he read in the *Washington Post* in February 1920 that Lucy's mother "announces the marriage of her daughter" to "Mr. Winthrop Rutherfurd of New York." He was plagued by a series of illnesses. His finances were in such poor shape that he had to depend on his mother more than ever. Demobilizing was a dull job after the excitement of 1917, even though he was able to take another trip to Europe, this time with Eleanor. And he suddenly lost his first and greatest mentor.

· · ·

Franklin and Eleanor were on their way to Europe, a few days after New Year's Day, 1919, when word was flashed to the ship that Theodore Roosevelt had suddenly died in his sleep from a coronary thrombosis at his home in Oyster Bay, a few hours after finishing another editorial, denouncing the League of Nations, for the *Kansas City Star*. For almost twenty years TR had either been president or been viewed as the next likely president. William Allen White had recently paid him a hospital visit to sound him out about running in 1920.

Five months earlier, shortly after his beloved son Quentin's death in July 1918, in an aerial dogfight with German planes in the skies over Reims, the Colonel had told his sister Corinne, "I have only one fight left in me, and I think I should reserve my strength in case I am needed in 1920." Indeed, TR, having returned to the Republican fold, had become the recognized leader of the opposition to Wilson. While Wilson found himself increasingly occupied with the peace treaty and the League of Nations, TR had been able to trumpet, one last time, his progressive agenda.

In a speech he gave to the Maine Republican Convention on March 28, 1918, he proclaimed that "we cannot afford any longer to continue our present industrial and social system, or rather no-system, of every-man-for-himself." It was impossible, he had concluded, to attempt to combine "political democracy with industrial autocracy"; the federal government had to take action, in the name of the "common good." It was "foolish," he pointed out, to object to large-scale business in the new era of telegraph and telephone, steam and electricity. Large-scale business had become "an absolute necessity." But, he went on, "the nation must be the master of the corporation."

The Bull Moose made radical calls for major social and economic change: steeply graduated taxes on excess profits; help for farmers, river valley developments, government development and control of waterpower; his own bill of rights for returning soldiers and higher education for all men and women who desired it; protection of the rights of labor, active government supervision of industry and labor, the right of workers to be "partners in enterprise" and share in profits as well as in management; public housing, permanency of employment, pensions, "insurance against accidents and disease," "day nurseries for the children of mothers who work in factories," and even "reasonable leisure." Just as Thomas Jefferson had felt that each citizen of Virginia was entitled to fifty acres of land, TR also believed that citizens had economic rights—rights not just *against* government, but new rights *through* government.

Roosevelt had successfully brought his progressive platform of 1912 "up to date," he assured William Allen White. All who cared to read or listen to him could now see in him a visionary whose profoundly progressive ideas and expansive view of democracy cohabited oddly with his hyper-nationalism and mistrust of "visionary" internationalist "schemes" like the League of Nations.

Now, in the autumn of 1918, still mourning Quentin's death and deeply concerned about the physical and mental war wounds of his son Archie, the old Bull Mooser, sixty-one years old, ailing and in considerable pain but refusing "to be reduced to doing nothing but talky-talky," for the last time rallied to the idea of recapturing the White House. He wanted at least to carry on the fight against Wilson's League. But he could not rally his failing body.

"The old lion is dead," Archie cabled his brothers. Hours later, as Edith and TR's sister Corinne Robinson somberly walked around the grounds of Sagamore Hill, they heard the unusual sound of airplanes. Looking up, they saw pilots dropping laurel wreaths over the dead hero's home. To the funeral in a small church in Oyster Bay, in January 1919, came family, friends, and even the foes—like William Howard Taft—who had loved him. The ceremonies were simple, the casket decorated with the cavalry flag of the Rough Riders. "Do you remember the *fun* of him, Mrs. Robinson?" asked a New York police captain.

. . .

Worst of all during these two years, FDR watched close up as Woodrow Wilson's dream of a League of Nations turned into a nightmare of tactical errors, vengeful opposition, and political disarray. The president had made his first mistake just before the off-year elections of 1918, when he called for a Democratic Congress, evidently forgetting as a political scientist that midterm congressional elections often went against a president no matter how good a job he was doing. The Republicans carried the House and—barely—the Senate, enabling Theodore Roosevelt to state, flatly and malevolently, "Our Allies and our enemies and Mr. Wilson himself should all understand that Mr. Wilson has no authority to speak for the American people at this time."

Wilson's essential strategy was to get a strong League of Nations accepted by the Allied leaders, to negotiate and compromise with them on territorial and other issues, and to assume that whatever he had to bargain away on such issues could be corrected later by action of a functioning League. So everything turned on a league-first strategy. But in the maze of global and national politics it was hard to maintain this priority, especially when American politicians harshly criticized the very "Great Power"

deals on reparations, colonies, frontiers, and the like that Wilson had swallowed to get his League.

FDR, from his front-row seat both in Washington and during his postwar trip to Paris and London, watched with chagrin as the president ran
into a political hornet's nest on arriving home with the proposed treaty.
Later impressions to the contrary, Wilson made repeated efforts, through
many face-to-face meetings with senators and others, to explain the treaty,
answer questions, and make adjustments. He met with pro-League Republicans, led by William Howard Taft, Charles Evans Hughes, and others,
to work out a bipartisan strategy. But Henry Cabot Lodge had his strategy too—to delay consideration of the treaty and the League, to wait for
war-kindled ideals to ebb in the postwar letdown, to give League opponents like William Randolph Hearst the chance to mobilize opinion against
the League, and to depend ultimately on the two-thirds vote in the Senate that the treaty would require.

Roosevelt watched as the somber scenario unfolded—as the Senate
split into three factions, pro-League, "reservationists" supporting Lodge,
and "irreconcilables," the last of whom Lodge skillfully exploited in delaying and blocking ratification; as the president made his fateful decision
to take his case to the people, in an exhausting western railroad tour during which he delivered impassioned speeches in twenty-nine cities; as he
suffered a stroke during his return home and then a more serious one that
left him an invalid for over six months; and as, after further infighting,
Lodge proposed a League so loaded with reservations that Wilson repudiated it.

And where was the ordinarily activist assistant secretary in all this?
Mainly silent and inactive, in contrast to his earlier strong support for
Wilson's League. Perhaps it was because he was still in the doldrums, but
mostly, perhaps, because he sensed that the Senate battle was a lost cause
and the issue would be decided in what Wilson would call the "solemn
referendum" of the forthcoming presidential election in 1920.

But for years there had never been anything better than a coming election to arouse a Roosevelt out of torpor and set his juices running. In 1918
FDR had been unable to run; he would have been seen as deserting his
navy post out of personal ambition. But now the war was over and Democratic party prospects were wide open. Earlier he had patched up relations
with Tammany, though bad feelings lingered on both sides. There was
some talk about FDR for president, but even Franklin was not that unrealistic. What about the vice presidency? Why not?

Seeking nomination by a party that had become "Wilsonized" both in its progressive economic policies and in its pro-League internationalism, FDR now presented himself as strongly in favor of both these postures. At the Democratic convention in 1920, he gave a seconding speech for Governor Al Smith of New York for president. During his rousing tribute to Smith he captured attention from the noisy delegates, especially when he promised that "the nominee of *this* convention will not be chosen at 2 A.M. in a hotel room!"—a reference to the alleged selection of Warren G. Harding by GOP leaders in a smoke-filled room in Chicago's Blackstone Hotel three weeks earlier.

Upon the unveiling of a huge portrait of Wilson, a demonstration broke out on the floor; FDR wrested the New York State banner from a Tammany guardian and paraded it down the aisle. The nomination went not to one of the national party celebrities but to Ohio governor James M. Cox on the forty-fourth ballot. And the running mate? FDR and his men had done the preparatory work; Al Smith seconded his nomination and even Murphy went along. So did the convention, for this perfect ticket balancer: young, a New Yorker, and a *Roosevelt*.

And Wilson, watching from the White House? Incredibly, this semi-invalid, unable to work or even talk for any length of time, not yet fully able to walk again, was hoping to be drafted for a third term—an unprecedented third term, at that. When word came to the White House that Cox had been chosen, this Presbyterian moralist burst into a stream of obscenities and profanities. Cox was a nonentity and a mediocrity, and as for Franklin, the president remembered him as affable and deferential but also a bit bumptious.

But Wilson's vision held, when Cox and Roosevelt together visited the White House.

"Mr. President," Cox said, "I have always admired the fight you made for the League."

"Mr. Cox," said Wilson, "that fight can still be won."

"Mr. President," Cox said a moment later, "we are going to be a million percent with you and your administration, and that means the League of Nations."

"I am very grateful," the president said in a faltering voice. "I am very grateful."

The two candidates made good their word, campaigning across the nation. Franklin threw himself into his own barnstorming with even more than his usual energy and éclat, speaking many scores of times during one eighteen-day twenty-state tour. He appeared to love every minute of it—except when his authenticity as a Roosevelt was challenged by Theodore Roosevelt Jr., still recovering from his war wounds. Franklin was "a maverick," said young Theodore, beginning an intrafamily feud that would last for decades. "He does not have the brand of our family." With the patriarch dead, the Oyster Bay Roosevelts were not in Franklin's corner.

The vice-presidential candidate encountered enthusiastic crowds, just as Wilson had in his pro-League tour, but Franklin was realistic enough to sense a losing cause. Harding swept the country with over 16 million votes to the Democrats' 9 million (and almost 1 million for the jailed Debs). It was one of the worst defeats in Democratic party history. Roosevelt's candidacy could not even tip New York to the Democrats. The debacle proved to be the death blow of a strong League of Nations.

4
A Meeting of Minds

By the time Eleanor Roosevelt crossed the Midwest on her husband's 1920 campaign tour, the endless red grasslands pictured two years earlier by Willa Cather in *My Ántonia* had long since vanished. In their place were farms, with houses dwarfed by gigantic barns, trackside grain elevators, and vast, rolling wheat fields, where in September and October the farmers were harvesting with huge steam-powered threshing machines.

During the four-week tour, Eleanor had plenty of time to gaze at the scenery of her country, as the private Roosevelt campaign car, the Westboro, pulled by regularly scheduled trains, steamed across the upper South and the plains (West Virginia, Kentucky, Missouri) west to Colorado. For the first part of the trip she had little to do but knit, read—often a book a day—write letters, and look out the window. Franklin had asked her to join him, probably to appeal to women, who were voting for the first time.

This was Franklin's second campaign tour in a month. During the first she had written him from New York, "Oh, dear! I wish I could see you or at least hear from you. I hate politics!" Probably still deeply depressed by the Lucy Mercer affair, she also hated the trip at first, was bored and lonely, and dined by herself in her stateroom.

She still lacked the social perspective that would enable her to understand the landscape that passed beyond her window. "I saw a great deal of our country on this trip which I had never seen before; though I had not begun to look at the countryside or the people with the same keenness which the knowledge of many social problems brought me in the future, still I was thrilled by new scenery, and the size of my own country, with its potential power, was gradually dawning upon me."

She did not know, however, about the desperate circumstances of many farmers, as they watched the prices of their products steadily declining. Nor was she aware that steep interest rates and the high cost of machinery were driving small farmers off their farms or forcing them into tenancy. Entire families struggling in the fields, exhausted farm women, uneducated children, inadequate housing and clothing—these were the reality behind the golden fields.

Instead, Eleanor worried about her own children, particularly James, who was homesick at Groton, not as well prepared academically as the other boys, and suffering from digestive disturbances. At one point Sara wired her that James had been so ill she had fetched him "home" from Groton for some grandmotherly nurturing at Hyde Park. For this Eleanor felt guilty and uneasy.

"This was the first time I ever remember not being on hand if one of the children was ill," she later wrote, "and it was very hard for me, but it was probably a very good thing for the children to learn that they could not always be my first consideration."

Franklin's performance was not entirely impressive. His political ideas were still rough, judging from some clumsy statements on his first western junket the previous month. In Butte, Montana, he had boasted of having at least twelve Latin American nations in his pocket—this in response to critics of the League of Nations who pointed out that England had six votes and the United States only one. In Centralia, Washington, he blundered into a conflict between members of the IWW, the International Workers of the World, and the American Legion, fervently but ignorantly taking the side of the latter. Eleanor might have been offended by this, as she had made her first tentative contacts with the women's labor movement that previous fall. She inwardly cringed when he spoke twice as long as scheduled; her main responsibility, she later remembered, was to tug at his coattail.

Yet the crowds that heard Franklin at the windy whistle stops along the tour liked his personality, if not his message. The manner that had not attracted his upper-crust classmates at Groton and Harvard did engage the broader audience he met while campaigning. Tall, lean, debonair, energetic, and confident, he struck many observers as having the good looks and charisma of a movie star or, in the words of the *New York Post,* "an idealized football player." Even the engineer of one of the regularly scheduled passenger trains that pulled the Westboro told a reporter, "Do you know, that lad's got a 'million vote smile' and mine's going to be one of them."

But the pace was grueling. "F. made 2 speeches & drove 26 miles over awful roads before we ever got any breakfast!" Eleanor wrote from Kentucky. "There have been two town speeches since then and at least one platform speech every 15 minutes all day!"

She was restless and uncomfortable in her role as candidate's wife. "I never before had spent my days going on and off platforms, listening apparently with rapt attention to much the same speech, looking pleased at seeing people no matter how tired I was, or greeting complete strangers with effusion." Also, "being the only woman was at times rather embarrassing. The newspaper fraternity was not so familiar to me at that time as it was to become in later years, and I was a little afraid of it."

Her boredom soon flamed into resentment. Her husband's days were spent out on the platform of the car, delivering up to twenty speeches a day, or meeting with politicians or campaign workers in different cities, or polishing phrases and honing policies with his team. In the evenings, to her dismay, Franklin and the other men relaxed by gathering at the end of the car and discussing the day's events over bourbon, cigars, and a game of poker.

The person who broached Eleanor's lonely isolation was her husband's assistant, Louis Howe. Eleanor had disliked Howe from the start when he went to work for Franklin in 1912. She and Sara shared a chilly annoyance with his rasping voice, messy cigarettes, and disheveled, gnomelike appearance; it was a rare bond between the two women.

Now, on the dusty, swaying, rattling train, Eleanor was alone in her stateroom when Louis knocked on the door and asked her opinion of a speech. Flattered, Eleanor found him easy to talk to. Their conversations soon ranged broadly over many topics, from poetry to national politics to the history of the towns en route. She began to appreciate his astute mind and piercing eyes. He became "Louis."

Once Eleanor began to know Howe and to welcome his visits, she felt much more connected. Soon Howe brought others with him into her stateroom, such as Stephen Early, who, on leave from the Associated Press, was serving the campaign as advance man.

"I had never had any contacts with the newspaper people before," she wrote later. "My grandmother had taught me that a woman's place was not in the public eye, and that had clung to me all through the Washington years." But "largely because of Louis Howe's early interpretation of the standards and ethics of the newspaper business, I came to look with interest and confidence on the writing fraternity and gained a liking for it which I have never lost."

She learned to understand the reporters' perspective, to appreciate their honesty and humor. And now she had allies. As "the newspapermen and I became more friendly, they helped me a great deal to see the humorous side. They would stand at the back of the hall when Franklin was making the same speech for the umpty-umpth time and make faces at me, trying to break up the apparent interest with which I was listening. When I followed my husband down the aisle and the ladies crowded around him and exclaimed over his looks and charm, they would get behind me and ask if I wasn't jealous."

On the way home to New York, Eleanor and Louis escaped from the campaign train to see Niagara Falls by themselves. There "Louis proved to be a very pleasant person with whom to sight-see," commented Eleanor, "silent when I wished to be silent and full of information on many things of which I knew nothing."

Soon Howe became a confidant and a bridge between her and Franklin, someone who understood and cared about what she thought and experienced. The campaign tour marked the real beginning of Eleanor's activism, which had its roots in her early settlement-house and Red Cross work and would ultimately see her emergence as an independent political figure in the 1920s.

Even though Franklin himself was not present, the "meeting of minds" between Eleanor Roosevelt and Louis Howe was also a key moment in his career. It marked the joining of two crucial personalities who would deepen and refine his political identity and inexorably propel him toward his great goal, the presidency of the United States.

5
Observing Leadership

FDR had been able to watch, close up, two of the master politicians of the early twentieth century, Theodore Roosevelt and Woodrow Wilson, and he had learned a great deal from them.

Uncle Theodore, his first mentor, taught a lot by sheer example—through his enormous enthusiasms, volcanic energy, face-to-face warmth, and force of expression. He dominated with hip and shoulder, sometimes literally leaning or pushing against a visitor to make his point. He also dominated by the force of his ideas, goals, and values and his utter commitment to them.

Doubtless FDR also saw the weaknesses of TR's strengths—the excessive moralizing, the self-righteousness, the explosive anger against those who opposed him. The preacher-president could hardly utter a sentence, especially in his letters, that did not invoke the loftiest of motives: "I would be unfaithful to all that is in me," he would declaim to a cowering stenographer, "were I not to ignore the cowardly way out," and so forth, "and fail to condemn in the most outspoken way," and so on. TR's self-righteousness, combined with his impetuosity, led him—a party man par excellence—to take the risky course of running as a third-party candidate in 1912 and splitting the GOP. Yet FDR had to admire his courage and idealism and his capacity for growth. And Franklin could also appreciate TR's skill as well—his skill at maintaining his independence within the Republican party until 1912 while keeping the benefits of sticking with it; his never-failing flair for catching the public eye; his courage in facing down, on occasion, some of the most formidable economic power wielders in the nation; his willingness, when all was said and done, to put his lofty goals before his consuming ambition, to risk the hatred of people even when he most wanted their love, and to suffer blows to his ego when he needed, above all, self-esteem.

Wilson was a different kind of mentor for Franklin, who never felt as close to the Democratic president as he had to Cousin Theodore. He felt at times put down by Wilson, rebuffed, ignored; he sensed none of the warmth, the glad-handing exuberance of TR; yet he admired his commander in chief both for his rhetorical leadership and his hands-on administrative management. In contrast to the contemporary and indeed many of the later historical portraits of Wilson, as chief executive the onetime college professor was purposeful, intellectually coherent, cogent and forthright in his directives—and not without human sensitivity. The lessons of this kind of leadership trickled through to his assistant secretary of the navy.

Probably FDR had learned something about his chief's long dedication to leadership, as well as his sense of the importance of followership. "The ear of the leader," Wilson had said, "must ring with the voices of the people."

Much more obvious to Franklin, at the end of Wilson's administration, were the president's "errors of leadership." But were these more apparent than real? It soon became conventional wisdom that Wilson was stubborn, dogmatic, inflexible in dealing with friend and foe. But the conventional wisdom about leaders was that they should be principled, purposeful, resolute, tenacious. What was stubbornness in the eyes of one observer was "sticking to his guns" in the eyes of another.

Of course, a skillful leader should know when to be flexible, when to hang tough. But there was a third element for Wilson and any other president: the intractability of the fragmented political system that gave opponents special advantages, as in the case of Lodge. FDR had not had to deal with the "checks and balances"—he had considerable executive leverage in the navy department, and Daniels dealt with Congress—but Wilson had to, almost every day of his presidency.

If pressed, FDR would have called himself neither an "idealist" nor a "practical politician" but a "realist," especially in international affairs. "People had talked much about internationalism," he told Drexel Institute graduates in May 1918, "of the day when nation will no longer rise against nation." But that day was not yet here, and would never be "as long as the nation endures." So much for Wilsonian idealism. Assistant Secretary Roosevelt prided himself for being a student of the great military strategist Alfred Thayer Mahan, but he was more impressed by Mahan's support for one of FDR's own immediate goals—concentration of the fleet—than by Mahan's broad theories about the influence of sea power on history.

As a realist, FDR concentrated on the specific problem, the immediate remedy, the practical outcome, without spending much time on long-run implications, objections of principle, or future choices or dilemmas on the shifting chessboard of politics and policy. The test was the quick result. Nor did he have a set of well-thought-out values, priorities of principle, or long-run goals aside from his own ambitious ones. He would have laughed off such talk, even if he understood it. His values were still essentially those of his parents: of home and family, of the Episcopalian faith, of rural life and needs. His concern for the plight of the farmer was genuine but increasingly time-bound as the nation became more urbanized and industrialized.

And as a realist he had a feel for the mechanics of power but little interest in its broader implications and dilemmas. "Young man," Henry Adams said to him one day, after Franklin had mentioned some immediate issue, while at lunch in Adams's mansion across Lafayette Square from the White House, "I have lived in this house many years and have seen the occupants of that White House across the square come and go, and nothing that you minor officials or the occupants of that house can do will affect the history of the world for long!" Franklin disagreed; he knew *he* could make a difference. But he hardly glimpsed the broader implications of Adams's comment—the mysteries of history and the ironies of power— even after Eleanor presented him with a copy of the (then) privately printed *Education of Henry Adams* shortly after the end of the war.

Celebrating his thirty-ninth birthday in January 1921, Franklin Roosevelt could reflect on his meteoric rise in the past decade, from a neophyte state senator to a national figure. If intellectually at this point he was still half formed and even shallow, politically he had become a seasoned and sophisticated campaigner and policy maker. Much would depend on another quality, his temperament—his buoyancy and energy, his "TR-type" ability to take defeats and hard knocks but push ahead, his ability to handle conflict and not be immobilized by it, his qualities of intuition and human sensitivity and imagination that lay beyond intellectual rigor or political calculation. He had met the tests of some of these qualities; even harsher tests lay ahead.

Chapter Four
REHEARSAL FOR THE PRESIDENCY

FRANKLIN D. ROOSEVELT,
Lawyer, Clubman and Statesman

Washington Herald, March 22, 1913.
(*Courtesy FDR Library*)

Defeat is one of the severest tests of leadership and one of the most unpredictable. Defeat can humble, ennoble, corrupt, steel, crush, or rekindle its victims. It tries their commitment and resolve, their opportunism and inconstancy. Defeat sets the stage for heroic action, whatever the final consequences: Napoleon's return from Elba, Britain's recovery after its 1940 rout in France, Lincoln's tenacity after his senatorial defeat, Grover Cleveland's recovery of the presidency after losing it in 1888, and—of course—Cousin Theodore's return to politics after his humiliating defeat for mayor of New York City, all aside from countless comebacks in the boxing ring and on football fields. How one recovers from a defeat can make the difference between a champion and an also-ran, lost to history.

Franklin and Eleanor's defeat in 1920 after their weeks on the campaign trail could hardly be classified as among the great vanquishments of the century. Still, it hurt. For the first time in ten years he would not be on a governmental payroll. And the Harding-Coolidge victory was so sweeping that Democratic party hopes would be clouded for some time.

And a man, even a Roosevelt, must earn a living. Through his social contacts in the yachting world, he lined up a job with Fidelity and Deposit, a surety bonding firm, whose business he boosted by using his political connections. After serving in a law partnership with two old friends, he founded his own with D. Basil "Doc" O'Connor, who would remain a partner and confidant for years. Soon he was representing business clients and even the American Construction Council, a peak association of the building trades. He plunged into a host of philanthropic, educational, and social activities: Lighthouses for the Blind, head of the Greater New York Committee of the Boy Scouts, president of the Navy Club (recreation for sailors). He became an overseer at Harvard and a leader in establishing the Woodrow Wilson Foundation.

Eleanor had suggested that Franklin hire a new secretary, twenty-three-year-old Marguerite LeHand, always called "Missy," to help deal with his correspondence. The young woman, who had worked in the Democratic headquarters during the presidential campaign, was initially reluctant to take the post, fearing the job would be too dull. "Oh, that's all right," Franklin assured her. "There'll be a lot besides legal briefs." Indeed there was; Missy would go on with Franklin to the governor's mansion and then to the White House.

...

A candidate's wife must also remake her life after a defeat, and Eleanor had to cope not only with Franklin's loss in 1920 but also with the wrenching failure in her marriage. She began by settling the children into their studies. She spent weekdays in New York with Franklin and the younger boys, then took the train to Hyde Park, where Anna and Elliott were studying with a new tutor and thriving on country life. James, meanwhile, had finally begun to enjoy Groton.

When her maternal Grandmother Hall died in the summer of 1919, Eleanor had wondered whether her grandmother might not have enjoyed a more fulfilling life, "some kind of life of her own." Since her youth, Eleanor admitted, she had been determined not to copy her grandmother's life, never to be dependent on family and children by allowing them to be the center of her interests. Two months after her grandmother's death, on her own thirty-fifth birthday, she had found herself alone in Washington; Franklin had sent a wire, her brother a book. The time had come for her to make friends and find meaningful work of her own.

New currents were coursing through Eleanor's life. Her friendship with Louis Howe was only the final catalyst in a process that had begun in her schooldays at Allenswood. Marie Souvestre had helped her recognize her own abilities and had challenged her to grapple with the issues of her time. The work in the Rivington Street Settlement had awakened her to lives of poverty and deprivation vastly different from her own. Her wartime work had taught her not only that she could handle tough jobs but that she also liked to help people. Louis Howe had shown her that her ideas were important; she would never again be able to live a purposeless life.

Now, in New York, all those experiences and thoughts were converging, and the numbness and repression brought on by the Lucy Mercer affair began to lift. Resettled in New York, freed from the social duties of a political wife, she was ready to seek out challenging and useful activity. "I did not look forward to a winter . . . in New York," she later recalled, "with nothing but teas and luncheons and dinners to take up my time. The war had made that seem an impossible mode of living." First, deciding that she needed some useful skills, she took courses in typing, shorthand, and cooking. It was a way "to remove the mystery from everyday things that had made her feel dependent, inadequate, out of control," in the words of her biographer, Blanche Wiesen Cook.

Very soon after Eleanor's arrival in New York, Narcissa Vanderlip, a Hudson Valley woman of wealth who was, as well, the head of the League of Women Voters of New York State, asked her to join the league board and take charge of writing monthly reports for other New York members on national legislation. The National League of Women Voters had been created in 1919 as a nonpartisan organization supporting reformist candidates within both established parties. Eleanor demurred with her customary self-doubts, but finally agreed after Vanderlip promised the assistance of "a very able woman lawyer," Elizabeth Read.

Though initially feeling humble and very inadequate, Eleanor was soon looking forward to her weekly appointments to discuss current legislation with the well-informed, intelligent, and analytical Read. Their working relationship developed quickly into a warm friendship. Eleanor often spent several evenings a week with Read and Esther Lape, Read's life partner, in their small East 11th Street apartment, dining elaborately and staying till late, discussing politics or art or reading poetry aloud. Eleanor had entered the world of the postwar, politically involved "New Women."

Her new friends' varied interests and serious attitudes toward their work, Eleanor later commented, "played a great part in what might be called 'the intensive education of Eleanor Roosevelt' during the next few years." Her horizons expanding as she spent stimulating hours with Read and Lape at their Connecticut estate as well as in New York, Eleanor eventually rented her own pied-à-terre on East 11th Street, a downtown refuge from the conventional uptown world of husband, children, and mother-in-law.

Through the League of Women Voters, Eleanor made other connections with women activists, discovering a plethora of meaningful issues. In 1920 and 1921 the group was unabashedly reformist, pushing for progressive ideas ranging from national health insurance and the abolition of child labor to membership in the League of Nations. Eleanor was enthusiastic about this agenda, and Lape soon recommended to Narcissa Vanderlip that she be recruited to do fund-raising. Eleanor would travel to Albany to attend the League's state convention in January 1921, where she would hear the state's governor, Nathan Miller, suddenly and unexpectedly attack the League and its legislative proposals, and she would travel to Chicago for the national convention, at which Carrie Chapman Catt urged the women of the world to work for peace.

Franklin sometimes gave political pointers to Eleanor, especially concerning internal power struggles within the League. At one annual meeting, Eleanor introduced a motion to condemn Calvin Coolidge, the vice president, for his gratuitous attack on women's colleges as hotbeds of radicals and Bolshevik propaganda.

In addition to her work for the League of Women Voters, Eleanor also continued to serve on several charitable boards, observing that her personal growth along with her education on social and political issues now made it difficult for her to stay aloof on boards with "no personal contact with actual work." And she was joyfully aware of her own gradual intellectual awakening: "I had begun to realize that in my development I was drifting far afield from the old influences. I do not mean to imply that I was the better for this. Far from it, but I was thinking things out for myself and becoming an individual."

Still, even as she explored new issues and new relationships, Eleanor had not broken with New York high society. She made time to lunch weekly with her mother-in-law's Monday Sewing Class, a group of socially prominent women whose mothers and grandmothers had enjoyed weekly lunches together since 1872. Few women in the group still did actual sewing; instead, members paid dues that went toward providing sewing work for other women in need of jobs. Garments sewn were distributed to charity. For Eleanor, it was a way to please her mother-in-law, for "it gave us a definite engagement together once a week."

Eleanor Roosevelt inhabited two worlds, the elite one into which she had been born and a new world of women activists of all classes. On the one hand, she experienced a heady new sense of freedom and engagement; on the other, she made sure that her sons followed family customs and left for Groton at age twelve, however painful the separation was for them and for her.

Even when a stern Eleanor complained that her children were being granted too many privileges outside the home, she remained loyal to certain traditions. Eleanor did not share her own liberation with her daughter and insisted that Anna make her debut in society at age eighteen, although the young woman protested fiercely against the stifling coming-out rituals in Newport. And though Eleanor herself always regretted not having had an American college education, she did not encourage Anna to attend college, agreeing instead with her mother-in-law's tradition-bound warning that a college education might predispose a young woman to spinster-hood. It was Franklin who pushed Anna to attend Cornell's College of Agriculture, which she left after a term. Four years later, Eleanor, by then a more resolute feminist, would maintain that the prejudice against women with college degrees was passing into oblivion along with other prejudices "that have their origin in the ancient tradition that women are a byproduct of creation." If emotionally she still felt herself a "lady," connected to certain traditions of the social elite, intellectually she was evolving in an entirely different direction.

As for her husband, at this juncture in his career Franklin had to deal once again with his mother Sara's hopes that he might turn away from politics, with all its compromises and crudities, and return to the benign world of Hyde Park leisure-class country squires and Hudson Valley aristocrats. For Sara Delano Roosevelt, it was the duty of the aristocrat to be better than other men, to serve as an example for the less fortunate to follow.

He could hardly forget a family confrontation on values at Hyde Park late in the war, after which Sara wrote him, "Perhaps, dear Franklin, you may on second thoughts or *third* thoughts see that I am not so far wrong." One could be "democratic as one likes," she went on, but "if we love our own, and if we love our neighbor, we owe a great example." She deplored the "trend to shirt sleeves, to the giving up of the old-fashioned virtues of family life, of tradition and dignity, to the tendency of some to be 'all things to all men.'" But Franklin, who had violated some of these old virtues in his adultery and politicking, had not carried on the dispute in writing, nor had Eleanor, a participant in the confrontation. In slightly more than a dozen years, he had moved from the narrow elite world of Hyde Park, Groton, and Harvard to become politician, legislator, bureaucrat, and war leader.

But while Franklin had demonstrated skill in dealing on equal terms with the shirtsleeved men of labor, the derby-hatted men of Tammany, and the uniformed men of Washington, his new postwar and postelection work in law, business, and philanthropy brought him back into close contact with his old New York social set. It was a charged-up environment of business, Wall Street, big money, society charities, splendid dinners for donors—and once again, as he mingled with wealthy industrialists, Franklin demonstrated his ability to adapt to a new context with the speed of a chameleon. Perhaps his mother had worried needlessly, for Franklin never lost his roots in Hyde Park. He could move with ease back and forth between the world of the Hudson aristocracy and the world of politicking because he had a strong sense of belonging and identity, never doubting that someday he would return to Springwood.

Thus, while politicking or while working for the League of Women Voters, neither he nor Eleanor gave up their social activities and ties. Franklin enthusiastically sponsored friends for admission to exclusive New York private clubs, socialized with elite Dutchess County families, and hobnobbed in Washington social circles, always recognizing that upper-class friendships not only cut across political party lines but that these ties of family and social rank also constituted a kind of Tammany-like machine that wielded its own power and influence.

How then did Franklin and Eleanor deal with political defeat? Especially defeat for the second highest elective office in the land—defeat at the hands of two run-of-the-mill politicians, Harding and Calvin Coolidge—defeat darkened by the gloomy knowledge that, historically, no American politician fades more quickly into obscurity than failed candidates for vice president?

Eleanor seized the opportunity to make a new life for herself. FDR, for his part, blamed defeat on forces beyond his control, so it was not a personal failure. The lighthearted quality some called lightweight served him well at this time. Despite a stinging sense of rejection, he put a good face on it, writing to a friend a letter headed "Franklin D. Roosevelt, Ex V.P., Canned (Erroneously reported dead)."

1
"The Most Trying Winter of My Entire Life"

Eleanor and her five children looked forward with particular excitement to their time at Campobello in the summer of 1921. Franklin would be vacationing with them longer than usual this year. They couldn't wait to share his exuberant love of the island, along with the hikes, sailing trips, and fishing expeditions he always led, just as Cousin Theodore had at Sagamore Hill.

After a few days together, however, a telegram arrived from Washington. The Senate subcommittee was about to release to the press its report on the Newport homosexual entrapment affair, a report Daniels termed "libelous."

Franklin demanded a chance to respond, so he left the island for the long train trip through the sweltering July heat to Washington.

On Monday morning, July 18, the subcommittee gave Franklin permission to examine the 6,000 single-spaced pages of testimony, saying his statement would be required by that evening. The release to the press would be delayed until that Friday, they promised.

The report was indeed damning. It found it "incredible" that Franklin could not have known that his Section A was asking young sailors to engage in homosexual behavior in order to entrap other men. If he did not know, the report went on, Franklin was "most derelict in the performance of his duty." However, the committee believed him to be a man of "unusual intelligence and attainments"; he had insisted on secrecy throughout the operation, and he had helped secure legal immunity for the operatives. Therefore, the report concluded, Franklin had been aware of Section A's methods, which meant he had lied before the Dunn court. He, along with Daniels, showed "an utter lack of moral perspective." His actions were "thoroughly condemned as immoral and an abuse of the authority of his high office."

Grim, determined, Franklin scribbled his answers and hurried over to the Capitol by eight o'clock that evening to read his statement to the subcommittee, but he arrived a few hours too late. The report had been released early. The headline in *The New York Times* read LAY NAVY SCANDAL TO F. D. ROOSEVELT . . . DETAILS ARE UNPRINTABLE.

The report pointed out serious weaknesses in Franklin's character: an initial lack of judgment compounded by a clumsy cover-up, errors that would destroy later politicians. As the week wore on, however, the story sank with hardly a ripple. FDR was not at that time a politician or a candidate, after all. And Americans, gorging on daily scandals in 1921, quickly moved on to the next course—vice squads busting up speakeasies and gambling dens; spectacular divorces involving millionaires and showgirls; accusations of graft in the 1919 World Series; politicians indicted for embezzlement or bribery; and the endless "rum cases" piling up. Franklin decided not to publish a major statement.

Shaken by the challenge to his character, drained by his effort to clear his name and save his career, and wounded by the senators' broken promises, Franklin was desperate to return to the sanctuary of Campobello. "Tell Louis I expect those boats to be all rigged and ready when I get up there and I am very greatly put out not to be there now," he wrote Eleanor. He welcomed the offer of his new boss at Fidelity and Deposit, Van Lear Black, to take him north to Campobello on Black's 140-foot steam yacht *Sabalo*. Missy LeHand noticed that he looked tired as they departed from New York on the three-day yacht trip north.

The entire family, the Howes, other guests, and several servants were waiting on the dock when the *Sabalo* finally glided in, late in the afternoon on Sunday, August 7. Now fatigued physically as well as emotionally, Franklin insisted on showing his boss a good time. In the morning he took Black and members of his party deep-sea fishing aboard the *Sabalo*'s tender. At one point he slipped and fell overboard into the frigid waters of the Bay of Fundy. "I'd never felt anything so cold as that water!" he later recalled. That evening he complained to Eleanor of feeling a little sluggish.

His pace, however, didn't slow, although the Black party may have wearied of the activity; they left the next day.

On Wednesday, Franklin awoke still feeling lethargic. Yet the children were clamoring for his long-awaited company, so they all, including Eleanor, set out for a long sail in their sloop, *Vireo*. Afterward, following a two-mile jog across the island and a dip in the icy ocean, Franklin noticed that he didn't feel the usual glow as he emerged from the sea. The group jogged home, where Franklin found the mail and newspapers had arrived. Too tired even to change from his wet bathing suit, he sat on the porch reading as the late afternoon began to cool.

All at once the fatigue hit and he began to shiver with a violent chill. White-faced, he said he was going up to bed without dinner. It was to be his last time climbing those stairs. In the morning, after a fitful, feverish sleep, he could hardly get out of bed, and his aching left leg gave way under him.

By now Eleanor was worried. She sent to Lubec for the family doctor, E. H. Bennett, who was mystified by Franklin's symptoms and finally concluded he had a bad cold. In the afternoon his right leg couldn't support him. By Friday, he could not stand; nor could he even hold a pen to sign a letter. His spirits plunged into a bleak depression that was completely uncharacteristic. He later told a friend that during the first weeks of the ordeal he even lost his faith in God, convinced he was about to die.

An elderly surgeon, Dr. William Keen, vacationing in Bar Harbor, arrived to see the patient, only to misdiagnose the problem as a blood clot in the lower spinal cord. He prescribed massage and announced that Franklin would be well in a matter of months.

The children returned from a camping trip to find their household shattered and their family life changed forever. Their usually noisy house had become a tense and silent infirmary. Upstairs lay their normally vigorous father, helpless, in severe pain and deep despair, completely paralyzed from the hips down. Outside the sickroom, both Eleanor and Louis were grim and preoccupied. The children were warned to play quietly, at a distance from their father. When they did occasionally glimpse Franklin, James later remembered, "He grinned at us and did his best to call out, or gasp out, some cheery response to our tremulous . . . greetings."

Monday, August 15, may have been the height of the crisis, when Franklin was "out of his head," Eleanor later wrote. Eleanor and Louis, drawn closer together by their devotion to the suffering patient, took turns sitting with him. In the following days the fever decreased and Franklin became closer to his usual self. Throughout it all, Eleanor maintained a determined air of cheerfulness. For Eleanor and Franklin, this ordeal demanded all their mental and spiritual strength. Together, they would survive.

Louis Howe, while assisting with the personal care, also took a practical approach. Not content with the diagnosis, he doggedly sought more information. He sent all the details of the case to Franklin's uncle, Frederic A. Delano, who consulted various doctors in New York and Boston. Infantile paralysis, poliomyelitis, was their common conclusion, and Dr. Robert W. Lovett of Boston was named as the leading authority on the illness. Lovett was contacted on vacation and persuaded to come to Campobello to see the patient. His diagnosis was immediate: the disease was indeed polio.

That the diagnosis was not made for two full weeks was not completely the fault of the elderly Dr. Keen. Although it was rampant in the early part of the century, polio was considered a disease of childhood, generally confined to congested, unsanitary, inner-city neighborhoods. It was rare for the polio virus to invade an upper-class family, and still rarer for it to attack a thirty-nine-year-old man.

Howe, always sensitive to his boss's political future, worked to keep news of Franklin's condition out of the papers. Polio, after all, was a dreaded illness, despite its low mortality rate: Americans were frightened, then as now, by disability. For Eleanor, silence about suffering was second nature, having learned as a child to keep family secrets. Even members of the extended family believed Franklin was recovering from a bad chill.

On August 31, Franklin was at the breaking point, convinced he was deteriorating even further. His mother Sara arrived the next day.

Entering the sickroom, she sensed a determinedly upbeat mood as she greeted her brave, handsome, smiling son. "He and Eleanor," she reported to her brother Frederic, "decided at once to be cheerful and the atmosphere of the house is all happiness, so I have fallen in and follow their glorious example. . . . Dr. just came and said, 'This boy is going to get all right.' They went into his room and I can hear them all laughing, Eleanor in the lead."

The days and nights somehow passed. It was decided to move Franklin to New York in mid-September. This maneuver was accomplished in secrecy, requiring all of Howe's ingenuity to avoid curious reporters. Franklin was stoic throughout the agonizing journey.

He remained at New York's Presbyterian Hospital for six weeks, under the care of an old Groton classmate, Dr. George Draper. Draper was not optimistic about Franklin's chances for recovery. The pain was still intense and the paralysis profound; Franklin could neither sit up nor extend his feet. Upon his discharge his medical record stated tersely: "Not improving."

In addition, Draper recognized the complex psychological factors involved in such severe cases, and he worried about the effect the hard facts of his condition would have on Franklin. "He has such courage, such ambition, and yet at the same time such an extraordinarily sensitive emotional mechanism," he wrote, "that it will take all the skill which we can muster to lead him successfully to a recognition of what he really faces without crushing him." Draper did not even examine Franklin's arms for a long time, because he did not wish to shake the patient's faith that his arms were unimpaired. Franklin himself wrote friends that he would walk out of the hospital on crutches in three weeks—in December he would predict he would be walking without a limp by spring. In fact, he left the hospital on a stretcher on October 28.

Life now changed in the brownstone on East 65th Street as radically as at Campobello. Everything centered around the invalid, with nurses and visitors streaming in and out at all hours.

For months Eleanor was too busy to experience her own pain or to confide in her equally unhappy daughter, Anna, scared and bewildered by her beloved father's condition, lonely at her new school. Eleanor later wrote, "I have always had a very bad tendency to shut up like a clam, particularly when things are going badly; and that attitude was accentuated, I think, as regards my children." In April, after "the most trying winter of my entire life," Eleanor finally broke down. She seemed a bottomless well of grief. But her breakdown brought her closer to her daughter, and an emotional understanding was finally born between the two, one that would deepen over time and become immensely important and satisfying to both.

Franklin continued to display the remarkable courage that sustained those around him as well as himself. Along with the day-to-day wearing on the spirit caused by adjustment to his condition, he was the focus of the tensions in the household. There were also terrifying setbacks, such as a relapse in November when his fever soared and his vision seemed in danger. In January his atrophied hamstrings contracted painfully, bending his legs and requiring plaster casts to force them straight again.

Yet he still believed he would recover fully, an attitude that determined the course of his future life. In the words of historian and rehabilitation psychologist Richard Thayer Goldberg, "He did not bemoan his fate or complain about his handicap; he refused to accept it, despite the classic admonition of health professionals to do so. He learned to circumvent the various restrictions imposed upon him by useless legs. He invented devices that provided him with greater mobility and access to the ordinary activities of life. He was a cooperative, uncomplaining patient, but he went his own way when his physician told him no further progress could be expected."

From his time in the hospital on, he cast a glow of optimism around his visitors. Whether from a stubborn refusal to be pitied or from simple, gallant good manners, he continued to present a bright, confident face to the world. He joked about his condition, he taught his sons the Latin names of his withered muscles, and he showed visitors how he could drag himself upstairs, chatting away while sweat streamed down his face. He continued to develop his upper-body strength, pulling himself around with a strap over his bed, exercising in the bath, roughhousing with the boys, even throwing a punch at unwary visitors. Through Louis Howe he stayed in touch with political contacts and business associates.

That June—1922—Franklin was trained to walk with braces and to rise from a sitting position. One doctor who worked with him at the time said, "He was the most charming man I've ever met. He had a charming personality. Whenever I saw him, he was always smiling. A lot of people committed suicide with infantile. I think by [that] time . . . he made his adjustments."

The family spent July at Hyde Park, where Franklin exercised on parallel bars set up on the lawn every morning and in a friend's heated pool in the afternoon. Water, he discovered, was therapeutic, supporting his limbs and making his weak muscles more effective. He regularly attempted to walk from the house down the circular driveway; his goal, the gate to the Albany Post Road.

Despite the exhausting exercise and the stubborn discipline, by the summer of 1923 his legs had shown no improvement since the onset of the disease. His face, arms, back, and digestive functions were normal, but he was still completely paralyzed from the hips down.

Yet his optimistic outlook held firm. "I am still on crutches," he wrote a friend in December 1923, "and cannot possibly play golf myself for a year or two."

2
The Education of Eleanor Roosevelt

Dr. Draper was convinced that Franklin needed to remain active. Eleanor and Louis, the two who knew Franklin best, agreed that in order to survive the ordeal of paralysis he required a positive, stimulating environment and continued involvement with the world. Van Lear Black had reserved Franklin's job for him, and Franklin repaid that loyalty by doubling the firm's business through his name and connections.

On his first visit since his illness to Fidelity and Deposit, in October 1922, he slipped and fell while making his way on crutches across the lobby. Bystanders gathered, shocked and helpless, while the chauffeur struggled to lift him up. Franklin looked up into the ring of horrified faces and burst into laughter. The crowd relaxed, and a burly young man helped Franklin to his feet.

Laughing at an experience that would have reduced many to an agony of shame—this illuminates Franklin's state of mind as he took hold of his life again. His aristocratic upbringing dictated that no one would be allowed to pity him. And his humanity, what would later be called "the common touch," engaged those around him and dissolved potential tensions.

Polio was not, as is so often said, the key to Franklin's later character, but it was the key to a number of elements in his makeup. Although recent biographers have focused on his disability, it did not, in fact, dominate his public image. He willed it not to. The force of his personality, the air of command and strength—these prevailed over any sense of weakness or incapacity. The shriveled legs so dwelt on by biographers were only a minor part of Roosevelt in the public view.

After months of concentrated exercise, he looked like a changed and newly powerful man, with the heavily muscled neck and shoulders of a wrestler, similar to the transformation TR underwent during his time in the Badlands. The physical discipline, however, was just the same concentrated attention Franklin had devoted in the past to play—to golf, fishing, collecting. The ordeal pulled together several preexisting strands of his personality, although others would not reveal themselves until much later. Thus the determined optimism that sustained him and others through the darkest days of the illness was the same cheery buoyancy that was condemned as shallow in his school and society days. The fortitude with which he fought the paralysis had been instilled in him by Sara when he was a child. His political confidence and charisma had expanded with his experience during ten years in the public eye. But the compassion that marked his presidential policies had not emerged by 1921 and would develop in response to the challenges of the next decade.

The optimism that served him so nobly in his illness was rather more disastrous in his new business career. Franklin was an enthusiastic, impulsive, even reckless investor. He put money—$5,000 was usually his limit—into varied schemes involving helium-filled dirigibles, lobsters, pine forests, vending machines, and devalued German marks. Only in a few of these ventures did he make a modest profit; for the most part, he lost his investment. Yet he continued to speculate playfully, as did tens of thousands of others.

For it was the 1920s, that most remarkable of times. Dubbed the Dollar Decade, it was a period when national income soared, industrial production almost doubled, and consumer spending shot upward. The stock market was booming; new millionaires were emerging every week, Republican presidents were protecting big industry with tariffs, entertaining tycoons at the White House, and otherwise keeping their hands off business.

But there were other stories to be told in the 1920s, stories of misery and squalor amid the plenty, of a reinvigorated Ku Klux Klan, of racism and red-baiting. And while the rich became richer, many of the poor became much poorer. Farmers had been left out of the boom; farm prices continued to sink, while equipment costs, freight rates, taxes, and farm tenancies rose. The bituminous coal industry, which had expanded during the war, collapsed in the early 1920s, leaving mines—and thousands of miners—idle throughout the Appalachians. Embattled factory workers were continually pressing owners for shorter hours, better working conditions, and higher pay, despite a huge rise in the value of stocks such as General Motors. Strikes—in factories, mines, and railroads—were long, violent, and often unsuccessful, as the government invariably threw its weight behind the employer. Membership in the International Ladies' Garment Workers Union dropped by more than half during the 1920s.

The Roosevelts were insulated by their wealth and by their focus on Franklin's illness from the social tempest of the early twenties. Sara still wanted Franklin to retire from the world and return to his tranquil childhood home at Hyde Park. She was deeply disappointed that he did not, and for this she particularly blamed Louis Howe, who seemed to her to embody all she hated of the swamp of politics.

Certainly Louis remained devoted to keeping her son's name politically current. When Franklin left Presbyterian Hospital on a stretcher just before the November election in 1921, a week later every victorious Democrat state assemblyman received a congratulatory letter signed with Franklin's name—a classic Howe touch.

Partly to keep Franklin involved and connected, Howe encouraged Eleanor to continue her political activities. Back in her familiar role as supportive and nurturing helpmate, Eleanor found it hard at first to think of anything she could do. In the spring of 1922, however, pursuing her interest in women's working conditions, she attended a luncheon of the Women's Trade Union League and decided to join the organization. The group had been founded in 1903 to improve working conditions for women and to help women workers organize themselves through union representation. Eleanor came to know Rose Schneiderman, the director of the New York League and a Lower East Side firebrand, as well as Marion Dickerman, an educator and former candidate for the New York State Assembly.

In June 1922, Dickerman's life partner, Nancy Cook, invited Eleanor to preside at a fund-raising luncheon for the women's division of the Democratic State Committee. Eleanor was soon part of a network of women involved in the League of Women Voters, the Women's Trade Union League, and the Democratic State Committee, where she served as finance chairman. With the ratification in 1920 of the Nineteenth Amendment providing for woman suffrage, it was an exhilarating time for political women.

She also became active in Al Smith's campaign to win back the governorship. Joseph M. Proskauer, Smith's campaign manager, recruited a dedicated team that included Eleanor and Frances Perkins, who had served as a labor commissioner in the New York Department of Labor during Smith's first term as governor. Both women traveled around the state, speaking to Democratic women's groups. In November, Smith won easily, on the record of his successful first term, the strength of his progressive platform, and the effectiveness of his campaign. He would go on to justify Eleanor and Franklin's faith in him by serving a brilliant second term. Women were elated when he appointed Frances Perkins to the new three-member Industrial Relations Board.

. . .

Life at home on East 65th Street was more harmonious by the fall of 1922. The house was calmer: Anna was back in her old room, the trained nurse had been discharged, and Elliott had joined James at Groton. Aside from his disability, Franklin was perhaps in better health than he had ever been, thanks to his regimen of exercise. He commuted to the office in a chauffeured car. That winter he traveled south to cruise and fish and loaf with Louis and Missy, working his muscles in the warm seas off Florida. Always, his aim was not simply to relax but to become well again.

Eleanor was happy in her new life and felt out of place when she visited Franklin on his houseboat, even though she brought Esther Lape with her. "I tried fishing but had no skill and no luck," she recalled. "When we anchored at night and the wind blew, it all seemed eerie and menacing to me. The beauty of the moon and the stars only added to the strangeness of the dark waters and the tropic vegetation, and on occasion it could be colder and more uncomfortable than tales of the sunny South led me to believe was possible." Eleanor was pleased that Missy LeHand was traveling with Franklin and serving as hostess. She herself was beginning to live a separate life, one that was rich, stimulating, and crowded with new friends and ideas.

Eleanor and Franklin were forging a remarkable partnership. Eleanor had seized the opportunity to quit the narrow social universe of the upper caste and make new friends, explore her own interests, and assert her own independent personality. With her growing sense of personal worth and strength she was able to welcome Missy LeHand, whose relationship with Franklin freed her of many duties. Out of the public eye, Franklin and she turned an unhappy marriage into a warm friendship, one based not on need but on respect, forgiveness, tolerance. As they directed their attention and energies away from the marriage, each was becoming the center of a different world.

For Eleanor, it was a New York world comprised of women friends, politics, and important issues. "I had dropped out of what is known as society entirely," she wrote. "Ever since the war my interest had been in doing real work, not in being a dilettante. I gradually found myself more and more interested in workers, less and less interested in my old associates." Along with Esther Lape she plunged into the campaign for U.S. membership in the World Court.

She started to make speeches, coached by Louis Howe. He was no easy tutor, telling her bluntly that she had to get rid of her self-conscious giggle. "Have something to say, say it, and then sit down." The other lessons he would teach her included "Never admit you're licked" and "If you have to compromise, be sure to compromise up!" She began to sense the realities of politics, seeing both its grime—the voters she drove to the Hyde Park polls on election day told her they often took money for their votes— and its glory, "hard work and unselfish public service and fine people in unexpected places."

Eleanor often minimized the importance of her work and her commitment to it. "You need not be proud of me dear," she wrote Franklin at one point. "I'm only being active till you can be again. It isn't such a great desire on my part to serve the world and I'll fall back into habits of sloth quite easily! Hurry up for as you know my ever-present sense of the uselessness of all things will overwhelm me sooner or later!" This striking self-deprecation— a retreat into the traditional role of "lady"? a denial of her own ambition? an attempt to repress her astounding energy?—was voiced at a time when her hectic schedule showed her to be deeply committed to issues of her own choosing. She apparently worried that her activity and growing reputation threatened her husband either personally or politically. Or perhaps she herself could not reconcile her enjoyment of work with her image of the patrician lady she had been brought up to be. Throughout her life, Eleanor would minimize the worth of her own contributions to society.

With Franklin confined to chair and crutches, Eleanor forced herself to take on more of the physical leadership of the family. She realized she would need to stand in for her husband in teaching the boys. "It began to dawn upon me that if these two youngest boys were going to have a normal existence without a father to do these things with them, I would have to become a good deal more companionable and more of an all-around person than I had ever been before." With her own kind of determination she persevered in learning to drive a car, despite two accidents. She also learned to ride a horse, lead family camping trips, and even to swim at the YWCA, finally conquering her childhood terror of the water.

. . .

Franklin, assisted always by Louis Howe, was maintaining his old ties and constantly forging new ones. He was still among the most prominent

Democrats in the state, even in private life and even with his disability. In April 1924, Boss Murphy died of a heart attack. That month Smith asked Franklin to head his New York campaign for the presidency, his first real political work in two and a half years.

The alliance between Smith and Roosevelt was based on mutual need. Their differences—religious, social, geographic—meant they could appeal to the entire spectrum of New York Democrats. Personally they got along well and respected each other's political talents. Smith had many virtues rare in a politician, primarily an unusual combination of integrity, progressivism, and efficiency. Privately, however, Roosevelt and Howe were doubtful that Smith could win the nomination. Smith was too closely identified throughout the country with the problems of New York State, and in particular, he was indelibly marked as a "wet [against Prohibition] and a Catholic," thus splitting the national party. But working with him just might win for Franklin the gratitude of tens of thousands of New York Democrats.

Franklin and Louis began energetically to comb state delegations to win votes for Smith. It was an education for both in the issues, machines, and electoral law that lay behind the shouting and dealing at the convention. The campaign also kept Franklin's name prominent, affording him thousands of new contacts. Ultimately, Smith asked Franklin to nominate him at the Democratic National Convention, to be held at Madison Square Garden in New York.

Eleanor was invited by Cordell Hull, the Democratic party's National Committee chairman (and FDR's future secretary of state) to take charge of a convention committee that would present planks "of interest to women" to the Resolutions Committee. She selected a panel of female experts that recommended membership in the League of Nations, creation of a federal department of education, establishment of a forty-eight-hour workweek, equal pay for women workers, ratification of the child labor amendment, and more.

She was already revealing a steely determination. That spring she had gone head-to-head with Boss Murphy in a fight over who would choose the women delegates-at-large from New York State to the national convention, the Tammany boss himself or the female party leaders. Eleanor, refusing to play politics the Tammany way, had threatened to expose Murphy's tactics to the women at the New York State convention and to the press and even persuaded Al Smith to support her. Murphy had to withdraw.

But more important, Eleanor was able to see that in the political arena it was essential to be able to rise above an ingrained desire for harmony and accept the inevitability of conflict; indeed, she began to understand that the very essence of politics was conflict and that she herself had the inner resources to engage in—and profit from—adversarial situations. "To many women, and I am one of them," she admitted to *The New York Times,* "it is extraordinarily difficult to care about anything enough to cause disagreement or unpleasant feelings, but I have come to the conclusion that this must be done for a time until we can prove our strength and demand respect for our wishes." It was of paramount importance for women to show their willingness "to fight to the very last ditch for what we believe in." A courageous political operative was born.

"There's one thing I'm thankful for," Eleanor had written Franklin. "I haven't a thing to lose and for the moment you haven't either."

. . .

In the late spring of 1924, the brownstone on East 65th Street was bursting with campaign workers, politicians, old political friends, and journalists as convention week approached. Eleanor would attend as one of the four delegates-at-large from New York State. Even James, then sixteen, would be part of the excitement, serving as a page. Staying with the family—for a longer time than they had expected—were a number of Eleanor's contacts, women activists from upstate New York.

Early in the week, Eleanor and her committee were supposed to present their recommendations to the Resolutions Committee. "This was to be a new step in my education." she wrote later, wryly. "I was to see for the first time where the women stood when it came to a national convention. I shortly discovered that they were of very little importance. They stood outside the door of all important meetings and waited." They waited, in fact, all night outside the locked room where the Resolutions Committee was deliberating. Most of the men inside could not accept an important role for women in politics. Three times they voted against even hearing the women's proposals; the final vote, at dawn, was 22 to 18. Furious at the exclusion of women from the circle of power, dismayed by the waste of three months' work, Eleanor was probably not very surprised—and certainly still fascinated. For the rest of the convention she gave receptions during the day and listened, knitting, in the New York delegation box during the noisy, sweltering evenings.

Despite this setback, Eleanor and Democratic politics clicked. And she had learned the importance of perseverance. Even after the women's defeat at the national convention, she wrote, "I took my politics so seriously that in the early autumn I came down to the state headquarters and went seriously to work in the state campaign." She relished her work. "Women must get into the political game and stay in it," she wrote. She was becoming a leader in the women's political community. Newspapers called on her for comments; her high-pitched voice could be heard on the radio as well as on the campaign trail.

The leisure-class culture that disdained work was left behind. Now the community of work and engagement began to reveal to her a deeper meaning of equality and solidarity. She saw that the class differences she once perceived between herself and others were superficial. "It always amuses me," she later wrote, "when any one group of people take it for granted that because they have been privileged for a generation or two, they are set apart in any way from the man or woman who is working in order to keep the wolf from the door. It is only luck and a little veneer temporarily on the surface, and before very long the wheels may turn and one and all must fall back on whatever basic 'quality' they have."

. . .

Franklin's nominating speech for Al Smith at the Democratic National Convention in Madison Square Garden was his first major public appearance since his own vice-presidential campaign, and by all accounts it was a magnificent performance. Written by Smith's campaign manager, Joseph M. Proskauer, with Roosevelt's additions, the speech came at the midpoint of an unusually hot, long, and bitter convention, marked by passionate orations for and against a platform plank to condemn by name the Ku Klux Klan and ugly vehement conflicts about Prohibition between "wets" and "drys" and, ultimately, between supporters of Smith and William Gibbs McAdoo, who had been Wilson's secretary of the treasury. The gulf between the urban Northeast and the rural South, the two traditional Democratic strongholds, was gaping perilously wide. With the party in disarray, the delegates were desperate for a hero. When Franklin appeared, painfully but gallantly making his way to the platform on his son James's arm, the crowd united in a thunderous ovation.

He took command of the moment. His tenor voice rang out boldly, through the crowded, smoky hall and out across America on radio, which was broadcasting the convention for the first time. "You equally who come from the great cities of the East and the plains and hills of the West," he said, "from the slopes of the Pacific and from the homes and fields of the Southland, I ask you in all sincerity, in the balloting on that platform tomorrow, to keep first in your hearts and minds the words of Abraham Lincoln: 'With malice toward none, with charity to all.'" Boldly he quoted William Wordsworth, describing Al Smith in words he had initially rejected as too fancy—"He is the Happy Warrior of the political battlefield."

The delegates went wild; for almost an hour they paraded, sang, chanted, and cheered. In the seventeen minutes of his speech Franklin had transformed himself in the public eye from a pathetic invalid into a powerful political presence. He had also won a vast personal victory through what was considered a generous tribute to Smith. Franklin, not Smith, seemed truly to be the Happy Warrior.

Praise flowed in. Walter Lippmann wrote him the next day, calling his speech "a moving and distinguished thing. I am utterly hard-boiled about speeches, but yours seemed to me perfect in temper and manner and most eloquent in effect. We are all proud of you." Journalist and editor Mark Sullivan deemed it "a noble utterance" that "belongs with the small list of really great convention speeches." A columnist in the *New York Herald Tribune* stated that Franklin was "the one man whose name would stampede the convention were he put in nomination." And the *New York Evening World* declared that "Franklin D. Roosevelt stands out as the real hero of the Democratic Convention of 1924."

Certainly neither Smith nor McAdoo emerged gloriously from the fray. After 103 ballots the delegates chose a lackluster compromise ticket—John W. Davis, a wealthy lawyer and former congressman from West Virginia, and Charles W. Bryan of Nebraska, brother of William Jennings Bryan—and went home exhausted. That summer Franklin reflected that the Democratic party would have to bide its time. "In 1920 . . . I did not think the nation would elect a Democrat again until the Republicans had led us into a serious period of depression and unemployment. I still think that forecast holds true. . . . Every war brings after it a period of materialism and conservatism." The primary goal in the meantime, he believed, was to restore party unity.

Sure enough, Davis and Bryan went down to defeat on November 4. In an election remarkable for its low turnout, Coolidge and his running mate, Charles Dawes, Harding's director of the budget bureau, won by nearly two to one—an even greater Republican landslide than Harding's victory in 1920. Al Smith, however, was reelected governor of New York. Eleanor had worked hard for him, believing that Smith had "an extraordinary flair for government" despite his lack of national appeal or expertise on foreign affairs.

Her ardor may have been increased by the fact that his opponent was New York State Assemblyman Theodore Roosevelt Jr., her own first cousin. Ted Jr., like Franklin, was trying to follow TR's political route; Ted Jr. had already been assistant secretary of the navy under Harding and now had his sights set on the governor's mansion in Albany.

For Eleanor, Ted Jr. had none of the political courage of his father; she saw in him a man bound to the interests of his class, nothing more than an agreeable young man, she noted, "whose public service record shows him willing to do the bidding of his friends."

With two women friends, she followed TR Jr. on the campaign trail around the state, riding in a strange vehicle on which was mounted a gigantic papier-mâché teapot, a reminder of the Teapot Dome scandal—in which Theodore Jr. had never been directly implicated. It was a "rough stunt" for which Eleanor would apologize years later in her memoirs. Nor was Eleanor's cousin lacking in political courage; he had been virtually alone in the Assembly in protesting against the refusal to seat five duly elected socialist representatives from New York City. But in the wake of Ted Jr.'s attacks on Franklin in 1920 and Eleanor's hounding of Ted, the two branches of the Roosevelt family considered themselves at war. Years later, after Ted Jr.'s death, there would be a kind of reconciliation. In 1956, Eleanor and her grandsons traveled to the American cemetery at Omaha Beach in France and visited the graves of her two cousins, buried side by side: Theodore Jr., dead near Utah Beach in 1944, and his brother Quentin, killed in action in France in 1918.

. . .

Despite his paralysis, Franklin continued to believe in the effectiveness of a water cure—"The water put me where I am, and the water has to bring me back," he once told a friend. But warm water, his doctors advised, would be more therapeutic than the ocean at Campobello. He and a friend, John L. Lawrence (whose legs were also weakened by illness), purchased a houseboat together and named her the *Larooco* (Lawrence, Roosevelt, and Company). For several winters Franklin traveled south with Missy LeHand and other friends to enjoy long, lazy cruises.

An acquaintance, George Foster Peabody, told him of the Warm Springs Company, a dilapidated resort hotel with a thousand acres of land near Bullochsville, Georgia. The main asset of the place was a natural spring, loaded with mineral salts and naturally heated to 89 degrees Fahrenheit, which fed a huge outdoor swimming pool. Franklin became riveted when Peabody said that a young man, crippled by polio, had spent three years there and now could walk with only a cane. He decided to go down there himself.

Franklin adapted easily to the place, single-mindedly fixed on its natural treasure. He found the water marvelously refreshing and thought he perceived an improvement even on his first day; he could slightly lift his right foot. After a few more days he could wiggle his toes, and before long he was able to walk around in water four feet deep "almost as well as if I had nothing the matter with my legs."

Exhilarated, Franklin decided to build a cottage on the premises so that he could enjoy Warm Springs every winter. He received local politicians, gave interviews to local reporters, presided over community suppers, and became deeply involved in plans for development of the resort.

As he grew fond of Georgia, he came to understand some of its problems. "One day, as I sat on the porch of the cottage in which I lived," FDR would later recall of his first year in Georgia, "a boy came over very nervously and shyly and said, 'Mr. Roosevelt, may I speak to you for a moment? We are having a commencement at our school on Wednesday. Do you think you could come over and say a few words and give out the diplomas?' I said, 'Certainly, I will be glad to come. Are you the president of the graduation class?' He said, 'No, sir; I am the principal of the school.' I said, 'How old are you?' 'I am nineteen.'

"Have you been to college?" FDR asked. "Yes, sir; I finished my freshman year at the University of Georgia."

"This is a pretty pathetic story when you come right down to it," FDR concluded. Life in Georgia was "a pretty tough game."

. . .

In 1926, Franklin's involvement in Warm Springs grew into a major personal and financial commitment. It was he who hired a manager and then doctors and therapists to work with the twenty-three patients at the resort. He sold at auction a group of his beloved naval prints to finance his trips south. He was anxious to purchase the place, for just under $200,000, a notion that Eleanor opposed. Louis Howe, on the other hand, perhaps responding to Franklin's excitement, perhaps convinced the springs would indeed restore his boss's legs, or perhaps drawn in by the humanitarian nature of the venture, was enthusiastic and supportive. Eleanor eventually realized that Franklin was deeply committed to the project. In 1926, he bought the resort, with plans to develop a country club centered around the springs.

Eleanor, meanwhile, had her own plans. Through her political activities she had grown close to Nancy Cook and Marion Dickerman. The three worked on many different projects, traveled extensively together, and corresponded faithfully when separated.

Now Eleanor wanted to build a cottage on Fall Kill, a stream on Franklin's property a mile and a half east of Springwood, their Hyde Park estate, and share it with her two friends. Franklin, who had developed a fond, avuncular relationship with Cook and Dickerman, joined in the project with enthusiasm; in fact, he may have suggested it. He financed and closely supervised the building of the stone cottage and its swimming pool during the summer of 1925, and it was completed by the following New Year's Day.

Val-Kill would become Eleanor's real home, a woman's sanctuary of books, art, music, picnics, and talk ranging from intimate confidences to vehement political debates. "The peace of it is divine," she wrote Franklin in 1926. One great advantage at Val-Kill was that Eleanor felt free of the overbearing presence of her mother-in-law. In Val-Kill she could entertain guests like political activist and unionist Rose Schneiderman, the Russian-Jewish immigrant whom she had not dared to invite to her mother-in-law's estate. As she developed personally and politically, she needed a place where she could be herself, pursue her own interests, entertain her own friends, even when they met with Sara's disapproval.

The creative energy generated by the three women soon found new outlets. Not far from the new cottage they set up the gray stucco Val-Kill Furniture Factory, to produce handmade reproduction furniture under the direction of the gifted and creative Nancy Cook. Their products were purchased by department stores, by nearby Vassar College, by the Warm Springs Company, and by their good friends. Also in 1925, Eleanor started a small newspaper, the *Women's Democratic News,* with Cook, Dickerman, Dickerman's friend Caroline O'Day, a wealthy Democratic activist, and Elinor Morgenthau, another Democratic activist and the wife of Henry Morgenthau (FDR's future secretary of the treasury), a Dutchess County couple who had become the Roosevelts' close friends.

In 1927 Eleanor agreed to help Marion Dickerman purchase the Todhunter School for Girls (at 66 East 80th Street) in New York City, where Dickerman had been vice principal. For Eleanor it was the fulfillment of a long-cherished dream: to be involved again in a school like Allenswood. Conscious of her lack of a college degree, she began to teach without pay, "as I would consider that I was being paid in experience." But it was soon obvious that teaching was her true and joyous calling—"the one thing that belongs to me," she told a reporter in 1930. Teaching brought together her sensitivity toward others, her love of learning, her interest in young people, and her vision of the future. She read widely and thought deeply to prepare her imaginative lesson plans, gave students challenging assignments, took them on field trips to Ellis Island and the Lower East Side, and demanded that they think for themselves as she had slowly learned to do. Her goal was to produce thoughtful, aware, responsible young women. Her students responded with energy and excitement. She quickly dominated the school in a manner reminiscent of Marie Souvestre. (Years later, in 1938, the friendship with Dickerman and Cook would end brutally and bitterly over a variety of misunderstandings and impugned loyalties, and she would sever all ties to the Todhunter School.)

It was well that Eleanor found satisfying work that was apart from politics and that she enjoyed the period she called in her memoirs "Private Interlude: 1921–1927," for in 1928 she would become a political wife again. Franklin was back in the game.

3
Albany Again: The Testing Ground

If Franklin Roosevelt had accepted his 1920 defeat with more than his usual equanimity, it was in large part because he saw inviting opportunities directly ahead. Governor Al Smith had been defeated for reelection in that same election year, and if Al chose not to bid again for the office, FDR could run for governor, the next crucial step, in his carefully planned political career. And if he won the governorship in 1922, he would gain that high office at the same age that Theodore Roosevelt had—forty.

For Roosevelt and Howe, the polio that had devastated FDR physically could not be allowed to crush him politically. It merely slowed down the time schedule. FDR would continue his physical rehabilitation and perhaps be able to walk with only a cane by 1932. That year he would run for governor, no longer an invalid, and four years later he would be primed to run for president. Meantime he would keep his political visibility by writing articles for newspapers, conducting a huge and diverse political correspondence, and giving well-publicized speeches. His electrifying speech for Al Smith at the 1924 Democratic convention was now a legend among many Democrats; he was scheduled to nominate the Happy Warrior again for president at the 1928 convention in Houston.

This slow and safe scenario collapsed in a few seconds during a long-distance phone call between FDR and Al Smith, a few weeks after the Houston convention, where Roosevelt had lauded Al as a man "who not only deserves success but commands it."

Even before Houston, Al Smith and state party leaders had urged FDR to run for governor immediately, to strengthen the whole Democratic ticket—and Al Smith's chances for president—in New York State. The appeals escalated as Democrats increasingly saw Hoover as an almost unbeatable candidate. FDR and Howe resolved to give a flat no to a draft appeal, no matter how forceful. Howe was especially adamant; he did not want the boss to be sacrificed to Al Smith's ambition.

"It's no use, Al," Roosevelt said when Smith phoned him on the morning of the New York State Democratic convention, asking him to run for governor of New York. But Smith decided to put on more pressure and turn the screws. "If those fellows nominate you tomorrow and then adjourn," Smith said, "will you accept the nomination?"

Roosevelt hesitated . . . and was doomed. He said he didn't know. That was all Al Smith needed; he broke off with a cry of triumph. The state Democratic party nominated Roosevelt the next day.

MESS IS NO NAME FOR IT, a chagrined Howe wired him. Why had his boss given in? It was partly because party leaders had acted as real party leaders should—they had drafted him—and he had accepted as a loyal party man should. It was also because he was conflicted, as people close to him were. GO AHEAD AND TAKE IT, his daughter Anna had telegraphed earlier. Eleanor too supported the run for the governorship. REGRET THAT YOU HAD TO ACCEPT BUT KNOW THAT YOU FELT IT OBLIGATORY, she wired her husband.

Back in New York, Roosevelt had barely a month to campaign. Some greeted him as a sacrificial lamb. "There is something both pathetic and pitiless" in the drafting of FDR, the *New York Post* judged. Republicans contended that the crippled candidate was not up to the job of governor, but Al Smith wisecracked, "We don't elect a Governor for his ability to do a double back flip or a handspring."

Soon FDR was off and running, answering whispers about his crippled legs by a vigorous campaign in the Theodore Roosevelt tradition. While he lacked Cousin Ted's mesmerizing passion, FDR attracted big and enthusiastic crowds as he traveled the old campaign routes from southwestern New York to Buffalo to Rochester down the Mohawk Valley to Albany, then down the Hudson to big rallies in Manhattan.

FDR's great "telephone gamble" paid off—but by a razor-thin margin. Out of 4,500,000 Empire State voters, he won by 25,000 votes. Despite Al's popularity in New York and FDR's repeated tributes to him on the campaign trail, Smith not only lost to Hoover but failed to carry his own state. Nothing could have been more deflating for the Happy Warrior.

Still, Smith carried many large cities by a small margin, and Democrats had even improved their percentage of votes in rural areas. But Democratic hopes that a Catholic scion of immigrants might draw millions of urban ethnics into the Democratic fold proved vain. Smith did trigger a surge in voting turnout, but as much among Republicans as Democrats. He had little appeal to African-Americans and even less to women, most of whom voted for Hoover.

After two trouncings in the polls, the Democrats had not learned by 1928 how to oppose. Aside from his positions on hydroelectric power and Prohibition, Smith hardly diverged from Hoover's moderate Republican stands. With a Southerner, Senator Joseph T. Robinson, as running mate, Smith was as captive to southern whites as earlier candidates for president had been.

Progressive Democrats, like Eleanor and Franklin, were disappointed. Despite their fondness for Al Smith, the election outcome demonstrated again the weakness of the Democratic party philosophically and organizationally. Eleanor Roosevelt's involvement in women's issues made her all the more aware of her party's failure to win over that huge constituency. And if FDR had a chance to look around the convention hall in Houston while nominating Smith, he might have noticed a haunting sight—the convention of a party that called itself the "Democracy" had cordoned off African-Americans behind chicken wire.

. . .

Two widely held maxims of American politics are that governorships are the best stepping stones to higher office and that they are the most reliable tests for it. In most of this century the former maxim has only occasionally been true, and the latter rarely. Franklin Roosevelt's governorship of New York from 1928 to 1932, however, *was* such a stepping stone and, even more, a testing ground—mainly because he wanted it so.

Ambition feeds on office, and office on ambition. Not a single major act in his governorship was taken by this man of towering ambition without close scrutiny of the effect it would have on his planned reelection campaign of 1930 and his planned presidential campaign in 1932. Thus he had to satisfy a national constituency at the same time as he sought to serve the citizenry of New York State. Daunting though this was, it was made easier by the fact that in governing New York he was governing a small nation-state larger than many other republics around the world. New Yorkers liked to boast that not only were they the largest state with the biggest city but that upstate Buffalo had more Poles than Warsaw, more Irish than Dublin, more Italians than Rome. With its huge industrial, financial, and agricultural base, its superbly located waterways, and its polyglot population, New York was a microcosm of the nation; with all the needs and demands ensuing therefrom, it was a macrocosm of crisis.

When Franklin Roosevelt's motorcade, preceded by the roar of police motorcycles, pulled up to the elegant Victorian portico of the executive mansion in Albany before hundreds of cheering spectators, a smiling Al Smith came bouncing down the steps, his hand stretched out to Governor-elect and Mrs. Roosevelt.

"God bless you and keep you, Frank," Al called out. "A thousand welcomes! We've got the home fires burning." Al gave Eleanor a hug, and the outgoing and incoming first ladies embraced. "I only wish Al were going to be right here for the next two years," FDR said. "We certainly will miss him." As the Smiths climbed into their departing limousine the crowd called out their good-byes to "Al," and as he drove off, holding aloft his brown derby, the onlookers broke out into a tearful "Auld Lang Syne."

It was a fine show of affection between the old pro and the younger one, a show that well concealed for the moment a rising tension between them. Behind his famous smile, Smith was a deeply embittered man. In his wrath he had cried out that he would never run for public office again— "I have had all I can stand of it."

This funereal note was but music to the ears of a dozen Democrats already eyeing the next race for the White House—most notably the new governor. Already there was much talk about FDR for '32, Al knew. It was mortifying enough that Roosevelt had won while he had lost; even worse that FDR had carried New York State while Al had not. And FDR owed him a lot. It was he, the Happy Warrior, who had asked FDR to give that famous speech in 1924, had talked FDR into running four years later, had created in New York a magnificent Democratic record on which FDR could run. And much as he liked his "protégé," he had always felt an indefinable distance between the Smiths and the Roosevelts.

Indeed, Eleanor, still a patrician, viewed Smith as from a different social orbit. Although she had forcefully condemned religious prejudice against the Catholic Smith, she revealed her own subtle class prejudices against him. Whereas Franklin, she noted at length in her memoirs, would spend money on a picture or on a first edition but would economize on food, clothes, and entertainment, Smith always wore expensive clothes, because they indicated material success. Deriding the "monumental desserts" that the cook in the Albany mansion served Governor Smith and his family, she emphasized that the traditional Roosevelt Sunday supper consisted only of scrambled eggs. Smith could not understand that a certain form of inconspicuous consumption could be the ultimate proof of privilege and entitlement—nor could he enjoy that sense of security with which upper-caste men and women were born.

FDR's antennae picked up Smith's feelings of resentment. But what could he do? One thing was to praise Smith's record without stint. Another was to confer with him at length about the transition to the new regime. Cross purposes quickly emerged as Smith tried to persuade FDR to keep some of his top appointees. FDR murmured soft replies of the type that first mystified politicians and later maddened them. But FDR had no wish to continue the Smith governorship. "I've *got* to be Governor of the State of New York and I have got to be it MYSELF." Otherwise, he said, tapping his chest, "something would be wrong in here." He was "awfully sorry," he went on, if it hurt Al. He had not had his last tangle with Smith.

As governor, FDR's first dramatic policy initiative concerned the most controversial economic issue facing New Yorkers, the control of electric power. Nothing was more likely to inflame the legislature. And nothing was more carefully calculated to win Roosevelt support from across the country, especially from the Midwest and West, where electricity was a burning issue.

The new governor moved fast and forcibly on the question of power over power. Great interests were involved—consumers, farmers, utilities investors—for New York State's electric power potential was the largest in any state outside the West Coast. Great ideas, too: private control versus public and, if the latter, how much, and, above all, control not simply over the production of power but over the highly profitable transmission of it as well. Earlier governors—notably Charles Evans Hughes and Al Smith—had been pitted against Du Pont, Mellon, and General Electric over sites and related issues.

With such momentum, FDR could afford to be bold. Ten weeks after his inauguration he proposed a new five-member body to circumvent the existing public service commission with authority to finance, build, own, and operate generating facilities on the St. Lawrence River. The power would be transmitted by private companies, but only at the "lowest rates to consumers compatible with a fair and reasonable return" on real cash investment.

"I want to see something done," he told the legislators. "I want hydro-electric power developed on the St. Lawrence, but I want the consumers to get the benefit of it when it is developed."

The *government* selling electricity—nothing could have more excited friend and foe. A "very brave step in the right direction," Senator George Norris of Nebraska commented, and there was no one, for both political and policy reasons, whose support Roosevelt prized more than that of the Nebraska Progressive. Norris added, however, that FDR had "stopped to change horses in the middle of the stream" by failing to demand outright public distribution of power. Outspoken socialists like Norman Thomas insisted that only a complete takeover of *all* the utilities could give the public cheap power. FDR was simply straddling the issue, Thomas maintained.

The more FDR became involved in the question of electric power, the more he saw its complexity and the more he resisted doctrinaire solutions. Despite his own concern with the issue, going back to his days in the New York Senate, he consciously set himself to learning more about it. He consulted with a host of legal, economic, and engineering experts, and not least with interested businessmen. One of these was Owen D. Young, the head of General Electric, a thoughtful industrialist and a New York Democrat much admired by both Franklin and Eleanor, who two years earlier had urged him to run for the Senate. After debating the issue by correspondence, Young sent the governor almost thirty pages of data and argument favoring regulation, not ownership. Experts tutored the governor on the mysteries of the reproduction-cost basis for utility valuation in setting rates, as against the prudent investment theory, which FDR came to favor because it would more likely thwart rate increases.

None of these complexities deterred the governor from keeping electric power at the top of his agenda. Appearing before the legislature on the first day of 1930, he angered the Republicans by sharpening his demand for state development of St. Lawrence power through the state financing of—and retaining title to—transmission lines. The Republican floor leader in the Assembly lambasted the governor not only for his position but for the "sneering and superior tone" of the message.

The struggle over electric power, characterized mainly by executive–legislative conflict and deadlock, continued during Roosevelt's governor-

ship. Slowly he came to believe that the solution to public power problems lay not in individual states, even New York, or in interstate compacts,
but in federal action, because power transmission crossed state lines. But
was federal action possible, with Herbert Hoover, the "Great Engineer"
and apostle of individual liberty and local control, in the White House?

Farm policies and programs lay even more heavily on FDR's mind
than public power; indeed, politically he saw cheaper power as mainly
benefiting farmers. Curiously, for a man who touted himself as just a farmer,
he was less optimistic and activist in this field than in most other policy
areas. Was it because he could not wring a profit out of his mother's farmlands at Springwood? Fearing the inexorable decline of the family farm,
he was yet puzzled as to what could be done about it. He launched major
investigations, talked with farmers at every opportunity, and conferred with
nearby friend and farmer Henry Morgenthau Jr., but few major policies
or programs emerged. The governor, sometimes cooperating with Republican legislators and sometimes opposing them, came up in 1929 with a spate
of specific proposals and measures, such as state aid to farm road costs,
minor tax relief, training rural leaders in state agricultural schools, and
ending franchise taxes on farm cooperatives.

None of this had much of an impact on the lives of the small farmers
of New York. At the height of the "prosperity" of 1929, their problems were
winning little sympathy across the country. FDR saw omens of future disaster, but few signals as to what action to take. Increasingly in farm policy,
as well as in other "typical" state problems of the day—crime and punishment, labor policy, old age security, health, and education—he was struck
by the limits on the extent that any state, even powerful New York, could
deal with these fundamentals. Thus, as Americans enjoyed "good times"
and favored simple solutions based on individual initiative and
local government, New York's governor was shaping possible lines of action for a future presidential administration—a Roosevelt administration.

As for the governor's wife, she had always been highly ambivalent about
FDR's victory in 1928, unwilling to give up her own independence along with
the issues that mattered to her. A political wife, Eleanor wrote in an article
on wives of great men, may keep her own opinions, "but she must keep them
to herself." She resigned as editor of the *Women's Democratic News*, though she
would continue to have a voice in the paper's policies.

Especially for a woman who no longer had small children and who was
already a grandmother (Anna's daughter "Sisty" having been born in 1927),
Eleanor felt it was of the utmost importance to embrace a political life "to

guard against the emptiness and loneliness that enter some women's lives after their children are grown." "If anyone were to ask me what I want out of life," she wrote, as if echoing her Uncle Theodore, "I would say—the opportunity for doing something useful, for in no other way, I am convinced, can true happiness be obtained." Eleanor's life would indeed be unusually full, with meaningful work, women friends—and even male companionship and affection, from her devoted bodyguard Earl Miller.

During Franklin's years as governor, she divided her time between hostess duties in Albany, her teaching responsibilities in New York City at the Todhunter School for Girls ("I really had for the first time a job that I did not wish to give up," she wrote), and her interest in key issues that concerned women: the five-day workweek, housing, education, and, more generally, women's political clout.

Women had been voting for ten years. But despite the vote, she wrote in a fiery article in *Redbook Magazine* in 1928, women had gained little real power and influence and were consistently "frozen out" of any real influence in their parties. The remedy? Women had to play the "hard game" of party politics just as men did. Within the existing political parties—not within a new woman's party—women had to unite, organize, and elect their own "bosses," who "would be in a position to talk in terms of 'business' with the men leaders." Such female bosses, like their male counterparts, would have political control over groups of women whose votes they could "deliver." From a young bride ignorant of the most basic principles of American government, Eleanor was evolving into a politician and strategist.

In the new industrial world, too, she felt that women with ideas and drive should play leading roles. Looking beyond the Val-Kill furniture factory, she would tell *The New York Times* in November 1930 that "there is no reason why we should not have a female Henry Ford." She would come to detest the complimentary expression, "She has the mind of a man." As she demanded later, "Can't a woman think, be practical and a good business woman, and still have a mind of her own?"

She did not shrink from offering political advice to Franklin, counseling him not to retain two of Al Smith's advisers, Robert Moses and Belle Moskowitz, whose "race," she remarked, had "nerves of iron and tentacles of steel!" Eleanor hardly needed to resort to the mean-spirited anti-Semitic clichés of her class to make arguments against the monumentally difficult Moses, who, according to historian Robert Caro, had a "visceral hatred" for FDR, or against Belle Moskowitz, who, FDR felt, had become "accustomed to running and planning everything." Franklin let Moses go as secretary of state but kept him on as chairman of the State Council for Parks and would support him in that position, realizing that Moses knew how to mobilize government to construct parkways, public parks, and beaches. When FDR complained to Moses that the new public beaches were virtually inaccessible to poor urban people, were segregated, and—unlike the rest of the park system—charged admission, Moses threatened to resign. Roosevelt backed down.

Eleanor also proposed to Franklin that he make Frances Perkins commissioner of labor. He responded positively to her support for women in politics, writing in an article of his own, in 1928, that had women over the years wielded more political power, "the unspeakable conditions in crowded tenement districts, the neglect of the poor," and other miscarriages of social and economic justice "would never have come about."

Eleanor still enjoyed teaching at the Todhunter School, a school for young girls of privilege; it was an elite insular institution that contradicted her commitment to public education, her earlier work in the Rivington Street Settlement, her belief in a meritocracy, and her assertion that the upper-caste world was a thing of the past. Giving tacit approval to a quota on Jewish students at the Todhunter School, she felt that "the spirit of the school" would be "different if we had too large a proportion of Jewish children." And the problem was not just quantity but quality. Jews, she said, were "very unlike ourselves" and had not yet become American enough. Still, she tried to inculcate in her students a social and political awareness, encouraging them, in the patrician tradition of noblesse oblige, to make community service a part of their lives.

During the summer of 1929, Eleanor, along with her two youngest sons, Franklin and John, and friends Nancy Cook and Marion Dickerman, toured European cities, showing the boys, at Franklin's suggestion, the battlefields and trenches, Quentin Roosevelt's grave, and some of the cemeteries. In the cities and towns of Europe, Franklin Jr. remarked, a generation of men seemed to be missing. "There don't seem to be any men of father's age." The trip, replete with the tensions of dealing with difficult adolescent sons, was not deemed a success.

. . .

As the stock market lurched and skidded, recovered, and then cascaded in sickening drops during the fall of 1929, Governor Roosevelt was as much perplexed as other "leaders of opinion." At first, like most established figures, he uttered reassuring statements and then was mystified as the tumbles continued. As late as December he was referring to the crash, in a letter to Howe and possibly with tongue in cheek, as the "recent little Flurry down town." In general he joined the reassuring chorus of wise men, saying that industrial conditions were fundamentally "sound." Brief market rallies early in 1930 strengthened his impression that the series of drops were just one more of the endless zigs and zags of the American economy—though far more serious than most.

Meantime he had an election to win, for even in big modernized New York the gubernatorial term was only two years. Despite odds heavily in his favor, FDR in effect campaigned long before his formal announcement. He very deliberately made his campaign a preview and test of a presidential one, mainly by emphasizing national issues while the Republicans sought to shift attention to state and local issues, such as FDR being soft on Tammany corruption. He experimented with media techniques too, using film—even the new talking movie—and radio in rented theaters. And he made his first "fireside chats."

He also campaigned by pretending not to campaign, and he did this on one of the oldest vehicles in American politics, the canal boat. Early in his first term FDR had discovered that the state had a small boat for inspecting canals. Why not take it over for his own inspection trips?

It was a comical and endearing sight: the huge torso of the chief executive visible across the flatlands, surrounded by family and crew packed into the narrow craft, as it moved sedately from lock to lock. During leisurely and frequent stops he talked with farmers and politicians, while Eleanor Roosevelt visited nearby hospitals, asylums, and other state institutions. On her return he queried her. Did the inmates actually get what the menus listed? Were the beds too close together or folded up, hinting of congestion? How did the patients seem to feel toward the staff? "We have got to de-institutionalize the institutions," the governor wrote Howe in the summer of 1929.

It was not exactly like the navy days, dashing about on a destroyer, Roosevelt laughed. But as he made his "sweeps" across the Genessee Valley, up the St. Lawrence, back down through the northern counties, and across the tier of counties north of the Pennsylvania line, he luxuriated in the seven-miles-an-hour pace as he watched the changing scenery. "I saw many people, too." He certainly did, said his Republican critics; he was just campaigning in the guise of inspecting.

He was, of course, doing both—and having fun. FDR had a capacity for jollity and playfulness that lightened up even the staid old executive mansion. The years 1929–30 were for Roosevelt a time for some serenity and tranquility—the last he would have until the final year of his life. The deepening Depression concerned him, and he took steps to alleviate unemployment and suffering in his state, but he insisted that the Hoover administration must shoulder the recovery effort. The coming Republican gubernatorial challenge concerned him, but he knew that everything was working in his favor, and his two years of campaigning paid off handsomely in a win by a margin of 725,000 votes over his run-of-the-mill opponent, former prosecutor Charles H. Tuttle, though the GOP hung on to its majorities in both chambers.

And in Albany the governor could always look a hundred miles or so to the south, to his home, his lawns and trees and gardens. And to his crops. This was serious business, but FDR had fun with it too. He and Morgenthau tried an experiment in squash as a cash crop, in a partnership they called "Squashco." He told Morgenthau that he had instructed Moses Smith, the Springwood farm supervisor, as to how the "common stock should be planted, whether it should be watered, whether the distribution should be wide or closely harrowed," and "whether it carries any bonus (besides bugs)." He left it to Morgenthau to decide whether he was talking about stock watering on his farmlands or on Wall Street.

PART II:
ACTION

Chapter Five
PEOPLE: PRIDE AND FALL

"Breadline—No One Has Starved" (detail), Reginald Marsh, 1932.
(*Courtesy Prints Division, New York Public Library*)

In 1929 the American people were nearing a time of economic and social trauma more devastating than anything they had known since the Civil War, seven decades before. That crisis had erupted amid the rumbling of guns after a long period of rising tension; this crisis struck like lightning, leaving darkened economic skies and withered aspirations. That crisis had dramatically both fired and crushed great expectations; this crisis relentlessly numbed hopes and blighted pride. Both crises left deep and lasting scars across the American landscape.

Republican politicians had told American voters during the 1928 campaign that they "had never had it so good," and they were right. Real income of workers was slowly but steadily growing during most of the decade. In the span of only five years, 1923–28, the average annual earnings of employed workers and farmers rose from almost $1,300 to more than $1,400. Wrote the former muckraker Lincoln Steffens in 1929: "Big business in America is producing what the Socialists held up as their goal: food, shelter, and clothing for all." But Americans were enjoying more than the mere essentials. They were feasting on a cornucopia of goods and services, from telephones and radios to Model T's and washing machines.

Amid all this abundance, of course, large "areas" of poverty festered across the nation. Both urban and rural poor lacked primitive goods and services: nourishing food, indoor plumbing, even running water and electricity. If only about 3.2 percent of the labor force was unemployed, this still amounted to over a million and a half jobless. As usual, women, children, and African-Americans made out far worse than white male workers. Major economic sectors—textiles in New England, miners in Appalachia, southern tenant farmers—shared little of the prosperity of the "roaring twenties." Curiously, union membership and successful strikes, which usually increased in prosperous times, declined in this decade.

But for the vast majority of Americans, the times looked good as well as felt good; they did not see poverty, save for the "hoboes" who might drift through the cities and the countryside. Millions of middle-class and working-class people were realizing the American dream; those millions who were not believed that with hard work and a bit of luck they could make it, or at least that their children could.

These were proud people, proud of making good, of owning a home or at least a car, of helping their children gain more schooling than they had, of not being beholden to anyone, perhaps not even a bank. Their beliefs shored up this pride: that common sense and hard work would lead to individual material success. Anyone relying on charity or government "handouts" was a failure. Any man willing to work could get a job if he really tried. America would always be the land of opportunity and the richest country in the world.

Most of all, they believed that the good times could be permanent. This was not just hope; it was attested to by President Herbert Hoover himself, who was not only a "great engineer" but a benevolent one, with a well-deserved reputation for dispensing relief to European civilians after World War I. "One of the oldest and perhaps the noblest of human aspirations has been abolition of poverty," Hoover declared, on accepting the Republican nomination for president in August 1928. "We in America today are nearer to the final triumph over poverty than ever before in the history of any land." Americans would soon "be within sight of the day when poverty will be banished from this nation." This was enough to make anyone proud to be an American.

1
Fear and Want

"I am convinced we have passed the worst and with continued effort we shall rapidly recover," declared Herbert Hoover in the spring of 1930, as the stock market appeared to recover from its wrenching collapse. But full recovery would not come for ten years. Instead, as vast numbers of Americans lost their jobs, a harrowing downward spiral began to reach into all corners of the economy. A spreading fear started to grip the minds of millions of people concerned about jobs, not their portfolios.

The Hoover White House sought to abate their fears. The president "used the word 'depression' because it sounded less frightening than 'panic' or 'crisis,'" according to Hoover's biographer David Burner. So earnestly did the president believe in maintaining confidence that he later attended a World Series game to demonstrate his own serenity. In fact, Hoover was not serene; he was in silent anguish. In his desperation he turned to any remedy that did not commit the federal government to spending big money. He set up an unemployment relief agency that mainly issued optimistic statements. Administration spokesmen also continued to issue rosy forecasts. The president even offered Rudy Vallee—the Frank Sinatra of the 1920s—a medal if he could "sing a song that would make people forget their troubles and the Depression." Businessmen gathering in their clubs sang forlornly, "Pack up your troubles in your old kit bag."

But economic troubles were piling up too fast to be packed away. As corporate investment in new plants and equipment fell off sharply from 1929 to 1931, wage cuts swept the nation, especially in textiles and coal mining. Hours worked per week plummeted, depressing wages even more. The big steel, automobile, and rubber companies cut pay rates between 10 and 20 percent. As huge numbers of workers were laid off, unemployment, which had run for years at around 3 percent, shot up to over 15 percent. The gross national product, or GNP, fell 30 percent in two years.

For most Americans such figures were abstractions; they could grasp only the close-at-hand, the palpable. There was little outright starvation; the poor and the jobless hunkered down, made do, lived off the land, borrowed, stood in breadlines, begged at restaurant doors, rummaged through garbage cans, or stole.

. . .

The president observed the mounting distress with rising frustration and irritation. He had felt confident that he could master this downturn, just as he had done ten years before when President Harding had appointed him to head a coordinated administration attack on the 1921 recession. He could not understand why no upturn took place.

He acted, but without imagination or conviction. Relying on voluntarism, he sought to induce business not to deflate, urging bankers to make credit more readily available and to use their banks' funds to safeguard threatened financial institutions. He set up a National Credit Corporation to pool private credit resources to help the banks. Not lacking in personal sympathy, but remote from people's sufferings, he persuaded Will Rogers to head up a Red Cross fund-raising effort, the American Friends Service Committee to supply food to coal miners' children, wealthy friends to give monetary aid to the unemployed.

Still, he would not ask the federal government, representing the combined resources and power of the whole nation, to come directly to the help of the poor and the jobless. Almost two years after the crash he set up an organization for unemployment relief but denied it resources, so that its head, Walter F. Gifford, had to say that the country would have to depend on community chest drives. The president did ask for federal spending for public works, but in an amount that would have slow and uncertain impact on unemployment. With the Depression escalating in severity, it was too little and too late.

Finally, in 1932, his fourth year in the White House, Hoover took a major step in winning from a supportive Congress an act setting up the Reconstruction Finance Corporation, capitalized at half a billion dollars and authorized to borrow up to two billion more to provide emergency funds to banks, life insurance companies, building and loan associations, railroads, and other enterprises. Six months later the RFC was given more money to finance state and local public works of a self-liquidating nature and to make temporary loans to states to alleviate economic distress.

But all this effort hardly touched the lives of the distressed. Hoover was still adamantly opposed to direct federal relief. This would, he feared, make the poor overly dependent on the government, would sap their enterprise and industriousness, and thus would be bad for their character. Instead, they could turn to the Red Cross or charitable organizations. "The sense of voluntary organization and community service in the American people has not vanished," Hoover told the press a year after the crash, and had been "strong enough to cope" with the need for the past year.

Where was leadership that could really cope? In the ancient monarchies of Europe, the king was the people's "father," the "baker" who saw to it that his people had bread. It was the monarch's duty to respond to his people's needs; it was a buttress of his legitimacy, and if he failed, his people would protest, agitate, and even revolt. Despite his personal concern, Hoover could not reach out to the people with economic help or even psychological rapport. He put the burden of action onto voluntary organizations, which were financially inadequate to the need, or onto state and local governments, whose tax resources were shrinking drastically.

In democracies such intense human suffering offers a grand opportunity to the opposition party to smite the party in power for its "callousness" and try to oust it. But the Democrats as a party, while exploiting Hoover's day-to-day mishaps, offered no militant, comprehensive set of alternatives. Nor did Franklin Roosevelt on his own, even though he was already calculating his and Hoover's chances in 1932. But there was a more personal reason. Even after a year of Depression, Hoover's standing was still high. People had not forgotten his brilliant leadership during World War I as head of the

Commission for the Relief of Belgium. Since then, Hoover had presented himself as a progressive Republican in the Theodore Roosevelt tradition and an admirer of the 1912 Bull Mooser. For TR's cousin, the president would not be an easy target, whatever his leadership failures.

2

Shame and Despair

In Albany, as hundreds of thousands of his fellow New Yorkers lost their jobs and their pride, Governor Franklin D. Roosevelt watched the gripping Depression through sympathetic eyes for those caught in its maw. He also watched it through his political spectacles, looking at its implications for 1932 and 1936. It became obvious that Hoover would not take forthright action. But what about Roosevelt? During the early Depression years he maneuvered almost as cautiously as President Hoover on this cloudy and complicated economic terrain.

As governor he had displayed an aversion to spending, pressuring his cabinet members to cut costs as much as they could. And in 1929, after the crash, he had joined the chorus of voices, led by Hoover, proclaiming that the economy was fundamentally "sound."

From the start, however, he was happy to take political potshots whenever Hoover offered a tempting target. When Frances Perkins, whom Roosevelt had appointed industrial commissioner, saw a presidential statement in January 1930 saying that employment was increasing and the economic situation improving, she knew Hoover was wrong. She was indignant because, as she wrote later, the statement "was going to hurt and grieve the people being laid off in great numbers. They would not understand, they would feel betrayed, they would feel that there was something wrong with them personally." A great despair, she feared, would enter their hearts.

After a laborious day of checking the data, Perkins called in the press and repudiated Hoover's rosy figures. Her story won front-page headlines across the nation. She was pleased, but later when she had a phone call from the governor's office she suddenly remembered, with consternation, that she had not cleared her bombshell with her boss. What if *he* repudiated *her*?

"Bully for you!" came the warm vibrant voice. "That was a fine statement and I am glad you made it." He added that he was glad she had gone ahead, because if she had checked with him, "I would probably have told you not to do it," and it was better to have it out in the open.

It was easy for Roosevelt to shoot from this kind of cover. But what alternatives could he offer to the Hoover palliatives?

One was unemployment insurance. Approaching the issue with a remarkable combination of seriousness and cautiousness, he studied the experience of other nations (but not other states; not one had legislated unemployment insurance); consulted authorities, including the noted British expert, Sir William Beveridge; and conferred at length with the indefatigable Perkins. He wavered for a time over some of the key questions, especially whether employees and not merely employers should contribute to the insurance system and whether plans should be financed through private insurance companies. Indeed, he remained cautious about the financing. Having been in the insurance and surety business himself, the governor told a critic of the program, "I am not a wide-eyed radical" and "the little tin god I worship" was the actuarial table.

Still, insurance was a long-run benefit. People needed immediate help in the face of the approaching winter of 1931–32, which economists were predicting would be the worst yet. Modern society, "acting through its government," FDR warned his fellow governors, "owes the definite obligation to prevent the starvation or the dire want of any of its fellow men and women who try to maintain themselves but cannot." After this bold statement he proposed a pay-as-you-go relief program that, he insisted, was not a "dole" or handout. He would raise funds not by borrowing but by raising the state income tax. For a time, with an eye to shifting political winds, he would proceed cautiously on relief.

To despairing Americans, the speeches of politicians like Hoover and Roosevelt were so remote from their lives that they hardly noticed. What they saw was the mean little economic world they now lived in; what they heard were stories about more suicides, often occurring quietly in homes, more thievery of food and small possessions. The Depression was biting deeper, reaching women and children who once had had some protection.

3
Anger and Impotence

People respond in diverse ways to internal pressures, to their raw feelings of stark fear and sheer want, burning shame and despair. Some internalize them, hiding their feelings from others and even from themselves; others explode in anger—anger against fate, bad luck, the rich, the government.

But as the Depression began to grip America, no rising of the masses, no expropriation of the capitalists, no overthrow of the government ever took place. Early on, in the spring of 1930, revolution did seem possible, as several thousands of people demonstrated in Chicago and San Francisco. These gatherings were unimpeded, but in Detroit, Cleveland, and other cities police tried to disperse the crowds with tear gas, and fierce street fights broke out. *The New York Times* reported the biggest struggle, in Manhattan: "The unemployment demonstration staged by the Communist Party in Union Square yesterday broke up in the worst riot New York has seen in recent years when 35,000 persons attending the demonstration were transformed in a few moments from an orderly, and at times bored, crowd into a fighting mob. The outbreak came after Communist leaders, defying the warnings and orders of the police, exhorted their followers to march on City Hall and demand a hearing from Mayor Walker." The *Times* story—a curious mixture of anti-mob bias and anti-police feeling—offered a graphic picture of screaming men and women, bloodied heads, sprawling bodies, and police battering protesters even as they fled.

These demonstrations, often led by Communists, aroused some concern for the jobless. But even more, as mob scenes were splashed on front pages across the country, they provoked anti-Communist fury, thus drawing some attention away from the victims. In the House of Representatives, Congressman Hamilton Fish, Franklin Roosevelt's old New York adversary, offered a resolution to create a special five-man committee to investigate Communist activities, which he said threatened the internal security of the nation. He was exceeded in indignation only by one Florida congressman, who urged that not only Communists but everyone not of white blood should be deported. Fish's resolution passed by an overwhelming majority—210 to 18—and became the origin of the House Un-American Activities Committee.

As the Depression tightened its grip on the poor, it appeared likely that the big demonstrations of spring 1930 would trigger even more massive upheavals. But anger seemed to atomize, erupting in thousands of isolated demonstrations, disruptions, lootings, riots. Desperate groups of men mobbed food trucks, invaded shops to demand food, battled with the summoned police. For a time these local spontaneous demonstrations became bigger, more numerous, and better organized. In Chicago several thousand jobless marched on relief centers to demand, with some success, three meals

The Lincoln funeral procession, Union Square, New York, April 1865.
In the circled window are Theodore and Elliott Roosevelt.
(Courtesy Theodore Roosevelt Collection, Harvard College Library)

TR's off-campus room, Cambridge.
*(Courtesy Theodore Roosevelt Collection,
Harvard College Library)*

TR at Harvard
*(Courtesy Theodore Roosevelt Collection,
Harvard College Library)*

TR (left) with his brother Elliott, sister
Corinne, and Edith Carow,
Oyster Bay, around 1876.
*(Courtesy Theodore Roosevelt Collection,
Harvard College Library)*

Interior of the Roosevelt mansion at
6 West Fifty-seventh Street.
(Courtesy Sagamore Hill National Historic Site)

TR (at center) with Thomas Platt (on right with beard)
at the 1900 Republican Convention.
(Courtesy Theodore Roosevelt Collection, Harvard College Library)

TR with his family at Sagamore Hill, August 1905.
(Courtesy Bettman/CORBIS)

TR at Grant's Tomb, 1904.
(Courtesy Brown Brothers)

TR during the 1912 campaign.
(Courtesy Theodore Roosevelt Collection, Harvard College Library)

Franklin Delano Roosevelt, age seventeen.
(Courtesy Franklin Delano Roosevelt Library)

Eleanor Roosevelt (center) with her cousins Muriel Robbins and
Helen Astor Roosevelt, Hyde Park, June 1903.
(Courtesy Franklin Delano Roosevelt Library)

Eleanor and FDR, 1905.
(Courtesy Franklin Delano Roosevelt Library)

FDR campaigning for the New York
State Senate, 1910.
*(Courtesy Franklin Delano
Roosevelt Library)*

Louis Howe, Thomas Lynch
(Poughkeepsie campaign volunteer), FDR,
and Eleanor during the 1920 campaign.
(Courtesy Franklin Delano Roosevelt Library)

FDR with Al Smith.
*(Courtesy Franklin Delano
Roosevelt Library)*

Eleanor with friends Marion Dickerman (at right) and (from left) Marion's
sister Peggy Levenson and Nancy Cook, 1926.
(Courtesy Franklin Delano Roosevelt Library)

FDR, Eleanor, and daughter Anna, Warm Springs, October 1932.
(Courtesy Franklin Delano Roosevelt Library)

a day and free medical aid. In March 1932, jobless Detroit workers, in a Communist-organized demonstration, marched on the Ford River Rouge plant, leaving four marchers killed and numerous men wounded.

But these upheavals never came to a head, to a national mobilization. Why not? Why did the American experience not parallel the European—the 1927 general strike in Britain, for example, or dramatic labor demonstrations in France or Germany? Partly it was the failure of Communist party activists to achieve enough organizing skills to mount massive efforts, partly the weakness of American socialists, who usually had to play second fiddle to the bolder Communist party. AF of L locals, depleted in membership and often broken in spirit, stood by, uninvolved if not hostile.

The jobless did make some effort to organize. Late in 1932 the Chicago Workers Committee, set up mainly by socialists to press for higher relief payments, called a meeting of "all Unemployed Leagues that we know of except the Communist Party's 'Unemployed Councils'" to form the Federation of Unemployed Workers Leagues of America. The resulting federation soon collapsed. The basic problem was simple: Usually the poor not only lacked money—crucial in a capitalist nation—but also education, skills, contacts, access, ideology, self-esteem, and motivation.

. . .

By mid-1932 the morale of the jobless and the poor was as low as the state of the economy. The unemployed felt licked. Novelist Sherwood Anderson saw a "breaking down of the moral fiber of the American man," because people were still apologizing for being poor and jobless. "We are less worried about revolution than we used to be," *The New Yorker* said in June. Rather than revolutionary, Americans were melancholy and hypochondriac. "People are in a sad, but not a rebellious, mood."

The poor were imprisoned in their hopelessness, apathy, despair. Most felt utterly impotent, finding nowhere to turn. The jobless and impoverished of Europe at least had massive organizations to turn to, the Labour Party in Britain and strong unions and left-wing parties in France and Germany; Americans had only the socialists, whose idealism and fervor were not matched by impact on policy, and the Communists, who were so tarred as subversive and "anti-American" as to lack political clout. Like Groucho Marx's joke about the man not wanting to join any club willing to admit him, many of the proud and patriotic poor would not join any radical organization willing to enlist them.

Worse still, wrote historian Cabell Phillips, was the knowledge "that there was nothing you or your boss or the governor of your state or the President of the United States could do about it. All the towers of wisdom on which you were accustomed to lean had crumbled. The roots of your faith in the American way and even, perhaps, in the benevolence of God, had begun to wither like a vine too long deprived of rain. You felt trapped, like an animal in a cage, as some malevolent force that you could neither comprehend nor fend off inexorably worked to destroy your whole scheme of life."

A dramatic failure illustrated their impotence. In 1924, not long after the post–World War I recession, Congress had passed—over President Coolidge's veto—a bill giving veterans a "bonus" based on the number of days spent in service, payable in twenty years. In 1932, Congressman Wright Patman of Texas introduced, in the face of opposition from the Hoover White House, a measure for immediate payment of the bonus, in recognition of the thousands of veterans who were jobless and unable to wait. The bill sounded as a bugle call to tens of thousands of veterans to muster in Washington, help put the bill through, and receive their checks.

And muster they did, perhaps twenty-thousand-fold, after long journeys in hundreds of boxcars. They gathered in unoccupied government buildings and encampments. They had a plaintive war chant:

> *Mellon pulled the whistle,*
> *Hoover rang the bell,*
> *Wall Street gave the signal,*
> *And the country went to Hell.*

The Republican Congress opposed the bill, Hoover refused to meet them, and when the "bonus army" stayed on in Washington, mockingly self-styled as the Bonus Expeditionary Force, he authorized their eviction. The "Force" was hardly an aggressive one. Interviewing men from all over the country, a *Washington Star* reporter found nearly all to "have one thing in common—a curious melancholy, a sense of the futility of individual struggle, a consciousness of being in the grip of cruel, incomprehensible forces." They refused to go home.

On a clear hot day in July 1932 a combat force emerged from the White House area and marched down Pennsylvania Avenue. Huddled along the way, the veterans confronted the majesty of the state: four troops of cavalry, four companies of infantry, a mounted machine gun squadron, several "whippet" tanks, all grandly headed by General Douglas MacArthur, attired in English whipcord breeches and service stripes, flanked by majors Dwight D. Eisenhower and George S. Patton Jr.

As the soldiers swept down the street, they forced the veterans out of their shanties with torch and tear gas. Swiftly and efficiently MacArthur's troops moved through the city, across the Anacostia Bridge, and into the main encampment area, where they routed men, women, and children out of their huts, leaving a smoldering ruin, three fatalities, dozens injured, an estimated thousand gassed.

The "president was pleased," the White House let it be known. In Albany, Governor Roosevelt, outraged as he read newspaper reports, told a visitor what Hoover ought to have done and what he—the governor—would have done. But he issued no statement. Earlier he had offered fares to New York veterans wishing to return home; few had accepted.

In Washington, young reporter Thomas L. Stokes reflected, after watching the army burn Anacostia, that this must be "the end of this country as we know it. The United States Army turned on American citizens—just fellows like myself, down on their luck, dispirited, hopeless. . . . So all the misery and suffering had come finally to this."

Hopeless.

Chapter Six
THE PRAGMATISTS:
MAKING IT WORK

BUDDIES

New York Herald-Tribune, October 23, 1932.
(*Courtesy FDR Library*)

As the Depression heightened, so did Governor Roosevelt's concern for the poor and the jobless. So did—perhaps even more—his presidential ambition. If his ambition intensified at a faster rate than his concern, FDR would have justified it in his usual breezy, pragmatic way: He could not act against the Depression unless he became president.

His apprehensions rose as well. As Hoover's popularity waned, 1932 looked like a sure thing for the Democrats, whetting the hopes and fantasies of potential rivals. Most worrisome and galling to the governor, however, was Al Smith's dog-in-the-manger posture. It was not clear that the Happy Warrior planned to run, only that he sought to snatch the prize from his successor. A friend of both men reported to Roosevelt that, questioned as to his attitude toward FDR, Smith admitted that his successor had been friendly and agreeable to him, but then Al had burst out, "Do you know, by God, that he has never consulted me about a damn thing since he has been governor? He has taken bad advice and from sources not friendly to me. He has ignored me!" His voice rising, Al went on, "By God, he invited me to his house before he recently went to Georgia, and did not even mention to me the subject of his candidacy."

For Roosevelt's rivals that was the rub—his disingenuousness. To friends, adversaries, and even family he contended that he was not only not running, he was not even *thinking* of running "in any shape, manner, or form," as he wrote a Democratic national committeeman. He had "no personal desire to run for a national office," he wrote a friendly senator. He had "no hankering, secret or otherwise, to be a candidate," he wrote a League of Women Voters activist and friend of Eleanor Roosevelt. He was "taking absolutely no part in any movement" on his behalf, he wrote party head Jouett Shouse, a friend of Al Smith's, virtually on the eve of throwing his hat into the ring.

What he was really doing was "the br'er rabbit" as he confided to "Uncle Henry" Morgenthau Sr.—he was biding his time. One result was that at a time when a despairing people needed a clarion voice for reform and recovery, Roosevelt was waiting, subordinating his principles to his presidential ambition. Even more, at a time when it was vital that the

Democratic party speak out in opposition to GOP policies, he objected to its national committee taking any public position on national issues. And why? Because it was contrary to "established powers and precedents," FDR wrote Smith. And why really? Because he feared that the DNC, under the domination of Smith & Co., would pass resolutions, especially for repeal of Prohibition, that might hurt FDR's campaign plans and posture.

Roosevelt had decided not to speak out forcefully, nor did he want his party to do so. But he still did not miss any item that might affect his campaign. When a Butte newspaper claimed that he had not dispensed with his wheelchair, FDR wrote the editor, "As a matter of fact, I don't use a wheelchair at all except a little kitchen chair on wheels to get about my room while dressing, before I am dressed, and solely for the purpose of saving time." He did not use one at all, he added, "in my work in the Capitol."

Even so, his adversaries might cruelly point out, a wheelchair could turn quickly and point in any direction. Roosevelt was so busy connecting with congressional leaders, governors, city bosses, newspaper publishers, and financiers in connection with his campaign, critics said, that he was unable to connect with the needs and hopes of the American people. But who was?

Not the intellectuals. In September 1932 fifty-three writers, including such eminences as Edmund Wilson, proclaimed the two major parties hopelessly corrupt; the socialists were do-nothings; capitalism was full of fatal contradictions; fascism was evil. They denounced the "disorder, the lunacy spawned by grabbers, advertisers, speculators, salesmen, the much-adulated, immensely stupid, and irresponsible 'businessmen.'" Much of this resonated with the needy. But what was the solution proposed by these fifty-three intellectuals? To support the "frankly revolutionary Communist Party" and its candidates.

Nor were the business leaders and their scribes speaking for ordinary Americans. By mid-1932 they were veering between mindless optimism and utter frustration. Advised the financier Roger Babson, "If you can't think yourself into a job, work yourself into one. Insist on working even without pay." Said Henry Ford of young vagabonds, "Why, it's the best education in the world for those boys, that traveling around!" Much better than years at school, he added.

Nor were the politicians leading the people. Declaimed Herbert Hoover, "We cannot squander ourselves into prosperity." Most of the Democratic party leaders were repeating conventional pieties about economics and morality. They offered no united opposition to Hoover Re-

publicans, no clear-cut alternatives. FDR was no exceptic
not quite place him. Sometimes he almost talked socialisn
marketplace, sometimes the need for a compassionate go
times the need for a balanced budget.

Eleanor was speaking out for women—their rights to employ..........,
proper housing, education, and union representation despite the Depression. Realizing that neither charity nor emergency relief of people's suffering was sufficient, in early 1932 she called for "great changes" and "new
solutions." She was beginning to present FDR with a liberal perspective,
so much so that his campaign manager, Sam Rosenman, found her too
assertive.

People reduced to the primal needs of food and shelter did not connect with established leaders. They had no political strategy, no battle plan.
They could only cry out, "Brother, Can You Spare a Dime?"

1
Ideologies and Practicalities

Even as the 1920s ended in Depression and despair, people were calling
it the Jazz Age. "The greatest, gaudiest spree in history," Scott Fitzgerald
had termed it prophetically. But it was much more than that. It was a decade of bitter political satire and scorching social criticism, a time when
skeptics and cynics punctured old myths and assailed reigning ideologies.

They had much to assail. Noted historian Charles A. Beard delivered
a body blow to American capitalism's most prized ideological possession,
its "sacred creed of rugged American individualism." Many economic leaders, Beard wrote, were exalting laissez-faire into a cult, "using the phrase
as an excuse for avoiding responsibility, for laying the present Depression
on 'government interference,' and for seeking to escape from certain forms
of taxation and regulation which they do not find to their interest." It was
necessary, Beard went on, to spell out calmly just who had been asking
the government for decades to intervene in the economy, and he proceeded
to do just that. Railroads, waterways, shipping, aviation, canals, highway
building, Commerce Department business development, the huge pork
barrel of military posts and public buildings, antitrust acts, the tariff, and
more—in all these instances, Beard said, businessmen had not only con-
doned governmental interference but demanded it, politicked for it. Business seemed to betray its most cherished beliefs.

Capitalism did not produce efficiently, railed economic theorist Thorstein Veblen; it sabotaged production, it exploited the poor. Scoffing at the capitalists and their way of life—especially their "conspicuous consumption" of furniture, works of art, clothes, and jewelry—he sharply differentiated between wasteful, profit-obsessed businessmen and potentially productive industrialists and technologists.

"Liberalism," as well as capitalism, was a spent force, asserted theologian Reinhold Niebuhr. He had been struck by the tragic contrast in "Motor City" between humans' moral codes as individuals and their mean and ugly behavior as collectivities—a contrast he summed up in the title of his most famous book, *Moral Man and Immoral Society*. Much of this difference he attributed to the chaos and cruelty of capitalism.

FDR did not really read the tomes of such men as Beard and Veblen; he did not really read books at all, though he did delve widely into history and biography during his long convalescence. Typically he leafed through books, picked thoughts from them, filed sentences away, and sometimes corresponded with the authors. One way or the other, he rummaged fruitfully through the ideas of people who were challenging orthodoxy. He also waded through widely read newspapers and magazines, noting especially the political items but not missing, with his quick eye, both the more serious and the more frivolous articles and columns.

While influenced by the general intellectual climate, Roosevelt could not ignore the writings of one man: Walter Lippmann.

FDR had known his fellow Harvard man since the war years, but he could hardly have known him outside Harvard and government social circuits, for Lippmann's was a more complex and distanced personality even than Roosevelt's. Intellectually curious and yet politically involved, socially charming and yet personally cool, idealistic and yet cynical, self-assured and yet insecure, aloof and detached and yet deeply committed to values he could not fully define, Lippmann had moved from youthful socialism to wartime nationalism to Wilsonian internationalism, only to become disillusioned by each. In every stage, though, he displayed a power of analysis, a philosophical depth, a liberal temper and generosity, and a mastery of expression that put him far above the ruck of journalists. His columns in the *New York Herald Tribune* were read avidly by politicians in all camps—and by the concerned public. "Lippmann scares me this morning!" James Thurber had one of his cartoon women exclaim to her husband in *The New Yorker*.

Lippmann's hero, leadership role model, and prototype president from early on to almost the end was Theodore Roosevelt, along with—though very secondarily—Woodrow Wilson. Compared to such heroes, Franklin Roosevelt in Lippmann's eyes simply did not measure up, at least during the Depression. FDR "just doesn't happen to have a very good mind," Lippmann wrote a friend in November 1931; "he never really comes to grips with a problem which has any large dimensions." The key for FDR was always political, but he was also just a "kind of amiable boy scout." A few weeks later Lippmann returned to the attack, and now publicly. Charming but slippery, carrying water on both shoulders, FDR was "a highly impressionable person without a firm grasp of public affairs and without very strong convictions," he wrote in his column. He was merely a "pleasant man who, without any important qualifications for the office, would very much like to be President."

When Howe sent this column up to FDR, the governor said nothing. Almost certainly it galled him to the bone. Much earlier, when Lippmann had criticized him for pussyfooting on public power and other issues, Roosevelt wrote a friend that in spite of Lippmann's "brilliance, it is very clear that he has never let his mind travel west of the Hudson or north of the Harlem!" Doubtless his reaction to the later onslaught was even more bitter. But he was still lying low. Right now he had to win a nomination and an election. Later on, once in office, he could settle what scores needed to be settled. But of course, once in power, he might not feel that scores needed to be settled at all.

. . .

And what of FDR's own philosophy? He was not much interested in ideas for their own sake but, rather, to the extent they could be put into practice. And even these more "operational" ideas he rarely discussed. Just as he preferred to shape his views by talking with people rather than reading books, so he based his broad philosophical beliefs on those of his heroes in American history. First of all he drew his beliefs from the teachings of Jesus Christ, from his disciples and interpreters over the centuries, and from the ministers he heard on occasional Sundays, especially in Hyde Park. His favorite hymn, all his life, was "Art Thou Weary, Art Thou Languid, Art Thou Sore Distressed?" Once, in later years when Eleanor asked him if he really believed in the church doctrines he had learned as a child, he responded, "I never really thought about it. I think it is just as well not to think about things like that too much."

He drew his political beliefs even more from his secular heroes, but these had changed during his first four decades of life. In his early years

his hero was his hero's hero, Theodore Roosevelt's Alexander Hamilton.
Just as TR admired Hamilton's style of strong leadership, his energy and
gusto, his defense of presidential power, and—of course—his New York
venue and statesmanship, so did FDR. Sometime during his convalescence
in the early twenties, however, FDR almost abruptly repudiated Hamilton
as his philosophical mentor and embraced Hamilton's fabled antagonist,
Thomas Jefferson. The switch seems to have been inspired by a book, as
well as by Cousin Theodore's death and departure from the ideological
battles. In 1925, Claude Bowers, a journalist and biographer of strong Democratic persuasion, came out with a biography, *Jefferson and Hamilton,* in
which the renowned Virginian did not suffer from the joint billing. In a
book review, evidently the only one he ever wrote, Roosevelt commended
Bowers for sketching Hamilton in his true colors as an aristocrat and foe
of democratic government. "Jefferson, eclipsed in the Cabinet by Hamilton,
the natural democrat against the natural aristocrat, began then"—in the
1790s—"the mobilization of the masses against the aristocracy of the few,"
wrote the book reviewer.

His TR-like repudiation of aristocracy and privilege and his embracing of Jefferson hardly focused FDR's political philosophy; on the contrary,
it enabled him to skip back and forth across the political and ideological
spectrum, much as Jefferson had during his long life of thought and action. While the great Virginian was always committed to liberty and equality, the noble ideals he had laid out in the Declaration of Independence,
these were so general as to allow a diversity of means to achieve them. In
the past century and a half, Jefferson's name had been invoked by Whigs
and Democrats, abolitionists and slaveholders, nationalists and localists,
and more recently by southern states righters, business free enterprisers,
Bill of Rights libertarians, and socialist and communist egalitarians.

So Jeffersonianism gave FDR just what he wanted doctrinally: a broad
canvas on which he could fill in his own shifting views and values, depending on election needs. But it also drained his political philosophy of rigor
and structure, of linkage of ends and means or a hierarchy of priorities. Thus
it was not that FDR had no ideology in the early 1930s but that his doctrinal
array was so soft and shapeless, so malleable in its central organization, as to
become a frail edifice of related and unrelated ends and means.

This was the way Roosevelt preferred it, as he faced the looming perils and unknowable choices of the approaching economic crisis, equipped
with a wildly swinging intellectual compass, a hazy ideology, determination, and hope.

2
The Deal and the Ideal

Roosevelt could hardly have anticipated that the first moral dilemma facing him in the campaign year would concern foreign policy. Save for the Democrats' routine flaying of the GOP over trade barriers—now the Smoot-Hawley tariff—international relations were a side issue in 1932. But hovering over the domestic battlefield was another ideology: the ideology of internationalism, of the centuries-old search for ways of organizing and ensuring peace among humankind. This ideology now took on the power of a lost cause, American failure to enter the League of Nations. Bitterness over this issue was almost as pervasive as the Vietnam war would become decades later.

As a candidate who had fought for the League side by side with James Cox twelve years earlier, FDR knew the power of this issue among his "Old Wilsonian" friends. He also knew its power for a host of Republican internationalists—men like Charles Evans Hughes and Henry Stimson—who supported some kind of league of nations but of course not *Wilson's* league. And FDR could not forget that his own No. 1 hero, Theodore Roosevelt, had also supported some kind of league—though again not Wilson's—and had rejuvenated a potent Republican brand of internationalism that still persisted, especially in East Coast press and public.

But from the West Coast, the day after New Year's Day 1932, there sounded a bugle call on a national radio hookup that threw a small panic into presidential aspirants' camps. William Randolph Hearst denounced FDR, Al Smith, Herbert Hoover, and any other candidate pledged to Wilson's "visionary policies of meddling in Europe's conflicts and complications" by joining the League of Nations. Hearst's candidate? John Nance Garner of Texas, Speaker of the House of Representatives, nominated by Hearst in front-page editorials in all his newspapers across the country.

This was a triple blow to Roosevelt. A Garner candidacy would stall a major effort FDR was making to pick up delegate support in the Southwest, especially in Texas. Hearst's blast fired up isolationist feeling in the West, where Roosevelt was wooing anti-League progressives like William Borah of Idaho. And Hearst helped produce a dangerous desertion from the League by Democratic presidential hopefuls.

An early deserter was Newton D. Baker, the most internationalist of internationalists and the darkest of dark horses. He did not favor "a plank in the Democratic national platform urging our joining of the League," he announced; he of course still favored American entry, which would come in time, but only after a majority of the American people came to support it. This weaseling statement left FDR in an exposed position, as the only pro-League man in the race. In a typically Rooseveltian maneuver, Jim Farley visited Hearst's *New York American* to report privately that Roosevelt had changed his mind about the League. And in a typically Hearstian ploy that made the publisher hated by all those who played politics by gentlemen's rules, Hearst blazoned Farley's visit on his front pages and, turning the screw tighter, pontificated that if Roosevelt had "any statement to make about his not being an internationalist he should make it to the public publicly and not to me privately."

Roosevelt was cornered. Onto his very next speech—at a New York State Grange convention in Albany—he tacked a complete surrender. Along with millions of his fellow Americans he had supported the League in 1920, he told the perhaps perplexed agriculturalists. But it had become a "mere meeting place" for European political talk without any action— in part perhaps because the United States had not joined at the outset. Therefore "I do not favor American participation."

FDR expected a firestorm, but probably not so close to home. Eleanor Roosevelt, who had her own internationalist ideals and her own avuncular and Wilsonian heroes, was disgusted and furious. She refused to speak to her husband for at least two days, despite Howe's efforts to explain to her the "facts of life." When FDR invited a longtime friend to make peace in the family, she refused to intervene with Eleanor or even to have lunch with FDR; "That was a shabby statement!" she said. Outraged complaints streamed in from other old Wilsonians, especially when it was learned that FDR was willing not only to junk the League to placate Hearst but even to oppose United States membership in the World Court.

"I had hoped you would understand," Roosevelt wrote an indignant friend. "Can't you see that loyalty to the ideals of Woodrow Wilson is just as strong in my heart as in yours—but have you ever stopped to consider that there is a difference between ideals and the methods of obtaining them?" The difference between himself and "some of my fainthearted friends," he went on, was that "I am looking for the best modern vehicle to reach the goal of an ideal while they insist on a vehicle which was brand-new and in good running order twelve years ago. Think it over! And for heaven's sake have a little faith."

His friends did not understand; perhaps they lacked the faith. In retrospect probably FDR—or at least Sam Rosenman, counsel to the governor—did too. In Rosenman's collection of FDR's 1932 speeches, compiled five years later, all Roosevelt's remarks on the League at the Grange convention were omitted.

Wilsonian idealists were not the only tormentors of Roosevelt's conscience during these preconvention days. Probably the most trying times for the candidate were caused by various Tammany and other New York City bosses—literally trying, because as governor FDR had the power to judge them and oust them. When he appeared to falter or delay in meting out justice, in part because he was hoping to minimize the bosses' opposition at the convention, New York City reformers denounced him for not summarily ousting the miscreants.

When two of the most prestigious of reformers—Rabbi Stephen Wise and the Reverend John Haynes Holmes—urged him to remove two Queens officials who had made off with many tens of thousands of dollars, FDR struck back at the anticorruptionists. In a public letter he upbraided Wise and Holmes for seeming to "care more for personal publicity than for good government." He was becoming convinced, he went on, that corruption and unfitness for office were "far less abhorrent to you than they are to me."

FDR's friends squirmed, even the faithful Howe. One of the few times in his public career that Roosevelt publicly lost his temper, the flap betrayed the strain on the candidate as he encountered pitfalls and brier patches on his journey toward the White House.

. . .

Nothing better reflected FDR's "pragmatic" and eclectic intellectual makeup than the diverse speechwriters and policy advisers he gathered around himself, many of whom would later be called the "Brains Trust." Until the campaign year he had been relying mainly on Howe, his law partner Doc O'Connor, and Sam Rosenman, a former state legislator and FDR's campaign manager—a disparate team to start with. Then he recruited Raymond Moley, not because Moley had a political philosophy— he was a self-proclaimed "pragmatist" too—but because Moley, an expert in criminal law administration, had a quick, inquiring, and yet disciplined mind, a cogency of speech and writing, and a grasp of political realities that FDR needed, especially in the handling of corruption scandals. Moley in turn recruited a fellow Columbia University professor, Rexford Guy

Tugwell, an expert in agricultural economics, a key issue for FDR. Then Moley gathered in still another Columbia faculty member, Adolf A. Berle Jr., who at thirty-seven had had a dazzling career: as a Harvard infant prodigy, a member of Brandeis's prestigious Boston law firm, an adviser to Wilson's Peace Commission in Europe, and an authority on the behavior and misbehavior of the modern corporation. He had even sandwiched in a three-year stint in Lillian Wald's Henry Street Settlement.

Outside this motley group revolved an even more diverse array of past, present, and would-be advisers—Wall Street financiers, noted industrialists, union chieftains, farm lobbyists, old-fashioned trust busters and populists, western and midwestern progressives of various stripes, and friends like constant correspondent Felix Frankfurter. These had occasional direct access to the candidate, much to the discomfiture of the inner circle, which was never sure when FDR was trying out his own thoughts on them or passing on those of the latest outsider who had caught his ear. What was lacking from both the inner and outer groups was perhaps more crucial. There was no socialist, no radical, no farm laborite, no egalitarian, no feminist, and certainly no African-American, who could challenge FDR's ideas. But one person did emerge, a philosopher and visionary who was a member of the inner group.

It was a heady experience for Tugwell to be plucked out of near obscurity to savor hours of dialogue with a man he had never previously met. But Tugwell was no small figure in the academic world. He wrote articles for ethics, economic, and political science journals; contributed to *The Nation* and *The New Republic*; and brought out, along with Stuart Chase, Paul Douglas, and other notables, a book on Soviet economics following a two-month visit to the U.S.S.R.

Tugwell would never forget his first encounter with Governor Roosevelt. Introduced to FDR and then breezily by him to Eleanor at the dinner table as "a Columbia professor," he immediately fell into a dialogue with his hostess, who wanted to know about his family and their farm and whether he knew about a land-retirement experiment carried out by the Cornell School of Agriculture. He did and thought well of it. She favored resettlement, she went on, of families that could no longer make a living on their farms—of which Tugwell approved—and she wanted to include similar resettlement of the urban jobless, which he said he didn't.

FDR, listening closely, pointedly interjected that at least the city people who were resettled would have something to eat, but Tugwell demurred—they couldn't eat unless they could grow the food, and he doubted that they could. All through dinner the spirited discussion continued; afterward, FDR, all the while talking, wheeled himself into the big living room and was smoothly shifted into a chair, still talking.

Then followed a typical evening's debate in the high-ceilinged executive mansion in Albany, with Roosevelt presiding and prodding, his guests listening, rebutting, and all the while sizing up one another. Tugwell saw a man with a massive head and torso that dwarfed his shrunken legs and poignantly unworn shoes. He noted the strong cut of Roosevelt's head, the jutting chin, high forehead, wide-set eyes, the whole mobile, expressive actor's face. A six-inch-long cigarette holder, with a quill stem and yellow end, much waved and constantly refilled, added to this portrait in animation.

FDR studied Tugwell too, a handsome man nine years his junior, almost too handsome with his curly hair and, according to some, soulful eyes. But he had a professional mien as well, and as Tugwell took over the evening, on invitation, his ideas came tumbling out with both clarity and gusto. And on this evening Roosevelt listened, as Tugwell went through the sordid economic history of the twenties, the tragic aftermath of the Depression, his Keynesian interpretation of the causes of the Depression, the maladjustment between a huge production spurt and consumer underconsumption, the gains from increased productivity that had gone to stockholders as dividends and not to workers as wages.

All this was familiar territory for FDR, but what Tugwell did, beginning that evening and during later conferences, was to confront the governor with the most drastic solution to the Depression, a combination of firm national economic planning and heavy government spending. FDR was opposed in principle to both these solutions. Both as a politician and as a product of conservative economics courses at Harvard, he was committed to balancing the budget. And he did not believe in comprehensive national planning but rather, if planning at all, in confining it to individual industries or economic sectors.

That night, by the time that Eleanor Roosevelt came in with drinks to call the discussion to a halt, posed a dilemma for Tugwell too—whether he should continue to advise a man who would listen to him but probably not follow his advice. Overnight, Tugwell wondered whether he had talked too much, had been too "teacherish." But in the morning, when Roosevelt shouted to him across the hall to come into his bedroom and the young economist found his host stretched out in his narrow bed in an old sweater, amid a small sea of crumpled newspapers, he found himself beguiled by the man himself. He enlisted for the duration, perhaps hardly knowing it at the moment, and certainly not knowing of the trials that lay ahead.

. . .

Roosevelt's speeches during the early months of 1932 revealed not only many cooks serving up each broth, but varied combinations of cooks supplying different menus from month to month.

He began his speaking campaign early in April with a radio talk that had ingredients from Moley, mainly, but also reflecting Moley's talks with Tugwell and others. Most of it was the usual opposition Democratic denunciation of Hoover and Smoot-Hawley, failed GOP economic policies, idle machines and men: "No Nation can long endure half bankrupt." But he proposed no drastic action; indeed, he denounced the idea that spending billions of dollars on public works would be anything more than a stopgap. But halfway through the talk his tone changed. "These unhappy times," he intoned, "call for the building of plans that rest upon the forgotten, the unorganized but the indispensable units of economic power, for plans of those like 1917 that build from the bottom up and not from the top down, that put their faith once more in the forgotten man at the bottom of the economic pyramid."

"The Forgotten Man!" Al Smith pounced on the phrase. It was a transparent effort "to invite class warfare," he told a Jefferson Day dinner in Washington. "I will take off my coat and fight to the end against any candidate who persists in any demagogic appeal to the masses of the working people of this country to destroy themselves by setting class against class and rich against poor!" Since FDR's talk as a whole had been moderate, this was Al's own demagogy at its finest—and clearly revealed that he was looking for a fight.

Five days later, in *his* Jefferson Day address, in St. Paul, FDR responded to his old comrade. It was the most measured, "statesmanlike" speech of the whole campaign. He made full use of the party deity, Jefferson, of course, but also Wilson and—in his usual style of party cross-dressing—Lincoln and Theodore Roosevelt. But the quotations were not random decorations; rather, they summoned the best of the American leaders' moral visions.

FDR said of Jefferson, "It was the purpose of Jefferson to teach the country" that "to build a great Nation the interests of all groups in every part must be considered, and that only in a large national unity could real security be found." He evoked a Jefferson who "was not only drinking in the needs of the people in every walk of life, but he was also giving to them an understanding of the essential principles of self-government."

Roosevelt quoted Lincoln, 1861: "'Physically speaking we cannot separate. We cannot remove our respective sections from each other nor build an impassable wall between them. A husband and wife may be divorced, and go out of the presence and beyond the reach of each other, but the different parts of our country cannot do this. They cannot but remain face to face, and intercourse must continue between them.'"

FDR did not fear to quote Theodore Roosevelt, even in a Jeffersonian speech, on the growth of class spirit "which tends to make a man subordinate the welfare of the public as a whole to the welfare of the particular class to which he belongs, the substitution of loyalty to a class for loyalty to the Nation. . . . This Government is not and never shall be government by a plutocracy. This Government is not and never shall be government by a mob."

And he quoted Woodrow Wilson on Jefferson, whose "principles are sources of light because they are not made up of pure reason, but spring out of aspiration, impulse, vision, sympathy. They burn with the fervor of the heart; they wear the light of the interpretation he sought, the authentic terms of honest human ambition."

These presidential tributes to the common life of the American people and to their supreme need for national unity perfectly framed Roosevelt's own message. He urged that there be "a real community of interest, not only among the sections of this great country but among its economic units and the various groups in these units; that there be common participation in the work of remedial figures, planned on the basis of a shared common life, the low as well as the high." FDR pleaded "not for a class control but for a true concert of interests."

Community, not class. A concert of interests—this was FDR's culminating theme and the phrase by which the address would be remembered. Thrilling to FDR's intoning of the term that Tugwell had invented, the economist reflected that Roosevelt was answering a question that had worried him: whether the governor "was weak on relations, on the conjunctural, the joining together of forces and processes, especially in the national economy." Still, concert, community, unity, harmony, nationhood were not enough in themselves. What higher values would they serve? The next major speech could answer such questions, and this was scheduled for Oglethorpe University, Georgia.

Laboriously Moley, Tugwell & Co. toiled over the speech drafts, enlisting in the process a host of experts on vital sectors of the nation's economic life. Then the speech team waited eagerly.

The Oglethorpe address was the most remarkable of the candidate's speeches in 1932. In compelling economic portraits, FDR said it was impossible to review the "history of our industrial advance without being struck by its haphazardness, the gigantic waste with which it has been accomplished, the superfluous duplication of productive facilities, the continual scrapping of still useful equipment, the tremendous mortality in industrial and commercial undertakings, the thousands of dead-end trails into which enterprise has been lured, the profligate waste of natural resources." Much of this waste was an inevitable by-product of progress in an individualistic society, he went on, but much of it "could have been prevented by greater foresight and by a larger measure of social planning." The climax of his talk brought words that would ring down through the corridors of New Deal history.

"The country needs, and, unless I mistake its temper, the country demands, bold persistent experimentation. It is common sense to take a method and try it: If it fails, admit it frankly and try another. But above all, try something. The millions who are in want will not stand by silently forever while the things to satisfy their needs are within easy reach."

Tugwell listened to these last words in amazement. They were not those of the brain trust; whose were they? The "ghostwriter," he discovered, was not from the inner circle; he was not even from the outer circle. He was Ernest K. Lindley, a reporter for the arch-Republican *New York Herald Tribune*. As Rosenman later told the story, FDR had been on an outing in Georgia with several of his newspaper cronies, who began to rib the governor about the moderation of some of his speeches, in sharp contrast to the activist, progressive portrait Lindley had drawn in his 1931 book *FDR: A Career in Progressive Democracy*.

"Well," said FDR joshingly, "if you boys don't like my speeches, why don't you take a hand at drafting one yourselves?" Lindley took the bait.

"I will," he said. And he did so, with the help of his buddies. The result was a hybrid—bold and glowing rhetoric, followed by virtually no concrete proposals; perhaps Lindley expected the brain trust to fill them in. The speech called for bold experimentation but also for "a larger measure of social planning." But planning for what? The speech was the ultimate expression of FDR's "pragmatism."

. . .

One more major speech lay ahead, the acceptance speech at the Democratic convention. The speechwriters' problems now dwarfed all the earlier ones. For if the speech were delivered, it would be the most important of all, setting the tone for the campaign and the presidency itself. But would FDR make it? The stakes now were higher, and the struggle among the advisers even sharper.

This was in part a power struggle, even more an intellectual one. Louis Howe waxed indignant over the Oglethorpe speech, as too radical or at least risky. The brain trusters, while remaining amicable save for Howe's jealousy of any and all rivals, tended to divide over the widening range of issues. And FDR continued to lend an ear to old-timer and newcomer alike—almost fecklessly, the inner circle thought.

As finally hammered out, the acceptance speech draft was far too long—9,000 words. Speechwriters, including FDR himself, manfully cut it down to 6,000 words, then 4,000. Even so, the draft on convention eve remained too discursive and fragmented because some of the linking ideas had been "brutally" excised. The "final" draft began with a pledge to "march along the path of real progress, of real justice, of real equality for all of our citizens, great and small." Soon it was condemning "wild radicalism," while adding that "[r]eaction is no barrier to the radical" but rather provoked him. Immediately, however, it condemned "improvised, hit-or-miss, irresponsible opportunism"—and then launched into remarks that were opportunistic and improvised.

But economics wasn't everything. To those hundreds of delegates flocking to Chicago and thrusting for repeal of the Eighteenth Amendment, the speech offered a frothy glass of champagne: "This convention wants repeal. Your candidate wants repeal. And I am confident that the United States of America wants repeal." To Democratic party conservatives it promised economy in government, with the time-honored pledges to abolish useless offices and eliminate unnecessary functions. To impoverished farmers it offered a sheaf of aids, including "reduction of the surpluses of staple commodities that hang on the market." To homeowners he promised lower interest rates; to farmers, reduction of their mortgages. To the destitute he promised "bold leadership in distress relief" by a Roosevelt administration. To all Americans, again and again, he promised "practical, immediate" action.

It was a politically practical draft: "pragmatic." But it was not practical in policy, as in its promise of both drastic economy and strong, direct federal action. So there it sat, in the safe files of the advisers, waiting to be brought to life or—as Rosenman feared—consigned to the wastepaper basket.

3
A New Deal?

The arresting story of FDR's 1932 convention fight for the nomination has been much told: how the Roosevelt forces arrived in Chicago with a big majority of delegates, pieced together state by state; how they were desperately short of delegate votes because of the rule stipulating that a candidate had to win two-thirds of delegate votes at the convention to be nominated; how Al Smith and other adversaries, who had slowed Roosevelt's momentum with major preconvention victories mainly in the Northeast, now maneuvered to bring him to a standstill in the voting and then trot out a dark horse; how those foes thought they could win when Roosevelt's vote increased by only a handful of votes in the second and third roll calls; how the exhausted, sweating delegates adjourned, expecting more long nights of balloting; and how the FDR forces, in a brilliant display of cross-country power brokering, marshaled the votes to put him over on the fourth ballot.

The dramatis personae were notable too: "Big Jim" Farley, the chairman of the Democratic party, hurrying around the convention floor and into the delegate caucuses to cash in his political chips; Louis Howe, tortured by asthma and gasping for breath, as he lay stretched out on the hotel floor, phone to his ear, while calling convention plays; the brain trusters trying to make sense of the frantic comings and goings, perfervid oratory, and chaotic scenes in the convention hall; Louisiana senator Huey Long grabbing every chance he saw to seize the limelight; the morose Smith lieutenants awaiting their opportunity to move; and, not least, the delegates themselves, peering through thick fogs of smoke, saturated with oratory, sitting in their seersucker suits on their red undertakers' chairs amid crumpled newspapers, thickets of signs, and trash.

The power brokers had not sweltered in the undertakers' chairs. They were on the phone trying to reach two men far from the convention floor: Garner in Washington and Hearst in San Simeon. The phone callers were unlocking a gridlock. The stark facts were that Hearst much earlier had plumped for the Texan for president, and the big California and Texas delegations were also now pledged to Garner. The FDR forces had been shopping the vice-presidential nomination around, but Garner's influence over two big delegations gave the Texan the upper hand for the vice presidency. But the chilling question was: Did Garner himself want the top job instead? Desperately the FDR loyalists, as well as the Smith and other camps, tried to reach Garner in Washington. But Garner was holed up in his Washington hotel and not taking phone calls.

At the crucial moment before the fourth ballot, Joseph P. Kennedy and other friends of Hearst warned the press mogul that if he did not accept FDR, the nomination could go to Smith, whom Hearst detested, or even to Newton D. Baker, the publishing mogul distrusted as an internationalist. Hearst got word to Garner that he was ready to support Roosevelt, at the same time that Democratic leaders like Sam Rayburn were urging Garner to break a deadlock that could imperil the whole party. The Texan, who lacked FDR's consuming ambition, OK'd the deal.

Politics is "funny," Garner told a mystified reporter.

And then came the climactic moment when, early in the fourth balloting, "California" was called and William G. McAdoo rose to ask permission to explain his state's vote. McAdoo, a victim of the 1924 deadlock that denied the nomination both to him and Al Smith! A hush spread over the throng as he made his way to the rostrum. "California came here to nominate a President," he trumpeted. "She did not come here to deadlock this convention." Wild cheers, resounding boos, and angry hisses erupted from the crowd as McAdoo proceeded to cast "the forty-four votes of California for Roosevelt."

Not present in Chicago was the most important actor of all, and it was he who would supply the delegates with their most memorable moments. On the face of it, Roosevelt had spent the convention hours virtually in a cocoon, as compared with his fellow delegates in the raucous convention hall. Surrounded by family members and secretaries in the gaunt old executive mansion in Albany, he had listened intently to the convention debate, calmly received telephone calls from his convention headquarters, and telephoned out on critical matters. Eleanor Roosevelt seemed equally composed as she knitted a sweater for Louis Howe.

In fact, Franklin and Eleanor Roosevelt were in deep anguish, in different ways, on the eve of their first great political triumph. Between the third and fourth ballots, as FDR, smoking cigarette after cigarette, waited for some word of a break in the deadlock, he had lost his nerve—or at least his optimism. Strangely, he had telephoned Newton D. Baker virtually conceding defeat and offering to help his fellow Wilsonian. Baker, appreciative but hesitant, lost his chance. Within an hour Roosevelt's spirits soared as he received reports of the impending Garner deal.

In much greater anguish was Eleanor Roosevelt. Her feelings had burst forth a day or so earlier, according to her friend Marion Dickerman, in a letter to Nancy Cook in which she expressed her fear that the White House would be a prison where she would serve a death sentence made up of endless receptions, formal dinners, and teas. She would rather run away, perhaps with her state trooper bodyguard and close friend, Earl Miller. It seemed as if Eleanor had lost her nerve, as Franklin had—but they had done so alone, separately.

During the convention a group of reporters set up a news bureau in the garage adjoining the executive mansion. Eleanor sent them sandwiches and coffee late on the first night of the convention, and the next morning she invited AP reporters Lorena Hickok and Elton Fay in for breakfast. Hickok noticed that Eleanor, though gracious, seemed pensive. "That woman is unhappy about something," she told Fay as they left.

Eleanor was indeed preoccupied, contemplating the enormous change that lay ahead. She had found real happiness in her teaching, her political work, her close friends. Her life was quite independent from Franklin's— and unconventional. She had crossed class barriers in her close relationship with her bodyguard Earl Miller and would overcome sexual stereotypes in an intimate friendship with reporter Lorena Hickok. Her understanding of humanity was deepening, along with her ties and commitments. How could she fit her complex life, her interests, and her activities into the formal protocol-ridden life of the first lady?

Two others close to FDR were also tasting bitterness at the moment of supreme triumph. Howe had taken last-minute and violent objection to the acceptance speech that had long been in preparation, largely, it seemed, because he thought the main author was his old rival for FDR's favor, Sam Rosenman. In vain Moley insisted that the speech was a product of the whole brain trust. Howe was adamant; he would write a whole new speech and hand it to the candidate. Amazed and upset, Moley had to reflect that Howe needed a "major role in the crowning oratorical triumph of his idol's career."

Spirits had lifted, at least in Albany, when the nominee, with Eleanor Roosevelt, four offspring, and staff took off in a Ford trimotor plane for Chicago. This trip too would become political legend, for FDR was breaking the custom that nominees gave their acceptance speeches weeks after the convention. Let this be a symbol of breaking foolish traditions, the speech had him saying. "You have nominated me and I know it, and I am here to thank you for the honor."

Fighting headwinds, the plane arrived late in Chicago, with an impatient convention waiting. After making his slow stiff-legged way through a huge airport crowd, Roosevelt had just been seated in the limousine when Howe slipped in next to him and presented his draft. Surprised at being so cornered, Roosevelt remonstrated—and then, wanting this devoted man, in his own way, to share the glory, said he would try to look at it "while we're riding down." And so he did, skimming the draft while waving to the street crowds cheering him as he neared the convention hall. He read enough to see that the solution was simple: to put Howe's first page on top of the brain trusters' draft.

Before a roaring crowd of rejuvenated delegates, the nominee called for a New Deal for the American people.

"Let us now and here highly resolve," he began, after invoking the memory of the "unquenchable, progressive soul" of our commander in chief Woodrow Wilson, "to resume the country's interrupted march along the path of real progress, of real justice, of real equality, for all of our citizens, great and small."

The Democratic party, he proclaimed, "by tradition and by the continuing logic of history, past and present, is the bearer of liberalism and of progress and at the same time of safety to our institutions. Wild radicalism has made few converts. The great social phenomenon of this Depression, unlike others before it, is that it has produced but a few of the disorderly manifestations that too often attend upon such times." Now he was back on the brain trusters' draft. "Reaction is no barrier to the radical," he contended, but rather a challenge, a provocation. He would offer a middle way between "blind reaction on the one hand and an improvised, hit-or-miss, irresponsible opportunism on the other."

In the spirit of Theodore Roosevelt but without invoking his name before this rabidly Democratic crowd, he invited "those nominal Republicans who find that their conscience cannot be squared with the groping and the failure of their party leaders to join hands with us." This was standard Roosevelt strategy going back to the 1912 party battle, but FDR went on to say something much more daring to a Democratic conclave, something that anticipated his later effort to realign the parties. "In equal measure," he said, "I warn those nominal Democrats who squint at the future with their faces turned toward the past, and who feel no responsibility to the demands of the new time, that they are out of step with their Party.

"Yes, the people of this country want a genuine choice this year, not a choice between two names for the same reactionary doctrine. Ours must be a party of liberal thoughts, of planned action, of enlightened international outlook, and of the greatest good to the greatest number of our citizens."

Roosevelt went on to discuss some policy issues, especially taxes (too high), repeal of Prohibition (he and they wanted it), unemployment (he favored public works), and agriculture (he would reduce farm mortgage interest). He would leave specifics for his later addresses. Even so, to the extent he discussed policy he took a cautious stand, in sharp contrast to his rhetoric. Thus government "must be made solvent" and public works should be made self-sustaining if possible; on farm policy "the Democratic party stands ready to be guided by whatever the responsible farm groups themselves agree on."

In ringing tones Roosevelt spoke out his climactic words:

"Throughout the Nation, men and women forgotten in the political philosophy of the Government of the last years look to us here for guidance and for more equitable opportunity to share in the distribution of national wealth.

"On the farms, in the large metropolitan areas, in the smaller cities, and in the villages, millions of our citizens cherish the hope that their old standards of living and of thought have not gone forever. Those millions cannot and shall not hope in vain.

"*I pledge you, I pledge myself, to a new deal for the American people,*" he proclaimed, in words that he did not italicize but that later events would. "Let us all here assembled constitute ourselves prophets of a new order of competence and courage. This is more than a political campaign; it is a call to arms. Give me your help, not to win votes alone, but to win in this crusade to restore America to its own people."

. . .

With such compelling rhetoric, and with a "standpat" Republican in the White House, the stage appeared to be set for a focused and coherent ideological confrontation between the two candidates, as well as for a tough political battle. From the start FDR was confident of winning. He had no need to run scared, dodging here and feinting there; he could even afford to be as bold as his acceptance speech suggested. For a time, to be sure, the Roosevelt camp was worried by two possibilities: that Al Smith, whose forces had quit Chicago in sullen anger before the victor arrived, would not come out for the nominee and might even oppose him; and that the burning issue of putting on trial and removing Mayor Jimmy Walker, the insouciant, high-living, but larcenous mayor of New York, might be thrown into FDR's lap to smolder there. But Smith finally came around enough to give his old ally a handsome endorsement, and Walker, after evading sharp questions by the governor—who had chosen to exercise his gubernatorial right to sit as judge as well as jury in the mayor's corruption trial—suddenly quit and fled the country, not to return until 1935. It was a relief to Roosevelt, who no longer had to decide between issuing "a hell of a reprimand" and removing the mayor, which might have alienated New York Tammany politicians. But luckily, FDR had emerged a star from the high-profile hearing. Now the campaign trail was clear and open.

President Hoover too was confident of winning, at first. He viewed Roosevelt as the weakest of the candidates who might have been chosen to run against him. He was proud of his record, his moderate conservatism, his refusal to truckle to the masses. And he had the support—even at a Madison Square Garden rally—of Edith Roosevelt, President Theodore Roosevelt's widow. Emerging from a decade of seclusion, dressed from head to toe in black, Edith introduced Hoover at the rally, to the rapturous applause of the audience. Hoover was no dinosaur; earlier he had even admitted that the book he had written of which he was so proud, *American Individualism,* was "a little out of date, as it was written when we were somewhat more exercised over socialistic and communistic movements than we need to be today."

So the stage appeared set—amid the worst crisis and the gravest test American capitalism had ever encountered—for a vigorous but principled running debate between some kind of moderate liberal and some kind of moderate conservative. Had not FDR himself said in his acceptance speech that never before "in modern history have the essential differences between the two major American parties stood out in such striking contrast as they do today"? But such a debate did not occur.

The main reason was Roosevelt's approach to the campaign, one that stemmed from his political philosophy, or lack thereof. This approach was best summed up by Tugwell, who watched Roosevelt closely while avoiding both hero worship and criticism. As those summer months were passing, he wrote later, "we had not fully realized how sharp a bend in history was being rounded. It can be seen now" that "old mistakes and neglects were demanding their consequences, and that the victims of a careless competitive system had reached the full stretch of their tolerance."

Tugwell talked with the candidate about this tension. At some moments "I thought Roosevelt saw how radical a reconstruction was called for; at others I guessed that he would temporize as the transition was made. I was right in this last. The New Deal was a mild medicine."

. . .

Why? Roosevelt had his reasons. He never forgot the hard lesson he learned from his two great mentors: from TR, when Cousin Ted took too strong a progressive line in 1912 to win, and from Wilson, when he took too strong a line for the League of Nations to beat the Lodge Republicans, a line that Cox and FDR had also embraced too tightly in 1920. But his main reason was "pragmatic"—to be able to feint and parry in the election campaign, to keep his opposition off guard and off track, and above all not to make campaign commitments that would compromise him as president, except on budget-balancing. What Tugwell and other brain trusters found philosophically or programmatically evasive and inconsistent and unprincipled, Roosevelt saw as politically and pragmatically adroit, self-protective, and effective.

Roosevelt never appeared to understand that the voters might wish to pass judgment on his economic and social views and his policy proposals *before* they went to their polling places. The great number of Americans were so passive during these months, because of their hopelessness —or perhaps so traumatized by their despair—that he hardly encountered a powerful demand from the populace for clear policies. But others were watching him closely. Heartland progressives like Robert La Follette Jr., George Norris, and Burton K. Wheeler, who served as links to old populists and Bryanites, had a tremendous stake in Roosevelt's keeping broadly to the left. As usual the radicals were divided, with the old muckrakers Lincoln Steffens and Matthew Josephson, authors John Dos Passos and Edmund Wilson, and academics Sidney Hook and John Dewey criticizing FDR as offering little choice to Hoover. And once again Norman Thomas was offering the socialist alternative.

No one watched FDR's course more closely or critically than the populist from Louisiana, Huey Long. Tugwell was sitting at a family luncheon with Franklin and Eleanor and staff when a telephone was brought in. It was Huey, and he was furious. In a voice loud enough to be heard around the table, he complained that Farley and Howe were ignoring him, that they were not giving him any election money, and that—his voice rising—"stuffed shirts" like Owen Young (the reform-minded head of General Electric) were seeing the candidate all they wanted while he, Huey Long—and who had swung the convention to Roosevelt if it wasn't Huey

Long?—was left out in the cold. He wanted to start campaigning. Why was Roosevelt delaying? In vain Roosevelt tried to placate him.

"You comin' down here?"

"No," said Roosevelt smoothly, "I don't need to; your country there is safe enough."

"Don't fool yourself. It ain't safe at all. You got to give these folks what they want. They want fatback and greens." No one was telling them that they would get help.

"They'll believe me if I tell 'em." Long would not quiet down. "Stop wastin' time seein' those Owen Youngs."

"The second most dangerous man in this country," Roosevelt told the group after he put down the phone. He was happy for them to tease the name of No. 1 from him: General Douglas MacArthur, the conqueror of the bonus marchers. But if FDR was patronizing to the truculent man he suspected would turn against him one day, he was also patronizing—rather than responsive—to leaders of millions of other desperate Americans. These millions included the tenant farmers and farm laborers and share-croppers who were not represented by the big farm lobbies in Washington. They included the impoverished veterans with whom FDR sympathized after their rout but whose demand for earlier payment of their bonus he would not support. They included the millions of workers not represented by an American Federation of Labor itself enfeebled by loss of member-ship in the Depression. They included the masses of immigrants whose only means of political expression often lay through the very machines, like Tammany, that FDR kept at arm's length.

The trouble with FDR, Henry Mencken had sagely observed, was that he had "so few fanatics whooping for him."

. . .

Franklin Roosevelt simply loved campaigning, and never more than in the weeks after the convention. He even "campaigned by sea" by rent-ing a yawl and, with three sons aboard, sailing up the coast of New Eng-land. He was trailed by a boat chartered by reporters and by a fancy steam yacht occupied at times by money men Jesse Straus, Joe Kennedy, and other "tycoons" and fat cats. He dropped into quiet harbors, politicked with the locals, repaired fences that had been damaged by the Al Smith forces in the preconvention campaign, and met with Colonel Edward House, a friend from his navy days, once famous as an intimate adviser to Wilson.

One purpose of the trip was to show FDR as mobile and active and as a family man with handsome, robust sons. Soon he planned a far more ambitious journey by rail, against the advice of aides who feared it might unduly fatigue him and, even more, that some incident might upset the applecart of a campaign already won. FDR would have none of that nonsense. He must show himself and his wife to the populace. And he had messages for an almost hopeless people. Also, the Hoover camp was beginning to bombard him, and "My Dutch is up," he told Farley, referring to his temper.

Using the bountiful materials stocked by the brain trust, Roosevelt devoted each major speech to a key topic. In Topeka he promised to reorganize the Agriculture Department; he favored the "planned use of land," lower taxes for farmers, federal credit for refinancing farm mortgages, and lower tariffs; and he came out for the barest shadow of a voluntary domestic allotment plan to deal with the pressing problem of farm surpluses. In Salt Lake City he laid out a broad plan of federal regulation and aid for the floundering railroads. In Seattle he unleashed a thunderous attack on high tariffs. In Portland he demanded full publicity about the financial activities of public utilities, regulation of the issuing of utility stocks and bonds, use of the prudent-investment principle in rate-making. In Detroit, amid some of the worst Depression despair in the country, he called for removing the causes of poverty—but he would not spell out the details because it was Sunday and he would not talk politics!

One speech—to San Francisco's renowned Commonwealth Club— on first reading excited observers on the left. Roosevelt spoke eloquently about the need for an economic constitutional order, about the role of government as umpire, with federal regulation as a last resort. The speech was studded with gleaming phrases about economic oligarchy, the shaping of an economic bill of rights, and every man's right to life, which the candidate defined as the right to make a comfortable living. But the implications of these ideas for specific programs were left vague.

Roosevelt was meandering, first right, then left, toward election victory. While he toured the streets and spoke from the back platforms of trains, fierce fights broke out in speech-drafting sessions between high-tariff and low-tariff men, among advocates of rival farm policies, between the budget balancers and the public-works spenders. These conflicts were reflected in the ambiguities and inconsistencies of the speeches—and in their overall moderation.

Here was no summons to a crusade, no fiscal strategy to meet the staggering problems of the jobless. Roosevelt had no *program* to offer, only an array of proposals—some well thought out, others vague to the point of meaninglessness—proposals without firm linkage to one another or to a dominant idea. On the whole FDR was remarkably temperate; there was little passion or pugnacity. From the White House, Herbert Hoover, now in deepening pessimism about his chances, launched a vigorous counter-offensive, denouncing what he called the radicalism and collectivism in Roosevelt's proposals.

Perhaps it was in response to this offensive, perhaps also to the increasing influence of conservative brain trusters as against Tugwell and Berle, that Roosevelt took his most definite policy stand of the election—and one that wholly violated his policy of avoiding commitments that might corner him in the White House. In Pittsburgh he roundly denounced Hoover for his two years of "unprecedented deficits" and promised—with only the tiniest of escape clauses—to balance the federal budget, adding: "I hope that it will not be necessary to increase the present scale of taxes."

Moderation appeared to pay off. On November 8, 1932, Franklin Roosevelt's long campaign for the presidency brought a sweeping victory: Roosevelt, 22,800,000 popular votes and 472 electoral votes; Hoover, 15,700,000 popular votes and 59 electoral votes; Thomas, 882,000 popular votes and no electoral votes. Hoover won only six states, all in the Northeast, including Pennsylvania and Delaware. In the Senate, Democrats would outnumber Republicans around two to one, in the House almost three to one.

. . .

He had done it. Long derided as a dilettante by his rich Republican friends, he had run the race of a wholly professional politician. Long accused of being an intellectual lightweight, he had used his brain trust to make some notable policy statements. Attacked for making sordid deals with the likes of Curley and Hearst and New York bosses, he had proved that the deals paid off in a splendid victory for the Democracy. Said to "lack spine," he had shown his determination to win.

And what had done it? Practicality, realism, common sense; shunning utopianism and even idealism; making the compromises that would help win a powerful office where perhaps such compromises would be costly.

Pragmatism had worked.

Chapter Seven
THE POLICY MAKERS:
STORMY PASSAGE

Messenger: " Mr. Litvinoff to see you, sir."
President Roosevelt: " Show him in."

London Daily Express, Fall 1933.
(*Courtesy FDR Library*)

Under one of the more antiquated rules of a stagecoach-era constitution, the new president could not enter the White House until four months after his election.

Who would lead during this transition period? Not Herbert Hoover—he had become a *roi fainéant,* a do-nothing leader, constitutionally responsible but politically impotent; not Congress, a lame-duck session convened in December, fragmented, rudderless, demoralized, many of its members repudiated by the November election.

In this vacuum, many turned to FDR to lead—and, indeed, to lead nobly. He himself had said, shortly after his election, that the presidency "is preeminently a place of moral leadership." "Luckily for him," wrote Walter Lippmann, "he has not made or had to make very many specific pledges to the voters which will rise to plague him. He has ample power. He is free to draw around himself the ablest and most distinguished men he can find. His goodwill no one questions. He has proved that he has the gift of political sagacity.

"If only he will sail by the stars and not where the winds of opinion would take him," Lippmann went on, "he will bring the ship into port."

Sail by the stars? The stars were silent and far away. The navigator lacked even a coherent political program for guidance, only a sheaf of promises. He had no grass-roots movement, with clear-cut goals, on which he could depend for direction and support. The very lack of "specific pledges" that Lippmann extolled robbed him of a policy mandate. The "pragmatism" of 1932 did not seem very relevant in the desperate climate of winter 1933.

The world scene had immensely darkened since the November election. On January 30, 1933, President Hindenburg of Germany named Adolf Hitler chancellor of Germany, in the wake of the Nazi leader's failure to win a majority in Reichstag elections—but in the wake also of the failure of socialist and centrist leaders to rally Germans against him. The Nazis were already laying plans for systematic persecution of Jews. In the Far East the Japanese government, after seizing control of South Manchuria, fending off League of Nations efforts to conciliate the issue, and ignoring a groundswell of popular support by Americans for an economic boycott of Tokyo, prepared to pull out of the League.

The Depression at home was closer and direr. Even since the low point of early fall, business activity had slumped to a quarter, perhaps a third, below normal. The jobless now numbered between ten million and thirteen million, at least one out of every five workers. As winter deepened, so did the popular mood: despairing inertia on the part of most; bitter anger on the part of many; desperate street protests on the part of a few—united, massive action on the part of none.

1
Strange Interlude: Piloting Without Power

During the transition period, President Hoover wanted President-elect Roosevelt to share some of the burden of decision making. Most immediately pressing in November was the long-festering war debt issue, which connected in turn with transatlantic economic relationships. Faced with British and French "bombshell" notes asking postponement of debt payments, Hoover hoped for support from Roosevelt. But FDR did not want to touch this sticky issue until he held office, for fear it might compromise his recovery program. Still, he accepted a Hoover invitation to discuss the matter in the White House.

Beneath a bipartisan array of presidential portraits, and amid a cloud of cigar and cigarette smoke, the two rivals and their aides somberly discussed the issue. For a time the men sparred over Hoover's proposal to turn the bombshell over to a (reconstituted) debt commission. Hoover thought he had FDR's agreement in principle; so the president reported to his secretary of state, Henry Stimson, adding that he had spent most of the time educating a very ignorant and "well-meaning" young man. Not *enough* time, perhaps: FDR shortly announced that responsibility for debt negotiations rested with the president. He would not touch this political tar baby.

Outraged, Hoover could find little solace in realizing that he had experienced what many others had and would—FDR's tendency to be affable, to nod as though in agreement, when he was merely trying to convey that he understood. Relations between the two leaders were left embittered.

Bitterness smoldered among the people as well. In mid-February, during a stop in Miami on the way back from a cruise, Roosevelt had just finished a warm little talk from his car when shots rang out from hardly ten yards away. The shots missed FDR but mortally wounded Mayor Anton J. Cermak of Chicago, who was talking with him. Roosevelt, notably calm, had Cermak put in his car. "Tony, keep quiet—don't move. It won't hurt you if you keep quiet."

"I do not hate Mr. Roosevelt personally," cried Joe Zangara, an unemployed bricklayer with a stomach full of ulcers and a gun bought at a pawnshop for eight dollars. "I hate all Presidents, no matter from what country they come, and I hate all officials and everybody who is rich." FDR remembered Cousin Ted saying, "The only real danger from an assassin is from one who does not care whether he loses his own life." Some weeks later, after Cermak died, Zangara was executed.

Drift, deadlock, defeatism, division within his own ranks as well as within the exiting Hoover administration, and now this act of violence. The four-month transition for Roosevelt was probably one of the most trying political phases of his life.

. . .

There was one euphoric moment during the transition months: visiting the Tennessee Valley.

Roosevelt's consuming interest in public power had not been limited to New York State and the St. Lawrence River. The potential of the Tennessee River had long excited him. He knew the tortuous political background: how Cousin Ted had vetoed a bill allowing private exploitation of power from the stretch of surging rapids at Muscle Shoals; how during the war President Wilson had authorized the building of a huge dam to generate power for producing nitrates for munitions; how the dam was uncompleted at war's end and sat idle for years as progressives led by Nebraska senator George Norris fought for public use of the dam and against private developers, including Henry Ford, who sought to buy it; how Coolidge and Hoover had blocked Norris's efforts, Hoover declaring that federal development of Muscle Shoals power would "break down the initiative and enterprise of the American people," destroy "equality of opportunity," and, indeed, negate "the ideals upon which our civilization has been based."

FDR also understood—perhaps even more important—the ideas that lay behind comprehensive valley or regional development. Here again Theodore Roosevelt had taken the lead, convening a White House Conference on Natural Resources in 1908, asking Congress for a permanent commission that would coordinate the work of the government on water-ways, and thinking in regional terms, especially about Appalachia. Another family member, FDR's uncle Frederic Delano, in spring 1930 gave his nephew a copy of the "Appalachian Report," urging him to read this study "prepared by your distinguished kinsman Theodore Roosevelt on the conservation and development of the Tennessee Valley." In fact it was on Appalachia alone and not the whole valley, and the work of many hands, but it did emphasize the regional approach.

And FDR knew the valley itself, embracing 41,000 square miles—and hence larger than many European countries—divided between mountain-ous northeast sections, peopled mainly by miners and mountaineers, and a southwest lower section occupied largely by cotton sharecroppers on flat alluvial lands. If he did not know the precise living standards of the people, he would know the reality of their dire needs and crushed hopes—large families, unschooled children, low spendable incomes half the national average, wretched housing, appalling mortality rates. Grim reality made the challenge and the potential all the greater.

So it was with vast pleasure and excitement that FDR went to Alabama late in January to tour the area by automobile in the company of daughter Anna and Senator Norris, and with both hope and pain that he looked up at the huge Wilson dam with the water roaring unused through its spillways. He and Norris became more eager with every step. "This should be a happy day for you, George," FDR said to the senator. Norris, tears welling in his eyes, responded, "It is, Mr. President. I see my dreams come true."

But realizing the dreams called for political and legislative action. Knowing well the sensitivities of the South to outside—especially "Yan-kee"—interference, FDR spoke to valley crowds whenever he could. At the end of the day, in Montgomery, he made much of his family's south-ern background—how one Roosevelt had married into a Georgia fam-ily, how some Roosevelts in the 1880s had called Confederate Navy veterans "pirates," but all *his* children just laughed heartily at "hearing brave officers of the Confederate Navy" so stigmatized. And he made clear that he was proud to stand in the "sacred spot" where Jefferson Davis had taken the oath as president of the Confederacy. But above all he wanted to explain his TVA idea to the South, and he did so in his usual simple terms.

"My friends, I am determined on two things as a result of what I have seen today. The first is to put Muscle Shoals to work. The second is to make of Muscle Shoals a part of an even greater development that will take in all of that magnificent Tennessee River from the mountains of Virginia down to the Ohio and the Gulf.

"Muscle Shoals is more today than a mere opportunity for the Federal Government to do a kind turn for the people in one small section of a couple of States. Muscle Shoals gives us the opportunity to accomplish a great purpose for the people of many States and, indeed, for the whole Union. Because there we have an opportunity of setting an example of planning, not just for ourselves but the generations to come, tying in industry and agriculture and forestry and flood prevention, tying them all into a unified whole over a distance of a thousand miles so that we can afford better opportunities and better places for living for millions of yet unborn in the days to come...."

Here was Roosevelt's answer, conscious or not, to Hoover's claim that federal development would mean destruction of "equality of opportunity."

. . .

A different set of satisfactions awaited Roosevelt in the final making up of his cabinet. Here he could indulge his penchant for rewarding friends —ignoring (and hence punishing) enemies—and for juggling and balancing, and at the same time seek to shape a competent ministry. But it was not to be a ministry of all the talents, for the new president would bypass some of the most experienced and highly regarded Democratic leaders such as Newton D. Baker, Norman Davis, Bernard Baruch, and John W. Davis, the 1924 Democratic presidential nominee.

Like most presidents, FDR wanted his own men. His easiest reward for loyalty went to Jim Farley for postmaster general. Others, too, had been "FRBC's"—For Roosevelt Before Chicago. His choice for secretary of state, Cordell Hull, was a Democratic party elder statesman, first elected to the Tennessee House of Representatives forty years earlier. A wily populist who had helped draft the federal income tax of 1913, Hull had served a stint as chairman of the Democratic National Committee in the early 1920s and had proved himself a low-tariff stalwart. White-haired, courtly, and long-suffering in public, Hull was noted for blowing up in private, demonstrating both a mountaineer's command of epithets and an inability to forgive or forget an enemy.

The second big cabinet job, treasury, went to William Woodin, another old Democratic warhorse, but one with extensive business as well as political experience.

The most daring and innovative appointment—a woman for the most "unwomanly" job of secretary of labor—was most put into jeopardy by the woman herself. Frances Perkins met every test of loyalty, competence, idealism, and commitment, but she believed, she wrote FDR, that the job should go to "someone straight from the ranks of some group of organized workers"—"to establish firmly the principle that *labor is in the President's councils.*" But FDR insisted.

For secretary of agriculture, Roosevelt would dearly have loved to pick good friend and neighbor Henry Morgenthau Jr., but Tugwell—and, more important, the major farm leaders—favored Henry Wallace, with his family background in agriculture and commitment to aiding midwestern farmers. For interior, FDR chose a man he had met only briefly, a zealous, public-spirited, and stubbornly outspoken Chicago lawyer named Harold L. Ickes; his was to be one of FDR's most durable—and perhaps most important—appointments.

In the end FDR's cabinet, like most American cabinets, was more a collection than a collectivity. It was mainly Democratic except for nominal Republicans like Woodin and Wallace and progressive Republicans like Ickes and Perkins; heavily political, interest-group oriented, with representatives of farmers, businessmen, and workers; and ideologically some indefinable combination of centrist, liberal, and even radical. It was a cabinet that FDR could easily dominate. Even so, he also made personal appointments of men who would share power as assistant secretaries and advisers, men like an old friend, William Phillips, and brain-truster Moley in the State Department; Rex Tugwell in agriculture; Morgenthau and others who would have direct influence in treasury. And beneath these levels were the hundreds, even thousands, of continuing federal officials who would variously elevate, administer, impede, and sabotage New Deal programs.

The most notable of the carryovers was indeed a near-celebrity, J. Edgar Hoover. Whatever doubts FDR had about Hoover's mixed record, his overzealousness, and his participation in the notorious Palmer raids on "reds" and "un-Americans" were overcome by the support Hoover could mobilize in high places—*very* high places. Supreme Court Justice Harlan Fiske Stone, hearing that Hoover's retention might be in doubt, wrote FDR's confidant Felix Frankfurter virtually a panegyric to the man. FDR told Frankfurter that he could assure Stone that "it is all right about Edgar Hoover."

The most influential holdovers were members of the old brain trust, especially Moley, Tugwell, and Berle, but no longer a "trust" as they were now ensconced in agencies. FDR's correspondents widened even further after he entered the White House, to include a host of labor leaders, farm politicians, newspaper editors, academics, southern notables, and state politicos, as well as old friends like James Cox, Colonel Edward House, Frankfurter, Josephus Daniels, and Norman Davis; Daniels's ambassadorial appointment to Mexico only seemed to enhance his cordial "Dutch uncle" relationship to "Franklin." Moley was worried by FDR's receptivity to ideas—many of them crank ideas, in Moley's view—that flowed in from all directions. The boss, Tugwell said, had a flypaper mind.

The president's advisers were conduits for countless other ideas and notions. Frankfurter and Berle passed on suggestions from Justice Brandeis, whose thoughts would become warnings as Roosevelt veered later toward "big government." Ideas pouring into the White House became grist for FDR's speeches. Unlike Theodore Roosevelt, who would brook little intervention in his speechwriting, FDR was heavily dependent on drafts written by a shifting array of in-house and out-of-house advisers that would later include the redoubtable team of Benjamin Cohen and Tom Corcoran, brilliant corporate lawyers from New York.

The president had a touching relationship with some of his advisers, notably Frankfurter; the two men visited often together and corresponded extensively, with unusual frankness—though FDR could depend on Frankfurter's lawyerlike discretion. And, strangely, FDR allowed Adolf Berle to address him as "My Dear Caesar" long after he became president, evidently without fear that a misplaced letter might play into the hands of Republicans who felt he was really acting like Caesar. Berle's claim that Caesar was "historically accurate"—a "supreme power, elective, subject to Senate and people"—would hardly have placated the critics. FDR counseled Berle as "your old Uncle Franklin."

. . .

Even as Roosevelt was making his final choices, events were moving ahead of him with shocking speed. Since November the economy had taken another sickening lurch downward, industrial production dropping to an all-time low. The most ominous signs, along with the ever lengthening lines of the jobless, were runs on banks, which began to close their doors, producing mobs of frantic depositors. By March 2, two days before FDR's inauguration, twenty-one states had shut down or curbed banking operations.

In his last days in the White House, President Hoover, now desperate, became more brazen than ever in urging his successor to abandon campaign promises, on the grounds that it was now *Roosevelt* who was causing the downturn. In a secret message to senators, Hoover admitted that he was calling on the president-elect for "abandonment of 90 percent of the so-called new deal." To this chutzpah FDR reacted with contempt.

2
The One Hundred Days: Uncharted Seas

The East Front of the Capitol, Noon, March 4, 1933.
Bareheaded in the cold, his face set and somber, the newly sworn-in president looks out on the huge crowd below him. The family Bible lies open at First Corinthians, chapter thirteen: "And now abideth faith, hope, charity, these three; but the greatest of these is charity."
The people standing below him, strangely silent and unsmiling, watch the president intently as, with his head back and jaw outthrust, he begins to speak. Perched on the icy branches of gaunt trees under a leaden sky are some who lack tickets: an old man in ancient, patched-up green tweeds; a young woman with red hair in a skimpy coat; an older woman in ragged clothes; a college student.

"This is a day of national consecration," the president said, having just scribbled these words into the start of the speech while waiting in the Capitol. He had sensed the lack of celebration as he waited outside the White House, which looked a bit seedy, its paint yellowing, for Herbert Hoover to join him for the trip to the Capitol; when he could not strike up a conversation with the glum president; when even the Marine Band seemed unable to evoke more than a few cheers from the throng.

"I am certain that my fellow Americans expect that on my induction into the Presidency I will address them with a candor and a decision which the present situation of our Nation impels. This is preeminently the time to speak the truth, the whole truth, frankly and boldly." In keynotes that would form headlines in newspapers across the country and around the globe, he spoke directly to the needs and hopes of the people.

Distress: The nation need not "shrink from honestly facing conditions in our country today," and the president spelled them out: values "shrunken to fantastic levels," the "withered leaves of industrial enterprise" lying on every side, farmers finding no markets, family savings lost, jobless workers facing "the grim problem of existence," others working for little pay.

Fear: "First of all, let me assert my firm belief that the only thing we have to fear is fear itself—nameless, unreasoning, unjustified terror which paralyzes needed efforts to convert retreat into advance."

But now hope: "In every dark hour of our national life a leadership of frankness and vigor has met with that understanding and support of the people themselves which is essential to victory. I am convinced that you will again give that support to leadership in these critical days."

And even happiness: "Happiness lies not in the mere possession of money; it lies in the joy of achievement, in the thrill of creative effort. The joy and moral stimulation of work no longer must be forgotten in the mad chase of evanescent profits. These dark days will be worth all they cost us if they teach us that our true destiny is not to be ministered unto but to minister to ourselves and to our fellow men."

Action: "This Nation asks for action, and action now. Our greatest primary task is to put people to work. This is no unsolvable problem if we face it wisely and courageously." The president reiterated his key campaign promises. "These are the lines of attack."

Above all, leadership: "If I read the temper of our people correctly, we now realize as we have never realized before our interdependence on each other." Without willingness to move "as a trained and loyal army willing to sacrifice for the good of a common discipline," no leadership was effective. This would make possible "a leadership which aims at a larger good." This he would offer, assuming "unhesitatingly the leadership of this great army of our people dedicated to a disciplined attack upon our common problems."

Was such leadership possible under the American constitutional system? The Constitution was so "simple and practical," the constitutional system "the most superbly enduring political mechanism" in the modern world, that it would meet the stress of Depression as it had of foreign and civil war. He expected that the "normal balance" of executive and legislative authority would work.

But then a surprise: In the event that Congress failed to follow his leadership or failed to lead on its own, "I shall not evade the clear course of duty that will then confront me. I shall ask the Congress for the one remaining instrument to meet the crisis—broad Executive power to wage a war against the emergency, as great as the power that would be given to me if we were in fact invaded by a foreign foe."

A warning of dictatorship? "We do not distrust the future of essential democracy. The people of the United States have not failed. In their need they have registered a mandate that they want direct, vigorous action. They have asked for discipline and direction under leadership." He would supply it.

. . .

"It was very, very solemn and a little terrifying," a somber Eleanor Roosevelt said at the end of the inauguration. More awed than exhilarated by the ceremony, the new first lady was startled by her husband's warning that he might have to "wage war."

The new president smiled his way through the hours of the inaugural parade, punctuated by tense conferences, as bulletins came in from the economically prostrate nation. But behind the laughter, behind the ever-resolute face, concealed from the inaugural paraders and cheering throngs, he had no false hopes about the burden he had just assumed. Four months earlier, after the evening's celebration at his New York headquarters of his defeat of Hoover, he had returned to his East 65th Street home, where his son Jimmy helped him into his bed—the same bed he had lain in for months after his polio attack. In a display of religious feeling rare even within his family, Roosevelt told his son that he was afraid of something else besides his old fear of fire.

"Afraid of what, Pa?"

"I'm just afraid that I may not have the strength to do the job. After you leave tonight, Jimmy, I am going to pray. I am going to pray that God will help me, that He will give me the strength and the guidance to do this job and do it right. I hope you will pray for me, too, Jimmy."

. . .

On returning to the White House after the inaugural parade, the new president took instant command. Having already sent his cabinet nominations to the Senate for quick confirmation, he watched their swearing in by Justice Benjamin N. Cardozo upstairs in his study. In a warm talk to his official family, and perhaps in awareness of its diverse makeup, he urged his cabinet to work together, as a team without friction, for the good of the nation. Later, after Eleanor and their children set off for the inaugural ball, FDR met with Louis Howe in the Lincoln study. For many minutes they discussed the problems and prospects ahead, while fireworks burst over the Washington Monument and showered gleams of light onto the facade of the Lincoln Memorial.

Now came "action and action now." The very next day, Sunday, March 5, amid a flurry of anxious conferences, the president prepared a proclamation, effective two days later, declaring a four-day national banking holiday. He summoned the 73rd Congress to convene in special session two days after that. The proclamation embargoed temporarily the export of gold, silver, and currency. FDR conferred with his cabinet again and with his aides, congressional leaders, and Republican holdovers from the Hoover administration. The advisers had forgotten how to be Democrats or Republicans, Moley wrote later. "We were just a bunch of men trying to save the banking system."

But no one really knew what to do—perhaps least of all Roosevelt—beyond halting the runaway financial situation. There was little thought of taking the banks over, nationalizing them, "socializing the banking system," as some urged, nor was there any other grand strategy. There was no master chart for the crisis: no party plan, election promise, or economic doctrine. The emphasis was on "swift and staccato action," in Treasury Secretary Woodin's phrase, but at the same time, in Moley's later recollection of the conferences, on the "stressing of conventional banking methods and the avoidance of any unusual or highly controversial measures."

Looming over the frenetic meetings was the question, What were the people thinking out there? How would they respond to the closing of the banks, their citadels of security? In fact, the people were doing just fine. Despite all the inconveniences and disruption, the American people were in an almost gala mood, joking about their predicaments, finding that they could get along—for a time—without ready cash. Even Eleanor Roosevelt, short of cash to pay the family's bill at the Mayflower Hotel in Washington, decided not to worry. People were reveling in a new sense of hope about the economy and about leaders who appeared actually to be *doing* something. And Roosevelt, with his incomparable skill at communicating, was determined to tell them the truth about the crisis. A week after closing the banks he gave his first national fireside chat.

"I want to talk for a few minutes with the people of the United States about banking—with the comparatively few who understand the mechanics of banking, but more particularly with the overwhelming majority who use banks for the making of deposits and the drawing of checks," he began. "I want to tell you what has been done in the last few days, why it was done, and what the next steps are going to be." He thanked his listeners for their "fortitude and good temper" during the bank holiday. He assured them that their money would be safe in the reopened banks, though there might be individual disappointments. And he thanked them for buoying up their president with their confidence. "Let us unite in banishing fear."

And so began the celebrated "One Hundred Days"—in fact and in legend.

The legend began early, grew rapidly, took firm root with the aid of historians, and set some kind of model for later presidents. It told of a president who wielded power as no chief executive had ever done. Operating from a broad party mandate and vague economic strategy, he unfolded a master policy program. This he presented to Congress, which supinely bowed to his will. The president led the people along his sure path, sharing his ideas and hopes with them in bimonthly fireside chats, and reaching out to the public through set speeches.

The story grew taller. In a series of dramatic proposals and actions, the president brought about a virtual revolution, saving the capitalistic system while fundamentally changing it, setting a radical course not only for the New Deal but for the next half century of liberal thought and action. Out of this emerged a picture for some of "Rooseveltian leadership," embracing and even surpassing the leadership heritage of Jefferson and Lincoln, Theodore Roosevelt, and Wilson, but in the minds of others, "Rooseveltian dictatorship," reminiscent of Napoleon or even Caesar.

A half century later the legend still lives—but now is challenged by the factual record, more prosaic yet ultimately more meaningful.

Roosevelt had no master plan, no grand strategy, aside from a belief in the crucial role of government in creating reform. On that score he was convinced that government must step in to help people where private enterprise had failed, and—because of the weakness and impoverishment of state governments—Washington must act. These recognitions were a big step forward, but the crucial question was, What would the federal government *do?*—and what it mainly did was to improvise a series of policies that had many consequences.

The chief result by far was to patch up failings and shortcomings in financial institutions and in their supervision by government. The bank holiday itself, which prevented further runs on banks and withdrawals of gold, was a rapid and dramatic but essentially preservationist cleansing of banks to rid them of their impurities and restore them in improved health to depositors. In one day, March 9, FDR presented to Congress—and Congress passed—his Emergency Banking Relief Act, which gave the president broad discretionary powers over transactions in credit, currency, gold, and silver and permitted sound banks in the Federal Reserve system to open only under licenses from the Treasury Department. The money panic was over.

FDR took other actions to strengthen—and in some cases reform—an ailing capitalism, in his effort to restore confidence to the business community at the same time as he sought to awaken hope among the people as a whole. His initial approach to public works was that they should be self-financing. His move to legalize beer and wine, greeted with an explosion of excitement and celebration in taverns across the nation, was designed also as a revenue act, imposing as it did a levy of five dollars per barrel. His proposals for securities regulation were widely viewed as reformist and even punitive, but they had the effect also of restoring confidence in the exchanges and exchangers.

The surest index to Roosevelt the conservative during the One Hundred Days, however, was his insistence on economy in government in order to "balance the budget." In retrospect it seems almost bizarre that the president, in the midst of dramatic presidential statements and emergency actions, would insist on carrying out his promise, made in Pittsburgh during the recent election campaign, to balance the federal books. Some thought he didn't mean it—just one more reckless promise—but the president was in dead earnest. He demonstrated this by selecting a zealous economizer, Lewis Douglas, as his budget chief. The initial approach to relief—the most human of problems facing the new administration—was to allot $500 million to be distributed by the states and municipalities. These were grants, rather than loans, and hence an improvement over the Hoover policy of loans, but the amount was minuscule compared to the dire wants and needs of the American people in the spring of 1933.

It was the veterans who took it in the neck. Lobbyists for the vets were eager to take the issue that had haunted Hoover back to the "more humanitarian" Roosevelt. The issue was non-service-connected benefits. All knew that tens of thousands more veterans received disability benefits than had actually been wounded; but these veterans, many of them hard up, believed the benefits were just compensation for all who had served. The Economy Act, given FDR's second-highest priority after the banking act, was passed by Congress hardly more than a week after inaugural day. This bill not only cut veterans' pensions and benefits but reduced up to 15 percent many federal salaries; it also reorganized federal agencies to save more money.

Why this emphasis on economy? It could not have been primarily its financial impact; the administration claimed only a half-billion-dollar saving, which turned out to be less than a quarter billion. The immediate reason was sheer political "practicality."

Bounding from bill to bill, trying always to conserve his congressional majorities, fearing that even one defeat could jeopardize impending measures, FDR had to attract conservative Democratic and Republican votes. He not only wanted to hold the confidence of business in general, he had to hold the support of those members of the financial community who might try a desperate flight of capital, or a "revolt of the capitalists," that could jeopardize the administration's entire economic program. And he could never forget the final failure of Cousin Ted, who in 1912 had reached too far.

Beyond all this lay FDR's temperament and intellect, in the early months of his administration. He was not in the mood to reconstruct or revolutionize, but rather to revise, reform, and restore. Restore what? Not the old dog-eat-dog individualistic laissez-faire capitalism of the past century, but twentieth-century capitalism as envisioned by TR and Woodrow Wilson. And he was still combining the TR and Wilson traditions: economic controls and conservation along with supervision and regulation of large corporations. Above all he was experimenting, "playing it by ear," just as he had promised, as he navigated the churning political seas.

Congress was a junior partner in all this, but still a partner. Nor was it merely a conservative force; some members of Congress, especially the Norris–La Follette–Wagner progressives in the Senate, often ranged to the left of the president. The House of Representatives liberalized FDR's home mortgage law, doubling the mortgage limit of $10,000, and Wagner amended the bill to provide a three-year moratorium on principal payments. Congress also exerted a form of pressure on the White House. Just as FDR had aroused hope and expectation among the people, so he did in Congress—and the members, expecting much of him, put pressure on him to deliver. The president timed some of his major proposals to meet the demands of a Congress hungry to act. When Senate Democrats had divided over the economy bill, he united them by a timely call for the immensely popular "beer bill" to legalize beer and light wines.

The president did not need to appeal to the people to put pressure on their senators and representatives. Indeed, contrary to the legend, he did not make a second fireside chat until eight weeks after the first. Nor did he tour the country stoking backfires for his friends and against his foes; he hardly left Washington during the first hundred days. He held twice-a-week press conferences, but early on he established a pattern of "press management," doling out information exactly to the degree he wished, timing announcements for maximum impact, brushing aside correspondents' questions with a casual "I don't know about that" when he did indeed know all about it.

How, then, did Roosevelt give such a firm image of steady leadership, even when he hardly ventured out of the White House? By dominating the headlines with a seemingly nonstop flood of actions, some planned and some makeshift—executive orders, proposals to Congress for major bills, statements on pending measures, bill-signing ceremonies, press conferences. The president did not need to speechify; *action,* usually real but sometimes symbolic, was his version of TR's bully pulpit.

Roosevelt directed his bully pulpit abroad too, but with far less positive impact than Uncle Theodore had. However absorbed in domestic needs and politics, he could hardly ignore the European scene. On the very day FDR took office, Adolf Hitler won election and promptly wiped out opposition parties, amid Nazi threats to annex Austria and the Polish Corridor, even at the risk of war. Already the Nazis were raiding and boycotting Jewish shops, driving Jews out of the arts and professions, and beating up Jews and dragging them through the streets. Appalled, Roosevelt nevertheless took no public stand. Rather, he joined British and French leaders in a campaign for disarmament, on the naive proposition, as FDR stated to Congress, that "the way to disarm is to disarm. The way to prevent invasion is to make it impossible."

The main concern of European leaders at the much-touted London Economic Conference was working on proposals for global economic cooperation, especially on proposals to limit production and stabilize commodity prices. To FDR's annoyance, the conferees were focusing unduly on short-term currency stabilization. Then, from the Europeans' standpoint, the president did everything wrong. He bargained on currency stabilization and then quit, he sent Moley to London with hazy instructions that conflicted with the equally hazy instructions Hull had brought earlier, and finally he sent a message harshly criticizing the diversion of the conference from its broader purposes.

This was the "bombshell message" that hit the world's headlines and stalemated the conference. Why such one-sided intervention, which struck some as the kind of thing a moralistic TR would have done, not the negotiating FDR? Some explained that the president was at Campobello Island with his family, Morgenthau, and Howe. Perhaps, it was even rumored, he was on edge, for that very evening Eleanor had upbraided him for serving a cocktail to son Franklin, now a teenager. "You can't scold me like that," FDR had protested. But the main reason for the "bombshell" lay much deeper. FDR was still in a nationalist mood, he faced a powerful isolationist bloc in Congress—and he dared not risk losing votes in the United States by challenging the "international bankers" of Europe.

So the august ship of state—composed of one mercurial activist president, an ever-shifting network of crew members inside and outside the White House, overworked cabinet members operating in their own troubled waters, a permanent bureaucracy facing daunting new tasks, majorities in Congress fired up by the New Deal spirit, and millions of Americans transfixed by the new leaders in Washington—tacked across the uncharted seas, to starboard and port and back. A vector run through its zigs and zags would doubtless have pointed to the right, but the ship was moving too fast for anyone to gauge the basic course between conventional liberalism and conservativism.

And even though in retrospect FDR was largely following "a bit right of center" directions, especially in his financial policies, the New Deal president was always lurking just behind the reviser and restorer. Three measures in the first hundred days would become part of the New Deal heritage: the Civilian Conservation Corps, the Tennessee Valley Authority, and the Agricultural Adjustment Act. The first two were closest to his heart of all the dozens of initiatives during that period.

How could he not be captivated by the CCC concept? He hoped to move a quarter million young men from street corners and unemployment lines into the nation's woods, to plant millions of trees, set up trails and fire lanes, and build protections against floods, soil erosion, pests, and diseases. Equally attractive to FDR the economizer, the young men would be paid only a dollar a day, and most of that would be deducted and mailed direct to their families; the whole operation, run by the army and financed out of existing funds, would not harm his economy drive. And by winning quick support from Congress, he could have the men in the woods by early summer.

The project had its own share of birth pangs. Secretary of Labor Perkins and some union heads objected to the dollar-a-day payment as undercutting local wage standards. Left-wing leaders objected to the military control. He could not believe the time had come, Norman Thomas declared, "when the United States should supply relief through the creation of a form of compulsory military service. Such work camps fit into the psychology of a Fascist, not a Socialist, state."

That was just "utter rubbish," Roosevelt told a press conference. "The camps will be run just like those in any big project—Boulder Dam or anything like that. Obviously, you have to have some form of policing. In other words, you cannot allow a man in a dormitory to get up in the middle of the night and blow a bugle." The reporters roared. "You have got to have order—just perfectly normal order, the same as you would have in any kind of a big job." But to mollify some of his critics he chose a Boston labor leader, Robert Fechner, as CCC director, who would work with the labor department (in charge of enrollment), the interior and agriculture departments (work direction), and the war department (outfitting and housing)— a typically Rooseveltian dispersion of functions.

Hidden away in the CCC measure was a provision that—fortunately for FDR—aroused little attention at the time but was a portent of intense governmental and political struggles to come. Proposed by the only African-American member of the House of Representatives, Republican Oscar De Priest of Illinois, the amendment read "that no discrimination shall be made on account of race, color, or creed" under "the provisions of this Act." Acceptance of this amendment by both houses was further testimony to the significant role of Congress—and of Republicans in Congress—during the first hundred days.

Roosevelt and Norris had thought and politicked so much about the Tennessee Valley proposal that its passage through Congress was relatively painless. What might have been the most controversial proposal, the socialization of key sectors of a huge river valley, aroused little opposition as socialism. Yet the TVA squarely met the classic definition: governmental ownership of a huge operation and employment of its operators, and FDR had already intimated that he proposed to extend such planning to a "wider field." But the people saw the TVA simply as a bold river valley development.

Perhaps the TVA, with its complex combination of development, conservation, flood control, power generation and transmission, diversification, and much else, simply defied easy definition, even short epithets. Norris asked the president, "What are you going to say when they ask you the political philosophy behind TVA?"

"I'll tell them it's neither fish nor fowl," FDR responded, "but whatever it is, it will taste awfully good to the people of the Tennessee Valley."

"Neither fish nor fowl" but tasting good to people—perhaps that was the best interim sketch of the New Deal of the first hundred days.

The archpins of the early New Deal were, inevitably, agricultural and industrial policy, though these imperatives often seemed lost in the hul-

labaloo as the media played up the "beer bill" and such short-lived policies as budget balancing. At first, far more interested in farm programs than
industrial ones, the new president had acted to "help farmers" within days
of taking office.

The passage of his farm bills presaged the legislative history of many of
the New Deal measures of the first hundred days. There was something old:
a continuation of the Hoover administration's effort to stabilize the buying
and selling of cotton, grain, and other commodities. There was something
new: giving direct benefits or rental payments to farmers in exchange for
voluntarily reducing acreage or crops. There was something so conventional
as to be widely accepted: providing cheaper credit to farmers by consolidating all government agencies lending to farmers and by refinancing farm
mortgages at lower interest rates. There was something so controversial as
to enflame major business interests: payment of the program not by general
taxation but by levies on the processors of farm products. There was something so conservative as to win the support of the big farmers' lobbying organizations: maintaining prices by reducing surplus crops of basic farm products
and the setting of "parity" prices. And there was something that would become crucial in the passage of most New Deal measures: the inability of
Congress to agree on key issues, followed by a wide delegation of authority
to the president to make the necessary judgments.

But dominating the making of farm policy were two other forces: Roosevelt's desire, based on a concern with farmers' needs born in his state senate days, to do something quickly, effectively, and dramatically about the
farm crisis in 1933; and the wider impact of the farm crisis itself. While
Congress deliberated at a much slower pace than Roosevelt hoped, farmers were still confronting falling prices and fearing worse to come. Milo
Reno, head of the Farmers' Holiday Association, was threatening a farm
strike. More radical farmers were dumping milk or burning corn, invading courtrooms to halt foreclosure proceedings, ganging up against eviction
sales, coming close to actually lynching a recalcitrant judge. Iowa authorities placed half a dozen counties under martial law, sent in the National
Guard, and collared over one hundred farm "rebels" in two counties.

It was not Milo Reno but Edward A. O'Neal, head of the Farm Bureau Federation, who warned earlier in the winter of "revolution in the
countryside" unless something was done for the farmer. Alarmed by the
tumult, unified by the president, pressured by farm lobbyists, and prodded by progressive senators like Norris, Congress finally passed the Agricultural Adjustment Act in mid-May, to Roosevelt's vast relief.

By this time a problem even more serious than that of the farmers was looming: Roosevelt's moderate financial efforts did not appear to be stimulating the national economy adequately. Unemployment remained critically high, and some even feared a new economic downturn, which would have struck a jarring blow to the New Deal program and hopes. Happily for the president, New Dealers and others both within the government and outside had been pondering a variety of proposals that could speed recovery. The thinkers and actors were so numerous, their ideas so eclectic and wide-ranging, their ideologies so diverse, their precise influence on thought and action so subtle and complex, that historians have been hard put to trace the origins of what became to FDR his most important measure, the National Industrial Recovery Act.

The ideas, in shifting clusters of combination and conflict, were coming to rough focus by May. A large number of industrialists, believing that "cutthroat competition" and depressed prices were the main obstacles to economic recovery, urged the suspension of antitrust laws so that "fair competition" codes could be drawn up by industrial trade associations in cooperation with the government. Approved by the president, these codes would be enforceable by law, with courts empowered to issue injunctions against violations. Doubtless each trade association, as Rexford Tugwell had urged in his 1933 book *The Industrial Discipline,* would have its own planning mechanisms.

FDR had good reasons to favor this notion. It resonated with Theodore Roosevelt's ideas of the New Nationalism and a nationwide approach to economic problems; FDR was well familiar with the long history of the idea of "self-government in industry" and "industrial self-discipline" in America and abroad; and he himself had headed a trade association, the American Construction Council, in the early 1920s. Far more remarkable, even staggering, was the support by leading industrialists of what inevitably would be a huge governmental intrusion into the economy and into their corporations' internal affairs. Men who in the 1920s had been uttering odes to laissez-faire, rugged individualism, and dog-eat-dog competition now were virtually begging government to help them stabilize production, sales, and, of course, profits in their industries.

A sharply contrasting idea had gained considerable momentum in the Senate: limitation of hours of employment to thirty hours a week. Backed by Alabama Democratic senator Hugo L. Black, this bill—essentially a share-the-work effort—was a significant counterpart to the efforts of the farm bloc to reduce farm acreage and production; it was the economics and politics of scarcity. Cool to the measure as too radical and too rigid, FDR nonetheless allowed Secretary Perkins to testify before the House Labor Committee in favor of the bill if it could be made more flexible. It had to accommodate rural industries, the man from Hyde Park reminded Perkins, and the special needs of canneries and dairy farms.

"There have to be hours," he told her, "adapted to the rhythm of the cow." Almost hysterical opposition from business to the measure, plus a reminder from the left-wing *Nation* that the workweek already had declined to about thirty-two hours, killed the proposal.

A better way of protecting the worker was already winning support in both Congress and the administration. If industry was to be given the right to organize, trade union leaders insisted, why should their employees not be guaranteed similar rights? A section of a draft bill numbered 7(a), stipulating that "employees shall have the right to organize and bargain collectively through representatives of their own choosing," had the cautious approval of the president, but when spokesmen for the National Association of Manufacturers urged FDR to modify this potent provision, he replied that not he but Senator Wagner was sponsoring it and they should see the senator from New York. Wagner proudly stood his ground.

As recovery faltered, it became more and more likely in the spring of 1933 that neither industrial nor labor cooperation, nor most of the other panaceas floated by one group or another, would quickly provide massive numbers of jobs. Sentiment rose in Congress, spearheaded by Wagner, La Follette, and other progressives, for a huge public works program. Once again the president was cautious. Still on his "economy kick," still pressured almost daily by Douglas to avoid unbalancing the budget, FDR resisted a Wagner plan for $5 billion in grants to public bodies. At a conference upstairs in the White House, the president, with Douglas by his side, went through a long list of proposed public works projects, dismissed most as unsound, and reduced the list to $1 billion. Within days, however, under pressure from Congress and from Perkins, Wallace, and Ickes, he accepted an overall figure of $3.3 billion.

During the first week of May, as feverish discussions rose to new heights of intensity at both ends of Pennsylvania Avenue, the several policy ingredients of the National Recovery Administration fell into place, with the thirty-hour week now excluded. In his second fireside chat, on May 7, the president spoke reassuringly of his partnership with Congress, the support he had received in both parties, and his observance of the constitutional separation of power between Congress and the president. He spoke modestly of "mistakes of procedure." What he sought, he said, was "the highest possible batting average," not only for himself but "for the team." Theodore Roosevelt, he said, had once told him, "If I can be right seventy-five percent of the time I shall come up to the fullest measure of my hopes."

Ten days later the president proposed the National Industrial Recovery Act to Congress. His brief message stressed planning—"for a great cooperative movement throughout all industry"—and public works. Despite all the momentum, the bill faced tough sledding in Congress. Lobbyists representing veterans, business, labor, and other interests pushed for weakening amendments, relevant or not. Congress on the one hand agreed on general provisions by delegating specific decision making to the president, while on the other hand warning of excess presidential power under the act. For several days a determined president and a stubborn Senate were locked in battle, with the upper house finally approving the bill by 46 to 39 votes, on June 16. Eleven Democrats voted against the president.

"The latter part of this session has been terrible," Senator Hiram Johnson wrote home. "We're all tired and many are disgruntled." But the president, tired but not disgruntled, had his bill, the archpin of recovery. Now he could head toward a vacation.

3
Eleanor: Sailing by the Stars

In the fall of 1932, as the Roosevelts were preparing to move into the White House, Eleanor had lamented the independent activist life she was leaving. "As I saw it," she later wrote, "this meant the end of any personal life of my own."

Uncertainties and questions gathered in her mind, but only once did she turn to Franklin for guidance. She meekly asked him if perhaps she might handle some of his mail, as Mrs. Garner would do for the vice president. FDR just looked at her "quizzically" and replied that the mail was Missy's department, and she might not welcome help.

Little guessing what an enormous impact she would make in her new role, Eleanor felt hurt and excluded. "My zest in life is rather gone for the time being," she dejectedly wrote Lorena Hickok, the reporter whom the Associated Press had recently assigned to cover Eleanor on a regular basis and who would become Eleanor's most intimate friend. "If anyone looks at me, I want to weep." As usual, her feelings of depression soon lifted.

Early in her husband's first term, it became clear that this was a new kind of first lady—because she was reinventing herself. As a host of urgent issues came to her attention, she quickly discovered that she had new power. Far from being a prisoner in the White House, pouring tea for ambassadors, Eleanor seemed to be everywhere at once. Just by going to a place or investigating an issue she could bring it into the full glare of nationwide publicity. She toured Washington's back alleys to publicize the conditions of the slums. Realizing that New Deal programs were geared toward men, she fought for the "forgotten woman"; she worked with Harry Hopkins to set up the women's division of the Civil Works Administration, providing, by the end of 1933, CWA jobs for 100,000 women. When she heard that farmers were slaughtering piglets, she intervened with the AAA (Agricultural Adjustment Act) administrator to ask that surplus food be given to the hungry; she lectured and wrote articles; she helped start a CCC-type camp for young jobless women; she gave a civics course at the New York Junior League; and she continually—and effectively—prodded her husband to appoint women to high government jobs.

Nor did she need to do her husband's correspondence. She found her own mail swelling to such proportions that it required the full-time attention of a large staff. In 1933 alone, she received over 300,000 pieces of mail, many of them personal requests for money, jobs, or used clothing.

Like the mail addressed to Franklin, each of Eleanor's letters told a wrenching story of struggle and suffering. Joseph Blin Jr., at sixteen the eldest of fourteen children, wrote two days before Christmas 1933 from Keegan, Maine, that because his father earned only $14 a week, "we can't spear any money to dress ourselves" and so his sisters could not attend school. The boy tried to get work but was turned away because so many married men couldn't find jobs. He had read that Eleanor was saving clothes and toys for the poor. "I don't ask you any toys," he wrote, "but I ask you clothes that you have to spear. It makes three years that we didn't see Christmas and my little sisters don't know what's Christmas."

As with Franklin's letters, the writers were proud people, bewildered by what had happened to their lives. A woman wrote, "Oh Mrs. Roosevelt we do not want charity. Now my husband is not lazy he has signed with PWA and a man who has never done any laboring work it comes very hard. But we are thankful for that but Mrs. Roosevelt you know $15 per week with 60 cents car fare is not much with six children to feed cloth and keep a roof over their head." These writers believed that Eleanor would care. "Your the first president's wife that looks for the poor," wrote Joseph Blin.

"We didn't write to other president's wife because they only try to owns money, but not you."

Care enormously as Eleanor did, these letters were answered with regretful notes from her secretary. "There are certain persons to whom Mrs. Roosevelt sends the clothing for which she has no further use," was the reply to Joseph Blin, "and she is very sorry indeed that she cannot comply with your wishes."

The mail handling was soon systemized. Eleanor's secretary, Malvina "Tommy" Thompson, would go through the heaps of letters first and sort them, setting aside whatever should go to Eleanor. Edith Helm, the social secretary, then attended to social correspondence, while other letters were rerouted to appropriate government departments.

Eleanor and Tommy quickly threw out the form letters used by the Hoovers and previous presidents dating back to the Clevelands. Eleanor felt strongly that her letters should be dealt with on an individual basis, and she or Tommy tried to attend personally to each. This meant that a heaping basket of mail constantly lay at Eleanor's elbow, and she and Tommy often worked long evenings to answer letters. Some answers Eleanor dictated; others she merely sketched out for Tommy to complete. A notable few found their way to a special basket at Franklin's bedside.

. . .

As first lady, Eleanor had made an impact from her first day in the White House, astonishing some elderly members of the staff by taking charge of her environment and her life. Decisive and energetic, she was too impatient to wait for someone else to run the elevator, preferring to do it herself. Pushing fussy furniture out of the way, she substituted sturdy pieces from the Val-Kill factory. In three days, wrote Associated Press reporter Bess Furman, she transformed the living quarters of the White House.

In the private wing on the second floor, suites occupied each corner, each comprising a large and a small room. Eleanor turned her large bedroom into a study and moved her bed into the small adjoining chamber, furnished in her favorite blue and looking out toward the Washington Monument. Franklin used the upstairs oval room as his study and slept in a small bedroom next to it. He liked having a lot of people around, and the White House was always full of the hubbub of family and guests. The recently separated Anna and her children, Louis Howe, and Harry Hopkins all lived with Eleanor and Franklin at different times, and the boys, at school or living independently now, were frequent visitors. Eleanor made one end of the grand hall into a cozy sitting room where the family and special guests had five o'clock tea. She wanted to make the White House a real home. "[I]t can be done in the White House just as well as in the plainest home," she told a reporter.

Even more than her physical surroundings, she was transforming the role of first lady.

"I simply will not have it!" Eleanor snapped, when Franklin urged her to permit the Secret Service to accompany her when she traveled. She continued to move about as she always had: on ordinary trains between Washington and New York, on city buses, on regularly scheduled airline flights. "No maid, no secretary—just the First Lady of the land on a paid ticket on a regular passenger flight," wrote humorist and social commentator Will Rogers in a letter to *The New York Times*. Plainly dressed in her typical "uniform" of tweed skirt, white silk blouse, and low-heeled shoes, unusually accessible and straightforward, proud of her "7-cent luncheons" of stuffed eggs, mashed potatoes, and prune pudding, Mrs. Roosevelt's feelings of security in her own social status—combined with her inbred sense of noblesse oblige—raised her above any need for conspicuous shows of rank. "I always thought when people were given great power it did something to them," one female reporter wrote to Eleanor. "They lost the human touch if they ever had it. To have been able to see you at close hand, demonstrating the exact contrary, means truly a great deal to me."

Still, as much as this egalitarian woman disliked formality and protocol, there was plenty of protocol to oversee, such as arranging who would sit where at official dinners. On a typical day she shook the hands of 500 people at a four o'clock tea, and another 400 an hour later. She endured these mind-numbing receptions by studying the faces of the people who filed by her. Every morning after a brisk horseback ride and breakfast at eight-thirty she met with the head usher and the housekeeper to supervise the operation of the White House, before plunging into the day's mail with Tommy Thompson.

Aside from protocol, the first months were uncertain. Nearly everything she was doing was tentative and exploratory. The purely ornamental role played by previous first ladies was not one in which she felt she excelled or could find meaning. Acting only as Franklin's helpmate would be a charade; it would bore her to the point of depression. Instead she would use her strengths—her intellect, energy, and empathy. She would lean on Louis Howe, and she would connect with Washington women.

Her growing network of women strengthened her, and she in turn gave women opportunities and exposure. She made the obligatory White House social calendar more personal and political by mixing guests of varied backgrounds and adding a few parties of her own, for the professional and political women of Washington. The annual Gridiron Dinner, when Washington newspapermen hosted the president and the cabinet, still excluded women journalists—and now Secretary of Labor Frances Perkins. Eleanor responded by throwing a women's party on the same night, for newspaperwomen and the wives of newspapermen and cabinet members. These "Gridiron Widows" parties became an annual tradition, including masquerades and satirical skits, and often lasted long after Franklin had come home from the Gridiron Dinner and gone to bed.

Even before the inauguration, Eleanor broke precedent by announcing that as first lady she would hold press conferences for women reporters only, an idea suggested by Lorena Hickok and seconded by Louis Howe. "Hick" had pointed out that this would help women hang on to their jobs, an argument that never failed.

Eleanor's press conferences started within a week after the inauguration in March. "I really beat Franklin," she said gleefully. "He isn't holding his first press conference until Wednesday!" At first, her remarks were scoffed at by men as being purely social in nature, but they quickly became an important instrument for Eleanor. She steered clear of obviously political issues, to avoid embarrassing Franklin, but she did not avoid the controversial subjects that mattered to her—particularly peace, women, and labor. According to AP reporter Bess Furman, Eleanor discussed such issues as "subsistence homesteads, work camps for single women, National Youth Administration projects, the mattress making and sewing of the women on relief, the paintings of WPA artists, and the guidebooks of WPA writers." Many of the sessions became educational in tone, as Eleanor held forth on how to serve frugal, wholesome dishes. She became friends with many of the reporters; she liked newspaper people, and these women were intelligent, energetic, and politically aware in the same way that she was. Throughout her years in the White House, until 1945, Mrs. Roosevelt would continue to hold women-only press conferences; the only man ever to attend one of them was the mischievous King George VI of England, in June 1939, who slipped in when no one was watching.

And there was time for fun: an Easter egg-rolling party for thousands of children and parents in the spring of 1933; a rose, a chrysanthemum, and a strawberry named after her; her friend Amelia Earhart piloting her to Baltimore. In contrast to her lifelong fear of the water, she adored flying.

. . .

Franklin was sometimes said to have the "common touch," but one of Eleanor's first acts as first lady illustrates her ability, despite her shyness, to relate to people whose lives were very different from hers. In the spring of 1932 she had followed the story of the World War I veterans who were demanding immediate payment of their veteran's bonus and living in squatters' shacks in Washington. She was horrified when the government evicted them with tanks and tear gas. In May 1933, the "bonus army" returned to Washington to demand from the new administration immediate cash payment of their bonuses, which FDR opposed. Louis Howe, now the president's secretary, took on the challenge, arranging for Fort Hunt, Virginia, an abandoned army camp twelve miles from Washington, to be spruced up for the bonus marchers.

The veterans arrived in rainy mid-May, in trucks and on foot, carrying knapsacks and suitcases, wearing pieces of old uniforms. They were transferred to Fort Hunt, where they were fed, put up in tents with electric lights and showers, furnished with blankets and mess kits, and given medical and dental care.

Howe talked daily with the leaders. FDR remained adamantly against paying a cash bonus but authorized Howe to offer jobs in the CCC forestry camps to 25,000 veterans. At first the marchers rejected this proposal because of the low CCC wages, a dollar a day. "To hell with the reforestation army!" one shouted.

To this tense situation Howe brought Eleanor, staying in the car while she ventured into the camp. The weary, cynical veterans squinted at the regal, willowy figure as she picked her way through the ankle-deep mud. They asked her who she was, and she told them, adding that she had wanted to see how they were getting on. The men guided her through barracks, hospital, and mess hall. She made an impromptu speech in the convention tent, first apologizing that she could not discuss the main issue of concern. Instead she reminisced about her work in the Union Station canteen in Washington in 1917 and her tour of the battlefields in Europe in early 1919. "I served many sandwiches and lots of coffee," she said. "I saw the boys when they came back and often I went to the hospitals, so I saw two sides of the war." This evoked a tremendous cheer from the men. "I would like to see that everyone has fair consideration," she finished, "and I will always be grateful to those who served their country." She and the men sang "There's a Long, Long Trail," and then she left.

"Hoover sent the army," one veteran commented, "Roosevelt sent his wife." A few days later the men drifted home, 2,600 of the veterans ultimately joining the CCC.

Although the police and Secret Service were vexed by her solo expedition, others admired her fearlessness. It wasn't what she said, but the fact of her going to the veterans that impressed people. Even though Franklin's way of dealing with the men was to drive by, wave his hat at them, and order up an unlimited supply of hot coffee, Eleanor's presence in the camp demonstrated that the administration cared and wanted to understand. She, not Franklin, was sailing by the stars. Wrote Josephus Daniels from Mexico, "It is such fine things as that which bring you the admiration of the American people."

Louis Howe's respect and admiration for Eleanor continued to grow. Once he appeared in her sitting room. "Eleanor," he said, "if you want to be president in 1940, tell me now so I can start getting things ready." Howe believed that women's increasing political experience and savvy over the previous ten years would allow a woman to be nominated for president in another decade. Eleanor, however, did not share his blithe optimism.

But she wanted to get out of the White House, to help bring change at the grass roots, to touch the lives of ordinary people. Franklin urged her to travel, to report back to him on conditions out in the country. She could not have found a more needy, a more challenging place than the mining hamlets of northern West Virginia. Of all her activities during 1933 and 1934, the one perhaps closest to her heart was her involvement in a remarkable experiment, the subsistence homestead projects, specifically the model community called Arthurdale.

. . .

The bituminous coal industry, which had boomed after World War I, skidded into a steep decline years before the stock market crashed. Production of soft coal plunged by 100 million tons during the 1920s; employment dropped by almost 150,000 men.

Scott's Run, Crown Mine, Bertha Hill, Pigeon Roost: the little hamlets straggled along the streams that carved their way through the coal-rich Appalachians. In the camps, listless adults drifted around like ghosts or drank to mute their frustration. Children grew up lethargic and half starved in shacks that were black with coal dust and overrun by rats, sharing one scant meal a day and a few pieces of clothing with numerous brothers and sisters.

The miners' shacks, reached by goat paths, clung to steep hillsides; slag piles and train tracks took up any level ground by the stream. Sanitation was nonexistent: the streams carried human and industrial waste through camp after camp before reaching the river. In the view of Williams Brooks, a prominent Quaker who worked in West Virginia resettling stranded miners, only slavery exceeded the coal industry in its degradation of human beings.

FDR had long been interested in agricultural planning and decentralization—moving industries and workers out of the congested cities into more healthful rural areas. In April 1933 he wrote Norris, "I really would like to get one more bill, which would allow us to spend $25 million this year to put 25,000 families on farms, at an average cost of $1,000 per family. It can be done. Also, we would get most of the money back in due time. Will you talk this over with some of our fellow dreamers on the Hill?"

The money came through, and the president set up the Subsistence Homestead Division as part of the National Industrial Recovery Act, assigning the division to the Department of the Interior under Harold Ickes. At FDR's suggestion, Ickes appointed M. L. Wilson head, and Clarence Pickett as assistant.

Wilson was a rare combination of pragmatist and idealist, an Iowa farm boy who taught at Montana State Agricultural College and then became an administrator in the AAA. He disliked cities. "This is no way for people to live [in city slums]. I want to get them out on the ground with clean sunshine and air around them, and a garden for them to dig in. . . . Spread out the cities, space the factories out, give people a chance to live." He envisioned a new world based on part-time farming; workers could produce food for their families on small farms while they earned cash wages in nearby factories.

Wilson and Pickett soon put specifics to their vision: The federal government would create "subsistence homesteads" where inhabitants could farm small plots and work in local industries. The government would purchase land and subsidize the building of homesteads; the settlers would purchase their homes over thirty years. In addition to the houses, the government would provide livestock, farm machinery, roads, water, clinics, schools, and sanitation.

The times seemed ripe for such a bold experiment, and preparations proceeded quickly. During the fall of 1933, sites were found for homestead communities ranging from a site near Dayton, Ohio, where the settlers would build their own homes, to Hightstown, New Jersey, where two hundred Jewish garment workers would move from New York City to establish a clothing factory. In Decatur, Illinois, an agricultural community comprised forty-six homesteads; in Georgia, farmers would be moved off worn-out lands to homesteads on better soil. Thousands of eager applicants were carefully screened for stability and responsibility. Because the first communities would serve as models, the first homesteaders had to have the potential to succeed—but could not, of course, be successful already.

Eleanor shared Franklin's interest in planned communities, but for different reasons. While Franklin saw the practical advantages of decentralization, Eleanor viewed the homesteads in more personal and idealistic terms. Here, she believed, was a chance to restore spirit and dignity to broken human beings by getting them off relief and helping them help themselves. And here was a model for other communities of how to establish a better life for their citizens.

With Quaker workers Alice Davis and Nadia Danilevsky as guides, she and Lorena Hickok—who had resigned from the Associated Press to work for Harry Hopkins in the new relief administration—visited the mining hamlets near Morgantown, West Virginia, in August 1933. They traveled in a battered car, going from shack to shack, talking with miners' wives and children about their health, their gardens, and their problems and taking detailed notes. In the idle, grimy camps Eleanor glimpsed a depth of degradation she had never imagined. "The conditions I saw," she wrote later, "convinced me that with a little leadership there could develop in the mining areas, if not a people's revolution, at least a people's party patterned after some of the previous parties born of bad economic conditions."

Eleanor told one story at a White House dinner, where a glistening table service and sumptuous food must have contrasted starkly with the scene she described. "In a company house I visited . . . were six children in the family, and they acted as though they were afraid of strangers. I noticed a bowl on the table filled with scraps, the kind that you or I might give to a dog, and I saw children, evidently looking for their noon-day meal, take a handful out of that bowl and go out munching. That was all they had to eat.

"As I went out, two of the children had gathered enough courage to stand by the door, the little boy holding a white rabbit in his arms. It was evident it was a most cherished pet. The little girl was thin and scrawny, and had a gleam in her eyes as she looked at her brother. Turning to me she said, 'He thinks we are not going to eat it, but we are,' and at that the small boy fled down the road, clutching the rabbit closer than ever." One of the guests at the White House dinner that night, William C. Bullitt, sent ER a check the next day, saying he "hoped it might help to keep the rabbit alive."

Eleanor's visit to Morgantown caused that area to be selected for a homestead. The government purchased the old Arthur estate just outside Reedsville, naming it Arthurdale. Eleanor became deeply involved in the subsistence homestead project as a whole, but by far most deeply in Arthurdale. It became an overriding interest over the next few years.

Louis Howe was another passionate advocate, and he pushed the model Arthurdale project hard. He may have felt the urgency of his own deteriorating health; by the next spring he would be almost completely bedridden. In addition he, like Eleanor and Clarence Pickett, felt it was imperative that the government act to relieve the misery, to prove it was not paralyzed in the face of this great crisis.

Much progress had been made by the time Eleanor again visited the Arthurdale site in late November. She declared herself "very much pleased." That visit, however, was probably the project's high point. Eleanor inspected the site of a planned factory where the homesteaders would be employed building post office furniture. The Mountaineer Crafts Cooperative was relocating at Arthurdale. Thirty-six families had moved into the old Arthur mansion to await the completion of their homes, and fifty prefab houses ordered by Louis Howe were due that week. Howe confidently promised that the first families would eat Christmas dinner in their new homes.

Then reality struck. The prefab houses turned out to be flimsy bungalows designed for Cape Cod summers, completely unsuitable for mountain winters. The first group of settlers spent the winter in the old Arthur mansion while the houses were refurbished at a cost that was twice what it would have been to build them from the outset of native stone. Critics seized the chance to jeer at the subsistence homestead scheme. Just when the government wanted to look competent, it looked inept.

Though Howe was blamed for the messy start, there were other mistakes. And because of the first lady's close connection to the Arthurdale project, every problem was magnified in the press. Most significant was the failure of any industry—always seen as the centerpiece of the community—to take hold.

A bill to set up a post office furniture factory was killed; a vacuum cleaner assembly plant operated for a year and then closed; a shirt manufacturer appeared briefly, as did a factory to build radio cabinets. Small companies could not start up while the national economy was still so depressed. Not until wartime did even half of Arthurdale's labor force find sustained work in private industry.

In the national press, attacks continued from both left and right. Communists claimed that the homesteads would institutionalize poverty. The United Mine Workers declared that miners would be "weaned" away, thereby weakening the union. Farmers who had spent their lives establishing their own farms resented the idea that coal miners and unsuccessful farmers should be given "completely cleared, stocked, and electrified farms." The right-wing *Saturday Evening Post* exposed the high costs of the Arthurdale project in an August issue. To the charge that the entire project was "Communistic," Eleanor responded heatedly. "Never in this country, to my knowledge," she declared, "has it been considered Communistic for an opportunity to be given to people to earn their own livings and buy their own houses."

Despite all the clamor, by the spring of 1934 the subsistence homestead movement was in full swing. Thirty projects had been approved. Former miners in the Appalachians, former steelworkers in Alabama and Ohio, farmers on worn-out Georgia farmland—all these were represented in the new homestead communities. And in the model Arthurdale community the rolling green hills were dotted with fifty new white houses by June 1934, already inhabited by former miners and their families. In front of each house was a newly planted garden, and in back was a barn for cows and poultry, with up to five acres available on each homestead for orchards and subsistence farming. Each house had four to six rooms, modern plumbing, electricity, a full basement, and a septic tank. A church, doubling as a community hall, occupied the village center. Near it were a library and a schoolhouse with playground and gymnasium. A few of the settlers worked at the craftsmen's association; a few others were employed in construction of buildings, but most stayed on relief while they planted their first crops.

Would the resettlement concept succeed? Subsistence homesteads, confessed Tugwell, the head of the new Resettlement Administration, would never be more than "small eddies of retreat for exceptional persons." The following spring he would tell the Senate Appropriations Committee that nine of the thirty-seven projects were financial failures.

Still, Eleanor would not give up. Despite all the problems, she remained deeply committed to the subsistence homestead idea. It was as if she believed the combination of money, creative leadership, and her own powerful will could fashion a new world. She made unannounced visits to the communities, intervened with Ickes and Hopkins, poured money of her own into Arthurdale, raised more funds among wealthy benefactors such as Bernard Baruch, and even went about pricing refrigerators for the miners' homes. She helped set up a school that was also a center where the entire community—from nursery children to adults—could become involved in theater, music, gardening, canning, animal husbandry, poultry raising, handcrafts, industrial arts, health care, and more.

But, years later, Eleanor would have to concede that the subsistence homestead project, and Arthurdale in particular, had failed. "Only a few of the resettlement projects had any measure of success," she wrote; "nevertheless I have always felt that the good they did was incalculable. Conditions were so nearly the kind that breed revolution that the men and women needed to be made to feel their government's interest and concern."

4
The Explorer: Midcourse Corrections

Like a boy bolting out of the last day of school, the president had signed the National Industrial Recovery Act and other bills in mid-June and immediately taken off to watch Franklin Jr. graduate from Groton and then to sail in the waters he knew so well and loved so dearly: from Buzzards Bay past Martha's Vineyard, Nantucket, and Provincetown to Gloucester. From this tiny Massachusetts port, after meeting with his old friend Colonel House and with Budget Director Douglas, he and James sailed up the Maine coast to Portland, where they were joined by Franklin and John. Occasionally taking the helm, FDR and his sons navigated through well-known waters to Campobello, which he could now visit without reliving the nightmare of 1921. Later, as he journeyed back south on the cruiser *Indianapolis,* he could recall happy days in the navy department.

He returned to a Washington enjoying a New Deal delirium. Dominating center stage was a dazzling New Deal impresario, General Hugh Johnson. A key figure in drafting the NRA measure and nursing it through Congress, Johnson had caught FDR's eye with his old cavalryman's gusto, bluntness, and loyalty to the commander in chief. "Square-jawed, thick-necked, red-faced, profane," as Arthur Schlesinger Jr. later pictured him, "he combined the qualities of a top sergeant, a frontier editor, and a proconsul." Like a good commander, FDR stood aside but saw everything.

And the general was a sight to see. Within days of taking over empty offices in the huge old Commerce Building that President Hoover had built as his showcase public work, the general was mobilizing public support through calls to arms, promises of victory, and denunciations of quitters, malingerers, and deserters. His enthusiasms spread through the country. Since the detailed work of drawing up codes proceeded slowly, employers were urged to subscribe temporarily to a blanket code pledging them to do business only with those displaying Blue Eagle signs reading WE DO OUR PART. To many Americans the NRA offered the excitement of war, with parades, banners, music; to others, it was a gigantic circus.

The NRA, as scholars have noted, came right out of Theodore Roosevelt and Herbert Croly's New Nationalism. Just as the New Nationalism, in Croly's words, meant "a drastic reorganization of the American political and economic system" that would substitute a "frank social policy" for the individualism of the past, the NRA too was founded on a new spirit of cooperation among government, industry, and labor.

It was Johnson's task to draw up strong codes for specific industries. This was tricky business. In exchange for agreements establishing standards of fair competition with rival entrepreneurs and thus eliminating "chiseling competitors" and sweatshop owners, businessmen would agree to wage-and-hour standards and protection for employees. Such agreements could violate the cherished antitrust laws, over which populists and progressives long had stood guard. The big issue was prices: Would the coded industries gang up against the consumer? Other questions soon arose: How much compulsion could NRA use, how were industries defined, what was the role of labor and consumers in code-making? The supreme goal of NRA was balance among employers, workers, and consumers, but the balance could easily be upset in practice.

For a time, sheer euphoria seemed to carry NRA along and many New Dealers with it. Hopeful that democratic self-discipline in industry was proving itself, the president was especially pleased that NRA appeared to be raising wages above the starvation level, cutting overlong hours, and—especially in the textile industry—abolishing child labor. Mainly amused, though sometimes appalled, by Johnson's flamboyant tactics, FDR didn't mind at all the credit he was getting as commander in chief of recovery. When Postmaster General Farley put out an NRA postage stamp, picturing the "honest" farmer, businessman, and blacksmith working together, Roosevelt claimed that the farmer looked like himself. As for the woman pictured, "Heavens, what a girl! She is wearing a No. 11 shoe, also a bustle, and if recovery is dependent on women like that I am agin recovery."

But as feelings both of economic crisis and of patriotic partnership ebbed, rips opened in the big NRA tent. Some businessmen never even went inside, most notably Henry Ford, who—typically—followed code provisions for wages and hours anyway. Some employers agreed to codes and then violated them. Most went along, but with increasing dismay, as competitors violated the codes and thus gained advantages. But the main problem still was prices. Long starved for profits, business now saw its chance at least to "stabilize" prices, which often meant boosting them. Achieving NRA's aim—neither hiking nor lowering prices but stabilizing them—required a fine-tuning that Hugh Johnson and the employers simply could not master, or often had no wish to.

Unexpectedly, given the NRA's central effort to recognize organized industry's needs for stability and profits, it was organized labor that remained most hopeful about its benefits under NRA. Those benefits turned on the delphic little Section 7(a), which was becoming a magic recruiting device at the hands of trade union leaders. Section 7(a) not only granted employees organizing and bargaining rights "through representatives of their own choosing" but went on to grant workers freedom "from the interference, restraint, or coercion of employers of labor" in designing such representation, and provided further that "no employee and no one seeking employment shall be required as a condition of employment to join any company union or to refrain from joining, organizing, or assisting a labor organization of his own choosing." Whether these provisions, which infuriated many corporation heads, could be turned into organizational power depended on the union leadership.

That leadership, especially in the person of John L. Lewis of the Mine Workers, felt fully up to the opportunity. "LABOR MUST ORGANIZE," read a labor handbill in Kentucky. "Forget about injunctions, yellow dog contracts, blacklists, and the fear of dismissal. . . . ALL WORKERS ARE FULLY PROTECTED IF THEY DESIRE TO JOIN A UNION."

In Lewis the employers—and Johnson too—met a man who would test their mettle. Elected head of the Mine Workers in 1920 at the age of forty, Lewis had established a reputation for militance, fortified by his massive figure, shaggy mane, Shakespearean rhetoric, and fiery face-to-face confrontations slyly mixed with pleasantries. He symbolized the new labor militance under NRA. Strikes almost doubled between July and August 1933; by September almost 300,000 workers were out, with thousands of militants manning picket lines. Johnson and other NRA officials stood aside, protesting neutrality, while unionists struck out on their own.

The president generally kept hands off worker-employer disputes. This was notably true when thousands of maritime workers on the West Coast, protesting antiunion activities, went on strike in May 1934. With the ports tied up, worker-employer relations hardened under the rival leaderships of the strong union leader, Harry Bridges, and an array of tough shipping magnates. The press played up the crisis, with the "communist" Bridges as a particular target. Vacationing at this time on the U.S.S. *Houston* headed toward Hawaii, FDR was happy to leave matters to his cabinet. Under rising pressure, Johnson, Attorney General Homer Cummings, and even Hull lost their heads and began to consider dire government action. Only Frances Perkins kept hers, skillfully fending off the extremists on all sides until longshoremen and employers agreed to arbitrate the issues and the strike petered out. The first woman cabinet appointee had brought a different kind of leadership to the world of industrial strife.

By mid-1934, only a year after NRA started, the Blue Eagle was fluttering amid heavy gales. Business was dissatisfied with prices and profits. Enforcement of code provisions was inadequate. Consumers felt left out. Small businesses saw large firms favored at their expense. Not only did big industry spar with "big labor," but fights erupted within each of these domains. Finally, as NRA became big and cumbersome, Johnson & Co. lost control of the situation by trying to establish codes for too many businesses. And as NRA declined, so did General Johnson, into fits of hyperactivity interspersed with withdrawal and into invective, self-pity, and drink.

Many Americans—and to a degree FDR himself—were content to see NRA relinquish its role as the key to recovery. Yet there was something poignant, even tragic, in NRA's decline. It had represented, after all, an effort to weld key economic groups into a great national partnership, to overcome despair and demoralization that had darkened the economic outlook, to plan ahead. It was an effort of the "ship of state" to move steadily through the currents and crosswinds, even to control the storms. It had curbed child labor and sweatshops, pressed for decent wages and hours. But it represented a voyage half completed; did it presage a New Deal half dealt?

. . .

Millions of Americans could hardly care less about the shenanigans, fights, and claims of the recovery agencies. For them the test of the New Deal was their own individual recovery. And here too the record was mixed. For some months, recovery had proceeded strongly. The Federal Reserve Board's index of industrial production almost doubled from March to July 1933 and then rested on a plateau for the next three months. Employment surged from almost 35 million in March to almost 39 million in October, with the number of jobless dropping from 15 to 11 million. But the rising indices appeared to become stuck in the autumn of 1933, according to economist Irving Bernstein; for months thereafter the economy seemed stagnant. From late 1933 until well into 1935, the index of industrial production bobbed up and down, but far below the base period of 1923–25.

Why this "boomlet and bust" during a time when many Americans felt a great and lasting surge of recovery? Part of that boomlet was illusion, rising from FDR's vigorous efforts and optimistic speeches; much of it was real, but based less on NRA programs than on an increase in federal spending even at the same time that Roosevelt was preaching economy. That spending came largely through farm aid, jobless relief, and public works. Each of those spending programs, however, was limited in economic impact, with farm aid going to the larger commodity producers and relief constrained by FDR's penurious spending policies early in the New Deal.

Public works spending was the acid test of recovery. New Dealers wanted it as a central recovery strategy; many Hoover Republicans backed major construction programs; members of Congress strongly favored public works, especially for their states and districts. NRA and PWA—Public Works Administration—had been married in the same June 1933 act that had appropriated $3.3 billion for public works. Johnson had ardently hoped and expected that he would run public works as well as the NRA, only to learn that the new secretary of the interior, Harold Ickes, would administer the works program. The general had been so crushed by this decision that, flushed with anger, he had protested to the president, who in turn asked Frances Perkins to calm him down and keep him away from the press. She did.

Johnson's behavior was so infantile as to be treated by historians as a sign of his later deterioration. But perhaps the general perceived that unless PWA spending was closely linked with NRA self-regulation, the impact of both would be sharply lessened. That is what happened, largely because of FDR's choice of Ickes to head PWA. As FDR doubtless hoped and Johnson feared, Ickes was far more eager to spend money honestly and cautiously than quickly and lavishly. A longtime Chicago municipal reformer who had battled both private and public privilege, he gained in FDR's eye by having supported Theodore Roosevelt and his progressive cause in 1912. His beady eyes mirrored his suspicion that in Washington he was entering a den of thieves. His bristling responses to project seekers and his obvious delight in his image as a curmudgeon led to suspicion that his main goal in Washington was to live up to his sobriquet of "Honest Harold," despite his stated objection to the name.

Eventually PWA would create—or help create—some of the most enduring public works in the country: the Triborough Bridge in New York, roads and bridges linking Key West to mainland Florida, modernization of the New York–Washington railroad connection, the port of Brownsville in Texas, Boulder Dam on the Colorado, and Grand Coulee and Bonneville dams on the Columbia. PWA spent billions on educational buildings, roads, bridges, subways, hospitals, courthouses—all without apparent fraud. And, at FDR's direction and to his infinite satisfaction, PWA built the aircraft carriers *Enterprise* and *Yorktown,* several cruisers, submarines, a veritable flotilla of heavy and light destroyers, and dozens of military airports, much to the annoyance of Senator Borah and other isolationists.

But the price of such major projects was delay, as Ickes laboriously reviewed major contracts and countless minor ones, shot back applications for revision, inquired into the financial lives of departmental employees as well as hopeful contractors. What should have been a heavy impact of these huge spending programs on relief and recovery was muted. While Johnson's NRA moved forward headlong with agreements, industry improvements, and euphoria, PWA lagged far behind. Millions of Americans took part in the economic transformation; millions of others had no part, no benefit.

. . .

New Deal euphoria—a mélange of affection and admiration for the president, satisfaction over progress in reform and recovery, and high hopes for more progress to come—appeared to ebb during 1934. "Do you not know this?" a California woman wrote him in October: "The masses who really are the people of the United States are still supporting you because of what *they hope you will do soon?* So far we recognize absolutely no fundamental benefits from your policies."

"By 1934, we really began to suffer," Malcolm X remembered. "This was about the worst depression year, and no one we knew had enough to eat or live on."

Increasingly, letters to FDR appeared to take a personal tone. "The Lord must have practiced making *fools* for a long time before he made you," wrote an Ohio woman in August. A man who described himself as a small property owner got right to his point: "Expunge the brains trust."

Even without reading such letters, Roosevelt knew, with his antennae always sharply attuned to public opinion, that for many Americans hope was giving way to the old depression feelings of fear, disillusionment, and emotions ranging from anger to a new passivity. How could he restore and maintain the momentum of 1933?

FDR was stymied by his own financial and political strategy, as well as by almost intractable economic and social conditions. He had been following a wavering, opportunistic strategy of "a little left of center," trying to create a national partnership that would transcend the old divisions between right and left. This partnership was not working well, as shown especially by the NRA. With redoubled fervor, conservatives and radicals moved on the New Deal flanks.

"All the big guns have started shooting—Al Smith, John W. Davis, James W. Wadsworth, du Pont, Shouse, etc.," FDR wrote to his friend William Bullitt late in August 1934. "Their organization has already been labeled the 'I CAN'T TAKE IT CLUB.'" He had far more personal sympathy with adversaries on the left, such as Norman Thomas, but almost equally limited sympathy with their ideas. With his fighting instincts aroused, he knew he must continue to push his program forward.

"During June and the summer there will be many new manifestations of the New Deal," he had written Colonel House in May 1934, "even though the orthodox protest and the heathen roar! Do you not think I am right?" "We must keep the sheer momentum from slacking up too much," the president went on, "and I have no intention of relinquishing the offensive in favor of defensive tactics." Hence, to the newly formed Securities and Exchange Commission, empowered to regulate the volume of credit in the trading of securities and to oversee the public disclosure of companies' financial reports, FDR appointed Joseph P. Kennedy as the new chairman in the spring of 1934, remarking in private, "Set a thief to catch a thief." "The days of stock manipulation are over," announced Kennedy as he began, during his brief tenure, to place the SEC on a firm footing. But there would not be "many new manifestations of the New Deal" later in 1934. What fresh and effective course could the New Deal follow?

An answer—provocative, unorthodox, outrageous—blew in from a far-off source: Spend more money, much more money. This came from a

British economist, John Maynard Keynes, whom FDR had never met but knew of favorably because of Keynes's support for the president's nationalist economic policies. In an "Open Letter to President Roosevelt" that Keynes wrote for the December 31, 1933, issue of *The New York Times*, the economist showed remarkable prescience in forecasting deepening economic troubles for FDR in 1934.

The letter was personal. "Dear Mr. President," it began. "You have made yourself the trustee for those in every country who seek to mend the evils of our condition by reasoned experiment within the framework of the existing social system. If you fail, rational change will be gravely prejudiced throughout the world, leaving orthodox and revolution to fight it out. But if you succeed, new and bolder methods will be tried, and we may date the first chapter of a new economic era from your accession to office." That is why he ventured to write from such a distance and from partial knowledge.

The letter was pointed. "At the moment your sympathizers in England are nervous and sometimes despondent. We wonder whether the order of different urgencies is rightly understood, whether there is a confusion of aims, and whether some of the advice you get is not crack-brained and queer." Almost everyone in London, he said, had a "wildly distorted view of what is happening in the United States." Some of them were sitting back and waiting for Roosevelt to fail.

Keynes was explicit. "You are engaged on a double task, recovery and reform—recovery from the slump, and the passage of those business and social reforms which are long overdue. For the first, speed and quick results are essential. The second may be urgent, too; but haste will be injurious" and long-range purpose better than immediate reform achievement. "It will be through raising high the prestige of your administration by success in short-range recovery that you will have the driving force to accomplish long-range reform. On the other hand, even wise and necessary reform may, in some respects, impede and complicate recovery."

He was prescriptive. As the "prime mover" in the first stage of recovery, "I lay overwhelming emphasis on the increase of national purchasing power resulting from governmental expenditure which is financed by loans," and not by taxing present income. "Nothing else counts in comparison with this. . . . In a slump, governmental loan expenditure is the only sure means of obtaining quickly a rising output at rising prices." Then, in a remarkable reference to what would be a momentous testing of his theories, Keynes added, "That is why a war has always caused intense industrial activity"—and why not use economic methods for "peace and pros-perity" instead of "war and destruction"?

"You can tell the professor," FDR responded coolly through Felix Frankfurter, who was at Oxford and had sent him an advance copy of the letter, "that in regard to public works we shall spend in the next fiscal year nearly twice the amount we are spending in this fiscal year, but there is a practical limit to what the Government can borrow—especially because the banks are offering passive resistance in most of the large centers."

It was FDR's "practicality" against Keynes's theory. Through most of 1934, Roosevelt would stick to his near obsession with cautious spending, with budget balancer Lewis Douglas still at his elbow preaching caution. A year later he was still skeptical of economists, complaining to Berle that "no two or two hundred or two thousand economists, businessmen, or politicians" could agree on anything except short-term policies.

Sail by the stars and not the winds of opinion, Lippmann had urged the president. But the helmsman was trying to find his way through stormy economic seas. Tacking back and forth, he was following known compass directions, familiar landmarks; he could not see much beyond the hori-zon. The seafarer would sail hour by hour, day by day. It was rather Eleanor Roosevelt who seemed to be guided by the stars, her own strong values of compassion and community. Both were now facing a mighty sea change that would emerge out of the wants and needs of the American populace.

Chapter Eight
THE POPULACE: ARMAGEDDON

"*Come along. We're going to the Trans-Lux to hiss Roosevelt.*"

Peter Arno, *The New Yorker.*

"Throughout the world, change is the order of the day. In every Nation economic problems, long in the making, have brought crises of many kinds for which the masters of old practice and theory were unprepared. In most Nations social justice, no longer a distant ideal, has become a definite goal, and ancient Governments are beginning to heed the call."

FDR was delivering his annual message to Congress early in January 1935, to the usual resounding cheers from the Democrats and polite applause from the Republican side. He had begun by calling for "useful cooperation" and "genuine friendships" between Congress and the White House. This would be a bit easier for FDR now, because of the remarkable victory he and his party had scored in the fall 1934 elections. Rather than the president's party losing in Congress, as was almost invariably the case historically (and would remain the case for at least another sixty years), the Democrats had picked up nine new seats in the Senate and thirteen in the House, thereby gaining more than a two-thirds voting power in each chamber.

Americans sought change, the president went on, "through tested liberal traditions, through processes which retain all of the deep essentials of that representative government first given to a troubled world by the United States." He referred to "rapid changes" in the machine age, especially communication. As FDR continued, however, it became clear that he was by no means happy with the pace of change in the United States, or even in its government. "Evils overlap and reform becomes confused and frustrated" on a piecemeal basis. "We lose sight, from time to time, of our ultimate human objectives."

The people, he admitted, were still suffering from "old inequalities, little changed by past specific remedies." Even more, "we have not weeded out the overprivileged" or "effectively lifted up the underprivileged." Both of these "manifestations of injustice" had "retarded happiness." The people had built wisely, but the nation must see "where we can do still better." He laid out a three-part program for security: security of livelihood, security of decent homes, and security against major hazards of life.

The legislators looked on with some astonishment. They were used to presidents claiming miraculous progress when they gave their message to Congress. But FDR's modesty was not a false one. Despite all the exciting initiatives and innovations of the past two years, he knew that real changes had come slowly and inadequately. Now the euphoric honeymoon was over. Now he would be tested for actual results, concrete progress. And he was wholly aware of compromises that had blocked or sharply curbed the extension of a new deal to millions still jobless, to tenant farmers and farm laborers, to African-Americans facing discrimination at every turn, to children and women working for five and ten cents an hour.

A setback in the summer of 1934 had reminded the president of the harsh limits of reform. Frances Perkins, along with Hopkins, Morgenthau, Wallace, and others, including her assistant solicitor, Thomas H. Eliot, had been drafting comprehensive social insurance programs that would become the Social Security Act. They were bold enough to consider adding health insurance to the program. When Perkins mentioned the need for some sort of health insurance in a radio talk, however, she touched off an uproar among doctors and their lobbyists. Soon the whole government retreated. The Perkins group dropped even the proposal for a future health insurance study, House members banished any reference to the subject in the social security bill, Perkins omitted the item from the group's report to the president, and FDR also buried it. Little could the president have expected, with his hopes for change, that the nation would still be debating proposals for health insurance in the year 2000.

There were other compromises with the needs of more vulnerable Americans. The plight of sharecroppers and tenant farmers deeply concerned New Dealers in the Department of Agriculture. Efforts to channel as much AAA money as possible into the hands of field-workers, and not merely landlords and planters, produced outbursts from the southern Democratic bloc in Congress; when young New Deal lawyers sought to strengthen the contractual rights of tenants against the landlords' rights to hire and fire, several of the militants were sacked. When Harry Hopkins and his assistant, Aubrey Williams, backed vocational training and "education in democracy" rather than mere handouts to students, Roosevelt favored the latter—though, typically, he kept Williams on.

What kind of leadership was Roosevelt offering? What kind of change had he made? Two years earlier, in his inaugural address, he had sought to banish fear, to offer hope and even happiness, to act and even attack. He had followed up with his crisis actions of the first hundred days. And he had followed up those first three months with brilliant displays of transactional leadership as he wheedled, persuaded, enticed, manipulated, compromised, horse-traded, placated, and mediated—as he led and followed, led and misled.

A "first-class temperament," old Justice Holmes had called him, probably thinking of TR as well, and FDR proved him right, laughing and jesting, telling long and somewhat imaginary stories, spouting ideas and instructions, all the time deploying his cigarette in its long jaunty holder. Calvin Coolidge, it was said, disposed of visitors by a country dodge: "Don't talk back to 'em." FDR outtalked visitors, advisers, agency heads, even visiting senators.

But FDR had also promised, in March 1933, a leadership that aimed at a larger good, a leadership devoted to a disciplined attack on common problems, a leadership of a trained and loyal army of followers willing to make sacrifices, a leadership that today we would call "transformational." Was he equipped mentally to do this? He was as undisciplined intellectually as his followers were politically, some believed. His judgments, Adolf Berle noted, were primarily instinctive rather than rational. He learned not from books but from people and the press, devouring newspapers "like a combine eating up grain," a friend noted. He was more a broker of ideas than a creator of them, more a processor than an originator. Rather than organizing his goals and ideas into some priority order, in the mode of a transforming leader, he played by ear and boasted of it. He was following no set course, left, right, or center.

Dazzling acrobatics, but with what impact on the lives of people—what *real* change as against ballyhooed change? To a considerable extent, in its first two years the New Deal had changed the nation's landscape with thousands of new school buildings, roads, housing projects, bridges, dams, conservation projects—and, even more, the first public works arts projects. Millions of persons had jobs, make-work, relief. But there was no fundamental alteration of the economic and social life of Americans, in part because FDR was not yet offering the transforming leadership that would make such basic change possible.

1
Winter of Discontent

During the early weeks of 1935, friends of FDR were mystified—as historians have been since—by a change in the ordinarily ebullient president. He was peevish, restless, even indecisive. Some thought he was drifting, that he had lost his way. Perhaps he was reflecting feelings among some of his entourage. Ickes appeared "discouraged and bitter," noted Tugwell, who in turn feared the president was "slipping."

From his mail, the polls, and his trips out into the country FDR knew that his own popularity remained high. But how to translate popularity into power? He suffered a stinging defeat—and Eleanor, a deep disappointment—in January when the isolationist Senate could not muster a two-thirds vote for United States membership in the World Court. Perhaps because he felt conscience-stricken for having deserted the League of Nations, FDR had pressed the upper chamber strongly for membership. It was with unusual asperity that he wrote Majority Leader Joseph Robinson that, as to the thirty-six senators who voted against the court, "I am inclined to think that if they ever get to Heaven they will be doing a great deal of apologizing for a very long time—that is if God is against war—as I think He is."

The economy was an even sharper disappointment. Despite much improvement during his two years in office, unemployment remained high, and national income—including not only urban people's income but that of the farmers whom FDR had so favored—remained less, embarrassingly less, than during Hoover's first year. The president admitted privately to an English acquaintance that the "unemployment problem is solved no more here than it is with you." Nothing could have been better political news for the GOP, flayed for years as the Hoover party of Depression.

And was even the *fear* of the Hoover days returning? "Things ain't too good," publicist Herbert Bayard Swope, an old friend of FDR, wrote to Jim Farley, who quoted the letter to Howe. "I am not referring now to business conditions. I am referring to a sense of fear that is beginning at the top, growing downward, and spreading as it goes," and taking the form of misgivings about the president. "It has not yet spread among the lower strata. There more hope exists than doubt; but the fermentation is beginning to work." After the New Deal had replaced fear with hope, was the reverse now perilously taking place?

Doubtless the political situation above all galled the president. For two years he had presided over what he pridefully viewed as a grand partnership of all the major interests and ideologies. To farmers and workers and other constituencies he had handed federal help; to liberals, major economic reforms; to Socialists, the TVA and other radical initiatives. And to business? The NRA had been an enormous concession to the age-old dream of industry and commerce for boosted profits and stabilized competition.

Above all, the president had preached and practiced budget-balancing, with *economy . . . economy . . . economy . . .* as his mantra.

FDR had tried to be conciliatory toward even the most hostile businessmen. In August 1934 his conservative foes had set up the American Liberty League, dedicated to "teach the necessity of respect for the rights of persons and property," the duty of government to protect initiative and enterprise, the right to earn and save and acquire property. Harry Hopkins, the federal relief administrator, quipped that the Liberty League, for "right-thinking" people, is "so far to the right no one will ever find it." It was, as New Deal historian William Leuchtenburg remarked, "transparently an upper-class front."

When FDR's old political friend and adversary Jouett Shouse wanted to discuss his ideas for the league, FDR had him in for a talk and was so charming and friendly that Shouse left feeling that FDR had almost endorsed the league, or at least its aims. To be sure, Roosevelt later joked with the press about the Liberty League's two commandments to protect profits and property, while ignoring the commandment about "loving your neighbor," but he was amiable in his comments as not to provoke the Liberty Leaguers.

In other ways too FDR had tried to demonstrate his conservatism, or at least his centrism. He had retained economizer-in-chief Lew Douglas as his closest financial adviser. He had kept his distance, at least publicly, from some of the more militant union leaders. Perhaps the most difficult sacrifice he made was when he declined to address a Jefferson Day dinner—that grand old Democratic party ceremony—on the grounds that he was trying to unite both Republicans and Democrats in a nonpartisan campaign for recovery. When a conservative adviser earlier had not only quit but evidently started to hold protest meetings, the president had scribbled a scorching reprimand, charging him with near-disloyalty—but he had never mailed it.

As Roosevelt read and heard of the furious denunciations of the New Deal during the summer of 1934, his reaction was one of anger against these ingrates. In 1933, businessmen had showered him with lavish praise, crediting him with saving the country. "If we continue to stand behind President Roosevelt," one such wealthy industrialist exhorted, "he will pull us through."

By mid-1934, as business conditions improved along with profits and stock prices, it was hard for FDR to understand the fury of the attacks against him, the emotion, the contemptible epithets and accusations.

When Roosevelt came to office, the nation's economic institutions were shattered; the banking system had crumbled, business confidence had collapsed. FDR was convinced that he had rescued the economic life of the country. But now that business interests were back on safe ground, they simply turned against him. Later, FDR would observe that the wealthy businessmen and industrialists were like the old gentleman saved from drowning who castigated his rescuer for not salvaging his silk hat.

Had FDR betrayed his own social and economic class, as many plutocrats had come to believe? "If by his class one means the whole policy-making, power-wielding stratum," remarked historian Richard Hofstadter, "it would be just as true to say that his class betrayed him." What was more, as a class they felt stung to have been displaced by a new elite—of intellectuals, visionaries, and brain trusters.

Historians trying to fathom the intensity of the conservative feeling against the New Deal gained some clues, in the 1950s and the 1980s, with the resurgence of conservatism as an expression of a profound and lasting American individualism—an unquenchable belief in individual liberty, protection against government. In the 1930s, critics of the New Deal had even defended child labor in the name of "rugged individualism." "The surest prescription for starting an American boy toward outstanding success," proposed the *Saturday Evening Post*, "is to let him go to work before he is fully grown."

Roosevelt, the supreme pragmatist, was fighting a full-blown ideology. The members of the Liberty League—many of the leading industrialists, financiers, and lawyers of the country—wanted nothing less than to destroy the New Deal in the name of laissez-faire economics.

But it was not all about money. Psychologists too were needed to explain the Liberty League and other conservative attacks on FDR. "I am convinced that the heart of their hatred is not economic," said one 1930s liberal. "The real source of the venom is that Rooseveltism challenged their feeling that they were superior people, occupying by right a privileged position in the world. I am convinced that a lot of them would even have backed many of his economic measures if they had been permitted to believe the laws represented the fulfillment of their responsibility as 'superior people.'"

In other words, the issue was not just businessmen's profits but also their psychological security—that is, their status and privilege, the freedom they had traditionally enjoyed to operate as they chose. Business was losing the power, real and symbolic, that it had enjoyed for decades, and hence was losing status. Financial and industrial leaders, as Walter Lipp-mann remarked in 1934, had "fallen from one of the highest positions of influence and power that they have ever occupied in our history to one of the lowest."

Recovery, the upper class was beginning to understand, would mean more than a healthy return to a strengthened status quo ante; it would mean real change. "Five negroes on my place in South Carolina refused work this spring," reported a stunned du Pont son-in-law; the men had found "easy jobs" with the government. What was more, "a cook on my house-boat at Fort Myers quit because the Government was paying him a dollar an hour as a painter." In their mansions, clubs, and commuter trains, members of the business elite were fuming. Their businesses would be doing pretty well if it weren't for *that man*. When someone said, "Well, let's hope somebody shoots him," all knew who the unnamed target was and agreed.

"Throughout the world, change is the order of the day," the president had declared. Later, he would remark that "the most serious threat to our institutions comes from those who refuse to face the need for change."

What was the hatred of the business elite for FDR if not a symptom of their resistance to change? Trying to hold on to old things and old ways, they cut themselves off from the changing mainstream, consoled if not revivified by their loathing of the scapegoat in the White House.

Before he took office, FDR had noted, "individual self-interest and group selfishness were paramount in public thinking. The general good was at a discount." Now the essence of the president's political agenda, as well as his moral mission, was to place the "general good"—and the interests of tens of millions of average Americans—back at center stage. When business leaders attending a meeting of the U.S. Chamber of Commerce attacked the New Deal, the president knew just how to respond. He lashed out at the speakers, noting that not one of them mentioned "the human side of the picture." A few people spoke in generalities, saying things like "We hate to see old people starve" and "We would not willingly throw people out of work." But such comments, FDR gibed, were "not exactly what you could call a constructive contribution." On the contrary, the chamber had a "one hundred percent record of opposition to things like factory inspection, excessive hours, child labor, old-age pensions, unemployment insurance," FDR wrote to a friend, adding that it was "year after year the same old story." Business leaders, one historian commented, had once been innovators; now they had become "sterile."

The loss of feelings of superiority and privilege in the business world had been confirmed by FDR's big win in the congressional races of fall 1934. But the battle lines were drawn. Business would now have to wait until 1936 to turn the tide.

Unfortunately for the conservatives who preferred, as Al Smith himself would write in an open letter to the New York Chamber of Commerce, "the leaders of the past" to the vast social experiments of "inexperienced young college professors," neither the U.S. Chamber of Commerce nor other business and banking organizations nor various conservative women's organizations nor the Liberty League made significant headway in organizing an effective opposition. The league's total membership climbed to only 75,000, even as it hurled reckless accusations at every New Deal program, labeling them "Fascist," "Socialist," "quackery," so many "monstrosities," and "calamitous blows" to the American way of life, so many steps toward tyranny and dictatorship. While defending "liberty," the American Liberty League had scorned equality, and that had constituted a fatal misreading of American history, American character, and the times themselves. One critic quipped that leaguers seemed to believe that the American Revolution had been "fought to make Long Island safe for polo players."

. . .

History is rarely neat and orderly. If it were, Roosevelt might have followed a more "logical" political course in 1934 and 1935. As fury mounted on the right, FDR might have been pushed by its blasts to the right of his centrist course. As hopes and expectations of the populace gave way to gusts of disillusion and anger, he might have been blown to the left. But FDR was not the puppet of ideological forces. Nor, as the political seascape darkened, did he act like a grand strategist who could command the storm. Rather, he would conciliate his challengers on the left and, if that failed, outlast them.

It was a measure of Roosevelt's remarkable outreach to other national leaders that he not only knew—but had friendly relations with and even made use of—both the Detroit radio priest Father Charles Coughlin and the former governor of Louisiana and U.S. senator since 1930 Huey Long, before they gained notoriety. After his pivotal role—as Long viewed it— of helping FDR win nomination in Chicago, the "Kingfish" exploited his access to the new president. When Long strode into the Oval Office, displaying a belligerent mood and keeping his straw hat on to prove it, removing it only to emphasize points by rapping the president's knee with it, Roosevelt responded with jocular pleasantries. But behind the president's banter was a growing determination to jettison him. This could most readily be done by sending Morgenthau's treasury agents into Louisiana to check on Long's casual approach to paying income taxes.

By 1935, after Long had given the New Deal some needed Senate support but was beginning to waver, the rupture between the two politicians was complete. Always an observant cynic, Long had begun to see through FDR's genial mask to the shrewd manipulative mind behind it. Roosevelt was like a scrootch owl, he had said earlier, slipping into the roost and gently "scrootching up" to the hen. "And the hen just falls in love with him, and the first thing you know, *there ain't no hen.*" Truculently, Long made it known that he would not be devoured by the New Deal.

Coughlin's early relationship with Roosevelt was even more bizarre than Long's. The priest had attached himself to the rising political fortunes of FDR, who in turn respected the potential power of Coughlin's radio audience and Coughlin's power over it. During 1933, Coughlin's praise of the New Deal was so lavish as to be almost embarrassing. "The New Deal is Christ's deal!" he intoned, while its foes uttered "damnable lies." At times, referring to FDR as "the Boss," he appeared almost to consider himself a member of the presidential circle. The White House continued to be unfailingly polite.

The president used charm and bonhomie with other leaders. In 1934 the old-time socialist and muckraker Upton Sinclair had decided to run for the Democratic nomination for governor of California on his EPIC program—End Poverty in California—which had won the backing of hundreds of thousands of people, including, to a certain extent, Eleanor Roosevelt. Receiving Sinclair at Hyde Park, FDR regaled him with stories, told him implausibly that his mother had read Sinclair's great opus, *The Jungle,* at breakfast, and declared himself in favor of Sinclair's plan of "production for use." Later, FDR refused to lift a hand for the Democratic nominee, while administration operatives, after trying in vain to persuade Sinclair to withdraw, perhaps made some kind of deal with Sinclair's Republican opponent, Frank F. Merriam, who retained the governorship.

As Long, Coughlin & Co. moved "left" in 1934, taking strongly populist stances on inflation, bank regulation, and related issues, their positions became too distanced from FDR's to be bridged by ancient presidential weapons of blarney, bludgeon, and boodle. Populist pressures were immensely enhanced by a man who had never met FDR, Dr. Francis E. Townsend. No large group in America had been hit harder by the Depression than the elderly, and few Americans had had more experience with their plight than this Californian, who had practiced medicine for years in the Black Hills and then in Long Beach. Late in 1933, Townsend concocted a scheme to give everyone over sixty a federal pension of $150 a month, provided they spent the money as they got it. This proviso hardly put a damper on the enthusiasm of his followers, who were only too eager to spend that kind of money—later upped to $200—to break out of their cycle of poverty.

The Townsend movement spread like a tidal wave through the West and then across most of the country, taking on millennarian and revivalist tones as Townsendites evoked the name of the Lord as well as His blessing.

If populist demagogues saw Roosevelt as increasingly standoffish, ungrateful, and hostile, progressive leaders found him more and more wily, opportunistic, and centrist. And if FDR found his old populist friends increasingly antagonistic and inflammatory, he saw some of his progressive allies as more and more self-righteous, individualistic, and independent. But he nurtured his friendly personal relationships with most progressives, especially with old supporters in the Senate like Wheeler, La Follette, and—always—Norris. To all he offered a politician's handshake along with a slight aristocratic distance.

For a time during the spring of 1935, FDR did not seem unduly disturbed by the "rupture on his left." He knew Long and Coughlin well enough, he felt, to doubt that they and the others could ever "lie in bed politically together." The president was coasting toward election year; only then would he try for "a new stimulation of united American action." Thus he would outwait Long and Coughlin. But would they outwait him?

Suddenly a hard gust from starboard stimulated action, but not the "united" one FDR sought. On May 27, 1935, the Supreme Court cut the heart out of NRA on the grounds of excessive delegation of power and overextension of the commerce clause. The decision came in the case of *Schecter v. United States,* the "sick chicken case," in which the Schechter brothers, in the business of selling diseased poultry below market price, successfully challenged NRA codes.

The right cheered; the left deplored, except for the demagogic left—"I raise my hand in reverence," exulted Huey Long, "to the Supreme Court that saved this nation from fascism." Four days after the decision, the president delivered his dissenting opinion at a press conference. While Eleanor Roosevelt sat listening, he preserved an icy affability as he quoted from piteous letters from the populace. He concentrated on the Court's narrow view of the commerce clause. It contradicted the economic interdependence of the nation, he said, adding—in a phrase promptly headlined in the press—that the High Court had turned back the Constitution to the "horse-and-buggy" days. As calmly and authoritatively as any justice behind the bench, the president spelled out his dissent for almost an hour and a half.

Behind the mask he felt chagrined and, even more, challenged. Although justices Brandeis and Cardozo had joined a unanimous Court, to FDR this was the Liberty League majority of the Court reflecting Hoover ideas after Hoover's rejection by the electorate. The decision hurt; it knocked the props out of his partnership with business. It knocked the guts out of the NRA itself: its price and wage stabilization, economic stimulation, child labor reform, and Section 7(a), assuring labor the rights to organize and bargain. It portended further judicial rebuffs to the New Deal. Still, FDR always came back to the personal aspect. So he had "deserted his class," as the conservatives claimed. Well, his class had deserted him.

. . .

Nothing stimulated FDR more than opposition, especially from the right. A week after the Court's beheading of the NRA, he sent to congressional leaders a list of nine bills, "things that I must get this session from the Congress." Thus began the Second Hundred Days.

He seemed almost a "new Roosevelt." After the "low-key interlude" earlier in the year, he threw himself into the legislative struggle. Administration contact men ranged amid the legislative rank and file, telling them as well as the leaders that certain bills *must* be passed. When they reported a balking congressman to the president, his big hand would move instantly to the telephone, and within moments he would be coaxing or pressuring or bargaining with the recalcitrant. Working until late at night, he and his aides, coordinating closely with friendly leaders on the Hill, stayed one or two jumps ahead of the opposition. Laboring in the stifling summer heat, FDR and Congress worked in a creative partnership.

July 5: The National Labor Relations Act. The product of a long struggle by Senator Robert Wagner and other Democrats, the act assured "employees the right of collective bargaining" and provided means for determining who was entitled to protect employees. Section 7(a) was reborn, soon to become more significant and more controversial than ever.

August 14: The Social Security Act. Long in the shaping, the measure "gives at least some protection," FDR said on signing, "to thirty million of our citizens who will reap direct benefits through unemployment compensation, through old-age pensions, and through increased services for the protection of children and the prevention of ill health." This landmark legislation, one of FDR's most enduring and transforming legacies, represented the very height of Roosevelt's ideas—the pooling of the interests of tens of millions of Americans into one vast program of mutual support.

August 24: The Banking Act of 1935. This concerned the organization of the Federal Reserve Board, the regulation of credit, and the reserve requirements of member banks. FDR had predicted a "knock-down and drag-out fight to get it through," and so it was. Opposition from bankers was expected, but even old Senator Carter Glass, father of the Federal Reserve System in Wilson's day, fought FDR's plan for "political control," as the Virginian dubbed it.

August 26: The Public Utility Holding Company Act. Aimed at curbing the power of huge utility holding companies over their operating subsidiaries, this act was guided through Congress by Wheeler, Rayburn, and Senator Alben Barkley.

August 31: The Revenue Act of 1935. Probably the most egalitarian of the measures, this act had been foreshadowed in mid-May when FDR shocked the business community by asserting that "great accumulations of wealth cannot be justified on the basis of personal and family security." He was taking up the same crusade that Cousin Ted had fought in 1906, 1907, and 1912, striking out at great fortunes. And, like Cousin Ted, he gave moral as well as economic reasons for his attack. After a sharp struggle, Congress hiked the rates for estate and gift taxes, raised the surtax rates for large incomes, laid a graduated tax on corporate income, and placed a special tax on corporations' undistributed earnings. This last provision aroused much anger in the corporate world. Heavier inheritance taxes were lost in the legislative labyrinth.

Perhaps the most important congressional action, at least in the short term, was the appropriation of $5 billion to establish the Works Progress Administration, designed to replace the sagging federal-state-local relief efforts with a huge national works program for jobless employables. At last FDR had reconsidered his commitment to a balanced budget and shaken off his economy fetish. Other bills and programs also gave the New Deal much greater range and depth: rural electrification, youth assistance, natural resource protection, farm credit, a motor carrier act, bituminous coal stabilization, a railroad retirement act. Thus the Second Hundred Days were but a part—though the central and key part—of the Second New Deal.

And budget director Lew Douglas resigned.

. . .

To explain Roosevelt's "lurch to the left" in 1935, some historians speculated that it was mainly due to his natural politician's desire to steal both the electricity and the electorate from Long and the others, and perhaps even to bring the populist leaders into his camp. If FDR harbored such hopes, he was soon disillusioned. Even though the Second New Deal — especially the big bills of the Second Hundred Days—brought many of the measures that populist leaders had long demanded, they did not appear to love FDR or the New Deal any more. Rather, their denunciations of the president became more and more shrill. It became abundantly clear that their aim was not to broaden or liberalize the New Deal but to displace it—and to replace its leader.

People were still thronging to hear the populists speechify. Huey Long was attracting huge crowds by the early months of 1935: 16,000 in Philadelphia, 5,000 in Columbia, South Carolina, more thousands in Pittsburgh, Nashville, Oklahoma City, the West. Crowds loved him for his antiestablishment antics, his bravado talk, his bizarre costumes—white flannels, pink necktie, and orange kerchief on one occasion in the Senate. He was aimin' to be president, he boasted. Why, he'd already written his presidential memoirs, *My First Days in the White House*. He'd run in 1936 as a third-party candidate, ensuring a Republican victory, and then run in 1940 as a Democrat. He had it all planned out.

Strutting around the Senate floor, he taunted his colleagues, lambasted the rich and the powerful by name, philosophized—he read Plato, he claimed—and filibustered. In June 1935, he filibustered for more than fifteen hours against an extension of the National Recovery Act—which he labeled variously as the "National Racketeers' Arrangement" and "Nuts Running America"—and in August another of his filibusters killed a supplementary appropriations bill for Social Security. He kept his base in Louisiana, establishing a virtual dictatorship there, in the heart of what Sherwood Anderson called the "beaten, ignorant, Bible-ridden, white South"—the Louisiana that Robert Penn Warren would illuminate in his memorable novel about Huey, *All the King's Men*—and was backing Share Our Wealth clubs across the country.

It was this movement, not Huey's antics, that worried the New Dealers. To call Long's bluff about his huge membership, Farley commissioned a secret public opinion poll. The results, even if unscientific, aroused trepidation; in a hypothetical presidential contest in the spring of 1935, Roosevelt won 54 percent of the total vote, an unnamed Republican candidate 30 percent—and Long 11 percent. In a real election, Farley concluded, the Kingfish could receive perhaps six million votes—enough to give him the balance of power in 1936.

But Long's message was as challenging as the movement. Behind all the antics was a consistent populist manifesto—yes, share the wealth. In Louisiana he single-handedly abolished the poll tax, hiked levies on business, spared the poor from the general property tax. As his national followership expanded, he called for a capital levy that would cut all fortunes down to around $3 million, and he would give every American family a start-up "homestead allowance" of at least $5,000 and then $2,000 a year, with pensions for everyone over sixty.

"Ev'ry man a king, ev'ry man a king," was now the war song of the Share Our Wealth clubs, with every man a millionaire.

. . .

For Father Coughlin the populist word was "equality." Late in 1934 he had announced the formation of his National Union for Social Justice. It offered a kind of populistic socialism: nationalization of oil, power, and natural resources; protection of organized labor; the annual wage; and radical monetary policies. For a while it was on again and off again with his old friend FDR. He applauded Roosevelt's plans for social security; "I believe in him as much as ever," he proclaimed. But soon he was denouncing the New Deal for out-Hoovering Hoover; he would not support a New Deal, he said, that "protects plutocrats and comforts Communists."

He was oddly inconsistent, wanting to nationalize utilities but opposing nationalization in general, demanding labor protection but through the Department of Labor rather than trade unions, broadening the tax base but lifting the burden from workers, attacking bankers by name, but increasingly they appeared to be Jewish bankers. He was consistent only as a purveyor of hate—against money lenders, advocates of birth control, internationalists, New Dealers, and of course Communists. Increasingly his silvery voice turned hard and impassioned as he denounced the Jews and above all Roosevelt—or was it Rosenfeld? Letters by the tens of thousands and dollars by the millions continued to pour into his busy offices at the parish in Royal Oak, a Detroit suburb.

The president was wrong in thinking that his populist rivals could not get along together. While they personally disliked one another as they competed for supporters, they threw many a bouquet at the rival camps. Roosevelt still had little fear that this crazy-quilt combination of radicals, along with their allies Dr. Townsend, Milo Reno, head of the Farmers' Holiday Association, and others, could put together a winning combination for 1936. The populists puzzled him more than they frightened him. Still of a pragmatic temper, he could not understand these doctrinaire programs, these strident voices, these purveyors of hate. And if he could not understand them intellectually, could he master them politically?

Alone at the helm, FDR was pursuing his kind of leadership: resourceful, opportunistic, "pragmatic," shifting dexterously from port to starboard and back, from liberal to centrist and back, from party leader to "president of all the people" and back, from chief budget balancer to big spender and back. He was consistent only in the Theodore Roosevelt tradition: a chief executive who also dominated Congress and his party. He was keeping afloat, but, some asked, was a more consistent course needed to reach the distant shore?

2
Followers as Leaders

While Roosevelt was dueling with Long and Coughlin and the others on the national stage, tens of millions of Americans at the grass roots and on cobblestone streets were still experiencing feelings of hope and expectation, frustration and despair, disappointment and anger. They were looking toward the president's rivals. Some people felt FDR was now a disappointment; they were listening intently to the messages of Father Coughlin and Huey Long.

As the nation's leaders competed for support from voters, the populace was not passive or inert. The rivals' overtures, however exaggerated or fraudulent, elevated the followers, empowered them. They felt *needed*, and they had choices. Even more, some were doing their own leading. They were talking to friends, writing to the newspapers, arguing in bars and over backyard fences, attending rallies—or boycotting them. They were leading with their feet.

Long could boast about his thousands of Share Our Wealth clubs, and he could run ads in local papers urging the "People of America" to get together to organize them, but it was local leaders who took the initiative, persuaded their friends and neighbors to meet, and oversaw election of local officers. Coughlin could organize local chapters and attempt to control them, but many chapters took on a life and direction of their own. Dr. Townsend could claim many thousands of Old Age Pension clubs, but when 12,000 of the elderly representing five thousand of these clubs met in Chicago late in 1935, the convention appeared to favor a third-party strategy that Dr. Townsend opposed.

Other protesting groups also struck out on their own. Galvanized by NRA's Section 7(a) and later by the Wagner Act, rank-and-file workers staged their own mass meetings, sent word that they wanted to be organized, or just organized themselves. Locals mushroomed. "You name the mill town," said a labor journalist, "and there was a local there," with names like the "Blue Eagle" or the "New Deal" local—even an "FDR" Local. Membership in the big national unions doubled, tripled, quadrupled. The new mass memberships burst through the old craft union boundaries of the American Federation of Labor and converted organizing committees into new union structures.

Farmers so embittered that they had dumped milk and burned crops in earlier years had mixed feelings about New Deal agricultural policies by 1934. But now they had another outlet—voting at their own "grain roots." In the spring of 1935 half a million farmers, participating in a referendum on whether to continue the wheat adjustment program of the AAA, balloted in favor by almost seven to one; hog raisers voted six to one to keep their program. Yet there was still discontent; many farmers, according to historian Donald McCoy, participated in the AAA "to get their share of what they felt were its dubious benefits." Still, voting could give farmers a heady feeling of telling their leaders what to do or not to do.

College and high school students, most of them voteless, were finding their own ways to protest: conventions, demonstrations, and "strikes." Young Communists and Socialists took over the American Youth Congress in 1934 to convert it into an anti–New Deal propaganda agency. Led by members of the Young Communist League and the Young People's Socialist League, the youthful militants attacked the Civilian Conservation Corps—composed of jobless members of their own generation—as "militaristic," the NRA as fascist, and other New Deal programs as inadequate at best. Their main posture was antiwar. In 1935 over one hundred thousand students walked out of their classrooms to "vote" in their own fashion—taking the Oxford Pledge not to back the government in any war it might declare.

Scraping through on parental support, tuition grants, and low-paid campus jobs, many students saw themselves as the lowest of the low, but they were not. The most desperate and demoralized persons—especially as they saw others gain WPA or private-industry jobs—were the continuing unemployed of 1934–35. They had no job to walk out of in protest, no classroom to desert. They could only protest with their feet and lungs—and late in 1934 over three hundred thousand did so in demonstrations in twenty or more states. They could also organize. Early in 1935, under the leadership of mainly socialist-led state federations, a Washington conference formed a "permanent nonpartisan federation" of the many organizations of the jobless that had sprung up locally, especially in eastern states. The new leadership of the conference was instructed to work with "unemployment councils" that had been formed largely by Communists.

. . .

In 1935 the followers were leading the leaders. The populace was telling the New Dealers that the reforms of the First Hundred Days were not enough, that the initial combination of reform, regulation, federal parsimony, and even experiments like the CCC and the TVA simply did not meet the huge and aching needs of tens of millions of Americans. They wanted things they could see and touch and embrace—pensions, WPA jobs, cheap electric power, higher wages through the right to organize, part-time jobs for students, help to small farmers, higher taxation of the rich in the hope it might mean lower taxes for the poor. The voters had warned the administration in the 1934 elections that they wanted more. Now they were insisting on more—and warning, too, that they could turn to other leaders.

For the White House it was a race against time, 1936 election time. By midsummer 1935 most of the "enduring" New Deal was in place—but how quickly would it respond to people's wants and needs? Some of the 1933 programs, such as benefits for the bigger farmers, had gotten under way quickly; others, such as Ickes's public works programs, were only now employing large numbers of construction workers. Harry Hopkins delighted the president by handing out WPA jobs with almost reckless speed. Other programs lagged but the laws had been passed and the money appropriated so that people could almost taste them in advance. By 1936, almost every major program that Townsend and Long, Coughlin and John L. Lewis had in effect called for, though in different sizes and forms, was in place, with varying degrees of impact.

The archpin of the second New Deal of course was social security—and the New Deal's main armament against the Townsend proposals, which would shift 40 percent of the national income to 9 percent of the people. The act was far more complex than Townsend's simple notion of "thirty dollars every Thursday" for the elderly and the jobless. The heart of the act was the creation of a national fund through taxes to pay retirees over sixty-five a modest monthly pension, the amount to depend on the number of working years during which the employee contributed. This was the federal program; the act also authorized grants to states to help them relieve the destitute blind and homeless and other deprived children, and it also set up a federal-state cooperative program of unemployment compensation, financed by taxes on payrolls. In 1939, the federal act was broadened to include domestic and agricultural workers (and hence more nonwhites and women) and also extended benefits to wives of living beneficiaries as well as to widows and children of deceased beneficiaries.

If the Social Security Act was a direct response to Townsend's battalions, the Revenue Act of 1935—"the Wealth Tax Act"—countered Long and Coughlin's demands for social justice, equality, and the leveling of income. FDR minced no words in calling for the measure, virtually echoing Cousin Theodore's denunciations of the "swollen fortunes" of the plutocrats; "Our revenue laws have operated in many ways to the unfair advantage of the few, and they have done little to prevent an unjust concentration of wealth and economic power." The act boosted the surtax on individual incomes over $50,000 and steeply graduated taxes on individual incomes above $1 million to a high of 75 percent on incomes over $5 million. Income taxes on small corporations were lowered, on larger corporations hiked.

But no program reached more to the heart of the New Deal than the Works Progress Administration, and no agency head exemplified the young New Deal leadership better than administrator Harry Hopkins, who delighted in accelerating the WPA so quickly that its employment shot up from around 200,000 in August 1935 to over 3 million six months later. The most dramatic and lasting aspect of the WPA was not simply the dollars spent and the jobless employed but its sheer scope and—strangely, for a program that was so often stigmatized as "make-work"—its lasting impact in many areas. Its projects ranged, according to historian Irving Bernstein, from "the construction of highways to the extermination of rats; from the building of stadiums to the stuffing of birds; from the improvement of airplane landing fields to the making of Braille books; from the building of over a million of the now famous privies to the playing of the world's great symphonies . . . from mosquito control to the serving of school lunches . . . sewing garments and rip-rapping levees . . . planting trees and planting oysters."

The story of the WPA was usually told in big figures—billions of dollars spent, 600,000 miles of roads built or repaired, tens of thousands of new bridges, several thousand new playgrounds and athletic fields and school buildings. But the real story was also written in the lives saved, the skills sharpened, the creative artists subsidized and sponsored. The theater and music and arts programs sustained run-of-the-mill artists and nurtured others who would become world famous. The Theater Project, under Hallie Flanagan, produced 924 plays for 20 million people; the Arts Project helped support Jackson Pollock, Willem de Kooning, Mark Rothko, Jacques Lipchitz, and others; the Music Project helped composers and subsidized concerts conducted by Arturo Toscanini and Igor Stravinsky; 5,300 artists in forty-four states were engaged to paint hundreds of murals. Murals, plays, guides, music scores, books, photographs, artworks—these would last forever.

The special needs of youth—and its political potential—were met by the National Youth Administration, a quasi-autonomous agency spawned by the WPA. Its main task was to provide financial help to young people from poor families in order to continue their schooling. While NYA provided the funds and set standards, schools and colleges carried out the programs at the local levels. The pay to the students was amazingly low—between $3 and $6 a *month* for high school students—but often decisive in keeping them in school and incidentally out of the job market.

The unsung heroines and heroes of the NYA and other agencies were federal employees, most of them earning less than $2,000 a year. Those employees—the "bureaucrats"—would not be remembered; they were too numerous, over thirty thousand in the WPA alone, and too anonymous. But these energetic, committed, often young workers made the difference.

The WPA—and, indeed, most of the great New Deal initiatives of 1935—provoked fierce media tempests. The newspapers played up the bungles, the "leaf-raking," the "boondoggles." The president paid little heed, and Harry Hopkins didn't give a damn. WPA workers, in a huge gang repairing a street with inadequate tools and little experience, stared with bewilderment at passing Buicks and Oldsmobiles filled with middle-class families who thumbed their noses and jeered at them. Doubtless the WPA workers wondered. They were *working*, not on the dole. Wasn't this what the rich wanted of them?

. . .

Some critics, whatever their positions on particular New Deal policies and programs, viewed Roosevelt's basic political and governmental strategy with alarm. For one thing, "interest-group democracy" treated the less organized groups unequally—notably farm laborers and sharecroppers—and left other groups completely out of its largesse. African-Americans shared relief and other benefits but suffered segregation and discrimination; they were denied the full benefits of NRA codes, admission to subsistence homesteads, and acceptance in training programs even of the "socialist" TVA. Critics attacked the whole philosophy and premise of "leadership by pressure group."

"Roosevelt is essentially a broker," wrote a journalist who was broadly favorable to his policies. "He has neither the will nor the power to move against the political currents of the day." Walter Lippmann, who had become disenchanted by both the president and his policies, likened New Deal programs to Louis XIV's protection of vested interests with the authority of the state. "Can the presidential system," asked Harvard political scientist Pendleton Herring in 1934, "continue as a game of touch-and-go between the Chief Executive and congressional blocs played by procedural dodges and with bread and circuses for forfeit?"

In part this was a fear that American government was changing into a jungle of competing agencies responding to a proliferation of factions—a fear that some of the founders had expressed a century and a half earlier. "Interest-group democracy," historian William Leuchtenburg aptly noted later, "had the tactical advantage of weakening opposition by incorporating potential opponents within the administration, but it also served to make the Roosevelt administration the prisoner of its own interest groups." The latter possibility raised the specter of a "broker state" that could become immobilized among the competing factions. What leadership, what device, what strategy could lift the New Deal out of such threatened *immobilisme*?

It was the first possibility—the co-option of protest groups by the administration—that most alarmed forces on the left. Radicals of all persuasions, Socialists, unionists, even Communists, could be enticed into the big New Deal circus tent by barkers' promises. Thus the protest activity of the jobless, which had begun with rent riots and street demonstrations during the Hoover years, shifted to national organizing in 1934 and 1935, with the creation of the Workers' Alliance of America, and then took the conventional form of lobbying and negotiating with governmental agencies in "bureaucratic minuets." The White House conceded relief recipients the right to organize—but not to strike.

The plight, as some saw it, of the Workers' Alliance epitomized the dilemma of a multitude of labor, left, and liberal grass-roots leaders during the early New Deal. Should they concentrate on an "economic" strategy and, if so, on militant street protest or strike action? Or should they stress political action and, if so, through "separatist" pressure groups and political parties, or should they play politics in the New Deal arena, in competition with other needful groups? Should they act politically within the two-party system—presumably within the Democratic party—or should they form a third party? Or should they reject party and electoral activity in favor of big protest movements—grass-roots action and cobblestone leadership?

Socialists, with their party that proudly and perennially presented Norman Thomas for president, and the largely Kremlin-dominated Communist functionaries, clung to third-party strategies. Both organizations had their counterparts in many countries around the world. Uniquely American, however, was the League for Independent Political Action, which was founded in 1929 to work for the formation of a new political party but never became more than a liberal/radical action group. With its roots in abolitionism and progressivism, LIPA gloried in its founding intellectuals: John Dewey as chairman, Paul H. Douglas of the University of Chicago as a vice chairman, *Nation* editor Oswald Garrison Villard as treasurer, Reinhold Niebuhr, Stuart Chase, and W. E. B. DuBois among its national committeemen. Calling in general for the democratization of industry and greater equalization of incomes, LIPA had proposed specific policies that anticipated much of the New Deal.

LIPA had come into its heyday during the Depression, when many deprived and depressed Americans accepted its radicalism. Its testing time came with the New Deal, which began to pass some of the liberal measures LIPA had advocated. After viewing Roosevelt's efforts skeptically for a year or so, and after forming a parallel organization, the Farmer-Labor Political Federation, LIPA began to denounce the New Deal at every turn.

Nothing "but failure can be expected from the New Deal," declared *Common Sense*, which had become virtually the LIPA house organ.

Where did John Dewey stand? Would not the great American pragmatist, the advocate of step-by-step, practical action, extol the efforts of Franklin Roosevelt, the Great Experimenter? Evidently not for long. "Experimental method is not just messing around or doing a little of this and a little of that in the hope that things will improve," Dewey wrote in 1935. What was needed now was "a coherent body of ideas, a theory that gives direction to effort," inclusively planned, cooperatively controlled, and socially directed action. New Deal tinkering, patching up, was hopelessly inadequate.

Pragmatism had been waylaid by its supreme advocate.

But if the ideas of Dewey and others were in transformation in 1935, so was much else in turmoil—radical groups, reform efforts, leadership itself. Perhaps not since the days of Theodore Roosevelt and of the muckrakers had there been such vitality and conflict and tumult in American intellectual and political life as in the days of the Second New Deal. In unions and in other organizations, leaders were overtaken and even engulfed by followers, who then became leaders. The New Deal administrators, once leaders, had become followers, and then, in the Second Hundred Days, leaders again. Some feared chaos, even anarchy, followed by dictatorship.

Amid these upheavals, amid these raucous battles between established and rising leaders, among rival leaders within groups, amid what seemed to be the dismemberment of America, was there any one leader who could rise above the tumult and stand for the whole nation, or for a majority of the populace, or at least for a party that occupied the executive and legislative branches? There was one man who might do so: Franklin D. Roosevelt, leader of the most inclusive organization, the Democratic party.

3
They Hate Roosevelt

With the Second Hundred Days climaxing in the August 1935 passage of the "radical" social security, tax, and reform measures, some observers expected that the country would settle down to a brief era of good feelings, at least until the start of the presidential campaign a year later. For a time Roosevelt encouraged these feelings. When newspaper publisher Roy Howard, head of the Scripps-Howard newspaper chain, wrote the president late in August that businessmen needed reassurance about future plans, FDR replied with soothing words. Now that the "basic program" had been passed, he wrote Howard, a "breathing spell" was under way.

Such a breather could not last long. In fact, animosity between Roosevelt and business was now so intense as to bar any lasting peace. In his letter to the president, Howard had minced no words. Many businessmen who had once backed FDR, he said, "are now, not merely hostile, they are frightened." They believed he had "fathered" a tax bill that aimed "at revenge rather than revenue—revenge on business." The break between Roosevelt and business, editorialized *Business Week*, "seems complete and permanent."

Many big businessmen not only feared Roosevelt, they hated him to a degree rarely seen in American history. They were used to differing with politicians, but often the politicians lacked power; they could be persuaded, negotiated with, offered genteel funding or even outright bribes. Roosevelt, in contrast, could not easily be persuaded and he had power—to regulate and tax and reform them.

And flay them. Like Cousin Ted, FDR possessed a bully pulpit, and like Cousin Ted, his target of choice was wealth.

In speech after speech, FDR lashed out at the plutocrats, often hammering away not just at excessive profits but at the "disturbing effects upon our national life that come from great inheritances of wealth and power." Such vast fortunes, he argued again and again, were "static" and "sterile," producing no "creative enterprise," bringing no benefits to society. His aim, he declared, was to encourage "a wider distribution of wealth."

"Mammon" had once ruled America, he thundered; he was not going to let the nation go back to those days.

FDR had put all his cards on the table. Members of the wealthy elite and upper class knew where he stood. Now they could give free rein to their burning hatred of the man from Hyde Park.

Even the son of Theodore Roosevelt chimed in. Repudiating his father's progressivism, Ted Jr. declared, at the 1935 Lincoln Day dinner of the National Republican Club, that the New Deal had "flouted the Constitution, emasculated Congress, assumed judicial powers, used the emergency legislation to break down important provisions of the Bill of Rights, and shaken the foundation of our liberty and democratic government." The young man, noted TR's old friend William Allen White, had taken to defending privilege, not democracy.

. . .

Hatred for Roosevelt signified more than rational opposition to his economic policies. It seemed to stem from the WASP establishment's horror of equality, from their fear of losing not only their privileges but, more important, their "sense" of privilege. It stemmed also from their belief in their own way of life. "If you destroy the leisure class," J. P. Morgan had warned a Senate committee, "you destroy civilization." As far as members of the upper class were concerned, FDR was threatening their very civilization. FDR's friend Cornelius Vanderbilt recalled that one society matron spent the entire summer of 1932 going from door to door, telling her friends that "society would snub Frank Roosevelt." It never dawned on her, commented Vanderbilt, "that the day 'Frank' Roosevelt was inaugurated, there would be nothing left of what she and hers had called society."

"Regardless of party and regardless of region," proclaimed *Time* magazine in April 1936, "today, with few exceptions, members of the so-called Upper Class frankly hate Roosevelt. . . . The cause of the active hatred," mused *Time,* "may be the ill-timed smile which accompanies his caustic criticism of the motives and morals of men who consider themselves upright citizens." But the origin of the hatred was more likely the talk of reform that had "deprived a class of U.S. citizens, who had some social security, of their feeling of security."

How to understand the incessant theme of Roosevelt hatred over dinner tables, at virtually every upper-class occasion? How to explain otherwise rational people seriously relating stories that the president was in fact insane, that the whole Roosevelt family was drunk most of the time, that White House visitors had heard FDR's strange, maniacal laughter? The loathing of Roosevelt could not be explained by New Deal policies alone, for as conditions for the wealthy 2 percent of the population improved, their extravagant, hysterical attacks on the president only increased. In truth, their morale, remarked former brain truster Adolf Berle, was "shattered"; they pitied themselves for their own "suffering" at the hands of the federal government and the president.

Why was Roosevelt so despised? "It would seem that we can forgive, or at least understand, an act of hostility from our enemy," one newspaperman explained, "but not from one of our own kind. Certainly if there is an aristocracy in the United States, the Roosevelts are of it," and so there could be "no forgiveness for their seeming disloyalty." He was a traitor to his class.

As *Time* had pointed out, not only had the president attacked the motives of the financial and industrial elite, assailing "a decade of debauch, of group selfishness," he had also battered the foundations of their self-esteem. Following in the footsteps of TR, FDR had exploded one of the most popular and deeply entrenched myths in America; he had dissociated the concept of wealth from the concept of virtue. Not only did he refuse to portray business leaders as virtuous men, he compared them to the fascist menace abroad. While countries dominated by "autocracy and aggression" threatened the United States from without, he charged that the nation was threatened by its own "resplendent economic autocracy" from within—economic autocrats who wanted nothing but "power for themselves, enslavement for the public."

Even as FDR was denouncing the plutocrats with what one historian termed "naked class appeal," he insisted that it was members of the upper class who were encouraging class antagonism, not he. *His* goal, he asserted, was to explode class distinctions and to place Hester Street and Park Avenue on an equal footing. "In the place of the palace of privilege we seek to build a temple out of faith and hope and charity." All Americans, he argued, whether farmers, industrial workers, or businesspeople, belonged "to the same class, for the simple reason that none of these occupations can survive without the survival of the others."

Looking back at centuries of American history, FDR discerned a clear pattern. "The underlying issue in every political crisis in our history," he explained, "has been between those who, laying emphasis on human rights, have sought to exercise the power of the Government for the many and those, on the other hand, who have sought to exercise the power of Government for the few." He would fight for "the many" and govern in the name of the sovereign people and the common good.

What the affluent members of the upper class could not understand, as they railed at the Benedict Arnold from the Hudson Valley, was that FDR had not betrayed the business and financial elite. How could he have betrayed that elite when he had never belonged to it? A member of the landed gentry that had lived in America for three centuries, he had been educated—by Cousin Ted as well as by Endicott Peabody—to believe that the noble, virtuous life was one of public service, not of maximizing profits. Roosevelt, not the wealthy businessmen and bankers, incarnated the values of the true American aristocracy. And those values had evolved from a belief in private charity and an aristocratic sense of noblesse oblige—the responsibility of the well-born to care for the less well off—to the conviction that only social legislation and government involvement could meet the needs of the people. But FDR's deep generosity and compassion, his simple decency and fairness, were apparently qualities that the plutocrats—clinging to their mantra of "rugged individualism"—could neither fathom nor embrace.

He was also a man of honor. In the opinion of brain truster Rex Tugwell, he always remained faithful to a "code of behavior" of honor and trust that had become an anomaly in the business world, replaced by double-dealing, fraud, blackmail, and cynical slogans like "business is business." When businessmen who paid lip service to the accepted "code" were exposed by Roosevelt as the violators of that code, "their indignation knew no bounds." According to Tugwell, they "hated and feared the reformer who wanted to improve their morals."

FDR had always enjoyed cruises on Vincent Astor's yacht *Nourmahal* in the company of men of his own social class and hugely wealthy Republicans; he had even been dubbed the "Knight of the *Nourmahal*" by Huey Long. Now he confessed that he was hurt by the attacks and comments of people of his own class. "I wish you could have heard the dinner conversations in some of the best houses in Newport," he wrote to a friend. And to an old Harvard classmate he confided, "Because of what I felt to be a very old and real friendship these remarks hurt."

Hurt feelings? FDR admitted that it was he who had "invited battle." "We have *earned* the hatred of entrenched greed," he would tell Congress. In attacking the plutocrats, he seemed as electric and aggressive as a boxer in the ring. When his press secretary, Steve Early, sent him a *New Yorker* cartoon showing a well-dressed upper-class Park Avenue couple calling to their friends inside an elegant private club, "Come along, we're going to the Trans-Lux to hiss Roosevelt," FDR's smiling response was "Grand."

There could be no progress, Franklin always believed, without conflict. "About a week ago I saw a very remarkable film," he told one audience, "a picture of the life of Louis Pasteur." He was especially impressed by the words of English chemist Joseph Lister. When people denounced Pasteur as a charlatan, Lister had said to his friend, "My dear Pasteur, every great benefit to the human race in every field of its activity has been bitterly fought in every stage leading up to its final acceptance." That was true, FDR observed, not only of science but of labor, business, and industry and "true of politics."

As for his hurt feelings, they could have been caused by remarks and actions of his own children. His son Elliott used his Texas radio stations to support the investigations of his mother's friends in the American Youth Congress conducted by the House Committee on "Un-American Activities" and to speak out against American interventionism in Europe and a third term for his father.

In June 1937, Franklin Jr. would marry Ethel du Pont, whose family was the financial backer of the Liberty League. With a few exceptions the du Pont family was packed with Roosevelt haters, and the president must have savored the irony of it, since at the wedding he had Harry Hopkins in tow. But the Roosevelts had tried to rise above politics and enjoy the du Ponts' festivities in Delaware. "The church was beautiful but the house—well, for a variety of reasons I found it a bit hard to swallow," admitted Eleanor to Lorena Hickok, adding that she "ran away for about an hour. . . . Well, it's over and the future will be what it will be."

FDR would never know that his youngest son, John, would become a Republican in 1952 and would spend his last years in the gated and guarded enclave of New York wealth called Tuxedo Park, choosing to live among people who had been railing hysterically against the class traitors TR and FDR for decades.

While remaining loyal to his children, FDR responded with anger and sarcasm to other attacks on him, scornfully dismissing the "values" of his wealthy critics and adversaries, sneering at the "gentlemen in well-warmed and well-stocked clubs" who claimed to be suffering "because their Government is spending money for work relief." These "gentlemen," he scoffed, knew nothing about the "battle-line of human necessity." He was especially contemptuous of those who felt that the government was depriving them of their "liberty." "I am not for a return to that definition of liberty," he held, "under which for many years a free people were being gradually regimented into the service of the privileged few."

Although the knee-jerk plutocrats loathed FDR, a few perspicacious patricians and multimillionaires joined forces with the New Deal: Averill Harriman, the son of the "czar" of the Union Pacific, became New York's National Recovery Administration chairman; Francis Biddle of Groton and Harvard headed the National Labor Relations Board; John Gilbert Winant joined the administration of the Social Security program; Henry Morgenthau, whose family had extensive Manhattan real estate holdings, served as secretary of the treasury; George Dern, whose family possessed mines in Utah, became secretary of war; William C. Bullitt, of the Pennsylvania Bullitt fortune, served as ambassador to France.

Still, the press joined in whipping up anti-Roosevelt hatred and hysteria. The entire Hearst publishing empire launched a full-scale assault against Roosevelt, intent on demonstrating Roosevelt's Communist plot to overthrow the U.S. government. The headlines screamed: MOSCOW BACKS ROOSEVELT and THE ENEMIES OF AMERICA WANT ROOSEVELT. Roosevelt was a "blood-brother of Lenin," wrote the sour journalist H. L. Mencken, who had complained in 1934 that New Deal programs were inane charity for the "congenitally worthless and unemployable." "Your goddamn university, Harvard," Mencken told a friend, "will have a lot to answer for to history for the Roosevelts." He branded FDR "the synthesis of all the liars, scoundrels, and cheapskates of mankind. If I were you," Mencken counseled, "I'd hand back my diploma."

The patrician FDR offered something to everyone. While some people hated him for betraying his class, others hated him simply because he belonged to that class. They accused him of having been born with a "silver spoon" in his mouth, his every wish granted; he knew nothing of real work, they claimed, for he spent all his time either vacationing or planning his next vacation. "You cannot take men," exclaimed one congressman, "who have inherited things from their forefathers, who do not know the value of a dollar, and have them run a great country like the United States." And to the pathological anti-Semitic crowd, FDR also offered something: a target for their hatred and paranoia. They raged that Roosevelt was Jewish on both sides of his family, that he was packing the administration with Jews, and that he was foisting on Americans his "Jew Deal."

. . .

While they hated and feared Roosevelt, the industrialist class did not see—they could hardly imagine—that Roosevelt feared *them* because they too had power. They controlled the big newspaper chains; they sought to wield influence over their employees, especially in the voting booth; they largely funded the Republican opposition; and, most galling to the president, their mentality dominated most of the members of the Supreme Court. The High Court *did* have power, as demonstrated by its judicial veto of progressive legislation. And with FDR too, fear led directly to anger.

Fears were not limited to the leaders on Wall Street and in the White House. Strangely, with the major New Deal measures in place and with rising employment in the wake of increased spending, millions of Americans were still frightened. Large numbers remained jobless; many were still

ill-paid and ill-housed. Many were still enthusiastic about the New Deal and its further promise; others were bitter. Many were still charging late in 1935 that the New Deal had not gone far or fast enough.

Letters were still pouring into the White House. The recovery still was making "the rich richer and the poor largely hopeless," wrote a Pennsylvania Republican who had voted for FDR in 1932. "You have not kept the faith," wrote a Delaware farmer. Others accused him of moving too fast and forcefully. One critic expressed it all in his salutation: "Dear Dictator Delano."

What was happening across the American political seascape? Roosevelt could see gathering storm clouds. Long and Coughlin were preparing for a showdown in 1936. Al Smith was leading an open and much publicized breakaway from FDR and the New Deal Democratic party. Farmers were as restless as ever, business-labor relationships more hostile than ever. With his great intuitive powers, FDR must have understood the fundamental forces at work: New Deal measures and partial recovery had only begun to satisfy the needy millions; revived hope had led to higher expectations, to a sharpened claim to entitlements, and now to heightened demands on him. The populace was taking the lead.

Would all the hate and fear simmering among Americans erupt in bloodshed? Labor and farm unrest had been limited and controllable, thanks especially to New Deal relief measures. But on September 8, violence exploded in the corridors of the Louisiana capitol, when a young doctor who hated Huey Long put a single fatal .32-caliber bullet into the Kingfish's stomach, then was gunned down by the senator's bodyguards.

So in September 1935, at the "height of the New Deal," FDR was not triumphant or exuberant; he was restless, irritable, and above all exhausted by the relentless pressures of negotiating with friend and foe on Capitol Hill. On a visit to Hyde Park, Walter Lippmann, who had grown ever more disenchanted with FDR, found him ill at ease, edgy, and lacking his usual buoyancy and self-assurance. Lippmann reported that when Eleanor joined them and spoke up on tax issues the two men were discussing, her husband said, "Oh, Eleanor, shut up. You never understood these things anyway!" Months later the president confided to Morgenthau, "I was so tired that I would have enjoyed seeing you cry or would have gotten pleasure out of sticking pins into people and hurting them."

It did not help matters that the Gallup poll—whatever its primitive techniques—reported that the president's support was down to about

50 percent, the lowest since inauguration. FDR read some of the critical letters still coming in; the editorials from a host of newspapers were more and more scathing as the election neared.

As Roosevelt was deploring violence at home, war clouds were thickening across the Atlantic. Hitler was expanding his army with unexpected rapidity and with predictable implications. And in May 1935, while FDR was heading into his Second Hundred Days of domestic policy, Mussolini launched a major attack on Ethiopia. The president wanted Congress to empower him to embargo arms against one or all belligerents in future wars, but key senators and representatives balked. For isolationists, this could be the road to war. The administration negotiated a compromise that prohibited all arms shipments—to aggressor and aggressee alike—but only for six months. This at least enabled the president to cut off arms to both nations without harming the Ethiopians, who could not import them through Italian-controlled ports anyway. But the six-month expiration meant that the whole issue would come up again in the early weeks of campaign year 1936.

. . .

Rising fear and anger at home, mounting violence abroad: September was indeed a somber time for FDR and New Deal supporters. Foreign policy presented no political dilemma for the president; he would campaign on a keep-out-of-war platform, as Woodrow Wilson had done twenty years before. But what strategy on domestic promises and policies? Powerful voices in the Democratic party, in the press, in the electorate, and even close to the administration—most notably Ray Moley—were urging him to move to the right, at least to the center. But then there was the populace—the millions who had voted for him and for a "new deal," the millions sticking with him, the millions still waiting for a real new deal.

More than ever, FDR felt the need to renew his connections with that populace face-to-face, to get away from Washington and find some kind of perspective, to try out some old and new themes of an almost philosophical character. Late in September his train pulled out of Union Station with a large presidential entourage on board—Eleanor Roosevelt, Missy LeHand, and Grace Tully; White House aides; the feuding Harry Hopkins and Harold Ickes—but sadly not including the longtime politico-in-chief, Louis Howe, so ill that he had been moved in August to the naval hospital, where he carried on his wily politicking. It was an ill-disguised campaign trip, coming to a climax in Los Angeles with a fifty-mile tour of the city. For the president it was a time to celebrate the New Deal and revitalize its goals.

In Fremont, Nebraska, he reminded farmers that he had never promised them a paradise, only to battle an intolerable situation "in every way that human effort and human ingenuity could devise." At the dedication of Boulder Dam, with Ickes standing happily next to him, FDR had the supreme satisfaction of celebrating the completion of "the greatest dam in the world," creating the largest artificial lake, 115 miles long. He stressed the national benefits of the project. In Los Angeles he reminded Californians that democracy "is not a static thing. It is an ever-lasting march." In San Diego, he said that the country could "summon our intelligence" to meet "the two most menacing clouds that hang over human government and human society . . . 'Malice Domestic and Fierce Foreign War.'" And he had two more supreme satisfactions: reviewing the fleet as commander in chief and embarking on a long ocean fishing trip, with Ickes and Hopkins —now less quarrelsome—still in tow.

During the last three months of 1935, in the wake of the strenuous congressional session, Franklin Roosevelt had time to ponder his strategic dilemma and his opportunities. Just how he did this we do not know, as he gave little indication, in public announcements or private correspondence, as to where he was heading. We know what he did *not* do: FDR was not one for laying out political flow charts, listing grand alternatives on index paper, or setting up priorities. More likely he mused from day to day, keeping his eye on mail and press comment and most of all remembering— remembering that it was the bold presidents who were the historically acclaimed leaders, that great leadership had responded to popular expectations and demands, that out of the chaos of public opinion great presidents had distilled the true temper of the populace.

He was aware, historically, of the pitfalls too. Cousin Ted had moved beyond the Republican party as he mapped the political tempests of 1912, then had broken with the GOP and spent years in the political wilderness. Woodrow Wilson had stuck with his party and with his ideals, only to see both lose out in the 1920 election. Abraham Lincoln had compromised over divisive slavery issues during his first two years in office, mainly to placate the border states, and then struck boldly with his Emancipation Proclamation.

History was only a suggestive guide, not a sure one. Above all, FDR had to face current political realities as well as possibilities. To the degree he had followed a grand strategy during his first two years, it was one of consensus, bipartisanship, of trying to placate all major groups and classes through the NRA and other programs, of mediating among interests right and left. The formula appeared to have worked, at least as measured by the 1934 congressional elections. Why change a winning game? He could move toward the center, pull some conservative Democrats back into the fold, hold his moderate Republican support, but still keep far enough left to preempt major threats from Townsend and Coughlin supporters as well as the followers of Huey Long, who were still mourning the loss of their hero. It was even possible, historian Frank Freidel surmised, that just as Theodore Roosevelt had used the fear of socialism to gain railroad legislation, FDR could capitalize upon fear of Long & Co. to bolster his program.

All this FDR could calculate, and did. But there were more fundamental factors at work, forces of ideology and emotion. He was still trying to hammer out a New Deal program that had not yet taken full shape; it must be both defended and expanded. And his feelings toward the opposition were hardening, moving from tolerance to irritation to anger and now to hate—hate spurred by fear that the combined opposition of money and media, the Republican party, and a conservative judiciary really might be able to bring the New Deal to a halt.

If it was partly hate of an uncompromising opposition that pushed him to the left, it was also Eleanor and those who loved him who were pulling him in that same direction. It became evident in polls that he was loved not simply as a charismatic leader but for his New Deal programs. Polls measuring explicit attitudes toward specific policies found Americans "voting" by huge majorities for social security, the WPA and other works programs, the TVA, and other supposedly controversial measures. Roosevelt sensed this from his private polling, from letters, and from his own special barometers for sensing the political winds. Americans who had been initially so enthusiastic for him, then disillusioned, were now feeling and tasting the New Deal. Increasingly educated by experience and observation, they were forming a powerful current that would steady the administration in a leftward course. The followers, more than ever, were becoming the leaders.

By Christmastime 1935, the president had set his course. And he had decided how to dramatize it—in his annual address to Congress, which, he insisted, should be delivered before the legislators in the evening, so he would have a maximum radio audience.

. . .

In a packed House chamber, amid wild cheers from the Democratic side, Roosevelt began his talk with conventional remarks—about power-seeking autocrats abroad threatening the peace of the world—and then shifted so adroitly to the "power-seeking minority" at home that his listeners hardly knew when the campaign talk began. Soon Democrats were applauding and Republicans sitting in stony silence, while the president, emblazoned by klieg lights and fronted by twenty-six microphones, threw out one challenge after another.

"In March 1933, I appealed to the Congress of the United States and the people of the United States in a new effort to restore power to those to whom it rightfully belonged." Now he had "returned the control of the Federal Government to the City of Washington."

In doing so, he had "invited battle." It had been necessary to drive "unscrupulous money changers" and incompetent "rulers of the exchanges" out of power. They had admitted their own failure and had abdicated.

"Abdicated? Yes, in 1933, but now with the passing of danger they forget their damaging admissions."

The president was delivering blow after blow.

"They seek the restoration of their selfish power. . . .

"They steal the livery of great national constitutional ideals to serve discredited special interests. . . . They engage in vast propaganda to spread fear and discord among the people—they would 'gang up' against the people's liberties. . . .

"Autocrats in smaller things, they seek autocracy in bigger things. . . . Give them their way and they will take the course of every autocracy of the past—power for themselves, enslavement for the public.

"Their weapon is the weapon of fear. I have said, 'The only thing we have to fear is fear itself.' That is as true today as it was in 1933. But such fear as they instill today is not a natural fear, a normal fear; it is a synthetic, manufactured, poisonous fear."

Having thrown down the gauntlet, FDR could hardly have been surprised that it would be picked up—and it was, by his old ally-turned-enemy, Al Smith. Decked out in white tie and tails, Al was the keynote speaker at a Liberty League dinner at the Mayflower Hotel in Washington. It was "the largest collection of millionaires ever assembled under the same roof," a reporter noted—though it reminded people of another millionaires' dinner, fifty years earlier at Delmonico's, when visiting British

Social Darwinist Herbert Spencer had instructed the upper class in the ethos of individualism and success.

The former governor of New York, introduced to the two thousand Liberty League diners as "Al Smith of America," lashed out for nearly an hour at the New Deal. In a voice full of New York street, he accused the New Deal of subverting the Constitution, violating states' rights, and squandering the taxpayers' money. Ironically, the man who had grown up in the tenements of the Lower East Side—and who now identified with the interests of America's wealthiest men—warned that the New Deal was fomenting class warfare. He wisecracked that if the young brain trusters wanted to "disguise themselves as Norman Thomas, or Karl Marx, or Lenin," it was all right with Al, but he would never allow them "to march under the banner of Jefferson, Jackson, or Cleveland."

Fairly standard anti–New Deal oratory it was, with a special sardonic twist from the 1928 Democratic standard-bearer. But Smith was not content with the resounding guffaws he won from his listeners. He evoked the red menace. There can be only one capital, he cried, Washington or Moscow, only one choice, between the "pure air of America" and "the foul breath of communistic Russia," between the "stars and stripes" and "the red flag of the godless Soviets."

Interestingly, the former mayor of New York, Jimmy Walker, returned from self-exile in Europe, now came out against his old mentor, Al Smith, and to the defense of Roosevelt, the man who had presided over his corruption hearing in 1932. "President Roosevelt has become the symbol of liberalism as opposed to reaction," Walker announced. "I shall always be on the side of the masses against their oppressors."

But Al Smith's invective paled beside that of another Smith late in January. Eager to seize Huey Long's mantle and mailing list after Long's assassination in September 1935, Gerald L. K. Smith was seeking to wed the Share Our Wealth movement to Dr. Townsend's forces and to Father Coughlin's National Union for Social Justice. A fiery speaker and unscrupulous demagogue, descended from three generations of fundamentalist preachers, Smith had been invited by Eugene Talmadge, the governor of Georgia who was conducting his own trial run for the presidency, to speak at Talmadge's convention in Macon.

Roosevelt, cried Smith from the rostrum, was an atheist, a cripple—and a Communist. He was "rapidly becoming the most despised president in the history of the country. He gave us the Russian primer and cursed the Bible. . . . He and his gang are in the death rattle." When this "minister of hate" called on his audience to pray for the defeat of the Roosevelt administration, according to historian Glen Jeansonne, everyone "dropped to the ground and prayed audibly."

Eleanor Roosevelt was a special target. Each delegate received a copy of *Georgia Woman's World* displaying a photo of the first lady "going to some nigger meeting, with two escorts, niggers, on each arm." "Negroes" had been invited to eat and even sleep in the presidential mansion, the paper said. Eleanor Roosevelt was "that female Rasputin in the White House."

. . .

FDR did not respond to these attacks, not even to these vituperative insults to his wife—not yet. Indeed, after his bugle call to the nation in his address to Congress, he shifted to another role he enjoyed—president of all the people. He even gave a "nonpartisan" talk to a big Jackson Day dinner and to three thousand local Democratic dinners, via radio across the nation. Many of his talks during the winter of 1936 were more "educational" than political, as though he were seizing this last chance to explain the New Deal to the voters who soon would be passing on it. And he appeared, at this time of political testing, to look for the lessons of history, of the presidential leadership of the past, and especially of Theodore Roosevelt.

It was convenient that the Theodore Roosevelt Memorial was dedicated during these days. FDR rose to the occasion with a glowing tribute to his cousin as conservationist, peacemaker, and explorer, and above all as progressive. He noted TR's capacity to face up to the "vast and complicated mechanism" of industrialism and labor-capital relationships. And who would continue the Square Deal thirty years later? FDR answered by quoting from *Pilgrim's Progress:* "My sword I give to him that shall succeed me in my pilgrimage, and my courage and skill to him that can get it."

Republicans suspected that he was trying to filch one of *their* heroes. FDR, unchastened, continued to invoke TR's name, the denouncer of "malefactors of great wealth," of the "wealthy criminal class," and the "lunatic fringe." But FDR knew that American history was more than just the Roosevelt family. He contrived also to pay tribute in these months to Carrie Chapman Catt, Abraham Lincoln, the Daughters of the American Revolution, Sam Houston, Thomas Jefferson (three times), and Robert E. Lee.

Having urged the nation in earlier days to rise above interest-group politics, the president showed his usual mastery of the practice. He greeted or otherwise recognized the Ancient Order of Hibernians, stock cattlemen, and stamp collectors; presided at every politically rewarding dedication; and spoke at centennial occasions, battlefields, and at both drought- and flood-afflicted areas.

Yet the president now had a strategy that transcended interest-group politics. He planned to shape a grand coalition not only of interests but also of ideologies, regional leaders, and religious groups, comprising a spectrum of centrists, liberals, and radicals. This coalition would be based on those whom the New Deal boasted of helping: formerly jobless workers, distressed farmers, abused consumers, young people without hope, small businessmen narrowly escaping bankruptcy, and even big businessmen who had benefited from the New Deal or were personally close to the president. The common unifying enemy would be the "Hoover depression," which the Democrats would continue to flay even though Hoover had no chance of being nominated.

Thus the coalition would rest on the "politics of the deed"—the millions the New Deal had helped, or at least promised to help in the future. It would rest on three years of over $5 billion spent on work projects and related help and another $4 billion on public works: roads, dams, sewers, school buildings. It would be the visible, palpable, politics of the CCC, the WPA, the Home Owners Loan Corporation, the National Youth Administration, aid to farmers—and, above all, the expectation of early social security checks.

And who would be the unifying force in the grand coalition? "There's one issue in this campaign," the president told Moley. "It's myself, and people must be either for me or against me." Not only would FDR have to symbolize the new bipartisanship and national unity, he must personally attend to coalition-building and fence-mending. He soothed business leaders by hosting a long White House luncheon for members of Commerce Secretary Roper's Business Advisory Council and promised again cuts in spending; he asked Ickes to call in Norris, Johnson, and other liberal Republicans to mobilize progressive support; he held his hand out to labor leaders; he placated Democrats who feared that he was deserting the party organization in posing as president of all the people.

But FDR knew that this strategy called for more than old-fashioned, face-to-face fence-mending. He knew he must tap the huge reservoir of votes in the big religious, civic, and economic organizations that stretched across the nation. Together he and Howe set up a whole separate campaign organization with the virtuous title of the Good Neighbor League, the function of which was to solicit support from top leaders: religious leaders such as Rabbi Lazarus, labor leader George Harrison of the Railway Brotherhoods, civic leader George Foster Peabody, women's leaders such as Lillian Wald. This organization of the forces of piety, uplift, and feminism, decked out in the demure garments of nonpartisanship, became an energetic vote-getting machine actually financed by the Democratic National Committee.

Such was the grand coalition-in-the-making, designed almost exclusively for Roosevelt's own reelection. But another grand coalition was forming in opposition, one that in the spring of 1936 appeared to have an awesome potential.

. . .

Historians have ably recorded how a "people's coalition" rose in the spring and summer of 1936—how Gerald L. K. Smith nourished a passionate desire to realize Huey Long's dream of a third party that would win the presidency in 1936, or 1940 at the latest; how Coughlin fell in with the plan and hand-picked for president one William Lemke, a North Dakota congressman who had won the heart of the Detroit priest by denouncing Wall Street and fighting for federal refinancing of farm mortgages; how the Union party was launched with the cautious support also of Dr. Townsend, who judged all candidates by the intensity of their support for his $200-a-month pension plan.

But this history, too, has tended to be taught "from the top down"— all the more tempting because of the personalities of the "populist big three." Behind their show of unity, Coughlin and Smith distrusted each other, sought to steal the limelight, and competed mainly in demonstrating their hatred for FDR. Smith could hold huge audiences rapt for hours, and Coughlin was not above tearing off his clerical collar and coat to denounce "Franklin Double-crossing Roosevelt." Far less known in retrospect was the intensity of feeling aroused among many millions of Americans who were turning, almost desperately, to any leader who could respond to their needs, assuage their fears, and find scapegoats for their crushed hopes and expectations.

Since the annals of the poor are poor, the populace left few documentary records. But in every possible way they demonstrated in the spring and early summer of 1936 that countless millions of Americans were seeking some kind of political voice and vehicle. They showed this by participating in Democratic party primaries so actively as to help hundreds of Coughlin-endorsed candidates to win nominations in Ohio, Michigan, and several other states in the Midwest and in the East. They showed it by flooding into Smith and Coughlin rallies by the tens of thousands and listening to the perfervid oratory past midnight. They showed it by flocking from all over the country to attend conventions as delegates: more than 11,000 oldsters at the Townsend conclave, over 10,000 at Coughlin's rally of the National Union for Social Justice. And in a quite different manner they showed it when, given a choice between hearing Coughlin or the New York Philharmonic on the radio, they "voted" for the former 187,000 to 12,000.

Still, if this was the politics of blighted hopes, it was also the politics of paranoia. Not only did Coughlin & Co. play up the insecurities of the jobless and the poor, they played down to ancient fears of the unknown, of the alien, of foreign creeds and doctrines—to xenophobia and anti-Semitism. The lines were drawn, Coughlin wrote in his journal *Social Justice* in June—the "Roosevelt administration, on one hand, bent on communistic revolution: on the other, a public opinion progressively enlightened, as never before, on matters of monetary finance."

The weapon of fear was still a multidirectional weapon. It could be aimed from the right as well. With such respectables as Al Smith, now an establishment figure, denouncing the New Deal as communistic, it was easy for the Republican party to load up its big guns. But who would fire them? Early in 1936 the GOP staged its usual quadrennial battle between its own right and left, as moderate progressives such as William Borah jousted with hard-core conservatives for the presidential nomination. And as usual they were ready to agree on someone at the party center. By May they had a front-runner, Alf M. Landon, governor of Kansas, practical businessman and family man, who had just the qualities of common sense, cautious liberalism, and rocklike soundness that Republican leaders hoped would appeal to Americans tired of White House antics and heroics.

Middle class by every test, Landon had the guileless face, the rimless glasses, and the slightly graying hair that made him a lookalike for a million other middle-aged American men. Later it would become fashionable to jest about Landon, but he was no joke to the Democrats in June 1936. For one thing, the GOP convention, eyeing the great prize of the presidency and the obvious appeal of the New Deal to millions of low-income Americans, voted through a moderately liberal platform. And Landon had proved himself no stick-in-the-mud; in 1912 he had deserted the Old Guard for the Bull Moosers. Thus the president would be running against a man

who had supported Cousin Ted—whom FDR had deserted that year for
Woodrow Wilson.

4
"I Welcome Their Hatred"

By July the 1936 campaign for the presidency appeared to be in full swing.
During the spring the Prohibition party had convened in Niagara Falls
and chosen Dr. D. Leigh Colvin for president. The Socialists had gathered in Cleveland and once again picked Norman Thomas. The Communists had met in New York City and selected Earl Browder. The
Republican National Convention had assembled in Cleveland and nominated Landon, with Frank Knox, Chicago publisher and old-time Bull
Mooser, as his running mate.

Politically the most inconspicuous contender during these weeks was
FDR, but he was hardly idle. He worked at length on the details of the
forthcoming campaign. He kept a close eye on state and congressional
contests that might affect his own race; most notably, he prevailed on his
old friend Herbert Lehman, who had managed to become both an effective and a popular governor of New York, to run for another term and thus
shore up the whole ticket in the Empire State. He kept a tight leash on his
White House and campaign staffs, including national chairman Jim Farley,
advising them in effect that saying nothing in response to attacks was usually better than saying anything. And he planned the Democratic convention—set for Philadelphia—down to the last detail.

This was to be a coronation more than a convention. Roosevelt supporters dominated it from start to finish; they wrote the platform and engi-
neered a convention reform that northern Democrats had long sought:
revoking the two-thirds requirement for presidential nominations. FDR
was in a combative mood. The original draft of the party platform promised to "rid our land of kidnappers, bandits, and malefactors of great
wealth," grouping together criminals and some businessmen. Following
a speechwriting session with Moley and Rosenman on the eve of the convention, the president began at dinner to taunt the magazine editor for his
growing conservatism. When Moley replied with equal heat, a furious
quarrel broke out, while Missy LeHand vainly tried to change the subject.
For the first and only time in his life, Rosenman recalled later, "I saw the
president forget himself as a gentleman."

If this quarrel betrayed FDR's intense but unexpressed anger at his conservative critics, his plans for his convention appearance revealed a longing to be impresario, director, scriptwriter, and star. The evening got off to a bad start when the president, making his slow, stiff-legged walk to the stage, spotted in the crowd the benign, bearded face of Edwin Markham. Reaching out to grasp the poet's hand, FDR was thrown off balance. Down he tumbled. Pulled back to his feet, shaken and angry, he snapped, "Clean me up." He quickly regained his composure as he was positioned on a huge stage behind closed curtains.

The curtains parted, amid an explosion of cheers and war cries from the ecstatic crowd, 100,000 strong. There stood the president, serene and smiling. After a few remarks about the need for bipartisanship and national unity, he proclaimed, "We have conquered fear." Even so, he noted the "clouds of suspicion" and "ill-will and intolerance" rising elsewhere in the world. Then he swung into his campaign stance, as a hundred spotlights set the president off sharply from the dark masses around him.

"The royalists of the economic order have conceded that political freedom was the business of the Government, but they have maintained that economic slavery was nobody's business." His voice came through clearly in the big arena. "They granted that the Government could protect the citizen in his right to vote, but they denied that the Government could do anything to protect the citizen in his right to work and his right to live." But freedom was "no half-and-half affair."

He taunted the "privileged princes" of new "economic dynasties," exploiting class conflict to the hilt. His voice rose in crescendo after crescendo. The economic royalists complained that the New Dealers were trying to overthrow American institutions; what they really feared was loss of their power. "In vain they seek to hide behind the Flag and the Constitution." The president's phrases cut through the frenzied cheering: "democracy, not tyranny ... freedom, not subjection ... against dictatorship by mob rule and the overprivileged alike. ..." He lowered his voice portentously.

"Governments can err, Presidents do make mistakes, but the immortal Dante tells us that divine justice weighs the sins of the cold-blooded and the sins of the warmhearted on different scales. Better the occasional faults of a Government that lives in a spirit of charity than the consistent omissions of a Government frozen in the ice of its own indifference.

"There is a mysterious cycle in human events. To some generations much is given. Of other generations much is expected. *This* generation of Americans has a rendezvous with destiny." He looked at the crowd.

"I accept the commission you have tendered me. I join"—the speaker waited out a clamorous roar from the crowd—"with you. I am enlisted for the duration of the war." FDR held his hands aloft like a prizefighter and made his slow trip back to his car. With the crowd still in a frenzy, he circled the field twice before his car disappeared into the night.

After this melodramatic declaration of war, press and people expected hostilities to escalate. So they did, on right and left, as the GOP opened up a heavy bombardment against New Deal spending, waste, regulation, and abuse of power, while radicals charged it once again with failing to live up to its promises of jobs, security, and welfare. But the generalissimo of the Democracy was not at his command headquarters. While campaign orators roamed the battlefront, he stayed quiet, even while Coughlin and Smith poured out their hatred of him at Dr. Townsend's convention. He gave no answer when Coughlin's National Union for Social Justice held its convention, where Gerald Smith denounced the "slimy group" of New Dealers "culled from the pink campuses of America with friendly gaze fixed on Russia." FDR was just lying low.

He resumed his little "nonpolitical" trips out into the country, especially to the seared drought areas. He made his "nonpolitical" dedications. He went sailing. He even visited Quebec. He gave an isolationist talk at the famous Chautauqua speaking ground, declaring, "I have seen war. . . . I hate war." He gave a fireside chat on conservation. He gave a speech at Harvard University at its tercentenary celebration that was pointed—but "nonpolitical." One hundred years earlier Harvard alumni were "sorely troubled," he said. "Andrew Jackson was president." On the 250th anniversary alumni were still troubled. "Grover Cleveland was president. Now, on the three hundredth anniversary, I am president."

But he would not campaign—yet. Ickes, eager to take the warpath himself, grumbled that the campaign was drifting: "The President smiles and sails and fishes," he complained to his diary, "and the rest of us worry and fume."

Eleanor Roosevelt, too, warned that the Republicans were moving quickly. Already a seasoned politico who relied on "outside sources," she fired off a memo to Farley, informing him that not only were the Landon headquarters set up and ready to work full-time but that the "whole spirit" in the Landon campaign "is the spirit of a crusade. My feeling is that we have to get going and going quickly." And she brought up crucial questions concerning the state of organization and readiness in the Roosevelt campaign. Who is responsible for studying news reports and suggesting answers to charges? she demanded. Who is in charge of research? Was there a tentative plan of strategy for the whole campaign? Her memo is all the more remarkable, given her ambivalence about another four years in the White House. "For the good of the country I believe it is devoutly to be hoped that [Franklin] will be reelected," the fifty-two-year-old first lady confessed to a friend, "but from a personal point of view I am quite overcome when I think of four years more of the life I have been leading!"

. . .

Lying low during the summer was not whimsy. He would make no political speeches until October, he wrote his old Wilson friend Colonel House in August. Of course it was difficult, he added, to "offset a Press in every one of the close States which is at least eighty-five percent hostile." FDR's percentage was probably not far off, and it took iron control to resist striking back at the highly partisan campaign coverage. But he was following his old intuition about not pushing the voters too hard or too long. Let the other fellows stick out their chins; he would pick his own time.

That time started at the end of September at the New York Democratic convention in Syracuse, where the president chose to rebut attacks by Hearst, Coughlin, and both Smiths—Al and Gerald—on the New Deal as communistic. He rejected communism and "any other alien 'ism.'" Turning the tables, he contended that it was the New Deal that had saved the country from a communist threat caused by the Depression. Indeed, New Deal liberalism was the best protection for responsible conservatism. "Reform if you would preserve."

Soon the president's campaign train was rolling through the Midwest at the glacial speed he preferred. This was the kind of politicking he liked best: short humorous back-platform talks to the locals, with a longer stop every few days for a major campaign address. He enjoyed bantering with his listeners—especially on one occasion in Emporia, Kansas, where he spotted editor William Allen White, longtime friend and admirer of Theodore, and of Franklin, too, part of the time. White had come out for his fellow Kansan, Alf Landon, even though he had admitted that "the stink of money was over the whole campaign." Now FDR described White "as a very good friend of mine for three and a half years out of every four."

White made his way through the crowd. "Shoot not this old gray head," he called out in mock alarm.

"Hello, Bill, glad to see you," FDR called back. Then to the crowd: "Now that I see him, I shall not say anything about the other six months."

The crowd applauded as the two men shook hands; then the train pulled
out.

Still, there was little occasion for mirth in the 1936 showdown. Radicals, populists, and conservatives bombarded the New Deal from every
sector. As an old campaigner, FDR was ready for the usual cannonading.
But he grew angrier over the course of this campaign. Landon's stance,
perhaps out of desperation, had become more and more reactionary, and
stridently so. Focusing their attack on the new social security program, the
Republicans not only criticized its method of financing—a fair campaign
point—but charged that recipients would have to put metal identification
tags around their necks, like those of dogs. The Hearst press even printed
front-page pictures of these imaginary dog tags. Millions of Republican
fliers openly jeered at the poor, accusing FDR of providing "Free lunch
to Hoboes, Relief Clients, Underprivileged Transients, and others who
won't work." Republicans were even touting Mrs. Alf Landon as the anti-
Mrs. Roosevelt; Mrs. Landon would be an old-fashioned stay-at-home first
lady, they promised. But the crowds wanted more of Eleanor.

As Roosevelt's militancy mounted during these October days, so did
that of the populace, and FDR in turn seemed to be further aroused by
their combativeness. Late in the month he set out on a swing through the
urban Northeast. That trip, FDR said later, brought out the "most amazing tidal wave of humanity" he had ever seen. There was something terrible about the crowds that lined the streets, he told Ickes; he could hear
persons crying out "He saved my home" or "He gave me a job." A seeth-
ing mass of 150,000 overran Boston Common; in Connecticut his entourage—including Eleanor—was almost stranded in jammed streets.

In Bridgeport, Connecticut, he saw signs saying THANK GOD FOR
ROOSEVELT. In Pittsburgh, crowds five and six deep lined the streets to
catch a glimpse of the president. In the wealthy districts, reported Senator
Guffey of Pennsylvania, houses were dark but servants stood in front of
mansions and cheered. Were America's socioeconomic classes at war with
one another? Or were candidates and parties simply doing what they are
supposed to do—offering voters stark, meaningful choices?

All of Roosevelt's own combativeness came to a white heat at the end
of October, before a fervent, wildly chanting crowd in Madison Square
Garden.

"For twelve years this Nation was afflicted with hear-nothing, see-
nothing, do-nothing Government," he trumpeted. Then the searing phrases:
"Nine mocking years with the golden calf and three long years of the

scourge! Nine crazy years at the ticker and three long years in the bread-lines! Nine mad years of mirage and three long years of despair." Power-ful forces were trying to bring back the doctrine that "that Government is best which is most indifferent."

As explosive cheers punctuated FDR's sentences, he deftly modified his text to catch the rhythm of the crowd. His voice had been in turn stern with indignation and sonorous with moral fervor. Now his tone hardened.

"Never before in all our history have these forces been so united against one candidate as they stand today. They are unanimous in their *hate for me—and I welcome their hatred*."

Thunderous applause burst from the crowd, died away, and then mounted again in wave after wave. It was more than hand-clapping. It was a guttural roar from the very belly of New Yorkers hungry for leadership. FDR began again, gently.

"I should like to have it said of my first administration that in it the forces of selfishness and of lust for power met their *match*." His voice rose; the words came faster, stronger. "I should like to have it said—" Cheers, cowbells, horns, clackers drowned out the words.

"Wait a moment!" Roosevelt directed. The old performer would not have his lines spoiled.

"I should like to have it said of my second administration that in it *these forces met their master*." The roars of the crowd swept the Garden like those at boxing knockdowns of old. FDR, like Cousin Ted before him, both mem-bers of the Dutch-American aristocracy, privileged products of Harvard, was declaring war on the financial elite and speaking out for the people and for their forgotten sovereignty.

FDR went on to answer those Republicans who, "silent about their own plans," had demanded that he list his. So he did, running through the New Deal achievements and repeating over and over:

"For all these things we have only just begun to fight!"

PART III:
CONFLICT

Chapter Nine
CHECKMATE?

New York News, January 31, 1937.
(*Courtesy FDR Library*)

O Grave, Here Is Thy Victory"

THE PRESIDENT
ELECTED AND ~~INAUGURATED~~
EVERY FOUR YEARS
BY THE PEOPLE

THE MEMBERS OF THE
HOUSE
ELECTED EVERY TWO YEARS.
THE MEMBERS OF THE
SENATE
ELECTED EVERY SIX YEARS
BY THE PEOPLE

THE SUPREMECOURT
APPOINTED BY PRESIDENTS
(DEAD OR REPUDIATED)
FOR LIFE

THE SUPREME COURT

"WELL, GENTLEMEN, IS ANY OF MY LEGISLATION BEFORE THE COURT, TODAY?"

THE SUPREME COURT OF THE UNITED STATES

Chicago Tribune, February 8, 1937.
(*Courtesy FDR Library*)

An avalanche of votes rolled across the nation. The president's militant, even aggressive tone, as in the Madison Square Garden speech, had helped mobilize an astonishing voting turnout of 83 percent. The Democrats won, and they won big. Their victory set off an avalanche of acclaim in the press. Suddenly Roosevelt was a political colossus, a superman, a miracle worker. All things, it seemed at this point, were possible for him.

The avalanche swept aside some old records. With 27.8 million votes to Landon's 16.7 million, FDR won the largest number of votes in presidential history. With an electoral college margin of 523 to 8 (Maine and Vermont for Landon), his electoral vote victory was the biggest in almost a century and a half. Not only had he cut down the vote for Coughlin's hand-picked candidate Lemke to under a million, his avalanche had rolled over the traditional left as well. Socialist Norman Thomas's vote declined from the near 900,000 of 1932 to under 200,000; the Communists stayed under 100,000. Even the Prohibitionists lost ground.

The people had won. After examining election returns and voting patterns, one analyst concluded that the New Deal "has drawn a class line across the face of American politics." "The rich were for Landon; the poor backed Roosevelt," a labor union official wrote. No longer could people credibly deny the importance of class, observed historian William Leuchtenburg. Another historian went even further, calling the election of 1936 "the closest that America had come to class warfare."

On trains leaving Grand Central Station for the wealthy suburbs of Westchester County or Connecticut, one commentator observed, "You would hear Mr. Roosevelt and the New Deal condemned with an intolerance and bitterness that would astonish any reasonable-minded man." But if you took a bus to New Jersey, "you would hear fanatical loyalty" to the president and to everything his administration was doing. "We've grown class conscious," a Detroit autoworker would say in 1940, as he explained why people like him voted for Roosevelt.

Landon had performed well in wealthy suburbs, but not well enough to make up for FDR's astonishing success in the nation's cities. In 1929, only 3 percent of voters in Pittsburgh were Democrats; in 1936, FDR carried every ward. In 1936, Chicago too was "polarized into political camps with definite class identities," reported historian Lizabeth Cohen. Only one group revealed no class cleavage. Rich or poor, Jews voted Roosevelt.

It was a victory not just for class but for party too, and the press gave the credit for the Democratic victory to the president. While the Democrats boosted their majorities in both houses of Congress and in state governorships and many legislatures, these wins were often attributed to FDR's enormous coattail influence. Although Jim Farley had patiently nurtured Democratic party organization and efforts across the country, he was extolled more for his electoral college prediction—"As goes Maine, so goes Vermont," went the quip—than for his leadership of the Democratic party.

FDR also saw this as a personal victory. Although he thanked Farley and others for their efforts, he could take enormous satisfaction in the decisions that only he could and did make. His timing, deciding to strike in the last few weeks despite much advice to campaign earlier, had worked out just as he had calculated. His making *himself* the issue had helped produce that avalanche of votes. He had crushed the Coughlin-Townsend-Smith-Lemke third-party effort. As for the Socialists, he liked Norman Thomas personally enough that he took no special pleasure in their discomfiture.

But he could take such pleasure in some other campaign outcomes. Next to his own victory, he was happiest about George Norris's win in Nebraska, against a Democratic party nominee whom the president publicly deserted in favor of his old friend. Progressives like Norris had won in a number of other states. And he had coped with a number of "political friends" who might have embarrassed him. When John L. Lewis, the head of the mine workers union, with a photographer in tow, visited him in the White House and proffered a check for a quarter of a million dollars, FDR—doubtless with thoughts of that photo appearing in scores of southern and other newspapers—had waved him away with a big smile. "Just keep it and I'll call on you, if and when any small need arises." That small need, in small increments, later in the campaign totaled far more than the labor leader's check.

With the applause of press and people still ringing in his ears, the president left late in November to receive the acclaim of millions of other Americans—Latin Americans. It was a measure of FDR's optimism about reelection that months earlier he had helped organize a special Inter-American Conference for the Maintenance of Peace to take place in Buenos Aires in December, for he would hardly have wished to attend as a lame duck. This also would mean a trip at sea, FDR's favorite kind of vacation, and the longest trip an American president had ever taken from Washington, FDR's favorite kind of "first."

He had fun on the way down, with fishing, horseplay, and the convening of Neptune's Court on the cruiser *Indianapolis* as it crossed the equator. "The Pollywogs were given an intensive initiation lasting two days," he wrote Eleanor, "but we have all survived and are now full-fledged Shellbacks." More enthusiastic letters followed to "Dearest Babs" and "Dearest Mama": "*You* have been given a *huge* silver tea set by the Brazilian government."

But what appeared to please and impress the president most was his reception in Rio and Buenos Aires. Hundreds of thousands of people, including children waving American flags, turned out to cheer and applaud the presidential procession. "There was real enthusiasm in the streets," he wrote Eleanor. "I really begin to think the moral effect of the Good Neighbor Policy is making itself definitely felt."

FDR believed—he had a right to believe—that these enthusiastic greetings were his reward for his most successful foreign policy program: hemispheric friendship and solidarity. He had worked with Hull for a reciprocal trade program with Latin American nations that had boosted imports of Latin American raw materials in return for United States sales of manufactured goods; he had abrogated TR's Platt Amendment of 1902, which gave Washington the right to intervene in Cuban disorders; he had pulled home the last marines from Haiti.

So the president returned home to more plaudits for a trip and a program that, however popular and noncontroversial, were sideshows next to grave events in Europe and the Far East. As Christmas 1936 approached, FDR could bask in both an election victory and a foreign policy program that he had personally shaped.

Within three months of his triumphant return from South America, within four months of his electrifying reelection victory, Franklin Roosevelt was embroiled in the most searing political crisis of his career, entangled in the most dramatic constitutional struggle in twentieth-century America.

1
The Fall: A Drama in Five Acts

Early in 1937, Franklin Roosevelt was completing a script for a bold act of leadership. Because he self-consciously viewed himself as playwright, stage manager, and star—the only star—and because he conceived this episode as a drama with hero and villains, historians may record it in that form—but must record also a scenario that went terribly awry for the scriptwriter.

Act One: *The Challenge*

January 20, 1937. Under a cold soaking rain, Franklin D. Roosevelt stands before Chief Justice Charles Evans Hughes to take the oath of office for his second term. They eye each other, Roosevelt's face stern and resolute, Hughes's wet whiskers quivering in the wind. As the rain drums on FDR's old family Bible, Hughes reads the oath with slow and rising emphasis when he comes to the words "promise to support the Constitution of the United States." At this point the president wants to cry out, Yes, but the Constitution as *I* understand it, flexible enough to meet any new problem of democracy, not the kind of Constitution your Court has raised up as a barrier to progress and democracy.

The president turns to face the crowd. Reading from rain-spattered pages, he reviews progress since the "stagnation and despair" of 1932. The crowd is settling down to the usual tribute to the New Deal and its future when the president's tone suddenly changes. He is talking about the "challenge to our democracy."

In this nation "I see millions of families trying to live on incomes so meager that the pall of family disaster hangs over them day by day.

"I see millions whose daily lives in city and on farm continue under conditions labeled indecent by a so-called polite society half a century ago.

"I see millions denied education, recreation, and the opportunity to better their lot and the lot of their children.

"I see millions lacking the means to buy the products of farm and factory and by their poverty denying work and productiveness to many other millions.

"I see one-third of a nation ill-housed, ill-clad, ill-nourished.

"It is not in despair that I paint you that picture. I paint it for you in hope—because the Nation, seeing and understanding the injustice in it, proposes to paint it out." How? He does not say. But while the chief justice listens attentively behind him, the president warns that the people "will insist that every agency of popular government use effective instruments to carry out their will."

A deceptive lull follows in Washington, as Roosevelt calls for public aid for flood sufferers in the Ohio and Mississippi valleys, addresses by radio the President's Fourth Birthday Ball for crippled children, and thanks on behalf of the nation Andrew W. Mellon's "magnificent gift" of his art collection. But he warns Frankfurter in mid-January, "Very confidentially, I may give you an awful shock in about two weeks. Even if you do not agree, suspend final judgement."

Act Two: *Shock and Recoil*

February 5, 1937. Amid the most dramatic secrecy, Roosevelt presents his "judicial reorganization" proposal to a joint meeting of cabinet members and congressional leaders. Only Attorney General Homer Cummings, who shaped the proposal with FDR, Solicitor General Stanley Reed, Rosenman, and one or two others know its contents. Press secretary Steve Early has seen the accompanying message to Congress only the afternoon before; the White House staff has reported for work at 6:30 A.M. to prepare hundreds of copies. The president is brooking no leaks.

In almost total silence, aside from a few comments by the president, the assembled leaders study the message to Congress. Most of it is pretty heavy reading, dealing with the federal courts' congested dockets, delays in justice that fall hard on the poor, the failure of the Supreme Court to hear 717 of the 867 petitions for review presented to it in the past year. But one sentence stands out from the pages as if neon-lit: the necessity "for the appointment of additional judges in all federal courts," *without exception,* "where there are incumbent judges of retirement age who do not choose to retire or to resign." Accompanying documents specify that retirement age as seventy—and everyone present knows that the "reactionary four" on the Supreme Court, and Justice Brandeis too, are over that age.

The president does not discuss the proposal with his cabinet and congressional leaders. After asking them not to take the documents with them when they leave, he is wheeled off to a press conference, where he spends over an hour explaining the proposal to avid reporters.

The group in the cabinet room breaks up, almost speechless. But in their limousine, driving back to Capitol Hill, the congressional leaders dourly calculate the political fallout. Suddenly Hatton Sumners, chairman of the House Judiciary Committee, bursts out, "Boys, here's where I cash in my chips." Soon, in the Senate, while the bill is being read, Vice President Garner stands in the lobby unsubtly holding his nose as he turns his thumbs down. Other members in both houses, including some liberals and progressives the president relies on, line up against the proposal.

A firestorm of criticism sweeps through the press, including some liberal organs. Many newspapers echo Herbert Hoover's warning that the president's real aim is to "pack the court," and that term is forever attached to the proposal. The most cutting criticism attacks the president for his "deceptiveness." Instead of directly confronting the problem of a conservative Court vetoing liberal legislation, the proposal stresses efficiency, speedier action, court modernization.

"And now you have blown me off the top of Vesuvius where you sat me some weeks ago," Frankfurter writes FDR from Cambridge. "Yes, you 'shocked me.'" The Harvard law professor proceeds to say every nice thing about FDR's "deft" handling of the issue, the seriousness of the situation, and so on, without actually expressing approval of the bill itself.

Act Three: *Confrontation*

As criticism continues in Congress and country, the president's advisers are telling him that this "efficiency" approach was *too* deft. FDR agrees. He puts all pretense aside in a speech important for both time and venue: a Democratic Victory Dinner on March 4, four years after his first inauguration. He pulls no punches.

"We are celebrating the 1936 victory. That was not a final victory. It was a victory whereby our party won further opportunity to lead in the solution of the pressing problems that perplex our generation. Whether we shall celebrate in 1938, 1940, and in 1944, as we celebrate tonight, will deservedly depend upon whether the party continues on its course and solves those problems. . . .

"We gave warning last November that we had only just begun to fight. Did some people believe that we did not mean it? Well—I meant it, and you meant it." He notes the ever-accelerating speed with which social forces now gather headway, the Supreme Court "vetoes" of laws designed to deal with those forces, the paralysis of the New Deal by court injunctions, the millions still waiting for democratic government to act. Once again he concludes with an appeal for the one-third of the nation "ill-nourished, ill-clad, ill-housed." Five days later the president gives a fireside chat in which he denies he wishes to "pack the court."

The president seeks to mobilize a majority not only in Congress but in the electorate from the kind of people who wrote him daily messages of appeal, protest, support, advice. The opposition is forming its own coalition, comprising not only Republicans and conservatives but also Southern Democrats, progressives with highly mixed feelings, and Americans who look on the Court as the guardian of their Bill of Rights liberties and their property rights. Indeed, in New England and elsewhere, "committees of correspondence" are forming to combat this executive autocracy, just as earlier committees rose against the British king. While the 1937 committees are recruited mainly from business and legal establishments rather than from the grass roots or cobblestones, they show the scope of the developing conflict.

And what is the populace thinking? The crude Gallup polls of the time indicate that public opinion is almost equally divided for and against the bill at the start, that support then begins to sink, only to rise again after the president's Democratic talk and fireside chat, then to drop again during the next few weeks. The decline of support in Congress is even more marked. Some members report their mail as running against the court plan ten to one.

Act Four: *Pulling Out the Rug*

As the impasse tightens, politicians maneuver for advantage. Gleefully watching the Democratic party discord, Republicans agree to withhold heavy attacks and allow the Democrats to fight both sides of the battle. Having planned that the court bill would go initially to the House, the administration now wants the Senate to handle it first. Garner heads a Senate delegation to urge the president to compromise on three Supreme Court justices rather than six. FDR: "No."

Inconspicuously but decisively, the main political action now is taking place in the High Court, not in Congress or the White House. FDR has no illusions about Chief Justice Charles Evans Hughes, who is far more a politician than a jurist. A longtime investigator of corruption, Hughes won the governorship of New York in 1906 during TR's second presidential term, won reelection, gained appointment to the Supreme Court in 1910, and then resigned from the Court to run against Wilson in 1916. Republican to the core, Hughes is an admired public servant among a host of leaders New York State had provided the nation. Now, challenged by the president, Hughes is dead set against the court bill. But as chief justice, what can he do about it?

Louis Brandeis supplies the key. A prestigious liberal reformer, the justice for years has been supplying advice and ideas to the administration through his friends Frankfurter, Benjamin Cohen, and Tommy Corcoran. But he knows when to get off the New Deal train, as he did when helping to demolish the NRA; he is even more opposed to the court bill. But Brandeis too knows that he cannot take overt action.

Now the plot thickens. Senator Burton Wheeler, who is heading the progressive opposition to the bill on Capitol Hill, learns that Brandeis is willing to meet with him on the measure at the justice's home. There Brandeis suggests that Wheeler advise Hughes, with Brandeis's imprimatur, to supply Wheeler with information directly rebutting FDR's case against tired old justices delaying justice. Within a day Hughes puts his data into Wheeler's hands, remarking genially, "The baby is born."

The "baby" creates a sensation when Wheeler presents it to the Senate Judiciary Committee. Factual and authoritative, Hughes's data are not questioned. But a far more dire threat to the court bill is being prepared within the bowels of the palatial Supreme Court building. Associate Justice Owen D. Roberts is switching sides on key issues, joining the liberals, thereby undermining the president's stand against the High Court. Suddenly in March the Court reverses a previous decision vetoing a state minimum-wage law. In the next few weeks the Court sustains the Frazier-Lemke Farm Moratorium Act, the Social Security Act, and—most dramatically—Wagner's National Labor Relations Act, all passed two years earlier and regarded by the legal establishment as probably unconstitutional.

"A switch in time saves nine," quips Harvard law professor Thomas Reed Powell, unforgettably. Roosevelt puts his best face on it. "Today is a very, very happy day for me," he tells a news conference after the Wagner decision comes down. He chortles over the discomfiture of the *New York Herald Tribune,* which had run an editorial titled "Thumbs Down on the Wagner Act" after a Liberty League lawyers' committee had held it unconstitutional, only now to endorse the switch with a new editorial, "A Great Decision." To the merriment of the reporters, he goes on, "Well, I have been having more fun."

But everyone, at least outside the White House, knows that the switches are vitiating the president's central argument about the reactionary High Court. Then comes a final blow: Justice Willis Van Devanter announces his retirement. FDR not only has a changed Court posture. He has a changed Court makeup.

Act Five: *Death and Defeat*

It is an indication of both the intensity and complexity of the court battle that neither side—none of the sides—seems to know by May 1937 what it has won or what it has lost and, hence, whether or not to quit the battle. Roosevelt may not be getting six new Supreme Court appointments or the proposed compromise of three new appointments, but at least he has one— Van Devanter's replacement. And all know who is slated to receive the first appointment: Majority Leader Joe Robinson, who day after day, week after

week, has been carrying on FDR's battle on Capitol Hill. For some time
the Arkansas senator has been urging the president to accept a compromise—two additional justices.

The Robinson situation presents FDR with a hard dilemma. He must
honor this political promise; besides, key support for a court bill in the
Senate depends on personal pledges to Robinson from friendly senators
who want to ensure that he actually receives the appointment. But there
could be a problem with the Arkansan. A loyal Democrat, he is also close
to, or at least indebted to, conservative senators, and his rulings on the
Court might reflect many years of compromise and concession. He appears
hardly likely to be a fighting New Deal judge. To appoint Robinson, even
along with another New Deal nominee, might produce a Court in which
a conservative could have the swing vote.

By the end of May, with the favorable Court decisions and the Van
Devanter resignation, Robinson is the key actor. Early in June the president tells the majority leader to settle for whatever he can get as a face-
saving compromise. Robinson returns to the fray with a bill that would
allow the president to nominate one extra justice for each member of the
Supreme Court over the age of seventy-five—but not more than one such
appointment each year. The fight even for this compromise goes badly.
Support for any significant court reform is dropping in Congress and in
the country.

Day after day Robinson works the Senate cloakroom, calling in his last
chips, exhorting, pleading, dealing, always counting. In his pajamas, on a
stifling night in Washington, *Congressional Record* in hand, he collapses and
dies alone in his apartment.

With his death dies any hope for significant court reform—and perhaps hope too for the New Deal and hence the well-being of that "one-
third of the nation" FDR had hoped to transform. The drama is over.

. . .

Why did he do it? How could the master politician of his time get into
such a political mess, suffer such a drubbing at the hands of his congressional and judicial foes? Perplexed, observers left the enigma to the "bar
of history" to solve. But historians have continued to be divided or ambiguous over the matter.

The most common explanation, then and since, has been sheer pride.
Intoxicated with his election triumph, FDR threw caution to the winds in
mounting first a flanking, and then a frontal, assault on the Court. Cer-

tainly hubris played some role in FDR's action, but not a major one. Before 1936, Roosevelt had won five elections, including the governorship twice and the presidency once, and he was not transported into unreality by winning a sixth. A longtime observer of the ups and downs of politicians, especially of both Theodore Roosevelt and Woodrow Wilson, he knew the price that could be paid for political overconfidence.

Nor does another popular theory—that his court plan was a spur-of-the-moment decision, quickly planned, poorly conceived, and hence badly executed—bear scrutiny. In fact, Roosevelt had been pondering judicial reform for years. He was aware of the brushes that other presidents had had with the High Court, and he remembered well TR's radical call in 1912 for popular referenda on judicial decisions. He had considered the experience of the British with reform of the House of Lords, the power seat of the law lords who served as Britain's court of highest appeal. He had pored over a number of alternatives to "court-packing," such as limiting the Supreme Court's jurisdiction or requiring a two-thirds vote of the Court to invalidate legislation. Most of these plans contained a fatal flaw: The Supreme Court itself would pass on their validity.

Roosevelt also thoroughly analyzed the most widely considered alternative—a constitutional amendment, which presumably would survive judicial hostility. Quite different types of amendments had been proposed: to grant Congress power to override judicial decisions; to abolish or curtail the power of the High Court to determine the constitutionality of acts of Congress; to bestow specific powers to Congress over such economic sectors as agriculture and industry; to set age limits on judges or grant them limited terms of office rather than lifetime appointments.

The president had absolutely no hope for the amendment route. Changing the Constitution was a slow process, usually taking many years. Those "howling their heads off" for the amendment process, he believed, did not know that as a practical matter no controversial amendment would ever pass. "Give me ten million dollars," FDR told a friend, "and I can prevent any amendment to the Constitution from being ratified by the necessary number of states."

If so many routes for court reform were blocked off, why did the president act at all? Why not let age and death slowly but inexorably do the job for him, as justices departed?

The answer lies less in hubris or recklessness than in the emotions of fear, anger, vengeance, vindictiveness—above all, a kind of righteous wrath. FDR's evocation of hatred in the campaign was no political gimmick. He meant it, and his anger did not abate following the election. After William Randolph Hearst made a postelection call of congratulations, telling FDR there were "no hard feelings" at the publisher's end, the president reported it to the cabinet with a show of angry contempt.

He was not in a forgiving mood. Rising in 1935 and climaxing in the Madison Square Garden speech, his indignation and wrath were of almost Moses-like dimensions.

"We are kindred spirits!" he wrote his old historian friend Claude G. Bowers two months after the election. "The unfair attacks of that part of the press which has no interest in reporting either the truth or the facts are enough to make any of us boiling mad. Some day we will have a chance to sit down together and plan our own form of revenge on Bert McCormick and the like." His feelings about reactionary publishers Robert McCormick of the *Chicago Tribune* and Hearst were significant. These were rich men of "good family," who had gone to the best schools. They were essentially businessmen—and it was the wealthy industrialists and financiers against whom FDR's wrath was directed.

It was a highly personal bitterness. If he had been a Marxist or some other kind of economic determinist, he might have waxed philosophical, viewing his foes as caught in a class culture and outlook that forced them to be reactionary. But FDR was no philosopher, and he hated his foes for their unfairness, social backwardness, political Toryism, and economic conservatism. These were men who should know better. Truly these were, in TR's memorable words, "malefactors of great wealth."

His anger was mixed with fear. He could beat them at the polls but he could not overcome their paying starvation wages to women and children, their antiunion policies, their stubborn opposition to changes like social security and regulation of finance, except through effective laws. And he could not gain such legislation in the face of a reactionary Court. To Roosevelt the "reactionary four" on the Court, with Associate Justice Owen Roberts as swing vote, were essentially agents of big business—but agents with power.

In his wrath, FDR made moral and political miscalculations. Instead of posing court reform as a key issue in his reelection campaign, out of fear that it might hurt him in marginal states, he lost the opportunity to use his election victory as a springboard to his court reform effort. Instead of playing up the high moral and political aspects of his proposal, as TR had done, FDR offered it to Congress as a problem of efficiency and competence. He refused to compromise when concessions might have brought him partial victory.

His miscalculations, however, have blinded historians to the courage and commitment he brought to a very fundamental problem of American democracy: a Court that failed to respond to current conditions and attitudes, blocking the overwhelming will of the majority. Americans call for courage and commitment, while deriding politicians who show such qualities but who nevertheless fail. In America—as TR and Wilson and now FDR discovered—when it comes to principle in politics, nothing fails like failure.

. . .

If the court fight brought out both the best and the worst in Franklin Roosevelt, the struggle brought out the best and the worst in the other key actors also.

Four reactionary justices based their socioeconomic decisions on ideological preferences, as they had every right to do, on a century and a half of judicial tradition—but they inflicted their prejudices on public policy long after the majority of the American people in election after election had repudiated their ideology. All four had stubbornly clung to their posts during FDR's first term, and he had no reason to expect that they would not do so during his second.

Chief Justice Charles Evans Hughes stubbornly and skillfully defended the institution he headed, but in doing so he not only projected the Court into the heart of a political struggle but used improper means in doing so. His report on the Court's actual efficiency, he said, was "in accord with the views of the Justices," but in fact he had consulted only two, Brandeis and Van Devanter. Most of the justices were in the city and three lived only a few minutes' walk from Hughes's home. Presumably Hughes feared he could not speak for a united Court.

Justice Roberts's role was mixed. He had the wit to be flexible at a time when the Court needed that quality, but his "switch in time," which he later defended on tenuous technical grounds, was mainly motivated by a desire to kill FDR's court plan. At best, Roberts's behavior suggested a man who was trying to have it both ways, to operate in the center and to be available someday for a chief justiceship at the hands of either party.

Justice Louis Brandeis, like Hughes, wanted to protect the Court's integrity and independence. But he too resorted to indirection and intervened enough politically to take some of the luster off his image as a noble and disinterested jurist.

The Democratic party failed as a governing or leadership entity. The party had feared to make the Supreme Court a key issue in its platform, and party chief Farley had urged Roosevelt not to make it a campaign issue. Democratic defectors on Capitol Hill could use the party's reluctance to take a clear stand on the High Court's conservatism as an excuse for deserting the party line: There was no party line.

The Republicans failed as an opposition party. Letting the Democrats fight it out was a good way to defeat the bill, but a poor way to enable the Republicans to fight for the Court and to pose alternative solutions, in the spirit of a "loyal opposition" that is both militant and constructive.

In a longer-run perspective, however, perhaps all the actors were the prisoners of a much more restrictive script—that of the Constitution of the United States and of the men who wrote it. The Framers built conflict into the very heart of the American system, with the hope that the states and the nation, and the three branches at both levels, would check and balance one another in order to protect individual liberty and prevent dictatorship. At the Democratic victory dinner, when Roosevelt demanded that the "team" of "three well-matched horses" pull as one to get the field plowed, he was misinterpreting the Constitution. The Framers had not wanted the three branches to pull as a team.

If FDR was saying, however, that in order to get the horses to stay in the tracks together at least long enough to get some of the field plowed, a large measure of civility was required, he was eminently right. But civility was in short supply during the winter and spring of 1937.

Perhaps, however, the president had made a strategic error at the very start, in stressing practical efficiency rather than overriding principle. In July 1937, a week after Robinson's death, FDR was in a more reflective mood when questioned by the press. He now talked about "fundamentals" and he reflected on a bit of history.

"There was a lot of feeling back in T.R.'s time about the need for judicial reform. It took the form, in the 1912 campaign, of the Progressive Party asking for all kinds of things like recall of judges and overriding of decisions by popular vote." That popular demand, FDR continued, had an "enormous effect" on the courts. "The courts listened and they legislated"—the correspondents laughed at this—"I mean they decided"—more laughter—and made their decisions on a judicial rather than a political basis. Then, during the Coolidge and Hoover years the courts, he said, went back to legislating.

FDR did not mention TR's open call for radical judicial reform in the election of 1912, compared to his own silence on the subject in 1936. But of course TR had lost, and he, FDR, had won.

2
Unneutral Neutrality

A brooding presence over the court fight lay three thousand miles to the east, in the German and Italian dictatorships, and ten thousand miles to the west, in the Japanese military's domination of Japan's foreign policy. Dramatic and evocative were cries from opponents that FDR's stab at judicial reform was a step toward further executive usurpation of power, on the road to dictatorship, European-style. Even as political passions slowly ebbed after FDR's defeat, his foes were worrying that he might seize on an "incident" abroad to divert popular attention from the ills at home to adventures far away. People in Washington had long memories—of Theodore Roosevelt's interventions in Latin America, of Franklin Roosevelt's emulation of his cousin in Wilson's navy department, of Franklin's eagerness to go to war with Germany in 1917.

His critics also knew that both the Constitution and precedent gave the president far more power in foreign than in domestic policy. Observing the collision of great nations, the Framers had recognized the need of the president to be chief foreign-policy maker as well as chief executive, chief of state, and commander in chief. But whatever constitutional power FDR had in foreign-policy making was more than vitiated by an even more potent force—political opposition. The power of isolationism in America held Roosevelt's foreign-policy making in a viselike grip during his first term. In a world clearly headed toward Armageddon, internationalists wondered, how long would this grip continue in his second term?

Much turned on the power of his isolationist opponents. And few political movements in American history have appeared so potent in the eyes of contemporary opinion as isolationism in the early and mid-1930s. The overwhelming majority of members of Congress feared to take any step that hinted of involving the nation in "foreign entanglement" or—fearsome thought—going to war. A Gallup poll in February 1937 showed 95 percent of the populace opposed to participating in another European war.

Powerful voices in Congress echoed this feeling: Republican William E. Borah of Idaho, progressive Republicans Hiram Johnson of California and Gerald P. Nye of North Dakota, and, in the House, members ranging ideologically from Hamilton Fish of New York, a former TR Progressive turned right-winger, to the populist radical Maury Maverick. Providing them with vociferous support were some of the most vocal of the press barons: William Randolph Hearst and his big chain of newspapers, Colonel Robert McCormick and his *Chicago Tribune,* and numerous publishers in the Midwest and West. The popular radio commentator Boake Carter piped his isolationist views into distant homes.

Some isolationists were secret anti-Semites, others not so secret. Senator Robert Reynolds, North Carolina Democrat and a rabid isolationist, told radio audiences that the Jews, because of their hatred of Hitler, were determined to force the United States into war. When his friend Senator James Byrnes of South Carolina, a friend also to Bernard Baruch and FDR, remonstrated with the North Carolina senator, Reynolds told him that all across the nation people were writing him about the Jews, and those views influenced his own attitudes on the subject. Byrnes urged Reynolds to "let the matter alone."

During the interventionist years through the later war and postwar years, historians often denigrated the isolationist movement. Even aside from some of the controversial figures connected with it, such as Coughlin and even unsavory proto-fascists like Gerald L. K. Smith, the chroniclers pointed to the extreme insular bias of many isolationists, their heavily ethnic makeup, their excessive disillusionment with the "folly" of intervention in World War I, the influence of immigrants who had fled Europe and hence shunned "the old country" or, conversely, came from Germany or Italy and felt protective of their homelands.

In longer perspective the isolationists appear to have demonstrated an intellectual power that almost matched their political strength. Opinion leaders such as Oswald Garrison Villard and Stuart Chase, prestigious academics like Charles A. Beard, respected radicals such as Norman Thomas, eminent Republicans—most notably Herbert Hoover—and up-and-coming young GOP leaders like Robert A. Taft of Ohio, contributed intellectual weight to the isolationist cause. In a category of his own, as America's number one hero, was Charles A. Lindbergh, who believed, as he said later, that if "our American ideals are to survive, it will not be through the narcotic of a foreign war."

Only in later decades, during and after the debate over Vietnam and other "foreign wars," did historians recognize that the essence of isolationism was not economic or ethnic or irrational but doctrinal, almost ideological. Bitterly disenchanted over Wilson's "war to end war" and war to "defend democracy," they had become fanatical over America's need to stay out of foreign quarrels, great power disputes, European "entanglements," power politics. Amid clouds of rhetoric they could quote George

Washington's admonition to "steer clear of permanent alliances," Jefferson's warning against entanglement in the "broils of Europe," James Monroe's "Doctrine." With reams of *Congressional Records* and committee reports they could cite precedent after precedent of noninterference, without harm to America's national interests. Often the isolationist argument crossed over into sheer fantasy, conspiracy theories, or the satanic nature of the war makers, but much of the debate was thoughtful and substantive.

. . .

And the president's reaction to the power of isolationism? Almost total submission. He never missed an opportunity publicly, and rarely in private communications, to promise that the United States would not become entangled in foreign quarrels or risk involvement in foreign wars. When very occasionally he tried a venture in "internationalism," as in his support of membership in the World Court, Senate rejection reinforced his cautiousness. His main scope was in his use of his executive power, most notably in recognizing the Soviet Union in 1933. He supported membership in the International Labor Organization only after Frances Perkins—with FDR's blessing but with no help from him—trudged from Johnson to Borah and to other isolationists to explain that the ILO had existed before the League of Nations and was not part of it.

But the president could neither ignore nor shield himself from the ultimate paradox of isolationism: A great nation with many foreign interests and connections may influence the rest of the globe as much by its inaction as by its participation. FDR had hardly taken office when he was drawn into the ill-fated London Economic Conference of 1933 and, far more portentously, faced worldwide repercussions from Japanese aggression in the Far East and from Hitler's seizure of power. Soon he was receiving personal reports from his own appointed envoys, who kept him in touch with the more subtle or long-range aspects of world politics: the balance of power in the French Chamber of Deputies, the foreign policy attitudes of British labor, the ominously silent power struggles within the Kremlin, the clash of Chinese warlords.

Reading long letters from his envoys—sometimes of several thousands of words—lunching with foreign ambassadors and visitors, quizzing his unofficial agents who had just seen a British prime minister or Mussolini or Hermann Göring, leafing through voluminous studies by State Department and other agency diplomats and economists, the president drank in information—rather indiscriminately, it was thought in the State Depart-

ment—from every available source. One of the most improbable of these
was a friend in Lima who somehow gained access to dispatches from the
British Foreign Office to diplomats in South America and relayed their
contents in detail to FDR. This informant also told the president that the
Foreign Office in turn had access to his and Hull's "most intimate communications" and distributed them to its entire foreign service so quickly
that Britishers in the field often learned about Washington policy sooner
than their American colleagues.

So Roosevelt was caught in an intellectual vise to some degree of his
own making. Both his official and unofficial correspondents and advisers
tended to be interventionist, and so was FDR, by heritage, experience, and
enthusiasm for TR's and Wilson's activist foreign policies. Politically he
would not challenge the isolationists, thus avoiding threats to his domestic program—and perhaps to his intermittent thoughts about a possible
third term. He was interventionist in thought but not in action. Rather than
taking leadership, if only through a program of forthright education of the
populace, he was waiting on events to do that teaching.

The test of FDR's cautious, opportunistic foreign-policy making would
come with crisis abroad, and that crisis was not long in materializing. Nor
did it come without warning. For months during 1935, Mussolini had made
clear his plan to seize Ethiopia. Isolationists in America had agreed to an
arms embargo but refused to authorize the president to discriminate between aggressor and victim. Presidential discretion, they warned, would
lead to entanglement in foreign machinations. Senators were not in the
mood to dicker. "I tell you, Steve," Senator Key Pittman, chairman of the
Foreign Relations Committee, wrote to presidential press secretary Early,
"the president is riding for a fall if he insists on designating the aggressor
in accordance with the wishes of the League of Nations." Three times he
warned that the president would take a "licking." He knew that FDR would
not run that risk, and he was right. The Congress duly passed a mandatory arms embargo by almost unanimous votes in both chambers, and FDR
duly signed the bill, while warning that the inflexible measure was more
likely to drag the country into war than to keep it out.

While various feeble efforts, in the League and in foreign ministries,
failed to deter Mussolini, his ground and air forces moved steadily to the
attack. A personal appeal from the president drew a long but negative response from the Italian dictator. In signing the neutrality bill, FDR urged
on Americans the "high moral duty" of not selling essential war materials
(such as oil) "to either belligerent"—a plea that had little effect on exporters.

Early in October 1935, as the president was beginning his long vacation cruise following the "second hundred days session," coded messages flashed to the *Houston* off San Diego: Mussolini's forces had started their invasion of Ethiopia.

. . .

The next foreign crisis facing the administration was in Spain. While Roosevelt was gearing up for his presidential campaign in midsummer 1936, what seemed at the time an obscure revolt broke out in Spanish Morocco against the recently elected Popular Front government in Madrid. Within a few weeks the revolt took on formidable proportions as the rebels seized Cadiz and Seville. Reports streamed in that Italian and German military aid was on its way to the advancing forces.

If FDR had any doubts about the background and urgency of the Spanish situation, he was thoroughly briefed before the end of August by his longtime close friend and envoy to Madrid, the historian Claude Bowers. There was "no possible justification for the rebellion in anything done by the legal, legitimate Government, voted in overwhelmingly a few months ago," Bowers informed his chief. Spain's president "is a republican, and a democrat, with no sympathy with doctrines we call 'subversive.'" He was trying to change his nation from a sixteenth-century state into a modern European nation and to end feudalism. Fearing communism as the alternative, he had sponsored plans for placing peasants on small farms and giving labor a living wage and civilized working conditions.

"He has no desire to interfere with the Catholic religion as a religion," Bowers reported, and church services had never been interfered with, but the Spanish president was "hated with fierce hate by the Church because of his public school policy, his expulsion of the Jesuits," and hated by the aristocracy because he would make "huge absentee landlords part with a portion of their lands" to create small farms. Bowers pictured the rebels as comprising Moors, the Foreign Legion, fascists, "Carlists—religionists," and key elements of the regular army.

And how did Roosevelt the foreign-policy maker in chief respond to the most sharply drawn moral issue of his first term? He had a marvelous opportunity to take a strong line, for he was scheduled to give a talk on peace at Chautauqua, the old speaking ground in western New York, where politicians—including Roosevelt—for years had been taking a high moral stance on peace and its preservation. Once again the Chautauqua audience heard the familiar catchwords about good neighbors and peaceful understanding. "We shun political commitments which might entangle us in foreign wars," the president told the crowd. "We avoid connection with the political activities of the League of Nations." But he was glad to say that "we have cooperated wholeheartedly in the social and humanitarian work at Geneva." Then he uttered, with some pardonable poetic license, words that would become memorable:

"I have seen war. I have seen war on land and sea. I have seen blood running from the wounded. I have seen men coughing out their gassed lungs. I have seen the dead in the mud. I have seen cities destroyed. I have seen two hundred limping, exhausted men come out of line—the survivors of a regiment of one thousand that went forward forty-eight hours before. I have seen children starving. I have seen the agony of mothers and wives." He promised to spend unnumbered hours planning how war might be kept from the United States.

"We believe in democracy," he concluded, "we believe in freedom; and we believe in peace." But what if those values came in conflict, as they were doing abroad at that very time?

Once again FDR felt himself in the grip of events. The Neutrality Act, which had been extended and revised early in 1936, did not apply to civil war, but he had little freedom of action politically. Gerald Nye, encouraged by his friend Secretary of the Interior Ickes, and in company with nine other members of Congress, telegraphed the president before the Chautauqua speech urging "every possible effort on the part of the government to prevent shipment of war supplies to Spain." Nye had promised Ickes that he would come out for FDR after the Chautauqua speech. Nye said later he liked the speech, but despite a personal meeting with FDR at Hyde Park, the North Dakota senator did not support him in the election.

The imperatives of the 1936 election were holding FDR in that foreign-policy vise. It was already clear that the Catholic hierarchy in the United States would support the rebels against the "Godless" "communist" Madrid government. The president dared not defy the Roman Catholic Church in an election that in late summer 1936 appeared to be close. "What an unfortunate and terrible catastrophe in Spain!" Roosevelt wrote to Bowers in September. But he would stick to "complete neutrality in regard to Spain's own internal affairs."

While FDR did nothing, while Britain and France dithered and delayed, Rome and Berlin acted quickly. Five days after the start of the army revolt, Mussolini pledged his aid and ordered army bombers to Morocco;

three days after that, Hitler promised aid to General Franciso Franco and soon sent transport planes with troops to Spain. Britain and France were quick to promise nonintervention. Foreign policy, FDR said in his Chautauqua speech, involved a "vast uncharted area" in which "safe sailing will depend on the knowledge and the experience and the wisdom" of the foreign-policy makers. If FDR was dragging anchor in navigating that sea, he had fumbled mightily in dropping that anchor in the first place.

3
Interventionist Nonintervention

Some hoped that Roosevelt's sweeping election victory in November 1936 would release him from his anchor's dragging effect. Surely now he would be less sensitive to the alleged power of isolationist fears and Catholic votes. But few could detect any major change in Roosevelt's foreign-policy making as his second term got under way in January 1937. The reason eluded many journalists at the time and historians since, partly because it was so simple. The reason was lack of reason itself—Roosevelt's inability to see his way clear through the eddies and crosscurrents, the tides and tempests, still besetting the globe.

What was the Führer up to: now, in the immediate future, in the long run? Envoys and journalists were interviewing the men around Hitler, and even Hitler himself, in desperate efforts to answer this question. The Führer was operating on three confusing levels. His party speeches were full of denunciation of the Versailles Treaty, the League of Nations, the communists, the Jews. Yet through his foreign office and diplomatic channels he dispatched mixed messages of conciliation, agreement for the Reich to take part in international conferences, willingness to bargain—but always provided that Hitler's expansionist claims were accepted ahead of time. And he was rearming.

As usual, actions spoke the loudest. From the very start of his rule, Hitler pressed a vast rearmament program. Soon he felt strong enough to pull Germany out of the League of Nations. Then, in March 1936, came Hitler's greatest gamble and the surest clue to his plans, his reoccupation of the Rhineland. This was followed immediately by a peace proposal, announced to cheering members of the Reichstag: a twenty-five-year non-aggression pact with France, demilitarization of the frontier (thus scrapping France's famed Maginot Line), and bilateral nonaggression pacts with Germany's eastern neighbors—save with Moscow. France hesitated in the face of the reoccupation and was lost; later it became evident that Hitler's troops would have pulled back if France and her allies had resisted.

Western leaders, including Roosevelt and Hull, were alarmed. But no one acted.

Some of FDR's own envoys and advisers also were realistically pessimistic about the prospects of peace. Ambassador William Dodd wrote from Berlin a series of warnings that "there is no prospect of a peace agreement except upon the basis of a solid Fascist-Nazi European front," that "Hitler and Mussolini intend to control all Europe," that Hitler was "simply waiting for his best opportunity to seize what he wants." Dodd, an old Wilsonian, did not presume to advise Roosevelt how to deal with a peace-obsessed people or a recalcitrant Senate, but he put the moral issue straight to the president: Was the Western world going to "give up the human system of Locke, Adam Smith, and Jefferson?" Was there any way "democratic countries can save the civilization" dating back to Luther, Erasmus, the Hollanders, and the English?

Roosevelt did not know the answer to these questions. In his 1937 inaugural address he spoke glowingly about the need to defend and enhance democracy, but not how to do so abroad. Shortly before that speech he received a message from his ambassador to Poland, John Cudahy. "The outstanding menace to peace, of course, is Hitler," Cudahy reported. "No one knows where he is going; probably he, himself, does not know." But Hitler did know, in strategic terms; it was the leaders of the democracies who did not.

. . .

If Franklin Roosevelt were a run-of-the-mill presidential politician, historians might deplore his plight—a host of foreign and domestic crises converging, often at the same time, during 1936 and 1937. Thus, while he was focussing on his reelection campaign in 1936, the civil war in Spain was coming to a head; while he was mired in the court fight in the summer of 1937, fighting broke out in the Far East. But for FDR this was no problem. A consummate juggler of policies, advisers, and opportunities, he seemed to glory in his skill at jumping from one crisis to another. Thus in 1937 he could deal with problems in the Far East as readily with his left hand as in Europe with his right.

Although FDR as a boy had not traveled in the Far East as he had in western Europe, he felt equally knowledgeable about both continents. It was rare for anyone even to mention China to FDR in a gathering without his launching into a long discourse about his ancestors' involvement in the China trade, complete with stories about the clipper ships. As a youth he had watched admiringly as Cousin Theodore demanded that western nations and Japan respect the Open Door policy in China, opportunistically promised noninterference with Japan's ambitions in Korea in exchange for Japan's noninterference in the Philippines, and negotiated a peace agreement between St. Petersburg and Tokyo following the Russo-Japanese war. And then TR's Nobel Prize!

FDR had long maintained a sympathetic concern for China. While governor of New York he followed Japan's aggression in Manchuria, in violation of earlier treaties and of the Covenant of the League of Nations. During 1932, as he campaigned for the presidency, Japanese forces strengthened their grip on southern Manchuria and Tokyo recognized the puppet state of Manchukuo. He watched with approval the efforts of Henry Stimson—TR's secretary of war and Hoover's secretary of state—to maintain the Open Door when Japanese forces attacked Shanghai and to force Japan's withdrawal, with League backing. And he watched disapprovingly when Japan withdrew from the League after the international body condemned its aggressiveness—even though the League also recognized Tokyo's "special interest" in Manchuria.

So FDR had inherited a mixed record of precedents and policies, agreements and disagreements, in Japanese-American relationships in March 1933. He promptly met with the outgoing secretary of state and readily agreed to maintain the "Stimson doctrine" of refusing to recognize Japanese conquests in Manchukuo. During his first term, as FDR jousted with the isolationists over neutrality, an almost silent war was waged between Japanese militarists and moderates over Tokyo's expansionist policies. To win popular acceptance of the heavy costs of the Manchukuo occupation, the military awaited only a pretext. Thus FDR was in the same paradoxical posture toward the Far East as toward Europe: The United States was a possibly decisive international presence even while preaching neutrality and nonentanglement. Hence the politics of Washington was all the more captive to the politics of other capitals.

The burgeoning Japanese forces in China needed only a spark to start another advance, and this came in July 1937 in a night fracas only a few miles west of Peking. Soon a huge ground war was under way. A month later an incident in Shanghai gave Tokyo the pretext for an attack on that metropolis. Washington's main response was to urge American civilians to depart the war zone and to send 1,200 marines to boost the small United States complement in Shanghai. Hull issued to the international community one more of his and FDR's perennial pleas for peace, for compliance with treaties, for noninterference in the internal affairs of other nations. The message was so general that even Japan responded affirmatively.

FDR could do little more. It was not only that the populace showed no great willingness to send troops, or even arms, to the much-admired Chinese. The neutrality law was a positive hindrance. There had not been a declaration of war, not even a severing of diplomatic relationships, between Tokyo and Peking. Even more, an embargo on arms shipments to the Far East would injure China without hurting Japan, with its big maritime commerce and industry. So Roosevelt did not even invoke the Neutrality Act.

Once again Washington was stumbling along with eloquent sermons, endless moralizing, and an already outmoded neutrality strategy, but also conscious of its direct stake in the huge Far Eastern area with which it had historic economic, diplomatic, and sentimental relationships. The result was a contradiction in terms, but not in FDR's opportunistic foreign policy—interventionist nonintervention.

The president had assumed that people were basically rational and that they would learn from events, if events were properly reported and interpreted. This called for educational leadership, which he was always ready to supply, whether in addresses to the nation, communications to foreign leaders, or advice to Washington officials. But people did not seem to be learning—from events or from his speeches. Mussolini now held Ethiopia, Hitler the Rhineland, and Franco most of Spain, but all this did not appear to change isolationist attitudes. On the contrary, people seemed more fearful than ever, more inclined to hunker down in the hurricane.

In the summer of 1937 the president decided to try again, this time to make the most dramatic speech of all. It would be as bold but as carefully considered as his court fight speeches earlier in the year. And he would choose a provocative venue: Chicago, the isolationist heartland, at a rostrum within a stone's throw of Bertie McCormick's Tribune Tower, the home of the reactionary "America First" newspaper that was widely regarded as the most influential organ in the Midwest.

Well over half a million people cheered the president early in October when he toured the city, dedicated the Outer Link Bridge, and drove down Lake Shore Drive to confront a crowd of around 75,000.

He began with the usual warnings and pieties. The world political situation had grown much worse; a "reign of terror and international lawlessness" had begun; the "very foundations of civilization" were "seriously threatened"; "innocent peoples" and "innocent nations" were being "cruelly sacrificed to a greed for power and supremacy"; if such conditions came to pass in other parts of the world, "let no one imagine that America will escape, that America may expect mercy"; there would be no safety from arms, authority, or science.

What to do? Now a parade of truisms: The "peace-loving nations must make a concerted effort in opposition" to treaty violations and other causes of "international anarchy and instability." But then FDR began to hint at something more novel, more definite. "There is a solidarity and interdependence about the modern world, both technically and morally, which makes it impossible for any nation completely to isolate itself from economic and political upheavals in the rest of the world." What was the president hinting at? Suddenly he came out with it.

"When an epidemic of physical disease starts to spread, the community approves and joins in a quarantine of the patients in order to protect the health of the community against the spread of the disease."

That was all. The president said nothing further about the nature of the quarantine, who would set it up, who would be quarantined, how it would be enforced, what implication it had for American neutrality. But this was the phrase seized on by the press at the time, emblazoned in headlines, elaborately scrutinized, lauded, and assailed, and endlessly analyzed and debated by historians ever since.

The crowd had roared its approval. Back on his train the president asked Grace Tully, "How did it go, Grace?" She mentioned the enthusiastic reception. FDR nodded, adding, "Well, it's done now. It was something that needed saying." But back in Washington, Secretary Hull and party leaders were silent. Isolationist congressmen threatened him with impeachment. A telegraphic poll of Congress revealed a heavy majority against common action with the League of Nations in the Far East. "It is a terrible thing," Roosevelt said later to Rosenman, "to look over your shoulder when you are trying to lead—and to find no one there."

What did Roosevelt mean? The reaction had been no more unfavorable than he would have expected. He was used to other "leaders" dragging their tails. Did he almost *want* a hostile reaction to fortify his own caution in an area where he knew he should be bold? The best test of his commitment to explicit action lay in his follow-up. Ordinarily the White House would issue reams of supporting explanation and argument, as it had in the court fight. President and cabinet members would take to the airwaves. And FDR would offer strong guidance to the press. Not this time.

The press conference the next day was the most revealing one FDR ever held, in its demonstration both of his own uncertainties and his skill at withholding explanation when he so chose. After FDR spent almost half an hour discussing domestic policies, a reporter asked if he would explain his foreign-policy address, off the record.

What did he mean by "quarantining," the reporter asked, and "how would you reconcile the policy you outlined yesterday with the policy of neutrality" laid down by Congress?

"Read the last line I had in the speech," FDR replied. He began looking through the *New York Herald Tribune* to quote it.

"Here it is," he said. "'Therefore America actively engages in the search for peace.'"

The still mystified reporter pressed on. "But you also said that the peace-loving nations can and must find a way to make their wills prevail."

"Yes?"

"And you were speaking, as I interpreted it, of something more than moral indignation. That is preparing the way for collaborative—"

"Yes?"

"Is anything contemplated? Have you moved?"

"No; just the speech itself."

"But how do you reconcile that? Do you accept the fact that that is the repudiation of the neutrality—"

"Not for a minute. It may be an expansion."

FDR repeated that this was all off the record.

"Doesn't that mean economic sanctions anyway?"

"No, not necessarily. Look, 'sanctions' is a terrible word to use. They are out of the window."

"Is there a likelihood that there will be a conference of the peace-loving nations?"

"No, conferences are out of the window. You never get anywhere with a conference—"

"You say there isn't any conflict between what you outline and the Neutrality Act," reporter Ernest Lindley asked. "They seem to be on opposite poles to me, and your assertion does not enlighten me."

"Put your thinking cap on, Ernest."

"I have been for some years. They seem to be at opposite poles. How can you be neutral if you are going to align yourself with one group of nations?"

"There are a lot of methods in the world that have never been tried yet."

The baffled reporters tried to zero in.

"Is a 'quarantine' a sanction?"

"No."

"Are you excluding any coercive action? Sanctions are coercive."

"That is exactly the difference."

"Better, then, to keep it in a moral sphere?"

"No, it can be a very practical sphere."

Practicality. Experimentation. Trial and error. Once again, "pragmatism" was in charge of Washington thinking, but ideology, backed up with naked power, was in charge in the foreign capitals that soon were carefully studying the president's remarks.

Chapter Ten
THE TWILIGHT OF THE NEW DEAL

Charleston Gazette (West Virginia), July 31,
(*Courtesy FDR Library*)

Buffalo News, January 4, 1938.
(*Courtesy FDR Library*)

"Dear Felix: I am glad you dug up those excerpts about T.R.," Roosevelt wrote Frankfurter in mid-December 1937. "Tooth nearly well. It did not touch the bone but was deep in the gum. Taking very good care of myself. I shall be delighted to have Borgese's book. I have heard much of him and I hope he will raise a dozen American-Italian children, all good citizens."

It was one of FDR's pithy little letters that revealed much and concealed much. The excerpts from press denunciations of Theodore Roosevelt just thirty years ago were especially heartening when Franklin Roosevelt faced still-rising hostility from conservatives. The attacks might have been made in the fall of '37.

"Those anxious and confiding Republican businessmen and editors who expected the President to utter a 'reassuring' word did not know their man," wrote the *New York Evening Post*, in August 1907. "His way of calming a nervous patient is to give another shock . . . radical . . . disturbing . . . disastrous." At the same time, the *New York World* demanded, "Always more law, more law—when will the President's clamor for legislation end? When will he give the legitimate business interests of the country a breathing spell?" TR's policies "threaten to paralyze every line of legitimate business," *American Business Man* complained a few months later.

FDR's tooth note was no run-of-the-mill dental complaint. He had suffered in November 1937 a deep molar abscess that inflamed the right side of his face and spread fever and pain to his whole body. His illness, which caused weeks of both postponed work and vacation, was treated in the press as some kind of gastrointestinal upset—one of the few references to the president's health by newspapers that continued to conceal the incapacity of his limbs, rarely raising any question about his health—except, in the rabid right-wing tracts, his mental health.

And his reference to Giuseppe Borgese, whom Frankfurter had portrayed as a "gift" from Mussolini, "one of those old-fashioned, capacious, versatile, continental fellows in the tradition of Goethe," reflected the president's concern for the antifascist intellectuals, artists, and scientists he was helping, in a guarded way, to escape from the dictator's persecution.

It was a cheery note that masked FDR's disappointments and anxieties. The final weeks of 1937 were some of the unhappiest of his life. Caught between his decidedly unneutral attitudes toward Nazism and his public neutrality, between his ad hoc interventionism and his professed non-interventionism, he felt helpless in the face of German and Italian aggressiveness in Europe. While the antifascist nations were weak and vacillating, the Axis was moving. In November, Japan had signed an anticommunist pact with Berlin and Rome, and there was nothing the president could do about it. And for every Borgese who could be rescued, thousands of Europeans lay at the mercy of fascist aggression and anti-Semitism.

The sting of his defeat in the fight over the Supreme Court still vexed him. And it was exacerbated by his appointment of Senator Hugo Black of Alabama to the vacancy Associate Justice Van Devanter had created. A powerful spokesman for southern populism, Black met all of FDR's criteria: relatively young, a non-Easterner, a committed liberal who nonetheless would gain approval from a Senate that otherwise had turned refractory. Then disaster: The *Pittsburgh Post Gazette* revealed that Black in his early political career had been a member of the Ku Klux Klan. A nine-day orgy of denunciation and recrimination followed as Black, who was vacationing and book-hunting in Europe, returned on a Cunarder to face the music. Mobbed by journalists on the boat, he bypassed the print press by taking to the radio—and an audience of tens of millions—to denounce his persecutors, to explain that he had joined and then *left* the Klan, and to stress that some of his best friends back home in Birmingham were Catholics and Jews. Through all this FDR never uttered a word, nor did he later.

A more serious carryover from the court fight were several bills that had been laid aside during the court melee: a major farm bill that would set up an "ever-normal granary" to store bumper crops in surplus years for later release in lean years, a fair labor standards act that would put a floor under wages and a ceiling over hours, a bill for reorganizing the executive branch, and a measure to establish planning machinery in the national government. The president had called Congress back into special session; Congress had debated the measures for weeks and had adjourned without passing any of them.

Roosevelt's great solace during such periods was threefold—family, close associates, and train and sea trips—and on occasion he combined all three. He thoroughly enjoyed taking his sons on fishing excursions, sometimes on Vincent Astor's yacht, the *Nourmahal;* he virtually took over the cruiser *Houston* as his personal vessel; and each year he scheduled spring and fall trips by railroad to Warm Springs. Eleanor, who did not relish ocean travel and would accompany him, if at all, no farther than the port of departure, could not understand Franklin's affinity for the "*Nourmahal* Gang" of wealthy yachtsmen.

Nor did she enjoy the male camaraderie that highlighted many of FDR's trips—the poker games, moderate drinking, loud laughing and joking and almost juvenile horseplay. There was much telling and retelling of hunting and fishing yarns. Missed shots and lost fish were noted, recollected, and derided. Roosevelt needed this kind of humor, needed it all the more because he could not hunt, or play tennis or golf, or fish except from a fixed position on a boat. Through camaraderie he could feel close to action that he could not share.

Sometimes he went beyond horseplay to jokes that had a sharp edge of cruelty. Earlier in the year, when he called in Joseph Kennedy to offer an appointment as the ambassador to the Court of Saint James, he stopped Kennedy as young Jimmy Roosevelt ushered him in.

"Joe," said FDR, "would you mind standing back there by the fireplace so I can get a good look at you?"

The puzzled Kennedy complied.

"Joe," the president went on, "would you mind taking down your pants?"

Incredulous, Kennedy did.

"Joe," said FDR, after staring at his bare legs, "you are just about the most bowlegged man I have ever seen." He would have to wear knee breeches and silk stockings and would be a laughingstock in the press. "You're just not right for the job, Joe." While the unflappable Kennedy smoothly replied that he would gain special permission to wear a cutaway and striped pants instead, and did so, the story, as told by James, lingered for years as a prime example of FDR's insensitivity. Few noted, however, that this was a man essentially lacking legs embarrassing a man who had them, bowed or not.

Surprisingly, given five years of heavy pressure on the administration, the top leadership of the New Deal was remarkably stable. All FDR's top cabinet appointees were still in their cabinet posts: Cummings as attorney general, Farley the postmaster general, Hull in State, Ickes in Interior, Perkins in Labor, Wallace in Agriculture, and Morgenthau in Treasury (having served almost from the start, after Woodin's death). Missy LeHand and Grace Tully, Early and McIntyre, served him in the Oval Office and oval study; Hopkins (aside from a long period of illness), and Cohen and Corcoran and Rosenman were still his close advisers; Frankfurter and a host of others were still his frequent correspondents. He puzzled, exasperated, mentored, chided, delighted, raised them up, and cast them down; but they stuck with him, and he with them.

He needed this fixity in his turbulent life; even more, he needed the fixity of his family. But his family was hardly a fixed entity. Louis Howe, who had become virtually a member of the family, was gone, though not the memories of his sardonic wit, his blunt advice to the president, his mentorship to Eleanor Roosevelt, and his penchant for staging elaborate family charades. Anna and the boys had been going through marriages and divorces. Anna, thirty-one years old in late 1937, was married to a newspaper editor and lived in Seattle. James Roosevelt, despite his mother's doubts about the idea, had agreed to serve as one of the president's assistants, and Franklin Jr. had married Ethel du Pont.

The president looked forward to the usual big family Christmas, but the family gathering would not be so big this year. Eleanor would be visiting Anna in Seattle; Elliott and his second wife would remain in Fort Worth, Texas; and FDR Jr. would leave with his wife during Christmas Day to join the du Ponts in Greenville, Delaware. This was the second year in a row that Eleanor had missed the White House Christmas festivities; the year before she had rushed to a Boston hospital where Franklin Jr. was ill. Now she was with Anna, who was recovering from an operation.

Still, on Christmas Day the president thoroughly enjoyed the early invasion of his bedroom by excited youngsters, watching the stockings opened in front of the fireplace, telephone calls to Eleanor and Elliott, and the traditional family dinner in the evening, with his mother sitting across from him. During the day he attended services at the Church of the Covenant. The sermon had hardly been soothing.

"It is Christmas Day in Spain," declaimed the young Reverend Mr. Peter Marshall, "and machine guns rattle in the hills. It is Christmas Day in China—and shrapnel is falling in the rice fields.

"Peace on earth! Goodwill toward men! Say the words over and over and you will be shocked at the hypocrisy of a world celebrating in solemn manner something it has not taken to heart." If the president looked unusually grave as he left the church on James's arm, could he have been reflecting that once again he had heard a sermon with no solution?

1
Cloudburst: The "Roosevelt Recession"

Realist though he was, the president could hardly have foreseen that 1938 would be the worst year yet for the democracies—that between March and September, two European countries would be lost to Hitler. Even less could he have predicted that 1938 would be the worst year yet for the New Deal, both economically and politically, and that he would have to spend far more time dealing with domestic problems than even with foreign crises during this dire period.

Economic storm signals had been mounting during 1937, but not to the degree that led FDR to see them as more than the usual ups and downs of the stock market and other indices. Earlier in the year conditions looked good, even compared to the boom year of 1929. The heavy spending in election year 1936, including payment of the veterans' bonus, had brought reemployment high enough so that the administration concluded it was now possible to slacken off on spending, even though around 10 percent of the workforce was still jobless and over four million families were still on relief.

But by the end of 1937, even this progress seemed threatened. There was a "Black Tuesday" on Wall Street in October reminiscent of Hoover days, a sharp fall in steel production, a surge in unemployment to a shocking height of ten million and still rising. Virtually all the other economic indices were alarming.

What to do? So pleased had FDR been by the 1936–37 "recovery" that he had felt he at last could redeem his repeated promises to balance the budget. And now his liberal advisers were saying that the drop in government spending to a trickle had drastically cut incomes and spending. But he was sticking to his budget-balancing philosophy. Even during the fall, as the crisis mounted, he was reassuring the ever-anxious Morgenthau that he was working on spending reductions.

Roosevelt kept his mask of self-assurance even while becoming more and more uncertain as to what course to take. In January 1938, he delivered his annual message: a substantive, thoughtful analysis of the underlying national problems in agriculture and business, a weighing of the pros and cons of different solutions, discussion of wages and taxes, an earnest restatement of the New Deal and of his unwavering belief in an activist government that has "a final responsibility for the well-being of its citizenship," and—once again—a call for a balanced budget. He resubmitted his 1937 legislative program and vowed he would not "let the people down." "Bert," FDR said to Republican leader Bertrand H. Snell after his talk, "as they used to say on the East Side of New York, 'that wasn't esking them, that was telling them!'"

If FDR was uncertain about the means to his goals, he was never uncertain about the goals themselves. His Jackson Day speech, on January 8, sought to remind his listeners of the true "morals of democracy"—the rule of the majority versus a handful of autocrats who claim vested rights to power. He urged Americans to join him in the spirit of Jefferson and Jackson, Lincoln, and Theodore Roosevelt to curb the power and privileges of small minorities, especially those businessmen who "will fight to the last ditch" to retain their autocratic control over the economy.

The struggle to enact New Deal legislation, for FDR, was part and parcel of the class warfare that had been going on since the battles between Federalists and Jeffersonian Republicans. "In our Nation today," he told the Jackson Day dinner crowd, "we have still the continuing menace of a comparatively small number of people who honestly believe in their superior right to influence and direct government, and who are unable to see or unwilling to admit that the practices by which they maintain their privileges are harmful to the body politic." There was no doubt about FDR's leadership role: "To serve the needs, and to make effective the will, of the overwhelming majority of our citizens and . . . to curb only abuses of power and privilege by small minorities."

But FDR discerned an odd twist. The cunning strategy of the plutocrats in their fight against the New Deal, he observed, was to convince the people that their true interest lay with the interests of big business, thereby blinding them to the reality of the class struggle. They were using, he declared, "an ancient strategy" whereby those would want to exploit or dominate a people "seek to delude their victims into fighting their battles for them." Thus the plutocrats hoped to convince people that the government's move against minority abuses was really an attack upon the exploited majority itself.

With these plutocrats there "is going to be a fight—a cheerful fight on my part"—but without "compromise with evil."

. . .

It was a good show of bravado, but in reality FDR was puzzled. While still talking budget-balancing, he began to consult business leaders, economists, and others about a change of strategy. Slowly he found himself immersed in a mortifying repeat performance, exploring virtually the same four alternatives that had faced him in 1933: economy, government-business collaboration, trust-busting, spending. It was trial by error all over again—long after the earlier experimentation had been assumed to lead to solutions.

A fierce backroom war broke out among his advisers. Facing again the chaos of king-of-the-hill business competition and boom-and-bust industrial production, the president was sorely tempted to return to the NRA idea—not the act itself—of government sitting down with business around a table to estimate future demand and supply and stabilize the market. Even though the president claimed he was seeing more businessmen than any other group, this idea never got very far—in part because at this point industry and government did not trust each other that much.

Far more popular with key White House advisers was the opposite course, a return to "trust-busting." Frustrated during the NRA days, advocates of Brandeisian economic decentralization were returning to the battle. They not only considered economic monopoly unfair and undemocratic, they also contended that inflexible prices and rigid structures had helped bring on the recession. FDR was responsive. In a message to Congress late in April 1938 he charged that blanket price increases, excessive price leadership, and other rigidities should be considered illegal. But, whatever the long-run desirability of fairer competition and freer markets, few could argue that future laws would have major impact on the still deep recession.

The question was, What could be done quickly? and another set of advisers had their answer: Spend, spend now, spend big. Harry Hopkins, recovered from "ulcers," was at hand with a readily available list of fine WPA projects. Ickes, who had glumly accepted the diminishing of his beloved Public Works Administration, also had his grander projects. Of a far different cut was Marriner Eccles, a Utah banker who had increasingly impressed the administration with his broad grasp of the economy in his chairmanship of the Board of Governors of the Federal Reserve System.

And there was still—and always—Treasury Secretary Morgenthau, day in and day out urging budget balancing with the certainty of the true believer. He had extensive support in Congress and in the business community. But opposing groups were active too. One hundred thousand people turned out for a relief demonstration in Detroit; three thousand youths mobilized in Washington to call for a "youth act" that would provide part-time jobs.

As the palace struggle over economic strategy was rising to its height, an unsolicited letter arrived for FDR from John Maynard Keynes. "You received me so kindly when I visited you some three years ago that I make bold to send you some bird's-eye impressions," Keynes began innocuously, and then proceeded to a blunt attack on the president's recent economic policies. Recovery was possible only through large-scale public works and other spending. Keynes, who moved amid Britain's business elite despite his views, warned the president away from secondary efforts, such as "chasing the utilities around the lot every other week." He even tried to improve FDR's understanding of those strange creatures, businessmen, who he said required different handling from politicians.

"They are, however, much milder than politicians, at the same time allured and terrified by the glare of publicity, easily persuaded to be 'patriots,' perplexed, bemused, indeed terrified, yet only too anxious to take a cheerful view, vain perhaps but very unsure of themselves, pathetically responsive to a kind word. You could do anything you liked with them, if you would treat (even the big ones), not as wolves and tigers, but as domestic animals by nature, even though they have been badly brought up and not trained as you would wish."

Roosevelt did not write back to Keynes; perhaps he reflected that British businessmen must be rather tamer creatures than the ones he knew in America. He turned the letter over to—of all persons—Secretary of the Treasury Morgenthau and signed the secretary's routine response.

Once again it was not general theory but specific conditions to which FDR did respond. In March the stock market's halting decline turned into a sudden sickening drop. Unemployment was still mounting. Secretary of Agriculture Henry Wallace and others in the administration were urging him to provide again, in Wallace's words, "that firm and confident leadership which made you such a joy to the nation in March of 1933." Even some business leaders were guardedly calling for spending.

Late in March the president journeyed to Warm Springs; on the way back he stopped off in northern Georgia to make one of his most bitter assaults on minority selfishness, making another declaration of war against the plutocrats.

Disagreeing strongly with Keynes's advice that it was a mistake to consider businessmen "more *immoral* than politicians," FDR excoriated the wealthy—as had Cousin Ted. The stock market slump seemed only to fan his anger. "Today, national progress and national prosperity are being held back chiefly because of selfishness on the part of a few," he declared. The nation could not permanently get on the road to recovery, he explained, if the methods of recovery were left to the discretion of those "who owned the Government of the United States from 1921 to 1933." Those same plutocrats who oppose progress, he asserted, believe in their hearts "that the feudal system is still the best system," and, he added, "there is little difference between the feudal system and the Fascist system. If you believe in the one, you lean to the other." After watching people standing to wave at him on the trip north, he turned to an assistant. "*They* understand what we're trying to do."

His mind made up, he decided to move quickly and vigorously. He urged Congress to pass a $3-billion spending program as soon as possible, and the legislators moved to comply. But now he had Morgenthau to contend with. In company with Hopkins and son James, he held an evening meeting with the obviously unhappy secretary shortly after the return from Warm Springs.

"We have been traveling fast this last week and have covered a lot of ground," the president challenged him, "and you will have to hurry to catch up."

Morgenthau said he doubted that he ever could.

"Oh, yes, you can," FDR said airily, "in a couple of hours."

It was a hard two hours. At the end Morgenthau said, "What you have outlined not only frightens me but will frighten the country." And, "How much is it going to cost?"

"Oh, we have all that . . . ," the president said, "we have all that."

During the following days, Morgenthau told his staff that he was more frightened than he had been since 1933. He infuriated FDR by informing congressional leaders, against his boss's wishes, that the new program would boost the 1939 deficit by at least $3.5 billion. He worked on Eccles and other administration advisers. And he threatened to resign.

"You just can't do that," FDR said. "You have done a magnificent job." If Morgenthau quit, he said, the Democratic party would be destroyed, a third party would come about, and the administration program would fail in Congress.

Besides, FDR added, if he resigned, Morgenthau would go down in history as having quit under fire. Morgenthau stayed.

. . .

Presented by Roosevelt with his new spending program, Congress responded with—for Congress—alacrity. The legislators had already voted a fresh $1.5 billion for Reconstruction Finance Corporation loans; to this the legislators joined the president's request for about $2 billion for direct spending, along with another $1 billion mainly for loans. Added to the administration's desterilization of gold reserves held by the Treasury, over $6 billion was soon being injected into the economy. Put into effect quickly by Roosevelt's eager spenders, the economy began to edge up again, though a large carryover of unemployment continued to drag recovery.

Congress also lived up to the old adage that lawmakers like nothing more than boosting spending and cutting taxes. In May, Republicans and southern Democrats took the lead in repealing the progressive normal tax and undistributed profits tax passed in 1936. The action distressed the president because it almost canceled the graduated tax on undistributed corporate surpluses and indeed repudiated the progressive tax principle by establishing a flat 15 percent on capital gains. But the president found some good items in the bill, especially its lightening of tax burdens on small business. In this dilemma he took a most un-Rooseveltian way out—for the first time in his presidency, as he announced to a West Virginia crowd, he would let a bill become law without his signature.

Congress also took the initiative on two measures less important in themselves than in their foreshadowing of the future. In May the Naval Expansion Act of 1938 authorized a $1 billion expansion of a "two-ocean navy" over the next decade, with increases for aircraft carriers, capital ships, and cruisers. And in the same month the House of Representatives established a committee to investigate "Un-American Activities," which came to be known as the Dies Committee after its chairman, the conservative Texas Democrat Martin Dies. Its task was to conduct probes into Nazi, fascist, communist, and other organizations deemed "un-American."

And there was a measure that both echoed political storms of the past and would precipitate more in the future. In 1906, at the height of Upton Sinclair's and the muckrakers' attacks on rotten meat in processing centers, Congress had responded to Theodore Roosevelt's call for reform with the Pure Food Act. Over thirty years later, after the act had proved ineffective in myriad ways, Congress replaced it with the Food, Drugs and Cosmetic Act of 1938. Toward the end of the Hundred Days in 1933, Roosevelt had approved a tough food and drug bill that Tugwell had brought to him—supported it, Tugwell felt, largely because of TR's 1906 leadership on the issue. But after that 1933 bill encountered a storm of opposition from advertisers and newspapers, as well as from drug and cosmetic makers, FDR's support faded away, and Tugwell was left exposed in the heavy crossfire. Now, in the 1938 act, Congress was strengthening the reach of regulation through the Federal Trade Commission, but the act left many gaps in coverage and loopholes for lawyers, which set the stage for more sharp struggles in the decades ahead.

What had happened to the four measures left over from the 1937 session? Congress finally passed one of them in February—the Agricultural Adjustment Act of 1938. Incorporating the "ever-normal granary" notion that Wallace had struggled for over the years, the bill authorized the secretary of agriculture to fix marketing quotas when surpluses of export farm commodities—notably corn, wheat, cotton, rice, and tobacco—threatened price stability; authorized acreage allotments to each farmer after two-thirds of the growers voted to approve the marketing quota in a referendum; and authorized the Commodity Credit Corporation to make loans to farmers on their surplus produce slightly below parity. The president was pleased by both the democratic, or plebiscitary, aspects of the measure, and by the near certitude that a major farm bill would now survive Supreme Court scrutiny.

The early and easy passage of the farm bill contrasted sharply with the plight of wages and hours, another of FDR's measures held over from 1937. Never had an FDR "must bill" received such a battering as the proposed Fair Labor Standards Act. Introduced in Congress in May 1937 by Senator Black and the co-sponsor, Congressman William P. Connery of Massachusetts, it met furious opposition at once, not only from southern legislators protecting their low-wage industries but also from organized labor, which feared that governmental protection would offer workers an easy alternative to union efforts. After more mangling in the Senate, the bill passed the upper chamber, only to become imprisoned in the House. A stalemate continued for months, as a conservative coalition stood firm in its demand for a north-south wage differential. Finally, in a tumultuous twelve-hour session, the House passed the bill by a decisive vote.

Now both chambers had passed the bill—but in two different versions. Southerners threatened filibuster, and labor warned it would oppose the bill if differentials were restored. Then, at last, a breakthrough; a conference committee skillfully negotiated a compromise.

When FDR signed the bill late in June 1938, exclaiming with a sigh of relief, "That's that!" it must have been with a sigh of disappointment as well. The early economic impact of the bill, which set a minimum wage of 40 cents an hour, would be minimal. Still, the forty-four-hour-week maximum, with time and a half for overtime, would lead to more and longer weekends for workers. And tucked away in the bill was a provision it had taken a century for the nation to adopt—a ban on labor by children under sixteen.

At least the wages-and-hours bill finally went through, however tattered. But on another of the carryover bills from 1937, executive reorganization, the president suffered a humiliating defeat.

On the face of it, administrative reform would appear to be the most widely popular of all FDR's proposals. For decades presidents, leaders of both parties, political scientists, and organization experts had been calling for an extensive overhauling of the executive branch. Businessmen wanted the government to be more "businesslike," and Americans eagerly swallowed reforms that would appear to foster efficiency and economy. Denunciations of "bureaucracy" had swelled during the New Deal years along with the bureaucracy itself. As FDR's agencies expanded, he too became more and more critical of the overlapping and lack of coordination. He wanted to put the chief executive's administrative machinery "on the same kind of an efficient basis" as "an industrial plant or a private charity or even the financial end of a church."

With such a consensus it was not surprising that FDR's recommendations were received with considerable support, despite some quiet hostility in Congress and general apathy, when he presented them in January 1937. He proposed to strengthen executive authority and responsibility by putting independent agencies under the line departments; to create two more such departments, Social Welfare and Public Works; to expand the White House staff; to substitute a director of personnel for the existing three-member Civil Service Commission; and to extend the merit system "upward, outward, and downward to cover practically all non-policy-determining posts."

Shunted aside during the court fight, these proposals marked time while the Supreme Court bill held the center of the stage. Not until late February 1938 did reorganization come before the Senate. The time was not auspicious. Memories of the outcries against "dictator Roosevelt" were ready to be reinvoked. Alarmed by the opposition's strength in Congress, Roosevelt, along with his chief politicos Hopkins, Corcoran, Farley, and Ickes, pulled out all the political stops, as they traded White House favors and patronage plums for congressional support.

Even the most hardened administration operatives could not have anticipated the hurricane of opposition to the reorganization bill. A "National Committee to Uphold Constitutional Government," launched by the conservative publisher Frank Gannett and his chain of newspapers, sent out almost a million letters urging protests to Congress. Father Coughlin, rallying from his 1936 setback, fulminated against the bill. A columnist warned of possible Hitlerism. Scores of "Paul Reveres," mounted on horses with banners reading NO ONE-MAN RULE, forayed up Pennsylvania Avenue toward the Capitol to save Congress from tyranny.

It was the Supreme Court fight all over again, but now with an almost hysterical edge. A proposal for minor executive reorganization had been converted into a lunge for dictatorship. FDR was so forced on the defensive that he took a course unusual for him—direct and quick repudiation of a charge at the height of battle, rather than using his own timing. Suddenly summoning reporters late at night at Warm Springs, he announced: "(a), I have no inclination to be a dictator; (b), I have none of the qualifications which would make me a successful dictator; (c), I have too much historical background and too much knowledge of existing dictatorships to make me desire any form of dictatorship for a democracy like the United States of America."

Perhaps this disclaimer helped the Senate to pass the bill despite the defection of as loyal a senator as Robert Wagner in the face of ten thousand telegrams of protest and reservations of his own. But the crucial test lay ahead, the House. Remembering the charges against him of "stubbornness" during the court fight, the president was willing to make concessions. Under the original measure Congress would have had power to veto presidential reorganization only by a two-thirds vote in both chambers; now the president agreed that only a majority vote would be required, thus making it easier for White House proposals to be defeated. In vain. Responding to pressures from administration agencies like the Veterans Bureau, as well as potent interest groups, the House of Representatives recommitted the bill to the hostile Rules Committee by an eight-vote margin.

When the president tried to accept defeat gamely by writing thank-you notes to Speaker William B. Bankhead and Majority Leader Sam Rayburn, he ran into a small White House rebellion. FDR should not take his defeat lying down, Ickes protested.

"Mr. President," Ickes said, according to his diary, "if I were you I would call a special meeting of my Cabinet. I would say to them: 'God damn you, I am not going to be satisfied with lip service with respect to this bill. I want every one of you to get out and line up every vote you can.'" As for that letter to Rayburn, Ickes said, Corcoran and Missy LeHand were opposed to such a conciliatory response to Congress.

The president toned down the letter but still sent it. No retaliation—yet.

2
The Disruption of the Democratic Party

On the face of it, Roosevelt appeared to accept his setbacks of early 1938 with good humor. After a White House visit in mid-May, Frankfurter wrote that he marveled at "the sense of serenity that everything about you conveyed." The Harvard law professor, who invariably flattered FDR, continued, with a kernel of truth, "With some knowledge of American history, I had the feeling that not since Lincoln has the White House had an occupant with such imperturbability of soul." Like Lincoln, he said, the president combined democratic faith, antiseptic humor, and largeness of view.

FDR seemed to be his usual cheery self in his repartee with the reporters, his self-assured and even cocky speeches, and his warm letters to personal friends. He resumed good relationships with some old allies—notably New York governor Herbert Lehman—who had deserted him in the fight over the Supreme Court. He was off on a cruise in July, he wrote William Allen White, "and I know the old health is holding up because I have not bitten off the heads of the office staff for months."

Behind this mask of breezy self-confidence, Roosevelt was a deeply frustrated and perplexed president.

Frustrated, because of the behavior of Congress. Of the "Big Four" carryover bills from 1937, the lawmakers had passed only one intact: the farm bill. The wages-and-hours bill had been terribly compromised, and Congress had virtually ignored his "must bill" for governmental planning machinery. But for FDR the most stunning disappointment of all was the defeat of the executive reorganization bill. It was a sharper challenge to his presidency than the court bill defeat; in that case, after all, he was intruding into the judiciary's domain, while on administrative reform the Congress was invading *his* turf.

It was a familiar story: FDR remembered visiting Theodore Roosevelt in the White House in 1905, TR stamping up and down in front of the fireplace in the oval room upstairs, muttering, "Sometimes I wish I could be President and Congress too."

How to deal with such deadlock? For a time the president's perplexity seemed greater than even his frustration. He was an old pro—he had served as state legislator, Washington politico, and governor; he knew all about the checks and balances, the game of politics, the pressures of interests, the give-and-take of executive-legislative relationships, the need for compromise in a democracy. Yet it was hard to comprehend how the huge Democratic and progressive majorities of 1932, 1934, and 1936 could have eroded so rapidly, especially on bills like wages and hours that came straight out of the progressive heritage represented by both Roosevelts.

FDR was so skilled in cloaking his deeper emotions that we will never know how in the spring of 1938 he was dealing, emotionally and intellectually, with his "dilemma of deadlock." We do know he tended to think not in terms of institutions, classes, and ideologies but of individuals, specific friends and foes, concrete situations.

This trait may throw light on the most daring, dangerous, and extreme political decision Roosevelt made during his entire political career—to try to purge the Democratic party of key congressional conservatives who had fought his programs.

Even his way of loosing this thunderbolt betrayed some mixed feelings and calculations on his part. In a long fireside chat late in June, he began by listing much that the 75th Congress had accomplished—not only two of the four carryover measures but bills to establish a new Civil Aeronautics Authority to supervise commercial aviation and air mail, to set up the United States Housing Authority for funding large-scale slum clearance and low-rent housing, and to authorize stepped-up spending programs for the Works Progress Administration, Public Works Administration, Rural Electrification Administration, Civil Conservation Corps, and other agencies. The president slyly noted that the Supreme Court had now shown willingness to cooperate with the two other branches "to make democracy work."

He then turned to himself. After the 1936 election, he said, he was told "by an increasing number of politically—and worldly—wise people that I should coast along, enjoy an easy Presidency for four years, and not take the Democratic program too seriously. They told me that people were getting weary of reform through political efforts and would no longer oppose that small minority which, despite its own disastrous leadership in 1929, is always eager to resume its control over the Government of the United States.

"Never in our lifetime has such a concerted campaign of defeatism been thrown at the heads of the President and Senators and Congressmen" as in the past year and a half. "Never before have we had so many Copperheads," he said, the people who in an earlier crisis had tried to make Lincoln give up his fight against slavery.

Having waxed congratulatory and militant, Roosevelt then became defensive as he discussed the economy. The fault, he said, lay with capital and labor, and with government too—but the last mainly for believing that industry and labor would make no mistakes and for delaying the passage of the farm and wage-and-hour bills. Once again the president denounced the businessmen who kept crying for restoration of "confidence" while showing indifference to the suffering of the people and thwarting all the efforts of the New Deal. More progress had to be made, and he would need help. The 1938 election would be a test of liberalism versus conservatism, and Democrats needed to distinguish between the two sides.

"As President of the United States, I am not asking the voters of the country to vote for Democrats next November as opposed to Republicans or members of any other party. Nor am I, as President, taking part in Democratic primaries.

"As the head of the Democratic party, however, charged with the responsibility of carrying out the definitely liberal declaration of principles set forth in the 1936 Democratic platform, I feel that I have every right to speak in those few instances where there may be a clear issue between candidates for a Democratic nomination involving these principles, or involving a clear misuse of my own name.

"Do not misunderstand me. I certainly would not indicate a preference in a State primary merely because a candidate, otherwise liberal in outlook, had conscientiously differed with me on any single issue. I should be far more concerned about the general attitude of a candidate toward present-day problems and his own inward desire to get practical needs attended to in a practical way." FDR complained of "reactionaries" who said yes to progressive goals but blocked specific action—this type he labeled as a "yes, but" fellow.

. . .

In this electrifying talk, which unleashed avalanches of praise and denunciation, the president made a double promise not to take part, as president, in either the primary or general elections of 1938. On the faulty premise that he could separate a part of himself out as party leader, he proceeded to violate the second promise and later the first.

Two weeks after his "purge" talk, the president was off in his air-conditioned railroad car for a long excursion to the West Coast, then a long sea voyage on his beloved *Houston,* thereafter to disembark in Florida for a final journey up the East Coast.

The railroad trip was mainly a delight, as FDR mixed patriotic and commemorative talks with praise carefully meted out to candidates on the basis of their cooperation with the New Deal. In Marietta, Ohio, he celebrated the sesquicentennial of the establishment of the "first civil government west of the original thirteen states," under the epochal Northwest Ordinance. In passing he made a glancing reference to Ohio senator Robert Bulkley, giving him as much support as Bulkley had to the New Deal, and only that much out of fear that an even less pro–New Deal candidate would win the primary.

The next stop, in Covington, Kentucky, brought a bit of comic opera. If there was any man Roosevelt wanted to protect rather than purge, it was Alben Barkley, a stalwart Senate leader and New Deal loyalist. Not only would a victory for Barkley prove New Deal support in this border state, but his defeat would mean the elevation of Senator Pat Harrison to Senate leadership—an outcome FDR so feared that he was in cahoots with John L. Lewis to help Barkley. The senator, however, was being challenged in the primary by Democratic governor Albert B. "Happy" Chandler, who had a big grin, a rousing platform style, a firm grip on his political organization, and dubious liberal and ethical credentials. While dignified Alben looked on, Happy seized his big chance by greeting FDR's train and adroitly sliding into the president's car and Barkley's intended place next to him. The governor took more than his share of the bows, while Barkley smoldered and FDR exhibited his usual sangfroid.

But Happy soon got his comeuppance when Roosevelt launched into a glowing endorsement of Barkley's long experience, national leadership, and legislative ability—a "son of Kentucky of whom the whole Nation is proud." He paid Chandler the dubious tribute that he "never came to Washington and went away empty-handed," but the young governor was not to be compared with the seasoned statesman. Claiming later that FDR at least hadn't "knocked him out," the irrepressible Happy tried at least to keep his thumb hooked into the president's coattails, but in a later talk FDR shook even that digit loose by hinting that Chandler had approached the White House with a deal in judicial appointments.

FDR's railway caravan zigzagged on and on across Kentucky, Arkansas, Oklahoma, Texas, Colorado, and Nevada, to California. The president made over thirty speeches—a measure of his determination to liberalize the

Democratic party as well as touch his own political bases. While he discussed many matters besides primary issues and candidates, he continued his judicious allotment of credits and discredits. In Oklahoma he praised Senator Elmer Thomas for his help on public works, without mentioning Thomas's mixed liberal record or repudiating Thomas's opposition in the primary. In Texas he smiled on Maury Maverick, who had aroused Garner's opposition for acting like a maverick, and he smiled too on twenty-nine-year-old Lyndon B. Johnson, who had won a special House election the year before. But he sent Senator Tom Connally, a court bill foe, into an icy rage by virtually ignoring him and—even worse—announcing his choice for federal judge of a man Connally had not favored.

It was becoming evident that, despite Roosevelt's claim that he would not make any single vote the litmus test, opposition to the court bill was a crucial strike against his support. In Colorado, Senator Alva Adams, another opponent of the bill, shifted uneasily from foot to foot while FDR ostentatiously ignored him. In Nevada the president snubbed Senator Pat McCarran, a stout New Deal foe, though the ever resourceful Pat managed to insert himself into the White House limelight by cheerleading the "Hurrah for Roosevelt" at every stop. In California he was reserved toward Senator William Gibbs McAdoo, merely referring to him as "my old friend," without any encomium, even though McAdoo was a longtime on-again-off-again political ally, and even though McAdoo's primary opponent was Sheridan Downey, a feared "radical" who had inherited the mantles of Dr. Townsend and Upton Sinclair by heading up a potent "$30 Every Thursday" movement.

Good news came to the president on the *Houston* even while he was cruising down the West Coast to the Panama Canal and north to Pensacola. Barkley won handsomely in Kentucky, as did Thomas in Oklahoma. While Adams too won in Colorado, and McCarran appeared certain to carry Nevada, Roosevelt had not been so involved in their races or cool to them for these to be marked as setbacks. It was the Barkley victory, with its implications for future New Deal leadership in the Senate, that won the crucial press attention.

. . .

As cheery as ever, deeply sun-tanned, evidently well rested, the president was the picture of self-confidence in Pensacola as he was piped off the *Houston* early in August 1938. Yet the most daunting phase of his "journey for liberalism" clearly lay ahead. For one thing, he was entering an area far different from the Midwest and West. Only a month earlier he had stated his "conviction that the South presents right now the nation's number-one economic problem—the nation's problem, not merely the South's." He listed the problems: wasted or neglected resources, soil abuse, absentee ownership of resources, farm tenancy, low farm income, and hence the heightened need for education, housing, health, and the protection of women and children. As a self-styled Georgia farmer he had in fact seen many of these conditions firsthand.

Too, he was entering a region whose liberalism was often as barren as its grown-over land. With some dramatic exceptions, the most intense opposition to the New Deal had been hoisted by southern businessmen, publishers, and members of Congress. The president was not about to ignore reactionary southern politicians, or snub them, or damn them with faint praise. He had come to help drive them out of office. This was the "purge." And no one symbolized and empowered southern reaction, in FDR's mind, more destructively than Senator Walter F. George, a mild, sixtyish, buttoned-up politico, whose longevity in the Senate had brought him the chairmanship of the Senate Finance Committee. Before a crowd of fifty thousand in Barnesville, Georgia, with Senator George sitting behind him, FDR told about his own coming to Warm Springs fourteen years earlier, how he found hospitality and health "in a pool of warm water," but how he had also found "one discordant note"—exorbitantly high electricity rates, four times the price of electricity in Hyde Park. This led him to the role of the Rural Electrification Administration (REA), the South as the number-one problem, and the need for southern leadership for definite action in Congress.

If the people of Georgia wanted such action, he said, they must elect "Senators and Representatives who are willing to stand up and fight night and day for Federal statutes drawn to meet actual needs"—"laws with teeth in them which go to the root of the problems; which remove the inequities, raise the standards, and, over a period of years, give constant improvement to the conditions of human life" in Georgia. FDR's tone was becoming more and more heavy and deliberate. Senator George, he said, was his friend, and a "gentleman and a scholar," but on "most public questions he and I do not speak the same language." George had neither the "constant active fighting attitude" that was needed, nor did he believe "deep down in his heart" in those objectives. Mixed cheers and boos arose from the crowd. FDR spoke slightingly of another aspirant for the Senate, former governor Eugene Talmadge, as a man merely of promises and panaceas, and strongly lauded the administration candidate, Lawrence Camp, an able young attorney.

On the platform, George rose to the occasion. "Mr. President," he said, "I want you to know that I accept the challenge." FDR replied blithely, "Let's always be friends."

Ignoring rising criticism throughout the South, FDR carried on. Next stop was South Carolina. The president had time for only a brief stop, but he did not waste the opportunity. Senator Ellison D. "Cotton Ed" Smith was having an unusual experience: He faced serious primary opposition for the first time in many years. Inveighing against the wages and hours bill, Cotton Ed had implied that, in his state, fifty cents a day was ample to support a family. After the usual back-platform homily, the president got in a shot at Smith as the train started to pull out: "I don't believe any family or man can live on fifty cents a day."

Roosevelt's remaining target was much farther to the north, in a border state still with a southern culture. He may have liked good old Walter George, but he despised his longtime foe, the urbane Senator Millard Tydings, who, he told a press conference, had run "with the Roosevelt prestige and the money of his conservative Republican friends both on his side," and he told the reporters that they could put this in direct quotes. Putting his biggest purge effort of all into the defeat of Tydings, the president lined up Maryland politicians behind Tydings's primary foe, Representative David Lewis. He asked the ambassador to Italy, Breckinridge Long, a wealthy Maryland politico, to provide some campaign money, and he personally stumped the state for two days in September.

FDR wove his attack on the privileged, reactionary minority into his praise of Representative Lewis. At a Labor Day address in Maryland, the president declared that the "cold-blooded few" who were "shortsightedly sure" that their interests lay in exploiting working people had adopted a strategy to divide and conquer, to turn working people against one another, making them "blind to their common interests," creating "a new class feeling among people like ourselves, who instinctively are not class conscious." The plutocrats, not the president, followed an ideology based on class. Lewis, on the other hand, had championed the Workmen's Compensation Act and old-age pensions and unemployment insurance; he symbolized, FDR assured the crowd, "the American tradition of equality."

3
The New Deal Half Dealt

It was all in vain. All three of FDR's main targets—George, Smith, and Tydings—won handsomely. "It's a bust," said Farley sourly, echoing the views of many party regulars, and a bust it was. Other anti–New Dealers or semi–New Dealers won. There was one bright spot: John J. O'Connor's defeat in Manhattan after a hard and concentrated effort by White House operatives. But the overall results were poor. "It takes a long, long time," FDR remarked during the purge campaign, "to bring the past up to the present."

The problem was the tenacity of the past, especially in the South. By 1938 anti–New Deal southern Democratic leaders no longer merely differed with FDR's liberalism. They had come to fear a president who seemed determined to curb their political power and the economic interests and racist attitudes they represented. FDR's pushing through the abolition of the two-thirds rule in Democratic presidential conventions had left southern Democrats with no veto power over the choice of his successors. And his sweeping 1934 and 1936 gains in Congress had left them without their old legislative veto power on Capitol Hill. This impotence led to fear, which in turn led to immense personal and political anger toward FDR and his White House "liberal cabal."

Inevitably, southern Democrats looked for allies. They had long held hands with conservative northern Democrats of the "old Cleveland party," but these "Bourbons" were few in number and even fewer in influence. What about combining with the Grand Old Party, with which many southern conservatives had been in de facto alliances, especially during and since the Supreme Court fight? It was not a new idea. In June 1936 the stoutly Republican *New York Herald Tribune* had urged the Republican convention to choose a conservative Democrat for vice president, and even Landon evidently was taken by the idea. That summer some "National Jeffersonian Democrats," as they liked to call themselves, broke with FDR. Republicans made overtures to the rebels, but party and ideological differences prevailed. "I am unable to see much difference between Roosevelt and Landon," said crusty old Carter Glass, the conservative Democratic senator from Virginia, "except that the former is a first-class New Dealer and the latter a second-rate New Dealer."

The court fight the next year not only eroded FDR's political prestige but also triggered renewed coalition efforts between southern Democrats and northern Republicans. GOP senator Arthur Vandenberg of Michigan wrote Landon that he might support a conservative Democrat heading a union ticket in 1940. Landon himself, noting that three years earlier he had said "we would not whip Mr. Roosevelt until we combined, as the Liberals and Conservatives did in England in 1929 against the Labor-Socialist party," still eyed this course after his 1936 defeat. But a redoubtable array of leaders stood in their path: Republican regulars, from national chairman John D. M. Hamilton down to county organizations, who believed that the GOP could win on its own in 1940—so why share power with *any* Democrats?

While conservatives were enjoying enticing notions of bipartisan coalition, FDR's own coalition had come under severe pressure. His somewhat tattered battalions still included union workers, farmers enjoying price supports, middle-class professionals (save for most physicians), southern Democrats "till the last dog dies," progressives in the TR and Wilson tradition, and numerous mercantile and financial leaders. But labor was still divided by disputes between craft and industrial unions; farm owners feared farm labor costs while tenant farmers and field laborers complained that agricultural benefits did not even trickle down to them; southern regulars were increasingly upset by Eleanor Roosevelt's—and FDR's?—friendliness toward African-Americans; and progressives were disunited as usual.

The progressives indeed posed a special problem for the president. Active in both parties, they had given him crucial congressional votes in 1933 and 1935. Several had later deserted him in the court fight, and others on executive reorganization and even the wages-and-hours bill. Two of the most loyal were senators George Norris and Robert La Follette. Two of the least were senators Hiram Johnson and William Borah. Others were hopelessly unpredictable in the eyes of White House tacticians. By 1938, progressive leaders and rank and file in both parties were eyeing Wisconsin as the showplace for a new progressivism that would attract liberals from both parties. Why not a new progressive party that would realign American party politics toward a clear-cut confrontation between a committed progressive and a stalwartly conservative party?

It was not Bob La Follette but his brother Philip, Progressive party governor of Wisconsin, who took the lead toward a new party. After several months of furious preparation, the governor announced the formation of National Progressives of America at a rally in the spring of 1938. If the arena decoration—including a party emblem of red, white, and blue—smacked somewhat of fascist mass meetings abroad, for many progressives across the country the new party offered new hope. But the reception among liberal and left leaders of all stripes reflected again their divisions. Senator Norris, perennial Socialist-candidate-for-president Norman Thomas, United Mine Workers head John L. Lewis, New York mayor Fiorello LaGuardia, *The Nation,* and *The New Republic* were not impressed.

Nor was FDR—but he responded with ridicule rather than reflection. "Did you know," he wrote Ambassador Phillips in Rome, "that Phil La Follette started his Third Party with a huge meeting in Wisconsin, the chief feature of which was the dedication of a new emblem—a twenty-foot-wide banner with a red circle and a blue cross on it? While the crowd present was carried away with the enthusiasm of the moment, most of the country seem to think this was a feeble imitation of the Swastika. All that remains is for some major party to adopt a new form of arm salute. I have suggested the raising of both arms above the head, followed by a bow from the waist. At least this will be good for people's figures!"

. . .

So it was some rather shaky New Deal constituencies that the president led into the fall election campaign of 1938. Instead of commanding a grand and united coalition, as in 1936, he spent much time putting out brush-fires. He found it necessary to defend Democratic governor Frank Murphy of Michigan against charges—made before the the new House Un-American Activities Committee—that Murphy had been a communist dupe when he refused to obey a court order to evict striking workers at a General Motors factory. He had to declare his support in California of Sheridan Downey as a real liberal despite the "$30 every Thursday" pledge, after the young Californian had beaten the old Wilsonian war horse, Senator McAdoo, in a turbulent primary. He had to tiptoe cautiously between Democratic regulars and pro–New Deal progressives. Political practicalities forced him to pay more attention than he would have liked to crucial state races, especially in New York, where Governor Lehman and Senator Wagner were seeking reelection.

It was widely assumed that the Democrats would lose ground on Capitol Hill in the 1938 elections. The Democratic majority had been so large—both houses were more than two-thirds Democratic—that Democrats had become prone to internecine struggles between conservative and liberal party members. And midterm elections almost invariably (save in 1934!) went against the incumbent president. But few—not even the realistic FDR himself—could have anticipated the electoral blow that fell on the Democratic party. Republican strength rose in the House from 88 to 169, and in the Senate by 8. The GOP lost not a single seat, while the liberal bloc in the House was halved. Many state races too went badly for the Democrats. Winning over a dozen governorships, the Republicans offered some fresher and younger faces to the nation: Leverett Saltonstall in Massachusetts, John Bricker in Ohio, Harold Stassen in Minnesota.

There were other happy portents for the GOP. A new face from a venerable Republican family emerged in Ohio as their next senator; Robert A. Taft, the son of Cousin Ted's vice president and successor, won handsomely. Wagner and Lehman both won in New York, but a brilliant and personable young district attorney, Thomas E. Dewey, came so close to beating the "unbeatable" Lehman that the challenger immediately became a "hot prospect" for his party's presidential nomination in 1940. And the GOP got rid of some possible future threats, as George Earle lost in Pennsylvania, Frank Murphy in Michigan, and—after his euphoric summer—Philip La Follette in Wisconsin.

As usual, the president refused to acknowledge defeat. The New Deal had not been repudiated, he told friends. The trouble lay in a lot of local conditions: factionalism, corruption, petty squabbles. After all, he noted, the Democrats still held big majorities in both chambers of Congress. He found other comfort in the results.

"Besides cleaning out some bad local situations, we have on the positive side eliminated Phil La Follette and the Farmer-Labor people in the Northwest as a standing Third Party threat," he wrote Daniels. "They must and will come to us *if* we remain definitely the liberal party." The president already had 1940 in mind. "Frankly," he went on, "I think the idea is slowly getting through the heads of people like Tydings and George and Bennett Clark that even if they control the 1940 Convention they cannot elect their ticket without the support of this Administration—and I am sufficiently honest to decline to support a conservative Democrat."

But what about the two years in between? "Will you not encounter coalition opposition?" a reporter asked at the first press conference after the election.

"No, I don't think so," the president said blithely.

"I do!" the questioner shot back, amid general laughter.

With his usual indomitability the president could hardly see that the reporter was right, that a new conservative coalition could block any major extension of the New Deal. And it was even harder for FDR to accept the fact that the New Deal had been stopped dead in its tracks—and at a point where the New Deal, by his own standards, had been only two-thirds fulfilled, at best.

Some of its failings were only too evident in 1938. Even after the stimulus given by the renewed WPA and PWA spending, many millions of Americans remained jobless. Tens of millions of family members were still in want. Later statistics would back up current observation: Hourly wages in manufacturing had risen by 1937 on the average only six cents above that in 1929. The percentage of women of working age in the labor force had barely risen since 1930.

. . .

Was it inevitable that the New Deal, like so many reform movements, would peter out after a few years? There were many reasons to think that this reform movement would not. It was led by a president and, increasingly, by a first lady who were absolutely committed to extensive, even transforming, change. This leader was enormously gifted as propagandist, politician, and hands-on practitioner. After much experimenting, the White House had worked out a comprehensive and relatively coherent policy agenda, which was ratified by the Democratic national party in its 1936 platform, on which in turn FDR campaigned for triumphant reelection. He had the support of a remarkably gifted and dedicated set of White House advisers, tens of thousands of local party activists, tens of millions of voters across the nation, and of Democratic majorities in Congress.

The South—where FDR made his boldest political commitment in 1938—was a special target for change for both Franklin and Eleanor Roosevelt, though they had somewhat different priorities. FDR's strategy for southern change emphasized economic measures. TVA and PWA building programs put southerners to work, including some African-Americans. Both Roosevelts were particularly hopeful about the role of young southerners. "They say that the Democratic Party can't be liberal because of the South but things are moving toward progression in the South," the president observed to TVA director David Lilienthal. The Old Guard leaders like Mississippi senator Pat Harrison, FDR went on, would be recalcitrant, but "the young people in the South, and the women, they are thinking about economic problems and will be part of a liberal group."

FDR's southern economic strategy was two-pronged. The South, he urged, must develop regionally, and this was possible only with industrialization. The South needed factories that based their strength not on low wages but on advanced technology and marketing and on paying wages that could create purchasing power as a basis for further economic development. The second prong pushed for integration of the southern economy into the national one. Nationwide thinking, planning, and action were essential for progress.

Though the president played up his affinity with the South as his second home and Georgia as his "second state," he did not resort to "southern charm" in addressing the South on its deep-seated economic problems. Better schools, better health, better hospitals, better highways would "not come to us in the South if we oppose progress—if we believe in our hearts that the feudal system is the best system." That a president who usually played his political cards with great caution could speak so bluntly was a measure of FDR's deep commitment to southern economic change.

Thus the "purge" was essentially a bold extension of a bold policy. Yet it was solidly grounded in economics. After concentrating relief and recovery funds in the South for several years, the president brought his economic strategy to its height in 1938 by staging a conference on the economic conditions of the south, composed of industry, labor, farm, government, and press representatives—and all southerners.

The conference's report thoroughly justified that label. Addressing fifteen topics, the "Report on Economic Conditions in the South" covered a dismal inventory from poor health care to deplorable housing, from soil depletion and other environmental neglect to economic backwardness, from sheer poverty to sheer human misery.

The report catalyzed feelings North and South. Not all southerners were opposed. Texas representative Maury Maverick, celebrated as the author of a definition of democracy as "liberty plus groceries," went right to FDR's point: "Let's join the United States." A handful of southern senators and newspapers applauded the report. But most of the top economic and political leadership in the Deep South reflected anger and indignation. The Southern States Industrial Council, which lobbied against higher wages for southern workers, said the report "did the South a grave injustice." Carter Glass and other senators denounced it. Northern liberals applauded the document, while Northern conservatives looked on FDR's whole enterprise as one more New Deal intervention against states' rights, the free market, and individual enterprise.

Franklin Roosevelt did not have to be a Marxist to assume that invigorating the South's economy was the first and indispensable step toward reforming its politics. The 1938 "purge" effort had soon followed on publication of the report. Here he ran headlong into an opposition that was even more backward and hidebound than the South's economy. He encountered states' rights ideas that would reserve crucial economic decisions for regional, state, and local politicians, who in turn drew their power from voting arrangements that excluded millions of poor whites as well as African-Americans; legislatures that overrepresented rural areas; Republican "opposition" parties that were in fact moribund; strong legislatures representing local and corporate interests, relatively weak governors, and powerful county Democratic committees responsive to local business pressures—in short, a politics of local oligarchies that barred intervention from the federal government and sometimes even state government. Years later the most acute student of southern politics, the distinguished southern political scientist V. O. Key, would conclude, "The South may not be the nation's number-one political problem," but "politics is the South's number-one problem."

Thus FDR was encountering a citadel of power all the more effective because it typically presented its battlements in the form of local institutions, laid-back southern pols, and a superficial southern charm. But even more potent was the ideology that undergirded all these arrangements and institutions—a pervasive and unrelenting racism. To challenge southern power inevitably was to evoke cries against "nigger-loving" outsiders, even on the part of some of the seemingly most genteel of southern gentlemen.

How to attack such a citadel? Roosevelt's answer had been to attack a few of the commanders, rather than the citadel itself. But the citadel, having been long abuilding, was rooted now in the southern economy, polity, and culture. During a few months in 1938 the president tried to mobilize small political forces, living off the land. FDR's trumpet call, at the gates of Jericho, disappeared into the air, unheard. The "purge" was a hopeless enterprise from the start.

How could the president, with his fine grasp of southern economics and with his long acquaintance with the South and with many of its politicos, stumble so badly? The answer lay in FDR's utterly personal reaction to the obstruction to the New Deal program the voters had endorsed by the tens of millions in 1936. He was angry, not at parties or institutions or "historic trends" but at *persons*—the individuals who stood in the way of justice and progress. Ever one to personalize politics, to think in terms of specific politicians, their strengths and their weaknesses, he took out his feelings on immediate targets, ones he hoped might be dissolved.

Close observers had never found FDR so aroused, so furious at "desertions," so bent on revenge, as he became after the court defeat. Farley found him, for weeks and months afterward, "smoldering against the members of his own party." George Creel, a longtime friend and close observer, wrote later that the president "took no pains to hide his anger." His "resentment crystallized into the desire to crush all who conspired against the throne."

Anger evoked anger. Senators, though often concealing their resentment, were furious over the president's highhandedness, as they saw it, during the 1937–38 conflicts. They could not ignore Roosevelt's handing out carefully measured plaudits, criticism, coolness, and nonrecognition, before and during the purge, much like a headmaster giving out rewards and reproofs. He was exacting a "high school girl revenge," complained a *Saturday Evening Post* writer. The president compounded all this by hitting recalcitrant legislators where it hurt, in their states and districts, by cutting off patronage and withholding federal aid projects. Southern politicians responded in the only way they knew how—by exploiting every veto trap, every malrepresentative institution, every special-interest device, every racist angle embedded in the southern political system.

FDR thought and acted in terms of specific situations, not vast systems. He probably did not realize, despite his long acquaintance with southern racial customs, how deeply embedded in racism was southern politics. Eleanor Roosevelt did have a clear sense of southern racism—and believed, even more than FDR did, in the need to approach the problem through economic measures as well as through social change and political reform.

4
Eleanor Roosevelt: The Other New Deal

Addressing three hundred members of the Junior League of New York City in November 1933, Eleanor had described a man most of her listeners could hardly imagine—a man who had been imprisoned for stealing food for his starving family. While in jail the man had been a model prisoner, but upon his release he declared to the warden that he would steal again if necessary.

"I wouldn't blame him," Eleanor confessed to her audience. "You would be a poor wishy-washy sort of person if you didn't take anything you could when your family was starving. Put yourself in someone else's position, thinking what right others have to more than they need when you haven't anything. Civilization is not going to last based on such conditions in various parts of the country."

Eleanor was speaking toughly and from the heart. Not many would have addressed decorous upper-class philanthropists in such a manner. But she knew this audience: Fear of social upheaval was a sure way to arouse the upper and middle classes to the need for reform. And when angry letters denounced her statement, as reported in the press, she calmly defended her position. "Revolutions do not start until great groups of people are suffering and convinced of the hopelessness of their cause getting a fair hearing. . . . Certain changes must come!"

Speaking out on controversial issues, working behind the scenes on others, inviting socially conscious groups to meet at the White House, tirelessly lobbying for the things she believed in—Eleanor was crafting a shadow New Deal. She could venture where Franklin could not go, politically as well as physically. She took stands on issues when he could not, listened to petitions he had to turn away, entertained ideas that were politically dangerous. Sometimes this meant waxing enthusiastic over utopian ideas the president shrugged off as ludicrous and impossible. But it also meant that, through his wife, Franklin could appease groups whose proposals he had to defer as well as come into contact with reformers, radicals, and a variety of civic leaders whom he would not otherwise have met. "Eleanor had a lot of 'do-gooders' to dinner last night," he would mention to a staff member the following morning, "and you know what that means."

It was not always clear when Eleanor had Franklin's direct support and when she was acting on her own, and both the president and the first lady preferred it that way. He could remain apart and gauge the political effect when she took a strong position; Eleanor, meanwhile, knew she had more influence when people thought her husband was behind her. On many issues he would explain to her what his policies were. In a talk to one group of women, Eleanor began, "I was talking with a man the other day, and he said . . . " When one member of her audience asked who the man was who had made such probing points, she replied, "Franklin."

She never forgot the mood she had sensed, like an ominous rumble of thunder, among miners in Morgantown, West Virginia. In other places as well, throughout America—in city slums, on impoverished farms, among the unemployed, the hungry, the bitter—men and women were still in want and despair and needed to know that the government was aware and concerned. Regarding young people in particular, "It was essential to restore their faith in the power of democracy to meet their needs, or they would take the natural path of looking elsewhere." Nothing, in her view, was more likely to bring on chaos and revolution than an indifferent or repressive government. As she saw it, the New Deal was a bulwark against communism.

One way Eleanor reached out to people was through her writing. Her daily column "My Day," begun at the end of 1935 at the invitation of the United Feature Syndicate, reached tens of thousands of readers. Her autobiography, *This Is My Story*, came out in 1938. In both she shared the homey details of White House life, some of which were not so different from her readers' own concerns. Offering a vision of wholesome values, of family love and solidarity, of caring and commitment, she provided reassuring glimpses of Franklin as the ideal father, serious and concerned yet capable of having fun, steady as an experienced captain piloting through stormy seas.

Eleanor was serious about her column, partly because of her admiration for the journalism profession and partly because it fulfilled her longing for the discipline of a job. She was under contract for five-hundred-word pieces six days a week and took great pains to meet deadlines, whether she was working, traveling, celebrating, vacationing, or nursing a sick family member. But she also understood the power of her column. Through her words, millions of Americans received a daily picture of a sane, caring, gracious White House. And occasionally she would disclose some new development that Franklin was not ready to publicize, forcing him to adopt the habit of warning her when their conversation was straying off the record. She donated most of her writing and speaking fees—for radio broadcasts and for lecture tours around the country—to the American Friends Service Committee.

So much did Eleanor journey around the country that one headline in the *Washington Post* announced MRS. ROOSEVELT SPENDS NIGHT AT WHITE HOUSE. "She travels—and how she travels—the U.S. 1 of middle-class psychology," *The Nation* reported, "and she combines in her person all those qualities that please and flatter it most." Her causes seemed almost endless: "Rural arts, housing, country life, WPA libraries, public health, community centers for Negroes, flood control, the eight-hour day for nurses, safety campaigns, white and black cooperation, education. But they are all sugar-coated with accounts of the dinners for the Supreme Court justices and Cabinet receptions which delight the hearts of people who would scorn her social views if they were presented by a solemn social worker."

Eleanor's top priority, in both her writing and her politics, was to include those who had been on the outside looking in at American prosperity: African-Americans, women, children. Perhaps, having grown up an outsider, she was especially sensitive to the injustice of leaving so many out of the American dream. One December evening in 1938, attending a dinner to raise money for European refugees, she heard speech after speech praising America as the land of the free. The next morning she roused the readers of her normally cheery column with a passionate question: "Are you free if you cannot vote, if you cannot be sure that the same justice will be meted out to you as to your neighbor, if you are expected to live on a lower level than your neighbor and to work for lower wages, if you are barred from certain places and from certain opportunities?"

Earlier in the year she had sounded a similar note, speaking on the seventy-fifth anniversary of the Emancipation Proclamation. "We still do tolerate slavery in several ways," she said. "Today we are facing another era in which we have to make certain things become facts rather than beliefs."

Although she spoke to white audiences about the injustice of discrimination, she sounded a different note when addressing African-Americans, stressing the importance of education and self-discipline. "Anyone in a minority group has got to strive to do a better job," she said, "not just for himself as an individual, but because it is going to help the whole group that he belongs to and because it is going to have an effect on what all the others are going to be able to do. Every time we fail, every time we do not do our best, we don't just let ourselves down, we let down all the others that we might help if we did our best and we did succeed."

Yet Eleanor's primary style was reactive; she would see a pitiful or unjust situation and respond to it, firing off a letter to the appropriate department head or congressman. Grace Tully, FDR's secretary, recalled a particularly heartrending letter Eleanor received from a destitute young mother. Eleanor was going out of town, but she asked Tully to take milk and eggs and other necessities to the woman, and on her return she grilled the secretary on the woman's circumstances: her health, the children's cleanliness, the condition of the apartment. Then Eleanor proceeded to visit the woman herself and invite her to Hyde Park, where she received instruction as a seamstress. Later, the woman was able to secure a job.

Eleanor helped Morgenthau and Hopkins when they needed $250,000 for milk for needy children in Chicago; she intervened on behalf of striking farmworkers in Arkansas, thirty-five of whom were jailed; she supported and protected women in her husband's administration, especially Secretary of Labor Frances Perkins, who often came under fire. Even the peanut vendor who stationed his cart near the White House was rescued by Eleanor from a sweep by the Washington police. "I would myself miss him on that corner," she wrote FDR's press secretary. "We had better let him stand at the White House gate."

In hundreds of cases, big and small, Eleanor followed her heart, believing that something should and *could* be done and she would be the one to do it. She had an unconquerable sense of responsibility, or, as she put it, "I had this horrible sense of obligation which was bred in me, I couldn't help it. It was nothing to be proud of, it was just something I couldn't help."

As a member of the privileged class that she herself blamed for the problems of the Depression, she felt she personally should do everything possible to correct the situation. She carried in her purse, Eleanor's friend and biographer Joseph Lash reported, a prayer attributed to St. Francis in which one asks God to grant "that I may not so much seek to be consoled as to console, to be understood as to understand, to be loved as to love."

No group was worse off than African-Americans. As early as mid-1933, when she had been involved in establishing the subsistence homestead in Arthurdale, a controversy had erupted over whether African-Americans would be part of the new community. Black families had been especially hard hit by the collapse of the soft-coal industry in West Virginia.

That fall Eleanor called a meeting of African-American leaders at the White House. Her guests included Walter White, head of the National Association for the Advancement of Colored People; Mordecai Johnson of Howard University; Robert Moton of the Tuskegee Institute, and others. It was the first time that such a distinguished group of Negro leaders had been invited to the White House to discuss issues of burning importance to them.

Hour after hour they bluntly described the crisis among American blacks to Eleanor, Clarence Pickett of the American Friends Service Committee, and the New Deal administrators present. The president joined them briefly around midnight. The leaders agreed that access by African-Americans to the programs and benefits of the New Deal was the most urgent need and that desegregation of the South would have to come second.

Out of that meeting grew Eleanor's approach to civil rights. Her emphasis would for many years be on equal opportunity, not desegregation. Education and literacy, housing, jobs, equal wages, and equal access to relief: These became her paramount goals. But even more pressing was the attempt to end mob violence against African-Americans. On civil rights in general, and on the issue of lynching in particular, Eleanor was far ahead of Franklin.

Lynching, the extremist nightstick of the white southern establishment, had taken the lives of scores of black men and women during the previous fifty years. Twenty-eight lynchings occurred in 1933 alone. In one case, a young black man was burned at the stake in Princess Anne, Maryland. The state attorney general, who fought to bring the mob of lynchers to justice, was almost lynched himself when he went to the scene. Walter White barely escaped a mob when he went to investigate another lynching.

Because southern states were unwilling to enact legislation against lynching, the NAACP had turned to the federal government. The Costigan-Wagner Anti-Lynching Bill, sponsored by Senator Rober Wagner of New York and Senator Edward Costigan of Colorado, slowly gained support during the early 1930s, winning endorsements from a number of state legislatures, along with church, labor, women's, and civil rights groups representing millions of voters. Filibusters, however, continually stalled Senate consideration of the bill. In April 1934 the bill was taken up in the Senate and was quickly condemned by southern senators, who claimed lynching was necessary "to protect the fair womanhood of the South from beasts." During the Senate debate, Senator Theodore Bilbo of Mississippi suggested that all Negroes be sent to Liberia along with Eleanor Roosevelt, who should be made "queen of the Negro nation." The bill barely hung on the calendar.

During the next few weeks, Walter White tried again and again to meet with the president to elicit his definite stand on the bill. FDR was cautious, concerned that public support of the bill would alienate the Democratic southerners he deemed so critical to passing his New Deal economic measures. In desperation White turned to Eleanor, who he knew was sympathetic to the plight of blacks. She immediately arranged an interview between White and the president.

Franklin was late for the meeting, but he arrived at last, ebullient and, as White later wrote, determined to postpone serious discussion by recounting a series of funny stories.

Finally White managed to turn the conversation to the critical issue at hand. To every objection the president raised to the anti-lynching bill, White had an answer. After a few minutes of this Franklin interrupted. "Somebody's been priming you. Was it my wife?"

White and Eleanor wanted to stick to the subject; even Franklin's mother, Sara, who was also present, told her son that she supported White. Franklin burst out laughing.

Then he got serious. "If I come out for the anti-lynching bill now," southerners would "block every bill I ask Congress to pass to keep America from collapsing. I just can't take that risk." Indeed, southern senators managed that spring to keep the bill from coming to a vote. And though the bill passed in the House of Representatives in 1937 and in 1940, it was defeated both times in the Senate.

Eleanor's and White's persistence on the anti-lynching bill exasperated the president. FDR discouraged Eleanor from speaking at a Carnegie Hall anti-lynching protest rally, warning her that if she spoke it would be "dynamite." But most of the time, she had carte blanche. "You can say anything you want," FDR allowed, adding, "I can always say, 'Well, that is my wife; I can't do anything about her.'" Some of FDR's advisers, particularly FDR's press secretary Steve Early, a Virginian, were far more upset. Early, who had barred African-American reporters from covering the president's press conferences, considered White provocative, "insulting," and a troublemaker. Eleanor had defended White by saying that although he indeed seemed obsessed with the bill, "if I were colored, I think I should have about the same obsession."

In early 1939, Eleanor attended the first meeting of the Southern Conference for Human Welfare, in Birmingham, Alabama. This group of eighteen hundred delegates viewed economic conditions in the South as the nation's biggest problem. Housing was desperately inadequate; public education was almost nonexistent for African-Americans, whose schools even had their own specially published textbooks. Sharecroppers and tenant farmers spoke up. Recommendations included more aid for education, extension of the Farm Security Administration programs, repeal of the poll tax, and more. Eleanor spoke on education and brought a letter of support from her husband.

Although the focus of the conference was economic, the reality of southern racism forced the group to address the issue of discrimination right at the start. The city of Birmingham insisted that the conference observe segregation laws and seat white and black delegates in separate parts of the hall. The organization reluctantly decided to comply, in order to proceed. But when Eleanor, accompanied by applause, walked into the hall and noticed the segregated seating, she sat down on the black side, next to her friend Mary McLeod Bethune, director of Negro affairs for the National Youth Administration. One of the officers sent by the sheriff tapped her on the shoulder and told her to move. Eleanor agreed to move her chair to the center line between the black and white delegates, and during the rest of the meeting she carried her little folding chair with her, always placing it in the middle of the room, in a race-free zone of her own.

"If the people of the South do not grasp this gesture, we must," wrote the weekly *Afro-American,* in praise. "Sometimes actions speak louder than words." Another group, the National Conference of Negro Youth, also officially thanked ER for her courage in Birmingham. If Eleanor was a bit less valiant than Rosa Parks, her gesture, in the context of her times, seemed eminently principled. She later would urge that, in defending equal rights and the preservation of civil liberties, "we must have courage; we must not succumb to fear of any kind."

But civil disobedience was not a possibility for a first lady, and even in the White House the segregation policies of Washington were observed. A few years earlier, in May 1936, Eleanor had invited the students and the staff from the National Training School for Delinquent Girls to a garden party at the White House. Though three-quarters of the girls were African-American, the White House served blacks in one tent, whites in the other.

Eleanor of course entertained African-American friends—like Mary McLeod Bethune and Walter White—in the private quarters of the White House, but the public White House was another story. At public functions, she bowed to segregation laws and even accepted—though reluctantly— Steve Early's dictum that black women journalists be excluded from her press conferences. Still, the young guests from the National Training School for Delinquent Girls clustered eagerly about the first lady, and Eleanor received praise from the African-American press for hosting the occasion. After the party, she called for a new rehabilitation program for the girls to replace the appalling conditions in the school.

Issues of racism, education, and economics were, Eleanor felt, all intertwined; for racism to end, "the Negro race as a whole must improve its standards of living and become both economically and intellectually of higher caliber." For long-term solutions to problems of race, she agreed with Franklin's emphasis on economic reform. "The economic situation," she wrote in 1940, "is the reason for much of our intolerance today." The country had to solve its economic problems "or we can never hope to wipe out intolerance." She suggested to Ralph Bunche, when he interviewed her for Gunnar Myrdal's book on American democracy and race relations, *An American Dilemma*, that often class—hence economic justice—and not race was the problem.

Another incident caused a firestorm, forcing Eleanor to assert herself again on the question of race. In 1936, she had invited Marian Anderson, the celebrated soprano, to sing at the White House. Three years later, in early 1939, Howard University wanted to present Anderson in concert in Washington's Constitution Hall, the largest auditorium in the city. The

Daughters of the American Revolution, who controlled the hall, refused
to let an African-American artist perform there.

Eleanor debated how to respond. In the past when she disagreed with
a policy or action of an organization, she had remained a member and tried
to influence it from within. But now she found herself in disagreement with
a group's basic tenet. "They have taken an action which has been widely
talked of in the press," she wrote. "To remain as a member implies approval
of that action." In a gesture that separated the woman she had become from
the woman she had been brought up to be, Eleanor resigned from the DAR.
Endicott Peabody, the headmaster of Groton and friend of TR and FDR,
wrote to voice support for her rejection of the "prejudice, I might say cruelty, with which we have dealt with the negro people. Your courage in
taking this definite stand called for my admiration."

The concert featuring Marian Anderson did take place—free and in
the open air—in a location charged with symbolic meaning: in front of the
Lincoln Memorial. Seventy-five thousand people heard Marian Anderson sing "America" and "Nobody Knows the Trouble I've Seen." "The
whole setting was unique, majestic, and impressive," Harold Ickes wrote
in his diary. But Eleanor was absent, fearful of antagonizing southern voters
and politicians even more.

To some extent, ER's attitudes toward race and prejudice were shaped
by her upbringing and her times. Her paternal grandmother, the mother
of Theodore and Elliott, had grown up in a slave-owning family in Georgia, and little Eleanor had heard her great-aunt Annie Bulloch Gracie de-
scribe plantation life and the slaves who slept at the foot of their masters'
beds. "I quite understand the southern point of view," Eleanor told southerners. When she used terms like "pickaninny" and "darky," that was part of
the intimate language of her family. When readers of the second installment of her memoirs protested against her use of the word "darky," Eleanor
responded that the word was used by her great-aunt as a "term of affection" and that she had "always considered it in that light," but she would
try to abstain from repeating the offense.

Still, the mentality of the times permitted only limited progress. Reply-
ing to people who criticized her for inviting and dining with Negro children in Hyde Park, she wrote that "eating with someone does not mean
you believe in intermarriage." At the National Conference on Fundamental
Problems in the Education of Negroes, she told delegates that education
for the Negro people should help them develop their special talents, for
"we know that there are in every race certain gifts." Among the "gifts" of

African-Americans, she could not resist mentioning "music and rhythm." And she entitled an article on race written in 1953, "Some of My Best Friends Are Negro."

But a few unfortunate choices of words and an occasional recourse to retrograde stereotypes cannot diminish ER's ardent commitment to equal rights. If she was less than an incendiary firebrand on race, she was more vocal, consistent, and brave on racial justice than anyone else in the administration, save perhaps Harold Ickes, who had been president of the Chicago chapter of the NAACP. "Sometimes it is better to fight hard with conciliatory methods," she wrote to a WPA teacher. "The South is changing, but don't push too hard." Within a few years, however, she would start to push harder.

. . .

While African-Americans were victims of the Depression and racism, American youths were also suffering. Three million American young people, Frances Perkins estimated, were out of school and unemployed. "I have moments of real terror," Eleanor confessed, "when I think we may be losing this generation. We have got to bring these young people into the active life of the community and make them feel that they are necessary." Only a "pretty poor" civilization, she wrote, does not provide a way for its young people to earn a living. FDR had considered the Civilian Conservation Corps and its reforestation camps adequate to meet those needs. Eleanor liked the CCC in theory but felt it was too militaristic; she wanted instead to put the spirit and idealism of young people to work in a mission to rebuild America.

Collaborating in 1934 with Harry Hopkins, still head of the WPA, his assistant Aubrey Williams, who had been a social worker in Alabama, and numerous young people, she conceived a two-year volunteer program. Young people who were out of school and jobless would work in government jobs or on public service projects—hospitals, settlement houses, schools, libraries—and live in camps. Hopkins and Williams asked her to present the idea to the president, fearing he would reject it for political reasons—that a government youth program seemed too much like the regimentation of youth under Hitler.

Franklin's response, according to Eleanor, was, "If it is the right thing to do for the young people, then it should be done. I guess we can stand the criticism, and I doubt if our youth can be regimented in this way or in any other way."

Not long after, the National Youth Administration was born, with an initial budget of $50 million in relief funds. "It was one of the occasions on which I was very proud that the right thing was done regardless of political considerations," Eleanor later wrote, pleased that "it turned out to be politically popular and strengthened the administration greatly."

Eleanor cared passionately about the NYA, checking monthly reports sent her by Aubrey Williams, who had become head of the department. But she was also aware of criticism—from the National Educational Association and from Republican politicians. Defending the NYA against critics who branded it ineffective and wasteful, Eleanor observed that although the program did not offer a fundamental solution to enduring problems, we "bought ourselves time to think" while providing "hope at a time when young people were desperate." She was also aware of criticism from within the program; she knew that when young people emerged from the work camps, they often could find no jobs. Some gravitated to the American Youth Congress, a turbulent body of youth agencies, rife with internecine conflict among socialist, communist, and democratic groups, that by 1936 had a decidedly radical, anti–New Deal outlook.

Convinced that "every shade of thought should be represented in every Youth Congress," Eleanor agreed to attend a meeting of the American Youth Congress in January 1936 and field questions. Though the questioners were hostile to New Deal "sops" and demanded an "American Youth Act" costing billions of dollars, a tactful, patient, and open-minded Eleanor remained unfazed, even when she was attacked for using "empty rhetoric" by the Young Communist League. Reminded by their brashness of her own children, she appreciated their determination to confront problems of unemployment, racism, education, and economic equality. One of the student leaders she met in 1936 was Joseph Lash, who became her lifelong friend and perceptive biographer.

While insisting that youth congress leaders take a more realistic approach to their proposals, she continued to speak to youth representatives—even inviting them to tea at the White House—about difficult subjects, for example discussing with pacifist youth the dangers of isolationism. The American Youth Congress, and the Popular Front of which it was a member, began actively to support the programs of the New Deal, no longer calling for enactment of the American Youth Act but instead lobbying for more support for the NYA.

But the right wing never let up; now they attacked her for her support of young people. When she attended the Second World Youth Congress, which took place at Vassar College—close to Hyde Park—in August 1938, the Roman Catholic Church, the Boy Scouts of America, and various right-wing groups charged that she was collaborating in a communist-dominated organization. For her part, Eleanor responded that she had "no doubt that there are many Communists among [the delegates], but they are not strong enough to rule the entire group." She had gone to the Congress "to find out what these young people are thinking about." They, after all, would have to solve the problems of the future.

The delegates' fairmindedness and mutual respect struck her. "The Chinese listened while the Japanese spoke; the boy from India spoke with the British delegates sitting not far away," she wrote. "I have been in lots of gatherings of adults who did not show that kind of respect for others' points of view." As one young delegate recalled, "She didn't go around talking down to us. She came right in to every session, sat with earphones like everyone else. Ate ice cream cones and [conversed] with hundreds of delegates. Never forget the time she became so interested in the story of a Chinese student that she ruined an expensive summer dress by letting ice cream goo drip all over it." At one evening's activities, she was greeted with a standing ovation. The young people, she wrote to Lorena Hickok, were "so earnest and full of hope" she would try to help them as much as she could. And she did—showing up uninvited, in December 1939, at hearings of the House Un-American Activities Committee, which had subpoenaed members of the American Youth Congress.

The National Youth Administration was not a fundamental answer, she told the American Youth Congress in the winter of 1939, but it was "something which has given us hope."

5
A Valley Transformed

If the New Dealers were treading heavy water by late 1938, and Eleanor Roosevelt's "shadow New Deal" was but a promise of things to come, Franklin Roosevelt could take enormous satisfaction in one program that appeared to be achieving the kind of social transformation—real change in people's lives—that he sought so ardently. This was regional development of the Tennessee River valley. He rarely seemed happier than when inspecting dams and homesteads and newly formed lakes in the "valley."

For FDR the TVA was a dream—a dream that embraced a multitude of visions, visions that illuminated a variety of plans, plans that laid out hundreds of practical actions, actions carried out with shovels and trowels—the dream of a people living harmoniously, productively, in a great river valley. The visions encompassed the protection and enhancing of mountains and rivers, forests and farmlands, life in communities and along streams and lakes. The practical tasks were innumerable, ranging from digging soil-erosion ditches to the building of enormous dams.

In a variety of ways, directly and indirectly, the TVA dream was the collective product of a stunning diversity of talents: Gifford Pinchot, TR's national forester, Bull Mooser, and Pennsylvania reform governor, who served as a personal link between the two President Roosevelts; Henry Ford, who wanted to buy and build Muscle Shoals and other dams, not only for his own industrial expansion but also to plant new towns and small subsistence farms along the Tennessee River in order to decentralize industry and restore small-town life; Morris L. Cooke, an expert in scientific management who had worked with Brandeis and Frankfurter, joined TR progressives as a foe of high utility and freight rates, and served as FDR's first head of the Rural Electrification Administration, which helped decentralize industry; social analyst Howard Odum at the University of North Carolina, who with colleagues there saw regional planning in the South as "salvaging marginal highlanders" and perhaps ushering in a "folk renaissance"; Lewis Mumford, literary and architectural critic, regional and urban planner, who for a time had high hopes for TVA but later turned against it for its failures, as he saw them, in large-scale regional planning, new town development, and decent housing.

Such diverse talents and interests—and those of scores of others of almost equal brilliance—guaranteed both that TVA would foster a multiplicity of theories as to how to unlock the human and economic potential of the valley and that it would provide a collective if divided leadership in carrying out the resulting policies and practices. This diversity of leadership was reflected in the three men FDR chose to head the Tennessee Valley Authority: Chairman Arthur E. Morgan, a widely experienced civil engineer, progressive educator, and visionary who saw TVA as a model for watershed multipurpose planning in the United States and around the world; Harcourt A. Morgan, another university administrator, an agriculturalist with special interest in cheap fertilizers, relatively cautious in his approach to social reform; and David E. Lilienthal, a much younger man than the other two, a Harvard Law School graduate who had much impressed Frankfurter, a disciple of the La Follettes, chairman of the Wisconsin Public Service Commission, and a biting critic of private utility policies and pricing.

Such dissimilar men, and the collective political and intellectual creativity that lay behind them, were indispensable for the task of carrying out the TVA's various interrelated functions: the making of cheap power, comprehensive flood control, reforestation, restoring soil and controlling erosion while retiring marginal land, building new homes and communities, creating lakes and other recreational venues, encouraging local small industries and handicrafts, and undergirding schools and libraries. The TVA idea "touches and gives life to all forms of human concerns," FDR said.

...

Who were the inhabitants of the Tennessee River valley? Northern TVA planners found the valley people as heterogeneous and individualistic as they had expected, but even more wanting and needy than they had imagined. "Battered old cars, dangling radio aerials, rust-eaten tractors, and abandoned threshing machines and hay balers scattered forlornly about"—this was the typical southern landscape described by agrarians like Frank Owsley. Cold statistics presented an even bleaker picture. Per capita income in the region was about half the national average. Less than 3 percent of the valley's farms were wired for electricity. Horribly eroded gullies, with their grassless and treeless banks, were the visible products of decades of overgrazing, overplanting, crops without roots, and general neglect.

The most telling human tragedy lay in the poor health of much of the valley people. Hookworm, pellagra, and malaria were widespread in the rural regions, black lung in the mining districts. The psychological toll was heavy too, for people displayed strange passivity in the face of suffering, leading to political apathy and what some local physicians termed a "chronic passive-dependency syndrome."

Deprivation was one of the few conditions that people of the region had in common; despite Washington impressions that a great river drainage area would show some economic and cultural coherence, the Tennessee River valley, reaching far out beyond its tributaries, encompassed a multitude of subcultures. The most striking difference lay between the hills and "hollers" of the Appalachians, the Piedmont areas fronting the eastern coastlines, and the rich meadows of the bluegrass regions lying hundreds of miles to the west. The region was peopled by Germans and other immigrant groups, as well as the more numerous Scotch-Irish, and by significant numbers of African-Americans, though far fewer than in the Deep South.

. . .

Could the valley be changed? What kind of leadership would be required? A host of architects, dam constructors, community planners, craftsmen, electrical engineers, road builders, and landscape designers moved into the valley to change the very physical appearance of the region. But from the start, planners knew that not things but people would need to change, in order to reach beyond even the TVA's lofty goals of higher pay, decent homes, cheaper power, and all the rest. But could *people* be changed?

To these questions, FDR and the TVA board were sensitive from the start. They had heard enough sermons about "do-gooders" trying to change people's lives. They knew, too, that overly intrusive programs would set off flash floods of indignant outcries about states' rights, northern interference in southern ways, and "socialism." But even more, these were leaders—not only Franklin and Eleanor Roosevelt but the people around them—who had a sense of people's needs, hopes, and longings. From the start, the TVA stressed administrative decentralization of policy making—and decision making—as a means of fostering local democratic participation. Moreover, the TVA decentralized itself, by establishing its headquarters not in Washington but in Knoxville, Tennessee.

As the TVA building programs proceeded smoothly, the figures began piling up: twenty-one large dams under construction within the TVA's first five years; flood-control programs so extensive as to contain twenty inches of rain a day for twenty days straight; an enormous channel-dredging program that opened up the Tennessee and its major tributaries to vessels drawing up to nine feet; creation of a string of lakes that offered vast new opportunities for swimming, boating, and fishing; support for regional school and library programs. The most visible of these programs was cheap electricity production from the burgeoning dams; well over a million farms were soon using electricity for the first time, at rates the TVA set at about half the national average.

Integrating these programs called for consummate teamwork in the field. Paradoxically (but perhaps inevitably), however, team spirit was notably lacking in Knoxville. From almost their first meeting, Chairman Arthur Morgan and David Lilienthal differed over central TVA strategy and even philosophy. For the chairman, the TVA was not primarily "a dam-building program, fertilizer job, or power-transmission job" but a comprehensive plan for a "designed and planned social economic order." To Lilienthal the production of electricity and its transmission though the TVA lines to the farthest hollows and hamlets was central to the goals of the entire project. Infuriated by Lilienthal's relentless support of power production, and alarmed by the intensity of the opposition of private utilities in the valley, Morgan complained to key members of Congress and eventually in a letter to *The New York Times* about Lilienthal's "intrigue" and malevolence. Refusing to back up his charges, Morgan was dismissed by FDR.

All this was a long way from the busy, bustling TVA world in its valley. By the late 1930s it was clear that the dream, the visions, and the multitude of plans were working effectively, in some cases with stunning impact on the valley's social and economic landscape. After visiting the region, Eleanor Roosevelt announced that "a more prosperous region would have been hard to find." Her typically rosy view is supported by the TVA's accomplishments—from power and flood control to malaria control to library bookmobiles, from recreational lakes to architectural design. "No other agency did so much to alter the mores of the region," concluded New Deal historian William Leuchtenburg.

Was the TVA then an act of transformational leadership on the part of the New Deal? If bringing people light for their reading and power for their washing machines, books into their homes and literacy so they could read them, low-cost recreation and community health programs, modern fertilizers and richer farmlands, protection from rampaging rivers and from erosion—if these and countless other programs amounted to a transformation in their lives, the TVA provided such leadership. But if this kind of leadership also required enduring changes in attitudes, class and race relationships, and cultural understanding and shifts away from parochialism and provincialism, progress could be neither so easily measured nor evaluated. Lewis Mumford and other social critics saw the TVA—from their own limited urban viewpoints—as a potentially magnificent social revolution that never quite came off.

In one other respect the TVA was a failure, mainly for no fault of its own. Just as its power production and distribution program was conceived as a yardstick by which the performance of private utilities across the nation could be measured, so the TVA as a comprehensive regional planning program was seen as an exemplar for other great river valley programs.

Later the president would propose seven more river authorities, most notably for the Missouri and the headwaters of the Mississippi. Congress rejected all these proposals, in part because of the TVA's internal troubles and its increasingly belligerent opponents, in part because, by 1939, Congress was more than ever in revolt against the Roosevelt administration.

So the dream of more TVAs would remain only a dream. In this respect the New Deal was not, literally, even one-half or two-thirds dealt, it was only one-seventh dealt. But in its own valley, on its own terms, the TVA was a stunning act of transformational leadership, as much on the part of the people in the valley as of its Washington and Knoxville administrators.

Chapter Eleven
THE NIGHTMARE BEGINS

"WARMONGER!"
David Low, *Europe Since Versailles*, 1940.

New York City Daily Worker, May 20, 1940.
(*Courtesy FDR Library*)

During 1938, as Franco drove toward Barcelona and cut the Loyalist defenses in two with the help of thousands of Italian troops and hundreds of Axis planes, the fascist success left a deepening scar on the democratic conscience. With an aching sense of helplessness, Americans were watching the slow murder of a democracy, along with the slaughter of tens of thousands of civilians. Idealistic young volunteers who had joined the Loyalist forces were encountering the grim realities of defeat, retreat, and death in battle. They saw that Soviet support of the Loyalists brought harsh communist control on the battlefields. And they were learning that "good" did not always win.

Feeling powerless to intervene in 1938, given the potent opposition within the Catholic hierarchy to the Loyalist cause, FDR felt even more distressed a year later by the impending Loyalist defeat but was still fearful of intervening in any major way. American opinion was intensifying, especially after the merciless bombing of the Spanish shrine city of Guernica by Axis planes. Still, the president felt his hands were tied—by the noninterventionist posture of Britain and France, by congressional obsession with "neutrality" and the foot-dragging in the State Department, and by the continued opposition of the Roman Catholic Church. He told Ickes that lifting the arms embargo on Spain would do no good, for munitions could not reach the Loyalists anyway, but when Ickes contended that such obstacles could be overcome, the president admitted that the problem was political—lifting the ban would mean the loss of every Catholic vote in the next election.

So the cat was out of the bag, a fuming Ickes wrote in his diary, "the mangiest, scabbiest cat ever."

If Ickes was the conscience of the cabinet regarding Spain, Eleanor Roosevelt was the conscience in the White House. As she saw Germany and Italy providing munitions to support Franco's Nationalist army, the Spanish war awakened her to the true power and threat of fascism—though she had been receiving reports on fascist persecution of Jews in Europe for several years without taking any action or making any public statements. She was especially stirred by the grim reports of foreign correspondent Martha Gellhorn from besieged Madrid.

"She seems to have come back with one deep conviction," Eleanor wrote in "My Day" in May 1937. "Something is happening in Spain which may mean much to the rest of the world."

Eleanor worked behind the scenes to evacuate Spanish children, help feed hungry civilians, and publicize Gellhorn's reports and a movie, *The Spanish Earth,* that Ernest Hemingway and Joris Ivens had made about the war. She soon became the target of angry criticism from the Catholic establishment, which supported Franco. Yet she longed to do more and felt frustrated by her husband's caution. "I wish that I were not in the White House at the present time and could be free to make some statement," she wrote Señora de los Rios, wife of the Spanish ambassador.

Along with Ickes, ER persistently entreated the president to lift the arms embargo against Spain. And when the State Department urged caution, Eleanor wrote bitterly to Gellhorn, "I gather that even our own State Department has people who are not very anxious to do much for the Loyalists. Strange how easily our profits affect our feelings for democracy!"

Years later, recalling the times when she had been most "annoyed" by Franklin's political caution, ER mentioned the Spanish Civil War. He wanted the Loyalists to succeed, she knew, but he justified his inaction by explaining that the League of Nations had asked the United States to remain neutral. He was "simply trying to salve his own conscience, because he himself was uncertain," Eleanor wrote. "It was one of the many times I felt akin to a hair shirt."

So it seemed to her in retrospect—but at the time she was even less forbearing. Leon Henderson remembered dining with her at the White House, the president as usual at the head of the table. Almost as though her husband were not there, she said to her guest, "You and I, Mr. Henderson, will someday learn a lesson from this tragic error over Spain. We were morally right, but too weak. We should have pushed *him* harder," nodding to her husband. Franklin Roosevelt remained silent.

1
The Living Nations Wait

March 12, 1938: Nazi troops invade and occupy Austria. Proclaiming *Anschluss,* Adolf Hitler parades before delirious crowds in Vienna.

The British and French governments issue mild protests and do nothing. The White House says nothing. Hitler has anticipated this; his only fear is the response of his ally Italy, which now borders on the annexed country. When word comes from Mussolini that he is accepting and friendly, Hitler is hysterical with relief. "Tell Mussolini," he exclaims over the phone to Rome, "I will never forget him for this! . . . Never, never, never, no matter what happens!"

March 16: Newspapers begin to report Austrian atrocities. Pro-Nazi mobs invade Jewish quarters, force men, women, and children out of their homes, rob and beat them, humiliate them in the streets, pillage their shops and homes. After Austrian police smilingly stand by, the authorities arrest hundreds of Jews.

Jewish and Protestant religious leaders in the United States urge immediate changes in immigration laws to allow rescue operations. The press calls for action. President Roosevelt takes no action but proposes an international conference on the refugee crisis; many nations accept, but the conference will not take place for several months.

May 3–9: Hitler visits Mussolini in Rome. After Hitler reviews goose-stepping Italian troops and other entertainments, the two dictators settle down for serious talk. A treaty is signed; Il Duce indicates that he will give the Führer a free hand with the next obvious target, Czechoslovakia.

There is no response from the Allies, except for heightened concern over Axis unity, no move toward the age-old means of countering hostile alliances—strengthening an anti-Hitler coalition that would include the Soviet Union.

May 28–30: Hitler summons his generals to proclaim to them his "unalterable decision" to smash Czechoslovakia soon.

Some senior German commanders dissent, contending that the Czechs have formidable defenses against Germany, that they could hold out until the British and French came to their aid, and that the Americans would eventually come in with far more power than in 1917. Hitler rejects these warnings. The Czechs refuse to be intimidated.

September 12: After brooding darkly for weeks in Berghof, his mountain lair, Hitler shouts to a huge and frenzied Nuremberg rally that he will end the "crimes" against the Sudeten Germans as he completes huge fortifications in the West. He does not threaten an immediate invasion of Czechoslovakia because British prime minister Neville Chamberlain has given every indication that Hitler can have what he wants—control of the Sudetenland and the dismemberment of Czechoslovakia—without a fight.

Chamberlain agrees to parley with the Führer in Berchtesgaden. After a three-hour meeting in the aerie, Chamberlain returns to London and meets with French premier Edouard Daladier. They agree on proposals for cession to Germany of all lands with populations more than 50 percent German. In Washington, where the State Department has been holding, in Berle's words, a "death watch" over Europe, Roosevelt is indignant but takes no public stand.

September 22: Hitler meets with Chamberlain in Godesberg to agree on final details for handing over the Czech territory. He shocks the prime minister by handing him a new ultimatum: The proceedings are too slow; he wants the key lands immediately, and more after a plebiscite.

A betrayed Chamberlain returns to London in dismay. The French call up a half million reserves; the British begin digging air-raid shelters. FDR invokes the 1928 Kellogg-Briand Pact, which pledges nations to solve conflicts by peaceful means, and urges more negotiation.

September 28: A truculent Hitler informs Britain that he will act within a day; he has already decided to mobilize and to attack Czechoslovakia. But he invites Chamberlain to meet with him at Munich.

To this sharp stick and small carrot, Chamberlain immediately caves in. He announces to a cheering House of Commons that he will meet with Hitler in Munich. A warm message arrives at 10 Downing Street from Roosevelt: "Good man." The meeting in Munich simply ratifies Hitler's demands, with a slightly slower timetable. Once again the Czechs are told they will have to go it alone if they do not accept Hitler's terms. In fury and despair they accept.

"I want you to know that I am not a bit upset over the final result," Roosevelt writes Ambassador Phillips in Rome. But in fact his reaction is much more mixed: tremendous relief that the immediate crisis is over, tempered by gnawing worries about the long-run prospect for peace in Europe. American press reaction is generally supportive but ambivalent. The *Richmond Times-Dispatch*, the *New Orleans Times-Picayune*, the *Washington Post*, the *Los Angeles Times*, the *Chicago Tribune*, and *The New York Times* are broadly favorable toward the pact, or at least toward Chamberlain's handling of the crisis. *The Philadelphia Inquirer*, the *Norfolk Virginian-Pilot*, William Allen White's *Emporia Gazette*, and the *Atlanta Constitution* are critical or skeptical. The New York *Daily News* praises Hitler's "significant gesture towards peace."

One Western leader defies this appeasement.

"We have sustained a total and unmitigated defeat," Winston Churchill protests to the House of Commons during a debate on the agreement. Feet stalwartly apart, chin sunk into his chest, thumbs planted in his waistcoat

pockets, looking up only to sweep the House with his cold stare, he pre-
dicts the future: "This is only the first sip, the first foretaste of a bitter cup
which will be proffered to us year by year unless, by a supreme recovery
of moral health and martial vigor, we arise again and take our stand for
freedom as in the olden time."

A cheering House of Commons gives Prime Minister Chamberlain
strong support.

. . .

Never in Roosevelt's presidency—perhaps never in his political
career—had his true feelings clashed so strongly with his public attitudes
and actions as during the crises of 1938.

Privately he was acutely aware of the likelihood of war. "Chamberlain's
visit to Hitler today," Roosevelt wrote Ambassador Phillips on September
15, "may bring things to a head or may result in a temporary postponement
of what looks to me like an inevitable conflict within the next five years." A
new crisis would come, he wrote Prime Minister Mackenzie King of Canada,
if Hitler did not live up to his promises. Hitler and Mussolini, he wrote his
envoy to Greece the following March, "are still on the warpath."

Publicly he made resounding speeches about aggression by the dictators and the threat of war in general. But his "even-handed" approach to
the Loyalists and the Fascists in Spain, his acceptance of the Munich pact,
and his repeated calls for negotiation and restraint among the European
powers drew a portrait of a man hopeful of peace, hopeful that dictators
would mend their ways, hopeful that reason would still prevail.

The president's ambivalence over rearmament showed itself most
unexpectedly in his treatment of the navy. Despite TR's delight in building and displaying big battleships, and despite expectations that his cousin
Franklin would build a "navy second to none," the president repeatedly
cut navy appropriations back or put expansion on hold during the middle
1930s. On the high seas, the navigator on the bridge was caught in many
crosscurrents: the isolationists' opposition to arms buildups, his own continuing hopes for disarmament, and his worry about excessive spending,
as against rising Japanese and German aggression, British and Japanese
abandonment of limitations under the old naval treaties, and pressure for
expansion from some members of Congress concerned about defense and
defense jobs. Not until the fall of 1938 was ship construction stepped up—
but precious planning and buildup time had been lost.

Privately the president came to believe, probably during late 1938, that the United States very likely would take part ultimately in the war that threatened. Harry Hopkins later asserted that, after he and the president had sat together listening to Hitler's Nuremberg speech, the "President was sure then that we were going to get into war." Increasingly, he pressed Congress and the army and navy departments for an arms buildup and greater military effectiveness; he could do this plausibly on the grounds that a stronger defense could keep America out of war, or at least keep the war out of America.

Publicly, the president's stance was that the United States must keep out of war, that he was neutral in action and policy toward the belligerents, and later that economic aid to the Allies was a way of keeping out of a shooting war. The pattern of his public remarks was a resolute expression for the need of leadership for peace, followed by a disclaimer of any intention to intervene.

. . .

The gap between Roosevelt's public policy and his private posture showed most poignantly and tragically in his concern over Jewish refugees and other victims of Nazism.

Of Roosevelt's personal concern over the plight of Jewish refugees there can be little doubt. While he had grown up in social circles where restrained but snobbish anti-Semitic remarks were common, he had rejected such talk along with many other upper-class attitudes. When he was attacked by the anti-Semitic right-wing anti–New Deal extremists for being Jewish and hence part of the all-purpose "international Jewish conspiracy," he merely answered candidly that in the distant past, his ancestors indeed "may have been Jews. All I know about the origin of the Roosevelt family is that they are apparently descended from Claes Martenssen Van Roosevelt."

FDR would never have uttered the banality "Some of my best friends are Jewish," but in fact they were: Morgenthau, Frankfurter, Baruch, Rosenman, Ben Cohen, and a host of others, warm personal as well as professional friends. These were upper-middle-class men, but over the years FDR had worked in Democratic party elections and activities with Jews and Catholics—though with few African-Americans—of diverse backgrounds.

However sympathetic FDR may have been to Jews, he felt that his power to help was limited. According to his ambassador to Berlin, William E. Dodd, FDR told Dodd in 1933 that the American government could play only a minimal role in helping Jews in Germany. FDR recognized that "the German authorities are treating the Jews shamefully," but he noted that it was not "a governmental affair. We can do nothing except for American citizens who happen to be victims. We must protect them, and whatever we can do to moderate the general persecutions by unofficial and personal influence ought to be done."

FDR was always political. For the next few years, the refugee problem for him was not what he thought but what the voters thought—and what the isolationists and restrictionists on immigration would permit.

It was also a period of virulent anti-Semitism in the United States. Gunnar Myrdal, the Swedish expert on American race relations, was convinced that anti-Semitism in America in the thirties was probably "somewhat stronger than in Germany before the Nazi era." The combination of isolationism and anti-Semitism—whipped up by Father Coughlin (whose rabidly anti-Semitic publication, *Social Justice,* would be shut down by the Catholic Church finally in 1942) and seconded by "national heroes" like the celebrated pilot Charles Lindbergh, by the people, and by bureaucrats in the lower echelons of the State Department where the issuance of visas could be effectively impeded—was a powerful stumbling block for a president who might have wished to provide more help to refugees from Germany and Austria. The quota law of 1924 had allowed for 26,000 immigrants to enter the United States from Germany each year, but regulations requiring immigrants to present proof of financial resources so as not to become dependent on the state had left immigration quotas unfilled.

In 1936 only 6,252 Jews were admitted to the United States; the following year, the number increased to 11,353. Between 1933 and 1937, as historian Sheldon Neuringer reports, 30,000 refugees entered the United States, whereas the quota would have allowed nearly 130,000. Neuringer adds that few Jewish spokesmen in the United States argued for filling the immigration quotas, worried as they were that Jewish charitable institutions might not be able to cope with more refugees and that additional refugees might aggravate already present anti-Semitism. But it was nevertheless true that the United States admitted more refugees than any other country.

In the face of such overwhelming popular support of low immigration quotas and restrictions on those quotas, FDR was willing after *Anschluss* (the political union of Germany and Austria) to merge the existing German and Austrian quotas to permit around 27,000 refugees to come annually to the United States. But he was unwilling to go beyond this concession—which, mild as it was, aroused protests in Congress. One representative in Congress berated the president for inhabiting "the warm fields of altruism" and was forgetting that one-third of Americans were "ill-clothed, ill-housed, and ill-fed."

FDR decided to leave the refugee problem to the Intergovernmental Committee on Refugees, established at the Évian conference in France, in the hope that the committee could persuade nations to share in the absorption of over half a million refugees. Predictably, the nations squabbled over their voluntary allotments, variously pleading unemployment problems, fear of German economic retaliation, or sheer opposition. Australia explained that it had no "racial problem" and had no desire to import one. The timidity, stupidity, and callousness of the international community left millions of Europeans open to extermination by the Nazis.

Early in November 1938, while the president was still pondering his setback in the congressional elections, word came to the White House of what would be called *Kristallnacht,* the "night of broken glass." Following the shooting of a German official by a deranged Jewish seventeen-year-old, Nazi chieftains unleashed S.S. and Gestapo thugs with a license to smash shop windows, wreck stores, and fire-bomb buildings belonging to Jews. Two hundred synagogues were burned, twenty thousand Jews arrested, hundreds murdered or badly mistreated. Jews were fined a billion marks as their penalty for the murder and charged with costs of repairing property.

FDR announced that the American public had been "deeply shocked," called home his envoy to Berlin—the only head of state to do so—and ordered that the visitors' visas of some 12,000 to 15,000 people be extended. But unlike fiery Cousin Ted, who had sent official protests to the Russian and Romanian governments in 1902, 1903, and 1906 condemning pogroms of Jews, Franklin planned no formal protest. Asked by reporters if he would urge that immigration restrictions be relaxed for Jewish refugees, he answered no, "we have the quota system."

. . .

If the inaction of the president can be understood in the context of the political tightrope he was walking, Eleanor's inaction—and silence—in regard to the plight of Jewish refugees before 1939 is harder to understand and excuse. To pleas for help in 1933 from Jewish refugees who painted the

situation in Germany for the first lady, Eleanor responded with cold re-
fusals. "Unfortunately, in my present position," she informed one desperate refugee, "I am obliged to leave all contacts with foreign governments
in the hands of my husband and his advisers." In her entire correspondence,
observes her biographer, Blanche Wiesen Cook, she never responded to
other requests for help with similar curtness.

To a woman who sent her an article about conditions in Germany's
first concentration camp in Dachau, Eleanor wrote, "My dear Miss Youngbar:
Unfortunately, what you have read is something which happens in Germany over which we have no control." ER, however, did not experience a
similar sense of the limitations of her political reach when it came to the
Spanish Civil War. Events in Spain would arouse her passionate involvement, inspiring her to write a steady stream of newspaper columns about
the bombings and suffering there; but reports of unspeakable anti-Jewish
violence, of concentration camps, and serious warnings of atrocities to come
appeared to leave her indifferent. Between 1933 and 1938, she "volunteered
no private or public response to reported atrocities" against European Jews,
comments biographer Cook.

Then, after *Anschluss* in 1938, confronting anti-Semitism in the United
States, ER wrote that she saw the future of the Jews tied to the future of all
races of the world. "If they perish," she concluded, "we perish sooner or
later." She lent her support to a variety of Jewish organizations and tried
to aid individual Jews, pursuing visas, helping reunite families, protesting
deportation proceedings, helping people find jobs and housing.

Finally, after *Kristallnacht,* Eleanor was no longer silent about conditions in Europe. "This German-Jewish business makes me sick," she wrote
to Lorena Hickok. "How could Lindbergh take that Hitler decoration!" she
fumed. Loosening restrictions on immigration quotas would now become
one of her causes. Once again, she would be the agitator, as historian Doris
Kearns Goodwin has pointed out, while Franklin would be the politician.

. . .

On the first day of January 1939, Mussolini accepted a German proposal to change their anticommunist pact into a military alliance. The Axis
powers were driving toward stronger collaboration, leaving Tokyo freer
to pursue its ambitions in eastern Asia. On the Ides of March, casually
breaking the six-month-old Munich agreement, Hitler occupied the rump
state of Czechoslovakia and put Slovakia under Nazi "protection." A week

later he seized the Baltic port of Memel in Lithuania. Snatching a bone thrown out by the Führer, Hungary gobbled up the Ukrainian province of Ruthenia.

The dictators were scoring triumph after triumph. Smashing the last Loyalist resistance, Franco took Madrid at the end of March and planned a triumphal parade. Early in April, Italy invaded and seized Albania. Japan occupied China's Hainan Island and laid claim to the Spratly Islands, covering huge areas southwest of Manila. Franco's Spain joined Germany, Italy, and Japan in the Anti-Comintern Pact.

To these diplomatic and military assaults the allies responded with alarm, appeals, gestures—and a modicum of action. Indignant but impotent, Chamberlain disavowed any obligation to protect Czechoslovakia against Hitler's grab. Alarmed now by Berlin's threats to Poland, the prime minister signed a mutual assistance pact with Poland, but he secured neither a Soviet guarantee of Polish boundaries nor the most vital safeguard: a firm alliance among Britain, France, and Russia to counter the unity of the Axis. FDR gave him little but moral support in such an effort. The navigator in the White House seemed uncertain, even bewildered by world events.

There was indeed little that the president could do in the face of anti-Hitler timidity and disunity in Europe. The test was his leadership in circumstances where he could act—most notably the refugees' plight. During 1939, ER worked closely with New Deal friends, including Ben Cohen and Judge Justine Wise Polier, in behalf of Senator Wagner's bill to admit—on a quota-exempt basis—twenty thousand German children to the United States, where Quakers and other humanitarians had guaranteed them homes. Anti-Semites and other "restrictionists" mounted a savage attack on the bill, which FDR would not publicly endorse. "It is all right for you to support . . . the bill," he telegrammed Eleanor, "but it is best for me to say nothing." With the failure of the president to speak out, the measure died. Other plans to help people leave Germany and Nazi-occupied countries also failed; schemes to resettle refugees in Baja California, Alaska, Africa, the Dominican Republic, and the Virgin Islands all came to naught.

"You know," an outraged Eleanor said to Judge Polier, "when I ask for help for the sharecroppers, the miners' children, the first people to come forward are the Jews." Why could people not help Jewish children now? "Because," Polier responded, "of the cruelty of the Christian world."

The worst blow to would-be refugees came from FDR's appointment of his friend Breckinridge Long to the post of assistant secretary of state for the Special War Problems Division, which handled visas, a position he held until 1943. The policy of the anti-Semitic Long, in his own words, was to "put every obstacle in the way" and use every administrative device possible to "postpone and postpone and postpone the granting of visas." Under Long, in 1941 the immigration quota went 50 percent underfilled.

Could the president have done more? Yes. He did not provide—and evidently did not seek to provide—the compelling moral leadership that could have broken through bureaucratic callousness, legislative resistance, popular ignorance, and apathy. Did his administration know about the Holocaust, about the imminent roundups of Italian Jews in 1943? Yes. But Roosevelt had to deal with reality as he saw it. He would eventually settle on the strategy—perhaps the only realistic strategy—of waging and winning a world war on three continents, without portraying that war as a "war to save the Jews." The mission would be broader than that, for it was a war to save the world. Nothing short of military power, as Holocaust scholar Lucy Dawidowicz suggested, could have saved the European Jews.

. . .

FDR's main excuse for evasion and inaction was still the anti-interventionist Congress—and fears, after 1940, of fifth columnists and spies. He still hoped that he could influence the legislators through persuasion, reasoning, education. "I do not belong to the school of thought," he told isolationist members of the Senate Military Affairs Committee during a long and candid discussion in the White House, "that says we can draw a line of defense around this country and live completely and solely to ourselves." But how to prevent Axis domination of the world? By strengthening America's "first line of defense" against Japan in the Pacific and against the dictators in Europe. This line of defense in the Pacific ran through a string of small islands that would enable the army and navy to keep Tokyo from dominating the Pacific and from cutting off U.S. access to South America, where the Nazis already were active. In Europe the first line of defense lay in Britain and France and countries dependent on them, notably Scandinavia, the Low Countries, and even Greece and Yugoslavia. Was the president saying, one of the Senate visitors asked, that the United States had a duty to maintain the independence of the nations he mentioned "by whatever efforts may be necessary?"

"No—no!" Roosevelt exclaimed. He then launched into a homily about how he had "probably" seen "more of the war in Europe than any other living persons," followed by an exaggerated version of his days on the Belgian, British, French, American, and even Italian fronts during World War I. "Therefore, you may be quite sure" of his personal conviction "that about the last thing that this country should do is ever to send an army to Europe again." The isolationists departed the session unconvinced.

Still concealing his bitterness toward the isolationists, at least in public, the president in mid-July tried once again a face-to-face appeal to key senators. After a plenteous serving of drinks and an hour of male bonhomie, the president said he should open the meeting with a prayer because Europe was on the verge of a world war. Soon Borah gained the floor.

There was "not going to be any war in Europe," at least not soon, he thundered. "All this hysteria is manufactured and artificial."

"Cordell," Roosevelt said, "what do you say to that?"

Almost in tears, Hull said that the senator should come to his office and look at the cables.

He had his own sources, "more reliable than those of the State Department," said Borah, and "there is not going to be any war." After desultory talk, Vice President Garner turned to the president. "Well, captain, we might as well face the facts. You haven't got the votes and that's all there is to it."

The president felt so frustrated by the legislative deadlock that he toyed with a bold device that had tempted earlier presidents in their times of bafflement over checks and balances: independent executive action. The former Harvard student who had told his mother in 1902 that he disapproved of Cousin Theodore for "his tendency to make the executive power stronger than the Houses of Congress," now, like TR, experienced the frustration of trying to provide strong leadership within a political system designed in the late eighteenth century to thwart just such leadership. Ickes and even Garner contended that the president had the authority to ignore the Neutrality Act under his constitutional powers as chief executive and as chief foreign-policy maker. If he failed to gain a new neutrality act, Roosevelt queried his attorney general, "how far do you think I can go in ignoring the existing act—even though I did sign it?" The president received little encouragement, and only two years after his court-packing defeat he dared not risk precipitating a new constitutional crisis.

Constricted both in his executive power and his legislative influence, the president spent many days in 1939 on rhetorical appeals and practical expedients. The most theatrical of his entreaties was also the most dramatically unsuccessful. In April he sent Hitler and Mussolini a forthright message in which he cited recent occupations and reports of plans for future aggressions. "Are you willing to give assurance," he asked the dictators as an added ploy, "that your armed forces will not attack or invade"—and then he listed thirty-one nations. Despite warnings from Henry Wallace that the "two madmen respect force and force alone," the president hoped that at least it would put the dictators on the spot. It did not.

The spring and summer of 1939 were filled with feelers, misunderstandings, secret negotiations, petty deals, rapprochements, diplomatic promises, and ordinary lies. But one fact dominated all the proceedings. The Axis and its possessions were united, despite internal differences; Hitler's adversaries were not. Suspicion of Russia pervaded allied diplomacy, while Moscow was determined not to bear the brunt of a Nazi onslaught alone. Even in the face of Berlin's threats to Poland, Warsaw appeared more fearful of Stalin's intentions than Hitler's.

It was the master Machiavellian in the Kremlin who rudely halted the diplomatic minuets. Forsaking ideology, abandoning his long castigations of the Nazis, Stalin responded to German feelers for "nonaggression" based on a division of Poland. A historic deal was cut. In mid-August 1939 announcement was made of the Soviet-Nazi nonaggression pact. As an astounded world reeled with dismay and recrimination, FDR sent yet another appeal, this time to Hitler, the president of Poland, and the king of Italy. While he had all but given up hope, he still failed to understand that Hitler did not plan on war only if diplomacy failed, Hitler *wanted* war.

Late in August a death watch settled over Washington and most of the world. A State Department official had the feeling of sitting in a house where someone was dying upstairs. "You saw," Berle grieved, "how delicate a fabric this thing we call modern civilization really is." At 2:50 A.M. on the first day of September 1939, the president was awakened by a call from Ambassador William Bullitt in Paris. German troops had invaded Poland; German bombers were swarming over Warsaw.

"Well, Bill, it's come at last," FDR said. "God help us all." Prepared for the news, the president could remember his Navy Department days; it was like picking up an interrupted routine. Two days later Ambassador

Kennedy in London notified the president that Chamberlain would make a war speech in two hours.

"It's the end of the world," Kennedy added, "the end of everything."

2
Illusions and Disillusions

Those who worked closely with FDR during the outbreak of the war marveled at his equanimity. After calmly relaying Bullitt's news to key cabinet members, he lay back in his bed and slept soundly until six-thirty, when Bullitt phoned to say that France would honor its pact commitment to Poland, after which FDR again went back to sleep.

Even as an "unknown and unknowable destiny yawned before mankind that morning," he told his cabinet later in the day, "I was almost startled by a strange feeling of familiarity"—a feeling that he had been through it before. During the World War I years, he recalled, the phone by his bedside had brought him "other tragic messages in the night." Now "the same rush messages were sent around—the same lights snapped on in the nerve center of government." From afar, Frankfurter noted FDR's "Lincolnian calm."

But there was one great difference with 1914. In that year Berlin was warring against Russia and the Allies; now the Russians were joining in the spoils. As the Nazis overran Poland, Moscow was planning to grab its half and secure other areas to consolidate its defenses against the perfidious West.

On September 3, 1939, Britain and France declared war on Germany. That evening the president gave a fireside chat that in twenty minutes summed up both the starkness of the moment and the deep ambivalence in his thinking. On the one hand, he restated more strongly than ever his determination to stay out of the war. "Let no man or woman thoughtlessly or falsely talk of America sending its armies to European fields." He was preparing a neutrality proclamation, he said. "I hope the United States will keep out of this war. I believe that it will. And I give you assurance and reassurance that every effort of your Government will be directed toward that end."

On the other hand, it was "easy for you and for me to shrug our shoulders and to say that conflicts taking place thousands of miles from the continental United States, and, indeed, thousands of miles from the whole

American hemisphere, do not seriously affect the Americas—and that all the United States has to do is ignore them and go about its own business. Passionately though we may desire detachment," every word that comes through the air, every ship on the sea, every battle affected that future.

Then he posed his ambivalence in its sharpest form. "This nation will remain a neutral nation, but I cannot ask that every American remain neutral in thought as well. Even a neutral has a right to take account of facts. Even a neutral cannot be asked to close his mind or his conscience."

Thus the president was asking the American people to share in his own dichotomy between thought and action. In doing so he was urging them to share his own capacity for divorcing talk from action when need be. But this was far easier for the master prestidigitator in the White House than for the populace. Americans increasingly were polarizing between those who wanted to aid the Allies to stop Hitler and those who wanted to escape Hitler by standing resolutely behind a barrier stretching up and down the Atlantic. They found it difficult to think one way and act another.

Even more, Roosevelt was telling the American people that they could have it both ways: They could indulge their consciences without making a commitment to action. He was giving them an easy way out of a moral commitment they might have to make—toward military action abroad. They could think interventionist, act isolationist. He was not only failing to mobilize potential interventionist strength that he might need some day, subject to Hitler's whims, he was demobilizing them morally and intellectually.

Why? FDR understood the gravity of the situation. He knew the peril to the Americas; he knew that Hitler might well crush the Allies as he had the Poles; he knew the dire peril to the Americas posed by a Nazi defeat of the Allies. But the answer was still political. Confronted by the propaganda skills and voting power of the isolationists, he did not dare take them on frontally. Rather, he would win small victories. And he scored a long-sought one when Congress by wide margins in both houses finally repealed the arms embargo in the beginning of November 1939.

The repeal was a tribute to FDR's skill in bringing around a number of internationalist Republicans such as Colonel Frank Knox, Landon's running mate in 1936, as well as anti–New Deal Democrats; even Al Smith gave a radio talk for repeal. At last the Allies, by paying "cash on the barrelhead," could obtain munitions from American ports—*if* they could raise the cash, obtain whatever arms Washington could spare, and evade German submarines and raiders infesting the long sea lanes to British and French ports.

Otherwise the president did what he could do as chief executive and chief legislator. He asked Congress for stepped-up arms programs, and the legislators grudgingly responded. He tried to energize the age-old navy and army bureaucracies and their operations. And he kept trying to cope with the refugee crisis in ways that would not arouse the isolationists.

Almost impotent in the face of the great decisions now in the hands of two men—Hitler and Stalin—Roosevelt underwent an autumn of fatigue and frustration, finding a little solace in thoughts about home.

Late in September 1939, the same month during which he was coping with the outbreak of war and the fall and dismemberment of Poland, he wrote detailed letters about preservation of the Vanderbilt, Odgen Mills, and other estates along the Hudson. At this time of turmoil he found some comfort in memories of a secure, calm, predictable patrician life. Could the Vanderbilt acres be used for a small forestry demonstration area? he wondered. Not long after, he wrote his old friend John Mack of Poughkeepsie about the inadequate water supplies of several Hudson towns. And always on FDR's mind as he followed history was the warming knowledge that his papers would go to the library being built at Springwood.

. . .

On the first day of December 1939, Soviet tanks and planes attacked across the Finnish border. Publicly the president expressed "profound shock" over what he privately called "this dreadful rape of Finland." But there was little he could do practically to help the beleaguered nation.

If the president could not stem communist advance abroad, at least he could denounce communist aggression at home. He had a most inviting target: a conference of the American Youth Congress in Washington in mid-February 1940. Under a cold rain several thousand youths marched up Constitution Avenue bearing placards calling for peace and schools, rather than more arms and aid to Britain. Swarming onto the South Lawn they confronted a president who had been told that Communists had taken over leadership of the organization and—especially since the signing of the German-Soviet pact—had dropped much of their earlier anti-Nazi militance. Eleanor had urged him to speak to the group face-to-face. Very well, he would do so, but on his own terms.

It was a most patriarchal venture. After his standard defense of New Deal economics, which fell hollowly on many working-class youths who had no jobs and expected none, the president noted that "you good people" were "getting pretty wet in this rain" and urged them to "go back to your rooms and change to dry clothes" before the next session. Then he shifted from the avuncular to the paternal. "Do not seek or expect Utopia overnight. Do not seek or expect a panacea—some wonderful new law that will give to everybody who needs it a handout—or a guarantee of permanent remunerative occupation of your own choosing." Coming from a president who year in and year out had promised security and jobs, this advice doubtless perplexed some of his rain-soaked listeners.

He lectured them further: Do not "as a group pass resolutions on subjects which you have not thought through and on which you cannot possibly have complete knowledge." He mentioned a local AYC council that had opposed loans to Finland because such action was an effort to force America into an imperialistic war.

"My friends, that reasoning was unadulterated twaddle based perhaps on sincerity but, at the same time, on ninety percent ignorance of what they were talking about."

The president saved his strongest words for the Soviets. He had had hopes for Russian communism, he said, because it might bring education and better health to millions in ignorance and serfdom, even though he abhorred the "banishment of religion" and "indiscriminate killings of thousands of innocent victims." But now his hope was shattered, or put in storage against a better day. The Soviet Union was "run by a dictatorship as absolute as any other dictatorship in the world. It has allied itself with another dictatorship" and invaded a tiny neighbor that sought only to live at peace "as a democracy, and a liberal, forward-looking democracy at that." A chorus of boos floated back toward Roosevelt through the rain.

"It has been said that some of you are Communists." As Americans they had a constitutional right to call themselves communists, to peacefully and openly advocate communism, "but as Americans you have not only a right but a sacred duty to confine your advocacy of changes in law to the methods prescribed by the Constitution"—"and you have no American right, by act or deed of any kind, to subvert the Government and the Constitution of this Nation."

The president's speech to the Youth Congress revealed more about the speaker than the audience. For a man who himself had often been called a Communist, it gave him a chance to assert his patriotism—and before an audience that gave him the perfect foil. It enabled him to be definite, didactic, emphatic, and preachy, at a time when he was still deeply ambivalent as to political and military strategy. But the speech assumed that Germany and Russia were common enemies, equally evil, equally dictatorial and militaristic, when in fact their global strategies were beginning to diverge. Russia, satiated with its occupation of eastern Poland, the Baltics, and Finnish frontier regions, and feeling more secure against attack from the West, was assuming an essentially defensive posture, while Germany was systematically preparing to attack.

. . .

Later the agonies of spring 1940 would be recalled as a single titanic Blitzkrieg that almost overnight inundated four small countries, broke the back of France, and threatened Britain with invasion. In fact the agonies of that spring spread out over sixty days, with the news relentlessly worsening with every report.

April 11: German troops invade Denmark and Norway by sea and air, routing an Anglo-French rescue force. *May 10:* German forces invade the Netherlands, Belgium, Luxembourg; defenses simply dissolve over the next two weeks. *May 14:* German troops launch their attack against France, smash through the "impassable" Ardennes and the "impregnable" Maginot Line, cut off rear communications, and open up a fifty-mile gap in the Allied defenses. *June 3:* British troops, cornered around Dunkirk, abandon France. *June 10:* Italy declares war on Britain and France. *June 13:* German troops occupy France. *June 17:* France asks for armistice terms, breaking its vow to Britain not to make a separate peace. *June 25:* German air raids on Britain intensify.

The Nazis not only crushed all the ground forces in their path, they also decimated the leadership ranks. Queen Wilhelmina of the Netherlands had fled to England. King Leopold of Belgium, having surrendered to Hitler without informing his allies, was now captive to the Nazis. Chamberlain, a broken and ailing man, had quit in the face of public and parliamentary demands that he "in the name of God, go." After a series of shifts a new "Vichy" government in France fell into the hands of Marshal Philippe Pétain, the "hero of Verdun." But new leaders arose. General Charles de Gaulle assumed leadership of the French resistance abroad. And Winston Churchill had taken command in Britain. Churchill's goals, in these desperate hours, were simple: to rally his country, if necessary, to face the enemy alone and to gain help from every friend overseas, especially from the industrial giant across the Atlantic.

Rally his nation he did: "We shall go on to the end, we shall fight in France, we shall fight on the seas and oceans . . . we shall fight on the beaches, we shall fight on the landing grounds, we shall fight in the fields and in the streets, we shall fight in the hills; we shall never surrender." And if Britain fell, the empire, guarded by the British fleet, "would carry on the struggle until . . . the New World, with all its power and might, steps forth to the rescue and the liberation of the Old." But reality overshadowed even stunning rhetoric. Britain, reported the American naval attaché in London, was "no more fortified or prepared to withstand invasion in force than Long Island."

Roosevelt did what he could to help Churchill; he expedited availability of aircraft, antiaircraft equipment and ammunition, and steel—though all cash-and-carry, of course, and subject to "our own defense needs and requirements." But the most important American move for Churchill in the long run was American rearmament, and Roosevelt repeatedly asked Congress for stepped-up appropriations for ships, planes, tanks, and guns.

The commander in chief had to look to the state of military organization as well. After long procrastination he moved to drop Secretary of War Harry Woodring, who had dragged his heels on making "surplus" war supplies available; renovated the old Council of National Defense; and established the National Defense Research Committee, involving such stellar scientist administrators as Vannevar Bush and Karl Compton of MIT and James B. Conant of Harvard. And—in perhaps his single most important administrative act—he asked Harry Hopkins, who had become his key personal assistant after a long bout with cancer, to move into the White House, where he would stay for over three years.

But still—despite Churchill's continued urgent pleas—no destroyers for Britain.

3
Leadership or Manipulation?

How to explain this Roosevelt who moved so cautiously at one of the titanic turning points of history? How to explain the leader whose rhetoric about the menace of Nazism almost matched Churchill's, while he rigidly stuck to his "keep out of war" stance, the leader who fully grasped the horrifying nature of Nazism, its threat to the United States, and his own belief that Americans must and would help destroy it—but refused to tell those Americans his true feelings? The man who had been so keen to make war in 1914 but now could not even send a few decrepit destroyers to Britain?

One answer lay in the frightful imponderables of defeat. Churchill begged him for destroyers; FDR delayed because he did not know if Britain—and its fleet—also would fall.

Another answer lay in the one political certainty of 1940—a presidential election—and the political imponderables that would come with it. The burning question for the public was whether FDR would run for a third term. He himself remained uncertain for most of his second term. Eleanor, who did not want to influence his decision, observed that he looked forward to the role of elder statesman, giving advice. Yet she saw no one else who was conceivable as a Democratic candidate, nor was Franklin seriously preparing anyone to succeed him. Sometime in the spring of 1940, without confiding to close friends or even to Eleanor, he decided to run.

In part this political decision sprang from his strategic indecision. His very lack of global control made domestic control all the more important, politically and psychologically. The terrain at home was daunting enough. He had to challenge the anti–third term tradition that had become sacred writ in American politics since 1796, when George Washington declined to run a third time for the presidency. He had to fend off Democratic rivals heating up with White House fever. And then he would have to beat the nominee of a resurgent Republican party bent on recapturing the office that earlier the GOP had dominated for eighty years.

Roosevelt assumed control through the most masterly display of deception and manipulation in his political career. He dealt with potential Democratic rivals not by being dismissive of them but by encouraging them and thus fragmenting the opposition. As usual he kept his cards to himself, not even intimating to his old friend Jim Farley, who after all was still head of the national Democratic party, that he would run. Men with only a faint hope for the presidency cautiously sounded FDR out, only to emerge from the oval study heady with the president's encouraging words. He talked up Cordell Hull, knowing full well that the elderly Tennesseean did not have the stomach—or the support—for the job. He smiled benignly on the candidacy of Vice President Garner, knowing that the "poker-playing, whiskey-drinking evil old man," as John Lewis called him, would never make it.

The president even manipulated the opposition party. In order to compose a "defense cabinet" during the June crises, he announced his selection of Republican elder statesman Henry Stimson for secretary of war and newspaper publisher and former Bull Mooser Frank Knox for navy. Planned and negotiated for many weeks, the appointments were announced on the eve of the Republican convention, arousing outrage among Republican regulars, as much against the two apostates as against the president. Otherwise the appointments aroused wide acclaim. It was a fine bipartisan gesture: The cabinet would gain two seasoned leaders, and national unity was strengthened in the face of external danger. As usual, it was hard to disentangle the manipulator's touch from the statesmanlike action—and that too was part of FDR's touch.

Still, the discombobulated GOP did quite well for itself in its convention in June, rejecting Robert Taft and other isolationists and choosing a new and charismatic figure on the political landscape, Wendell L. Willkie. A former Hoosier Democrat, Willkie had gained national notoriety as head of the Commonwealth and Southern Utility Company, from whose corporate headquarters he had bombarded the TVA, especially its control of power distribution. His open, rumpled, laid-back appearance concealed a quick keen intellect, a sophisticated lifestyle, volcanic energy, and a genial wit. And his exciting come-from-behind triumph in the convention roll call propelled him instantly onto the national battlefield.

By the time the Democrats convened in mid-July, rank-and-file party members were perplexed and ambivalent. Most of them were relieved that FDR appeared ready to run again, if only because of the lack of realistic alternatives. They nominated Roosevelt and, with some reluctance, approved his choice of Secretary of Agriculture Henry Wallace as his running mate.

The convention had one other job to do, approving the party platform, and here again the president took full control. The platform committee, chaired by Senator Wagner, had written a plank stating, "We will not send our armed forces to fight in lands across the seas." By telephone the president had added the words, "except in case of attack."

. . .

During late summer and early fall 1940, while Democrats and Republicans battled each other for the electoral backing of the American people, British and German pilots battled for air supremacy over the exposed ports and beaches of England. The Battle of Britain ended in a glorious victory for the defenders, a victory that would come to be seen as one of the great turning points in history. The battle in America ended in a victory for the Democrats—but a victory so flawed that it contained the seeds of further indecision and delay.

Roosevelt had begun by reassembling his brilliant speechwriting team of old—Rosenman, Hopkins, and Berle, now assisted by playwright Robert Sherwood, poet Archibald MacLeish, and Felix Frankfurter, who did not allow his judicial robes to hinder him from sending in a stream of advice and ideas. FDR attacked not Willkie but the big business interests for which he claimed Willkie was a front, and even more the reactionary and isolationist GOP congressional wing, which in fact suspected Willkie's internationalism. Willkie shifted his portrait of FDR from the dawdling, cautious president to that of a warmonger. For his part, Roosevelt created his own bogeymen in the form of the three anti–New Deal GOP congressmen, Martin, Barton, and Fish, a line he used so often that crowds began to pick it up and chant with him: MARTIN—BARTON—AND *FISH!*

Roosevelt evaded stands on acute policy issues—notably the draft—that might further inflame isolationists, especially those like Joe Kennedy in his own party.

But he could not evade the war. As hundreds of German planes poured bombs on English airports, factories, railroads, and entire cities, Churchill sent a STRICTLY SECRET AND PERSONAL plea to FDR: "It has now become most urgent for you to let us have the destroyers, motorboats, and flying boats for which we have asked. The Germans have the whole French coastline from which to launch U-boats, dive-bomber attacks upon our trade and food"—and he still feared attack by sea. No longer worried that the British navy could fall into Nazi hands, the president could evade no longer. In a brilliant move, he and the British devised a "horse trade"; in exchange for granting the overage destroyers, Washington gained ninety-nine-year leases on a string of naval and air bases stretching from Newfoundland to Bermuda and south into the Caribbean.

With this issue removed, the campaign continued its downward spiral. The issue was not aid to Britain, continuing the New Deal, or even defense policy, but peace—peace—peace. Willkie and Roosevelt outbid each other in promises not to go to war. As Republicans stepped up their attacks on FDR as a warmonger, Willkie appeared to be moving ahead in the polls. Frantic Democrats begged FDR to renew his pledges for peace. The president responded.

"It is for peace that I have labored," he told a Philadelphia crowd, "and it is for peace that I shall labor all the days of my life." He called Joe Kennedy home from his London post, invited him to a "family supper" where he listened sympathetically to Kennedy's complaints against the State Department for bypassing him in London, and, with the help of the first lady and others present at the supper, persuaded the hitherto reluctant Kennedy to give a radio talk for the ticket. In Boston, with Kennedy in the audience, Roosevelt made his strongest pledge for peace.

Very "simply and very honestly," he called out to a roaring crowd, he gave assurance to parents that their boys in training would be well housed and well fed. "And while I am talking to you mothers and fathers, I give you one more assurance. I have said this before, but I shall say it again and again and again: Your boys are not going to be sent into any foreign wars." This time he omitted the phrase "except in case of attack."

"That hypocritical son of a bitch!" exclaimed Willkie, listening on the radio. "This is going to beat me."

Perhaps it did. As Willkie pressed the "warmonger" issue, as Republican radio commercials warned of "your boy dying on some battlefield . . . crying out, 'Mother! Mother!'" polls showed Willkie at first overtaking FDR, who then simply outpromised him. Even so, the outcome was in doubt. Listening to returns at Hyde Park, FDR evidently saw some unfavorable report that put him into a brief funk. He had Secret Service man Mike Reilly close his study door and guard it against any visitors, including Morgenthau and Eleanor Roosevelt herself. Perhaps it was the "mothers of America" who helped him beat Willkie by 27 million popular votes to 22, and 449 electoral votes (38 states) to 82. Whatever the peace issue, however, he had gained his biggest margins in the large urban areas and among the poor, as in days past.

4
A Christian and a Democrat

Persons close to Roosevelt in 1940—and historians ever since—have wondered why the president who privately expected war publicly promised peace. Was it to appease an isolationist population and thereby win the 1940 election? Was it to dupe anti-interventionist Americans into gradual intervention?

But were most Americans really neutral toward the "Europeans' war," opposed to aid to the Allies, convinced that America lay safe behind its Atlantic barrier? Evidently not, though it was partly a question of timing. While an October 1937 *Fortune* survey found 62 percent of the American respondents neutral in their view of Germany, still 56 percent favored a boycott of German goods after Munich, 61 percent after *Kristallnacht* in

November 1938, and 65 percent after the Nazi seizure of Czechoslovakia in March 1939. If FDR was willing to "accept" Munich, most Americans were not. When Europe went to war in the fall, over 80 percent interviewed by a national poll blamed Germany for the war, and a month later a *Fortune* poll found well over 80 percent hoping the Allies would win.

In February 1939—after Munich but before the Czechoslovakia grab— almost 70 percent of the respondents favored supplying Britain with arms and ammunition in case of war. By May 1940, a Princeton poll showed more than one-third of the respondents willing to underwrite a British victory even at the risk of war, well over one-third against military intervention but favoring more American aid to the democracies, and less than a third holding out for isolationism. Four months later the isolationists measured fewer than one-eighth, and slightly more than half the respondents saw the defeat of Hitler as more important than staying out of war.

After the fall of Poland, in September 1939, a national poll found over 60 percent of respondents expecting that, if victorious in Europe, Germany would eventually attack the United States. After the fall of France over 40 percent feared an immediate attack. Another 20 percent expected a Nazi effort to seize territory in the western hemisphere.

The liberal onetime isolationist press was shifting with the impact of events. While its publisher, Senator La Follette, clung to his "unilateralism," *The Progressive* in Wisconsin prophetically noted, after the fall of Poland, "If Hitler defeats England and the British fleet is destroyed, what becomes of our splendid isolation, with Hitler on the Atlantic side and Japan and Russia on the Pacific side?" *The New Republic* sacked its increasingly isolationist columnist, John T. Flynn, and was soon urging support of the democratic cause.

Thus people and press were taking the lead toward interventionism, not Roosevelt. The president waited for events to educate the people. Yet "events" were the actions of other persons, mainly the Nazis and the fascists, but also of European leaders and their followers, American publicists, party politicos, pacifists, and ministers, priests, and rabbis. Were these the true leaders?

Roosevelt appeared daunted by some force that seemed to rise above politicians and publicists; it was not the size of the isolationist forces so much as their intensity of feeling, their political activism, their isolationist *ideology* that gave him pause politically. Before the power of this ideological tempest, the navigator retreated into the havens of concession and compromise; from these havens he could sally forth when events—and other leaders who created events—made possible his renewed voyage to war.

. . .

This isolationism was well represented in the Congress that had convened in January 1939, following Roosevelt's setbacks in the fall congressional elections. Embracing this large faction, but even broader, was a reinvigorated conservative coalition emerging from that election. Of 260 Democrats left in the House, 40 or 50 were cool or hostile to the administration. Roosevelt faced a bleaker prospect in the upper chamber. Of 69 Democrats left in the Senate, between 20 and 30 could be expected to block or water down New Deal measures.

If the conservative coalition expected moderation in return, the president gave his answer—at least in bold rhetoric—within a week of the convening of the new Congress. Captivating a typically boisterous Jackson Day dinner audience, he launched a stream of fighting phrases.

"Millions who had never been Democrats gave us the power in 1932, and again in 1936, to get certain things done. And our party can continue in power only so long as it can, as a party, get those things done which non-Democrats, as well as Democrats, put it in power to do. . . . We Democrats . . . have to act as a party in power. And we cannot hold the confidence of the people if we cannot avoid wrangling except by agreeing to sit still and do nothing. . . . If we deliver in full on our contract to the American people, we need never fear the Republican Party so long as it commands the support" of the American Liberty League and the like.

In a lower key, in this rousing address, Roosevelt made some remarks with long-run implications. "If there are nominal Democrats who as a matter of principle are convinced that our party should be a conservative party—a Democratic Tweedledum to a Republican Tweedledee—it is on the whole better that the *issue be drawn within the party, that the fight be fought out,* and that if the Tweedledums are defeated they join the Tweedledees."

Once again, despite the failure of the purge—or perhaps because of it—FDR was seeking a fundamental change in American party combat. He was demanding a showdown fight within the Democratic party, just as surely as Theodore Roosevelt had demanded and gotten a showdown within the GOP in 1912. But TR had deserted his party; Roosevelt was asking conservative Democrats to desert theirs.

But the showdown never happened. Instead, a stalemate began to intensify in Congress that would dominate policy making for two years.

The anti–New Deal coalition in Congress was not strong enough to "repeal the New Deal," but it was able to thwart its extension, harry it with investigations—especially of "reds" in New Deal agencies such as the National Labor Relations Board—and curb some of its spending.

The president followed up his speech with new initiatives and revised old ones. Never giving up on his environmental interests, he sent to Congress a comprehensive study of the energy resources of the nation and—amid the growing threat of war in early summer 1939—urged Congress to pass legislation conserving reindeer herds in Alaska. He called for better housing for middle income groups, with limited response on the Hill. In an area only marginally touched by the federal government—people's health needs—he helped engineer a national health conference that led to proposals for a modest national-state-local health program. These became part of a national health act proposed by Senator Wagner, but this bill made little progress against the opposition of the American Medical Association and its Washington lobbyists.

As the president watched his power as chief legislator ebb away in the presidential-congressional deadlock, he exploited all the more fully his authority as chief executive. The most potent of these was the appointive power, and nothing more clearly reflected FDR's continuing commitment to New Deal goals than his second-term appointments. His selection of Hopkins for secretary of commerce had been seen by business as a calculated affront to business leaders, who had long looked on the cabinet post as a place for building "confidence" in the free enterprise system. Hopkins's later selection as, in effect, FDR's chief of staff had hardly alleviated business anxiety.

Roosevelt's appointments of a string of "New Deal" Supreme Court justices and lower federal court judges, most of them relatively young, showed that the president would leave a "Roosevelt stamp" on the judicial system for years, just as Theodore Roosevelt's selection of Oliver Wendell Holmes Jr. and others had done. FDR's elevation to the Court of William O. Douglas, who had antagonized Wall Street as the hard-hitting chairman of the Securities and Exchange Commission, testified to the president's continued support of some kind of "trust-busting."

It was FDR's appointment of Felix Frankfurter to the Supreme Court's "Jewish seat" that set some businessmen's teeth on edge. Not that some did not like him personally; Frankfurter had developed many friendships in the business world during his long years on the Harvard Law School faculty. But Frankfurter, who had become a legal celebrity for his great briefs for reform measures and for his criticism of the Sacco-Vanzetti trial, symbolized to many businessmen what they perceived as the radical and perhaps foreign aspects of the New Deal. It was partly for this reason that a group of wealthy and influential Jews, including *New York Times* publisher Arthur Hays Sulzberger, called on the president to warn him against a Frankfurter appointment. It might bolster anti-Semitism at a difficult time in Europe, they said. FDR's reaction to this was one of "revulsion." He nominated his old friend and adviser to the High Court in January 1939; the Senate confirmed him without a dissenting vote. But on other judicial appointments, the presidential-congressional stalemate continued, a stalemate in which key elements were ideology, checks and balances, and senators' power over their fiefdoms.

. . .

"You know," Frances Perkins had said to Eleanor one day in Albany, "Franklin is really a very simple Christian."

ER pondered this remark for a moment, and then said, "Yes, a *very simple* Christian."

Both women were concurring with the public view of FDR. Many of his most stirring speeches were really sermons spelling out his ideas of good and evil. His most notable talk—his Inaugural Address of 1933—abounded in biblical allusions. But by 1939, Hitlerism, with its direct attack on basic human morality and decency, its assault on the underpinnings of civilization itself, was forcing people to reassess their religious and political views. What about Roosevelt?

His conventional Christian views gave him little practical help in the face of the Nazi attack. Christianity preached turning the other cheek, love among human beings, and above all peace. But it was also the religion that professed divine punishment and eternal damnation of those who practiced evil. While the president responded rhetorically to the overwhelming number of Americans who believed in Christ as the apostle of peace, he was secretly taking a few steps—and planning for more—toward military confrontation. Thus, while on the one hand he was mouthing great principles, he was, on the other hand, taking the most practical and expedient steps in the name of those principles—but with little actual connection between the two. Rhetoric simply became detached from reality.

Roosevelt had been shifting back and forth between loftily urging peace and conciliation to Europeans engaged in a life-or-death struggle and stern warnings about the threat of Hitlerism. As the European struggles reached their climaxes in 1940, this position became increasingly problematic. A ferocious and powerful ideology was forcing Roosevelt to choose. Theologians like Reinhold Niebuhr were shifting from pacifism to interventionism, but Roosevelt was not reading philosophers like Niebuhr with his view of "moral man and immoral society," perhaps had not yet heard of him. He did not know of Kierkegaard and his doctrine of the natural sinfulness and helplessness of man. Hence it was hard for Roosevelt yet to see that, in Hitler, Western democracy had more than the historic aggressive, even bloody, ruler. This was a very different leader, representing a very different ideology of racism, militarism, and anti-Christianity. Roosevelt would wait for events to teach him, or at least to pose the issues more sharply.

So when Eleanor, with a certain look on her face, called FDR a *very simple* Christian, she may have meant that the man she knew clothed his moral stances in pieties; or she may have seen him as a man armed with sword and shield but too simple in his faith to comprehend the true powers of darkness enveloping the world.

Chapter Twelve
THE GRAND STRATEGISTS' WAR

The New York Post, October 13, 19
(*Courtesy FDR Library*)

Japan Times & Advertiser, December 20, 1941.

The impact of crisis can be crippling and paralyzing or catalytic and creative, depending on the leadership confronting it. In the weeks after his reelection triumph of 1940, as Americans beheld a Britain still reeling from the blows of the Luftwaffe and increasingly hamstrung by savage U-boat attacks on its shipping, Franklin Roosevelt created a bold new program that would transform the European war and serve as the central United States strategy for decades after the war. This program was first called Lend-Lease.

Early in December, in what Churchill called one of the most important letters he ever wrote, the prime minister warned the president that unless more help came, "we may fall by the way." The moment was approaching "when we shall no longer be able to pay cash" for ships, artillery, tanks, planes, and small arms. Appealing to FDR's honor and morality, Churchill pleaded that "it would be wrong in principle and mutually disadvantageous in effect if, at the height of this struggle, Great Britain were to be divested of all saleable assets so that after victory was won with our blood, civilization saved, and time gained for the United States to be fully armed against all eventualities, we should stand stripped to the bone."

Speaking from a smoldering London, Churchill appealed by radio to Americans mesmerized by his growling cadenzas. "We do not need the gallant armies which are forming throughout the American Union." He would never need them—never. "Give us the tools, and we will finish the job." Churchill's ambassador to Washington was even more blunt. "Well, boys," he told reporters, "Britain's broke; it's your money we want." But facts more than words were shaping the view of Americans as they heard nightly radio reports and witnessed films and newspaper photographs of valiant Britishers holding out in their burning and blasted cities.

Churchill's "most important letter" reached the president while he appeared to be in a most unmilitant mood, during days of playing poker and watching movies on a Caribbean cruise. For many hours, propped up at the rail and contemplating the calm waters, he pondered the prime minister's warning. "Then," Hopkins reported later, "one evening, he suddenly came out with it—the whole program. He didn't seem to have any clear idea how it could be done legally. But there wasn't a doubt in his mind that he'd find a way."

The "whole program"—massive "loans" of guns and ships that the British could repay at war's end—Roosevelt described enthusiastically to a press conference on his return to Washington. "Now," he said cheerily, "what I am trying to do is to eliminate the dollar sign. That is something brand new in the thoughts of practically everybody in this room, I think—get rid of the silly, foolish old dollar sign." Suppose a neighboring home caught fire, and he had a length of garden hose. "If he can take my garden hose and connect it up with his hydrant, I may help him to put out his fire. Now, what do I do? I don't say to him before that operation, 'Neighbor, my garden hose cost me $15.'" FDR didn't want the money, he wanted his garden hose back after the fire. Not a single correspondent asked him how the munitions—the garden hose—could be returned if used or smashed up.

The president kept on the offensive. Four days after Christmas 1940 he told Americans in a fireside chat that they themselves must be the "arsenal of democracy." But Congress was the key target. If Churchill's letter was the most important he ever wrote, Roosevelt's annual message to Congress early in the new year, 1941, was the most important he ever gave, in its enunciation of lofty goals and the means to achieve them.

American security had never been so "seriously threatened from without as it is today," he told a crowded House chamber. He warned of appeasement, of dreaming that "America, single-handed, and with one hand tied behind its back, can hold off the whole world." He warned that those "who would give up essential liberty to purchase a little temporary safety deserve neither liberty nor safety." He warned that the future of all the American republics was today in serious danger. He warned that rearmament was not proceeding fast enough. And he asked Congress for authority and funds to manufacture additional war supplies that he could turn over to those "nations which are now in actual war with aggressor nations."

Suddenly his tone changed. He was talking about the future, about values, about a "world founded upon four essential human freedoms.

"The first is freedom of speech and expression—everywhere in the world.

"The second is freedom of every person to worship God in his own way—everywhere in the world.

"The third is freedom from want—which, translated into world terms, means economic understandings which will secure to every nation a healthy peacetime life for its inhabitants—everywhere in the world.

"The fourth is freedom from fear—which, translated into world terms, means a worldwide reduction of armaments to such a point and in such a thorough fashion that no nation will be in a position to commit an act of physical aggression against any neighbor—anywhere in the world.

"That is no vision of a distant millennium. It is a definite basis for a kind of world attainable in our own time and generation."

The chamber roared its approval, but some Republicans sat on their hands. Eleanor Roosevelt was so disappointed in the lukewarm Republican reception that she devoted a whole column to her husband's address. "Surely all of us can be united in a foreign policy which seeks to aid those people who fight for freedom and, thereby, gives us the hope of present peace for ourselves and a future peace for the world founded on the four great principles enunciated today." The nation could ill afford "to have any partisan differences, no matter how we may differ on the details of achievement."

1
Toward War: Leading and Misleading

In a dazzling display of leadership, the president asked congressional leaders for lend-lease legislation while telegrams and letters of support were still flooding Capitol Hill and the White House. Patriotically designated H.R. 1776, the bill authorized the chief executive to "sell, transfer title to, exchange, lease, lend" or otherwise dispose of any defense article "to any country whose defense the president deems vital to the defense of the United States." A vast and unprecedented grant of power to the executive, the bill by his request would limit neither the kind nor the amount of aid he could give and left him free to decide whether repayments could be in kind or property or "indirect."

The bill instantly polarized Congress and the nation. Speaking for the America First Committee, which had become the most formidable anti-interventionist organization, General Robert E. Wood, the Sears, Roebuck head, denounced the president for demanding not just a blank check but a "blank checkbook with the power to write away our manpower, our laws, and our liberties." Roosevelt expected this kind of attack, but he boiled over when the ineffable Senator Burton K. Wheeler of Montana called lend-lease "the New Deal's triple 'A' foreign policy—it will plow under every fourth American boy." This FDR regarded, he said at his next press conference, "as the most untruthful, as the most dastardly, unpatriotic thing that has ever been said. Quote me on that."

In the midst of the furious debate occurred a one-day strange interlude: the president's third inaugural. The speech was almost anticlimactic after the stirring addresses earlier, but the president wanted a bipartisan moment. While the throng in the Capitol Plaza shivered in the January cold, he offered a brief but eloquent "nonpolitical" paean to democracy. But neither he nor his speechwriter, Archibald MacLeish, could resist the opportunity to respond to Anne Morrow Lindbergh's much publicized tract, *The Wave of the Future,* presenting her and her husband's argument that Americans must adjust themselves to the inevitability of a new order in Europe.

"There are men," the president responded, who believe that "tyranny and slavery have become the surging wave of the future—and that freedom is an ebbing tide."

But Americans did not believe this, insisted the presidential navigator, who had learned much about waves and tides. "Eight years ago, when the life of this Republic seemed frozen by a fatalistic terror, we proved that this is not true. We were in the midst of shock—but we acted. We acted quickly, boldly, decisively." And "we" would do so again.

The crowd came to life as the inaugural parade marched down a flag-bedecked Pennsylvania Avenue. The New Deal was there with uniformed NYA women and CCC men, doggedly trying to order their ranks, and the new army and navy, showing off some of their finest marching men. Despite the war abroad, it was also a time for jubilation—as the top-hatted FDR waved and laughed while the scout cars and mobile guns went by, his little dog Fala jumped into the president's seat for the ride and had to be ousted, and the rented top hat of retiring Vice President Garner kept falling off his patch of white hair. But the marching contingents were pitifully small compared to the massive parades in Berlin and Rome—and many in the crowd knew that, somewhere out there, army recruits were training with wooden guns and simulated tanks.

. . .

The lend-lease debate immediately resumed on Capitol Hill. Isolationist spokesmen derided aspects of the bill. Lending arms, said Senator Taft in a rare quip, was like lending chewing gum—you didn't expect it back.

The bill passed with the convincing majorities FDR wanted: 60 to 31 in the Senate, 317 to 71 in the House. In Parliament, Churchill hailed the measure as "the most unsordid act in the history of any nation."

For the prime minister it was but a step, though a step crucial to survival. "I would like to get them hooked a little firmer," he confided to a fellow Englishman, "but they are pretty well on now." Actually, the Americans were far from "on." In 1941 only 1 percent of British arms and munitions came through lend-lease.

The debate unleashed by lend-lease did not end with its passage. Strong feelings remained, so much so that in later years Americans who had witnessed fervent argument all the way from the early New Deal years to Vietnam and Iran-Contra could not recall disputes that divided friends, families, neighborhoods, and the whole nation as deeply and heatedly as the debate of 1941. In April, Colonel Lindbergh began to denounce the administration at America First rallies; to a press conference, goaded by a reporter, FDR compared him to Clement L. Vallandigham, a "Copperhead" antiwar leader during the Civil War. The indignant colonel resigned his commission.

. . .

It is not by speeches and parliamentary resolutions that the great questions of the day are decided, German chancellor Otto von Bismarck had announced in the nineteenth century, but by "blood and iron." Adolf Hitler had learned from the master. During late 1940 and early 1941, he was exerting force at every point he could along thousands of miles of battle lines. While FDR was campaign speechifying in October, German troops began to occupy Romania. Mussolini invaded Greece from Albania. Having humbled the Low Countries, Norway, France, and Poland, the Axis partners were now poised to conquer southeastern Europe. But the Italians were confounded by the Greek resistance.

Hitler did not wait. With his usual massive forces he invaded Greece and Yugoslavia early in April. Belgrade's army surrendered within two weeks, the Greeks within three. German airborne troops readied plans to seize Crete, an advance post in the Mediterranean. Hitler's naval attacks on the Atlantic and other lifelines were scoring frightening successes. When Italian troops invading Egypt were forced back into Libya, with huge casualties, Hitler came to their aid, pushing British troops back toward Egypt east of Tobruk, and in a brilliant military feat German airborne troops overwhelmed British forces in Crete.

Day after day, White House aides brought Roosevelt news of these jolting setbacks. Roosevelt felt "shackled"—by the intractable military situation in Europe, by the divisions within his own administration between interventionists like Stimson and Ickes and more cautious officials, and above all by public opinion polls reflecting overwhelming sentiment against war and against sharply stepped-up aid to Britain. He took "safe" steps, authorizing British ships to be trained on American docks and pilots on American airfields, transferring a few coast guard cutters to the Royal Navy, putting Greenland and the bulge of Africa under U.S. Navy surveillance. In a speech late in May proclaiming an "unlimited national emergency," he announced the "blunt truth" that the Nazis were sinking merchant ships at more than three times the capacity of British shipyards to replace them. But aside from stepping up American shipbuilding, he offered little follow-through. Given the mixed state of public opinion, he would wait on "events"—especially a provocative "incident." But here was another shackle: Berlin had no desire for an incident in the Atlantic—indeed, it sought to avoid one—because Hitler at this point did not want a showdown with the Americans.

But Hitler was still making events. For weeks, London and Washington had been picking up intelligence that the Wehrmacht was readying a massive attack against Russia. At dawn, June 22, 1941, a tide of German troops, tanks, and guns burst across the eastern border and engulfed Soviet rifle divisions in a holocaust of flame and death.

The Nazi assault on Russia—which later would be seen as the most momentous single event of the war—did not immediately reshape global strategy. For Berlin it was an intensification and broadening of its advance to the east. For Moscow it was a fight for sheer survival; but at least it would be a war against a single foe. Moscow and Tokyo had signed a nonaggression pact in April that, for a time at least, was to the advantage of both; later they could resume their old-time rivalry. For Churchill it was also a fight for survival, now economic as well as military; by a superb irony, he was in the same situation FDR had been in months earlier: How much military aid did he dare send to an ally if it might fall into the hands of victorious Nazis? Churchill sent as much aid to the Soviets as he could, consistent with his own survival needs.

And Roosevelt? The Nazi invasion did not centrally affect his global strategy because he had no global strategy, only an array of precautions, responses, initiatives, and alternative plans. He was adhering to an Atlantic First approach—all aid to Britain short of war. This policy drew from a long heritage of Anglo-American friendship; it could readily be administered by two capitals used to working with each other; it suited FDR's temperament, met the needs of the Britishers, and was achieving a momentum of its own. But it was not a grand strategy embracing the full range of worldwide diplomatic, and political, and economic as well as military power, potential as well as existing. Above all, FDR's tactical efforts were negative in that they could achieve full effect only in the event of war. But Hitler would not give the president a pretext for war—and without one Roosevelt did not dare to declare it.

Why then did not the president—assuming he now expected some kind of global war involving the United States—turn to a Pacific First emphasis, even strategy? Surely there were compelling arguments for such a drastic shift. During 1941, Japan had been pressing its merciless occupation of China and was moving offensively to the south, culminating in the seizure of French Indochina. Chiang Kai-shek was warning that continued resistance to Japan depended on large military and economic aid from Washington.

The answer lay in a common heritage, longtime Anglo-American unity, the orientation of the American "establishment" and the press toward western Europe, and above all the need to support America's old ally against the nation that had become a global menace. If that was the case, however, then a wholly opposite strategy posed itself: Appease Tokyo in whatever way and degree necessary, above all avoiding a showdown, until the Nazis were defeated and Washington could turn—someday—to the rescue of China and the other threatened Asian nations.

Standing in the way of such a drastic alternative was a powerful force—public opinion. Many of the same Americans who so vocally opposed intervention against Hitler strongly favored intervention against Japan. Polls early in 1941 showed almost 60 percent of Americans favoring some kind of American action to keep the Japanese out of the Dutch East Indies. Americans would not "die for Danzig" or even Paris, one commentator noted, but evidently they would for the Moluccas and Java. At summer's end 1941, the president was informed that over two-thirds of the public was ready to risk war with an overly aggressive Japan. A pacific policy in the Pacific was out of the question.

. . .

For weeks in the fall of 1940, Secretary Hull had been negotiating the transcending question of China with Japanese envoys, without resolution. Despite the increasing military domination of Japanese war policy and despite FDR's sinking hopes, Roosevelt and Hull continued negotiations, in order to ensure that the "first shot" would be fired by the Japanese. They

did not know that on November 1 the Japanese high command, at a long
and stormy meeting, had decided on war if negotiations continued to falter. The president proposed a compromise, which failed, and appealed at
the last minute directly to Emperor Hirohito—but by then the Japanese
carriers were headed for Pearl Harbor.

In the final days the president appeared to be almost fatalistic. "It is
all in the laps of the gods," he told Morgenthau.

2
Europe First, Asia Second

AIR RAID PEARL HARBOR—THIS IS NO DRILL.
Reading the first flash at the Navy Department, Knox burst out,
"My God! This can't be true, this must mean the Philippines!" He tele-
phoned the president, who was sitting at his desk in the oval study chat-
ting with Hopkins about nonmilitary matters. There must be some mistake,
Hopkins said. Surely the Japanese *would not* attack Honolulu. No, said
Roosevelt, it was just the kind of unexpected thing the Japanese would do.
He appeared relaxed, like a man who had just got rid of a heavy burden.
Japan had taken the question of war out of his hands.

A phone call from Churchill: "Mr. President, what's this about Japan?"
Yes, it was true; "we are all in the same boat now." Hanging up, the prime
minister allowed himself a moment of pure exhilaration. So he had won,
after all. Yes, after Dunkirk, the fall of France, the threat of invasion, the
U-boat struggle—after seventeen months of fighting without allies—the
war was won. The war would be long, but all the rest would be "merely
the proper application of overwhelming force": the force of British determination, American technology and resources, and vast Russian manpower.

The president had no time for exultation. As the shattering specifics
trickled in, his early composure gave way to tension and anger. That evening, gray with fatigue, the president finally let down his own guard back
in his study, pounding his fist on the table and exclaiming to correspondent Edward R. Murrow that American planes had been destroyed on the
ground—"on the ground, by God, on the ground!"

Later, Pearl Harbor would spawn a host of conspiracy theories, particularly that the president had invited the attack on Pearl Harbor, knew
that it would take place, and even used his fleet as bait. In fact it was a classic
example of the confusion theory. Washington and Pearl Harbor had an

overload of conflicting intelligence items, a mixed bag indicating that the Japanese were attacking south, or north, or east, or not attacking at all. Washington was also confused by the expectation that Tokyo would follow the Nazi strategy of attacking weaker nations first, then encircling the larger. But FDR was facing a different enemy, with its own tempo, its own goal, and its own way—a sudden disabling blow.

Still, at the end, despite all the confusion, the president had triumphed in two major ways. War had come in a way that instantly united the country. And, he could believe, he had acted in a democratic way. America had not struck first.

. . .

The day after the attack a solemn and composed president slowly made his way to the rostrum of the House of Representatives amid round after round of applause.

Gripping the podium, he looked up at the throng. "Yesterday, December 7, 1941—a date which will live in infamy—the United States of America was suddenly and deliberately attacked by naval and air forces of the Empire of Japan." He reviewed the timing of the negotiations and the attack and reported on the "many American lives" lost and the severe damage to military facilities. Then he called the roll of other nations and islands attacked by Japan: Malaya, Hong Kong, Guam, the Philippines, Wake, Midway.

Now the president's voice rose in indignation. "No matter how long it may take us to overcome this premeditated invasion, the American people in their righteous might will win through to absolute victory. . . . With confidence in our armed forces, with the unbounding determination of our people, we will gain the inevitable triumph. So help us God."

Japan had struck. What would Germany do? To the amazement of chancelleries around the world, Hitler immediately declared war on the United States, an act that was in part rational calculation, in part heroics. But beyond all rational calculation lay Hitler's xenophobia and racism. The Führer had only contempt for Americans, half Judaized, half negrified, by no means a warrior race. For months he had publicly held his temper in the face of Roosevelt's threats and provocations. Now he could pour out his hatred to a boisterous, roaring Reichstag, asserting that he considered Roosevelt mad, just as Wilson was. Roosevelt had brought no improvement to his country; rather, strengthened by the Jews around him, he had turned to war as a way of diverting attention from his failures at home.

Germany wanted only its rights. It would secure its rights "even if thousands of Churchills and Roosevelts conspire against it."

. . .

For Roosevelt the pieces of conflict had at last fallen into place; the nations had chosen up sides. Hitler had done him an immense favor by declaring war on the United States, further unifying the American people and proving the president's longtime argument that the aggressive dictators of the world were united in their global ambitions.

As the gaming board of war now expanded, players on both sides faced momentous questions of strategy. For a time, at least, the game would be one of chess, in which the master players would have full control over their queens and rooks and pawns as they maneuvered for position and power. For a time the leaders would be too involved in military crises to think about issues that lay beyond the chessboard.

But one person in the White House already was thinking about the longer run. As 1942 dawned, Eleanor Roosevelt wrote in "My Day":

"The English-speaking peoples will, probably, when peace first comes to this earth, have to bear a heavy burden. They must lighten that burden as quickly as possible, through the participation of all the free countries in this hemisphere. Liberated people in other parts of the world must join with us as soon as they can, if we are to have a program which expresses the hopes now hidden in the hearts of people throughout the world."

3
Command Leadership

Within a year of Pearl Harbor and the staggering defeats of early 1942, Americans felt a swell of optimism about the war's outcome. December 7, 1941, had been avenged at Midway. Allied forces were counterattacking at key points along Tokyo's huge perimeters. British and American troops were securely ensconced in North Africa, the RAF had fought off the worst of the Luftwaffe's air attacks, and the Red Army was starting an epic counteroffensive that would trap and destroy hundreds of thousands of Nazi troops.

These successes would open up new strategic possibilities and dilemmas, but at this point the crucial factor was not strategy but supply.

If the armies of yesteryear traveled on their stomachs, as Napoleon used to say, now they were traveling on ships, planes, landing craft, tanks, and jeeps. As the global counteroffensives fostered needs beyond anything ever dreamed of in even the biggest wars, General Logistics took command.

Ships—from huge cargo carriers to tiny landing craft—were the top priority. Shipyards that had languished during depression and recession burst into round-the-clock activity. Bosses and workers began to compete with rival concerns over quick completion rates. Using hundred-ton prefabricated sections, they first shaped the hull; installed bulkheads and engine assemblies; added strakes and fantail, decks and other superstructure; and finally mounted antiaircraft guns, along with last-minute welding, riveting, and electrical wiring.

Shorter and shorter became the elapsed days from keel laying to outfitting with lifebelts, until, in a burst of production glory, the cargo ship *Robert E. Peary* was built and launched in four round-the-clock days. The ships would have plenty to carry. Four weeks after Pearl Harbor, the commander in chief set production goals of 60,000 planes, including 45,000 bombers, dive-bombers, and pursuit planes; 45,000 tanks in 1942 and 75,000 tanks in 1943; 6 million deadweight tons of merchant ships in 1942 and 10 million the next year; and, over the two years, 55,000 antiaircraft guns. America would become more than ever the "arsenal of democracy."

FDR's uplifting oratory pointed the way, but everything depended on what would happen in the factories of America. At first some employers held back. Months after Pearl Harbor, the automobile industry was still turning out passenger cars. But the military setbacks of early 1942 fostered a crisis feeling that brought manufacturers together in a huge combined effort. Soon workers by the hundreds of thousands were flocking to war production centers. Under the supervision of local entrepreneurs and assembly line experts, skilled workers were helping in the crucial task of conversion: typewriter factories turning out machine guns, electric toaster plants making gun mounts, pot and pan makers assembling and loading flares.

In 1943, steelworkers produced twelve tons for every American soldier, as production of locomotives quintupled, of aluminum quadrupled, of industrial chemicals tripled. The work had to combine huge output with great precision. Hence production depended on the nation's unrivaled stock of highly precise, special-purpose machine tools; to build one Ford B-24 bomber, two million parts had to be exquisitely fitted together. A special effort was made to spread work out to small subcontractors, with the result that towns that had flourished back in the days of Yankee tinkerers, and then declined in the face of huge new industrial combinations, boomed once again.

Constantly bombarded by appeals from Hollywood stars to boost production, always reminded how directly their output related to battle successes, industrial workers were made to feel that they were production soldiers. But out on the war fronts the real soldiers often felt like production workers. Rarely did they fight with pistols and fists in typical Wild West fashion. Rather, they wormed along on their bellies as they ran into strong points, manhandled their light weapons into position, poured in machine-gun fire, and pushed on; or, if enemy defenses held, they paused, asked for bigger tools such as tanks, waited, called for heavy mortars and artillery, released a new barrage of metal and fire, waited, even called for planes for air strikes. Government and press glorified the "tough elite" troops who acted as the "cutting edge" of war; more typically, that cutting edge was a ragged, almost invisible line of men in shapeless work clothes, cursing and bitching while with grimy hands they operated the machines of war.

. . .

Within a year of Pearl Harbor, Americans were undergoing the early phases of a vast economic and social transformation as they mobilized for total war. The very face of the earth began to change as factories expanded, new roads crowded with heavy traffic radiated out from the mushrooming war plants, and outlying pastures gave way to trailer homes amid thickets of shiny cars, jalopies, and pickup trucks. People were flocking into these areas as men—and, increasingly, women—took jobs in factories desperately trying to meet stepped-up defense demands. They were part of the biggest "fast" migration in American history, the vanguard of some 15 million of the civilian population who left their home areas and streamed into Detroit, Los Angeles, and scores of other cities. Hundreds of thousands of African-Americans were leaving their southern homes, migrating into northern and western cities, often moving into tenements and shanties just deserted by migrating whites. These migrants were the new Okies—men and women with jobs but little else.

America was changing, here swiftly, there more slowly, elsewhere not at all. Some feared that migration and other social forces might get out of hand. Was anyone in charge overall? One man assumed he was, the commander in chief. He tried to keep up with the pace of things by reorganizing the government, reshuffling agencies, setting up the War Production Board under Donald Nelson, a Sears, Roebuck executive. Businessmen moved into Washington to run the industrial mobilization agencies. He needed men who could "deal with industry's intricate structure and operation," Nelson said—naturally businessmen and industrialists. Suddenly, hitherto unknown men became "czars" of mobilization, at least in newspaper headlines.

While FDR delegated considerable authority to the mobilization commanders, he kept the reins of fiscal policy in his own hands. Buttressed by his presidential spending power under the Constitution, and by huge congressional appropriations, he and a small group of advisers simply took command of the distribution of tens of billions of dollars, including their division between "war" and "domestic" needs. As priorities became the watchword, new agencies set the priorities, consulting congressional committee chieftains as need be. FDR continued to talk economy as government spending soared to undreamed-of heights. His first true war budget, for 1943, was $59 billion.

The president's direst home-front fear was war inflation. In the spring of 1942 he warned Congress that "to keep the cost of living from spiraling upward"—an injunction he repeated seven times—the nation "must tax heavily," keeping corporate and personal profits down; fix ceilings on prices paid by manufacturers, middlemen, and consumers; hold down salaries and wages; stabilize farm prices; boost the sale of war bonds; and discourage credit and installment buying. For a man who had not been in a grocery market for twenty, perhaps thirty, years, Roosevelt had an uncanny capacity to think in terms of a housewife shopping in Hyde Park or Poughkeepsie.

With vivid memories of World War I profiteering—and of the isolationists' exploitation of the issue ever since—Roosevelt and Morgenthau were determined to curb the rise of "war millionaires." In his spring 1942 anti-inflation charge to Congress, he stated that no American ought to have an income after taxes of more than $25,000 a year—a clear carryover from his New Deal campaigns against the "forces of greed."

. . .

FDR was reinventing TR's war on the plutocrats. Although his stated aim was economic—to lessen the wide "discrepancies between low personal incomes and very high personal incomes"—like TR, he brought a moral agenda to the issue of taxation.

At first asking all Americans for "cooperation and restraint and sacrifice," he then gave more thought to the idea of sacrifice and decided that "sacrifice" had a negative resonance. "I have never been able to bring myself to full acceptance of the word 'sacrifice,'" he explained, noting that "free men and women, bred in the concepts of democracy, deem it a privilege rather than a sacrifice to work and to fight for the perpetuation of the democratic ideal." And so the concept of "privilege" was reinvented, transferred from the domain of the wealthy elite to that of hard-working citizens contributing mightily to the war effort. "Here at home," he told Americans in a fireside chat, "everyone will have the privilege of making whatever self-denial is necessary, not only to supply our fighting men but to keep the economic structure of our country fortified and secure during the war and after the war." Discerning a new form of democratic "privilege" that would replace the old sense of entitlement and privilege of the plutocrats, FDR was joining Cousin Ted in a moral crusade for equality.

The proposal to cap incomes at $25,000 was greeted with howls of indignation as socialistic. The *New York Herald Tribune* termed it "a blatant piece of demagoguery," but Frankfurter wrote the president that Theodore Roosevelt would have said, "Bully!"

The president imposed his proposal for a $25,000 cap by executive order, and Congress killed the order. Month after month, Congress argued over the president's other economic stabilization programs, while lobbyists for all the usual interests lobbied as hard as ever. Farm lobbyists led the attack in defense of commodity prices. As inflation pressures mounted, FDR became increasingly impatient and angry. In the fall he took a daring step. In a message on September 7 he asked Congress "to pass legislation under which the president would be specifically authorized to stabilize the cost of living, including the prices of all farm commodities."

Then the president added a most remarkable challenge. If Congress did not act by October 1, "and act adequately, I shall accept the responsibility, and I will act." Mortified by this threatened exercise of unprecedented presidential power, Congress glumly set to work and produced a bill on October 2. But the president had to wait another three weeks for a tax bill: one, as it turned out, that would reduce personal exemptions, lift the top surtax on individual incomes a little, raise the top excess-profits rate sizably, and boost a number of excises on luxuries and scarce goods—but raise only $7 billion in new revenue. Morgenthau despaired of ever achieving "total war on taxes."

. . .

Increasingly in 1942 and 1943, the domestic front as well as the military fronts were under the control of command leadership. The president and his small group of economic advisers were making crucial domestic decisions, just as the commander in chief and a small group of admirals and generals were making epochal military decisions. And the president, acting as legislator in chief as well as chief executive, won applause whenever he acted decisively. In July 1942, when it was necessary to cut back the merchant ship program to build more landing craft, Roosevelt authorized cancellation of almost $150 million in contracts, resulting in the abandonment of a big shipyard under construction in New Orleans. It was the "practical thing" to do.

The command leaders were virtually all men, although Frances Perkins managed to hold on in her own domain. Even the first lady could be shut out. Eleanor began work at the Office of Civilian Defense early in September 1941. She worked well with New York mayor Fiorello LaGuardia because the mayor, a noted fire buff, concentrated on emergency alert systems, air-raid shelters, and fire equipment while she dealt with problems of civilian morale, nutrition, medical care, and housing—somewhat like her old-time concerns at Arthurdale and the priorities of the New Deal. Thus she was thinking about—and trying to act on—precisely the long-term social and psychological problems that men were neglecting as they tried to meet day-to-day "practical needs" of war workers. The work was exhausting. "I think Mrs. R. is overtired," her worried secretary Malvina Thompson told Esther Lape, "because she falls asleep night or day, when she is not concentrating on work. I don't think she has had enough sleep for weeks and weeks."

Inevitably Eleanor had to pay the price of idealism. Demagogues in Congress attacked her for appointing "pinks," even "downright reds," to the OCD. When she brought Mayris Chaney, a professional dancer, into the OCD, the House of Representatives voted to deny funds for the teaching of "fan dancing." She was mocked for sponsoring lunch-break calisthenics and square dancing on the roof of OCD headquarters. Never before, she wrote later, had she had such an unfavorable press, and she was even more saddened by the attacks on Chaney and others. "To know me," she said, "is a terrible thing."

The first lady could hold out against attacks from Capitol Hill but not against desertion by her husband. Two months after Pearl Harbor, with his typical disingenuousness, FDR confided to Francis Biddle that he would like his wife to quit OCD. Ten days later she resigned. But what would the first lady do now? "There is a great change in Mrs. R.," Tommy

Thompson wrote Esther Lape. "There is a frustration too at not having any specific work for the war."

. . .

A week after Pearl Harbor the president had offered a glowing tribute to the Bill of Rights on the 150th anniversary of the ratification of the "people's charter" on December 15, 1791. Prepared well before the outbreak of war, the radio address had been converted into an attack on Hitler and his perversion of individual rights. The propositions the Nazis advanced in place of "Jefferson's inalienable rights," said FDR, were these:

"That the individual human being has no rights whatsoever in himself or by virtue of his humanity; that the individual human being has no right to a soul of his own, or a mind of his own . . . or even to live where he pleases or to marry the woman he loves; that his only duty is the duty of obedience, not to his God, not to his conscience, but to Adolf Hitler; and that his only value is his value, not as a man, but as a unit of the Nazi state."

FDR went on to make his own eloquent tribute to individual liberty, to the "great upsurge of human liberty" springing from the Bill of Rights, to the fixed determination "of this generation of our people to preserve liberty." Despotic rule could only come, he declaimed, "if those who have inherited the gift of liberty had lost the manhood to preserve it."

Earlier in that same year of 1941 an "individual human being" working in Washington heard that FBI agents had been asking questions of friends and acquaintances about her in her neighborhood. Her name was Edith B. Helm. They were questions, set out in the FBI manual, about an official's— or a job applicant's—perceived behavior: Did he or she drink? throw loud parties? live beyond his or her means? receive foreign magazines, even the *Daily Worker?* Inevitably, after the G-men made their rounds, the neighborhood was full of suspicion—especially if an applicant did not actually get a job.

There was something a bit unusual about this individual, however— she already had a job, in the White House, as social secretary to the first lady. Mrs. Roosevelt at once protested vociferously to both her husband and to the attorney general. J. Edgar Hoover wrote her a personal letter of explanation. The FBI had not known of Mrs. Helm's identity or job; if it had, "the inquiry would not have been initiated." This smooth answer might have worked, but at this point ER discovered that the personal life of another of her aides, Malvina Thompson, was also being checked out. Once again she remonstrated with Hoover, adding, "This type of investigation seems to me to smack too much of the Gestapo methods." She went on to question the efficiency of Hoover's organization.

Eleanor Roosevelt was one of the few persons—perhaps the only person—of high status who had the courage to challenge J. Edgar Hoover. She had of course the protection of her husband, her administration friends, indeed of her "constituency." But how much courage would FDR show in defense of her "individual liberty," or that of the average citizen, in times of stress? Hoover drew much of his power from an enormous number and variety of wiretaps that netted him information on persons' lives, correspondence, visitors, political discussions, bedroom talk. The FBI also bugged rooms and intercepted letters.

When Senator Norris called him the biggest publicity hound in America, Hoover denounced the "smear campaign" being conducted by various "anti-American forces." While citizens far less powerful than a United States senator—union leaders, black activists, radicals—were targeted by the hundreds, Hoover also aimed at the top. The FBI monitored Vice President Wallace's telephone conversations, wiretapped his friends, opened their mail and photographed letters from the vice president, and kept him under surveillance during official trips, including his 1943 Latin American tour.

And where was FDR in all this? Put in the crassest terms, he had an implicit deal with Hoover. The director, albeit on a selective basis, gave the president information he needed on both his friends and enemies, including his own administration officials. Hoover had the Bureau check out telegrams he received from the White House opposing "national defense." In return, the president in effect guaranteed Hoover's job security and helped him with the job. When the Supreme Court sharply limited wiretapping and Attorney General Robert Jackson prohibited it, Hoover, exploiting fears of Nazi spies on the loose, persuaded Roosevelt to instruct Jackson to authorize the use of listening devices against persons suspected of "subversive activities."

Roosevelt also rewarded Hoover with an occasional letter of thanks (perhaps ghost-written), to which the FBI head responded with fawning gratitude. The president and the director never challenged each other. And Hoover never dared challenge Eleanor Roosevelt as long as her husband was president.

. . .

While hundreds, perhaps thousands, of Americans were subject to suspicion, loss of privacy, and in some cases jobs, over a hundred thousand Japanese-Americans lost their individual human rights.

Japanese-Americans were herded en masse into concentration camps. Routed out of their homes some weeks after Pearl Harbor, tagged like train baggage, they were sent off to assembly centers, surrounded by guards and searchlights, loaded onto trains, and shipped with drawn blinds to Arizona and California deserts, Utah flatlands, and Arkansas lowlands. There they lived in tarpaper barracks and—grandmothers and children alike—used communal showers and toilets.

After the war, Americans who really believed in the "First Freedom" could not understand why this docile and industrious population, long rooted to the California soil, could be uprooted and imprisoned. It was easy to blame the army, but the military in California were slow even to find security reasons for the evacuation. The basic cause clearly was racial, but the white population in California did not appear to explode spontaneously in hysteria at once after the infamous attack at Pearl Harbor. Rather, the racist feeling seemed to be whipped up by members of Congress, newspaper publishers, and government officials who ordinarily would be expected to be forces for moderation, if not for liberty.

Who would stand up now as a sentinel of freedom? Virtually no one, aside from dedicated civil libertarians and a few conservatives like Senator Robert Taft. Not Walter Lippmann, that self-appointed guardian of individual liberty against New Deal big government, who said in effect that constitutional rights faded away on a battlefield. Not Attorney General Biddle, so proud of his ancestry of Randolphs as well as Biddles, so secure in his old friendship with FDR. As the official guardian of the Constitution, Biddle was opposed to relocation but could not muster the spunk to fight it. And not the columnists, beneficiaries of the First Amendment. "Personally, I hate the Japanese," said one. He had a plan: "Herd 'em up, pack 'em off, and give 'em the inside room in the Badlands."

And not Eleanor Roosevelt. The "conscience of the White House"— so vocal and outraged about the suffering of republicans in faraway Spain— now fell silent. Had FDR insisted that she support the policy of internment? As historian Allida Black discovered, it was a most contentious subject between them. When he asked her to visit some of the camps, after some internees rioted, she complied. Her visit to a concentration camp in Arizona in 1942 inspired the prisoners with hope. "This great lady, coming out to tell us not to lose faith," commented one woman decades later, moved by the memory of the comfort Mrs. Roosevelt brought to the traumatized Japanese-Americans.

The Grand Strategists' War

The internment of Japanese-Americans anguished Eleanor. The nation "knew so little and cared so little about them," she wrote her friend Joseph Lash, "that they did not even think about the principle that we in the country believe in: that of equal rights for all human beings." In private, she joined Dillon Meyer, director of the War Relocation Authority, and Harold Ickes in proposing the closing down of the camps, a suggestion rejected by FDR. But in public, in her newspaper column, she reported only on the Japanese-American prisoners' attempts to beautify their pitiful plots of desert land, not on the paramount issues of racism and the unconscionable suspension of these citizens' civil rights.

And certainly not the commander in chief, who, because there was no clarion call of protest, was never confronted by a set of compelling alternatives to internment. During the few days when he had to make up his mind he was inundated with some of the worst news of the war—from the Philippines and Singapore and elsewhere. For him it was simply a matter of immediate safety and practicality. It was the "pragmatic" thing to do. It would be much later before Americans would come to realize that the Japanese relocation was not only one of the cruelest and most unprincipled but also most unnecessary and impractical acts of American leadership in World War II.

Command leadership had met its first test after Pearl Harbor. It had reached far beyond the ordinary battle lines of war, far beyond the struggle for industrial mobilization, to rout out and imprison a hundred thousand of its own people. It had done this almost casually, as a mere incident of war, without major debate within the military, without any confrontation between civilian and military power, with no more reflection or pangs of conscience than if the decision instead had been about moving an army corps from the West Coast to the East. Decades later the episode would be almost universally condemned by libertarian conservatives and First Amendment liberals alike. But where were the outcries of conscience and protest at the time?

. . .

It was not the Japanese relocation itself but its bland acceptance that showed the extent to which the nation was submitting to the influence of the so-called military and industrial complex that would dominate American life for years to come. The president was both a shaper of this change and a product of it. Or perhaps he was hardly aware of it, when he criticized the "pettiness" of Congress and its lack of "fighting leadership" or when he barred publishers (not correspondents) from visiting war theaters, mainly because of his keen dislike of Colonel McCormick of the *Chicago Tribune* and Henry Luce of *Time*.

At least much of this kind of presidential assertiveness was publicized, if only by word of mouth. Something else—infinitely more significant—was happening in dead secrecy.

For some time before and after Pearl Harbor, a small group of command leaders had been shaping a weapon of unimaginable horror. It would become the atomic bomb that, within half a decade, would be dropped without warning on a far-off city called Hiroshima.

The making of the atomic weapon was first shrouded in so much secrecy, and then the A-bomb exploded with such devastation as it ushered in a "new era," that two vital aspects of its origins have been all but forgotten: First, the early theoretical work was highly international, and, second, it was widely shared—and not only within a narrow scientific community. A sunburst of theorizing in physics, symbolized most publicly by Albert Einstein, was lighting up remarkable new paths in scores of areas, including radar, rocketry, and the mysteries of the atom. Brilliant young physicists, some of them hardly through with their graduate studies, shared their ideas and their excitement at international scientific conferences, in scholarly journals, and in laboratory visits and talk.

These scholars came from many countries: Marie Curie of France, Otto Hahn of Germany, New Zealand–born Ernest Rutherford of England, Niels Bohr of Denmark, Leo Szilard of Hungary, Enrico Fermi of Italy. They epitomized the internationalist spirit so crucial to scientific progress. By 1933, the year that both FDR and Hitler came to power, scientists had penetrated into the heart of the atom and glimpsed many of its elements and behaviors, its tendencies toward stability and disintegration, and its awesome destructive potential. But 1933 brought changes in the global community of "open" science. Nazi civil service laws drove German Jews out of their universities; scores followed Einstein's earlier departure to the United States. And as Hitler and Mussolini rattled their arms, physicists in other countries drew into a defensive and more secret posture.

Their fears were not imaginary. Not only did the Hitler regime close off its scientific community, in defiance of the old standards of free and unlimited communication, but two physicists at the Kaiser-Wilhelm Institute, Otto Hahn and Fritz Strassman, along with others, were doing advanced work in fields that might lead to the development of atomic weaponry. The idea that Hitler might someday command such a weapon staggered the imagination. When American and refugee scientists realized they must arouse Washington to this peril, they found penetrating the Washington bureaucracy almost as daunting as penetrating the atom. Two navy lieutenant commanders listened with stony politeness and incomprehension early in 1939, as Fermi tried to explain the discoveries. Szilard convinced Einstein that the only way to get action in Washington was to go to the top, with a direct appeal to the commander in chief, who was noted for his openness to new ideas and experiments.

Dr. Alexander Sachs brought Einstein's warning letter into the Oval Office, but during Sachs's long explanation, FDR's interest seemed to flag. Sachs managed to wangle an invitation to breakfast and there surprised FDR with the story of Napoleon's rejection of Fulton when the inventor of the steamship tried to interest him in the idea. FDR was quiet for a few moments, thinking, and then exclaimed, "Alex, what you are after is to see that the Nazis don't blow us up," and called in his aide, General Edwin Watson: "Pa, this requires action."

Command leadership, however, was not at this point very commanding. It had been months before Sachs could bring in Einstein's letter, more months passed before there was any "action," still more months before the first research funds were released. But as the Axis threat intensified, so did the Allied effort. After Churchill and Roosevelt met in June 1942 and the prime minister readily agreed that the United States would assume the main burden of the atomic project, the president set up the Manhattan Engineering District two months later. James Conant warned that the Germans might be a year ahead of the Allies. "Three months' delay might be fatal."

As the project moved ahead, secrecy intensified. Atomic scientists were sequestered in Chicago and then at Los Alamos. Knowledge of the program was restricted to a tiny circle of scientists and army men. And as the military dimensions of the project were limited to a few command leaders, the opportunity to consider its *moral* dimension was confined within a tiny circle.

Chapter Thirteen
THE PEOPLE'S WAR

JUST DON'T BE SURPRISED, THAT'S ALL

Herblock, 1942.
(*Courtesy FDR Library*)

On the eve of 1943, the Roosevelts held their usual New Year's Eve party at the White House for family and close friends. As the midnight hour struck, the president raised his glass of champagne and offered his usual toast to the United States, but this year he added, "and to United Nations victory." Earlier that evening the guests had watched a film about Nazi villainy in North Africa, Vichy collaborators, and three escapees from occupied France starring Ingrid Bergman, Humphrey Bogart, and Paul Henreid. The film was *Casablanca*.

Was FDR, always a great tease, sending a cryptic message to his intimates? Nine days later Roosevelt and Hopkins and their party traveled by train to Miami, destination Morocco. The trip had all the makings of a Hollywood propaganda film—except it was probably the most decisive meeting that the president would ever attend.

FDR treated the journey as a first-class holiday, Hopkins noted, telling his favorite old yarns and not losing his composure when one of the sailors carrying him slipped and the commander in chief landed on his rear. The two men laughed about the "unbelievable trip" even beginning. It would be the first time this president—or any president—traveled by air. Roosevelt went to see for himself, to speak for himself—above all, Hopkins reflected, he just wanted to make the trip. He seemed to Hopkins as excited as a sixteen-year-old as the Pan American clipper taxied out of the harbor on the first leg to Africa. The president, hunched over by a window, missed nothing as the plane flew over the Citadel in Haiti and the one-hundred-mile-wide Amazon River mouth. After hops to Natal, then eighteen hours to Gambia and a night on the cruiser *Memphis* at this old slave post, he flew on over mountains and desert to Casablanca.

Agreeably settled in a commodious villa, the president soon was presiding over a wartime conference that seemed at times more like a combination reunion and old home week. FDR greeted his close comrade-in-arms Churchill, the combined British and American chiefs of staff who had been meeting for three days—and Lieutenant Colonel Elliott Roosevelt, in from his air force reconnaissance unit; Lieutenant Franklin D. Roosevelt Jr., summoned from an Atlantic Fleet destroyer; and Hopkins's son Robert, ordered in from a Tunisian foxhole.

All the hail-fellow-well-met camaraderie under Casablanca's sunny skies could not camouflage irksome divisions in the Allied camp. The problem was not only the "natural contrariety of allies," as Churchill called it, but the inevitable rivalries of services and ambitions over strategies and tactics, within both the British and American camps. The Casablanca conferees did not differ over the vital importance of the big jobs ahead: winning the shipping battle of the Atlantic, mounting an invasion of Europe from the west, massively helping Russia, pushing on up from the Mediterranean, meantime sustaining joint operations with China and pressing the sea-air-ground effort in the Pacific. The problem lay in priorities, the very essence of strategy.

While Roosevelt's generals and admirals still felt torn between European and Asian needs, they agreed under General George Marshall's leadership on the top priority: a massive cross-channel attack through France in 1943. Fresh from their successes in North Africa, and with half a million troops at their disposal, the British looked eagerly toward Sicily and points north and east. While some of the Americans wanted to get on with the fight immediately in the Mediterranean, most of Roosevelt's planners—especially Marshall—feared that Italy would be a sideshow draining troops from the cross-channel buildup.

Whatever worries the other chiefs might have had about such drainage, Churchill did not share. Rather, he saw Italy as a superb opportunity both to attack the allegedly "soft underbelly" of the Axis in the Mediterranean and to use southern Italy as a base for all sorts of opportunities. But Churchill's first target was FDR. Before the conference he instructed his chiefs "not to hurry or try to force agreement, but to take plenty of time; there was to be full discussion and no impatience—the dripping of water on stone."

Churchill knew his man. Attracted by all the tactical advantages of an Italian strategy, the opportunistic Roosevelt agreed to give the Mediterranean the immediate top priority. Despite British assurances that a successful Mediterranean strategy would make the cross-channel attack more assured of succeeding, it was also clear that an Italian campaign would delay the big attack from 1943 to at least 1944. This possibility—and the fact that other priorities like Asia were accordingly diminished—left Hopkins and the military depressed; Roosevelt seemed content to seize the tactical opportunities of the moment.

The stepped-up Mediterranean priority and the lowering of other alternatives raised some dire political problems that the two leaders would have to face during 1943. For Roosevelt, far more than Churchill, the key political issue was unconditional surrender. Whatever his vagaries on other political matters, FDR for months had been making clear that the Axis nations would be compelled to surrender without negotiations or conditions. Roosevelt would risk neither a repetition of the problems of the World War I negotiated peace nor disunity among Moscow, London, and Washington.

Churchill had wholly agreed with the doctrine in principle, but he was already wondering at Casablanca whether an exception might be made for Italy. Then the president sprung a surprise on the prime minister when he suddenly announced at a press conference that the "elimination of German, Japanese, and Italian war power means the unconditional surrender by Germany, Italy, and Japan." That did not mean the destruction of their populations, FDR added, but rather of the "philosophies in those countries which are based on conquest and the subjugation of other people."

Was the president's sudden announcement a result of the thought "popping in his mind," as he later contended, or, more likely, a calculated ploy to secure Churchill's adherence publicly to applying the doctrine to Italy? The prime minister, who was taken by surprise only by FDR's unilateral announcement, not by the doctrine, gamely backed up the president.

A more immediate political problem for the two men was a matter of prickly personality more than political strategy, and its name was Charles de Gaulle. De Gaulle and General Henri Giraud were still vying for leadership of the Free French. FDR had come to despise de Gaulle for his pretensions as the sole anti-Vichy leader, his stubbornness, and—not least —the liberal and radical support he had aroused back home as *the* heroic leader of the French Resistance.

Invited to Casablanca to meet and harmonize with Giraud, de Gaulle came grudgingly but they stalled for two days, while FDR notified Secretary Hull in Washington that he and Churchill had "delivered the bridegroom," Giraud, but "our friends could not produce the bride, the temperamental lady de Gaulle," who showed no intentions of "getting into bed" with his rival. Then FDR, like a wily marriage broker, brought the two together, maneuvered them into shaking hands for the camera, and helped patch up an agreement between the two generals for "permanent liaison."

Another of FDR's ventures with the French connection proved more fruitful. Despite a packed schedule at Casablanca, he hosted a banquet for the sultan of Morocco, a prime leader in Morocco's struggle for independence from France. A longtime critic of French colonialism, the president took extraordinary pleasure in supporting that struggle and offering aid in Morocco's economic development. The sultan, who would assume the throne as King Mohammed V, would never forget the president's warmth and hospitality. Nor would his thirteen-year-old son, rushed out of his Rabat school that day to attend the banquet—and who later, as King Hassan II, would support the United States decade after decade, through the Cold War and North African turbulence.

Altogether, FDR's Casablanca week, in January 1943, was one of the most enjoyable and fulfilling of his entire life. He was in the fullness of his vigor and virtuosity as he presided, mediated, bargained, stage-managed, manipulated, roared with laughter, and denounced with high indignation. The conference proclaimed some noble objectives, agreed on important short-term goals, and fine-tuned military operations.

But it was only a partial success, largely because of one man who did not join the happy few who were there. Stalin, though invited, declined because, he said, he had a war to fight.

Reeling from the casualties the Russians were suffering in stalling the Germans, Stalin had called for a second front in western Europe that would provide some relief from the German attack on Russia. He had sent his toughest negotiator, Foreign Commissar Vyacheslav Molotov, to Washington on May 29, 1942, to present his second-front demands face-to-face. Molotov wanted a straight answer. What was the president's position on a second front? It had to be 1942, the Russian insisted, not 1943, because by 1943 Hitler would be master of Europe and the task would be infinitely more arduous. Roosevelt and Churchill skillfully dangled the bait of a big invasion in order to keep the Russians in the war without making a final commitment about an attack in 1942, and without offering Moscow anything more than a series of half promises that in the end did not result in a flat promise—or in an invasion. The upshot: The Russians would continue to take horrendous losses while London and Washington would take their time. FDR even had to tell Molotov that lend-lease supplies to Russia would have to be reduced from 4.1 million to 2.5 million tons in the coming year. Pacific war needs were eating away at supplies.

And so, in January 1943, with no second front having been created in 1942, Stalin was in no mood to join his allies in Casablanca. But in Morocco, for the moment, Roosevelt and Churchill could bask in tasks well done, and bask they did. Churchill insisted on driving with Roosevelt to Marrakesh, where he said they could get an incomparable view of the Atlas Mountains. After climbing to the top of a tower, the prime minister urged the president to come up, and soon, his legs dangling, he was hoisted up on a chair composed of the arms of servants. So Casablanca ended, as it had started, with a Hollywood touch of comradeship and dramaturgy.

1
A People Mobilized

Command leadership tightened its grip on the people's lives during 1942 and 1943. The commander in chief imposed curb after curb on people's buying, spending, consuming, traveling. He shuffled and abolished war agencies under his war powers, occasionally refused to carry out congressional legislation he opposed, and despite the venerable separation of powers, enjoyed the counsel and cooperation of at least three of his appointees to the Supreme Court. War agencies penetrated ever more deeply into the daily lives of Americans. More millions of men, and some women, came under the male hierarchical discipline of the military. People groused, swore—and submitted.

For millions of Americans it was a time to make sacrifices for a high moral purpose. For millions of others, it was a time to carry on business as usual. Net income per farm doubled during the war years; the after-tax profits of corporations almost doubled. In a time of desperate need for production, producers were in the driver's seat.

Millions of workers too were producers, but their experience was quite mixed. For years, FDR's approach to labor had been personal, paternalistic, supportive, and manipulative. As the war production effort intensified he continued to be paternalistic and supportive, but now he had to depend more on institutions. Chief of these was the National War Labor Board, with tripartite representation but dominated by the four public members—particularly William H. Davis and Wayne Morse—who took on the heavy responsibilities of both holding down spiraling wage rates and settling strikes.

During 1942, as walkouts continued even after Pearl Harbor, the board had searched for a formula that would accommodate both the opposition of business to an enforced "closed shop" and labor's demand that the bosses not use the war for union-busting drives. The board reshaped an old formula, maintenance of membership, under which members had had to stay in their unions for the life of the contract, into "maintenance of voluntarily established membership," under which employees had ten or fifteen days to quit the union before membership was final. Thus did the board seek to reconcile liberty with order and equality.

Surprisingly, in the face of hostility to strikes on the part of the public and especially soldiers overseas, and despite a "no-strike" pledge by labor and extensive mediation and conciliation agencies, walkouts not only continued but escalated during the war years: from approximately 2,000 in 1942 to 3,700 in 1943, to nearly 5,000 in 1944. The president, bypassing some of his agencies, fought a long and bruising battle with Lewis, who was unpopular with the military and much of the public—"John Lewis, damn your coal-black soul!" cried the soldiers' paper, *Stars and Stripes*—but had the absolute loyalty of the union men who mined the coal.

"FDR walked with consummate skill the tightrope between angry workers and an irate public," judged historian William O'Neill. "In a no-win situation, he lost almost nothing," ensuring a steady supply of coal while protecting the effort against soaring wages.

. . .

What about *un*organized Americans: women, blacks, children, "aliens"?

Entering the 1930s with abysmally low wages—on the average half to two-thirds that of men—women had ended that decade in a scarcely improved position. The New Deal had indeed been less than half dealt for working women. NRA codes endorsed sex differentials 14 to 30 percent lower than for men. Most relief and work programs employed less than 10 percent women. CCC camps were set up for young men by the hundreds; despite Eleanor Roosevelt's intervention, only eighty-six were set up for women. Women's organizations such as the General Federation of Women's Clubs and the Women's Trade Union League had no clout, historian Irving Bernstein concluded, and could be safely ignored.

From 1940 to 1945 the number of women in the labor force shot up from less than 13 million to more than 19 million. With women flooding into war plants and services in tight labor markets it was expected that their wages would rise, but these still lagged behind men's. Some unions resisted (and even struck against) women taking jobs that might leave veterans out in the cold when they returned from the front. There were many stories about "Rosie the Riveter" and other heroines of production, and defense work did give many women a heightened sense of self-esteem that lasted into their postwar lives. But somehow the glory rarely translated into higher wages and better working conditions.

When mothers suffered deprivations, so did many children. Schools were often congested, sometimes to double their capacity. Some schools were so crowded that many children did not even attend. Lack of child care and of extended families left youngsters to their own devices as parents worked graveyard shifts. Millions of children with working parents were left at home without adequate care. There were federal subsidies for child care under the Lanham Act and under Emergency Maternal and Infant Care programs, but they were rarely adequate. Eleanor Roosevelt appealed to the heads of industry to provide day-care facilities for workers' children. A pioneering model was set up in one shipyard in Oregon, but there were no statewide or nationwide programs for toddlers. Some youngsters had neither schools nor home care nor day care. By mid-1943 almost 2 million girls and boys under eighteen worked on farms or in factories, usually at much lower pay than adults. Children were hardly a political pressure group.

Nor were African-Americans, outside of a few northern cities and a few "colored" unions. Even before Pearl Harbor, black leaders were finding once again that the white power structure could not be altered from the inside if you lacked both access to money and the right to vote; it had to be challenged from the outside. In April 1941 the National Negro Council had urged the president to abolish discrimination in all federal agencies by executive order. Meetings of Walter White and other black leaders, even with friends like union leader Sidney Hillman, who had joined the Office of Production Management, had brought little but promises. Then White, A. Philip Randolph, the revered head of the Brotherhood of Sleeping Car Porters, and other black leaders threatened a march on Washington, to take place on July 1, 1941, unless action was taken against discrimination in war plants.

Eleanor Roosevelt was the only real friend African-Americans had in the White House. Presidential aides Early and McIntyre were Virginians with conventional southern attitudes. FDR himself viewed "Negro rights" with a mixture of personal compassion, social paternalism, recognition of pervasive racism in Congress, and a practical awareness both of blacks' importance to the defense effort and their potential influence at the ballot booth. The general policy of the administration, to the extent it had one, was "separate but equal," in the armed forces, in civilian agencies, and—

at least by exhortation—in war industries, but the separation usually thwarted the equality. Now the black leadership was demanding that FDR live up to his 1940 campaign promises and make good on his words about "equal opportunity."

Apprehensively Roosevelt watched the escalating plans for Randolph's march on Washington. Typically, he tried to head it off not by open opposition but indirectly—in this instance through his wife, who had by now been backing black activists for years. "I feel very strongly that your group is making a very grave mistake," Eleanor wrote to Randolph three weeks before the planned march. She feared that it would "set back the progress which is being made, in the Army at least, towards better opportunities and less segregation." It might arouse even more "solid opposition" from "certain groups" in Congress.

It took iron resolve on the part of African-American leaders to stand up against their friends as well as their foes, but Randolph and his comrades were determined not to retreat without an executive order against discrimination. Calling Randolph and White to the Oval Office, FDR tried all his arts from persuasion to rhetoric. "What would happen if Irish and Jewish people were to march on Washington?" he asked, and answered the question himself—the rest of the American people would resent it.

But the president was beginning to weaken. He arranged a meeting of Eleanor, NYA head Aubrey Williams, and New York mayor Fiorello LaGuardia with black leaders in New York. After Randolph and White threatened a march on the New York City Hall as well, they negotiated an agreement that the president would sign. The march was called off.

It turned out to be both a symbolic and a hollow victory for African-American leaders. Symbolic, because at last blacks had a law—or at least an executive order—against discrimination, and an agency—at least a presidentially established one—to give the law some enforcement. Hollow, because the impact was very limited. The president set up a Commission on Fair Employment Practices within the defense bureaucracy but without any real policing power. He appointed a six-member board headed by Mark Ethridge, publisher of the Louisville *Courier-Journal* and a strong civil-rights advocate, and composed mainly of white members. Its staff consisted of a half dozen field investigators. But the main problem was the sheer intractability of the problem: a corporal's guard was trying to breach the citadels of Jim Crow. Training and jobs were linked in a vicious circle: Employers turned away blacks because they had inadequate training; training classes were closed to blacks because of an alleged lack of jobs.

But some lessons had been learned. The president had learned that African-American leaders were deadly serious and would not cave in even to his persuasiveness and his power. Black leaders had learned that the "power system" could be breached only with militance and persistence. Southern leaders learned that a Democratic administration could, when the chips were down, turn against segregationist southerners. As for the segregationists, they revealed their fanaticism. Eugene ("Bull") Connor, then and for years afterward head of Birmingham "Public Safety," charged that the Fair Employment Practices Commission was causing disunity, that venereal disease was the number one Negro problem, and that the Ku Klux Klan would be revived.

"Don't you think," Connor demanded, "one war in the South" had been enough?

. . .

Across the nation, by 1943 the war was triggering an explosion of excitement, an outburst of volunteerism, and an outpouring of grass-roots participation without parallel in the American experience. This eruption rose far above class attitudes, racial tension, ethnic feelings, and interest-group self-protectiveness, as the American people responded as one nation to calls for a mass movement of activists. Towns held meetings, citizens formed committees, blocks elected captains, people sent off aluminum pots and pans to be made into airplanes.

Was the government not only triggering but fully unleashing the huge potential of people at home? Not in the eyes of many women. It was largely under their own initiative, rather than on government demand, that millions of women flocked into Red Cross centers, volunteered for the Women's Ambulance and Defense Corps of America, served as security guards and couriers for the armed services, and organized their own groups. After Pearl Harbor a poll reported that 68 percent of the respondents favored a labor draft for women under thirty-five—almost three out of four women polled favored it—but Congress would not vote for something so radical.

Women, and many men as well, were simply moving beyond the government in their zeal to contribute. But for many women this was not enough; they wanted to serve in the armed forces. Only after Republican congress-woman Edith Nourse Rogers of Massachusetts demanded that women be allowed to serve in the U.S. Army was the Women's Army Auxiliary Corps—soon to become known as the WAACs—set up to do clerical and other non-combatant work. Ten thousand women promptly volunteered.

The war experience of African-Americans was more mixed and complex. For hundreds of thousands of blacks the war meant migration—from south to north, from civilian to military life—that for some represented major turning points in their lives. But many faced the same problems of discrimination in the heavily segregated armed forces that they had encountered in civilian life. They did find educational opportunities in military service or with some defense programs that they had earlier been denied. Whatever fraternization they might have achieved with white military personnel overseas, however, quickly ended on returning home.

No sector of American life underwent greater change than education. "We ask that every schoolhouse," the president said, "become a service center for the home front." The schools took up the challenge with an array of efforts from bond drives to courses in Asian geography to paramilitary youth organizations. Some universities and schools came near to closing as male students and teachers were drafted and women left for factory and other war work. In 1943–44, liberal-arts graduates were fewer than half and law school graduates only one-fifth the prewar level. Science adviser Vannevar Bush estimated to FDR that science lost 150,000 college graduates and 17,000 advanced-degree graduates to the war.

As education was disrupted and protests streamed in from educators, Roosevelt sought a short-term solution. Stimson and Knox responded with the Army Specialized Education Program and the Navy V-12 program. By the end of 1943 the two programs had used idle college buildings at about 500 institutions to provide training for about 300,000 men. Students marched alongside ivy-covered buildings, uniformed officers took over classrooms, science professors worked on bomb technology and battle medicines in their laboratories. This augmented federal wedge in education would lay the groundwork for an ever greater federal role in the postwar years.

Heroic participation in the battle of the home front did not spring spontaneously out of the hearts and minds of civic patriots. It was mightily abetted by the most intensive, comprehensive, and sophisticated propaganda effort Washington had ever mounted. The main effort began with massive war bond campaigns. In charge of the effort, Treasury Secretary Morgenthau followed the shrewd insight "to use *bonds* to sell the *war*, rather than vice versa." Hollywood stars, radio commentators, singers, famous bands, musicians—even violinist Yehudi Menuhin playing Mendelssohn's Concerto in E Minor—were enlisted in the cause. As against the negative propaganda of World War I, much of the publicity produced or supervised by the Office of War Information under Elmer Davis struck the key themes of the global conflict, backed up by FDR's unmatched skill at conveying war aims and peace goals to the public.

. . .

Perhaps never had the American people been so psychologically and emotionally aroused and fulfilled as they were during these war years. They had a heady sense of participation, of working with others, of taking on new tasks and accomplishing them, of pursuing a clear-cut goal—beat the Axis—as a first step to postwar peace and security. Paradoxically, never had the American people as a whole had their material needs so well satisfied. Despite rationing, tens of millions enjoyed higher wages, better clothing, more food, improved health care, and more job training than ever before; many had better housing and recreation, though under crowded conditions. These millions included huge armies of military men and women, who had considerable job security too, for a time.

One reason for this well-being was the continuation of the New Deal programs into the war—programs often enlarged rather than dropped. Eleanor Roosevelt was insistent that the social welfare measures for economic security and civil rights continue in some form. To her, this was what young people in particular were fighting for. When a public housing project for Negro defense workers in Detroit, the Sojourner Truth project, came under attack by white politicians, Eleanor intervened on the defense workers' behalf and the Michigan national guard was called up, to assure black tenants the right to live in the housing project.

And Franklin Roosevelt, despite a public announcement of his shift from "Dr. New Deal" to "Dr. Win-the-War," in fact continued in the former capacity as well. If it was necessary to bootleg New Deal measures to the American people under patriotic labels, this was wholly acceptable to him.

Never indeed had so many Americans had it so good in so many ways. But these tens of millions did not include a million war casualties and the families who suffered over their deaths and wounds. And for the millions who were fighting in distant lands, the war was not just the "organized bore" that soldiers called it but an agonizing hell.

2
The Soldier and the Prince

By 1943 the leaders of all the armies in Europe—American, British, German, Russian—were proclaiming that they were leading "people's wars": crusades for Freedom and Equality. Among those who were doing the actual fighting rather than talking, however, few were tasting either of these lofty aims. None had expected much freedom in their armed forces, of course, but the vast majority of fighting men and women experienced equality only in their common misery.

The grossest inequality lay between soldiers on the Soviet front and on the Anglo-American fronts: an inequality of death. Compared to the fierce Soviet defensive battles of 1942 and the huge offensives that lay ahead, American and British forces fought only limited battles in 1943, as they inched their way up the Italian boot past Naples. The postponement of the cross-channel invasion left the Soviet Union still with the brunt of the fighting. Hurling masses of troops and tanks against the enemy, the Russians suffered staggering losses that were beyond anything known in the history of warfare: 6 million military deaths from all causes, 10 million civilians killed, 25 million left homeless.

Within the American military as a whole there was an inequality of death; the chance of being killed on the average was less than one in fifty, but that chance radically escalated among rifle companies, armored battalions, combat engineers, medics, and tank destroyer units. It did not help to be an officer, except above the company-grade level.

Enlisted troops did not expect to share the creature comforts of officers—anyway, in combat areas everyone felt deprived—still, they did expect equality of recognition. But rewards for good conduct or great courage were grossly unequal. Combat air crews received more campaign stars than combat soldiers; headquarters personnel won more ground army medals than riflemen.

Servicewomen fared poorly compared to men. The original WAAC, which had been poorly trained and deployed, gave way in 1943 to a new Women's Army Corps (WAC), placed directly under the general staff. Still, women were ridiculed as unsoldierly, slandered as promiscuous, caricatured as unfeminine, and employed in some of the most unfulfilling tasks—except by General MacArthur, who called them "my best soldiers."

African-Americans predictably faced the old problem of segregation and discrimination, even in a new war for freedom and equality. The administration had planned to draft fewer blacks than whites, proportion-ately—and these mainly for service units. But manpower needs combined with black protests impelled the administration to boost blacks to the same level as whites in the army, a hike of around 10 percent. Inch by inch the army retreated from its discriminatory policies, appointing the first African-American general and promising to put some black combat units into the field. The main obstacle was not public opinion but rather foot-dragging within the services on the part of officers who vilified blacks as badly edu-cated, unskilled, and undisciplined.

Why not then abolish all-black units and integrate? This aroused all the usual fears—of race riots in camps, of violence in southern military towns, even of black-white conflict during combat. The army sent some black combat units overseas, the little U.S. Coast Guard commissioned ten times more black officers than the navy, and as units became shuffled and reshuffled along the tortuous battlefronts, some de facto integration occurred.

Many lesbians and homosexuals faced the worst of circumstances. They had no equivalent to black and women's organizations to fight for their rights on Capitol Hill. Some became combat medics or hospital per-sonnel or chaplain's aides; others were subject to witch hunts, thrown into "queer stockades" or brigs, sent home on "queer ships." Only toward the end of the war did the army begin to alter its hard-line policy, as it or-dered cases of discharged self-confessed homosexuals to be reviewed and their readmission to the army authorized.

And then there were those who lost their freedom for good. By the end of 1943 the American death toll was averaging around 5,000 a month; a year later it was rising to between 12,000 and 18,000 GIs each month. Of the 16 million Americans serving in all branches of the armed forces, losses totaled 1 million casualties, including 300,000 battle deaths and 100,000 other fatalities. But American losses paled next to the 6 million military deaths and 10 million civilian deaths suffered by the Soviets. In all lands tens of millions were left bereaved, widowed, orphaned, or coping with return-ing veterans who were physically or psychologically maimed by war.

. . .

Could anything justify such stupendous losses, such endless suffering and heartbreak? It would be "inconceivable—it would, indeed, be sacrile-gious—if this Nation and the world did not attain," Roosevelt declared in his State of the Union speech to Congress in January 1943, "some real, last-

ing good out of all these efforts and sufferings and bloodshed and death."
Victory in the war was the immediate task, but freedom from fear and
want—enlarging people's security throughout the world—would be the
ultimate victory.

"After the first World War we tried to achieve a formula for permanent peace, based on a magnificent idealism," the president continued,
referring to the League of Nations. "We failed. But, by our failure, we have
learned that we cannot maintain peace at this stage of human development
by good intentions alone." The Allies, "the mightest military coalition in
all history," must remain united to build world peace. "The people have
now gathered their strength," and nothing now could stop them.

Bold and timely in rhetoric but also scarred by Wilson's—and his own—
defeat in 1920 on the issue, the president during 1943 was caution itself in laying
plans for a United Nations structure and organization. In 1942, he, Churchill,
and Stalin had jointly composed a "Declaration of United Nations" which
was signed by twenty-six nations, declaring that they would preserve human rights and justice in the world. Now, trying to gather support and avoid
the debacle of the League of Nations, FDR had even allowed some Republicans to jump ahead of him; in April, Wendell Willkie had published *One
World,* an instant best-selling account of his travels to Russia and China and
a plea for United States cooperation to preserve postwar peace. GOP legislators were planning to draft their own statement on the issue. The president
let Hull and a group of State Department experts move ahead—very quietly—on postwar peace planning. In Congress, J. William Fulbright and other
Democrats were restive. The Arkansas senator asked FDR to support his
resolution favoring international machinery with power adequate to maintain
peace, but the president would not take the lead on this innocuous resolution.

Indeed, FDR's ideas on UN organization were still evolving. Early in
the war he had strongly favored UN domination by the Big Four—with
Britain, China, Russia, and the United States as the "Four Policemen"—
but State Department planners and many American liberals and internationalists favored one universal organization with effective representation
of smaller nations. Already tough questions were rising, FDR knew—of
the method of representing smaller nations, of a Big Four veto, of the nature of the world security force—questions that aroused for FDR disturbing
echoes of the controversies that had helped kill the League of Nations.

In these hopes and fears the president had a partner in Eleanor Roosevelt. She too had lived through the euphoric and then lacerating days of
1919 and 1920, and she fully shared her husband's central concern for a strong

FDR and Herbert Hoover at 1933 Inauguration.
(Courtesy Franklin Delano Roosevelt Library)

FDR, Warm Springs, December 1933.
(Courtesy Franklin Delano Roosevelt Library)

FDR, Ruthie Bie, and Fala,
February 1941.
*(Courtesy Franklin Delano
Roosevelt Library)*

FDR and Winston S. Churchill, 1943.
(Courtesy Franklin Delano Roosevelt Library)

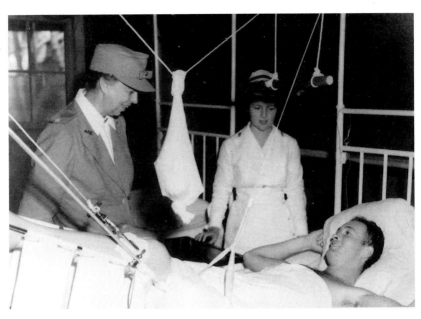

Eleanor during her trip to the South Pacific, 1943.
(Courtesy Franklin Delano Roosevelt Library)

FDR and Eleanor at Val-Kill, 1943.
(Courtesy Franklin Delano Roosevelt Library)

FDR campaigning with Secretary of the Treasury Henry Morgenthau, Jr.,
near Hyde Park, November 1944.
(Courtesy Franklin Delano Roosevelt Library)

FDR and Eleanor with their grandchildren at the White House, January 1945.
(Courtesy Franklin Delano Roosevelt Library)

Anna and Eleanor at FDR's funeral, Hyde Park, 1945.
(Courtesy Franklin Delano Roosevelt Library)

Eleanor at the UN, 1947.
(Courtesy Franklin Delano Roosevelt Library)

Eleanor holding the Universal Declaration of Human Rights, 1948.
(Courtesy Franklin Delano Roosevelt Library)

Eleanor and Adlai Stevenson, 1960.
(Courtesy Franklin Delano Roosevelt Library)

Eleanor with John F. Kennedy, 1961.
(Courtesy Franklin Delano Roosevelt Library)

(Courtesy Franklin Delano Roosevelt Library)

Eleanor Roosevelt's funeral, Hyde Park, 1962. From left: Lady Bird Johnson, Jacqueline Kennedy, President John F. Kennedy, Lyndon B. Johnson, Harry S. Truman, Bess Truman, Dwight D. Eisenhower. (*Courtesy World Wide*)

United Nations. She usually deferred to FDR on matters of political strategy—indeed, she asked him not to share any military secrets with her—but the first lady, in Joseph Lash's words, "was haunted by the fear that the system of privilege and inequality within and among nations that had led to two world wars would inevitably breed more wars, despite a military victory, if the old division between haves and have-nots survived."

Eleanor's concern for postwar peace, and her ideas about it, were strengthened and focused by her wartime travels. She had eagerly accepted Queen Elizabeth's invitation to visit England in fall 1942. Normally the most courageous of women, she had felt her fears rising during the transatlantic plane trip, especially in regard to her strenuous itinerary and a stay in Buckingham Palace. But the king and queen met her at Paddington Station and made her feel comfortable in their palace, which she used as a base from which to tour bombed-out buildings in London, air-raid shelters, and army camps. She complained to General Dwight Eisenhower, then commander of U.S. forces in the European theater, when she discovered that the GIs were wearing cotton socks instead of wool. Code-named "Rover" by the American embassy because of her constant motion, she gave speeches about the war and received numerous members of deposed European monarchies—doubtless with the ardent acquiescence of her husband.

As she extended her travels, ultimately to the Pacific—New Caledonia, Samoa, Bora Bora, New Zealand, Australia, and Guadalcanal—and as she hosted VIPs in Washington such as Madame Chiang Kai-shek, Eleanor Roosevelt became more outspoken in her views about peace. Having challenged Churchill to his face on Britain's 1930s policy toward Spain, she had no reluctance later in attacking his colonialism and his hope that he could return to the prewar world. The United States must join with "liberated people" around the world who were expressing the hopes for freedom and justice hidden in their hearts, she wrote in "My Day." She wanted to extend the Four Freedoms, just as FDR did, but in her own way. People assumed—incorrectly—that when the first lady held press conferences, her remarks might forecast the president's position on some issue. Still, she conveyed her views to him well enough through her reported speeches, evening talks with visitors they both hosted—and not infrequently by accosting him while he was still abed of a morning.

. . .

Franklin and Eleanor Roosevelt were, at heart, Soldiers of the Faith. If she could call him "a very simple Christian," he could justly say the same of her. They differed in the nature of their faiths—his grounded more in orthodox Episcopalian doctrine, hers more in her own individualized spirituality. But as fellow soldiers of the faith they could believe that they were fighting for clear and definite goals: world peace (through a United Nations organization), liberty and equality and security at home (through implementation of the Four Freedoms), and human rights around the globe (through means to be worked out after the war).

But far more than his wife's, FDR's faith ran up against the hard rocks of reality—of intractable circumstances, the caprices of Fortune, stubborn institutions. So he had to battle not only for a global ideology of peace and freedom but also guard the interests of his nation in a tumultuous and impious world. As a "Christian and a Democrat"—FDR's summation of himself—he possessed a moral credo that was a patchwork of attitudes and instincts about honor, decency, good neighborliness, and noblesse oblige. But such attitudes and instincts were often hard to translate into clear directives, explicit policies, or specific operations.

The result was often a profound gap between Roosevelt's moral code and his day-to-day practice, between his lofty ends and his dubious means, between his magnanimity and his Machiavellianism. Because men were "bad," and would not observe their faith with the leader, "so you are not bound to keep faith with them," the Florentine "Prince of Darkness" wrote. FDR consciously did not embrace such cynical realpolitik, but in promising the public peace, in the most cardinal case, and following measures that would lead the country into war, he had resorted to manipulation and deception. His lofty dreams and his "practical" compromises, moreover, not only collided with one another; they also inflated the significance of each other, for the higher he set his goals and the lower he pitched his improvisations, the more he widened the gap between the existing and the ideal and thus raised people's expectations while failing to fulfill them.

If Roosevelt was both idealist and realist, the reason lay not only in his own intellectual and political habits but also in his society and its traditions. Americans have long embraced both moralistic and realistic tendencies, the first symbolized by men as diverse as Jefferson and William Jennings Bryan, the second by the "tough-minded" men—Washington, Monroe, the two Adamses—who directed the foreign policy of the republic in its early years. If Roosevelt's goals were somewhat mixed and murky, they were shaped by liberal values and internationalist impulses so widely shared and diluted as to supply little ideological or programmatic support for politicians. Inevitably FDR faced the classic dilemma of the democratic leader: He must moralize and dramatize and simplify in order to lead the public, but in doing so he may raise false hopes and expectations, including his own, the deflation of which in the long run may lead to disillusionment and cynicism.

On the day that France was invaded by Germany, June 5, 1940, a preoccupied FDR had agreed to meet once again with American youth leaders in the White House. It was a candid three-hour conversation—on a horrendous day for the world—about the critical issues facing the United States. In response to the young people's criticism that he had abandoned the New Deal, subordinating burning social issues to the national defense, FDR thoughtfully, perhaps wistfully, invoked the memory of Lincoln.

"I think the impression was that Lincoln was a pretty sad man," FDR told his small audience, "because he couldn't do all he wanted to do at one time, and I think you will find examples where Lincoln had to compromise to gain a little something. He had to compromise to make a few gains." Lincoln, he explained, was "one of those unfortunate people called a 'politician'"—an idealist forced to play the game of compromise and pragmatism. Maybe one of the young people present "would make a much better president than I have," FDR concluded. But "if you ever sit here you will learn that you cannot, just by shouting from the housetops, get what you want all the time."

FDR could not escape history. American foreign policy had been shaped by two diplomatic strategies. One was a diplomacy of short-run expedience and manipulation, of balance of power and spheres of interest, of compromise and adjustment, marginal choices and limited goals. The other was a diplomacy—almost a nondiplomacy—of world unity and collective security, democratic principle and moral uplift, peaceful change and nonaggression. Too, the institutional arrangements in Washington—the separation of decision making between the State Department and the military and in their access to the White House; the absence of an integrating cabinet or staff; the institutional gaps in Congress among legislators specializing in military, foreign, and domestic policies; and indeed the whole tendency in Washington toward fragmented policy making—all reinforced the natural tendency of the president to compartmentalize.

. . .

The "diplomatic-political" year of 1943 posed weighty issues for FDR that variously brought out the realist and the idealist in him, or often a combination of the two.

As a leader of the "people's war," the president continued to put his main faith in the creation of a permanent United Nations designed to keep the peace after the war. All the Big Four leaders endorsed this visionary idea in principle; the question was where they placed it in their priority list of war goals. It was clear that the main threat to a strong UN would be the age-old carving out of spheres of interest by the big powers. Still aware that the Big Four would need to police the world for some time, the president by 1943, as historian Frank Freidel noted, was concluding that the UN should be a single worldwide body, with regional councils subordinate to it. This was a move toward Cordell Hull's universalism. Republicans at home, under Vandenberg's leadership, were also moving toward a stronger UN. Early in November 1943, the president led representatives of forty-four nations at the White House in signing an agreement creating the United Nations Relief and Rehabilitation Administration. Nations, he proclaimed, "will learn to work together only by actually working together."

3
The Power of a President

It was the greatest concentration of power the world had ever seen, Churchill had remarked, as he looked around the conference table in Teheran in late 1943; history lay in the hands of the three leaders, Roosevelt, Churchill, and Stalin. One evening, after sparring with Stalin and listening to Roosevelt trying to placate the Russians, Churchill was of a different mood. "Stupendous issues are unfolding before our eyes, and we are only specks of dust that have settled in the night on the map of the world."

The three men were at the height of their brute military power. In the east, Stalin commanded the biggest infantry-tank forces ever mobilized; in Britain, Churchill and Roosevelt had marshaled the most powerful amphibious force in history. Yet both the latter men—Churchill especially—were filled with trepidation about the capacity of their armies to cross the English Channel and take on a still-mighty Wehrmacht.

The Allies were now paying the price for their two-year delay in mounting the cross-channel attack. While London and Washington were taking their time in building up their attack force, the Germans were feverishly fortifying possible invasion sectors. Hitler, now fighting a defensive war on his eastern front while trading space for time, was shifting hundreds of thousands of troops into France. A defensive system that in 1942 probably would have allowed invading forces to seize and hold staging areas in France, for further advances, was now strong enough to hold off all but the mightiest of invasions.

The Germans had made good use of their time. By the spring of 1944 they had built a vaunted "Atlantic Wall" stretching, in uneven strength, hundreds of miles from Belgium to Spain. Installing millions of underwater obstacles to smash landing craft, they had heavily mined beach areas, set up nests of barbed wire covered by carefully placed machine guns and mortars, built pillboxes and gun emplacements deep into the ground. They sought to deceive the invaders with dummy headquarters, ground movements on fake missions, and false radio reports.

But the Americans had a clear edge in technological innovation, a leadership edge provided more by civilians than soldiery. American industrialists and inventors had pioneered in a variety of weapons, but most notably in developing craft that allowed troops to cross miles of rough water, move over reefs, land vehicles safely on rocky beaches, and return. Together with the British they had developed radar, tank landing ships longer than a football field, and smaller craft, which would open bow doors, lower ramps, and disgorge masses of armor. But the true genius was Andrew Higgins, who conceived and built the famed LCVP—Landing Craft, Vehicle and Personnel—made largely of plywood, thus saving on metal, and able to run its square bow up on a beach, back off, turn in a shallow draft, and return to the mother ship for another load.

The Germans were pretty clever too. To thwart gliders, Field Marshal Erwin Rommel—the "desert fox" who had fought brilliantly in North Africa and who was now organizing German defenses against an Allied invasion—devised "asparagus": ten-foot logs protruding from potential glider landing fields and topped with shells to smash the light craft. His technicians designed "S-mines" that jumped up and exploded at waist level. There was nothing the invading troops feared more.

Yet as a military leader, Roosevelt far outrivaled Hitler by 1944. The Führer was brilliant but erratic. He had won remarkable victories through an audacity that repeatedly caught his foe by surprise. He had shown persistence, but often to the point of irrationality, on the Eastern Front. He browbeat generals, shifted them about, and let incompetent Nazi party functionaries gain influence in the military. And strangely, in contrast to his reputation as a man of power and decision, he could be irresolute. In supervising the defense of France he had vacillated between concentrating armor near the beaches or inland and ended up by dividing his panzer divisions between both.

On military matters, FDR was orderly, focused, directive, persistent. Despite pleas to divert resources to other efforts, such as rescuing endangered nations or populations, he stuck strategically with "Atlantic First." As commander in chief he husbanded military resources in all theaters until the enormous industrial and military power of the nation could be marshaled. Despite endless temptations to strike elsewhere, he stuck firmly to an overall strategy of the cross-channel invasion.

At the level of grand strategy, FDR's "soldierly" qualities paid off. He helped gain a maximum Soviet contribution to the bleeding of German ground strength through military and economic aid to Moscow. He brought Allied troops into Europe at just the right time to share in—and claim— military victory. He found the right formula to obtain the most military help from the Russians without letting them, if they wished, occupy much of western Europe. He remained on good terms with his generals and admirals, encouraged them, listened to them, but always insisted on keeping the reins of top power in his own hands. He picked the right military leaders early on—Stimson and Knox in 1940, Marshall later on, MacArthur and Nimitz and Eisenhower—and stuck with them.

Normandy was the acid test of all this—and the crucial test of that test was that the cross-channel invasion was never in fact in danger of defeat. There were moments of tough decisions, of immediate peril, of second thoughts, but the invasion went on with the power and momentum of a dreadnought. The Germans fought skillfully. But they were dealing not simply with conventional invasion forces but with a tide so strong and overpowering it simply overflowed the German strongpoints and swept on. Perhaps the most telling comment came from an American infantryman.

"It seemed so organized," said Private John Barnes of the 116th Infantry after attending a briefing, "that nothing could go wrong, nothing could stop it. It was like a train schedule; we were almost just like passengers. We were aware that there were many landing boats behind us, all lined up coming in on schedule. Nothing could stop it."

The commander in chief was confident too, though cautiously so. While the invaders were still crossing the channel, FDR offered a D-Day prayer that asked Almighty God to lend stoutness to our sons' arms and warned that their "road will be long and hard. For the enemy is strong. He may hurl back our forces. Success may not come with rushing speed, but we shall return again and again."

But after furious battles and bloody stalemates on the beach the tide did move with rushing speed. With most of the Seine River bridges down and highways bombed out, the Germans had all the predictable difficulties in bringing up reinforcements. After dislodging Germans from their hedgerow defenses in Normandy, U.S. forces reached the west shore of the Cotentin Peninsula within two weeks of D-Day, captured Cherbourg a week later, and by the end of the month had landed almost a million troops, half a million tons of supplies, and more than 150,000 vehicles in France. In another two weeks the Americans had executed a wide flanking maneuver, were ready to break out from Saint-Lô, and were heading toward the liberation of Paris.

Rommel, whom Hitler had assigned to the Western Front with special responsibilities for coastal defense, had been right to believe that the first day on the beaches would be decisive. But he had been wrong, too: The decisiveness turned on countless decisions made and resources marshaled over a two-year period—above all, the decision to cross the English Channel.

. . .

Earlier in 1944, at a press conference, a reporter mentioned rumors in the anti-Roosevelt press that the election would be called off. "How?" the president shot back.

"Well, I don't know. That is what I want you to tell me."

"Well, you see," FDR said, "you have come to the wrong place because—gosh—all these people around town haven't read the Constitution. Unfortunately, I have."

Hitler had evidently read the Constitution too—or at least he knew an election was approaching in November 1944. He had told his key commanders in the West, while emphasizing the vital necessity of a successful defense, that stopping the invasion would not only deliver a crushing blow to the enemy's morale but would "prevent Roosevelt from being elected—with any luck he'd finish up in jail somewhere."

So the president had his own two-front conflict: winning reelection while in the midst of winning a war. This was not a problem that faced Stalin, of course, or even Churchill. Britain, a seedbed of democratic practice, was postponing its general election during the war, as it had in World War I. But there was, to many Americans, something almost exalted in the idea that democratic procedures must stand even in great crisis. Yet it seemed strange, too, that people united behind the supreme goal of victory must suddenly pit gladiators against one another in the domestic arena. It soon became clear that "wartime unity" would have little impact. The 1944 election would be just as bitter and hard fought as earlier ones.

Curiously, the war against Hitlerism appeared to sharpen racism and reaction at home. Early in 1944 the president called for a soldiers'-vote bill—"the right of eleven million service people stationed around the world to cast their votes for federal candidates by name, or, if they did not know their names, by checking the party preferred." The message hit Congress like a declaration of war. Senator Taft, his face red and his arms flailing, charged that Roosevelt was planning to line up soldiers for a fourth term as he had WPA workers for his second.

"Roosevelt says we're letting the soldiers down," a senator complained. "Why, God damn him. The rest of us have boys who go into the army and navy as privates and ordinary seamen and dig latrines and swab decks, and his scamps go in as lieutenant colonels and majors and lieutenants and spend their time getting medals in Hollywood. Letting the soldiers down! Why, that son of a bitch."

Southerners feared that a soldiers'-vote act would override the poll tax and enable blacks to vote. In the House, John Rankin of Mississippi pointedly read off the names of Jewish New Yorkers backing FDR's proposal. "Now who is behind this bill?" Rankin harangued the House. "The chief publicist is *PM*, the uptown edition of the Communist *Daily Worker* that is being financed by the tax-escaping fortune of Marshall Field the Third, and the chief broadcaster of it is Walter Winchell—alias no telling what."

"Who is he?" asked a Republican member helpfully.

"The little kike I was telling you about the other day, who called this body the 'House of Reprehensibles.'" Scores of members applauded Rankin at the end of his talk; no one protested.

Despite all the oratory about national unity, deep feeling against the administration was evident in the country as well as in Congress. A British observer noted that while Churchill had the backing of a united nation, FDR moved in an atmosphere of political bitterness, industrial discord, racial tension, press opposition, Democratic party defections—and of "enmity against him" of an intensity and persistence without parallel in England.

Certainly the president's own party was in some disarray, except over the question of whether FDR should run for a fourth term. Almost all of the liberal and centrist elements in the party wanted their proved vote-getter at the head of national and state tickets. FDR was willing. Was

Eleanor? "I dread another campaign," she confessed in a letter to Lorena Hickok, "& even more another 4 years in Washington, but since he's running for the good of the country I hope he wins."

When FDR almost casually announced that he was available for a fourth term, there was nothing like the controversy that had boiled up over his third-term venture four years before. Still, tension remained high, not only with congressional conservatives but with leaders of the liberal wing on the Hill. It took a tax bill early in 1944 to trigger a Democratic revolt in the Senate.

For months the president had been trying to obtain a major revenue increase from Congress. The Treasury Department had estimated that in the new fiscal year income payments to individuals would run about $152 billion and that the goods and services available could absorb only about $89 billion of that figure. An inflationary gap of many billions threatened the nation's stabilization program. As zealous as ever to be seen as "fiscally responsible," the president pressured the congressional Big Four—Vice President Henry Wallace, Speaker Sam Rayburn, House Majority Leader John McCormack, and especially his loyal supporter Senate Majority Leader Alben Barkley—to push through a strong bill. When after Barkley's best efforts Congress came up with an inadequate tax bill marred by provisions for "special interests," the president dug in his heels.

He could not resist some sloganeering. It was, he said, "not a tax bill but a tax relief bill providing relief not for the needy but for the greedy."

At this Barkley boiled over. After consulting with his wife and congressional friends, he took the Senate floor before packed galleries to denounce the president's veto and announce his resignation as majority leader. FDR's message, he cried, was a "calculated and deliberate assault upon the legislative integrity of every member of Congress." The sequence was predictable. The president urged him not to resign, Barkley did so anyway, his Senate Democratic colleagues unanimously reelected him, the nation's press was delirious over the rebuff to the president, Congress overrode his veto by heavy majorities in each house, FDR and Barkley made peace, and Barkley's role as majority leader remained unchanged.

All was well again—except for the setback to stabilization.

. . .

Far more divisive even than taxes was the burning issue of FDR's choice of running mate. The stakes were high. Many people who noticed the president's thin face and sunken eyes—the cost to his health of wartime leadership, high blood pressure, and cigarettes—suspected that if FDR won the election he might not live to complete his fourth term. And then his running mate would be the next president of the United States. Most liberal Democrats, including Eleanor Roosevelt, asked simply, Why not keep Vice President Henry Wallace? Word leaked out that FDR was looking favorably on Hull, Barkley, Justice Douglas, Senator Harry Truman, or even an "outsider" like Ambassador Winant in London or industrialist Henry Kaiser. Names rose and fell like stocks on the Exchange. Finally, the talk turned to Harry Truman. The president liked him for his personal loyalty and legislative support even while the senator was chairing a committee that investigated governmental failures on the home front. He was a stalwart midwestern Democrat, from the politically doubtful border state of Missouri. The president did seem worried about Truman's age and sent someone out to check it, but by the time word came back—the senator had just turned sixty—the subject seemed to have been forgotten. In the deepening haze, Harry Truman got the nod.

To symbolize his lofty position "above party politics," FDR had taken an inspection trip across the country while the delegates nominated him and Truman in Chicago. The president accepted the nomination in a speech from a naval base in San Diego. He would not campaign in the usual sense, he told the delegates by radio. "In these days of tragic sorrow, I do not consider it fitting." But as usual FDR left himself a way out. He would feel free to report to the people "to correct any misrepresentations."

What about the Republicans? They were determined not to repeat the catastrophe of their 1940 convention, when party stalwarts Thomas E. Dewey and Robert A. Taft had led in the early balloting, only to be outrun on the sixth ballot by that interloper, Wendell Willkie. Now, four years later, Dewey easily won the nomination after an impressive preconvention campaign, choosing as his running mate Governor John Bricker of Ohio, a genial conservative who could placate the Republican right. "The Dewey-Bricker ticket is not going to be a pushover," Eleanor warned in a note to her friend Joe Lash. "It is part of the fight of the future between power for big moneyed interests & govt. control & more interest on the part of the people in their govt."

Of all his election foes, FDR had the least liking or respect for this Republican nominee. Dewey had almost beaten Herbert Lehman for the New York governorship in 1938 and had won impressively in 1942. Articulate and handsome, he had used the governorship as a dugout from which he bombarded FDR's war leadership. Liberals scoffed at Dewey as the man on the wedding cake, the only man who could strut sitting down, the boy orator of the platitude. Publicists called him another Theodore Roosevelt, whom ten-year-old Tom and his father had backed in 1912. He was something of a look-alike, with his short bulky frame, mustache, and vim and vigor, and he represented the eastern internationalist wing of the GOP.

Nothing could have galled FDR more than this comparison. For him, Tom Dewey was no Theodore Roosevelt.

Certainly Dewey was no militant TR in the early weeks of his campaign. At the request of General Marshall, based on security grounds, he had agreed not to make the president's advance knowledge of Japanese codes before Pearl Harbor a campaign issue, even though Dewey had learned independently of the code-breaking and viewed Roosevelt as guilty through ineptitude of enabling the Japanese to make their surprise attack. But when Dewey fell back on his basic campaign issue—FDR's bungling leadership of the war—he won little support in the aftermath of the triumphant Normandy landing, and the advances of MacArthur and Nimitz in the Pacific.

In desperation, Dewey resorted to a device that seemed out of character for him—simple red-baiting. By the end of the campaign he had called FDR the dupe of radical labor leaders and Communists and charged flatly that "the Communists are seizing control of the New Deal, through which they aim to control the Government of the United States." Conservative Republicans carried on this attack but made a special point of FDR's unbridled spending. One of them, a Michigan congressman, charged that when Fala had been mistakenly left behind on one of the president's sea voyages, a destroyer had been sent back to retrieve the Scottie at the taxpayers' expense.

And Roosevelt? He was lying low. For many weeks he followed his traditional strategy, staying away from the campaign trail on the pretext that he was too busy with the war to do any politicking. Then, only a few weeks before election day, he opened a campaign that would become legendary in American political memory.

He began with a speech to a Teamsters union dinner. "Well, here we are together again—after four years—and what years they have been! You know, I am actually four years older, which is a fact that seems to *an-noy* some people," but there were "millions of Americans who are m-o-o-r-e than *eleven* years older than when we started in to clean up the mess that was dumped into our laps in 1933!"

Having given poor old Herbert Hoover one more pounding, the president then lauded "the enlightened, liberal elements in the Republican

Party" that were trying to bring it up to date. But the Old Guard Republicans were still in control. Could the Old Guard pass itself off as the New Deal? No "performing elephant could turn a handspring without falling flat on his back."

Soon he had the crowd roaring, as he delivered his barbs, shifting from deadpan innocence and rolled-up eyes of mock amazement to biting ridicule to gentle sarcasm. Then came his rebuttal of the Fala story, his dagger lovingly fashioned and honed, delivered with a mock-serious face and in the quiet, sad tone of a man much abused. "These Republican leaders have not been content with attacks on me, or my wife, or on my sons. No, not content with that, they now include my little dog, Fala. Well, of course I don't resent attacks, and my family doesn't resent attacks, but Fala"—being Scottish—"*does* resent them!" Some reporters saw this as a turning point in the campaign.

Roosevelt was also determined to demolish a whispering campaign about his health. He could do this only with action, not words—most conspicuously by showing himself to millions of persons, especially in the largest city in the nation. Doffing his old gray campaign hat, under a cold pouring rain that drenched his navy cape and plastered down his hair, he drove in an open Packard through Queens to the Bronx, then to Harlem and mid-Manhattan and down Broadway. Eleanor Roosevelt was in the procession behind; at her apartment in Washington Square he rested, then returned to the drive, still under a downpour. Countless onlookers for the rest of their lives would never forget the president's cheery face, his upflung arm and sleeve, the rain dripping off his fedora.

The legend ended with victory, FDR carrying thirty-six states, almost as many as he had won against Willkie. But there was another side to this legend.

Roosevelt had appeared to have everything going for him in this wartime election. As commander in chief he was presiding over splendid victories east and west. The country was prosperous from war spending. People could "shoot with their votes," for nothing would have strengthened Hitler's resolve more than the repudiation of his despised enemy. And FDR clearly outcampaigned Dewey. But FDR won the popular vote with a margin a million and a half less than in 1940. It was the closest election in popular votes since Wilson. If one in every twenty-five voters had balloted for Dewey instead, FDR would have gone down to defeat.

Why this outcome? War weariness? Too much government? Revulsion against casualties, especially following the Normandy attack? Dewey's red-baiting? A resurgence of isolationism? Some analysts had a simpler explanation—the soldiers' vote, or lack of it. The legislation FDR had urged was greatly weakened in Congress. Only a fraction of men and women in service actually voted. Millions of mobile war workers were disenfranchised by state restrictions requiring weeks of residence. The low voting turnout carried a message: A nation fighting for democracy had given a poor demonstration of it in 1944.

4
The Transformation of a President

In January 1944, Franklin Roosevelt gave the most radical speech of his life, ushering in a year of his most transformational leadership. Such leadership requires a strategy of *real change*, embracing alterations in the well-being and happiness of a whole people, measured by their supreme historic and continuing values, expressed in their daily needs and wants, hopes and expectations—real change, executed in a planned and purposeful series of interlinked and mutually supportive actions by the whole nation.

Roosevelt a radical in the last year of his war leadership? This notion defies conventional wisdom and most historical scholarship, and the attitude of FDR himself. Did not the president himself announce the demise of "Dr. New Deal" and his replacement by "Dr. Win-the-War"? Historians have taken this switch seriously, as a natural course for a nation that had to turn from partisan New Deal reform to a united, nonpartisan, nonideological war effort.

Little noticed have been two aspects of FDR's famous metamorphosis. It was not a long-considered shift but an "item" that came up almost inadvertently after a press conference and that FDR felt he had to explain at the next meeting with the reporters. But his explanation consisted almost entirely of detailing how he was *not* abandoning the New Deal, only adding wartime "doctoring" to it. And he implied that the New Deal would need to be extended after the war.

The second factor was Eleanor Roosevelt. Within a few days of Roosevelt's press conference she publicly disagreed—in her "My Day" column—with any dropping of "Dr. New Deal." "I . . . could not help feeling," she wrote later, "that it was the New Deal social objectives that had fostered the spirit that would make it possible for us to fight the war."

It was obvious, she continued, that "if the world were ruled by Hitler, freedom and democracy would no longer exist." Her views hardly surprised FDR. She had been pestering him at every opportunity to push even harder for New Deal measures—social services, civil rights, opportunities for women—during the war, and she was constantly looking ahead to the postwar world.

But it was the president himself who made clear he wished to advance, not jettison, the New Deal. He did this in his State of the Union address, January 11, 1944. He considered this speech so important that, when an attack of the "flu" (as he called it) kept him from presenting it in person, it was duly read by a clerk, with the president delivering it over the radio in the evening to reach the widest possible audience. After dealing in his usual strong terms with war issues, he suddenly switched to postwar planning at home. We could not be content, he said, with any fraction of the people, one-third or one-fifth or one-tenth, "ill-fed, ill-clothed, ill-housed, and insecure." He briefly enumerated—and endorsed—Bill of Rights liberties but added that, as the nation and the economy had expanded, "these political rights proved inadequate to assure us equality in the pursuit of happiness."

Then the most remarkably philosophical words from this very "pragmatic" president: True individual freedom "cannot exist without economic security and independence. 'Necessitous men are not free men.' People who are hungry—people who are out of a job—are the stuff of which dictatorships are made."

He climaxed his speech with a "second Bill of Rights," the explicit and specific rights "to a useful and remunerative job in the industries or shops or farms or mines of the Nation . . . to earn enough to provide adequate food and clothing and recreation . . . of farmers to raise and sell their products at a return which will give them and their families a decent living . . . of every businessman, large and small, to trade in an atmosphere of freedom from unfair competition and domination by monopolies at home or abroad . . . of every family to a decent income . . . to adequate medical care and the opportunity to achieve and enjoy good health . . . to adequate protection from the economic fears of old age and sickness and accident and unemployment . . . to a good education."

FDR had expanded the notion of individual rights beyond freedom of expression—and expanded, for the rest of the century, the responsibilities of the State: The government, he believed, had the obligation to guarantee citizens' economic well-being.

During the months that followed, the president took every possible opportunity to establish these rights by executive action, explicit messages to Congress, and appeals to the people. But he did much more than this. He expressed these rights in terms of basic values, he established priorities among these values, he interlinked policies with values, and—boldest of all—he proposed a radically new political strategy.

His paramount value—his top-priority goal for Americans—was security: personal security at home and national security abroad. To advance the latter he continued to press for a strong United Nations that could enforce peace. Personal security called for millions of new jobs, governmental guarantee of employment, plus the usual "New Deal" protections of wage levels and unions. "Jobs. *Jobs,*" FDR said to reporters. "It's a good old Anglo-Saxon word."

His second great value was liberty—yes, *after* security, because without security there could be no liberty. He would not desert the "first" Bill of Rights, however, to fight for the "second." The needy simply were not free. Economic, social, and moral security were interlinked. And in fighting Nazism, Americans were counterattacking the ultimate in oppression, the crushing of every kind of personal, economic, and political liberty.

FDR's third supreme value was equality, by which he meant not equality of condition but of opportunity. This constituted most of his practical domestic agenda for 1944: public health programs that would include the poor, better education especially in financially starved rural schools, extending rural electrification to poorer farm families out in the backcountry, tax policies for the needy instead of the "greedy," a national service act that would equalize contributions to the war effort, fair employment rights for blacks. On this last count the president called for the extension and strengthening of the Fair Employment Practices Commission, but he dared not push very hard because of the FEPC's manifest unpopularity with conservative Democrats and Republicans in Congress.

If these values, and their ordering, added up to "life, liberty, and the pursuit of happiness," this was no accident. This Jeffersonian president clothed his goals in the historic values of the great Virginian and the other founders and heroes of the onetime Republican party of Jefferson and Madison that had continued as the Democratic party of Jackson, Van Buren, and their successors. And these values were linked. Survival—order and security—first, but not at the expense of liberty and equality.

He wanted, FDR said, to attain "a stronger, a happier, and a more prosperous America."

How to achieve such magical goals? First of all, by winning elections,
and FDR spent most of 1944 doing just that. But by that year he had come
to realize that his goals were imperiled not just by conservative opposition but by the structure or organization of American party politics, specifically by a "four-party" system that pitted conservative Democrats allied
with Republicans against a majority of Democrats allied with a few liberal
Republicans. He had discovered that tinkering with the system was not
enough, that sudden proposals such as his court-packing plan could mis-
carry, that the "purge" of 1938, and his proposed bills, failed because of the
powerful alliance of southern and northern conservatives.

So it was that FDR in early summer 1944 responded to a "feeler" from
Willkie, who was blocked by Tories in his own party. What about uniting
liberals in both parties? FDR liked the idea, he told his political confidant
Rosenman. "We ought to have two real parties—one liberal and the other
conservative." Why not start party realignment right after the election?
FDR sent Rosenman to New York to work out specific plans with the 1940
GOP nominee. After a two-hour meeting Rosenman reported back to a
hopeful president. But then something went wrong—worry on Willkie's
part that FDR might be using the idea as just an election-year ploy,
Willkie's diminished standing in the GOP. The two leaders agreed to wait
until after the election. A month before that election, Willkie died. With
his death passed an opportunity to reconstitute the very bases of American party and electoral politics.

Perhaps FDR was justified in his caution. He needed that southern
Democratic vote in November. His 1944 "fighting liberalism" had run the
risk of losing centrist support. He had urged a big turnout, especially by
housewives and working women. He had called for a stronger soldiers'-
vote bill. Over and over again he appealed to the "people," like most candidates, but with a special urgency. As commander in chief, he said, he had
no superior officer—only the people. They could command him to report
for another tour of duty, or they could discharge him. In November they
reenlisted him for the duration—but by so close a margin as to give FDR
pause.

But the American people had done something else. If FDR had led
them, they had led him, not only because he needed their votes but because they shared his vision. No one close to him expressed and symbolized the needs and hopes of the popular majority that sustained him more

than Eleanor Roosevelt. While the couple's marital relationship remained
as unromantic as ever, their political and moral partnership strengthened
during the war. So did FDR's partnership with a majority of the American
people.

. . .

As the war in Europe came to a climax, Roosevelt hoped to engineer
a supreme act of transforming leadership. This leadership he would offer
at the next Big Three summit meeting, to take place at Yalta early in 1945.
The timing seemed ripe for historic achievements around the peace table.
By the end of January 1945 the Russians had captured Warsaw and Budapest
and overrun East Prussia. In France, after Allied attacks from the north
and south had driven the Wehrmacht back toward its homeland, the Germans had powerfully counterattacked in the Battle of the Bulge, but the
Allies were now mobilizing for another great push eastward, while maintaining heavy air attacks. MacArthur's troops were closing in on Manila,
while Admiral Chester Nimitz's navy planned daring island attacks close
to the Japanese homeland. In Yalta, FDR would join Churchill and Stalin
and old comrades on their three staffs: Vyacheslav Molotov and Andrei
Vishinsky; Hopkins, William Leahy, and Marshall; Anthony Eden and the
British military chiefs.

Few at Yalta underestimated the fateful nature of this conference—
fateful not because there would be new solutions to new problems but
because all the great strategic questions rising from previous diplomatic
and battlefield successes would come to a head on the shores of the Black
Sea. Volumes would be written about the Crimea conference, but few
would emphasize what to Roosevelt was the transcending question because
it would affect the outcome of all the others.

That question was the power and scope of the new United Nations. That
the Big Three would establish an international organization was taken for
granted, but FDR had learned enough from the demise of the League of
Nations to know that leaders could piously support the idea of a world peace
organization and at the same time support provisions that could cripple it.
He had won an election mandate in the fall for a "strong UN"—but how to
transform that mandate into actual strength? To serve as peacekeeper, the
UN would need armed forces. How would member nations supply these,
how far would their writ extend, who would control them, to what extent
would the Big Three—with China, the Big Four—have central control, and
to what extent would that control be shared with the other, smaller nations?

These questions were the top priority for Roosevelt at Yalta, but he had other priorities that could not be separated from the first. By far the most important of these was Soviet participation in the final assault on Japan. That Stalin would take part was never in doubt, if only to share the spoils of victory. The brutal question was how much and how soon—only after the Allies had suffered the bloodletting of an invasion of Japan, or early enough to share the burden? What price would Stalin exact to come in early and powerfully?

And then there was the thorny problem of a compromise formula for Poland—and another refractory matter, colonies, about which FDR could do little. He had long been conducting a half-serious, half-bantering debate with Churchill about the future of the Empire. But FDR would no more challenge Churchill about the future of India than he would Stalin about the future of Poland. Rather, he took out his anticolonial feelings on France, which was hardly in a position to demand control of an Indochina lost to the Japanese. When the subject even of postwar trusteeships came up at the conference, Churchill rose to the height of Churchillian oratory: "Under no circumstances," he proclaimed to the conference, "would I ever consent to forty or fifty nations thrusting interfering fingers into the life's existence of the British Empire."

As the transactions continued at Yalta, as the leaders brokered and traded, as compromises were dealt out on scores of issues, FDR had one great consolation that hardened his commitment to his priority. Having lived through a lot of history and learned from it, he knew that international conferences came to many settlements that would eventually be swept into the dustbin of history. What *must* last would be the international machinery for patching up the failures, making new compromises, and enforcing year-to-year peace efforts. That would be the job of the new United Nations, the essence of which emerged intact from the conference despite such obstacles thrown up by Stalin as extra votes for the Soviet Union.

So when the president reported to Congress, on returning from Yalta, that the conference "ought to spell the end of the system of unilateral action, the exclusive alliances, the spheres of influence, the balances of power, and all the other expedients that have been tried for centuries—and have always failed," he was not indulging in vainglory or naïveté. He was talking about the "only hope on earth" of maintaining world peace. He was harking back to the Wilsonian idealism and practicality that he had once embraced, had abandoned in the 1920s, and now was making the very foundation of his postwar hopes. By a great act of transforming leadership—before Yalta as well as during the conference—he had done all he could to justify and build on the transactional leadership of all three leaders on the shore of the Black Sea.

"Twenty-five years ago," the president said, in concluding his hour-long report to Congress on Yalta, "American fighting men looked to the statesmen of the world to finish the work of peace for which they fought and suffered. We failed them—we failed them then. We cannot fail them again and expect the world to survive again."

FDR had no rosy hopes that peacekeeping, so central to his thoughts in the post-Yalta days, would be self-executing, that the nations would set up the new organization and enforce the peace according to formula. Leadership was crucial—and he had no false modesty about his own indispensability, nor real worries about being around. Later it was noted that he took some actions, such as putting certain of his affairs in order, that indicated he was anticipating an early death, but these were no more than any prudent man in his sixties would take. FDR to the end was too much the optimist, the activist, the enthusiast to dwell more than momentarily on his mortality.

5
Triumph: FDR's Last Hundred Days

On Christmas Eve 1944, while GIs were valiantly defending Bastogne in the Battle of the Bulge, the president spoke to the nation from Hyde Park, addressing especially the soldiers around the globe who were so far from home. Later in the evening, sitting in his old rocker with gifts piled high behind him, he read "A Christmas Carol" to his flock of grandchildren.

"Next year," said Elliott's new wife, Faye Emerson, "it'll be a peace-time Christmas."

"Next year," said Eleanor Roosevelt, "we'll *all* be home again."

In three and a half months Franklin Roosevelt would return home for good. And because he was a "dying man" during these final days, a legend grew of a vacant, befuddled president, deserting his New Deal at home and outmaneuvered by Churchill and Stalin abroad. In fact, all that FDR had worked for finally was coming together for him during the "last hundred days." The vast military effort was reaching its culmination as the Germans were thrown back from their Ardennes effort; the Russians began their grand offensive; U.S. forces landed in the Philippines and captured Manila.

On the diplomatic front, Roosevelt achieved the foundations of Big Three solidarity that he believed would be crucial after the war. His double feat at Yalta—winning Moscow's promise to join the Pacific war against Japan and to make a commitment to the United Nations—achieved his crucial war and postwar goals. His was by no means a solo performance; grand strategy had been a vast collective effort of hundreds of diplomats and soldiers in the United States and abroad. But FDR had supplied the indispensable top leadership.

There were of course some uncertainties. With the war against Japan only now coming to a peak, China remained a dubious ally. Moscow would join the war against Japan only after the Allies had taken their bloodletting in the home islands, and might make only a token commitment to the United Nations. At home, Americans were becoming war weary and might slacken off during the slow shifting of troops from Europe to Asia. Women and blacks were still facing discrimination; children living in trailers and shacks were still suffering inadequate nourishment and schooling.

Little notice was given, amid the calls for wartime unity and bipartisanship, to an ominous development: the rise of a presidential quasi-dictatorship. Having compromised unduly with congressional isolationists before the war, FDR rode roughshod over the lawmakers after Pearl Harbor, demanding that they vote through huge bills and funding under deadlines he set, incidentally establishing precedents that future and more dictatorial presidents might exploit.

. . .

Through his last hundred days and for about a year before, Roosevelt's medical symptoms were alarming to all except FDR himself. In March 1944 the president had appeared so gray and weary during the weeks after he returned from the Teheran conference that he was persuaded to have a checkup at the Bethesda Naval Hospital. Dr. Howard Bruenn, a young cardiologist, found him suffering from hypertension, hypertensive heart disease, and cardiac failure in the left ventricle of his enlarged heart. After consultations among several specialists, including Dr. Frank Lahey, the president was put on a program of digitalis, reduced smoking, a low-fat diet, and "reduced tension." For a time, at least, FDR was a good patient, even cutting down on smoking; presumably no one sought to explain to him how tension could be reduced in a wartime White House.

Increasingly, during the last year, people around Roosevelt noted his gaunt features, sagging facial muscles, trembling hands, half-open mouth. His blood pressure was erratic but generally high, touching 240/130 in September 1944 (a "normal" blood pressure for a man his age would have been around 140/90). At times he was unduly passive, drowsy, unfocused, sometimes sleeping ten hours at night without feeling fully rested in the morning. Then he would snap back, as cheery and bouncy as ever. During his ups and downs, the White House failed to inform the public of his poor health, but photographs betrayed his wasted features.

People visiting FDR—especially after not seeing him for a few weeks —were alarmed by his appearance. They were much quoted in later memoirs, leading to allegations that FDR in the final months had "impaired mental functioning" and was largely "disconnected" with reality, especially at Yalta. But few of these later diagnoses noted the difference between an activist's literal physical condition and his day-to-day behavior. Despite his longer vacations and reduced working hours, FDR continued to work intensively until the end, especially in March 1945 after his return to the work that had accumulated during his trip to Yalta.

If he appeared vacant and unfocused at times, he knew how to focus on the key problems. Charles E. Bohlen, the Soviet expert at the State Department, noted at Yalta that while the president's "physical state was certainly not up to normal, his mental and psychological state was certainly not affected. He was lethargic, but when important moments arose, he was mentally sharp." Yes, FDR was ill at Yalta, but he was "effective."

Roosevelt and his doctors later were accused of concealing the gravity of his illnesses. That they did. But even though the press almost never published photos of FDR in a wheelchair, the public knew he was crippled— that he could not walk alone, that he had to use a cane and the arm of a son or aide, that he would have to use a wheelchair back and forth to the Oval Office. In a less prurient age they did not need photographs. Thousands had seen him moved in and out of automobiles; millions had watched him swing his stiff legs back and forth, in a rocking motion, as he moved to a podium. Angry millionaires had called him "that cripple in the White House"; Gerald L. K. Smith had called him a Communist *and* a cripple.

The crucial denial was not Roosevelt to the public but Roosevelt to himself. For years he had clung to his determination to walk again, after the early reaction of despair and anger. Finally he had accepted his disability by minimizing it—playing swimming games with children at Warm Springs, ocean sailing and fishing, traveling as far as he wished. He would adopt expedients. Dinner companions watched in amazement as two large men, their hands under his shoulders, would bodily lift him away from the table while Roosevelt, still talking without a break, was seated in his wheel-chair. It was significant that he did not wait for his guests to leave before they watched this operation; he was minimizing the procedure to himself, not to them.

During the crippling Depression, he had led the American people out of their own fear and shame, despair and anger, to new hopes and expectations and actions. He had done the same for himself. For FDR the final test was indeed action, performance, achievements. And during no year of his life was he more active and effective than in the year and a half—and especially the last hundred days—before his death. There were the "historic achievements": international conferences from Teheran to Yalta, military conferences with admirals and generals in the Pacific and in Europe, the selection of Harry Truman as his new running mate, his winning of a fourth term in a hard-fought campaign. There were also his policy triumphs: vetoing a tax bill "not for the needy but for the greedy"; gaining a public health service act; extending New Deal measures such as rural electrification; pressing for the Bretton Woods agreement, which set up an International Monetary Fund and an International Bank for Reconstruction and Development. But the most important measure was the GI Bill of Rights, which, by providing money for tuition, books, and living expenses for up to four years of education for all World War II veterans, opened up the middle class to tens of millions of American families. This bill, FDR's last sweeping assault on the class system, would transform the postwar nation.

He also had the time and energy for an amazing variety of lesser matters—not only lesser matters of state but people and things that especially interested him: sending "Clemmie and Winston" a clipping alleging a direct link between Mrs. Churchill and the Mormons, with additional comments by FDR as to his "very high opinion of the Mormons"; corresponding at length with various dispossessed European royalty; urging Cordell Hull to consider "Basic English" as the language of diplomacy; making plans for the FDR Library in Hyde Park; urging on Shah Mohammed Reza Pahlevi of Iran the reforestation of denuded mountain slopes FDR had seen from the air on his trip to Teheran; instructing his Hyde Park people about growing Christmas trees; thanking a woman friend for darning socks for the inaugural after what he called "THE DIRTIEST CAMPAIGN IN ALL HISTORY"; writing Secretary Ickes of his great elation that the Gridiron Club Dinner had abandoned dressing in "white weskins" and white ties; warning Isador Lubin, off to Moscow to discuss reparations, "to be sure to keep your rubbers on!"

As commander in chief he still had to make day-to-day decisions, especially with Churchill. But the long-planned strategies were now culminating in victory after victory. Even while the Allies were closing in on the German heartland, American amphibious forces were closing in on the Japanese. When, early in April 1945, marines captured Iwo Jima and the Tenth Army gained a secure foothold on Okinawa, two things were clear: Allied troops could defeat Japanese forces dug into terrain much like that of the Japanese home islands; and the cost in casualties—a total of 60,000 killed and wounded on those two small islands—would make it necessary to plan both a conventional and a nuclear military strategy against Tokyo.

The president had to keep a close eye on safeguarding the peace arrangements on which he had set his heart. This meant keeping Stalin on board the planning of the United Nations organization and keeping China in the war. Chiang Kai-shek continued to be obdurate on such matters as compromises with the Chinese Communists in their capital of Yenan, and Stalin turned downright surly when he suspected, because of a confusion of incidents in a bungled local surrender on the Italian front, that the Anglo-Americans were attempting some kind of separate peace and hence violating the unconditional surrender agreement. FDR in turn was angry enough to cable Stalin: "Frankly, I cannot avoid a feeling of bitter resentment toward your informers, whoever they are, for such vile misrepresentations of my actions or those of my trusted subordinates." But he had to be careful with Stalin too. Moscow could still disrupt United Nations planning by sending a second-rate official to the initial meeting planned for San Francisco, by using its veto power, or by overindulging in sphere-of-interest power politics in Poland and elsewhere.

. . .

Franklin Roosevelt was far more a "living" than a "dying" president in his final days. He had outlived people close to him: Missy LeHand had died in the fall of 1944 after a long illness, and Louis Howe long before that. Pa Watson succumbed to a stroke on the trip back from Yalta. Harry Hopkins was too ill to help out now, and Cordell Hull had resigned as secretary of state in the fall. Pitching in to fill the gap were his secretaries—most notably Grace Tully, who with her Oval Office mates supplied the continuity, and the good cheer, that FDR needed. But only one woman could take his place at ceremonial occasions, travel with him on campaign trips, greet endless lines of guests at huge White House receptions: Eleanor Roosevelt.

More than ever, though, the first lady was not content with being simply first lady. She was using her influence wherever she could, especially during Roosevelt's long absences abroad and in Warm Springs. After the 1944 election she had pressed her husband to fulfill the domestic reform promises he had made; sounding like her Uncle Theodore, she urged on him his *moral* obligations to do so. She hoped, she told him, that he would not go abroad to receive huge popular demonstrations—precisely what FDR *did* want to do.

Healthy herself at sixty, convinced that her husband should not be treated as an invalid, as Wilson had been, Eleanor Roosevelt pressed her views on her husband—against State Department officials who she felt were soft on fascism, against Jesse Jones as the proposed secretary of commerce because of Jones's connections with anti–New Deal Democrats in Texas, against "die-hard Southern Congressmen." She urged him to choose Wallace again in 1944 for vice president, but he was not responsive.

She eagerly wished to accompany him to Yalta, but he wanted Anna to go instead, and she gamely accepted her exclusion. She was thrilled to hear later that the Big Three had agreed on the United Nations organization. "All the world looks smiling," she said.

Franklin Roosevelt could still share his dreams with Eleanor, telling her shortly before his April 1945 trip to Warm Springs, "You know, Eleanor, I've seen so much now of the Near East and Ibn Saud and all of them, when we get through here, I believe I'd like to go and live there. I feel quite an expert. I believe I could help to straighten out the Near East."

"Can't you think of something harder to do?" she asked, teasingly.

"Well, yes"—in a serious tone—"it's going to be awfully hard to straighten out Asia, what with India and China and Thailand and Indochina. I'd like to get into that."

"Does *that* sound tired to you?" Eleanor asked, in reporting FDR's remark to her friend Margaret Fayerweather. "*I'm* all ready to sit back. *He's* still looking forward to more work."

She realized, however, that Franklin was more weary and irritable than ever and she was pleased that he planned on a long spring stay in Warm Springs, taking his cousins Laura Delano and Margaret Suckley with him. He would have a long rest, without a wife around to "bother" him with problems of state. He would have nondemanding companions. Did she have a premonition that someone else would be there?

In the summer of 1941, Roosevelt had renewed his friendship with Lucy Mercer Rutherfurd again, despite his longtime promise to Eleanor that he would not. After Lucy's husband died in the spring of 1944, their meetings became more frequent. He asked Anna to make the arrangements. So eager was FDR to resume the relationship that he was willing to compromise Anna's relationship with her mother. And so strong was Anna's desire to please her father that, after her first flush of anger, she had agreed to help provide him with the companionship he so obviously craved.

Lucy was the perfect listener, as Franklin hour after hour reminisced about olden times in Washington. Over the next nine months he and Lucy had perhaps a dozen meetings, with Anna and others usually present. He went driving with Lucy out in the country, visited her occasionally at her summer estate in northern New Jersey, and in mid-March hosted Lucy in Washington over a ten-day period, during which FDR and Eleanor celebrated their fortieth wedding anniversary at a small family luncheon with old friends. Franklin and Lucy made plans for her to join him at Warm Springs, where he would have his portrait painted by an artist friend of hers.

On April 12, 1945, Eleanor was busy with her usual Washington chores when word arrived that Franklin had died at Warm Springs. He died among his chosen close companions, giving dictation to Grace Tully, watching Lucy as she observed the painting take form, with his cousins nearby.

It was Eleanor's painful task to inform Harry Truman of the dreadful news. Truman, staggered, asked her what he could do for her. "Is there anything we can do for *you*," she said, turning the question back to him, for "you are the one in trouble now." She cabled her sons overseas: "He did his job to the end, as he would want you to do." Remembering to recognize the White House ushers and doormen, she hurried off after the swearing-in ceremony to Warm Springs. Through all this she was somber, self-controlled, seemingly tearless.

Then, as if by some awful script of fate, she discovered that Lucy had been with her husband at Warm Springs. She remained composed then, and on the long slow trip on the funeral train to Washington. In the White House she gazed down at the open casket, then slipped a gold ring from her finger and placed it in her husband's hand. Now she confronted Anna. She was so upset, Anna later recalled, that forgiveness seemed impossible. Eleanor had been betrayed by her father, by her husband—and now by her daughter? But she steadied herself for the funeral ceremonies ahead.

During his working vacation at Warm Springs, the president had completed a speech for Jefferson Day: "The work, my friends, is peace. More than an end of this war—an end to the beginning of all wars. Yes, an end forever, to this impractical, unrealistic settlement of the differences between governments by the mass killing of peoples.... The only limit to our realization of tomorrow will be our doubts of today. Let us move forward with strong and active faith."

For Eleanor Roosevelt, there was work to do—and *that* was her work.

PART IV:
CHANGE

Chapter Fourteen
THE ENTIRE WORLD HER FAMILY

"I don't see how Mrs. Roosevelt does it!"

The Washington Post, April 10, 1944.
(*Courtesy FDR Library*)

A grieving crowd of Franklin's fellow patients at Warm Springs, many of them children, made their way to the roadside in their wheelchairs to watch the hearse pull away. In Atlanta, where the funeral party caught the late morning train for Washington, stunned and weeping throngs of people lined the viaducts as church bells tolled. Young and old, rich and poor, Americans drew close to share their sorrow.

During the long train ride across the South, escorting the flag-draped coffin from Warm Springs to Washington, Eleanor lay awake all night. She gazed out at the knots of mourners gathered in the spring darkness at every way station and country crossroad, and she thought about Franklin's life and death and her own future.

"My husband and I had come through the years," she wrote later, "with an acceptance of each other's faults and foibles, a deep understanding, warm affection, and agreement on essential values. We depended on each other." Now that creative partnership was over; that confident, magnetic, elusive personality was gone from her side. Suddenly she felt at sea. "I find that mentally I counted so much on Franklin," she confessed to her friend Joseph Lash, "I feel a bit bereft." She had depended on his wisdom, and now she felt she had lost this "backing," she told Elinor Morgenthau. "I think we had all come to think of him as able to carry the world's problems and now we must carry them ourselves."

What would she do with her private life? She knew what she did *not* want to do. On the train that night, she made "certain definite decisions": She would never again run an elaborate household, live in the big house at Hyde Park, cease being useful in some way, or let herself feel old. She would divide her time between the little cottage she had made out of the furniture factory at Val-Kill and her apartment at 29 Washington Square West in New York City.

A regal figure in black, a focal point for the grief of millions of people, she bore herself with calm dignity through the White House funeral and the burial at Hyde Park and then began packing to leave Washington, her home for the last thirteen years. With feelings of melancholy and uncertainty, she rode for the last time in the White House elevator—the same elevator she had energetically operated by herself, to the consternation of the staff, on her first day there in 1933. Life would change, but her life had always been full of change. Facing the future without her husband, her children grown, she felt a special closeness to the thousands of women whose husbands would not come home from the war. Her secretary, Tommy Thompson, was fortunately with her, and that made an enormous difference, but there was still "a big vacuum," she wrote, "which nothing, not even the passage of years, would fill."

The shock of FDR's death was followed by elation over victory in Europe. Americans would rejoice at V-E Day and then cope with absorbing hundreds of thousands of soldiers, uprooted and transformed by war, many bewildered or bitter about changes that had taken place on the home front in their absence. Reconversion to a peacetime economy would be a long and complex process—and there were still hundreds of thousands of GIs in the Pacific.

Like the nation, the sixty-one-year-old widow was at a turning point. She was already a survivor. Her husband had died prematurely at the age of sixty-four. Harry Hopkins left the government after Roosevelt's death, only to die eight months later at the age of fifty-five. She still felt the loss of Louis Howe and Missy LeHand. The Depression and the war had taken their toll. Franklin especially had devoted his energy and his life to a country in need of help. And as the country grew stronger, Eleanor mused, he grew weaker and died. But from the ordeal the United States had emerged more powerful and productive than ever before.

Now, without a Roosevelt at the helm, the followers would have to become the leaders. "Many leaders and many peoples must do the building," Eleanor wrote in her "My Day" column, just days after Franklin's funeral. "It cannot be the work of one man, nor can the responsibility be laid upon his shoulders, and so, when the time comes for people to assume the burden more fully, he is given rest."

During the first months after her husband's death, Eleanor put her life in order, taking care of Franklin's estate, turning the big house over to the government, and purchasing Val-Kill and 825 acres for herself. Going through Franklin's belongings one day, she came across a little watercolor portrait of him, painted by Lucy Mercer Rutherfurd's friend, Madame Elizabeth Shumatov. Rising above painful memories, she asked Franklin's cousin Margaret Suckley to send it to Lucy.

Her life would be simpler now. Taking stock of her financial situation, she completely revised her personal budget. No longer would she need the servants, the wardrobe, the entertainment expenses that went along with being first lady. From now on she would finance her modest lifestyle through her own earnings by writing and speaking.

Even Fala, Franklin's Scottie, had to readjust. When he heard the wailing sirens of a police escort arriving at Hyde Park one day in 1945, his ears perked up and his little legs straightened out. He expected to see his master coming down the drive once again—not General Eisenhower, who had journeyed there to lay a wreath at the president's grave.

Some friends urged her to run for office. "You would be unbeatable," Harold Ickes told her. A friend who was a theatrical producer offered to manage her career. President Truman proposed that she go to San Francisco as a special delegate to the United Nations Preparatory Commission. Others asked her to head the National Citizens' Political Action Committee. All these offers she rejected.

One thing was clear: She would not neglect what she considered her real work but would write and speak her mind as before on issues large and small. After only a week's hiatus she went on with her column—and would continue to do so, six days a week, until the end of her life. Now she was truly writing as herself, not as first lady. "Father never told me what to write or what not to write," she remarked to her son Elliott, "but naturally I was always aware that whatever I wrote might bring repercussions, so I conserved myself. I don't feel any such inhibitions now. I write as I please."

Some newspapers stopped running "My Day," but many continued to carry it. Millions of people were still drawn to her unpretentious, wide-ranging column. Whereas journalists like Walter Lippmann and Arthur Krock appealed to the educated elite, she happily observed to her daughter, "a fifth grader can read me, so more people read me!" She wrote about the war, women's rights, migrant farmworkers, literacy, the preservation of historic landmarks in New York City, unionization of domestic employees, social mobility. Readers loved her columns about everyday postwar American life, about the virtues of frozen vegetables and homemade butter, her garden, and the adventures of Fala, but more and more she began to tackle complex national and international issues: the Murray-Wagner Full Employment Bill, the plight of American Indians, the House Un-American Activities Committee, national health care, segregation, the atomic bomb, world security. One column advocating cooperation with the U.S.S.R. became a small cause célèbre, and she found herself having to write more columns defending and clarifying her views.

And Harry Truman seemed to need her. Old Roosevelt hands and newcomers from Missouri surrounded the president, jostling for position in the new administration. Steering amid the chaos, he used Eleanor as a lodestar. He sought her opinions on issues and her insights into the people closest to FDR, and he trusted and relied on her.

Just a month after Franklin's death, Truman confessed to Eleanor, in an eight-page handwritten letter, his difficulties dealing with Churchill. Eleanor of course understood that Churchill was "a gentleman to whom the personal element means a great deal." She responded at length to Truman, urging him to develop a personal relationship. Talk to him about books, she suggested, and "let him quote to you from his marvelous memory everything from Nonsense Rhymes to Greek tragedy." Stunned by the length of Truman's letter to her, she also begged him to have his secretary type his letters.

She wrote to the president every week, offering comments, suggestions, and warnings, using every opportunity to talk about domestic politics—fair employment practices, the poll tax, party jobs for women—and foreign issues. Truman always responded promptly, in longhand, urging her to write again and often making an effort to respond to her suggestions. When she sent him a letter she had received about violence and discrimination against Japanese-Americans, Truman replied that "this disgraceful conduct almost makes you believe that a lot of our Americans have a streak of Nazi in them." He followed up by instructing the Justice Department to investigate all such cases and turn evidence over to state and local authorities. The two leaders whose support he needed most, Truman admitted to Secretary of State James Byrnes, were Eleanor and Henry Wallace.

Then, as Truman came into his own and developed his own presidential priorities, his responses to Eleanor increasingly became courteous, slightly aloof defenses of his own policies. He would not give an enthusiastic endorsement, as she had urged in a three-page letter and in a subsequent meeting, to the Murray-Wagner Full Employment Bill, which would have increased public works projects and provided jobs for all people "able to work and seeking work." Nor was he open to her ideas about increasing wages and controlling prices, ideas she got from Chester Bowles, the new director of the Office of Economic Stabilization. And when Truman threatened to halt a mine workers' strike by seizing control of the mines and halt a strike by railroad trainmen and locomotive engineers by drafting the strikers into the army, Eleanor's support for her husband's successor dwindled. "I hope that now you will not insist upon a peacetime draft . . . of the strikers," she wrote Truman. "That seems to me a dangerous precedent."

Eleanor would have to write, argue, and fight for Franklin's legacy, for economic justice, and for peace—on her own.

Decades earlier, her family and their insular upper-class social set had comprised Eleanor's universe. But her world had expanded and evolved. Her closest friends—Lorena Hickok, Louis Howe, Elinor Morgenthau, Earl Miller, Malvina Thompson, Walter White, Pauli Murray, Mary McCleod Bethune, Joseph and Trude Lash, and later David Gurewitsch, the people who, she said, were "part of your laughter, part of your joy"—were hardly the kind of patricians with whom her class-bound parents or mother-in-law would have associated. On the contrary, she rejoiced in what she called the American "bloodless revolution" that, since the Depression, had contributed to a redistribution of the nation's wealth, leaving "fewer people at the top." Even the borders of her own upper-class Protestant identity began to fade as she excitedly contemplated ties between the Roosevelt family and the Sephardic Jews of early New Amsterdam. "The history of New York City includes the story of many Jews and intertwined with their story is that of many other New York families, among them my own Roosevelt ancestors."

Over the years, as she struggled to overcome her prejudices and rise above racism and anti-Semitism, as her empathy deepened, as her deep sense of duty expanded, her feelings of community had broadened to encompass all those in need. More and more she looked beyond the nation's borders to see the connections, similarities, and interdependence among all peoples. Now on her own, the entire world would become her family.

1
United Nations

Picking up the telephone in her Washington Square apartment, Eleanor heard President Truman's familiar midwestern voice. The president asked if she would agree to be a delegate to the first organizational meeting of the United Nations General Assembly in London the following month. It was December 1945, the season of hope.

Partly out of respect, partly to please her admirers, Truman wanted Eleanor to serve in his administration in some way.

"Oh, no! It would be impossible," she blurted out. "How could I be a delegate to help organize the United Nations when I have no background or experience in international meetings?" Self-doubts still plagued her—despite her accomplishments and fame.

"You have to do it," Franklin Jr. advised. Tommy Thompson urged her not to decline the offer without considering it carefully, and President Truman assured her that there would be plenty of people to help her. The United Nations was "the one hope for a peaceful world," she realized—and, moreover, it represented Franklin's legacy. "I knew that my husband had placed great importance on the establishment of this world organization," she wrote, admitting that she "felt a great sense of responsibility." After talking it over with Tommy, her children, and other close friends, Eleanor decided to accept—though with "fear and trembling."

Four distinguished men were also members of the American delegation: Secretary of State James Byrnes, Assistant Secretary of State Edward Stettinius, Senator Tom Connally of Texas, and Senator Arthur Vandenberg of Michigan. There were also five alternates: Representative Sol Bloom from New York, the chairman of the House Foreign Affairs Committee and the ranking Republican on the committee; Charles Eaton of New Jersey; Frank Walker, former chairman of the Democratic National Committee; John Townsend Jr., former chairman of the Republican National Committee; and John Foster Dulles, who advised Governor Dewey on foreign affairs during the 1944 campaign. The advisers who came along were also noteworthy: a young State Department hand, Alger Hiss; political scientist Dr. Ralph Bunche; Leo Pasvolsky, who had been Cordell Hull's aide; and Adlai Stevenson, not yet governor of Illinois.

It was a stellar lineup—but it was Eleanor who captured the headlines. Her appointment made the front page of *The New York Times*. When one senator voted against her confirmation in the Senate, it was also front-page news. Theodore Bilbo of Mississippi not only protested her nomination, he blasted her stand on civil rights, boasting that his reasons for opposing her were "so long that he was writing a book about them." Several senators leaped to her defense. Mr. Bilbo's opposition was, one senator remarked, "a splendid compliment to Eleanor Roosevelt."

On December 30, 1945, all the delegates but one traveled in a special train from Washington to New York, along with 120 advisers, secretaries, and technical experts. At Pennsylvania Station they posed for pictures and then traveled in a motorcade, sirens wailing, to the pier on West 50th Street where the *Queen Elizabeth* was docked. When the fanfare was over, Eleanor arrived alone at the pier. The skies were leaden and rainy, and without Tommy or any friend for company she felt lonely and "heavyhearted."

In her stateroom, however, lay a pile of documents to be read in preparation for the first meetings. She immediately set to work, though the blue sheets marked SECRET made for dull reading, almost putting her to sleep.

Dozens of personal messages had also poured into her stateroom. Poet Archibald MacLeish, who had been a speechwriter for FDR, wrote to say that "millions of your fellow citizens are profoundly thankful to the Almighty God that you are a member of the Delegation." Carrie Chapman Catt sent a prayer: "We, O Lord, have determined to kill no more men by war, and with Thy help we shall succeed." NAACP leader Walter White, reporter Drew Pearson, her old friend Esther Lape, and many others sent thoughtful and eloquent letters of praise and warm appreciation.

Entrusted with their hopes, Eleanor plunged into her new work. She was apprehensive but also deeply excited. As first lady, she had devoted herself to a dizzying, disparate array of duties; now she faced a single, vitally important task, a clear focus for her passion, her vision, and her humanity.

. . .

The *Queen Elizabeth* was a fitting vessel to carry the delegation of Americans to the first meeting of the United Nations. Built as a luxury liner, it had been converted to wartime use; with blacked-out portholes and gray camouflage paint, it had transported troops to Europe. Since V-E Day the huge vessel had been ferrying the soldiers home. Now a ship of peace, the great liner left the dock at 4 A.M. on the last day of 1945, but had to drop anchor just off Staten Island in a heavy fog.

The course for the United Nations would also be clouded and uncertain. Roosevelt, Stalin, and Churchill had hammered out the initial agreements in the face of a common enemy, at a time of unprecedented global upheaval. With the end of the war, however, national aspirations revived, and the bonds of common interest began to dissolve. During 1946 in particular, international relations would chill into the frozen entrenchments of the Cold War.

During the last half of 1945, when tension had grown between the United States and the Soviet Union, American liberals like Eleanor had had to come to terms with Soviet encroachment in Eastern Europe. For them, the Soviet Union was like, in the words of historian Alonzo Hamby, "an individual who had been gravely injured by an assailant and was attempting to build a fence around his home to safeguard against his attacker's return." American liberals compared Soviet dominance in Eastern Europe to American dominance in Japan and on the Pacific islands and dismissed the idea that the Soviet government was truly totalitarian. Above all else, they were convinced that the Soviet Union had to participate in the United Nations for that organization to be effective and for peace to be possible. "If we learn to trust them," Eleanor said in early October, "perhaps they'll trust us."

But a meeting of the Big Three foreign ministers in London had broken up in anger in the beginning of October 1945, with nothing achieved. One major stumbling block had been the Soviet demand that the West recognize the new puppet governments in Bulgaria and Romania. In December, Secretary of State James Byrnes traveled to Moscow and there, along with other initial agreements on control of atomic energy and American occupation of Japan, accepted Soviet domination over Bulgaria and Romania. Byrnes's action angered Truman, but it undoubtedly kept the Soviets at the bargaining table—which a month later had become the General Assembly of the United Nations.

The gulf between the West and the Soviet Union was widening. But so was a new one between the United States and Great Britain. On the one hand, the British wanted to rebuild Europe along democratic free-enterprise lines; on the other, they wanted to preserve the remnants of their empire, keeping all the remaining jewels of Britain's imperial crown, and for this they needed a massive influx of American aid. Eleanor Roosevelt, Henry Wallace, and other liberals warned Truman not to align with England and thereby tip the balance of the Big Three. "Great Britain is always anxious to have someone pull her chestnuts out of the fire," Eleanor remarked, noting, "though I am very fond of the British individually and like a great many of them, I object very much to being used by them."

Three mighty forces exerted pressures and counterpressures on the nations trying to forge the fragile alliance of the United Nations: the Cold War, the anticolonial movement, and the development of atomic weapons. Eleanor had spoken out on all three issues as they emerged, calling for a maturity of vision and an effort of trust, courage, and generosity. She urged that communication and trust be maintained between the United States and the Soviet Union. Foreseeing small countries struggling to throw off the manacles of colonialism, she objected to Churchill's vision of an Anglo-American alliance dominating the postwar world. And she called on the United States to entrust its discovery of atomic power to an international agency. She did not speak for all Americans, but she did speak for hopeful liberals who believed in the basic goodness of human nature and were convinced it was possible for human beings to shape and guide the destiny of nations.

Aboard the *Queen Elizabeth* she studied the documents that the State Department had prepared for the delegation, talked with delegates and alternates, and attended all the shipboard briefings, even those for reporters. Reading was her main activity, all day, with breaks for meals and walks around the deck. And she got to know her fellow delegates, particularly the silver-haired and steely Arthur H. Vandenberg.

Senator Vandenberg had been apprehensive about Eleanor's appointment to the delegation. A staunch conservative Republican, he had opposed many New Deal reforms but supported others. Though he had been an outspoken isolationist in the 1930s, once the United States entered the war he had given full support to FDR's policies. For his part, Franklin had come to respect Vandenberg as a man of principle. The senator had initially opposed the idea of an international organization, but when Franklin asked him to go to San Francisco, promising him that he could vote exactly as he felt was right, Vandenberg became one of the strongest supporters of the UN. Still, he was fearful of giving up U.S. atomic secrets to an international authority. Outspokenly anti-Soviet, he would be instrumental in shaping the postwar policy of the United States.

As she was walking to her cabin on the *Queen Elizabeth*, Eleanor ran into Vandenberg. "Mrs. Roosevelt, we would like to know if you would serve on Committee Three," he said. Who had appointed Vandenberg the leader of the group? Eleanor wondered. Had the members been making decisions without her? And what in the world was Committee 3? Though puzzled, she said yes, she would serve on that committee, but would he please furnish her as much information as possible on its goals?

Committee 3, it turned out, was concerned with humanitarian, educational, and cultural questions. Had the other four delegates conspired to relegate her to a minor role? Did they not respect or trust her judgment? "Here's the safe spot for her—Committee Three," she imagined them saying. "She can't do much harm there!" But after immersing herself in the documents of Committee 3, she saw things differently. "I began to realize that Committee Three might be much more important than had been expected," she wrote. "And, in time, this proved to be true."

London was sleety and grim. From the window of her taxi, Eleanor peered out at a city devastated by war. Even in central London she saw bombed-out buildings, gaping holes in the ground, downed trees. And times were hard. Rationing had become even stricter than during the war. The bath towels in her hotel, she frowned, had been cut in half, and the linen was worn. But London welcomed her warmly. Bouquets of flowers, a welcome note from her friend the queen, and piles of letters and invitations flooded her suite at Claridge's. Immediately upon her arrival she began receiving a stream of visitors; old friends, members of the staff of the American embassy, everyone wished to make her feel comfortable. And, of course, along with the invitations were hundreds of requests for help in obtaining American citizenship.

People felt an electric sense of anticipation about the launching of the United Nations. On the day of the opening session of the General Assembly, Eleanor filed in with the other delegates to Westminster's Central Hall. The American delegation was seated next to the Soviet delegation, and Eleanor mistakenly took the seat of V. V. Kuznetzov, who proposed that she simply join the Soviets: an amiable beginning.

The delegates elected as president of the General Assembly Paul Henri Spaak, the foreign minister of Belgium. In his acceptance speech, he took note of the presence of one distinguished delegate "who bears," he intoned, "the most illustrious and respected of all names. I do not think it would be possible to begin at this Assembly without mentioning her and the name of the late President Roosevelt."

The United Nations and Mrs. Roosevelt were news. *The New York Times* covered everything from the serious—the thorny issues under discussion, from the makeup of the Security Council and election of a secretary-general to the permanent location of UN headquarters—to the frivolous—delegates' living accommodations. Almost every day Eleanor dashed to the BBC studios for interviews, one time bumping into famed newscaster Edward R. Murrow.

The most sought-after guest at London parties was Eleanor Roosevelt. She dined with the king and queen and their daughters, Elizabeth and Margaret, playing charades with them after dinner. She lunched with the Churchills and other English political leaders. She was the keynote speaker in the Albert Hall at a ceremony welcoming the UN delegates. Hundreds of people lined the sidewalks outside of Westminster's Central Hall to applaud her arrival just after nine every morning, and they waited for hours to cheer her when she left. "For two days I've had no voice," a fatigued Eleanor whispered.

Amid all the excitement, her old insecurities resurfaced. She "walked on eggs," she said, during daily briefings, committee meetings, and General Assembly sessions, confessing to Anna that her contributions were "very insignificant." The only woman in the U.S. delegation and one of only six women—out of 750 delegates—in the entire organization, she felt left out by the men. She invited the five other women, most of them former schoolteachers, from Byelorussia ("White Russia"), the Dominican Republic, Great Britain, New Zealand, and Norway, along with the women alternates and advisers, to her rooms for a meeting. They found they shared common concerns—most of all, about the lack of women in important positions in the UN. They brainstormed on ways to motivate and train women to take on roles of power and responsibility, even issuing a "manifesto" urging governments to encourage the participation of women in national and international affairs.

Oddly, Eleanor was noncommittal toward the formation of a permanent UN commission on the status of women to implement equal rights. Women should not be studied as a separate category, she felt. On the contrary, she wanted them brought into the United Nations at every level, part of every decision, working with men to build the UN. She herself, her friend Joseph Lash remarked, "preferred to do her politics with the men."

Her adviser, Durward Sandifer, in the tradition of Louis Howe, furthered her education in diplomacy and tactics, giving her an important lesson in leadership. She often "lagged behind," he sternly pointed out to her, when it was time to vote. "The United States is an important country," he insisted. "It should vote quickly because certain other countries may be waiting to follow its leadership." So she made a point of making up her mind before a vote was called for—and of voting "with alacrity." She admired the meticulous work of the head of the U.S. delegation's Preparation Committee, Adlai Stevenson. The background information he provided "made all the difference in our ability to work with the others," Eleanor said. But she did not hold an equally high opinion of the official American delegates. The "boys" treated her with condescension, and she found them undiplomatic, "rude and arrogant." On some occasions, they created "suspicion" among foreign delegates; on others, they appeared overly cordial. She felt that the American delegation, under the leadership of James Byrnes, was trying too hard to be conciliatory. Other countries "would be reassured if they saw that we had convictions and would fight for them." Byrnes, moreover, seemed "afraid" of his own delegation. It was not that he was leaving her out of meetings, she noted in her diary; all the delegates felt left out.

...

Two harsh letters were entering the American vocabulary and consciousness: DP, for Displaced Persons. DPs included survivors of German concentration camps, people who were physically and mentally ravaged, homeless and hopeless; people whose homes had been destroyed in the fighting; Spanish Republican refugees; and tens of thousands of people who did not want to return to countries under Soviet control—Ukraine, Byelorussia, Poland, Czechoslovakia, Latvia, Lithuania, and Estonia. Stateless exiles in limbo, they had been herded into DP camps. Especially, the first tide of defectors from communism posed a new and politically delicate challenge for the framers of the United Nations.

The debate on refugees began on January 28, 1946. "It was ironical perhaps," Eleanor wrote, "that one of the subjects that created the greatest political heat of the London sessions came up in this 'unimportant' committee to which I had been assigned." The source of the heat was the Soviets. They insisted that all refugees from their satellite countries be returned home. Their rhetoric was heated too. Any war refugee who did not wish to return to his country of origin, the Yugoslav delegate judged, was simply a traitor. The West, on the other hand, felt that refugees should have the right to choose whether or not to return to their countries. Although the commitee was divided, its chairman, Peter Fraser of New Zealand, had to present a majority report to the General Assembly. The report was immediately challenged by the U.S.S.R., which insisted on mandatory repatriation.

John Foster Dulles, acting on behalf of the American delegation, asked Eleanor to make a public presentation at the General Assembly of the American position. Her ideological opponent was the Soviet delegate, Andrei Vishinsky, a hard-nosed Stalinist prosecutor at the Moscow purge trials and a debater skilled in using the weapons of wit and ridicule. The confrontation between Vishinsky and Eleanor "led to one of the most dramatic episodes of the Conference," Dulles said later, "a debate where Mrs. Roosevelt, with moving simplicity, pleaded for tolerance, and where Mr. Vishinsky, with the explosive power of a great prosecutor, denounced tolerance as a dangerous weakness."

There was no such thing as unconditional liberty, Vishinsky exploded. "It is impossible to have unlimited freedom. It is impossible in the interests of society. It is impossible in the organization of the UN. Freedom is limited by life itself, and without this principle there can be no society;

there can be no society of states." Tense and excited, Eleanor walked to the rostrum. Speaking without notes, she turned the tide with simple words about tolerance, freedom, and the rights of human beings. A savvy tactician, she knew that the South American countries held the swing votes, so she also talked about Simón Bolívar and his stand for the freedom of the people of Latin America.

At 1 A.M. on February 13, after more than six hours of debate, the General Assembly voted 31 to 10 to adopt the refugee resolution sponsored by the United States and Great Britain, rejecting Soviet, Yugoslav, and Polish amendments. The resolution recognized the refugee problem as an international one, refused forced repatriation, and recommended a special committee to examine the problem.

"I feel I must tell you that when you were appointed I thought it terrible," a happy Dulles said to her afterward, "and now I think your work here has been fine!" "So—against odds, the women move forward," a pleased Eleanor penned in her diary. The other American delegates shared Dulles's respect. One morning, when Mrs. Roosevelt was a few minutes late to a delegation meeting, Senator Vandenberg remarked to a group of his colleagues that "Mrs. Roosevelt is doing a splendid job. She has made a fine impression on all the other delegations. I want to say that I take back everything I ever said about her, and believe me, it's been plenty."

2
Flight to Palestine

"I realize quite well that there may be a need for curtailing the ascendancy of the Jewish people," Mrs. Roosevelt had written to her German friend from Allenswood, Carola von Schaeffer-Bernstein, in September 1939. "But it seems to me it might have been done in a more humane way by a ruler who had intelligence and decency."

"The ascendancy of the Jewish people"? A "decent" Hitler? Her mindless words leave one as speechless as she herself became when she visited DP camps in 1946 and saw for herself the results of efforts to curtail the "ascendancy" of the Jews.

As soon as the United Nations session ended, early in 1946, she flew to Germany. Nine months after the end of the war, 98,000 stateless refugees still lingered in abjection in German barbed-wire holding pens. What she saw in the camps moved her so deeply that at one point she was overcome, wordless, she who was usually able to cope with any situation. The Jewish camps in particular she would never forget.

"There is a feeling of desperation and sorrow in this camp which seems beyond expression," she wrote in "My Day." "An old woman knelt on the ground, grasping my knees. I lifted her up but could not speak. What could one say at the end of a life which had brought her such complete despair?" In the camps she met children who had wandered in alone, unable to remember their own names. One man, looking far older than his years, murmured, "They made us into soap."

"It was everybody's fault," her old friend from Allenswood blithely announced. But Eleanor ridiculed her friend's comment that "we never knew what was going on in Germany," contemptuously dismissing the postwar German myth that "there were no Nazis. They all hated Hitler."

In Eleanor's heart and mind, the "ascendancy" of the Jews had been displaced by her new understanding of the "weight of human misery." In her 1952 introduction to the American edition of *The Diary of a Young Girl* by Anne Frank, Eleanor wrote that the diary made her "intimately and shockingly aware of war's greatest evil—the degradation of the human spirit."

The Holocaust transformed Eleanor's thinking. She no longer viewed Jews from the vantage point of an anti-Semitic American upper class. Now their victimization aroused her empathy. In a "My Day" column in the fall of 1945 she described the "miserable, tortured, terrorized Jews who have seen members of their families murdered and their homes ruined, and who are stateless people, since they hate the Germans and no longer wish to live in the countries where they have been despoiled of all that makes life worth living." The world was letting these "emaciated, miserable" people die, at the rate of fifty a day, "while we sit comfortably."

Jewish refugees, she recognized, "naturally" wanted to go to a secure homeland, to their own community, to Palestine. "It seems to me urgent that these people be given permission to go to the home of their choice," she wrote in "My Day" in 1945. "They are the greatest victims of this war." Eleanor's new cause was the state of Israel. "I knew for the first time," she later said, as she recalled her visit to the DP camps, "what that small land meant to so many, many people."

"I do not happen to be a Zionist," Eleanor informed President Truman that same year. A slow convert to the concept of a Jewish state, she felt that Zionism yielded to Nazi dogma—to the idea that the Jews were a people apart. She saw Judaism as a religion, not as the defining characteristic of a people. "I don't lump people together," she wrote to Joseph Lash in 1944. "I don't think of them except as individuals whom I like or dislike." In 1943 she had still believed that Jews could continue to live all over the world—"They are the great names in so many nations," she had written in "My Day." But where could homeless Jews, rejected by one European country after another, now go other than to Palestine?

Palestine must "be made a Jewish state," Theodore Roosevelt had proclaimed in 1918. Three decades later, his niece would come to agree.

. . .

While the UN delegates were meeting in London in January 1946, a small ship packed with one thousand Jewish refugees was rocking in the Mediterranean Sea off the coast of Palestine. British planes and a destroyer had quarantined the ship before it was able to dock in the port city of Haifa.

Eleanor knew the background. Jews had been emigrating from Europe and Russia to Palestine for a hundred years. After Britain seized Palestine from the Turks in 1917 during World War I, London issued what became known as the Balfour Declaration, guaranteeing a Jewish homeland. The League of Nations then gave Britain a mandate to develop Palestine toward eventual independence. But two decades later, independence seemed no closer, the dream of a Jewish homeland still a dream. In 1939, the British government issued a White Paper limiting Jewish immigration to Palestine to seventy-five thousand total over the next five years. Zionists everywhere protested in vain. So diligent were the British in restricting immigration that, by the end of the war, the seventy-five thousand immigrants to Palestine approved by the White Paper had still not been admitted.

Arabs, meanwhile, objected to the prospect of a massive immigration to Palestine by their traditional enemies—and fellow Semites—the Jews. FDR had come away from a meeting with the Saudi Arabian king, Ibn Saud—on a destroyer in the Mediterranean on his way back from Yalta in early 1945—with the feeling that the king was closed to change. And the huge oil resources in Saudia Arabia made Western nations reluctant to alienate any friendly Arab ruler.

During the war, both Great Britain and the United States—ignorant of conditions in Nazi Germany and indifferent to Jewish suffering when they did know—had drastically reduced Jewish immigration. Only in 1942, after word filtered out of Europe about the Nazi plans for a "final solution," did world sentiment begin to change, ever so slowly. British Home Secretary Herbert Morrison then proposed that Britain take in a small number of refugees, from one to two thousand, but only on the condition that they be sent to the Isle of Man and stay there as long as he deemed necessary. Neither children and elderly people with relatives in Britain nor Jewish orphans were allowed to immigrate to Britain. In Washington, officials in the State Department dragged their feet, dismissing the ghastly news from Europe as fantastical.

So what was the alternative for Jews facing the gas chambers other than illegal immigration to Palestine? While governments were paring down their immigration quotas, hundreds of thousands of Jews desperately tried to leave Europe. Thousands of them streamed into Palestine from Europe by secret routes—by banana boat and leaky freighter across the Mediterranean, by train through Turkey, on foot across the Syrian desert. An underground organization called Brichah, Hebrew for "flight" or "escape," assisted them. Sadly, the perils they encountered while fleeing to Palestine were often caused not by Nazi officials but by Royal Navy ships.

After the war, Truman sympathized with the plight of displaced, homeless European Jews. Several times during 1945 he called on London to admit as many Jews as possible into Palestine. But momentum flagged in November when he agreed to a British proposal for an Anglo-American Committee of Inquiry to study the problem. "I am very much distressed that Great Britain has made us take a share in another investigation of the few Jews remaining in Europe," Eleanor wrote to Truman. "If they are not to be allowed to enter Palestine, then certainly they could have been apportioned among the different United Nations and we would not have to continue to have [their deaths] on our consciences."

Eleanor and other liberals were deeply disappointed. But Truman did authorize entry into the United States of 39,000 displaced persons at a rate of 3,000 per month, starting in May 1946. In June 1948, Congress passed the Displaced Persons Act, allowing the entry into the United States of 205,000 refugees over two years. Some in Congress opposed the bill on the grounds that it allowed "the scum of all Europe," along with loafers and revolutionists, to enter the country. Since discrimination against Jewish refugees still existed, an amendment to the act added another 136,000 visas.

In late April 1946, the Anglo-American Committee issued a unanimous report advocating the immediate admission of 100,000 Jews to Palestine and urging that Palestine become a binational state, dominated neither by Jews nor by Arabs. In view of the hostility between Arabs and Jews, it favored continuance of the British mandate. However, the British government backtracked, deciding not to follow the committee's recommendations. Foreign Secretary Ernest Bevin, who earlier had promised to implement any unanimous recommendation, now asserted that the only reason Truman wanted Palestine to take Europe's Jews was because Americans did not want any more Jews in New York City.

When the British deported to Cyprus all Jewish "illegal" immigrants, penning them once again into detention camps, Eleanor exploded. "We sit safely and smugly in the United States and read of new detention camps in Cyprus," she wrote. "I cannot bear to think of the Jews of Europe who have spent so many years in concentration camps, behind wire again on Cyprus." The Labor-Socialist government in Great Britain, she fumed, might just as well have been a Tory government. The situation was "a mess" that should be turned over to the United Nations. The right of the Jewish people to a homeland had still not been recognized by the international community.

In February 1947, Britain handed over the whole problem to the United Nations. Eleanor had lost confidence in Ernest Bevin, and she had lost patience with the British government. The American government, too, did little but utter pious, "unctuous" words. Meanwhile, in May 1947, in the United Nations, Andrei Gromyko rose to declare his support for the Jewish dream of statehood, demonstrating the kind of leadership that the Western Allies lacked. But his bold move led only to the establishment of yet another committee—the United Nations Special Committee on Palestine (UNSCOP)—to visit the British mandate of Palestine and report to the regular session of the Assembly in September.

A dismayed Eleanor charged that Anglo-American interest in oil was behind the delay; for his part, Truman felt that the question of a Jewish homeland was "a basic human problem" he would handle "in the light of justice, not oil." But Eleanor had no patience for more committees, more reports, more debates, more roadblocks. The world had tacitly given its support to the idea of a Jewish homeland, she wrote in "My Day," and now the world was "obligated" to see it through—but with "every consideration" given to the economic and religious rights of Arabs. And she warned against Great Britain's continuing to maintain law and order in Palestine.

Her fears were justified. Britain stepped up its policy of intercepting ships carrying illegal immigrants. Now, instead of taking them to Cyprus—where 1,700 Jewish children, so many undersized political hostages, were still languishing behind barbed wire in detention camps—the Royal Navy actually returned three shiploads of Jewish refugees to Hamburg, Germany. "The thought of what it must mean to those poor human beings seems almost unbearable," Eleanor wrote in "My Day." "They have gone through so much hardship and had thought themselves free forever from Germany, the country they associate with concentration camps and crematories. Now they are back there again. Somehow it is too horrible for any of us in this country to understand."

British authorities had interfered with Jewish refugees one time too many; during the summer of 1947 world opinion did an about-face. The UNSCOP report, issued in time for the meeting of the General Assembly in September 1947, called for termination of the British mandate and for partition of Palestine into two separate states, Jewish and Arab, joined together in an economic union, with Jerusalem a separate entity under the direct trusteeship of the UN. Still a member of the United States delegation, Eleanor was not enthusiastic about partition but she backed the UNSCOP recommendations.

"She impressed me as having an open mind on every subject other than Palestine," her assistant Durward Sandifer told Joseph Lash. "She was not open to persuasion on that issue." Indeed, when Arabs protested against the United Nations partition resolution in 1947, Eleanor announced that their protest was no longer seasonable. "It seems to me that that decision has come a little too late and that all of us must abide by the plan which has been offered by the majority of a commission of the United Nations," she told a friend, adding that the plan for partition of the British mandate of Palestine into two homelands, one for the Jews and one for the Arabs, "will not hurt the Arabs, in fact they will profit by it, but we do not always like what is good for us in this world." Later on, she sternly advised Arabs to "accommodate themselves and stop looking backward." But mutual accommodation would not be reached so easily.

As Arab opposition to the UNSCOP recommendations mounted, Truman wavered. The White House and the State Department seemed to be at war with each other. "Experts" in the State Department, focused on Arab oil, opposed the UNSCOP majority report, while George Marshall, who was appointed secretary of state in 1947, and President Truman supported it. The entire administration was ravaged by charges of anti-Semitism, pandering for votes, and playing into Soviet hands. In November 1947, the General Assembly voted 33 to 13 to approve partition, with ten nations abstaining. The support of the U.S.S.R. and its satellites had assured passage.

But the turmoil was not over. Arab nations protested the partition plan. And in the United States, the government, concerned about a possible war with the Soviet Union, believed that America needed Arab oil to fuel both the Anglo-American military and the Marshall Plan. Worried that the Arabs might turn toward the Soviets, Washington bowed out of the UNSCOP recommendation for an international security force in Palestine and placed an embargo on the shipment of weapons to the Middle East. In March 1948, the United States gave up on partition and called for UN trusteeship over Palestine until the conflict between the Arabs and the Jews—escalating violence and terrorism on both sides—could be resolved.

Eleanor considered the idea of trusteeship a betrayal of the UN resolution and a shattering reversal of U.S. policy. *The New York Times* agreed with her, accusing the Truman administration of caving in to pressure. "A land of milk and honey now flows with oil," the *Times* editorialized, "and the homeland of three great religions is having its fate decided by expediency without a sign of . . . spiritual and ethical considerations." "It was one of the worst messes of my father's career," Margaret Truman said.

Sensing that she had become "a cog in the wheels," Eleanor offered her resignation from the U.S. delegation to Secretary of State Marshall. For Truman, her departure would have been disastrous, and he begged her not to resign. Eventually the trusteeship scheme was forgotten.

Despite a long and tumultuous labor, the Jewish state was indeed being born. On May 11, 1948, Eleanor informed Marshall that she had heard that the U.S.S.R. wanted to be the first nation to announce diplomatic recognition after the declaration of statehood scheduled for May 18. And she mentioned her fear that the United States would "lag behind and again follow instead of lead." But after stormy White House meetings with his senior staff, and without alerting the U.S. delegation to the UN or most of his administration, Truman decided that the United States would be the first nation to recognize the new country—before the Soviet Union. "A new country asking for recognition," commented Truman's aide Clark Clifford, "it doesn't happen every day." So new was the country that it still had no name.

When the members of the American delegation received news of Washington's recognition of the Jewish state, they thought it was a joke. But laughter quickly evaporated when they realized they had been bypassed by the White House. Marshall sent his head of UN affairs, Dean Rusk, to New York to keep them from resigning en masse. Eleanor erupted in anger, outraged by the way the matter had been handled: the last-minute haste, the secrecy, the lack of consultation. "Much as I wanted the Palestine State recognized," she wrote Truman, "I would not have wanted it done without the knowledge of our representatives in the United Nations who had been fighting for our changed position."

The former first lady did not shrink from calling Secretary of State Marshall on the carpet, now accusing the Truman administration of vacillation. "Several of the representatives of other governments have been to talk to me since, and have stated quite frankly that they do not see how they could ever follow the United States' lead because the United States changed so often without any consultation. There seems to be no sense of interlocking information between the United States delegate [sic] and the State Department on the policy-making level. This is serious because our acts which should strengthen the United Nations only result in weakening our influence within the United Nations and in weakening the United Nations itself.

"More and more," she concluded, "the other delegates seem to believe that our whole policy is based on antagonism to Russia and that we think in terms of going it alone rather than in terms of building up a leadership within the United Nations."

. . .

At the same time, the presidential election of 1948 was approaching. And it was not at all clear whom Eleanor would support.

Eighteen months after Truman took office, the Republicans had swept the House and Senate. For the first time in sixteen years, the GOP controlled Congress. The congressional "Class of '46" included the virulent anticommunist senator Joseph McCarthy of Wisconsin. A year later McCarthy would be joined in battle against "Communists" by Representative Richard M. Nixon of California. As hostility was increasing between the United States and the Soviet Union, some Americans' fears about anything and everything—inflation, unemployment, crime—coalesced in the fear that Communists were working to destroy the United States government and the American way of life. Anticommunist senators and State Department "experts" urged a hard-line power-politics approach to foreign policy—so many sheriffs facing down desperadoes in the OK Corral.

In his foreign policy, Truman had swung back and forth between traditional Wilsonian idealistic internationalism and Cold War realpolitik. On the home front, he issued Executive Order 9835, requiring investigation of the political activities of government employees and job applicants. This "Loyalty Program" horrified Mrs. Roosevelt. "If a wave of hysteria hits us, there will be very little protection for anyone who even thinks differently from the run-of-the-mill." Was the United States on the way to becoming as repressive as the Soviet Union? "Political conditions in the U.S.S.R. today still do not recognize the right of individuals to think differently. Only here and in other free democracies can we criticize our Government and have the freedom to think independently. It is, I believe, a very precious freedom, but it requires of us something more than apathetic citizenship. We must really believe in democracy and in our objectives. We cannot live in fear of either Fascism or Communism. We have to be certain that the majority of our people recognize the benefits of democracy and therefore are loyal to it."

While Truman veered to the right, Henry Wallace, who had served as FDR's vice president during his third term and then as secretary of commerce under Truman, tried to steer a liberal course. But when Wallace called for a peace treaty between the United States and the Soviet Union, Truman branded him a dreamer and labeled his supporters "a sabotage front for Uncle Joe Stalin." Thus breaking with the "anti–Cold War forces," Truman allied himself with the anticommunist Cold Warriors, from Secretary of State Brynes to Undersecretary of State Dean Acheson.

Now, in the fall of 1948, Truman was facing a formidable challenge in the Dewey-Warren ticket and had lost a good deal of support to Wallace, who was running for president as a third-party candidate. The break between Truman and Wallace dismayed Eleanor. She had always admired Wallace's idealism and progressivism, but the former first lady was first and foremost an organization Democrat who had always believed in working within the Democratic party. About Wallace, she minced no words. "As a leader of a third party he will accomplish nothing," she wrote bluntly in "My Day." "He will merely destroy the very things he wishes to achieve. I am sorry that he has listened to people as inept politically as he is himself."

Could Truman win? Along with many others, Eleanor had doubts. Though buoyed by the Marshall Plan, she disagreed with Truman's Cold War stance, his refusal to provide American soldiers to a UN police force, and his arms embargo in the Middle East. And why was he unable to attract more women to his programs?

No, she would not endorse Truman in the 1948 election because, as she later wrote to Frances Perkins, he was "such a weak and vacillating person." "The Democrats will lose I think this year," she wrote to Joseph Lash.

Truman's ten-point civil rights program and the civil rights plank of the 1948 Democratic platform were not enough to swing her over to the president's side. Nor would she entertain the idea of running for vice president herself, as the only person who could, in Clare Boothe Luce's words, "restore" the "Roosevelt mantle" to Truman. While tight-lipped about Truman, Eleanor did express enthusiasm about Republican Margaret Chase Smith's run for the Senate. In September, she happily endorsed Chester Bowles and Adlai Stevenson as governors of Connecticut and Illinois respectively; Hubert Humphrey and Paul Douglas for the Senate; and Helen Gahagan Douglas of California for the House of Representatives. But no words of support for Harry Truman.

Meanwhile, the Roosevelt children, especially James, were trying to mobilize people to draft Eisenhower as the 1948 Democratic presidential candidate. In California, Truman grabbed James. "Here I am trying to do everything I can to carry out your father's policies," he shouted. "You've got no business trying to pull the rug out from under me."

Finally, only four weeks before the election and after remaining noncommittal for months, Mrs. Roosevelt sent Truman an open telegram from Paris, where she was attending the UN session. "I am unqualifiedly for you as the Democratic candidate for the Presidency." Mrs. Roosevelt "had to be dragged kicking and screaming into the campaign," Truman groused. Still, the grande dame had spoken.

3
Agenda: Human Rights

Armed with a pocketful of change for the subway, Eleanor journeyed from her apartment on Washington Square all the way uptown to Hunter College in the Bronx, five days a week for three weeks in May 1946. Only once did she get lost in the maze of underground tunnels, where people routinely stopped her to say, "We loved your husband."

The UN Economic and Social Council had asked her, as a member of the American delegation, to serve on a new committee that, for three weeks at the UN's interim headquarters on Hunter's Bronx campus, would plan for the permanent creation of a Commission on Human Rights. The permanent commission would hold its first session in early 1947 at Lake Success on Long Island and then move to Geneva. Its eighteen delegates, aware that Eleanor's immense prestige was one of their greatest assets, unanimously elected her their chairwoman. Her task would be to guide the permanent commission in the creation of a Universal Declaration of Human Rights.

For the next two and a half years, between May 1946 and December 1948, Eleanor had her work cut out for her. Hardly a legal scholar skilled in the history of rights or in drafting rights legislation, she profited from the invaluable assistance of John Humphrey, a Canadian who had just been appointed the head of the Division of Human Rights in the UN Secretariat. Humphrey's "first real test" turned out to be a weekend as Eleanor's guest at her Val-Kill cottage. "Nothing could have been more simple and more friendly than the way she received me," Humphrey wrote. "Within minutes I felt completely at ease and was talking to her as naturally as if I had known her all my life. Simplicity and the knack of giving other people confidence often go with greatness. Mrs. Roosevelt had both."

The United Nations in 1947 comprised fifty-five diverse nations, all at different stages of political, economic, industrial, and social development. How could one common standard of rights and freedoms be agreed upon? Could Soviet-style economic claims on the state—rights to work and to an adequate standard of living—be acceptable in Western-style capitalist economies? Could the American Enlightenment view of the sanctity of the individual and individual rights be reconciled with other nations' communitarian visions of the primacy of the rights of the group as a whole? Were the political rights that James Madison identified and enumerated in 1789 relevant in Third World cultures emerging from colonialism in the mid-twentieth century?

While sipping tea in Mrs. Roosevelt's Washington Square apartment, Dr. Pen-chun Chang of China, vice chairman of the commission, whose country was engaged in ferocious civil war, Charles Malik of Lebanon, the rapporteur, and John Humphrey realized that they would not be able to agree on a working draft of a declaration of rights, so far apart were they philosophically. Instead they assigned to Humphrey the task of preparing a draft. Humphrey's draft was later revised by the French delegate, René Cassin, and Cassin's text became the second working draft. The drafts were discussed, debated, and modified at meeting after meeting: first by an eight-member drafting committee, then by the full commission, and finally by the entire General Assembly. "I was no Thomas Jefferson," Humphrey confessed, but he did have access to a plethora of models and documents.

Words mattered. Every word of every article in Humphrey's draft was scrutinized and debated at length. The United States would not, for example, say that it would "guarantee" full employment but it could promise to "promote" it. And just what did the right to work really mean? Must an individual accept any assigned work? And the language, Eleanor insisted, had to be simple, clear, and free of legalese; she objected to an article stipulating that everyone has a right to a "legal personality" but approved wording saying that everyone has the right to recognition everywhere as a person before the law. Rights were defined and redefined, interpreted and reinterpreted, as members negotiated, persuaded, argued, speechified, and compromised.

The document must not state that everyone has a right to primary, secondary, and higher education, complained Madam Hansa Mehta, the representative from India. Why, the Indians were struggling just to provide elementary education for India's citizens, she explained. Just as the Soviet Union voiced objections to certain political rights, the United States harbored reservations about certain economic rights. Soviet representative Vladimir Koretsky protested that the basic characteristic of the drafts before the committee was "their tendency to liberate man not from persecution but from his government, from his own people. That meant putting him in opposition to his own government and to his own people." Humphrey acknowledged that one purpose of the declaration was indeed to protect individuals from their governments. "If human rights did not mean that," he huffed, "it did not mean much."

"There must be a great deal of Uncle Ted in me," Eleanor admitted, "because I enjoy a good fight." She did indeed lose patience with one of the Soviet delegates, Alexei P. Pavlov. "His words rolled out of his black beard like a river," she wrote, "and stopping him was difficult." After listening to one too many of his numbing speeches, Eleanor waited for him to take a breath and then slammed down the gavel. Everyone near her jumped. "We are here," she announced, "to devise ways of safeguarding human rights. We are not here to attack each other's governments, and I hope when we return on Monday the delegate of the Soviet Union will remember that! Meeting adjourned!" Pavlov was often provocative and out of order, Humphrey felt, but he also thought that Eleanor sometimes treated him unfairly.

One State Department adviser found Mrs. Roosevelt's performance a mixture of "naïveté and cunning." Occasionally, when proceedings became extremely argumentative, she defused the situation by assuming a nonprofessional, quasi-amateur style. "Now, of course, I'm a woman and don't understand all these things," she would say to an antagonist, and then proceed to outline the American position.

Perhaps Eleanor was not always a good chairman, Humphrey conceded, but ultimately "she was more sinned against than sinning; and when she made a mistake, it was usually because she had been badly advised by her state department assistants." These assistants sometimes overstepped their duties, Humphrey observed, in advising her how to conduct meetings. Once he was tempted to leave the chamber, embarrassed by her treatment of Dr. Pavlov. "I did not want the commission to think that the chairman was getting her advice from me," he wrote.

At times, Eleanor was under stress. She had even developed a case of shingles. "I used to think I had reached the limits of my patience in bringing up five children," she would later quip, "but I was mistaken. It took much more patience to preside over the Commission on Human Rights."

As she herself admitted, she was driving her committee mercilessly, but no one worked harder than she herself. Reading glasses perched on her nose, her head adorned with the UN simultaneous-translation headphone, a stack of memos and briefs in front of her and her advisers seated behind her, she oversaw all the debates and discussions, focusing all her energy solely on producing a document that would articulate the fundamental and universal rights of all human beings.

The partnership between Eleanor and Franklin had not ended with his death; on the contrary, she was continuing to further his ideals, especially the Four Freedoms and his proposal, introduced at the UN preparatory conference in September 1944 at Dumbarton Oaks, that a statement of human rights be included in the new UN charter. But now their roles were reversed. Franklin had always been the pragmatic politician, wheeling and dealing to get his programs through, while Eleanor had been the conscience, the idealist. Now she too had to learn to compromise and negotiate to achieve her ends. So while she was still an idealist who believed that "every step forward is the result of somebody who dreamed dreams," she also knew that one need not be afraid of going forward too fast: "You'll be slowed up by circumstances anyway." The experience on the rights commission changed her, her son Elliott believed, and taught her "the business of give-and-take." "Previously she had scorned such compromising as lack of principle," he wrote. But she came to recognize "that every question was many-sided, not a clear-cut matter of right or wrong."

During all the discussions about human rights, Eleanor never forgot that human rights concerned not abstract masses but individuals, in all their fragility. "My interest or sympathy or indignation is not aroused by an abstract cause," she explained at the age of seventy-five, "but by the plight of a single person whom I have seen with my own eyes." The problems of individuals—and her empathy for those individuals—led her to an awareness of human needs and of the significance of those problems for the community, the country, and finally the world. One day, in New York, she saw a homeless man, drunk or ill or asleep, sprawled on the sidewalk. "People glanced at him and hurried by," she wrote in "My Day." "And the next day, at Lake Success, as we argued about human rights at a committee meeting, I wondered how many human rights that poor man had."

The fall 1947 session convened in gray, cold Geneva, where a raw wind blew steadily down the lake. The full commission had two weeks to go over the document prepared by the drafting committee. A melancholy Eleanor was determined to be home for Christmas. She decided to impose a grueling schedule, with evening meetings that ran into the early morning hours. She saw to it that the commission finished its work. Now she and all the delegates could go home for the holidays.

. . .

Eleanor was trying to keep her family together. She was proud of her children—her daughter, Anna; her sons, all of whom had served in the military during the war—especially, she admitted, when they could rise to be their "best selves." She always looked forward to a family Christmas. "I like to have people I love around me!" she happily told her friend David Gurewitsch just before Christmas 1947. She had already done her Christmas shopping and "nearly all plans and orders are given so Xmas should be no strain, just pleasure."

She would spend Christmas Eve with Joe and Trude Lash and then return to Val-Kill, not forgetting the Yule logs, the Christmas stockings, the traditional family toast to the United States of America, nor would she forget to dash over to the Wiltwyck Training School to read Dickens's *Christmas Carol* to the wayward boys. Hyde Park was beautiful. There was no snow but it was clear and cold; ice was forming on the pond. At night she would stand on her porch, looking at the stars, "so bright and near."

In summertime, whenever possible, she gave Fourth of July picnics at Val-Kill; she would benevolently watch children munch on hot dogs and hamburgers; and then, with family and friends listening, she would read aloud the Declaration of Independence and the Bill of Rights. One year the Soviet cultural attaché and his wife joined the Roosevelt family. Someone asked Eleanor if she was trying to indoctrinate the Russians by reading the Declaration of Independence. "No, no," she replied, "I was only trying to indoctrinate my grandchildren."

Still, it was a full-time job getting along with her troubled brood. "I have often differed with my children," she once remarked to her son Elliott, adding that she had come to understand that there were always "two sides to every story." In the wake of Elliott's new book, *As He Saw It*, putting an anti-British and pro-Soviet spin on FDR's views, Eleanor's remarks were generous. But the problems of her children were more serious than mere disagreements. Life had been difficult for the offspring of famous parents preoccupied with nothing less than the fate of the planet. "Where was the guidance you should have had from Father and equally from me?" Eleanor asked Elliott. "Anna and Jimmy suffered just as you did. *Nobody* was willing to devote the time to provide you with a proper upbringing." For Elliott, Eleanor was "a figure of tragedy, consumed by guilt" for the "misdeeds" of her children.

Family holidays would not remain happy occasions for long. Once John and Elliott nearly came to blows, finally turning their hostility against their mother. "My children would be much better off if I were not here," a heartbroken Eleanor sighed. During one Thanksgiving at Val-Kill, Elliott's third wife, the actress Faye Emerson, slashed her wrists and was rushed to a hospital. Elliott, the most troubled of the children and the one who reminded Eleanor of her equally troubled brother Hall, would find stability in New York, helping his mother run Roosevelt Enterprises, which produced a variety of radio and television interview programs hosted by Eleanor and occasionally also by her daughter. But when Elliott resorted to selling off not only some of his mother's most treasured possessions but even Sara's Campobello house and "Top Cottage," the Hyde Park retreat that FDR had designed for himself, Eleanor terminated Roosevelt Enterprises, straining her relationship with Elliott.

Anna too was suffering. She fell ill, and she and her second husband, John Boettinger, separated. He would commit suicide in 1950. Perhaps the most successful son, Franklin Jr., divorced Ethel du Pont, remarried, and was elected to the New York House of Representatives in 1949. James, married to his second wife, was the California state Democratic party chairman and would run unsuccessfully for governor of California in 1950. And John, the not so "secret Republican" who had wandered from job to job, moved east from California with his wife in 1952, also joining Roosevelt Enterprises. Eleanor was concerned that he and his wife Anne drank and that Anne was suicidal.

Sadly, by 1961 Eleanor would give up on family reunions. The children had had one stormy confrontation too many with one another and with her. Her time on the earth was "limited," she told Anna, and her children's "rude" and unrestrained quarrels made her too unhappy. "I have determined to hold no more 'reunions,'" she sadly but resolutely informed her daughter and sons. "I will make every effort to go and see each one of you as often as I can."

For the mother of five children, grandmother to many, and a famous first lady of the world engaged in dozens of projects, it could still be a lonely life. Eleanor had so much love to give and so many frustrated needs for closeness and intimacy. Just as she had bestowed her love on Lorena Hickok in the 1930s, the center of her emotional life in the 1950s would be not her children but rather her new friend David Gurewitsch, a Russian-Jewish doctor who had studied medicine in Switzerland and practiced in Israel and then in the United States. Much has been written about Eleanor's passionate attachment for Lorena Hickok, but there were other deep attachments too.

"David, my dearest," she wrote in 1956, "you are always in my thoughts and if that bothers you I could hide it . . . love me a little and show it if you can." A ladies' man, David was married while he knew Eleanor, then divorced, and remarried again—and there was also a crucial age difference separating him and Mrs. Roosevelt. "I'm not stupid dear and I never forget that twenty years lie between you and me but I love you deeply," ER wrote to Gurewitsch, closing her letter with the words "my whole heart is yours." "If you can find it in your heart now & then," she humbly wrote him, "to want me a little & to ask for my presence it would help my self-respect." Her love for the younger doctor was unrequited, though he accompanied her on some of her travels and though their families and lives became intertwined. Eleanor would give the wedding reception for David and his new wife, Edna. "I need you both very much," she wrote to Edna. The three would soon buy and share a house on East 74th Street, living on separate floors.

Eleanor's deep ability to love and give of herself to others, combined with her lifelong sense of duty, ultimately found their expression in her work, her selfless, passionate, tireless, unceasing commitment to political and humanitarian causes.

. . .

Just as the draft of a Declaration of Human Rights was beginning to take shape, public opinion in the United States was cooling toward the idea. Southern segregationists were hardly in the mood for extending human rights to black citizens. They were all the more alarmed in 1946 and 1947 when they learned that the National Negro Congress and the NAACP had submitted petitions to the United Nations describing widespread human rights violations in the United States. Blacks were suffering from discrimination in employment, education, health, and housing; they were forced to attend segregated schools, eat in segregated restaurants, travel on segregated buses, swim at segregated beaches, and drink from water fountains labeled COLORED. Eleanor herself had avoided issuing a pronouncement on the explosive petitions, claiming that people already "know where I stand."

But when the Georgia House of Representatives approved a "white primary bill" barring blacks from voting in Democratic primaries, it was the last straw. "The United Nations Commission on Human Rights has before it the creation of a subcommission on discrimination," Eleanor wrote. "Are we going to put ourselves in the position of having the world think of us as a backward nation? A nation that discriminates and takes away political rights from a large group of its citizens?" The retrograde racist action in Georgia "affects the standing of the United States in the world family of nations."

Southerners were not alone in their opposition to a universal declaration of human rights. Joining them was the president of the American Bar Association, Frank Holman. In 1948 he launched a campaign to turn public opinion against any human rights treaty, complaining that not only were foreigners sitting on the rights commission, why, there were even three Russians! As for the declaration itself, its language was "indefinite and elastic" and would only "promote state socialism, if not communism, throughout the world." Crusading against the treaty in the Senate was John Bricker of Ohio, who suggested that "Mrs. Roosevelt's lack of legal training" might be responsible for the "dangerously inept draftsmanship" of the covenant.

All over the world the postwar mood was taut and jittery. Americans and Russians alike wanted control and security. The postwar drift to the right in the United States, the Cold War atmosphere of hostility and suspicion, and the anticommunist witch hunts of the 1950s furnished the background against which Eleanor and her colleagues struggled to build bridges.

Mrs. Roosevelt was entirely aware that some of the basic freedoms of American citizens were being violated by anticommunist investigations and by the newly instituted "loyalty oaths." Just as, a decade and a half earlier, FDR had warned against fear, Eleanor too announced that fear was the most dangerous force of all. "What is going on in the Un-American Activities Commission worries me," she admitted in a "My Day" column in 1947. "Little people have become frightened and we find ourselves living in the atmosphere of a police state, where people close doors before they state what they think or look over their shoulders apprehensively before they express an opinion."

But the Cold War began to suck Eleanor in, in spite of herself. It was a tense time: In June the Soviet Union had blockaded Berlin.

The French delegate to the rights commission, René Cassin, invited Eleanor to speak at the Sorbonne in the fall of 1948 on "The Struggle for the Rights of Man." President Truman and Secretary of State Marshall urged her to accept.

Huge, expectant crowds awaited ER's arrival at the Sorbonne, giving her a tumultuous welcome "the like of which I have never seen," commented John Humphrey. Eleanor spoke in French to an auditorium filled to capacity, with many more standing listening outside. "Of course, the French language lends itself to oratory," she smiled. After some extemporaneous, witty remarks, Eleanor charged that the Soviet Union's different view of human rights was at the root of the world's troubles. In private, too, she had expressed frustration with the Russians, telling friends that "the Russians attack furiously in every committee. They seem to want to see nothing accomplished until one wonders whether they should be barred from contacts until they want them enough to try to cooperate."

. . .

After two and a half years of labor, the human rights commission's work was finally complete, and in December 1948 the General Assembly adopted the Universal Declaration of Human Rights without a single dissenting vote. Forty-eight nations voted in favor of the declaration; no countries voted against; eight abstained (the Soviet Union and five Eastern European satellites along with South Africa and Saudi Arabia), and two were absent. Mrs. Roosevelt alone received a standing ovation.

The document is stunning—as fresh, luminous, and inspiring for the reader today as it was in 1948. The preamble announces the faith of the United Nations in "fundamental human rights, in the dignity and worth of the human person, and in the equal rights of men and women." The member nations committed themselves, not to immediately enact and enforce these rights and freedoms, but rather to "promote respect" for them by teaching and education and by adopting progressive measures.

In thirty crisp and concise articles, the declaration recognizes the rights of all individuals to life, liberty, and security of person. There shall be no slavery or servitude. No one may be subjected to torture or cruel punishment. All people are equal before the law. No one may be arrested arbitrarily; the accused have the right to a fair and public hearing and the right to be presumed innocent. Every individual possesses the right to a nationality or, for those without a nationality, to the protection of the United Nations. Everyone has the right to asylum in other countries from political persecution. Individuals may enjoy freedom of travel and movement; they may leave their countries and also return to them. They may own property. They possess freedom of thought, conscience, and religion. They have the right to express and promulgate their opinions, and they may assembly peacefully. People have the right to a government whose authority comes from periodic and "genuine" elections decided by universal and equal suffrage and by secret vote.

And people have social and economic rights too: the right to enter into a marriage of their free choosing and to found a family. People have a right to privacy. Elementary education must be compulsory and free; higher education must be equally accessible to all on the basis of merit. People have the right to work, to join trade unions, to have equal pay for equal work, to have just remuneration. They have the right to a decent standard of living that includes medical care, necessary social services, and protection against illness and disability, and they have a right to security in old age. Mothers and children have a right to "special care." And vacations too—"rest and leisure"—are a right, not a privilege. Omissions? The declaration did not recognize the need of "nondominant" groups—minorities—to be protected, since everyone would supposedly be treated equally and alike. For Mrs. Roosevelt's part, the three most important rights were the rights of freedom of thought and of conscience and the right to take effective part in the government of one's country.

The few dollars Eleanor used for subway tokens to Hunter College in the Bronx were well spent.

. . .

It was one thing for nations to agree on universal human rights. It was another thing to enforce them. According to the UN Charter, the United Nations had no power to intervene in the domestic affairs of any nation. Early on, Eleanor had decided to expedite the creation of a declaration of rights by persuading the commission's members to produce two separate documents: one a declaration of rights, the other an implementation covenant that would have the force of law on ratifying states. A nonbinding declaration of rights, she reasoned, could pass sooner than a binding one. Ultimately, the commission decided to produce a three-part bill, consisting of a declaration, recognizing and defining all the human rights; a covenant, or treaty, to be signed by the individual nations; and measures for implementation.

In 1949, it was time for Eleanor to turn to the problem of implementation. Was there any way to enforce the new declaration of rights without challenging the sovereignty of member states? Australia had proposed an International Court of Human Rights, while the Soviet Union insisted that sovereign national institutions be the only ones to enforce rights—a position with which the U.S. Senate agreed. Southern segregationists opposed any type of binding treaty for fear the United Nations would assist blacks seeking redress for human rights violations in the United States.

The Truman administration was divided and ambivalent about a covenant that would oblige nations to protect enumerated rights, including socioeconomic rights. Southern Democrats were already prepared to bolt the party over Truman's attention to domestic civil rights issues. Experts in the State Department knew that the Senate would never ratify a covenant that denounced racial discrimination. Nevertheless, when Eleanor wrote Secretary of State George C. Marshall in spring 1948, urging the United States to support both the declaration and covenant, Marshall agreed, as long as the covenant itself stayed faithful to existing constitutions, laws, and practices—a caveat with which the Soviet Union fully concurred.

Eleanor did not have her heart in the debate on international implementation. She was disappointed that the United States and Great Britain were proposing that only states—and not individuals or groups—would have the right to bring complaints before the implementation body.

Moreover, the United States had insisted that the one covenant enforcing the principles of the declaration become two separate covenants, one covering political and civil rights and the other covering economic and social rights. Eleanor argued forcefully in support of this position, though she herself believed that economic justice and political justice were inseparable. While the Soviets held that civil and political rights were "illusory" without economic and social rights, Eleanor was obliged to defend the American stand that economic and social rights could not be achieved until civil and political rights had been established. In any case, she knew well that a covenant enforcing economic and social rights would not make it through the U.S. Senate.

In the 1950s, the United States was hardly in a progressive mood. At best, the country was in a holding pattern, consolidating the gains of the New Deal. The struggle for an implementation convenant began to weary Mrs. Roosevelt. "All of us feel that the collective intelligence of mankind should be able to save the world from suicide, and yet nothing seems to indicate that such is the case," she wrote, striking a pessimistic, tragic chord.

For her part, Mrs. Roosevelt candidly admitted that the Declaration of Rights itself had "no legal value." But, she added, it "should carry moral weight." For the next half century, the declaration would continue to grow in moral weight, serving as the anchor for UN resolutions against apartheid in South Africa and Namibia and a variety of other abuses of human rights, and justifying military intervention to protect civilians from slaughter and from human rights abuses.

By September 1999, more than thirty years after her death, the declaration's "moral weight" had become powerful enough to justify military enforcement of human rights. On the opening day of debate in the General Assembly in 1999, Secretary-General Kofi Annan stated that nations that flagrantly violate the rights of citizens would no longer be permitted to shield themselves behind the excuse of national sovereignty. "Nothing in the Charter precludes a recognition that there are rights beyond borders," Annan declared. Some Third World countries disagreed. The Algerian representative protested that international "interferences can only occur with the consent of the state concerned," asserting that Algerians "remain extremely sensitive to any undermining of our sovereignty." But the secretary-general perceived a moral imperative that outweighed national sovereignty. There was, he asserted, a "developing international norm in favor of intervention" to protect civilians from slaughter and from abuses of their human rights.

The Universal Declaration of Human Rights survives as a remarkable, almost miraculous document—nations of vastly different traditions all recognizing certain specific principles of fundamental human dignity. At the beginning of a new century, Eleanor's work still stands at the center of the planet's moral conscience.

Chapter Fifteen
FACING THE FUTURE

"OF COURSE I KNOW—IT'S MRS. ROOSEVELT"

Herblock, 1954.
(*Courtesy FDR Library*)

Striding to the podium at the Republican National Convention to second the nomination of General Dwight Eisenhower for president of the United States was none other than John Roosevelt, FDR's youngest son, still acting out his ambivalence toward his late father.

Conservative and moderate Republicans at the 1952 convention were bitterly divided between "Mr. Republican," Senator Robert Taft, the son of TR's successor in the White House, and General Eisenhower. Ike was lukewarm about the presidency. What did the general who accepted the German surrender in 1945 have to gain as president? How could he top his role as supreme Allied commander in Europe during the war? But Ike had a sense of public service—and he also had the votes.

Eleanor Roosevelt was worried. Ike would be the tool of big business, she felt, but his running mate, Richard Nixon, worried her even more. Two years earlier, Nixon had run for the Senate from California against Eleanor's friend, Congresswoman Helen Gahagan Douglas. Not only had Nixon implied that Douglas was a Communist, his campaign organization had mailed out thousands of postcards from a fictitious "Communist League of Negro Women" exhorting people to VOTE FOR HELEN. The red-baiting Nixon had even turned Douglas's friendship with Mrs. Roosevelt into a campaign issue. When Nixon won, ER hoped that Douglas would challenge the election results. The idea of this man "who would do anything to get elected" in the White House alarmed the former first lady. If Nixon should ever find himself in the Oval Office, "very, very serious times would develop for this country," she feared. "I regard Mr. Nixon as a very able and dangerous opportunist."

When Eleanor arrived at the Democratic National Convention in 1952, the band burst into "Happy Days Are Here Again," the theme song of the New Deal. The crowd went wild. The cheering stopped only when the chairman banged the gavel. "Will the delegates please take their seats," he beseeched. "Several million people are waiting to hear the First Lady of the World." ER then went on to speak about the importance of the United Nations. "I'm sure the Democratic party has been in power too long," Eleanor had written Lorena Hickok in 1951, but reminding her friend that the alternative was "even worse!"

Who could beat Ike? Truman would not run again. Adlai Stevenson, the witty, intellectual, liberal-minded governor of Illinois, had little yearning for the White House; he enjoyed being governor, and he felt Ike was unbeatable. Still, the party drafted Adlai, and he accepted the nomination. As his running mate, the convention chose Senator John Sparkman of Alabama, whose record on civil rights caused fifty black delegates to walk off the convention floor.

No presidential debates took place that year. Ike refused to debate Stevenson, preferring instead to evoke the specter of communist "infiltration" in Washington. Ike even endorsed for reelection to the Senate Joseph McCarthy, the high priest of Republican right-wing extremism, brandishing his weapons of fear.

While Eisenhower electrified his audiences by declaring that he would "go to Korea," the Stevenson campaign found itself caught in the middle by a party taking ambiguous stands on federal fair employment legislation as well as on civil rights. Though Eleanor made suggestions for Adlai's campaign strategy that were, according to economist and Stevenson speechwriter John Kenneth Galbraith, "far more acute" than anything his professional advisers had to suggest, the Democrats nevertheless wound up offering neither a galvanizing message nor a foreign-policy alternative to Cold War assumptions about containment. And it was an uphill struggle to oppose the man Stevenson himself called "a national hero who has been a household word in every family in America for ten years." As for Senator McCarthy, Stevenson limited himself to criticizing "those" who, obsessed with anticommunism, were undermining freedom in America, but he would not mention McCarthy by name. Ironically, Stevenson's victories were all in the South: Alabama, Arkansas, Georgia, Kentucky, Louisiana, Mississippi, North Carolina, South Carolina, and West Virginia.

. . .

Shortly after Eisenhower's big win, Mrs. Roosevelt, as a courtesy, tendered her resignation from the UN delegation. The new president quickly and coldly snapped it up, sending her a few pro forma words of gratitude. The new administration was washing its hands of the UN's human rights covenants—and of Mrs. Roosevelt. "The General has a thorough distrust, distaste, and dislike for Eleanor," FBI man Louis Nichols reported to J. Edgar Hoover.

Although Eisenhower himself was not an isolationist who scorned internationalism, the right wing of his party was, and he was not tempted to waste political capital by standing up for an international declaration of rights. Secretary of State John Foster Dulles announced in April 1953 that the United States was ending its active support for the two human rights covenants along with the treaty on the rights of women and the convention on genocide. "We have sold out to the Brickers and McCarthys," Eleanor fumed in "My Day." The world would have to wait until 1966 for the General Assembly's approval of the Covenant on Civil and Political Rights. In December 1952, Mrs. Roosevelt gave her last speech at the UN, using the bully pulpit one more time to promote women's rights and urge that women wield more power in national and international decision making. How cruelly disappointed she would have been to learn that in a 1984 UN publication, *The United Nations and Human Rights,* her name does not appear. Only the "boys" receive credit, the chairwoman's years of work expunged.

On the east side of First Avenue stood the United Nations. On the west side of the avenue was housed the American Association for the United Nations. Eleanor had only to cross First Avenue to reach her new office and another new beginning. One of her first columns in 1953 announced her plan to begin work the following Monday at the AAUN. This was the kind of work that energized her: building something from scratch, using her considerable organizational skills, as she had in the old days for the Women's Committee of the Democratic National Committee. The only hope for human rights—in the face of a proposal in the Senate for a constitutional amendment prohibiting the president from signing any human rights treaties—was to educate the public, to show people what was really going on in the UN.

. . .

In January 1953, just as Eleanor was preparing to begin work at the AAUN, a major feature story on her by A. M. Rosenthal appeared in *The New York Times Magazine.* Mrs. Roosevelt had been the UN's "chief tourist attraction," Rosenthal observed. But now, with her resignation from the UN, she could speak freely, after years of having to put her husband's policies or those of the American delegation first. What would she say? First and foremost, she wanted to talk about the Russians.

No Soviet delegate she knew of, she told Rosenthal, had ever been persuaded to change his view by an opponent or ever indicated that he would take an opponent's view seriously. Soviet delegates, in her mind, were afraid to negotiate. "They don't speak as free people," she remarked.

"They just say what they have been ordered to say and that's all. If they ever did give any signs of acknowledging a point, why, they wouldn't last long." She was even less optimistic about delegates from Soviet satellites, who toed the line even more scrupulously. An Eisenhower-Stalin summit meeting might be the answer; she saw no other forum in which real decisions could be made and real changes launched.

Also in early 1953, Eleanor's book *India and the Awakening East* was in the final stages of preparation. "You, Mrs. Roosevelt, do not care what happens to the children of Asia; they are colored," a Pakistani delegate had scolded. "The children of Europe are white." So off Eleanor went to Asia in 1952. It was a frantically hurried trip. After brief stops in Lebanon, Syria, and Jordan, she toured Israel for six days. "I'll be walking on eggs in the Arab countries," she predicted, "because they know I believe in Israel, but so far with the Arab press I've got by." In Israel she witnessed "a determination and a sense of dedication that filled me with confidence. So much spirit, so much resolve, cannot possibly be without result."

But Pakistan and India called her. Huge throngs of people treated her like a queen, kneeling as she passed. Though the problems in Pakistan were, she felt, "staggering," she enjoyed the trip immensely, especially when she realized that she was traveling in her father Elliott's footsteps from the Taj Mahal to Mt. Everest, from Bombay to Calcutta, from Nepal to Kerala. She toured farms, mills, factories, schools, housing projects, and hospitals, in what *The New York Times* called an "immensely popular and effective one-woman goodwill mission." To her daughter she confessed that the poverty in India was "below anything we know," yet "the spirit, religious life & dignity of these people is also something astounding." One photograph in her book showed her teaching the Virginia reel to a group of Muslim women in Pakistan. Did she have any regrets about her trip? she was asked. Only that she let herself be persuaded out of riding an elephant. And were there any questions for her? Yes. Why had the United States not aided India—and Indochina—in their struggle for independence? The Soviets, in contrast, had been much more supportive in the anticolonial struggle.

In 1953 Eleanor made another voyage to the Far East, where she visited Hiroshima and met women in the fledgling Japanese women's movement. Other stops included Hong Kong, New Delhi, and Istanbul (where she managed to visit three mosques before breakfast), Athens, and finally Belgrade. Here she had a longer visit, because she wanted to learn firsthand about President Tito's non-Soviet brand of communism. She visited

Bosnia-Herzegovina and Montenegro, and spent a weekend with Tito and his wife at their summer home on the Adriatic island of Brioni.

A youthful, vigorous, pioneering spirit energized Yugoslavia, she observed at a press conference. The young people, on whose faces there was "no dull expression as they approached their work," especially impressed her. Tito's policies reminded her of the New Deal, but there was a difference. "What happens in America comes from the people up," she observed, "and here what happens comes from the top down."

A genuine improvement in the world, she was convinced, had to come from the bottom up, from the people. This was why she would now devote herself to educating and organizing through the AAUN. "Instead of having used all that energy apprehending Communists," she had remarked to A. M. Rosenthal earlier that year, "if we had put it into teaching people to recognize Communism and what it was, why then we needn't have been afraid. People could have defended themselves.

"This business of acting frightened," she went on, "that is one thing I hate."

1
The Only Thing to Fear

On Broadway in 1952, Arthur Miller's *The Crucible* was opening. His play about the seventeenth-century witch trials in Salem, Massachusetts, was his creative response to different witch trials taking place in Washington.

That year, the dark-jowled Senator Joseph McCarthy was at his apogee. He embodied the currents of fear that had been circling the globe since World War II, the paranoia, suspicion, and misunderstanding that colored relations between Moscow and Washington, between Washington and China. Shortly after the war, the House Un-American Activities Committee had begun its inquisitorial task of exposing and ferreting out alleged Communists in the United States government and in the film industry. "We find ourselves living in the atmosphere of a police state," Eleanor wrote in "My Day," denouncing the investigations as "ludicrous" and excoriating the big Hollywood producers for being too "chicken-hearted" to speak up for the freedom of their industry.

McCarthy had created his first big sensation by charging that the State Department, under President Truman and Secretary of State Dean

Acheson, was infested with more than two hundred "known Communists." Though the charge was not substantiated, some Americans panicked. Was the government rotten with treachery?

In 1950, the nation was witnessing more revelations and scandals—the imprisonment of eleven Communist leaders for advocating the violent overthrow of the government, followed by the spectacular trial and conviction of former State Department official and New Deal adviser Alger Hiss for committing perjury about passing secrets to a communist spy. Eleanor, trying to resist the anticommunist hysteria, would admit only that Hiss had probably lied but not committed treason.

The most basic freedom in a democracy, the freedom to dissent, was coming under assault, Eleanor declared. People had become "afraid to be themselves, to hold convictions, to stand up for them," she told a meeting of Americans for Democratic Action in 1950. She went on to chide the members of the ADA, an organization she had helped found, for yielding to "the contamination by association" mentality. Three years later, when McCarthy launched an attack against the ADA, Eleanor agreed to serve as its honorary chairman, successfully facing down McCarthy's threat of an investigation.

"Actually some of the gentlemen in the Committee [on Un-American Activities] are a little annoyed with me," ER remarked with sly understatement, "because I have expressed my disapproval of some of Mr. McCarthy's methods." Though the "gentlemen" of the committee had never asked her to appear before them, she stated, she "would be very glad to do so." But the "gentlemen" hardly had the courage to take on Eleanor Roosevelt.

. . .

Was McCarthy a loose cannon, a loudmouth, a potential despot? As far as conservative Republicans were concerned, he was a useful and helpful ally. He could fight their reelection battles for them, and he did; he was asked to speak for more Republican candidates than all the other senators combined. The 1950 elections toppled at least five anti-McCarthy senators. Though other forces were at work as well in these defeats, the perception was that opposing McCarthy meant committing political suicide. McCarthyism even played a role in the erosion of support for the human rights treaties, which were improbably attacked as Soviet efforts to undermine the American system. Even the Marshall Plan, designed to strengthen and rebuild Europe, had to be presented to the American public as a means to combat communism in Europe. By the time Eisenhower was inaugurated, McCarthy controlled the Committee on Government Operations and commanded formidable support in the Senate. He was "a very bad man to cross politically," warned *The New York Times.*

McCarthy did not limit himself to slur and sly innuendo in denouncing those he considered Communists. Instead he hurled accusations that were as specific as they were reckless and unfounded. Skillfully manipulating the media, he made major pronouncements just before deadline, using the shock value of his accusations to produce two-inch headlines. The newspapers blazoned his charges on page one and buried his retractions among the classifieds. Even senators who disagreed with his incriminations let him have his way. Just by making accusations, Eleanor sadly observed, McCarthy was "able to obtain the result that he desired." Even students, once so vocal in expressing their opinions, she noted, were now fearfully shunning political involvement.

Nor were Eleanor's own friends immune from attack. When accusations of being a communist sympathizer were hurled at Mary McLeod Bethune, the African-American leader who had worked in the National Youth Administration under FDR, Eleanor expressed her dismay. "There are moments when I listen to Senator McCarthy and hear about an un-American activities committee," she wrote in "My Day," "when I wonder where our freedoms are going." She was equally "appalled" the following year when she learned that the committee was about to investigate the African-American political scientist and statesman, Dr. Ralph Bunche, who had won the Nobel Prize in 1950 for his mediation in the Middle East.

"I despise what Senator McCarthy has done," Eleanor retorted sharply in "My Day," after a reader attacked one of her columns. "My devotion to my country and to democracy is quite as great as that of Senator McCarthy." She minced no words: "I do not like his methods or the results of his methods and I would like to say to my correspondent that I think those of us who worked with young people in the thirties did more to save many of them from becoming Communists than Senator McCarthy has done for his fellow citizens with all his slurs and accusations." Just as she despised the way the Soviet Union sought to control people's minds, she abhorred McCarthy's attempt to impose a new anticommunist conformity in America. "He would use the same methods of fear to control all thought that is not according to his own pattern—in our free country!" McCarthy incarnated the "greatest menace to freedom we have," Eleanor told the FDR Young Democrats of City College in New York.

"McCarthy's methods, to me, look like Hitler's," she warned, "and perhaps that's why the people here who are accustomed to the methods of people like Hitler and Stalin display such an interest in him." Not only did McCarthy, like Hitler, divide the world into good and bad while manipulating people's most submerged fears, he even resorted to book burning. His aides Roy Cohn and David Schine, as Eleanor's biographer Allida Black noted, confiscated and burned books in American libraries overseas. President Eisenhower, in a speech at Dartmouth College, criticized "book burning"—but the next day called McCarthy to reassure him that the president had not targeted him in his remarks!

How could the president stoop to such cowardice? Eleanor demanded. And how could McCarthy be stopped? Only when American politicians begin "to serve as leaders" would the reign of terror cease, she wrote in *McCall's* magazine.

No other liberal—not the cautious Stevenson, not John Kennedy, who evaded the question, not Robert Kennedy, who worked as a researcher on McCarthy's staff, not Hubert Humphrey, who sought passage of the Communist Control Act of 1954—possessed Eleanor's courage to take on the Senate's bully. People, she said, had to "stand up and be counted," state clearly "the harm that McCarthyism did to our country," and then oppose him "actively." While politicians and presidents cowered in silence, one elderly woman spoke out for freedom and the Bill of Rights.

2
Civil Rights: 1956

"Is your blood white, black, or yellow?" demanded the American Red Cross when Americans donated their blood—and duly recorded the "color" of the blood on the donor cards. Only in 1950 did the Red Cross cease classifying blood by race. "Human blood is all alike, regardless of race," Eleanor hotly asserted in a "My Day" column.

For decades Mrs. Roosevelt had been helping black Americans—tenant farmers, sharecroppers, African-American WAACs—and fighting for their causes: the inclusion of blacks on juries, affordable and integrated housing, desegregated neighborhoods. Again and again, desperate people turned to her for help. As historian Alan Brinkley remarked, after her husband's death Eleanor continued to symbolize liberal hopes, not so much early New Deal hopes that concerned reshaping the capitalist world and breaking up concentrations of economic power, but hopes that "centered more around visions of a generous system of welfare and social insurance" and racial equality. In the decades after the war, the focus of American liberalism had shifted, as Brinkley noted, from economic reform to a "preoccupation with 'rights'" and with the "liberties and entitlements of individuals."

Indeed, the rights of African-Americans were the top priority on Eleanor's agenda. She boldly compared racism and segregation to fascism, provoking a wild outcry against her. The first lady was aiding the enemy, people protested. Could not Hoover and the FBI silence her?

Mrs. Roosevelt early on had won notoriety for "coddling" the Negroes. When photographs in newspapers around the country showed the first lady serving refreshments in an integrated canteen in Washington where blacks and whites danced together, people again were outraged; the president's wife dared to threaten "racial harmony." At the height of the civil rights movement, the FBI file on Mrs. Roosevelt contained thousands of pages; the FBI's director, J. Edgar Hoover, suspected that she had "Negro" blood.

"I do not believe I have interviewed anyone about whose sincerity I am more impressed," Ralph Bunche reported about ER to the sociologist Gunnar Myrdal. In the postwar world, predicted Myrdal, there would be a "redefinition of the Negro's status in America." The war had started the process of altering the lives—and aspirations—of African-Americans. After 1941, when FDR established fair hiring rules in the military, many blacks entered military service or found work in war production. Higher wages created higher self-esteem, higher expectations. Freedom movements in Africa added to the sense of hope and possibility. But white racism, rooted in the power structure, stood in the way of economic progress. No wonder some blacks—W. E. B. DuBois, Paul Robeson, and Richard Wright—had joined the Communist party in the 1930s and 1940s, ER pointed out. It was virtually the only organization open to and supportive of them.

In 1945, Mrs. Roosevelt had joined the board of directors of the NAACP, acting as intermediary between the NAACP and the Department of Justice and often conferring with NAACP counsel Thurgood Marshall. She also worked in the NAACP's legal affairs committee. After that committee became the NAACP Legal Defense and Education Fund in 1950, she would serve as its vice president in 1951.

For the NAACP's Walter White, Mrs. Roosevelt was the indispensable woman—the person he continually consulted on questions relating to policy and strategy—in tackling housing, education, apartheid, colonialism, and other problems. He always included her recommendations in his reports. But progress seemed agonizingly slow.

Then, suddenly, light.

ER was appearing on the *Tex and Jinx* morning television talk show when the news came in of a unanimous Supreme Court decision. It was May 17, 1954. The decision in *Brown v. Board of Education of Topeka, Kansas* declared segregation in public schools unconstitutional. There would be massive resistance to desegregation throughout the South—along with the emergence of a reinvigorated Ku Klux Klan and numerous White Citizens Councils. The lynching in 1955 of fourteen-year-old Emmett Till, who was visiting Mississippi from Chicago, was an extreme and gruesome example of the violence raging through the South. But the wheels of desegregation were finally in motion, and they would not be stopped.

Though a major battle had finally been won, ER knew that desegregated schools, while important, meant little if neighborhoods and housing remained segregated. Indeed, she felt all civil rights—in the North as well as in the South—depended on integrated housing. She had thrown her support to a variety of slum clearance and low-income housing bills and spoken at rallies voicing support for people who encountered resistance to their moving into white neighborhoods.

"Discrimination in housing must be wiped out," she exclaimed after the *Brown* decision, for without that, "we cannot possibly have integrated schools." But what was the real fear? Eleanor wondered. Why were southerners so alarmed by the idea of integration? Was it equality they feared? She intuited that white southerners' dread and anxiety could only be explained by their horror of mixing the races, of intermarriage. "I realize that that is the question of real concern to people," she wrote in "My Day," three days after the *Brown* decision was handed down. Two years later, she returned to that same subject. "Marriage is purely a personal matter," she wrote. "While people of the same color and race generally prefer to marry each other, there have been mixtures of races just as there have been mixtures of religions." The only issue that mattered, for the survival of the nation, was that of giving "all citizens full equality before the law and equal dignity as human beings." And again in her last book, *Tomorrow Is Now,* she would call the fear of intermarriage "a red herring if I ever saw one." Why, it was nothing but "sleight of hand" to "distract our attention from inequalities in wages, in living quarters, in education, that are an ineffaceable disgrace to us as a people."

Day after day, the struggle for integration and equal rights went on. When an airport restaurant in Houston, Texas, refused to serve the Indian ambassador to the United States, insisting that he eat in the small room reserved for "coloreds," ER took to the pen. "How could an ambassador be treated in this way? A better question is: How could any human being be treated in this way?"

. . .

"A few days ago I met Mrs. Rosa Parks," ER wrote in "My Day" in the spring of 1956. "She is a very quiet, gentle person and it is difficult to imagine how she ever could take such a positive and independent stand."

On December 1, 1955, on a crowded bus in Montgomery, Alabama, after a long day at her tailoring job, Rosa Parks, a forty-two-year-old seamstress who had been active in the NAACP for years, refused to move from the four-person seat she was sitting in so that a white man could sit there alone. "I felt that I was not being treated right and that I had a right to retain the seat that I had taken," she wrote later. "The time had just come when I had been pushed as far as I could stand to be pushed." She was arrested for breaking the segregation code and taken to jail.

Although her action was unplanned, black activists were ready to respond, especially members of the Women's Political Council. They called for a massive boycott of Montgomery's buses by the city's fifty thousand black citizens. People would travel to work, often for hours, on foot, on mules and bicycles, in cut-rate taxicabs and horse-drawn wagons—but not on segregated buses.

It took a year, but the boycott achieved its goal of desegregating Montgomery buses. Just as important, it inspired the black community to organize, it galvanized the nation, and it produced visionary leaders: Martin Luther King Jr. and Ralph Abernathy, activists Jo Ann Robinson and E. D. Nixon. "Gandhi's theory of nonviolence seems to have been learned very well," Eleanor wrote in a "My Day" column praising the "dignity and calmness" of black citizens.

Mrs. Parks and Mrs. Roosevelt met in Eleanor's New York apartment in May 1956. Eleanor was deeply impressed by the woman who had stood up to the white power establishment in Montgomery. "I suppose we must realize that these things do not happen all of a sudden," she wrote. "They grow out of feelings that have been developing over many years. Human beings reach a point when they say: 'This is as far as I can go,' and from then on it may be passive resistance, but it will be resistance."

"This is what seems to have happened in Montgomery, and perhaps it will happen all over our country wherever we have citizens who do not enjoy complete equality. It may be that this attitude will save us from war and bloodshed and teach those of us who have to learn that there is a point beyond which human beings will not continue to bear injustice."

Later that month, ER joined Rosa Parks at a huge Madison Square Garden civil rights rally, where both women electrified the crowd. Dr. King was supposed to speak as well, but the pressure of events forced him to stay in Montgomery.

In October 1956, Mrs. Roosevelt invited Dr. King to her apartment in New York. HAVE BEEN MUCH INTERESTED IN WHAT YOU ARE DOING IN MONT-GOMERY, she wired him. WOULD BE DELIGHTED IF YOU CAN COME TO SEE ME. Perhaps she hoped among other things to talk with him about the 1956 election. But he was unable to come, and the two corresponded for more than a year before they finally met. King sought her support when Southern Christian Leadership Conference leaders were jailed; she asked for his help to commemorate the first organizing of farmworkers. He called on her to help salute civil rights leader A. Philip Randolph at Carnegie Hall; she asked him to help honor another civil rights leader, Aubrey Williams.

Momentum for progress in civil rights was in the air. But could that momentum survive the electoral politics of an upcoming presidential election?

. . .

The lightning rod was the controversial, pioneering New York congressman Adam Clayton Powell.

The Supreme Court's decision on desegregation in *Brown v. Board of Education* was clear. What was less clear was how—and if—that decision would be enforced. The NAACP wanted the federal government to enforce *Brown* by any means necessary, withholding money, even sending in troops. Then Adam Clayton Powell, an African-American, had an idea. He introduced a rider on a federal school construction bill that would disqualify any segregated school—in effect, nearly every southern school—from receiving federal funds. But for some politicians it was more important for school construction to go forward than for funds to be withheld from noncompliant schools.

"I think if I were a member of Congress," Eleanor wrote liberal Representative Richard Bolling, who opposed the amendment, "I would feel obliged to vote for the bill and prevent the amendment from being introduced if possible. I am, however, not a member of Congress nor a candidate for office. I have, therefore, an obligation, I think, to live up to the principles in which I believe. I believe that it is essential to our leadership in the world and to the development of true democracy in our country to have no discrimination in our country whatsoever. This is most important in the schools of our country. Therefore I feel personally that I could not ask to have this bill passed without an amendment since unless the situation becomes so bad that the people are worried about all education, I fear nothing will be done in the area of discrimination."

Eleanor and Powell had a history. In October 1945, Powell had cabled the White House, irate that his wife, pianist Hazel Scott, had not been allowed to perform in the Daughters of the American Revolution's Constitution Hall. Truman deplored the DAR's racism, but Bess Truman went ahead and attended a DAR tea the next afternoon, explaining that she had to go because she had already accepted the invitation.

Representative Powell contrasted Mrs. Truman with Eleanor. "From now on, Mrs. Truman is the last lady," he snapped. "The excuse given by Mrs. Truman doesn't bear up when compared with Mrs. Eleanor Roosevelt's withdrawal from the DAR in 1939." Not only the DAR but all of Washington's theater owners adhered to the city's segregation policy, Eleanor pointed out in "My Day" two days later, calling on the public to work for change.

. . .

Two Democratic presidential candidates in 1956, Governor Averill Harriman of New York and Senator Estes Kefauver of Tennessee, supported both the 1954 *Brown* decision and the Powell amendment. Harriman, who had served as ambassador to the Soviet Union and had been at Yalta with FDR, had the backing of Truman—as well as the NAACP.

One presidential candidate equivocated on civil rights; he was opposed to the Powell amendment and remained silent about the lynching of Emmett Till in 1955. This was Adlai Stevenson. He had the backing of Mrs. Roosevelt.

Stevenson's reaction to the landmark *Brown* decision was curiously "remote," remarked his biographer, John Martin. Ten days after the decision was handed down, Stevenson stated that "the South has been invited by the Supreme Court to share the burden of blueprinting the mechanics for solving the new school problems of nonsegregation." A curious reaction, expressing "no praise of the decision, no call for all to support it," Martin mused. What could be done to implement the Supreme Court's decision, Adlai was asked two months later. "My goodness," he blurted out, "this is a monstrous order," going on to suggest that people offer their "advice, counsel, and help and certainly [their] understanding." Again his remarks were "long and fuzzy," Martin concluded.

In 1956 *Look* magazine took a shot at getting a straight answer. What would he do as president should a southern state refuse to comply with the Supreme Court decision? Stevenson's speechwriters had suggested that he state that any president "will act promptly and vigorously to fulfill his duties under the Constitution." But he rejected those words in favor of his own. "I cannot foretell what a President would or should do in the hypothetical circumstances you suggest."

Well, what *did* he believe on civil rights? He did not believe that southern racism could be changed by "a stroke of the pen," and he disapproved of "punitive (or coercive) action by the Federal Government." Progress would have to be made "gradually," he told a crowd of African-Americans in Los Angeles.

Gradually? "To Negro Americans 'gradual' means either no progress at all, or progress so slow as to be barely perceptible," a deeply disappointed Roy Wilkins, the new head of the NAACP, wrote to Stevenson. But Mrs. Roosevelt wrote back to Wilkins, informing him that she had examined Stevenson's record as governor. His "stand on civil rights is the correct one in every way," she told him. "We will need great wisdom and patience in the next few months, not hotheaded bursting into print." But Wilkins threatened to urge blacks to vote for Eisenhower, and an angered ER resigned from the board of the NAACP—only to withdraw her letter of resignation after a personal talk with Wilkins.

But doubts about Stevenson lingered. Senator Lehman of New York wrote to him to express his "sense of disquietude" over Stevenson's emphasis on "gradualism" and "education." "These are words," Lehman explained, "which have been used by apologists for discrimination and injustice for many years." Progress in the South had not been the result of education but rather the result of judicial fiat, he correctly pointed out. Stevenson did not agree. "True integration," he felt, requires "changes in the hearts and minds of men." Tensions in the South would have to be reduced over time, so that moderate southerners could work out their own problems, step by step. And on the Powell amendment Stevenson held his ground. "Punitive action by the federal government," he stated, "may actually delay the process of integration in education." Even Arthur Schlesinger Jr., one of Stevenson's advisers, termed the governor's attitude one of "almost grudging espousal of the civil rights cause."

For her part, Mrs. Roosevelt attempted to minimize the differences between herself and Stevenson. His foray into gradualism and incrementalism was "unwitting," she decided. There existed no real "cleavage," she told black leaders, between herself and Stevenson. President Eisenhower, moreover, did not support the Powell amendment either, she pointed out. "Yet the papers and the Negro leaders have not attacked the President. Why this discrimination?" In any case, the Powell amendment failed to pass.

Adlai was her man. For Eleanor, he towered as the "inheritor of the beliefs of President Roosevelt," she told audiences. "He is the one candidate who represents the thinking of my husband." She admired his intellect, integrity, eloquence—and appreciated his willingness to follow her advice.

During the summer of 1956, Democratic National Committee chairman Paul Butler asked Eleanor to help develop a civil rights plank for the national convention, one that would keep the South in the party. But was it possible to mollify southern segregationists, who were threatening a walkout, and also appeal to northern liberals? Americans for Democratic Action and the NAACP were pushing for a firm statement in favor of federal action in support of *Brown*.

"I don't look forward to it," she confessed to Stevenson, admitting her ambivalence about working on the civil rights plank. "I have spent endless hours in the UN discussing the value of words, and I think that is what we will have to do in this case. It is essential for the Democratic party to keep the colored vote in line, so you can't take away the feeling that you want to live up to the Supreme Court decision and go forward, and that this can't be done in one fell swoop. Desegregation of schools in the South must follow a number of steps." As she had feared, exhausting, contentious committee meetings lasted until the early hours of the morning. One day, upon Eleanor's invitation, Martin Luther King Jr. offered a prayer at the beginning of the session, while, later in the day, Circuit Judge George Wallace, who would become governor of Alabama in 1962, lectured committee members on the evils of integration.

The final plank would declare that Supreme Court decisions were "the law of the land," but it rejected including a pledge to "carry out" the Court's decisions. Many liberals were dissatisfied: The plank did not even specifically mention *Brown v. Board of Education*, nor did it urge federal enforcement of the decision. Ironically, southerners were dissatisfied as well. Despite all the compromises, all five southern members of the committee voted against the plank.

But Eleanor was pleased. "Pretty good wording on both the planks on education and civil rights," she wrote Joseph and Trude Lash. "It won't be strong enough for Harriman, but I think it actually says all that needs to be said & would allow for any action one could take & still I think it won't divide the party." Her top priority? To keep the party together long enough to elect Stevenson, who then would presumably use his presidential powers to produce change.

Arriving at the Chicago airport for the Democratic National Convention, Eleanor was immediately whisked off to a press conference where she "had to face more reporters and more cameras" than she had ever seen before. Truman had just endorsed Harriman, and for the first time Mrs. Roosevelt publicly opposed the former president. Her press conference was "an adroit and ruthless performance," Arthur Schlesinger Jr. commented. Wearing a large Adlai campaign button, she admonished Truman for endorsing Harriman, insisting that "we must have a candidate who is prepared to go forward." The following day the former president and the former first lady met for lunch. With news-hungry reporters eavesdropping from the next table, the two Democratic leaders respectfully agreed to disagree. Truman fully supported Harriman; in addition, he told Eleanor, he wanted "to make this convention do some real thinking about issues."

Mrs. Roosevelt worked the delegates for Adlai. "I visited a number of delegations during the day with Stevenson," she wrote in her column on August 15, also mentioning that "people keep asking me if women get into smoke-filled rooms at a convention. I have yet to find any room really smoke-filled."

Finally, on the convention floor, it was Eleanor's turn to address the crowd. She gave what journalist Edward R. Murrow called "the greatest convention speech I have ever heard."

"I want victory," she declared, "and I believe we will have it in November, but I want even more that each and every one of you, as you go back to your communities, take the message of what you want that victory to mean." The party had had great leaders, "but we could not have had great leaders unless they had had a great people to follow. You cannot be a great leader unless the people are great.

"There are new problems," she went on. "They must be met in new ways. . . . It is a foolish thing to say that you pledge yourself to live up to the traditions of the New Deal and the Fair Deal: Of course you are proud of those traditions; of course you are proud to have the advice of the elders in our party, but our party is young and vigorous. Our party may be the oldest democratic party, but our party must live as a young party, and it must have young leadership. It must have young people, and they must be allowed to lead. They must not lean on their tradition. They must be proud of it. They must take into account the advice of the elders, but they must have the courage to look ahead, to face new problems with new solutions.

"Could we have the vision of doing away in this great country with poverty?" she asked. "It would be a marvelous achievement, and I think it might be done if you and I, each one of us, as individuals, would really pledge ourselves and our party to think imaginatively, of what can be done at home, what can make us not only the nation that has some of the richest people in the world, but the nation where there are no people that have to live at a substandard level. That would be one of the very best arguments against Communism that we could possibly have."

The speech expressed her strategy as well as her vision; she was telling the party that it did not have to remain tied to Harry Truman. The next day she left for Europe to meet her grandchildren.

The convention went on to pass the civil rights plank, but Eleanor was now experiencing doubts. "I may have been very wrong in my stand on the platform," she wrote her friend David Gurewitsch, worried that she might have made an ill-considered moral compromise. Still, her work had its desired effect: A southern bolt was averted, and Adlai Stevenson was nominated.

His acceptance speech, people generally agreed, was a letdown. It was still "the old Stevenson, the literary critic, the man obsessed with words and with portentous generalization," commented Schlesinger. For Schlesinger, who worked for Stevenson, the campaign of 1956 was "an ordeal" and "no fun at all."

Would Eleanor stay in Europe with her grandchildren or return home to campaign for Stevenson? If she remained in Europe, her friends warned, her support for Stevenson would seem only lukewarm. She finally decided to send her grandchildren on ahead while she returned to the United States and plunged into the contest.

She coached her candidate, giving him ideas on issues, making suggestions on what to talk to women voters about, and offering tips on delivery. "If you can speak to the mass of people as though you were talking to any one individual in your living room at Libertyville, you will reach their hearts and that is all that you have to bother about."

And she traveled. She was everywhere at once—making speeches, appearing on television, flying back to New York from Michigan to appear with Stevenson in Harlem and flying out to Wisconsin the next morning. The travel was exhausting but Eleanor loved every minute, assuming that it would be the last campaign in which she would participate so wholeheartedly, night and day. Fellow Democrats thought she was magnificent; some voters thought she was the best thing in the Democratic party.

What did she say about civil rights?

In 1948, she had admitted once believing that racial justice could be the result of incremental progress. "I felt that we could take time about it," she had written. "I felt that there was time, and that we needn't move too fast, that we could do it step by step, and gradually." But her thinking had changed. After the war, she could no longer assume that meaningful change could be made incrementally.

But in 1956 she did another about-face. "We must use patience," she urged, in a campaign speech for Stevenson. "We can't do everything at once, nor as quickly in every place, but we must move and we must show that we really intend that every citizen shall have equality of opportunity."

Why the switch back toward incrementalism from a belief in transformational change?

The two political parties had not realigned, as FDR had wanted, along ideological principles and agendas. The Democratic party still comprised southern segregationists and northern liberals, virtually forcing any national candidate to walk a political tightrope. Eleanor was trying to adopt Stevenson's gradualist line to keep the party together—and play politics the way FDR had, sacrificing some things to gain what she thought most important. In the White House, she had been the idealist and Franklin the pragmatist. When she had prodded him to support the anti-lynching bill, he had brushed her off, fearing that losing southern Democrats would jeopardize passage of key New Deal programs.

Now, in the 1950s, while southern blacks were arduously winning integration, Republicans were relishing the division in the Democratic ranks. "They would like to see the party completely divided," Eleanor wrote Stevenson, "and I don't know that there is any way one can hold it together and live up to one's convictions, but somehow I think understanding and sympathy for the white people in the South is as important as understanding and sympathy and support for the colored people." Accordingly she reminded her "My Day" readers that she herself had southern blood and that her paternal grandmother—TR and Elliott's mother, Martha Bulloch—had grown up on a slave-owning plantation. Not unlike Stevenson, she had become a practiced tightrope walker.

While she trekked from town to town, making her stump speech for Adlai, French and English planes were bombing Egypt over the Suez Canal and the Israelis were invading the Sinai Desert. Egypt had nationalized the Suez Canal that year, provoking Israel, France, and Great Britain to protect that economic lifeline. Just a few days before the election, Eleanor used her "My Day" column to attack Ike's handling of the Middle East situation. "How could we have had worse leadership than that which brought us to this present situation?" she demanded. It mattered little that the leadership was that of Secretary of State John Foster Dulles, not Eisenhower, who was recovering from a serious heart attack.

Violence had also erupted in Europe. Tens of thousands of Hungarians had taken to the streets to protest against their Soviet-controlled government. In a response consisting of massive, violent repression, the Soviets deployed their tanks, killing thirty-two thousand people. Eisenhower decided to remain neutral, fearing that American support for the Hungarian freedom fighters would precipitate a third world war in Eastern Europe. An experienced man of war, Ike had become a man of peace, and the reason was that he carried a new burden—the horrifying possibility of atomic war. For Eleanor, Ike was "one of the weakest Presidents we have ever had." But the people liked Ike.

He won, again, by a landslide. Stevenson carried only seven states, one fewer than in 1952. Only Missouri and six southern states voted for him, not one northern state. More African-Americans went Republican than in any election since 1932. "No one could have done more," Mrs. Roosevelt wrote to console him, suggesting that "the love affair between President Eisenhower and the American people is too acute at present for any changes evidently to occur." Still, the Democrats won control of both houses of Congress, suggesting that the country had not moved to the right but that Stevenson had not offered voters a convincing message.

Had Eleanor proved herself to be a savvy power broker, preventing a divided convention, promoting civil rights, and ensuring Stevenson's nomination, as historian Allida Black suggests? Or did she compromise convictions that she had held for decades? In any case, equivocation on civil rights had not paid off. On the contrary, her waffling cost her respect among civil rights leaders. Scholars Joanna Schneider Zangrando and Robert L. Zangrando found that Mrs. Roosevelt's conservative stand "helped to convince a number of young black militants that the New Deal forces of the 1930s and the progressive, reformist mentality of the early twentieth century—which Eleanor Roosevelt so amply represented—were not wholly reliable."

Still, whatever shortcomings she may have possessed, whatever compromises she may have made, she was setting her own priorities and agenda, defining her own responsibilities and duties, following her own moral principles. She remembered that as a young girl her "chief objective" had been to do her duty, "not my duty as I saw it," she explained, "but my duty as laid down for me by other people." And as a young wife in Albany she had also "looked at everything from the point of view of what I ought to do, rarely from the standpoint of what I wanted to do." Now, in the 1950s, on her own, she was following her own inner compass, her own sense of true north.

. . .

"Dear Mrs. Roosevelt: You have not answered my questions, the amount of Negro blood you have in your veins, if any."

Eleanor's blood comprised the subject of her "My Day" column a few weeks after the election. "I am afraid none of us know how much or what kind of blood we have in our veins," she wrote, "since chemically it is all the same. As far as I know, I have no Negro blood, but, of course, I do have some Southern blood in my veins, for my Grandmother Roosevelt came from Georgia."

The struggle for the universal recognition of red blood was evidently not over, but even after Stevenson's defeat, Eleanor was hopeful about the future. In a Christmas Eve column, she applauded the triumph of the Montgomery bus boycott and the Supreme Court order banning segregation. And for the first time she mentioned Martin Luther King Jr., who had urged "calm dignity and wise restraint"—two Gandhian traits Eleanor believed in.

In 1957, a civil rights bill proposed in Congress sparked debates that revived passions that had been smoldering since the Civil War. Right on cue, Senator Strom Thurmond of South Carolina tried to kill the bill with a filibuster of 24 hours and 18 minutes, the longest on record. Southern segregationists hoped to water down the bill, first by striking out Section III, which allowed the Justice Department to use various legal tactics to aid individuals whose civil rights had been violated; and, second, by proposing an amendment requiring that civil rights violations be tried before a jury—which of course meant an all-white jury. "The whole point of the

Southerners' fight for the jury trial," Eleanor informed her readers, "is that they know a white jury will not give Negroes the right to vote." The jury trial amendment passed but Section III was voted down.

The Civil Rights Act of 1957 was the first civil rights legislation enacted since Reconstruction, but many Americans longed for more. "Our people are not going to be satisfied with crumbs such as this civil rights bill gives them," Eleanor fumed. "It will bring us no peace, but it is better to pass it and see what we can achieve with even this slight change." She then went on the attack, targeting Senator Lyndon B. Johnson of Texas and Senator Richard Russell of Georgia, also a Democrat. They would find that they had won, she warned, "a costly victory—because this fight for civil rights is not going to stop. . . . Vice-president Nixon and Senator Johnson," she concluded, "both are trying to fool the people, white and colored people alike."

When Johnson objected to this accusation that he had been trying to "fool the people," Mrs. Roosevelt stuck to her guns. "I understand your extremely clever strategy on the Civil Rights Bill," she scolded, repeating that "it would be fooling the people to have them think this was a real vital step toward giving all our people the right to vote or any other civil rights."

After her attacks on Russell, Johnson, and Nixon, and especially after her furious criticism of Mississippi Senator James Eastland, the chairman of the Judiciary Committee, the atmosphere heated up. All the newspapers in the Scripps-Howard chain except one dropped her column—though other papers, such as the *New York Post*, would start printing her column for the first time. When she traveled to Texas for a speaking engagement, the White Citizens Council demanded that she leave the Lone Star State "immediate." When she refused to be intimidated, people picketed her talk. In North Carolina, dynamite went off near the church where she was speaking. Even the FBI cautioned her against appearing in Texas.

Neither criticism nor hatred inhibited her. Just as FDR had exclaimed that he "welcomed" the hatred of his political enemies, his wife also explained that although she knew she was "fanatically" disliked by many people, "it seems to me that I cannot afford, as a self-respecting individual, to refuse to do a thing merely because it will make me disliked or bring down a storm of criticism on my head." She did not mind being unpopular or standing alone, she wrote, preferring that to the "comfortable anonymity of the herd." During the summer of 1957 she would launch still more attacks on Arkansas governor Orval Faubus and on the Eisenhower administration.

African-Americans' patience was wearing thin. "Human beings have a break point if denied an outlet for their emotions and convictions," she warned. In the 1930s she had limited her outrage—and her courage—over segregation to placing her folding chair in a free zone, in the aisle between the segregated white and black audiences. In the 1950s, such a mild protest no longer seemed sufficient. For how long would oppressed people be content with nonviolent protest?

Now she lent her name and her money to causes the NAACP felt were too explosive to touch. She supported the Southern Conference Education Fund, standing undaunted when the SCEF was denounced by Senator Eastland for harboring Communists and conspiring to subvert American "social traditions," and equally undaunted when the NAACP, also fearing guilt by association with Communists, tried to convince her to leave the SCEF. Instead, she publicly encouraged the SCEF agenda, hosting fund-raising events and publicizing their causes in her column. She admired their activist stands on school desegregation, integration of southern hospitals and professional schools as well as their responses to the lynching of Emmett Till and to other murders and miscarriages of justice.

One case the NAACP refused to touch concerned two seven-year-old black children in North Carolina. The two little boys kissed—or were kissed by—a little white girl, and were sentenced in 1958 to twelve and fourteen years in prison for "rape." The boys' lawyer called Eleanor for help. Why hadn't he already called her? she demanded. Around the world the affair became a cause célèbre. In the Netherlands, several thousand students at the Roosevelt High School in Rotterdam signed a petition demanding freedom for the two boys. Eleanor delivered the petition to the president. Ike responded—and the children were released, their records destroyed.

Was the American political system failing? There seemed to be no politicians on the horizon, Eleanor felt, who were trying "to draw out the best in the people instead of the worst."

On *Meet the Press* in October 1957, Eleanor talked about American politics. The Eisenhower administration struck her as "a businessmen's Administration." But more critical, Americans seemed to have grown "passive" about democracy, she told the reporters. Citizens had come to an impasse, taking democracy "for granted," unsure of the "things that we believe in and that we are ready to die for, or to live for."

The Democrats? The party was lacking an ideology, a sense of "where it was actually heading." But when asked whether the Democratic party would be better off if it could divest itself of its southern wing, she skirted the explosive issue that FDR had tried in vain to tackle. "You can't remove the civil rights problem," she replied, observing that "not only the Democrats have it, but the Republicans have it." Finally, Marquis Childs, a reporter who had covered the White House during the Depression, asked her whether she would be a candidate in 1960.

"I am seventy-three years old," she laughed. "Wake up."

3
Eleanor, the Party Broker

"The Negroes are going more and more to the Republicans," Mrs. Roosevelt warned Senator Lyndon Johnson early in 1960, urging him to push for stronger civil rights legislation. "Those that we can count on as Democrats need a real achievement on the part of the Democrats to point to as a reason for backing the Democratic Party." It was "absolutely necessary" for congressional Democrats to take a strong, principled stand.

Time seemed to be running out. Mrs. Roosevelt appeared more and more willing, noted her friend Joseph Rauh, the national chairman of Americans for Democratic Action, to support civil disobedience. Her heart was in the South—with the student protesters. "I had the most wonderful dream last night," she said one morning to her secretary, Maureen Corr. "I dreamt I was marching and singing and sitting in with students in the South."

Was segregation in the United States significantly different from apartheid in South Africa? Eleanor wondered gloomily, while congressmen debated and senators filibustered civil rights legislation. Democratic congressmen were missing crucial votes on civil rights. They were being outmaneuvered by Republicans who would call for a vote in the evening after the Democrats had left for dinner. And the Democrats seemed more intent on dinner than on sticking around for crucial votes. But in May, the Civil Rights Act of 1960 was passed, strengthening the 1957 act with greater powers for judges to help blacks register and vote and with criminal penalties for bombing and bomb threats. Finally, some hope.

It was another election year.

Was there anyone on the political horizon who had the stuff of a Washington, a Lincoln, a Wilson, or a Roosevelt, reporter Mike Wallace had asked Mrs. Roosevelt in 1957. "At the moment the only person I see those beginnings in is Adlai Stevenson," she replied. But why then had the American people rejected Stevenson twice, and the second time more severely than the first? Wallace shot back. Perhaps, she mused, it was his "inability to quite put the things he believes in the language or in the emotional way that will come home to the average human being." In 1955 she had conceded that Stevenson was "remote"; now she confessed that he was no great communicator. But still, he was her man—and he would be again in 1960. Given that Stevenson was a "better campaigner in 1952 than in 1956," she wrote in "My Day," perhaps, if nominated again in 1960, he would campaign as he did in 1952.

She was lukewarm toward the other candidates. When Lyndon Johnson was invited by James Roosevelt to a Memorial Day ceremony at FDR's grave in Hyde Park, Eleanor had tried to avoid him and his wife, Lady Bird. Since then, her feelings had mellowed a little—she had congratulated him for his work on the Civil Rights Act of 1960—but she would not support him for president. Senator Stuart Symington of Missouri? No. Senator Hubert Humphrey of Minnesota? No.

John F. Kennedy? The idea of supporting Kennedy for president was "radically against her political instinct," commented John Kenneth Galbraith, who knew them both. Recalling Mrs. Roosevelt's antipathy for Joseph Kennedy, Galbraith remarked that "Eleanor's adverse feeling was very deep; it extended automatically to [Kennedy's] son." Joe Kennedy, moreover, was a close friend of McCarthy, according to Eleanor's biographer, Allida Black, who notes that McCarthy had even refused to campaign for young Kennedy's senatorial rival, Henry Cabot Lodge Jr.

Did anti-Catholic feelings also play a role in her lack of interest in Kennedy? For years she had been criticized by Catholics for her stands on divorce and birth control. She had feuded publicly with New York City's Cardinal Francis Joseph Spellman, though they had finally extended olive branches to each other. Years ago, she had supported the Catholic Al Smith for president. But perhaps she did worry, her son Elliott remarked, that a Catholic president might be more loyal to the pope than to American citizens. Her friend Joseph Lash reflected that perhaps "somewhere deep in her subconscious was an anti-Catholicism which was a part of her Protestant heritage," but she herself conceded, according to Lash, that it was a greater liability to have lost the presidential election twice than to be a Catholic candidate.

In 1956, the young senator from Massachusetts, hoping to be a vice-presidential candidate, had sought Mrs. Roosevelt's support. He assumed that she would endorse him again as she had in 1952 when he ran against Lodge, the grandson of TR's close friend. But what had he done from '52 to '56? Sitting facing each other on twin beds in her hotel suite at the 1956 convention, she grilled him.

"Just where do you stand on McCarthyism, Senator?" she asked.

Recovering from back surgery, he had not been present at the Senate vote to censure McCarthy. As far as she could tell, he had been—and still was—equivocal.

"I do not see how I can possibly support you, Senator," she told him bluntly. "McCarthyism is a question on which *everyone* must stand up and be counted. You avoid committing yourself, while your brother Robert was actually on the McCarthy staff. I am surprised that you ask help from *me*. Good day!"

Eleanor's feelings had not changed. But at Galbraith's suggestion, in late 1959, Mrs. Roosevelt appeared with the young senator on her TV interview program, *Prospects of Mankind,* produced by her friend Elinor Morgenthau's oldest son, Henry. Both participants were interesting and cordial. But upon being asked afterward if she would support Kennedy for president, she left no one in doubt: *certainly not.* Though the young man had written *Profiles in Courage,* she told an ABC-TV interviewer, she was not certain that he himself possessed the "independence" necessary to have courage.

"It is obvious to me," she wrote in 1960 in "My Day," "that more and more people are joining the bandwagon for Stevenson." She realized that many delegates supported Kennedy; therefore, it was all the more imperative for Stevenson forces "to get into the convention and make a noise about their choice. Perhaps it is well, then, to make all the noise they can now!" Refusing to see that support for Stevenson was crumbling, she was furious when former Stevenson advisers such as Arthur Schlesinger Jr. and John Kenneth Galbraith came out for Kennedy in June.

What was likely to happen at the convention? Mrs. Roosevelt wondered. She imagined a scenario according to which Lyndon Johnson would block Kennedy from the nomination, followed by Kennedy's throwing his support to Stevenson. Then Kennedy would take second place on a Stevenson ticket, and that Stevenson-Kennedy ticket would gain her seal of approval. "A Stevenson-Kennedy ticket would give confidence to the world," she enthused, "in a way that no other ticket I can think of would do." She went on to urge convention delegates to bombard Senator Kennedy with "pleas" to run as Stevenson's vice president. "It would not only be the best for the country but for our political party, too."

But was Stevenson even interested? He would "serve [his] country and [his] party whenever called upon," he tepidly announced, then added, "I am not a candidate." His waffling and indecisiveness grated upon his most loyal supporters.

That did not stop Eleanor from drumming up support for him. She informed reporters at a press conference at the Los Angeles convention that Kennedy was unlikely to command Negro support; she wheeled and dealed for Adlai at the convention; she called Chicago mayor Richard Daley, asking him to throw his support to Stevenson; she visited eleven state caucuses.

Finally, at the last minute, Stevenson began to work in earnest for the nomination. But it was too late. "I could have murdered him," said Eleanor's friend Agnes Martin, after Stevenson made a few lame and flat remarks in lieu of a speech at the convention.

People applauded wildly when Mrs. Roosevelt, the Democratic icon, entered the convention hall in Los Angeles, taking her seat in the Stevenson box, adorned with a banner announcing ALL THE WAY WITH ADLAI. It was she who gave the seconding speech for Stevenson. When it became clear that Kennedy would be the party's nominee, she hurriedly left the hall for the airport—"almost in tears," a friend observed. But Kennedy was anxious to speak with her before she left Los Angeles. From the convention hall, he called her at the airport. She brushed him off. He could communicate with her through her son Franklin.

Angry and disappointed—was she a sore loser too? The whole convention, she scolded, was a "circus" and a sham. "The noise, bands, balloons," she snapped, were manufactured and controlled. The culprit? The "party bosses" who had controlled Kennedy's nomination so tightly. Why, one of them had even thrown away a large box of telegrams all in favor of Stevenson. She recalled that it was in protest against the bosses of the Republican machine that her Uncle Theodore had started his Bull Moose party. Political conventions, she fumed, "are as obsolete as outmoded machinery. . . . We cannot again permit the political bosses to dictate who the nominees are to be." The whole system was "intolerable."

"How was it possible that in the 1960 conventions the choice of candidates was made without regard to the wishes of the American citizens?" she demanded, unwilling to believe that the primaries and convention had been fair and that a majority of Democrats wanted Kennedy and not the two-time loser Stevenson.

JFK knew he needed the endorsement of the woman who was the "conscience" of the Democratic party—and the conduit to Stevenson supporters and ADA liberals. And he had reason to fear her ambivalence toward him. When, at a Democratic fund-raiser, she praised the party platform more than the presidential candidate himself, *The New York Times* ran a headline announcing SHE'LL BACK DEMOCRATIC TICKET DESPITE SOME MISGIVINGS. But Eleanor needed JFK too. Should he be elected, she wanted him to find a prominent position in his government for Stevenson—perhaps Secretary of State?

Kennedy's aide and speechwriter Theodore Sorensen asked Eleanor's friend Hyman Bookbinder to arrange a meeting, and she agreed: It would be at the Roosevelt Library in Hyde Park, on August 14, following a ceremony commemorating the twenty-fifth anniversary of the Social Security Act.

And so the young senator came courting to Hyde Park. It was an inauspicious day. Eleanor's granddaughter, the daughter of her son John, had just died after falling off a horse, but Eleanor told Kennedy to come anyway. Comparing their meeting to Napoleon and Czar Alexander's meeting on "their raft at Tilsit," he skillfully set about mending fences. Eleanor requested that JFK quote Stevenson in his campaign speeches and advised him to come out more strongly for civil rights and stop trying to placate the South. Kennedy agreed.

Three days later, the readers of "My Day" learned firsthand about Mrs. Roosevelt's meeting with John Kennedy. "Mr. Stevenson has a more judicial and reflective type of mind," she mused. Still, the grande dame of the Democrats was slowly coming around to Kennedy. He was "likable, charming," and "anxious to learn," she judged, though he tends "to arrive at judgments almost too quickly." He struck her as "hard-headed"; "he calculates the political effect of every move." But she believed that he wanted to leave a record of helping his own countrymen as well as "humanity as a whole."

"I have enough confidence in him now to feel that I can work wholeheartedly for his election." The senator from Massachusetts finally had her endorsement.

Would she campaign for him? "Whether I will take any trips or become more involved," she told friend Mary Lasker, "will depend on whether or not I am happy with the way he progresses as a person in the campaign." But she did travel for him, stumping for him in California, West Virginia, Chicago, New York, and elsewhere.

And she kept her readers informed about the race. The second Kennedy-Nixon debate was better than the first, she wrote in her column. although it "did not give either side a clear-cut advantage over the other."

In the third debate, Nixon improbably attacked Truman for having used "bad language." Ike's vice president would tolerate no "lapses in language." A surprised Eleanor wrote that she refused to "join Mr. Nixon in his virtue." The patrician Mrs. Roosevelt could only smile when Nixon, the self-proclaimed "commoner," portrayed himself as a "paragon of virtue." "He reminds me too much of a little story we used to laugh about in our family for many years," she wrote. "My mother-in-law, like Mr. Nixon, felt that no gentleman ever used bad language. When by chance my husband said 'damn' in front of the children, she would draw herself up and say: 'Franklin never used to use bad language. He has learned it from his little boy Johnny, whom you, Eleanor, allow to spend so many hours in the stable!'" "Good" or "bad" language, Eleanor felt, was not "really a criterion by which we choose the best man to be President of the United States." Two decades later, when the Nixon White House tapes were released, Americans would learn firsthand about Richard Nixon's own memorable brand of language.

When JFK squeaked to victory, by a mere 113,057 votes (but by 303 votes in the electoral college to Nixon's 219), had Eleanor's help made the difference? Perhaps. In any event, the young president would need "all the youth and energy and health" he seemed to possess, she wrote right after the election, to meet the world's problems.

On a blustery day in January 1961, Eleanor found herself once again witnessing the inauguration of another president of the United States. She had declined to sit in the presidential box, her son Elliott reported, for that would have meant sitting near JFK's father, Joe Kennedy. Instead she sat in the bleachers beneath the podium, wrapped in an old army blanket. Inauguration day, Eleanor wrote Lorena Hickok, "was cold & beautiful & the ceremonies impressive. I thought the speech magnificent, didn't you? I have reread it twice."

The young president paid off his debts, asking Adlai Stevenson—a man he couldn't "bear being in the same room" with, according to Jacqueline Kennedy—to serve as the American ambassador to the United Nations. He appointed Mrs. Roosevelt to the American delegation to a special

General Assembly session, later to the advisory council of the Peace Corps, and, in 1962, to chair his Commission on the Status of Women. "The commission will try to make its influence felt concerning women's problems," Eleanor told her "My Day" readers, "not only in the Federal area but in state and local areas and in industry as well as in women's home responsibilities."

Eleanor was back in her old role of sending long letters of advice to the White House. She had been listening on the radio to JFK's last press conference. Wasn't it "too sophisticated for the average person to understand?" she wondered. It really did not take the place of a fireside chat. And then there was the matter of the president's voice. "I wish you could get someone like my old teacher to help you deepen and strengthen your voice on radio and TV," a motherly ER proposed to JFK. "It would give you more warmth and personality in your voice. It can be learned, and I think it would make a tremendous difference." JFK agreed. It would be difficult to change nature, he said, but he would attempt "to nudge it."

It was wonderful, Eleanor felt, to have "so young, intelligent, and attractive a First Lady." She wrote Jacqueline Kennedy about the pressures and challenges of being first lady and later commented on the importance of "image" in leadership. Neither the president nor his wife can ever "give way to apprehension," she observed. "If the country is to be confident, they must be confident."

But her principal focus was policy. She wrote to JFK about Berlin, disarmament, Vietnam, migratory farmworkers. When she learned that only nine of his first 240 appointments were women, she sent him a list of competent women. And, as always, she was a benevolent, loyal friend and advocate for African-Americans.

Would Mrs. Roosevelt bring "the necessary pressure and persuasion" on President Kennedy on civil rights? Martin Luther King Jr. wrote to ask. Eleanor complied, sending King's articles to JFK and urging the president to intervene in voting rights disputes and in protecting civil rights workers. When King was arrested in Albany, Georgia, in July, she asked Robert Kennedy to intercede for him. And when the president delayed an executive order integrating federally financed public housing, she lobbied Robert Kennedy.

. . .

"When you cease to make a contribution you begin to die," Eleanor had written a friend in 1960. Now the only thing slowing her down was her health. In 1960 her close friend and doctor, David Gurewitsch—with whom she still shared a house on East 74th Street—had diagnosed aplastic anemia.

Still, in her mid-seventies Mrs. Roosevelt continued to do her daily column, now published in about forty newspapers; she wrote a monthly "question and answer" column for *McCall's*, and still interviewed guests on her TV show.

At seventy-five, she had begun a two-year stint teaching a seminar in international law and international organization at Brandeis University. She would catch an evening flight out of LaGuardia Airport, spend the night in Boston, and make her way the next morning, without car or driver, to Brandeis to teach her class. When her secretary in New York, feeling that Mrs. Roosevelt looked tired, arranged for a limousine to meet her at the airport in Boston, Eleanor fumed. "Don't ever do that again," she ordered. So astonishing and inspiring were her energy and commitment to a multiplicity of causes that in 1959 she was asked to write an article for *Harper's* on "Where Do I Get My Energy?" The opening sentence read, "My uncle, Theodore Roosevelt, was known for his remarkable energy."

"I think I have a good deal of my Uncle Theodore in me," Eleanor said on her seventy-seventh birthday, "because I could not, at any age, be content to take my place in a corner by the fireside and simply look on. Life was meant to be lived. . . . One must never . . . turn his back on life."

Four hundred hot dogs, twenty-five quarts of ice cream, and one hundred comic books were ready when the boys from the Wiltwyck Training School visited Val-Kill. People were still Eleanor's life. One day, when friends arrived for a small luncheon at Val-Kill, they found that a delegation of two hundred "colored" ladies had also been invited. Her patrician Hudson River neighbors objected to the activities and guests—from Leonard Bernstein and Harry Belafonte to Allard Lowenstein—of the ex–first lady. Once, when picnicking with some friends on the Hudson River grounds of Mrs. John Henry Livingston, she and her friends were ordered to leave. For the patrician set, Eleanor was persona non grata.

"Everything was grist to my mill," she wrote, explaining that she never let slip an opportunity to increase her knowledge of people and conditions. Open to everyone and everything, she did not even balk at making a television commercial for margarine. "I'll do it," she decided. So what if she would be "bitterly criticized," she thought. Her $35,000 fee would pay for many CARE packages. For that amount of money, she noted, "I can save 6,000 lives." And she insisted on including in her commercial a reminder to her television audience that there were hungry people in the world.

Slightly stooped, carrying her own suitcase, taking buses, planes, and trains, uninterested in fashion, valuing friends from all walks of life, an aging Eleanor Roosevelt incarnated the engaged citizen in a participatory, inclusive democracy. In February 1962 she traveled to Europe, making a quick trip to Israel and stopping in Switzerland for some winter fun with family and friends.

She was selfless and heroic to the end. In May 1962, six months before she died, an already ill and suffering Eleanor, horrified by reports of violence against nonviolent protesters in the South, left her sickbed to convene the ad hoc Committee of Inquiry into the Freedom Struggle in the South. Prominent leaders joined her in her inquiry into the lack of judicial protection for Freedom Riders. For two grueling days, they listened to people testify about the lack of police protection for demonstrators, police violence, excessive sentencing, and excessive bond for nonviolent protesters. When the committee's lawyer, ADA head Joe Rauh, objected to the public naming of corrupt judges, urging the committee to go into executive session, Mrs. Roosevelt declared that judges too should be held accountable for their actions, and the names were entered into the public record.

Chairing the committee was "one of the most difficult experiences" of her life, she confessed in her last book, *Tomorrow Is Now*. It was "intolerably painful" to learn that what was happening in the United States "was the kind of thing the Nazis had done to the Jews of Germany." But in America, the issues once again concerned class as well as race. The greatest brutality, she held, was committed by "whites whose economic condition was little better than that of the Negroes." Violence against blacks constituted "the only way in which they could proclaim their superiority."

Her heart was broken by the case of Ronnie Moore, who sat in at a lunch counter, was jailed for three weeks, arrested again, and jailed for two months with a higher bond set. But each case was worse than the last. Negroes praying and singing attacked with forty-seven tear-gas bombs and by police dogs; a white boy, the son of a minister, threatened with castration for protesting the expulsion of a black girl from a high school. Making matters worse, she complained, the violence was being ignored by newspapers and television. The Kennedy administration was doing too little to protect civil rights workers and Freedom Riders in the South.

A social revolution had begun. Its goal, she said, was to provide "all our people with an equal opportunity to enjoy the benefits that have been the privileges of a few." This revolution would not level society down, but bring all up. Poor, underprivileged people would be socialized and educated to share in the privileges of the elite. "Too often, it is true," she wrote, "Negroes from underprivileged areas move into apartments or neighborhoods and, because they have been taught no better, clutter the hallways with filth and arouse reasonable resentment and alarm in the white tenants." The function of "democratic living," she asserted, "is not to lower standards but to raise those that have been too low." She advised Martin Luther King to "help some of the underprivileged Negroes prepare themselves to fit in to better surroundings."

Mrs. Roosevelt had left the insular world of the patrician elite far behind. When Theodore Roosevelt first ran for the New York State Assembly in 1881, he too had turned his back on the upper-class world of beauty, refined manners, and ceremonial observances of etiquette. "Etiquette," Eleanor wrote one month before she died, "is not just a matter of knowing how a lunch or dinner should be served, or what the 'proper' behavior is in this or that situation." True "manners," she remarked, meant something else entirely. "The basis of all good human behavior is kindness," concluded Eleanor, the democrat whose heart and compassion had grown and deepened over the decades.

But she was growing weary. During the summer of 1962 she was hospitalized. Trying to concentrate, she struggled to dictate her last book, *Tomorrow Is Now.* "I can't work," she admitted one day to her secretary. "I don't understand it." Work ceased for the day.

How could she resist making one more trip back to Campobello, where a bridge joining Maine and Canada was being dedicated as a memorial to FDR? That final exhausting trip, made against the advice of her doctor, was followed by two autumn months in and out of the hospital in New York City, surrounded by friends and family. Her disease, as it turned out, was not aplastic anemia but a rare bone-marrow tuberculosis, diagnosed only in October.

There was so much work yet to be done! From her sickbed, just a month before she died, she still expressed her outrage against reactionary politicians. In particular, senators Everett Dirksen of Illinois and James Eastland of Mississippi aroused her fury. "These are evil men," she exclaimed in "My Day," "who combine together to scratch each other's backs." Not only were they blocking Americans from registering to vote, she told her readers, they were even blocking legislation on government testing and regulation of pharmaceutical drugs. Just like Uncle Ted a half century earlier, she denounced "those who consider free enterprise more sacred than human lives."

One afternoon she dragged herself to a campaign rally for a candidate for the New York State Assembly, becoming faint after her short speech. She sent advice—and a contribution—to Robert Morgenthau, her friends' son, advising him how to "humanize" his campaign for governor of New York against Nelson Rockefeller, who was being aided by her Republican son John. Requests and offers were still coming in. Would Eleanor consent to run for the Senate, New York congressman Emanuel Celler's secretary called to ask. Celler planned to propose on a Sunday morning television program that Eleanor run for the Senate as the Democratic candidate from New York. "I don't believe in old people running," she responded. Nor would she give any more big parties, she announced in September. The fourteen people who were coming to breakfast the following morning, in Mrs. Roosevelt's mind, were not a big party.

But her disease was taking over. From her hospital room where she spent her seventy-eighth birthday in October, she arranged for a children's party to take place in her apartment. She felt helpless and angry, Trude Lash wrote—frustrated about her own powerlessness, furious about the measures doctors were taking to keep her alive in her great pain. She pleaded with Dr. Gurewitsch to "let her go." Joseph Lash offered to read the newspapers to her. "It'll never come together," she murmured. "Nobody makes sense." Adlai Stevenson was one of the last to visit her, but she probably did not recognize him.

On November 7, 1962, Eleanor Roosevelt died. She was buried next to Franklin, in the rose garden at Springwood. She wanted a plain oak casket, covered with pine boughs. No flowers, she insisted. President and Mrs. Kennedy, Attorney General Robert Kennedy, General Eisenhower, President Truman, Vice President Johnson, Governor Rockefeller, Senator Lehman, Frances Perkins, James Farley, Marian Anderson, Mayor Wagner, Adlai Stevenson, and hundreds of relatives and friends came to Hyde Park to mourn.

EPILOGUE:
A CENTURY OF REFORM

New York News, August 28, 1938. (*Courtesy FDR Library*)

"Don't be snobs!" Theodore Roosevelt had exhorted Groton schoolboys as young Franklin sat transfixed by his cousin's charge. It was the first moral lesson that the future twenty-sixth president of the United States would instill in the thirty-second. It would not be forgotten.

But why was TR speaking with such vehemence about "contemptible snobs" when he could have regaled the boys with his stories of big game hunting in the West or nabbing crooks in Manhattan? TR loved adventure, but even more he loved wielding power—for a moral purpose. And that moral purpose was wed to his defiance of his own class.

Critics of TR, like Richard Hofstadter, make no concession to TR's "betrayal" of his class. They see his attacks on the rich for living corrupt and evil lives and exploiting the poor as sheer bombast. They scorn him for being selective in his class targets. He railed against rich men, like John D. Rockefeller, who lacked a family background of education and refinement, while finally making peace with—and indeed honoring—J. P. Morgan, who collected books and art. He chose easy targets, such as those guilty of "rotten frivolity," in the knowledge that they could not retaliate politically. And as for snobbism, some accused him of being "cold and priggish," as Edmund Morris reported.

In the final analysis, though, the test of Theodore Roosevelt's presidency lay not in oratory or epithets but in his active leadership for transformational change based on his moral values and sense of social justice. His leadership was crystallized in a series of ground-breaking laws: the Elkins and Hepburn acts, significantly strengthening the Interstate Commerce Act; the establishment of a new department of Labor and Commerce; the Newsland Act financing irrigation projects in arid states; the Pure Food and Drug Act of 1906; the Meat Inspection Act of the same year; and, throughout, his antitrust efforts resulting in forty-four suits against monopolies.

If TR was disloyal to a class, it was to a class he considered to be greedy and frivolous and utterly lacking in either national vision or social responsibility. What then was he loyal *to*? First and foremost, to his country, he would say, and if that sounded banal or fatuous to turn-of-the-century people, for him it had a special meaning: the security and survival of the United States of America. And if this too was dismissed as a platitude, TR would offer a spirited rebuttal: No other public value—justice, liberty, opportunity, the pursuit of happiness—would be possible in a nation that did not survive. Equality too; TR would have shuddered at being called an egalitarian, but that value also lay at the heart of his great "Square Deal" reform proposals, both economic and political.

In pursuing these supreme values TR was in almost constant conflict, from his earliest days in the New York legislature to his fight for progressivism in 1912 and his call for early United States intervention in World War I. But he demonstrated over a span of three decades that conviction and courage, rather than continual compromise and consensus, were both the engines of social betterment and the empowerment of his highest values.

. . .

However much he admired Cousin Theodore's militancy and heroics, Franklin in his early years did not share TR's love of conflict. He fitted easily into the life of Groton, despite some teasing, and then moved smoothly into the world of Harvard. There he lived and dined mainly with friends from his own social class. Caught between his hero worship of TR and his family's Democratic party heritage, he rooted for TR in election contests but then ran for office as a Democrat because a Democratic seat opened up. (If a Republican opportunity had appeared first, he most probably would have grabbed that, thus giving the nation two Republican Roosevelts.) Later, Hofstadter labeled him "the Patrician as Opportunist"— a title that seemed justified, at least for a time.

Everything seemed to come readily to FDR during his early years in politics. He won acclaim for taking on Tammany in the state senate but suffered little embarrassment when the fight petered out. He supported Woodrow Wilson in 1912, without incurring Cousin Theodore's wrath, then moved urbanely into just the position he wanted in the Wilson administration. He and Eleanor continued their social contacts with the patrician world even as Wilson was shaping the "New Democracy."

Even in the turbulent days of the "first New Deal," FDR acted more as a unifying force than a controversial leader. He presided over a "concert of interests" that offered aid to business, labor, and agriculture. He dexterously brokered deals among political and economic factions. Constantly experimenting, he shifted from one policy to another so adeptly that he gave the impression of a steady, determined leadership.

All this ended within two years of taking office. People's hopes and expectations had soared, only to be brought to earth by continuing joblessness and poverty. The New Deal suddenly seemed less than half dealt. Neopopulist followers of Long and Coughlin and Townsend, radical farm leaders and socialists and utopians, mobilized across the country. Business leaders founded the Liberty League as an attack dog against the president. The "concert" of interests was now emitting raucous noises.

Just when did class warfare begin to disrupt FDR's grand coalition of all the interests? New Dealers could argue that it started with the founding of the Liberty League by du Ponts and other tycoons in August 1934. Conservatives could contend that it started when Roosevelt put through the "radical laws" of 1935. All would agree that the battle was joined at the opening of election year 1936, when Al Smith charged the New Deal with socialism or worse in his speech to the Liberty League, shortly after FDR had bombarded Congress with a militant State of the Union speech.

Class war had been declared. It was never clear-cut; dissident elements operated behind the lines. Each side accused the other of fomenting the war; each claimed to represent the interests of the whole nation. Respectable conservatives charged Roosevelt with being a "traitor to his class," the ultimate sin. The war came to a climax in the 1936 election, with FDR's ringing words, "They are unanimous in their hatred of me—and I welcome their hatred!"

Class war was fought not only in speeches and elections but through institutions. In the president's view, the Supreme Court that struck down his New Deal laws spoke for upper-class interests, as did the Democratic legislators who joined the GOP in obstructing his proposals and in starving his New Deal agencies.

In a democracy Roosevelt could not—would not—obstruct conservative thought or action, but could he realign the two major parties to accord more ideologically with the growing socioeconomic conflict? His attempted purge of the conservative southern Democrats, a rational though highly risky effort to give voters a meaningful choice between liberal and conservative candidates, ultimately failed. Then, through his agents, FDR sought to negotiate a union of liberal Republicans and progressive Democrats to form a powerful majority party of workers and farmers, northern and southern liberals, progressives and Farm Laborites.

It was this failed effort at party realignment that brought FDR most dramatically back to the unfinished business of TR. For Cousin Theodore had hoped that his newly founded Progressive party would forge Wilson

Democrats, Bull Moose Republicans, and La Follette progressives into a clearly liberal and militant party that could fight on even terms with Old Guard Taft Republicans allied with "Tory" Democrats.

FDR hoped the post–New Deal elections, as in 1912, would turn on clear confrontation between liberal and conservative values. In this respect, at least, the president did his part in advancing the Four Freedoms as a dramatic restatement and modernization of the calls in the Declaration of Independence for life, liberty, and the pursuit of happiness, and even more explicitly in proclaiming his "Economic Bill of Rights," which laid out the agenda of liberal Democrats for the Truman, Kennedy, and Johnson presidencies ahead.

The American people were not passive bystanders amid the class war between rich and poor. They were participants. Perhaps FDR's greatest success lay in helping them to define for themselves their true interests. And they knew where the president stood. Letters poured into the White House reflecting people's grasp of the liberal-conservative values in conflict, where the right-wing opposition stood, where *they* stood.

"Dear Mr. Roosevelt," wrote Eva S. Conners, when the ideological battle was heating up in January 1935. "You, a man born to wealth and social position, come so close to us who are poor and distressed in these hardest of times. Mr. Roosevelt—may I salute you with a new and rather slightly different title, *President of the People* of the United States."

. . .

"President of the people!" Nothing would have warmed the president's heart more. But it was precisely this kind of attitude—and FDR's response to it—that underlay presidential scholars' later criticism of Franklin Roosevelt and of Theodore Roosevelt too. Writing in the 1980s and 1990s with a longer perspective, some critics held that FDR's presidency in particular had been too personalized, overly keyed to popular demands, too willing to detour around institutions such as Congress or political parties, and that FDR, like TR, had been too eager to concentrate power in himself.

Thus political scientist Theodore Lowi charged that "Roosevelt and the New Deal had put an end to the constitutional regime of balanced and limited government, transforming the American state into a presidency-centered system." Historian Sidney Milkis accused Franklin Roosevelt of bypassing the Democratic party and hence hastening the general decline of the American two-party system. Political theorist Michael Sandel saw FDR as striking a "terrible blow to the republican tradition" by treating

Americans as consumers rather than citizens, by catering to people's material wants and needs rather than elevating them to some higher moral purpose.

How would both Roosevelts have answered such critiques? First, that they brought victories to their parties rather than harming them. Second, that the vital need was to raise the incomes of poor Americans without worrying that this might have hurt their character. And finally, that civic virtue can hardly survive amid poverty and desperation.

But one criticism by the post–New Deal scholars FDR would have found particularly baffling: that he compromised too much with American conservatives, big business, the upper-class. He might have been content to remind his critics that the economic royalists hated him and he welcomed their hatred.

. . .

When Franklin D. Roosevelt was accused of class betrayal, his attackers seemed to assume that such betrayal was the greatest of disloyalties—or indeed that it was the only disloyalty a politician could be guilty of. In fact, humans have many potential disloyalties. People can betray a spouse, a family, a neighborhood, an employer, or an employee. They can be disloyal to their religion, political party, social cause, or ideology, to their community, region, nation—and to their world. And what about disloyalty to oneself, to one's better nature?

People cannot be equally loyal to all the above. They must make choices, even rank their loyalties in a rough set of priorities. Theodore Roosevelt was disloyal to his political power base, the Grand Old Party. FDR was disloyal to his wife and perhaps disloyal to his country, in agreeing to the blueprint for the postwar peace in Europe, as some critics charged.

And Eleanor Roosevelt? She would be disloyal to her class and occasionally to her family as her loyalty to the widening circle of friends she fashioned during the postwar years grew. But above all she would be loyal to the world community—especially to those in all lands who shared her belief in human rights.

She saw the eclipse of the small elite world of privilege mirrored in her husband's family. "The revolution in our social thinking appears, in capsule form, to my eyes, in one family I know well—my own," she wrote in her last book, *Tomorrow Is Now.*

"My mother-in-law belonged to the established world of the last century. She accepted its shibboleths without questioning. To her these things were true.

"When she died, in September 1941, my husband felt strongly this ending of an unshakable world behind him. And yet, he told me, it was probably as well for his mother to leave us at that time. She was immersed in her old world and the new one was alien to her. The adjustment for her would have been impossible.

"To my mother-in-law, for instance, there were certain obligations that she, as a privileged person, must fulfill. She fed the poor, assisted them with money, helped them with medical expenses. This was a form of charity required of her.

"The point of view that she simply could not accept was my husband's. He believed—as I trust most civilized people believe now—that human beings have rights as human beings: a right to a job, a right to education, a right to health protection, a right to human dignity, a right to a chance of fulfillment."

Like her Uncle Ted and her husband Franklin, Eleanor worked for decades to substitute for the privileges of the few the rights and claims of the many, to conceive help for those in need not in terms of the charitable gestures of the few but in terms of government action for tens of millions.

Sometimes History, despite its unpredictable twists and turns, exhibits a breathtaking logic. Not only was Eleanor Roosevelt the inheritor and embodiment of both TR's and FDR's idealistic calls for security, peace, and justice, she went far beyond them. Whereas neither TR nor FDR put First Amendment rights at the top of their own priority lists, Eleanor championed individual civil liberties. Eleanor Roosevelt pursued just the right combination of vision and practicality needed to help establish the United Nations Declaration of Human Rights on a firm foundation.

In the process she became a world politician—indeed, a world leader. She well knew, from her years in Albany and Washington, that it was not easy to persuade parochial politicians to take strong positions for universal human rights. She appealed to the "peoples" of the world, much as Woodrow Wilson had tried to do—unsuccessfully—four decades earlier. Reform must come also from below, from the people, she felt, and not merely from the top. Followers must become leaders.

As a practical politician as well as a moral leader, Eleanor Roosevelt had only to look at her own country to sense the problem of carrying out human rights in an "advanced Western nation," knowing as she did that the task was far more difficult for the peoples of impoverished countries torn by religious, racial, and ideological hatreds. Could the United States serve as a model for these countries? She had only to recall the racial bias in the United States Senate to grasp the difficulty of bringing about real change in her own country, change that FDR had tried to foster by proclaiming the South as America's number-one economic problem, and by trying—unsuccessfully—to oust the South's racist politicians in the Senate.

So she plunged back into the human rights struggle in her own country. And once again she was confronted with Political Man, American style. Her good friend Harry Truman sponsored and backed her in her human rights leadership but then veered into a militant anticommunist stance that violated her ideals of understanding and tolerance among nations. Dwight Eisenhower casually shut her out from her human rights leadership. Enchanted by Adlai Stevenson personally, by his wit and eloquence, she came to see the lack of iron in his leadership, especially on civil rights issues. And although she eventually managed to accept and support John Kennedy, despite his own compromises on McCarthyism, she never fully rose above her antagonism to Kennedy's father and Joe Sr.'s alleged influence on his son.

The former first lady also had to confront the frailties of a political system that had thwarted both her uncle and her husband as well as other political leaders: fragmented government, powerful congressional factions, presidential-congressional deadlock, low-voltage executive agencies. Her special nemesis was the U.S. Senate, holder of the treaty-ratifying power. While she echoed Uncle Theodore's war cry, "I enjoy a good fight," often the fighting was not clear-cut but rather a battle of guerrilla armies of legislative factions and party politicians entrenched in the thicket of government branches, special interests, and popular attitudes. She had to summon all her experience—and her dubious willingness to make compromises—to tread her way warily through these encampments.

Eleanor Roosevelt was a woman of fierce loyalties: to her country, to her Democratic party (which, however, she probably would have deserted, as TR did the GOP, if her party had become an essentially racist party dominated by southern reactionaries), and above all to the moral values set forth in the Declaration of Universal Rights. She was loyal to the oppressed women of the world, and especially to African-Americans in their quest for equality and justice.

The "First Lady of the World," admirers called her—a tribute she would have declined. She was never named Woman of the Year. What she really became in the end was *the* woman leader of the twentieth century.

. . .

Today we take it for granted that such ambitious and politically committed persons as the three Roosevelts would inevitably enter electoral politics. But during the early lives of all three, descending into the vulgar world of office-seeking was simply déclassé. After all, there were genteel alternatives. Why not serve as public leaders in nonelective positions? This is the path that many of their forebears had taken; TR's father had been a fine public servant who had shunned the political process that he believed had degraded democracy. Then too, the two presidents could have taken a completely nonpolitical path such as that of the banker Willard Straight, or the brilliant jurist Oliver Wendell Holmes Jr., or educators like Charles W. Eliot of Harvard, or diplomats in the State Department. Each a gifted writer, all three Roosevelts could have written memorable books or become famous journalists like Walter Lippmann. But they chose the hard rough-and-tumble world of electoral politics—a dangerous arena in which a politician could fail with just one major defeat at the polls.

When the three Roosevelts followed the political path shunned by most members of their class, they faced not only harsh election contests but also the huge opportunities that American politics offered to the ambitious. That all three were remarkably skilled political operators is beyond dispute. Whatever their noble causes, they were never above the brokering and negotiating and all-night horse-trading that characterizes nine-tenths of American politics. Their masterful election campaigning speaks volumes. TR would undoubtedly have won another presidential term if he had run in 1908; FDR and Eleanor won two gubernatorial and four presidential elections; after the war, Eleanor had a mixed track record in politics, winning with Truman in 1948 and Kennedy in 1960, losing with Stevenson twice in the 1950s.

But the crucial test of democratic politics goes beyond brokering deals and even winning elections. It is the test of transformational leadership—the capacity to bring about fundamental change that meets the aching wants and needs, the burning hopes and expectations of the people during critical moments in a nation's history.

At those moments, great changes surge outside government; and the first question is whether public leaders can even cope with the massive changes produced by private-sector leaders. This was the test for the founding fathers in the 1780s and 1790s and for Lincoln and his fellow Republicans in the Civil War era. The vast industrialization of America during TR's time threatened to leave the government impotent while the great decisions were made by tycoons. The terrifying economic collapse of 1929 confronted the federal government with a massive crisis of a sort that the presidency had never confronted—indeed, FDR had noted the "ever-accelerating speed with which social forces were gathering headway" in his plea to modernize the court. The horrendous crushing of human rights under fascism and communism and even capitalism confronted Eleanor Roosevelt and her fellow internationalists with the desperate need to frame a global creed of moral conduct.

Still, in the end, historians ask the challenging question: Who really took the leadership, the politicians or the people? Populists, laborites, city reformers, trustbusters were active long before Theodore Roosevelt's presidency; muckrakers prodded TR on even as he moved to the left in his presidency. Farm laborites, urban radicals, old progressives, Socialists, Communists, and neopopulists like Huey Long were mobilizing grass-roots protests years before FDR's "lurch to the left" in 1935. Wilsonian idealists, human rights defenders, and peace activists had been crusading for a generation before Eleanor Roosevelt's leadership in framing the Universal Declaration.

The genius of the three leaders lay in their recognizing the needs of the people early on, sensing their political mood, mobilizing their support, and then—above all—*acting.* And that is what these three leaders did. By doing so, they transformed American society and reshaped history for the United States and the rest of the world. The impetus and momentum of their leadership carried over through the administrations of John F. Kennedy, Lyndon B. Johnson, and Jimmy Carter—up until the rise of Reagan conservatism. For a hundred years—from 1881, when TR first ran for the New York State Assembly, until 1981, when Carter left office—the three Roosevelts charted the course of progressive reform in America.

. . .

Yes, sometimes History exhibits a breathtaking logic, as it did in knitting these three family members into a century-long fabric of leadership. Sometimes History is the destroyer of leadership, amid a hail of bullets. Sometimes History is the Great Stage Manager, pushing actors forward to the front of the stage, leaving them to the applause or the catcalls of the audience. Above all, History is the Great Moralist, judging leaders according to the values they govern by. Theodore Roosevelt of the Square Deal, Franklin D. Roosevelt of the Four Freedoms, Eleanor Roosevelt of the Universal Declaration would have wished above all to meet this test of history. These three Roosevelts met that test.

NOTES

Prologue

1 *Lincoln's funeral procession:* Carl Sandberg, *Abraham Lincoln: The War Years* (New York: Harcourt, Brace & Co., 1939), 4:396–99.

1 *Theodore Sr. and Lincoln:* Carleton Putnam, *Theodore Roosevelt: The Formative Years, 1858–1886* (New York: Charles Scribner's Sons, 1958), 42.

1 *"Once, when I felt . . .":* Theodore Roosevelt, *An Autobiography* (New York: Macmillan Co., 1913), 14.

1 *"But, Mother . . .":* ER, "My Day," 13 January 1953, in *Eleanor Roosevelt's My Day,* David Elmblidge, ed. (New York: Pharos Books, 1991), 3:4.

2 *historians put in antithesis; Lincoln was "stirred . . .":* TR, "Lincoln the Practical Idealist," 22 September 1905, in *The Works of Theodore Roosevelt,* ed. Hermann Hagedorn (New York: Charles Scribner's Sons, 1926), 11:206, 207.

3 *"beneficiaries of privilege":* "Nationalism and Democracy," in *The Works of Theodore Roosevelt,* 17:104.

3 *"principles of Lincoln . . .":* TR, speech of 31 December 1912.

3 *"Inherited economic power . . .":* FDR, 19 June 1935, quoted in Gustavus Myers, preface to the 1936 edition of *History of the Great American Fortunes* (New York: Modern Library, 1936), 22.

3 *"social revolution":* Eleanor Roosevelt, *Tomorrow Is Now* (New York: Harper & Row, 1963), *What I Hope to Leave Behind: The Essential Essays of Eleanor Roosevelt,* ed. Allida M. Black (Brooklyn, N.Y.: Carlson Publishing, 1995), 184.

3 *myth associating wealth and virtue:* See James MacGregor Burns, *Roosevelt: The Lion and the Fox* (New York: Harcourt Brace Jovanovich, 1956), 240.

One: TR, Reformer or Regular?

8 *"I have become acquainted . . .":* TR to Martha Bulloch Roosevelt, 23 October 1876, in *The Letters of Theodore Roosevelt,* ed. Elting E. Morison (Cambridge, Mass.: Harvard University Press, 1951), 1:19.

8 *TR goes to Harvard:* David McCullough, *Mornings on Horseback* (New York: Simon & Schuster, 1981), 198–99.

8 *"I most sincerely wish . . .":* TR, quoted in Carleton Putnam, *Theodore Roosevelt: The Formative Years, 1858–1886* (New York: Charles Scribner's Sons, 1958), 136.

8 *TR asks mother about his friends' families:* TR to Martha Bulloch Roosevelt, 23 October 1876, in *Letters,* ed. Morison, 1:19.

8 *"did not seem very refined":* TR to Anna Roosevelt, 15 October 1876, in *Letters,* ed. Morison, 1:17.

8 *intermarried clans:* Frederic Cople Jaher, "Nineteenth-Century Elites in Boston and New York," *Journal of Social History,* 6:1 (Fall 1972), 53.

9 *"just as cosy . . .":* TR to Martha Bulloch Roosevelt, 29 September 1876, in *Letters,* ed. Morison, 1:16.

9 *servants:* McCullough, *Mornings on Horseback,* 168.

9 *quite satisfied:* TR to Martha Bulloch Roosevelt, 23 October 1876, in *Letters,* ed. Morison, 1:18.

9 *food at Commons:* TR to Martha Bulloch Roosevelt, 6 October 1876, in ibid., 1:20.

9 *no minorities in TR's class; description of his "set":* McCullough, *Mornings on Horseback,* 199, 203.

9 *"I stand 19th . . .":* TR to Anna Roosevelt, 13 October 1879, *Letters,* ed. Morison, 1:41–42.

9 *"perfectly willing . . .":* Putnam, *Theodore Roosevelt: The Formative Years,* 131n.

10 *"He puzzled us . . ."; "tenacity in argument . . .":* Richard Welling, *As the Twig Is Bent* (New York: G. P. Putnam's Sons, 1942), 32.

10 *"great fun"*: TR to Anna Roosevelt, 13 October 1878, in *Letters,* ed. Morison, 1:35.

10 *"little supper . . ."; Sunday drives:* TR to Corinne Roosevelt, 10 November 1878, in *Letters,* ed. Morison, 1:36, 35.

10 *horse and buggy:* TR to Anna Roosevelt, 29 September 1879, in *Letters,* ed. Morison, 1:41.

10 *"dearest on earth"*: TR, quoted in Edmund Morris, *The Rise of Theodore Roosevelt* (New York: Coward, McCann & Geoghegan, 1979), 95.

10 *"I remember so well . . ."*: TR, Private Diary, Library of Congress.

10 *"as if nothing had happened"*: Quoted in McCullough, *Mornings on Horseback,* 189.

10 *"loyalty and manliness"*: Richard Welling, *As the Twig Is Bent,* 33.

10 *"My Sunday School . . ."*: TR, Private Diaries, quoted in Putnam, *Theodore Roosevelt: The Formative Years,* 142.

11 *"Theodore, you have the mind . . ."*: Corinne Roosevelt Robinson, *My Brother Theodore Roosevelt* (New York: Charles Scribner's Sons, 1921), 50.

11 *skating on Fresh Pond:* Richard Welling, *As the Twig Is Bent,* 31–32.

11 *bellicose TR:* See Putnam, *Theodore Roosevelt: The Formative Years,* 144, 179.

11 *swindler:* TR, Private Diary, 13, 19, and 28 April 1881.

11 *TR shoots neighbor's dog:* TR, Private Diary, 9, 22, 24, 26 August 1878.

11 *"My ordinary companions . . ."*: TR to Edward Sanford Martin, 26 November 1900, in *Letters,* ed. Morison, 2:1443–44. Italics added.

11 *"For the next two years . . ."*: TR, Private Diaries, 1 September 1878, quoted in Putnam, *Theodore Roosevelt: The Formative Years,* 150.

12 *"things livened up"; "Now look here, Roosevelt"; "the real thing"; "oblivious to all . . ."*: Putnam, *Theodore Roosevelt: The Formative Years,* 140, 138.

12 *soles of boots burning:* Putnam, *Theodore Roosevelt: The Formative Years,* 138; Richard Welling, *As the Twig Is Bent,* 34.

12 *presents papers:* Morris, *The Rise of Theodore Roosevelt,* 109.

12 *"I had no more desire . . ."*: TR, *An Autobiography* (New York: Macmillan Co., 1913), 29.

12 *"I cannot possibly conceive . . ."*: TR, Private Diaries, 30 June 1879.

13 *debating at Harvard; "almost no teaching . . ."; "real civilization" and "lawless individualism"; work that lay ahead:* TR, *An Autobiography,* 28, 30–31.

14 *Lee family:* Cleveland Amory, *The Proper Bostonians* (New York: E. P. Dutton & Co., 1947), 20.

14 *"I have been in love . . ."*: TR to Henry Davis Minot, 13 February 1880, in *Letters,* ed. Morison, 1:43.

14 *"Really you mustn't feel melancholy . . ."*: TR to Martha Bulloch Roosevelt, 8 February 1880, in *Letters,* ed. Morison, 1:43.

14 *"Please send my silk hat . . ."*: TR to Martha Bulloch Roosevelt, 11 January 1880, in *Letters,* ed. Morison, 1:42.

14 *Alice Lee, Sara Delano:* See Betty Boyd Caroli, *The Roosevelt Women* (New York: Basic Books, 1998).

14 *"never took his eyes off her . . ."*: Rita H. Kleeman, *Gracious Lady: The Life of Sara Delano Roosevelt* (New York: D. Appleton-Century Co., 1935), 101.

14 *"I am going to try to help . . ."*: William Roscoe Thayer, *TR: An Intimate Biography* (Boston: Houghton Mifflin Co., 1919), 20.

15 *"the happiest year . . ."*: TR, Private Diary, 31 December 1880.

15 *"Jolly little dinners"*: TR, Private Diary, 13 December 1880.

15 *"I sat between . . ."*: Ibid., 3 December 1880.

15 *"every living individual"*: Ibid., 8 December 1880.

16 *pioneers and revolutionaries; "an old vintage"; a "strange apathy"; "our society was a 'little set'"; "leaving one's card"*: Edith Wharton, *A Backward Glance* (New York: D. Appleton-Century Co., 1934), 55, 5, 95, 79, 61, 93.

16 *"compact" society:* ER, "Women Have Come a Long Way," *Harper's Magazine* 201 (October 1950), in *What I Hope to Leave Behind: The Essential Essays of Eleanor Roosevelt,* Allida M. Black, ed. (Brooklyn, N.Y.: Carlson Publishing, 1995), 275.

16 *Weber's analysis of an elite caste:* Max Weber, "Class, Status, Party," in *Class, Status, and Power,* ed. Reinhard Bendix and Seymour Martin Lipset (Chicago: Free Press, 1953), 71.

16 *labor a "disqualification" for status:* Weber, ibid., 72.

16 *consumption of time "nonproductive":* Thorstein Veblen, "The Theory of the Leisure Class," in *Class, Status, and Power,* ed. Bendix and Lipset, 41–44.

17 *"Society is an occupation . . ."; Ward McAllister, dismayed at their eclipse:* Quoted in Frederic Cople Jaher, "Style and Status: High Society in Late Nineteenth-Century New York," in Frederic Cople Jaher, ed., *The Rich, the Well Born, and the Powerful: Elites and Upper Classes in History* (Urbana, Ill.: University of Illinois Press, 1973), 279, 261, 263.

17 *"the Morrises . . ."; "most refined people . . .":* Putnam, *Theodore Roosevelt: The Formative Years,* 13–14.

17 *crossed paths but did not merge:* Jaher, "Style and Status," 270.

18 *"a sacramental character":* Veblen, "The Theory of the Leisure Class," in Bendix and Lipset, eds., *Class, Status, and Power,* 44.

18 *"a sterile aristocracy":* H. G. Wells, *The Future in America* (New York: Harper & Brothers, 1906), 134.

18 *Higginson and Pepper; Who's Who; Roosevelt, Wharton, Rutherfurd; "The Four Hundred would have fled . . ."; no art, profession, or trade:* Jaher, "Style and Status," 275, 267, 277, 276. 279.

18 *richesse oblige:* Arthur Meier Schlesinger, *New Viewpoints in American History* (New York: Macmillan Co., 1922), 96.

18 *plutocrats shunned fashionable society:* Jaher, "Style and Status," 276.

18 *listed in Social Register:* Jaher, "Nineteenth-Century Elites . . . ," 54.

19 *more philanthropically inclined:* Ibid., 65.

19 *"Gentleman":* TR, quoted in Cleveland Amory, *Who Killed Society?* (New York: Harper & Brothers), 327.

19 *plate glass business:* H. W. Brands, *T.R.: The Last Romantic* (New York: Basic Books, 1997), 5.

19 *"comfortable though not rich":* McCullough, *Mornings on Horseback,* 205.

19 *TR's biographers (Pringle and Harbaugh); comparative standard:* Edward Pessen, "Social Structure and Politics in American History," *American Historical Review* 87:5 (December 1982), 1296.

20 *"could not and would not endure . . .":* Wharton, *A Backward Glance,* 313.

20 *"Why is it . . .":* TR to Anna Roosevelt, 22 April 1886, in *Letters,* ed. Morison, 1:99.

20 *"To be a man of the world . . .":* TR to Henry Cabot Lodge, 7 February 1886, in *Letters,* ed. Morison, 1:94.

20 *"certainly very unhealthy . . .":* Quoted in Joseph P. Lash, *Love, Eleanor: Eleanor Roosevelt and Her Friends* (Garden City, N.Y.: Doubleday & Co., 1982), 9.

20 *Elliott's short story:* Geoffrey C. Ward, *Before the Trumpet: Young Franklin Roosevelt, 1882–1905* (New York: Harper & Row, 1985), 270, n. 2.

20 *"as much as I enjoy loafing . . .":* TR Sr., February 4, 1862, in McCullough, *Mornings on Horseback,* 28.

20 *"the first American to drive . . .":* TR, quoted in McCullough, *Mornings on Horseback,* 138.

20 *"My father was the best. . .":* TR, *An Autobiography,* 12.

21 *Sunday evenings at Newsboys' Lodging House:* Corinne Roosevelt Robinson, *My Brother Theodore Roosevelt,* 5.

21 *TR meets Governor Brady:* See Corinne Roosevelt Robinson, *My Brother Theodore Roosevelt,* 6; and Theodore Roosevelt, *An Autobiography,* 13.

21 *"It has been a pathetic experience . . .":* See Frederic Cople Jaher, *Doubters and Dissenters: Cataclysmic Thought in America, 1885–1918* (New York: Free Press of Glencoe, 1964), 144–45.

21 *"money-getters and traders":* Arthur M. Schlesinger Jr., *The Vital Center: The Politics of Freedom* (Boston: Houghton Mifflin Co., 1949), 19.

21 *"Fastidiousness":* Jaher, *Doubters and Dissenters,* 150.

21 *Henry Adams's anti-Semitism; takes refuge in the Middle Ages:* Jaher, *Doubters and Dissenters,* 152, 155.

21 *upper-crust men turn to politics; "Not all men of a certain class . . .":* Gerald W. McFarland, "The New York Mugwumps of 1884: A Profile," *Political Science Quarterly* 78:2 (1963), 41, 44.

22 *"theory that any class of men . . .":* Dixon Ryan Fox, "New York Becomes a Democracy," in Alexander C. Flick, ed., *History of the State of New York,* quoted in Pessen, "Social Structure and Politics in American History," 1312.

22 *"aristocratic revolt . . .":* Schlesinger, *The Vital Center,* 19.

22 *Republican Mugwumps refuse party loyalty:* Michael E. McGerr, *The Decline of Popular Politics: The American North, 1865–1928* (New York: Oxford University Press, 1986), 54–55.

22 *"We want a national set . . .":* Geoffrey Blodgett, "Reform Thought and the Genteel Tradition," in H. Wayne Morgan, ed., *The Gilded Age* (Syracuse, N.Y.: Syracuse University Press, 1970), 57.

22 *Curtis and Storey; "an organized class":* McGerr, *The Decline of Popular Politics,* 53.

22 *"We want a government . . .":* Carl Schurz, quoted in Eric F. Goldman, *Rendezvous with Destiny* (New York: Alfred A. Knopf, 1952), 24.

22 *"an ignorant proletariat . . .":* Francis Parkman, quoted in Stanley P. Caine, "Origins of Progressivism," in Lewis Gould, ed., *The Progressive Era* (Syracuse, N.Y.: Syracuse University Press, 1974), 19.

23 *Boss Tweed; "good to the poor":* Goldman, *Rendezvous with Destiny,* 13–14.

23 *Mugwumps and injustices of Gilded Age:* Richard Hofstadter, *The Age of Reform: From Bryan to F.D.R.* (New York: Alfred A. Knopf, 1959), 142.

23 *government by the elite:* Jaher, *Doubters and Dissenters,* 142.

23 *Parkman on limiting suffrage;* New York Times: McGerr, *The Decline of Popular Politics,* 46–47.

23 *board of finance idea; "business practices":* Ibid., 49, 65.

23 *"corporative administration . . .":* Martin J. Schiesl, *The Politics of Efficiency: Municipal Administration and Reform in America, 1800–1920* (Berkeley, Calif.: University of California Press, 1977), 8.

23 *Theodore Roosevelt Sr. supports Tilden Commission:* McGerr, *The Decline of Popular Politics,* 49–50.

24 *"oligarchy of wealth" and rest of reform agenda:* Ibid., 50, 43.

24 *occasional fringe rebellions;* Brooklyn Daily Eagle; *Mugwumps ridicule Eliot; "disappointed" Americans:* Blodgett, "Reform Thought and the Genteel Tradition," 64, 73–74, 56, 72.

24 *"Almost immediately after leaving Harvard . . .":* TR, *An Autobiography,* 62.

24 *"Every moment of my time" . . . :* TR, Private Diary, 6 January 1881.

24 *going to Morton Hall:* TR, Private Diary, 15 March 1879, quoted in Morris, *The Rise of Theodore Roosevelt,* 142.

25 *"merely meant that the people I knew . . .":* TR, *An Autobiography,* 63.

25 *"men of cultivated taste"* and *"clubs of social pretension":* Ibid.

25 *Max Weber:* Quoted in E. Digby Baltzell, *The Protestant Establishment: Aristocracy and Caste in America* (New York: Random House, 1964), 19.

25 *"no distinction of class . . .":* Woodrow Wilson, *The New Freedom: A Call for the Emancipation of the Generous Energies of a People* (Garden City, N.Y.: Doubleday, Page & Co., 1913), 15.

25 *"companionable and clubable"; "qualities as gentlemen . . .":* Baltzell, *The Protestant Establishment,* 14.

25 *Max Weber on clubs:* Weber, "Class, Status, Party," in Bendix and Lipset, eds., *Class, Status, and Power,* 74.

26 *"lack of interest . . .":* TR speaks to press, 9 October 1882, in *Letters,* ed. Morison, 1:57n.

26 *"People of means . . .":* TR, 1885, quoted in Schiesl, *The Politics of Efficiency* (Berkeley, Calif.: University of California Press, 1977), 10.

26 *"petty"; "degeneration . . .":* TR to Edward Sandford Martin, 30 July 1903, in *Letters,* ed. Morison, 3:536.

26 *Atlantic Monthly article:* TR, "The College Graduate and Public Life," 1890, in *The Works of Theodore Roosevelt,* ed. Hermann Hagedorn (New York: Charles Scribner's Sons, 1926), 13:36–46.

26 *"administer their offices . . .":* Quoted in Schiesl, *The Politics of Efficiency,* 13; Richard Welling, *As the Twig Is Bent,* 41.

26 *"instinct of political realism":* Schlesinger, *The Vital Center,* 19.

26 *"In good city districts . . .":* TR to James Bryce, 5 February 1888, in *Letters,* ed. Morison, 1:138.

27 *"who are sometimes rough . . .":* TR, "Morality and Efficiency" [July 1894], in Theodore Roosevelt, *American Ideals and Other Essays, Social and Political* (New York: G. P. Putnam's Sons, 1897), 38.

27 *"When I went into politics . . .":* TR, *An Autobiography,* 68.

27 *conspicuously, histrionically masculine:* Bruce Miroff, *Icons of Democracy: American Leaders as Heroes, Aristocrats, Dissenters, and Democrats* (New York: Basic Books, 1993), 161ff.

27 *"strenuous" life:* Arthur Schlesinger Jr., *The Vital Center,* 21.

27 *"Such words as national honor . . ."; "Thrift and industry"*: TR, "American Ideals" [February 1894], in Theodore Roosevelt, *American Ideals,* 12–13.

27 *a knight politician:* TR, "Morality and Efficiency" [July 1894], in Theodore Roosevelt, *American Ideals,* 43.

27 *synthesis of statesman and politician:* Miroff, *Icons of Democracy,* 175.

28 *"social rallying point . . ."; "racing stable":* TR, "Machine Politics in New York City" [November 1886], in Theodore Roosevelt, *American Ideals,* 119–20, 123.

28 *Murray gets TR nominated to Assembly:* William Henry Harbaugh, *Power and Responsibility: The Life and Times of Theodore Roosevelt* (Farrar, Straus & Cudahy, 1961), 18–19. See also Putnam, *Theodore Roosevelt: The Formative Years,* 241–49.

28 *independent in municipal matters:* TR, Private Diary, 4 November 1881.

29 *"We have been . . .":* TR to Francis Markoe Scott, 30 October 1884, in *Letters,* ed. Morison, 1:84–85.

29 *"Neither Joe Murray nor I . . .":* TR, *An Autobiography,* 69.

29 *"bitterly opposed":* TR, Private Diary, November 22, 1881.

29 *"my friends are standing by me":* TR, Private Diary, November 26, 1881.

29 New York Times: Morris, *The Rise of Theodore Roosevelt,* 152.

29 *"Too true! . . .":* TR to Charles Grenfill Washburn, 10 November 1881, in *Letters,* ed. Morison, 1:55.

29 *support of family friends; TR's gratitude:* David McCullough, *Mornings on Horseback,* 252–53.

30 *positive response to TR's new position:* William H. Harbaugh, *Power and Responsibility,* 19.

30 *"dude":* Frederic Cople Jaher, "Style and Status: High Society in Late Nineteenth-Century New York," 267.

30 *"His hair was parted . . .":* Quoted in Morris, *The Rise of Theodore Roosevelt,* 161–62. He cites *Kansas City Star,* 12 February 1922.

30 *"There are some twenty-five Irish Democrats . . .":* TR, *Letters,* Appendix 1, Diary of Five Months in the New York Legislature, entry of 12 January 1882, 2:1470.

30 *negative view of Republican members: Letters,* ed. Morison, 2:1469–73.

30 *liked most of his "fellow members . . .":* TR, Private Diary, 10 January 1882.

30 *six-mile spin and barroom brawl: Chicago Press,* 9 May 1895, Reel 454, TR Papers, Library of Congress.

31 *allies had to "sit on his coattails":* Quoted in Morris, *The Rise of Theodore Roosevelt,* 170.

31 *"that most dangerous . . .": New York World,* 3 March 1883, quoted in Howard Lawrence Hurwitz, *Theodore Roosevelt and Labor in New York State, 1880–1900* (New York: Columbia University Press, 1943), 263.

31 New York Sun *and* Harper's Weekly: Quoted by H. W. Brands, *T.R.: The Last Romantic,* 137.

31 *"It was contrary to the principles of political economy . . .":* TR, *An Autobiography,* 88.

32 *Cigarmakers' Union bill:* TR, *An Autobiography,* 88–91.

32 *"must not be deprived of their liberty":* TR, editorial in the *Outlook* for 24 September 1910, in Theodore Roosevelt, *The New Nationalism* (New York: Outlook Co., 1911), 247.

32 *designed to weaken Tammany control: Letters,* ed. Morison, 1:65n.

32 New York Times: Quoted in Brands, *T.R., The Last Romantic,* 137.

32 *"tide of corruption"; support of city's leaders: Letters,* ed. Morison, 1:58n.

33 *conversation with family friend; Tenement Cigar Case; would take more "to shake me out":* TR, *An Autobiography,* 85–86, 88–92, 90.

33 *"wealthy criminal class":* TR, quoted in *Albany Argus,* 3 March 1883.

33 *"The light has gone out . . .":* TR, Private Diary, 14 February 1884.

33 *"She was beautiful . . .":* TR, memorial on the death of his first wife, in Wayne Andrews, ed., *The Autobiography of Theodore Roosevelt* (*Supplemented with Other Writings*) (New York: Charles Scribner's Sons, 1958), 24.

33 *"I think I should go mad . . .":* TR to Carl Schurz, 21 February 1884, in *Letters,* ed. Morison, 1:66.

34 *single-issue third parties:* James MacGregor Burns, *The Workshop of Democracy* (New York: Vintage Books, 1985), 208.

35 *corrupt machine politician:* McGerr, *The Decline of Popular Politics,* 58.

35 *"an overwhelming rout":* TR to Anna Roosevelt, 8 June 1884, in *Letters,* ed. Morison, 1:70.

35 *"We can take part in no bolt"*: TR to Henry Cabot Lodge, 12 August 1884, in *Letters,* ed. Morison, 1:77.

35 *"Republican by inheritance and education"*: *Boston Herald* interview, in Morris, *The Rise of Theodore Roosevelt,* 280.

35 *"scorn and contempt . . ."*: TR to Henry Cabot Lodge, 24 August 1884, in *Letters,* ed. Morison, 1:80.

35 *TR's second marriage:* See Morris, *The Rise of Theodore Roosevelt,* 313–14, 359–60, 368. He cites Sylvia Jukes Morris, *Edith Kermit Carow Roosevelt* (then in ms.).

37 *"a millionaires' meeting"; "industrial slavery"; "to prevent the strong . . ."*: Morris, *The Rise of Theodore Roosevelt,* 348, 351; he cites Alexander De Alva, *A Political History of New York State,* 4:71.

37 *"radical reformer"*: Morris, *The Rise of Theodore Roosevelt,* 353.

37 *"capacity for steady, individual self-help . . ."*: *New York Star,* 28 October 1886.

37 *"prevented those of us whose instincts . . ."*: TR, *An Autobiography,* 87–88.

37 *"the worst capitalist . . ."*: TR, "Our Poorer Brother," 1897, in *The Works of Theodore Roosevelt,* ed. Hagedorn, 13:160.

37 *fair-minded Hewitt:* Allan Nevins, *Abram S. Hewitt* (New York: Harper & Brothers, 1935).

37 *TR disposes of the 1886 mayoral campaign:* TR, *An Autobiography,* 144.

38 *"I would like above all things . . ."*: TR to Henry Cabot Lodge, 5 March 1889, in *Letters,* ed. Morison, 1:154.

38 *class in TR's biography of Morris:* Theodore Roosevelt, *Gouverneur Morris* (Boston: Houghton Mifflin, 1888), 9–19.

39 *"As long as I was responsible . . ."*: TR to Henry Cabot Lodge, 29 June 1889, in *Letters,* ed. Morison, 1:167.

39 *"Here I am back . . ."*: TR to Henry Cabot Lodge, 22 July 1891, in *Letters,* ed. Morison, 1:256.

39 *Blum pointed out:* John Morton Blum, *The Republican Roosevelt* (New York: Atheneum Publishers, 1972), 18.

39 *a warm welcome:* See Morris, *The Rise of Theodore Roosevelt,* 711; and Blum, *The Republican Roosevelt,* 56. See also *The Education of Henry Adams* (Houghton Mifflin Co., 1918), 332.

39 *TR like an express locomotive:* Morris, *The Rise of Theodore Roosevelt,* 473. (Morris gives no reference for this but notes that Henry Adams, among others, made the comparison.)

39 *"I do wish the President . . ."*: TR to Henry Cabot Lodge, 28 July 1889, in *Letters,* ed. Morison, 1:175.

40 *"My career is over . . ."*: TR to Henry Cabot Lodge, 29 June 1891, in *Letters,* ed. Morison, 1:254.

40 *1894 mayoralty race:* TR to Anna Roosevelt, 22 October 1894, in *Letters,* ed. Morison, 1:407.

40 *"useful citizen"*: TR to Anna Roosevelt Cowles, 25 February 1896, in *Letters,* ed. Morison, 1:516.

40 *"the only thing I am afraid of . . ."*: TR to Anna Roosevelt Cowles, 9 March 1896, in *Letters,* ed. Morison, 1:520.

40 *"still ignorant . . ."*: TR, *An Autobiography,* 186.

40 *"English-speaking race"*: TR to Henry White, 30 March 1896, in *Letters,* ed. Morison, 1:523.

40 *no place for racial discrimination:* TR, *Thomas Hart Benton* (1887), in *The Works of Theodore Roosevelt,* ed. Hagedorn, 7:79ff.

40 *mingling with diverse people:* Gary Gerstle, "Theodore Roosevelt and the Divided Character of American Nationalism," *Journal of American History* 86:3 (December 1999), 1300ff.

41 *"I think it a good thing . . ."*: TR to Anna Roosevelt, 14 April 1895, in *Letters,* ed. Morison, 1:442.

42 *headlines:* May and June 1895, Reel 454, TR Papers, Library of Congress.

42 *Napoleon: New York Journal,* 8 June 1895, Reel 454, TR Papers, Library of Congress.

42 *"mischief"*: TR, *An Autobiography,* 188.

42 *social reform, fair play, and decency:* TR, *An Autobiography,* 220.

43 *"a specially notable figure . . ."*: *The Outlook,* June 1895, Reel 454, TR Papers, Library of Congress.

43 *"one of the first young men . . ."*: *The Basis,* 11 May 1895, Reel 454, TR Papers, Library of Congress.

43 *Bradley Martin ball:* TR to Anna Roosevelt Cowles, 31 January 1897, in *Letters,* ed. Morison, 1:577.

43 *Bradley Martins flee to England:* Lloyd Morris, *Incredible New York: High Life and Low Life of the Last Hundred Years* (New York: Random House, 1951), 242.

44 *TR's reforms on Police Board:* See Jay Stuart Berman, *Police Administration and Progressive Reform: Theodore Roosevelt as Police Commissioner of New York* (Westport, Conn: Greenwood Press, 1987).

44 *"Are you working . . . think of it"*: Lincoln Steffens, *Autobiography*, quoted in H. Paul Jeffers, *Commissioner Roosevelt: The Story of Theodore Roosevelt and the New York City Police, 1895–1897* (New York: John Wiley & Sons, 1994), 158–59.

44 *"violated with impunity . . ."*: TR, reported in *The New York Times*, quoted in Morris, *The Rise of Theodore Roosevelt*, 503.

44 *"shrieking with rage"*: TR to Henry Cabot Lodge, 20 July 1895, in *Letters*, ed. Morison, 1:469.

44 *"If I were asked . . ."*: Quoted in Morris, *The Rise of Theodore Roosevelt*, 513. He cites unpublished letter, 5 November 1895, in Theodore Roosevelt Birthplace, New York City.

45 *"A dangerous and ominous jingo"*: Leon Edel, *Henry James: The Master: 1901–1916* (J. B. Lippincott Co., 1972), 265.

45 *"ferocious jingo"*: TR to Anna Roosevelt Cowles, 9 March 1896, in *Letters*, ed. Morison, 1:520.

45 *"Life is strife"*: *Chicago Tribune*, 23 February 1895, quoted in Morris, *The Rise of Theodore Roosevelt*, 526.

45 *"cult is nonvirility"*: TR to Henry Cabot Lodge, 19 January 1896, in *Letters*, ed. Morison, 1:509.

45 *"servile in their dread . . ."*: TR to Anna Roosevelt Cowles, 26 January 1896, in *Letters*, ed. Morison, 1:510.

45 *"flabby" and "timid"*: TR to Henry Cabot Lodge, 29 April 1896, in *Letters*, ed. Morison, 1:536–37.

45 *"grimy"*: TR to Anna Roosevelt Cowles, 28 June 1896, in *Letters*, ed. Morison, 1:545.

45 *"harassing"*: TR to Henry White, 30 March 1896, in *Letters*, ed. Morison, 1:523.

45 *"stormy"*: TR to Henry Cabot Lodge, 6 May 1896, in *Letters*, ed. Morison, 1:537.

45 *McKinley might fail in a crisis:* TR to Anna Roosevelt Cowles, 20 June 1896, in *Letters*, ed. Morison, 1:543.

45 *Bryan and bimetalism:* See Daniel J. Boorstin, ed., *An American Primer* (Chicago: University of Chicago Press, 1966), vol. 2, 573ff., for text of Bryan's speech.

45 *"You shall not crucify . . ."*: Bryan, quoted in John Milton Cooper, *Pivotal Decades: The United States, 1900–1920* (New York: W. W. Norton & Co., 1990), 20.

45 *"semianarchistic . . ."*: TR to Cecil Spring Rice, 5 August 1896, in *Letters*, ed. Morison, 1:556.

46 *"the leaders of the Terror . . ."*: TR, "The Menace of the Demagogue," speech of 15 Octrober 1896, in *The Works of Theodore Roosevelt*, ed. Hagedorn, 14:264–65.

46 *resemblance to Jefferson:* TR to Cecil Arthur Spring Rice, 5 August 1896, in *Letters*, ed. Morison, 1:553.

46 *"genuine fanaticism"*: TR to Anna Roosevelt Cowles, 26 July 1896, in *Letters*, ed. Morison, 1:550. See also TR to Cecil Arthur Spring Rice, 8 October 1896, in *Letters*, 1:562.

46 *"greatest crisis"*: TR to Anna Roosevelt Cowles, 8 November 1896, in *Letters*, ed. Morison, 1:566.

46 *Mahan; larger and more powerful navy:* H. W. Brands, *T.R.: The Last Romantic*, 236–37.

46 *"intensely interested"*: TR to Anna Roosevelt Cowles, 21 February 1897, in *Letters*, ed. Morison, 1:582.

46 *first-class navy:* TR to William Sheffield Cowles, 5 April 1896, in *Letters*, ed. Morison, 1:524.

46 *"half a dozen battleships"*: TR to Anna Roosevelt Cowles, 1 March 1896, in *Letters*, ed. Morison, 1:519.

46 *"futile sentimentalists"*: TR to Henry Cabot Lodge, 29 April 1896, in *Letters*, ed. Morison, 1:535.

46 *"deep and damnable alliance . . ."*: *The Autobiography of William Allen White* (New York: Macmillan Co., 1946), 297–98.

47 *"all the great masterful races . . ."*: TR, "Washington's Forgotten Maxim," address of June 1896 to Naval War College, in *The Works of Theodore Roosevelt*, ed. Hagedorn, 13:184.

47 *"poured into my heart . . ."*: White, *Autobiography*, 297.

48 *TR cablegram to Dewey (25 February 1898):* Quoted in Joseph Bucklin Bishop, *Theodore Roosevelt and His Time* (New York: Charles Scribner's Sons, 1920), 1:95. See also, *Letters*, ed. Morison, 1:784–85.

48 *"McKinley has no more backbone . . ."*: Quoted in Henry F. Pringle, *Theodore Roosevelt: A Biography* (Harcourt, Brace & Co., 1931), 178.

48 *"I shall be useless on a ship"*: TR to Robert Bacon, 5 April 1898, in *Letters*, ed. Morison, 2:812.

49 *"What on earth is this report . . ."*: Quoted in Morris, *The Rise of Theodore Roosevelt*, 612.

49 *"Are you afraid to stand up . . . ?"*: TR, *The Works of Theodore Roosevelt*, ed. Hagedorn, 12:306.

49 *"the most famous man in America"*: Morris, *The Rise of Theodore Roosevelt*, 665. He cites *New York World*, 28 August 1898.

49 *five thousand or more:* Richard Morris, ed., *Encyclopedia of American History* (New York: Harper & Row, 1982), 344.

49 *Rough Riders have heaviest loss:* Morris, *The Rise of Theodore Roosevelt*. For a general account, see also Anastasio Azoy, *Charge! The Story of the Battle of San Juan Hill* (New York: Longmans, Green, 1961).

50 *"overjoyed"*: TR to Gustav Adolf Von Goetzen, 7 February 1899, in *Letters,* ed. Morison, 2:935.

50 *"The good people in New York . . ."*: TR to Henry Cabot Lodge, 31 July 1898, in *Letters,* ed. Morison, 2:863.

51 *Platt chooses TR over Black:* G. Wallace Chessman, *Theodore Roosevelt and the Politics of Power* (Boston: Little, Brown & Co., 1969), 11–12, 16.

51 *Jewish Republican club:* TR to Lemuel Ely Quigg, 21 October 1898, in *Letters,* 2:887n.

51 *"make war on Mr. Platt . . ."*: Quoted in Morris, *The Rise of Theodore Roosevelt*, 668.

51 *"consult with me and other party leaders . . ."*: Quoted in Harbaugh, *Power and Responsibility*, 109.

51 *"It seems to me . . ."*: TR to John Jay Chapman, 22 September 1898, in *Letters,* ed. Morison, 2:877.

52 *"The speech was nothing . . ."*: Billy O'Neil, quoted in *Letters,* ed. Morison, 2:885n.

52 *"I have played it with bull luck . . ."*: TR to Cecil Arthur Spring Rice, 25 November 1898, in *Letters,* ed. Morison, 2:888.

52 *"we could do no greater harm . . ."*: TR to Sherman S. Rogers, 1 February 1899, in *Letters,* ed. Morison, 2:928.

52 *TR on unnatural relationship of business and politics:* TR, *An Autobiography*, 289.

53 *franchises and Marshall:* TR, Gubernatorial Message, "The Taxation of Franchises," 22 May 1899, in *The Roosevelt Policy: Speeches, Letters, and State Papers,* ed. William Griffith (New York: Current Literature Publishing Co., 1919), 1:3–6.

53 *"I had heard from a good many sources . . ."*: quoted in Harbaugh, *Power and Responsibility*, 115.

53 *"to my very great surprise . . ."*: Ibid., 117.

53 *"improper corporate influence . . ."*: Ibid.

53 *"communistic"*: *Brooklyn Daily Eagle,* quoted in Harbaugh, *Power and Responsibility*, 119.

54 *city water supply:* Howard Lawrence Hurwitz, *Theodore Roosevelt and Labor in New York State,* 265.

54 *teachers "responsible for the upbringing . . ."*: TR, quoted in William Henry Harbaugh, *The Life and Times of Theodore Roosevelt,* rev. ed. (New York: Oxford University Press, 1975), 121.

54 *inheritance taxes:* TR, Gubernatorial Message, 3 January 1900, in *The Roosevelt Policy,* ed. Griffith, 1:11.

54 *"As for my impulsiveness . . ."*: TR to Lemuel Ely Quigg, 21 February 1900, in *Letters,* ed. Morison, 2:1200.

54 *"many of the worst and most dangerous laws"*: TR, Gubernatorial Message, 3 January 1900, in *The Roosevelt Policy,* ed. Griffith, 1:18.

54 *"generous indignation . . . callous disregard"*; *"emotional side"*: TR, Gubernatorial Message, 3 January 1900, in *The Roosevelt Policy,* ed. Griffith, 1:21, 22, 20.

55 *"has a harder time than the man . . ."*; *be a mother:* TR to Helen Kendrick Johnson, 10 January 1899, in *Letters,* ed. Morison, 2:904–6.

55 *"odious aristocracy"*: Susan B. Anthony, quoted in Arthur Meier Schlesinger, *New Viewpoints in American History* (New York: Macmillan Co., 1922), 98.

55 *"You have evidently entirely failed . . ."*: TR to Percy S. Landsowne, 7 December 1900, in *Letters,* ed. Morison, 2:1455.

55 *removing the head of "Lunacy Commission":* TR to Peter Manuel Wise, 7 December 1900, in *Letters,* ed. Morison, 2:1458; TR to Philip Bathell Stewart, 31 December 1900, in *Letters,* 2:1464.

55 *"highest type"*: TR to Thomas Collier Platt, 13 August 1900, in *Letters,* ed. Morison, 2:1382.

55 *"You are not entitled . . ."*: Frank Davis Ashburn, *Peabody of Groton* (New York: Coward-McCann, 1944), 341.

56 *"After supper tonight . . ."*: FDR to his parents, 4 June 1897, in *FDR: His Personal Letters, Early Years,* ed. Elliott Roosevelt (Duell, Sloan & Pearce, 1947–1950), 110; cited elsewhere in this

chapter as *FDR Letters.* See also Frank Freidel, *Franklin D. Roosevelt: The Apprenticeship* (Boston: Little, Brown & Co., 1952), 46.

56 *"wild with excitement"*: Ward, *Before the Trumpet: Young Franklin Roosevelt,* 195.

56 *"Please don't make any more arrangements . . .":* FDR to his parents, 28 May 1897, *FDR Letters, Early Years,* 105.

56 *"There were lovely mornings on horseback . . .":* McCullough, *Mornings on Horseback,* 142–43.

56 *life at "Tranquility":* Morison, *Chronology of the Governorship,* 1498–1504.

57 *"meeting room of a board of directors"; "great games there":* TR to Winthrop Chanler, 23 March 1899, in *Letters,* ed. Morison, 2:970.

57 *"The fact is that the little fellow . . .":* TR to Alexander Lambert, 29 March 1898, in *Letters,* ed. Morison, 2:804.

57 *"queer little fellow . . .":* TR to Tiffany & Co., enclosing letter to "My dear Sir or Madam," 2 February 1899, in *Letters,* ed. Morison, 2:929.

57 *"I want results!":* TR to Seth Low, 3 August 1900, in *Letters,* ed. Morison, 2:1374.

58 *"Don't any of you realize . . . ?":* Margaret Leech, *In the Days of McKinley* (Harper & Brothers, 1959), 537; also see Arthur Schlesinger Jr., *The Vital Center,* 22.

58 *"big-monied men with whom . . .":* Quoted in Harbaugh, *Power and Responsibility,* 133.

58 *"We stand on the threshold. . .":* TR, "The Administration of William McKinley," Speech of 21 June 1900, in *The Works of Theodore Roosevelt,* ed. Hagedorn, 14:345.

58 *"make a first-class lover . . .":* Quoted in Morris, *The Rise of Theodore Roosevelt,* 728. He cites *New York World,* 22 June 1900.

58 *"corporate interests of the United States . . .":* Quoted in Harbaugh, *Power and Responsibility,* 139.

59 *"most righteous foreign war . . .":* Ibid., 140.

59 *"It is of vital importance . . .":* TR to Winthrop Chanler, 26 July 1900, in *Letters,* 2:1364.

59 *"McRoosey and Kinvelt!":* H. Wayne Morgan, *William McKinley and His America* (Syracuse, N.Y.: Syracuse University Press, 1963), illustration following p. 116.

Two: Reform in a Silk Hat

61 *TR reassured about McKinley:* TR to Cummins, 7 September 1901, in *The Letters of Theodore Roosevelt,* ed. Elting E. Morison (Cambridge, Mass.: Harvard University Press, 1951), 3:140.

61 *TR learns of assassination:* Hermann Hagedorn, *The Roosevelt Family of Sagamore Hill* (New York: Macmillan Co., 1954), 116–18.

61 *"I told William McKinley . . .":* Mark Hanna, quoted in Mark Sullivan, *Our Times: America Finding Herself* (New York: Charles Scribner's Sons, 1927), 2:380.

61 *TR plans to carry on McKinley policies:* TR to Maria Longworth Storer, 4 October 1901, in *Letters,* ed. Morison, 3:158; TR to Henry Lee Higginson, 30 November 1901, in *Letters,* ed. Morison, 3:203.

61 *"It is a dreadful thing. . .":* TR to Henry Cabot Lodge, 23 September 1901, in *Letters,* ed. Morison, 3:150.

61 *TR encouraging dangerous ideas:* See TR to Lucius Nathan Littauer, 24 October 1901, in *Letters,* ed. Morison, 3:181n.

62 *TR on southern indignation:* Ibid., 3:181.

62 *"idiot or vicious Bourbon element . . .":* TR to Curtis Guild, 28 October 1901, in *Letters,* ed. Morison, 3:184.

62 *"I am very glad . . .":* TR to Albion Winegar Tourgée, 8 November 1901, in *Letters,* ed. Morison, 3:190.

62 *"I would not lose . . .":* TR to Lucius Nathan Littauer, 24 October 1901, in *Letters,* ed. Morison, 3:181.

62 *Booker T. Washington:* See Lewis L. Gould, *The Presidency of Theodore Roosevelt* (Lawrence, Kans.: University Press of Kansas, 1991), 22.

62 *TR never invites another black man:* TR to Littauer, in *Letters,* 3:181n.

62 *"social recognition":* TR to John Hay, 18 September 1902, in *Letters,* ed. Morison, 3:326.

62 *government intervention:* See John M. Blum, "Theodore Roosevelt: The Years of Decision,"
in *Letters,* ed. Morison, Appendix, 2:1493.

62 *"Porcellian man":* TR to Richard Derby, 29 May 1901, in *Letters,* ed. Morison, 3:80.

62 *TR in sympathy with McKinley:* William Henry Harbaugh, *Power and Responsibility: The Life
and Times of Theodore Roosevelt* (New York: Farrar, Straus & Cudahy, 1961), 149–50. He quotes
The New York Times, the *Tribune,* and the *Sun.*

63 *depression, unemployment, and strikes; Coxey:* Stanley P. Caine, "The Origins of Progressivism,"
in Lewis L. Gould, ed., *The Progressive Era* (Syracuse, N.Y.: Syracuse University Press, 1974),
21–22, 24.

64 *Social Gospel movement; Buffalo meeting; emergence of new organizations:* Ibid., 13–14, 31, 26.

64 *tax system . . . public transportation:* Ibid., 28–30.

65 *"But now whin I pick . . .":* Quoted in James MacGregor Burns, *The Workshop of Democracy* (New
York: Vintage Books, 1985), 345; Finley Peter Dunne, "National Housecleaning," in Louis
Filler, ed., *Mr. Dooley: Now and Forever* (Academic Reprints, 1954), 244–45.

65 *writers denouncing societal evils:* Burns, *The Workshop of Democracy,* 347–48.

66 *isolationism vs. role in international affairs:* John Braeman, "Seven Progressives," *Business History
Review* 35:4 (1961), 582.

66 *immigrants and immigration:* Richard Hofstadter, *The Age of Reform: From Bryan to F.D.R.* (New
York: Alfred A. Knopf, 1959), 179.

66 *racism not on agenda:* Gould, ed., *The Progressive Era,* Introduction, 10. See also Thomas K.
McCraw, "The Progressive Legacy," in Ibid., 191–92.

66 *historians suggest discarding terms:* Peter Filene, quoted in David M. Kennedy, "Overview: The
Progressive Era," in *Historian* 37 (1975), 464. See also Gould, *The Progressive Era,* Introduction, 8.

66 *a real movement:* Kennedy, "Overview: The Progressive Era," 465.

66 *sense of moral responsibility:* Hofstadter, *The Age of Reform,* 206.

66 *White on sacrifice, on "quickening sense," on TR:* Hofstadter, *The Age of Reform,* 212, 167, 214.

66 *"possessed a hold . . .":* "The Republicans Under Roosevelt and Taft," in Gould, *The Progressive Era,* 61.

67 *"Teddy was reform in a derby . . .":* Quoted in Eric F. Goldman, *Rendezvous with Destiny* (New
York: Alfred A. Knopf, 1952), 165.

67 *"satellite":* William H. Harbaugh, *The Life and Times of Theodore Roosevelt,* rev. ed. (New York:
Oxford University Press, 1975), 164.

67 *Godkin:* Burns, *The Workshop of Democracy,* 159.

67 *"living in luxury . . .":* Bellamy, *Looking Backward* (Boston: Houghton Mifflin Co., 1898), 8.

67 *"laughing-stock and a menace":* TR, "The College Graduate and Public Life," 1890, in *The
Works of Theodore Roosevelt,* ed. Hermann Hagedorn (New York: Charles Scribner's Sons,
1926), 13:37.

68 *"contempt and anger . . .":* TR to Cecil Arthur Spring-Rice, 3 July 1901, in *Letters,* ed. Morison, 3:107.

68 *"the antics of the Four Hundred . . .":* TR to George Brinton McClellan, 2 August 1905, in *Letters,* ed. Morison, 2:1299.

68 *"Each of us has been able . . .":* TR to Cecil Arthur Spring-Rice, 3 July 1901, in *Letters,* ed. Morison,
3:108.

68 *displacement of old capitalist class:* Henri Pirenne, "Stages in the Social History of Capitalism,"
in Reinhard Bendix and Martin Lipset, eds., *Class, Status, and Power* (Chicago: Free Press,
1953), 501–502.

68 *coal barons et al.:* Arthur Meier Schlesinger, *New Viewpoints in American History* (New York:
Macmillan Co., 1922), 94.

68 *Josiah Strong:* Ibid.

68 *kings had not dreamt of:* Lloyd, quoted in Hofstadter, *The Age of Reform,* 141.

68 *"new privileges and pretensions . . .":* Schlesinger, *New Viewpoints in American History,* 100.

68 *"going as far as we ought . . .":* Theodore Roosevelt, *An Autobiography* (New York: Macmillan
Co., 1913), 88.

69 *"representatives of predatory wealth"*: TR, "Campaign Against Privilege," 31 January 1908, in *The Roosevelt Policy: Speeches, Letters, and State Papers,* ed. William Griffith (New York: Current Literature Publishing Co., 1919), 2:715.

69 *"deep and damnable alliance . . ."*: TR, quoted in Burns, *The Workshop of Democracy,* 329; see also, *The Autobiography of William Allen White* (New York: Macmillan Co., 1946), 297–98.

69 *"property rights against human rights"*: TR, *An Autobiography,* 463.

69 *"bucking bronco"*: H. H. Kohlsaat, *From McKinley to Harding* (New York: Charles Scribner's Sons, 1923), 98.

69 *"I must frankly tell you . . ."*: Quoted in Burns, *The Workshop of Democracy,* 331.

69 *"Go slow"*: Harbaugh, *The Life and Times of Theodore Roosevelt,* 155.

69 *"the first step toward controlling . . ."*: TR, *An Autobiography,* 467.

70 *"overcapitalization"*: Harbaugh, *The Life and Times of Theodore Roosevelt,* revised ed., 155.

70 *violent contrast between rich and poor:* TR, "The Control of Corporations," in *The Works of Theodore Roosevelt,* ed. Hagedorn, 16:63.

70 *"riot of individualistic materialism"*: TR, *An Autobiography,* 462.

70 *J. P. Morgan description:* Burns, *The Workshop of Democracy,* 331.

70 *Morgan bailed out Cleveland administration:* H. W. Brands, *T.R.: The Last Romantic* (New York: Basic Books, 1997), 437.

70 *Morgan indignant:* See Harbaugh, *The Life and Times of Theodore Roosevelt,* 150.

70 *"represents an effort on my part . . ."*: TR to Elihu Root, 5 December 1900, in *Letters,* ed. Morison, 2:1450.

70 *"tremendous whack . . ."*: Jean Strouse, *Morgan: American Financier* (New York: Random House, 1999), 440.

70 *TR-Morgan-Knox talk:* Quoted in Burns, *The Workshop of Democracy,* 332; also, Joseph Bucklin Bishop, *Theodore Roosevelt and His Time* (New York: Charles Scribner's Sons, 1920), 1:184–85.

71 *"swollen fortunes"*: TR, "Legislative Actions and Judicial Decisions," 4 October 1906, in *The Works of Theodore Roosevelt,* ed. Hagedorn, 16:71.

71 *"predatory capitalists"*: TR, "The Puritan Spirit and the Regulation of Corporations," 20 August 1907, in ibid., 16:81.

71 *"Bourbons"*: TR, "Legislative Actions and Judicial Decisions," 4 October 1906, in ibid., 16:73.

71 *"oppose and dread . . ."*: ibid., 16:70.

71 *"protect labor . . . shackle cunning and fraud"*: TR, *An Autobiography,* 464.

71 *not the method but the power:* Ibid., 465.

71 *"the most powerful men in this country . . ."*: TR to George Cortelyou, 11 August 1904, in *Letters,* ed. Morison, 4:886.

71 *government has not yet devised the proper method:* TR, *An Autobiography,* 470.

71 *description of northeastern Pennsylvania:* Jay Parini, *Anthracite Country* (New York: Random House, 1976).

72 *dangers of the mines:* Irving Stone, *Clarence Darrow for the Defense,* quoted by Harbaugh, *The Life and Times of Theodore Rooseevelt,* rev. ed., 167.

72 *salary increases for operators:* Ibid., 168.

72 *"There cannot be two masters . . ."*: Mark Sullivan, *Our Times: America Finding Herself* (New York: Charles Scribner's Sons, 1927), 2:423.

72 *telegram from Seth Low:* Ibid., 2:427.

72 *operators seem recklessly indifferent:* Arthur M. Schaefer, "Theodore Roosevelt's Contribution to the Concept of Presidential Intervention in Labor Disputes," in *Theodore Roosevelt, Many-Sided American,* ed. Natalie A. Naylor, Douglas Brinkley, and John Allen Gable (Interlaken, N.Y.: Heart of the Lakes Publishing, 1992), 214.

72 *"Christian men to whom God . . ."*: Burns, *The Workshop of Democracy,* 333.

72 *newspapers' response to Baer letter:* Sullivan, *Our Times,* 2:427.

73 *"We have come out of the strike . . ."*: TR to Anna Roosevelt, 22 July 1894, in *Letters,* ed. Morison, 1:391.

73 *"wisdom and courage"; "Benedict Arnold":* TR, "American Ideals," 1895, in *American Ideals and Other Essays* (New York: G. P. Putnam's Sons, 1897), 8.

73 *"My men here are hardworking"*: TR to Anna Roosevelt, 15 May 1886, in *Letters,* ed. Morison, 1:100.

73 *engineers, firemen, and pump men:* Harbaugh, *The Life and Times of Theodore Roosevelt,* rev. ed., 268.

73 *Woodrow Wilson:* Ibid., 169.

73 *"I am at my wits' end . . .":* Quoted in ibid., 170.

74 *only one man had behaved:* Ibid., 172.

74 *"the preservation of law and order . . .":* TR to Benjamin Bishop, 18 October 1902, in *Letters,* ed. Morison, 3:356.

74 *the titans forget:* TR to Robert Bacon, J. P. Morgan's partner, 5 October 1902, in *Letters,* ed. Morison, 3:340.

74 *"an attitude of arrogance. . .":* TR to Robert Bacon, 7 October 1902, in *Letters,* ed. Morison, 3:344.

74 *"rights in the matter"*: TR to Winthrop Crane, 22 October 1902, in *Letters,* ed. Morison, 3:362.

74 *"I feel most strongly . . .":* TR to Mark Hanna, 3 October 1902, in *Letters,* ed. Morison, 3:337.

74 *"some constitutional reason . . .":* Harbaugh, *The Life and Times of Theodore Roosevelt,* rev. ed., 176.

74 *Schofield and Quay:* Sullivan, *Our Times,* 2:436; TR, *Autobiography,* 515.

75 *"narrow, bourgeois commercial world"*: TR to Winthrop Crane, 22 October 1902, in *Letters,* ed. Morison, 3:365.

75 *"utter absurdity"*: TR to Winthrop Crane, 22 October 1902, in *Letters,* ed. Morison, 3:366.

75 *"I at last grasped the fact . . .":* TR, quoted by Harbaugh, *The Life and Times of Theodore Roosevelt,* rev. ed., 178.

75 *"nothing that you have ever written . . .":* TR to Finley Peter Dunne, 20 October 1902, *Letters,* ed. Morison, 3:357.

75 *"My dear Mr. Morgan . . .":* TR to J. P. Morgan, 16 October 1902, in *Letters,* ed. Morison, 3:353.

75 *"Now that the strike is settled . . .":* FDR to Sara Delano Roosevelt, 26 October 1902, in *FDR, His Personal Letters, Early Years,* ed. Elliott Roosevelt (New York, Duell, Sloan & Pearce, 1947–1950), 481. Cited hereafter in this chapter as *FDR Letters.*

76 *John F. Kennedy:* James MacGregor Burns, *The Crosswinds of Freedom* (New York: Vintage Books, 1990), 651.

76 *"I am President . . .":* Quoted in Bruce Miroff, *Icons of Democracy: American Leaders as Heroes, Aristocrats, Dissenters, and Democrats* (New York: Basic Books, 1993), 189.

76 *TR and strikes in Arizona and Colorado:* Miroff, *Icons of Democracy,* 189.

76 *"inevitably sympathize with the men . . .":* TR, *An Autobiography,* 518–19.

76 *Roosevelt Corollary:* See David Gerth Hardin, "The Development of the Roosevelt Corollary to the Monroe Doctrine," BA thesis, Williams College Department of History, 1977. See also, Dexter Perkins, *Hands Off: A History of the Monroe Doctrine* (Boston: Little, Brown & Co., 1955).

76 *"If a nation shows. . .":* Harbaugh, *Power and Responsibility,* 194; TR to Elihu Root, 20 May 1904, in *Letters,* ed. Morison, 4:801. The principles of the Roosevelt Corollary were first set forth in a letter by TR to Elihu Root that Root read at a Cuban anniversary dinner in New York. In his annual message to Congress six months later, TR reemphasized them.

76 *"brutal wrongdoing . . .":* *Encyclopedia of American History,* ed. Richard Morris (New York: Harper & Row, 1982), 295.

77 *Britain's abandoned claim:* Henry Kissinger, *Diplomacy* (New York: Simon & Schuster, 1994), 38.

77 *"sophistication matched by no other"*: Kissinger, *Diplomacy,* 41.

78 *"Under no circumstances . . .":* Burns, *The Workshop of Democracy,* 334.

78 *"watch out for me"*: Harbaugh, *The Life and Times of Theodore Roosevelt,* rev. ed., 208.

78 *FDR joins Republican party:* Kenneth S. Davis, *FDR: The Beckoning of Destiny, 1882–1928* (G. P. Putnam's Sons, 1971), 144.

78 *"Last night there was . . .":* FDR to his parents, 31 October 1900, Elliott Roosevelt, ed., *FDR Letters, Early Years,* 430–31.

78 *"My father and grandfather . . .":* FDR, Address at the Jackson Day Dinner, 8 January 1938, in Samuel I. Rosenman, ed., *Public Papers and Addresses of Franklin D. Roosevelt* (New York: Macmillan, 1941), 1938, 38. Cited hereafter in this chapter as *PPA.*

78 *"We think the lover . . .":* TR to ER, 29 November 1904, in Franklin D. Roosevelt Library, Roosevelt family correspondence, Box 20, folder 11. Hereafter cited as FDRL.

79 *"Only some utterly unforeseen . . .":* TR to ER, 19 December 1904, in FDRL, Roosevelt family correspondence, Box 20, folder 11.

79 *"Well, Franklin . . .":* Quoted in Nathan Miller, *Theodore Roosevelt: A Life* (New York: William Morrow & Co., 1992), 410.

80 *"carried their way of life around them . . .":* James MacGregor Burns, *Roosevelt: The Lion and the Fox* (New York: Harcourt Brace Jovanovich, 1956), 7.

81 *dinner invitation from Mrs. Vanderbilt:* William D. Hassett, *Off the Record with F.D.R., 1942–1945* (New Brunswick, N.J.: Rutgers University Press, 1958), 124.

81 *"had already formed . . .":* Eleanor Roosevelt, *This I Remember* (New York: Harper and Brothers, 1949), 43.

82 *FDR's room decorations at Harvard:* Geoffrey C. Ward, *Before the Trumpet: Young Franklin Roosevelt, 1882–1905* (New York: Harper & Row, 1985), 214.

82 *FDR's reaction to rejection by Porcellian:* Quoted in Ward, *Before the Trumpet*, 236; Frank Freidel, *Franklin D. Roosevelt: The Apprenticeship* (Boston: Little, Brown & Co., 1952), 57.

83 *FDR's courses and grades at Harvard:* Freidel, *Franklin D. Roosevelt: The Apprenticeship*, 54, 58n., 60, 60n.

83 *"like an electric lamp . . .":* Quoted in Davis, *FDR: The Beckoning of Destiny*, 140. He cites L. L. Cowperthwaite, "Franklin D. Roosevelt at Harvard,"*Quarterly Journal of Speech* 38 (February 1952), 37–41.

83 *Davis, on FDR's mind:* Davis, *FDR: The Beckoning of Destiny*, 140.

84 *"Dearest Mama . . .":* FDR to Sara Delano Roosevelt, 12 January 1904, in *F.D.R.: His Personal Letters, The Early Years*, ed. Elliott Roosevelt, 523.

84 *FDR's "geniality"; "a kind of frictionless command":* Quoted in Davis, *FDR: The Beckoning of Destiny*, 163; he cites *Harvard Alumni Bulletin*, 23 April 1928. Also quoted in Freidel, *Franklin D. Roosevelt: The Apprenticeship*, 66.

84 *research help from his mother:* FDR to Sara Delano Roosevelt, *FDR Letters, Early Years*, 464–65.

84 *"very democratic spirit":* Davis, *FDR: The Beckoning of Destiny*, 153.

84 *"its duty by the community":* Arthur M. Schlesinger Jr., *The Crisis of the Old Order* (Boston: Houghton Mifflin Co., 1957), 324.

85 *"they lack progressiveness . . .":* Ibid., 323.

85 *"Much has been given you . . .":* Frank Davis Ashburn, *Peabody of Groton* (New York: Coward-McCann, 1944), 176–77.

85 *patrician:* See J. William T. Youngs, *Eleanor Roosevelt: A Personal and Public Life* (Boston: Little, Brown & Co., 1985), 14.

85 *Patriarchs' Balls insufficiently exclusive:* Ward, *Before the Trumpet*, 264.

85 *"You have no looks . . .":* Blanche Wiesen Cook, *Eleanor Roosevelt* (New York: Viking, 1992), 1:62.

85 *"to have me out of the way":* ER, *This Is My Story* (New York: Harper & Brothers, 1937), 11.

86 *"She is such a funny child . . .":* Cook, *Eleanor Roosevelt*, 1:71.

86 *"I was always disgracing . . .":* ER, *This Is My Story*, 17.

86 *"a maniac . . .":* Cook, *Eleanor Roosevelt*, 1:65.

86 *New York Herald:* Cook, *Eleanor Roosevelt*, 1:67.

86 *"acquired a strange and garbled idea . . .":* ER, *This Is My Story*, 16.

86 *"No one bothered me":* Ibid., 17.

86 *"My father was back . . .":* Ibid., 19.

87 *Elliott takes Eleanor for a walk:* Ward, *Before the Trumpet*, 285.

87 *ER helps father and uncle:* ER, *This Is My Story*, 27.

87 *ER's father's funeral:* Ibid., 34.

87 *"the only person in the world . . .":* Ward, *Before the Trumpet*, 287, n7.

87 *happy evenings:* ER, *This Is My Story*, 42.

87 *grandmother said no:* ER, "Where I Get My Energy," *Harper's*, January 1959, in *What I Hope to Leave Behind: The Essential Essays of Eleanor Roosevelt*, Allida M. Black, ed. (Brooklyn, N.Y.: Carlson Publishing, 1995), 44.

87 *upper-crust lives:* Elliott Roosevelt and James Brough, *An Untold Story: The Roosevelts of Hyde Park* (New York: G. P. Putnam's Sons, 1973), 30.

87 *"elegant leisure":* ER, "The Ideal Education," *The Woman's Journal* 15 (October 1930), in *What I Hope to Leave Behind,* ed. Black, 296.

87 *"early loves":* ER, *This Is My Story,* 360.

87 *"greater social organization . . .":* ER, "The Ideal Education," in *What I Hope to Leave Behind,* ed. Black, 296.

87 *"Social life was very important . . .":* ER, "Where I Get My Energy," in *What I Hope to Leave Behind,* ed. Black, 44.

87 *"I remember how . . .":* ER, "Values to Live By," *Jewish Heritage* 1 (Spring 1958), in *What I Hope to Leave Behind,* ed. Black, 50.

88 *"not my duty as I saw it . . .":* ER, *The Autobiography of Eleanor Roosevelt* (New York: Harper & Brothers, 1958), 412.

88 *"Eleanor, my darling Eleanor":* Ward, *Before the Trumpet,* 292.

88 *ER's visits to Oyster Bay:* ER, *This Is My Story,* 50.

88 *fearful that ER would be a bad influence:* See Cook, *Eleanor Roosevelt,* 1:92.

88 *"social graces . . .":* ER, "Women Have Come a Long Way," *Harper's Magazine* 201 (October 1950), in *What I Hope to Leave Behind,* ed. Black, 276.

88 *"intellectually emancipated":* Ibid.

88 *"starting a new life . . .":* ER, *This Is My Story,* 65.

88 *"very little interest in public affairs":* Ibid., 69.

88 *"Though I lost some of my self-confidence . . .":* Ibid., 85.

88 *"come out":* Ibid., 96.

89 *"carrried away . . .";* *"temptations":* Marie Souvestre to ER, 5 October 1902, quoted in Cook, *Eleanor Roosevelt,* 1:122.

89 *portrait on her desk:* See Cook, *Eleanor Roosevelt,* 1:123.

89 *"utter agony":* Ward, *Before the Trumpet,* 306.

89 *"New York Society was really important":* ER, *This Is My Story,* 103.

89 *"just a group of girls . . .":* Ibid., 107.

89 *"terror":* ER, "Values to Live By" 1958, in *What I Hope to Leave Behind,* ed. Black, 50.

89 *ER at settlement house:* ER, *This Is My Story,* 108.

89 *"feller";* *little girl taken ill:* Ward, *Before the Trumpet,* 319.

89 *"kind to the poor . . . conventional pattern":* ER, *This Is My Story,* 3–4.

89 *ladies of ER's class:* Jean Bethke Elshtain, "Eleanor Roosevelt as Activist and Thinker: The Lady, the Lie of Duty," in *Halcyon* 8 (1986), 93–114; see also Anne Firor Scott, *The Southern Lady: From Pedestal to Politics, 1830–1930* (Chicago: University of Chicago Press, 1970).

90 *"Sat near Eleanor":* Cook, *Eleanor Roosevelt,* 1:133.

90 *"No other success in life . . .":* TR to FDR, 29 November 1904, quoted in Joseph P. Lash, *Eleanor and Franklin* (New York: W. W. Norton & Co., 1951), 138.

91 *"Everyone is talking about Cousin Theodore":* FDR to Sara Delano Roosevelt, 7 September 1905, in *FDR Letters: 1905–1928,* 84.

92 *"There is a craze . . .":* Lewis L. Gould, "The Republicans Under Roosevelt and Taft," in Gould, ed., *The Progressive Era,* 67–68.

92 *"We do not intend that this Republic shall ever fail . . .":* Harbaugh, *The Life and Times of Theodore Roosevelt,* rev. ed., 233.

92 *TR infuriating conservatives:* John Morton Blum, *The Republican Roosevelt* (New York: Atheneum Publishers, 1972), 86–105.

92 *"process" of corruption:* Richard L. McCormick, "The Discovery That Business Corrupts Politics: A Reappraisal of the Origins of Progressivism," in *American Historical Review* 86:2 (April 1981), 265.

92 *description of sausage manufacturing:* Upton Sinclair, *The Jungle* [1905] (New York: Signet Classics, 1960), 98.

Notes 593

93 *"Organize!"*: Upton Sinclair, *The Jungle*, 340.
93 *"I would like a first-class man . . ."*: TR, quoted in Harbaugh, *The Life and Times of Theodore Roosevelt*, rev. ed., 248.
93 *"hideous"*: See Ibid., 249.
93 *government report on meat:* Mark Sullivan, *Our Times*, 2:541.
93 *"revolting"*: TR, message to Congress, 4 June 1906, in *The Roosevelt Policy*, ed. Griffith, 2:386–89.
94 *"Mary had a little lamb . . ."*: See Sullivan, *Our Times*, 2:541.
94 Washington Post *editorial:* 20 June 1906, quoted in Sullivan, *Our Times*, 2:548.
94 The World's Week *editorial:* Ibid., 2:551.
94 *"gross injustice."* TR, Message on Employers' Liability Law, 31 January 1908, in *The Roosevelt Policy*, ed. Griffith, 2:699–702.
95 *"rudimentary"*; *"moralistic"*: Harbaugh, *The Life and Times of Theodore Roosevelt*, rev. ed., 259.
95 *"the foundation on which to build . . ."*: TR, Speech of 2 May 1907, in *The Roosevelt Policy*, ed. Griffith, 2:492.
95 *"great and genuine detriment; . . . I would not apply . . ."*: TR to Raymond Robins, 12 August 1914, in *Letters*, ed. Morison, 7:797–98.
95 *"If ever our people . . ."*:TR, Speech of 21 October 1907, in *The Roosevelt Policy*, ed. Griffith, 2:634.
95 *ideals "worth sacrifice";"splendidly eager":* TR, Speech of 7 July 1905, in *The Roosevelt Policy*, ed. Griffith, 1:284.
95 *two-year industrial service:* TR to Raymond Robins, 12 August 1914, in *Letters*, ed. Morison, 7:798.
95 *chaotic individualism:* Herbert Croly, *The Promise of American Life* (New York: Macmillan Co., 1909), 23.
95 *good businessman equals good citizen:* TR, *An Autobiography*, 86.
96 *Congress mandates use of IN GOD WE TRUST:* TR to Roland C. Dryer, 11 November 1907, in *Letters*, ed. Morison, 5:842. We are indebted to Arthur Schlesinger Jr. for bringing this letter to our attention.
96 *"campaign against privilege"*: TR, Message to Congress, 31 January 1908, in *The Roosevelt Policy*, ed. Griffith, 2:710.
96 *"slow process of education . . ."*: TR to Raymond Robins, 12 August 1914, in *Letters*, ed. Morison, 7:797.
96 *"an ethical movement"*: TR, Message to Congress, 31 January 1908, in *The Roosevelt Policy*, ed. Griffith, 2:729.
96 *"The transmission from generation to generation . . ."*: FDR, 19 June 1935, quoted in Gustavus Myers, preface to the 1936 edition of *History of the Great American Fortunes* (New York: Modern Library, 1936), 22.
96 *"wealthy men of enormous power"*; *"cut out rottenness from the body politic"*: TR, Message to Congress, 31 January 1908, in *The Roosevelt Policy*, ed. Griffith, 2:734, 736.
96 *"those rich men whose lives are corrupt . . ."*: TR, Message to Congress, 31 January 1908, in *The Roosevelt Policy*, ed. Griffith, 2:719.
97 *banks were forced to close:* Harbaugh, *The Life and Times of Theodore Roosevelt*, rev. ed., 297.
97 *"certainly held responsible"*: TR to Alexander Lambert, 1 November 1907, in *Letters*, ed. Morison, 5:826.
97 *"those conservative and substantial businessmen"*: Quoted in Burns, *The Workshop of Democracy*, 351.
97 *"dishonest dealing"*: TR to George Cortelyou, 25 October 1907, in *Letters*, ed. Morison, 5:822.
97 *"The trouble is . . ."*: TR, quoted in Harbaugh, *The Life and Times of Theodore Roosevelt*, rev. ed., 302.
98 *"far more satisfactory to work"*: Ibid., 163.
98 *Root on TR and on the "enjoyment of wealth":* Ibid., 221.
98 *"I do not see very much of the big-moneyed men . . ."*: TR to Cecil Arthur Spring-Rice, 3 July 1901, in *Letters*, ed. Morison, 3:108.
98 *"I have not a doubt . . ."*: TR to Edward Sandford Martin, 30 July 1903, in *Letters*, ed. Morison, 3:536.
98 *"We bought [TR] . . ."*: Edward Wagenknecht, *The Seven Worlds of Theodore Roosevelt* (New York: Longmans, Green & Co., 1958), 102.

98 *"Our whole effort . . ."*: TR, Message to Congress, 31 January 1908, in *The Roosevelt Policy*, ed. Griffith, 2:719.

98 *"worst revolutionaries"*: TR, *An Autobiography*, 525–26.

98 *"violent and extreme radical"*: TR to Marshall Stimson, 27 October 1911, in *Letters*, ed. Morison, 7:422.

98 *appointment of Straus:* Harbaugh, *The Life and Times of Theodore Roosevelt*, rev. ed., 212.

98 *"I grow extremely indignant . . ."*: TR to Lyman Abbott, 29 May 1908, in *Letters*, ed. Morison, 6:1042.

99 *"stand on exactly . . ."*: TR, "True Americanism" [April 1894] in *American Ideals and Other Essays*, 29.

99 *"traitor to his caste"*; *"on the side of capital"*: Albert Bushnell Hart at Farewell History Lecture, Harvard (1926), quoted by Edmund Morris, *The Rise of Theodore Roosevelt* (New York: Coward, McCann and Geoghegan, 1975), 144.

99 *"It is very gratifying . . ."*: Lewis L. Gould, "The Republicans Under Roosevelt and Taft," in Gould, ed., *The Progressive Era*, 69.

99 *"Oh, if I could only . . ."*: Frank Friedel, *Franklin D. Roosevelt: The Apprenticeship*, 86.

99 *"not as a straitjacket . . ."*: Quoted in Davis, *FDR: The Beckoning of Destiny*, 215.

100 *"in entire sympathy . . ."*: Quoted in Burns, *The Workshop of Democracy*, 335.

100 *"could carve out of a banana . . ."*: Harbaugh, *Power and Responsibility*, 162.

100 *TR using arts of bargaining, rewarding:* Burns, *The Workshop of Democracy*, 352.

100 *"While President . . ."*: TR to George Otto Trevelyan, 19 June 1908, in *Letters*, ed. Morison, 6:1087.

100 *"They have raved against trusts . . ."*: TR, quoted by Sullivan, *Our Times*, 2:406.

100 *"criminal rich"*: Harbaugh, *The Life and Times of Theodore Roosevelt*, rev. ed., 326.

100 *"public-relations"*; *"charade"*: Hofstadter, *The Age of Reform: From Bryan to F.D.R.*, 246, 256.

100 *"the type of Progressive leader whose real impulses . . ."*: Ibid., 240.

101 *"pseudo-progressive"*: Daniel Aaron, *Men of Good Hope: A Story of American Progressives* (New York: Oxford University Press, 1951), ch. 8, "Theodore Roosevelt and Brooks Adams: Pseudo-Progressives."

101 *muckrakers speech:* TR, "Muck-Rakers," 14 April 1906, in TR, *The Roosevelt Policy*, ed. Griffith, 2:367–78.

101 *denounced socialists:* TR, "Latitude and Longtitude Among Reformers," *Century*, June 1900, 214, quoted in Howard Lawrence Hurwitz, *Theodore Roosevelt and Labor in New York State, 1880–1900*, 275.

101 *"must act . . ."*: TR, "Morality and Efficiency" [July 1894] in *American Ideals and Other Essays*, 37.

101 *"'The Radical Movement . . .'"*: Mentioned in Hofstadter, *The Age of Reform*, 264.

101 *"raise himself . . ."*: TR to Upton Sinclair, 15 March 1906, in *Letters*, ed. Morison, 5:178–80.

102 *Mugwump cult of "character":* Caine, "The Origins of Progressivism," in Gould, ed., *The Progressive Era*, 20.

102 *"I am no more to be frightened . . ."*: TR to Jacob Riis, 18 April 1906, in *Letters*, ed. Morison, 5:212.

102 *"I too am a dreamer . . ."*: TR to Charles Dwight Willard, 28 April 1911, in *Letters*, ed. Morison, 7:256.

102 *TR on Lincoln:* "Washington and Lincoln," in *The Foes of Our Own Household*, in *The Works of Theodore Roosevelt*, ed. Hagedorn, 19:51ff.

102 *George Roosevelt's conversation with TR:* Quoted in Hofstadter, *The Age of Reform*, 253; See also Nicholas Roosevelt, *TR: The Man as I Knew Him* (New York: Dodd, Mead, 1967).

102 *no effective solutions:* Richard L. McCormick, "The Discovery That Business Corrupts Politics: A Reappraisal of the Origins of Progressivism," in *American Historical Review* 86:2 (April 1981), 272.

102 *"results":* TR to Seth Low, 3 August 1900, in *Letters*, ed. Morison, 2:1374.

102 *"temperamentally disposed to act"; morally indignant:* Harbaugh, *The Life and Times of Theodore Roosevelt*, rev. ed., 222.

103 *"I don't think that any harm comes . . ."*: Quoted in Harbaugh, *The Life and Times of Theodore Roosevelt*, rev. ed., 321.

103 *"unless he could find . . ."*: TR, *An Autobiography*, quoted in Miroff, *Icons of Democracy*, 179.

103 *"Sarah Knisley's Arm":* Mentioned in Thomas K. McCraw, "The Progressive Legacy," in Gould, ed., *The Progressive Era,* 190.

103 *climate for reform as resource:* Hofstadter, *The Age of Reform,* 254, 256.

103 *Perkins on TR:* Frances Perkins, *The Roosevelt I Knew* (New York: Viking Press, 1946), 9–10.

104 *second message:* 31 January 1908, in *The Roosevelt Policy,* ed. Griffith, 2:703–5.

104 *third message:* 31 January 1908, in *The Roosevelt Policy,* ed. Griffith, 2:710.

104 *"representatives of predatory wealth . . .";* "*law-defying*"; "*brutally indifferent . . .*"; "*extraordinary violence*": See TR, *The Roosevelt Policy,* ed. Griffith, 2:715, 719, 734, 721.

104 *"moral regeneration";* "*Federal Government does scourge sin*": TR, *The Roosevelt Policy,* ed. Griffith, 2:724, 722.

105 "*underbred*": TR, Letter to the Department of State, 2 December 1908, in *The Theodore Roosevelt Treasury: A Self-Portrait from His Writings,* ed. Hermann Hagedorn (New York: G. P. Putnam's Sons, 1957), 176–77.

105 "*Lily White movements*": Lewis L. Gould, "The Republicans Under Roosevelt and Taft," in Gould, ed., *The Progressive Era,* 65.

105 *Brownsville incident:* Burns, *The Workshop of Democracy,* 353.

106 "*diplomatist of high rank*": London *Morning Post,* after 1907 Hague Conference.

106 *Japanese "ask too much":* TR to Kermit Roosevelt, 25 August 1905, in *Letters,* ed. Morison, 4:1317.

106 "*When I feel gloomy . . .*": TR to Cecil Arthur Spring-Rice, 24 July 1905, in *Letters,* ed. Morison, 4:1285.

107 *TR's protests against Jewish pogroms:* Arthur D. Morse, *While Six Million Died* (New York: Random House, 1968), 107.

108 *Robert B. Roosevelt:* Ernest Schwiebert, ed., *Superior Fishing* by Robert Barnwell Roosevelt (St. Paul, Minn.: Minnesota Historical Society Press, 1985), xiiff. See also Nathan Miller, *Theodore Roosevelt: A Life* (New York: William Morrow & Co, 1992), 51–52.

108 *TR stalks out of Gridiron Dinner:* George Mowry, *Theodore Roosevelt and the Progressive Movement* (New York: Hill & Wang, 1960), 213.

108 *TR's conviction that the nomination could be his:* Burns, *The Workshop of Democracy,* 353.

108 *FDR attends Columbia to be near Hyde Park:* Ward, *Before the Trumpet,* 257.

108 *houses sold to Hillel Foundation:* ER, *This I Remember,* 18.

109 "*made no effort to overcome . . .*": Quoted in Geoffrey C. Ward, *A First-Class Temperament: The Emergence of Franklin Roosevelt* (New York: Harper & Row, 1989), 62.

109 "*He will not find himself*": Earle Looker, *This Man Roosevelt* (New York: Brewer, Warren & Putnam, 1932), 48.

109 *FDR's first job and salary arrangement:* Ward, *A First-Class Temperament,* 64.

110 "*unpaid bills";* *chloroforming dogs:* Robert D. Graff, Robert Emmett Ginna, and Roger Butterfield, *FDR* (New York: Harper & Row, 1963), 47; Ward, *A First-Class Temperament,* 71n.

110 "*Everybody called him Franklin . . .*": Quoted in Davis, *FDR: The Beckoning of Destiny,* 213.

110 *FDR's law partner's pronouncements:* Ward, *A First-Class Temperament,* 77.

111 "*an entirely dependent person . . . fairly conventional . . .*": ER, *This Is My Story,* 138.

Three: Two Roosevelts Move to the Left

113 *FDR on seeking political office:* Quoted in Kenneth S. Davis, *FDR: The Beckoning of Destiny* (New York: G. P. Putnam's Sons, 1971), 213–14.

113 *TR's example turns FDR away from high society:* Frank Freidel, *Franklin D. Roosevelt: The Apprenticeship* (New York: Little, Brown & Co., 1952), 85–86.

114 "*desire to outshine Ted*": Geoffrey C. Ward, *A First-Class Temperament: The Emergence of Franklin Roosevelt* (New York: Harper & Row, 1989), 499.

114 *Vanderbilt on a political career:* Cornelius Vanderbilt, *Farewell to Fifth Avenue* (New York: Simon & Schuster, 1935), 242.

116 "*You bet I do*": James MacGregor Burns, *Roosevelt: The Lion and the Fox* (New York: Harcourt, Brace & Co., 1956), 33.

116   *"I'm not Teddy..."*: Quoted in Freidel, *Roosevelt: The Apprenticeship*, 93; he cites *Poughkeepsie News Press*, 27 October 1910.

116   *ER on FDR's public speaking:* Eleanor Roosevelt, *This Is My Story* (New York: Harper & Brothers, 1937), 167.

116   *FDR on the Hudson Valley:* Ward, *A First-Class Temperament*, 121–22.

117   *women and reformers:* James MacGregor Burns, *The Workshop of Democracy* (New York: Vintage Books, 1985), 275–78.

118   *FDR's margin of victory:* Davis, *FDR: The Beckoning of Destiny*, 242.

118   *"every hour of the 24"*: Quoted in Ward, *A First-Class Temperament*, 122.

118   *SDR's tally of election:* Ibid., 123.

118   *"Every one of our friends..."*: Cornelius Vanderbilt, *Farewell to Fifth Avenue*, 244.

118   *FDR and ER's living quarters in Albany:* Ward, *A First-Class Temperament*, 125, 158.

119   *Van Buren and the Albany Regency:* James MacGregor Burns, *The Vineyard of Liberty* (New York: Alfred A. Knopf, 1982), 371–72.

119   *Description of FDR:* Ward, *A First-Class Temperament*, 130–31; see also Davis, *FDR: The Beckoning of Destiny*, 247–48, and *New York Times* feature article by W. Axel Warn, 22 January 1911.

119   *"finely chiseled face..."*: Davis, *FDR: The Beckoning of Destiny*, 247.

119   *"Are you an admirer..?"*: Ward, *A First-Class Temperament*, 140.

119   *Boss Sullivan on FDR:* Ernest K. Lindley, *Franklin D. Roosevelt: A Career in Progressive Democracy* (New York: Blue Ribbon Books, 1931), 78.

119   *FDR on the Democratic party:* Quoted in Davis, *FDR: The Beckoning of Destiny*, 247.

120   *"swap stories like soldiers..."*: Ward, *A First-Class Temperament*, 135.

120   *FDR's proposal to William Barnes:* Ibid., 148.

120   *Song taunting FDR:* Quoted in Ibid., 151.

121   *FDR on "Murphy and his kind":* Davis, *FDR: The Beckoning of Destiny*, 259.

121   *"somewhat shocked..."*: ER, *This Is My Story*, 180–81.

122   *ER's lack of knowledge of politics:* ER, "Wives of Great Men," 1 October 1932, *Liberty 9*, reprinted in *What I Hope to Leave Behind: The Essential Essays of Eleanor Roosevelt*, ed. Allida M. Black (Brooklyn, N.Y.: Carlson Publishing, 1995), 215–16.

122   *"I believe that at that time..."*: Frances Perkins, *The Roosevelt I Knew* (New York: Viking Press, 1946), 10.

122   *"rarely talking..."*: Ibid., 11.

122   *"an awfully mean cuss..."*: Quoted in Perkins, *The Roosevelt I Knew*, 12.

123   *"gone back on their promises..."*: TR, quoted in William H. Harbaugh, *The Life and Times of Theodore Roosevelt*, rev. ed. (New York: Oxford University Press, 1975), 365.

123   *"I am ready and eager..."*: Theodore Roosevelt, *The New Nationalism* (New York: Outlook Company, 1911), xiv.

123   *"We have passed the time..."*: TR, *The New Nationalism*, 51.

124   *TR on labor's right to organize:* TR, Speech of 10 September 1910, in *The New Nationalism*, 223–24.

124   *"Of course, it is outrageous..."*: Ibid.

125   *TR's speech in Osawatomie:* TR, Speech of 31 August 1910, in *The New Nationalism*, 3–33.

125   *"national need..."; "left-wing statist"; "not care a rap"*: TR, quoted in Martin J. Sklar, *The Corporate Reconstruction of American Capitalism, 1890–1916* (Cambridge, Mass.: Cambridge University Press, 1988), 353, 352, 356.

125   *"drift along..."*: TR to John St. Loe Strachey, 26 March 1912, in Elting E. Morison, ed., *The Letters of Theodore Roosevelt* (Cambridge, Mass.: Harvard University Press, 1951–54), 7:532.

125   *"come 180 degrees..."*: Nell Irvin Painter, *Standing at Armageddon: The United States, 1877–1919* (New York: W. W. Norton & Co., 1987), 258.

125   *"startled"*: Lodge to TR, quoted in George E. Mowry, *Theodore Roosevelt and the Progressive Movement* (New York: Hill & Wang, 1960), 144.

125   *"waving the red flag"*: Quoted in John Allen Gable, *The Bull Moose Years: Theodore Roosevelt and the Progressive Party* (Port Washington, N.Y.: Kennikat Press, 1978), 11.

125   Denver Republican: Quoted in Harbaugh, *Life and Times of Theodore Roosevelt*, rev. ed., 368.

126 *"thirsty sinner"*: see editor's note, TR to Elihu Root, 14 February 1912, in *Letters,* ed. Morison, 7:504n.

126 *"My hat is in the ring . . ."*: TR to Herbert Spencer Hadley, 29 February 1912, in *Letters,* ed. Morison, 7:513.

126 *"sordid baseness . . ."*; *"sensible and honorable men . . ."*: TR to Root, quoted in Harbaugh, *Life and Times of Theodore Roosevelt,* 371.

126 *"dangerous crank"*: TR to H. Rider Haggard, quoted in Hermann Hagedorn, *The Roosevelt Family of Sagamore Hill* (New York: Macmillan Co., 1954), 308.

126 *Corinne on TR's loneliness:* Corinne Roosevelt Robinson, *My Brother Theodore Roosevelt* (New York: Charles Scribner's Sons, 1921), 267.

126 *"their number is legion . . ."*; *"has the reputation . . ."*: Robert Grant, quoted in Harbaugh, *The Life and Times of Theodore Roosevelt,* rev. ed., 391.

127 *some representatives of big business support TR:* See George Mowry, *Theodore Roosevelt and the Progressive Movement* (New York: Hill & Wang, 1960), 203.

127 *"I am with you"*: Brooks Adams, 2 May 1912, quoted in TR, *Letters,* ed. Morison, 7:551n.

127 *Caesar:* Brooks Adams, 1, 22, 25 May 1912, quoted in TR, *Letters,* ed. Morison, 7:551n.

127 *George Perkins offers support:* Harbaugh, *The Life and Times of Theodore Roosevelt,* rev. ed., 383.

127 *"You could not advise me . . ."*: TR to Hermann Henry Kohlsaat, 16 March 1912, in *Letters,* ed. Morison, 7:526.

127 *final blow for some conservative businessmen:* See Mowry, *Theodore Roosevelt and the Progressive Movement,* 217.

127 *Dred Scott and Bakeshop cases:* TR, "Criticism of the Courts," editorial in *Outlook,* 24 September 1910, in TR, *The New Nationalism,* 252, 254.

127 *"For the past thirty years . . ."*: TR to Herbert Croly, 29 February 1912, in *Letters,* ed. Morison, 7:512.

128 *TR on Justice Taney:* TR, "The Record of the Democratic Party," 30 October 1884, in *The Works of Theodore Roosevelt,* ed. Hermann Hagedorn (New York: Charles Scribner's sons, 1926), 14:55.

128 *"absolutely reactionary"*: TR to Hiram Warren Johnson, 27 October 1911, in *Letters,* ed. Morison, 7:421.

128 *"unusually good . . ."*; *"against these abuses"*: TR to Henry Lewis Stimson, 5 February 1912, in *Letters,* ed. Morison, 7:494.

128 *"for the rule of the many . . ."*: TR to Joseph Moore Dixon, 21 March 1912, in *Letters,* ed. Morison, 7:529n2.

128 *"My dear fellow . . ."*: TR to Henry Cabot Lodge, 1 March 1912, in *Letters,* ed. Morison, 7:515.

128 *"corporation attorneys on the bench"*: TR speech, "The Recall of Judicial Decisions," quoted in Harbaugh, *The Life and Times of Theodore Roosevelt,* rev. ed., 399.

128 New York Times: Quoted ibid., 397.

128 *many thoughtful lawyers:* Ibid., 399.

129 *"honest and genuine democracy"*: TR to Joseph Dixon, 8 March 1912, in *Letters,* ed. Morison, 7:521.

129 *"I have scant patience . . ."*: TR, quoted in Sklar, *Corporate Reconstruction of American Capitalism,* 353.

129 *"so that the people may jointly do . . ."*: TR to Joseph Dixon, 8 March 1912, in *Letters,* ed. Morison, 7:521.

129 *TR on Lincoln:* TR to Joseph Dixon, 8 March 1912, in *Letters,* ed. Morison, 7:522.

129 *"He had a feeling for social justice . . ."*: ER, "My Day," 25 October 1958, in *Eleanor Roosevelt's My Day,* ed. David Elmblidge (New York: Pharos Books, 1991), 3:182–83.

129 *"two radically different views . . ."*; *"entrenched privilege . . ."*: TR to Joseph Dixon, 8 March 1912, in *Letters,* ed. Morison, 7:522–23.

129 *"to take from some one man . . ."*: Osawatomie speech, quoted in Sklar, *Corporate Reconstruction of American Capitalism,* 353.

129 *"We must not repeat . . ."*: TR to Arthur Hamilton Lee, 21 March 1912, in *Letters,* ed. Morison, 7:530–31.

129 *"sordid money interests . . ."*: TR to John St. Loe Strachey, 26 March 1912, in *Letters,* ed. Morison, 7:532.

130 *"wise, progressive leadership . . . extremists of progress . . . with all fervor . . ."*: Ibid.
130 *"applied ethics"*: TR to Henry Rider Haggard, 28 June 1912, in *Letters,* ed. Morison, 7:567.
130 *"demagogue," "egotist," "fathead," "puzzlewit"*: See TR, *Letters,* ed. Morison, 7:541n.
130 *"fool" and "blackguard"*: TR to Arthur Hamilton Lee, 14 May 1912, in *Letters,* ed. Morison, 7:544.
130 *guinea pig*: H.W. Brands, *T.R.: The Last Romantic* (New York: Basic Books, 1997), 712.
130 *"Roosevelt was my closest friend"*: Taft, quoted in Brands, *T.R.: The Last Romantic,* 707; see also TR to Oscar King David, 28 April 1912, in *Letters,* ed. Morison, 7:537n.2.
130 *"He is essentially a fighter"*: Root, quoted by Harbaugh, *The Life and Times of Theodore Roosevelt,* rev. ed., 402.
130 *seventy votes short*: Ibid., 405.
130 *"I'll name the compromise candidate"*: TR, quoted by Harbaugh, Ibid. 405–6.
130 *"swindled nomination"*: TR to Edwin A. Van Valkenburg, 16 July 1912, in *Letters,* ed. Morison, 7:576.
131 *"My loyalty . . ."*: TR to Augustus Everett Willson, 14 February 1912, in *Letters,* ed. Morison, 7:503.
131 *"By rejecting Roosevelt . . ."*: Arthur M. Schlesinger Jr., *The Vital Center* (Boston: Houghton Mifflin Co., 1949), 23–24.
131 *"By 1932 . . ."*: Lewis L. Gould, "The Republicans Under Roosevelt and Taft," in Lewis L. Gould, ed., *The Progressive Era* (Syracuse, N.Y.: Syracuse University Press, 1974), 82.
131 *"privileged classes seldom . . ."*: Brooks Adams, quoted in Schlesinger, *The Vital Center,* 23.
132 *TR's "Confession of Faith"*: Gable, *The Bull Moose Years,* 82–85.
132 *"waving red bandannas"*: Burns, *The Workshop of Democracy,* 371, cites George E. Mowry, *Theodore Roosevelt and the Progressive Movement* (Madison, Wis.: University of Wisconsin Press, 1946), 164.
132 *"Progressives meant to help . . ."*: Painter, *Standing at Armageddon,* 269.
132 *TR at the convention*: Burns, *The Workshop of Democracy,* 370–72.
133 *"deeply prized", "confused thinker"*: TR to Arthur Hamilton Lee, 5 November 1912; TR to Florence La Farge, 13 February 1908, in *Letters,* ed. Morison, 7:633, 4:942.
133 *It had been a century . . .*: Subsection taken substantially from Burns, *The Workshop of Democracy,* 370ff.
133 *Wilson's position*: Burns, *The Workshop of Democracy,* 372–73.
134 *"laying the foundations . . ."*: Schlesinger, *The Vital Center,* 177–79.
134 *John Wells Davidson*: See Harbaugh, *The Life and Times of Theodore Roosevelt,* rev. ed., 420.
134 *Brandeis attacks Progressives*: See Gable, *The Bull Moose Years,* 120–21.
134 *TR on women and "Negro" rights*: Gable, *The Bull Moose Years,* 66ff., 267; see also Burns, *The Workshop of Democracy,* 375.
135 *"The hazards of sickness . . ."*: "TR and Universal Health Insurance," *Theodore Roosevelt Association Journal* 19:4 (spring–summer 1993–94), 21.
135 *"only a few supporters . . ."*: Gable, *The Bull Moose Years,* 118.
135 *small sums from average Americans*: Ibid.
135 *A thousand delegates*: See William Allen White, *The Autobiography of William Allen White,* ed. Sally Griffith (Lawrence, Kans.: University Press of Kansas, 1990), 252.
135 *"In my estimation . . ."*: TR to Frederick Jackson Turner, 4 November 1896, in *Letters,* ed. Morison, 1:564.
135 *"privilege . . . Western expansion"*: TR to William Edward Dodd, 13 February 1912, in *Letters,* ed. Morison, 7:501.
136 *FDR's transformation*: Davis, *FDR: The Beckoning of Destiny,* 263–65.
136 *FDR and conservation*: Keir B. Sterling, Richard P. Harmond, et al., eds., *Biographical Dictionary of American and Canadian Naturalists and Environmentalists* (Westport, Conn.: Greenwood Press, 1997), 680.
136 *FDR's "new theory"*: Quoted in Davis, *FDR: The Beckoning of Destiny,* 266.
137 *Josephus Daniels on FDR*: Quoted in Ward, *A First-Class Temperament,* 183.
138 *William Jennings Bryan on corrupt politicians*: Quoted in Burns, *The Workshop of Democracy,* 369.
138 *FDR's wire to ER*: Quoted in Ward, *A First-Class Temperament,* 184.
138 *Howe declaring FDR would be president*: Blanche Wiesen Cook, *Eleanor Roosevelt: 1884–1933* (New York: Viking, 1992), 1:199.

138 *Howe working for FDR:* Alfred B. Rollins Jr., *Roosevelt and Howe* (New York: Alfred A. Knopf, 1962), 61.

139 *TR speaks after being shot:* Burns, *The Workshop of Democracy*, 376.

139 *"forty-one minutes":* *Times* reporter, quoted by Hagedorn, *The Roosevelt Family of Sagamore Hill*, 324.

139 *demonstration in Madison Square Garden:* See Hagedorn, ibid., 324–25.

139 *"We recognize..."*: TR, quoted in George Mowry, *Theodore Roosevelt and the Progressive Movement*, 278.

139 *polling data for TR:* See Gable, *The Bull Moose Years*, 141ff.

139 *75 percent of popular vote; "radical politics":* Sklar, *Corporate Reconstruction of American Capitalism*, 349–50.

139 *"rather blue":* Edith Roosevelt, quoted in Hagedorn, *The Roosevelt Family of Sagamore Hill*, 327.

139 *no regrets:* TR to Charles Dwight Willard, 14 November 1912, in *Letters*, ed. Morison, 7:647.

139 *cutting loose from the Republican party:* TR to Gifford Pinchot, 13 November 1912, in *Letters*, ed. Morison, 7:642.

140 *Howe takes out advertisements:* Ward, *A First-Class Temperament*, 197.

140 *Oyster Bay family wounded by FDR:* Ibid., 186.

140 *"All respectable society..."*: TR, quoted in Brands, *T.R.: The Last Romantic*, 710.

141 *"I have just come from Boston..."*: TR quoted in Hagedorn, *The Roosevelt Family of Sagamore Hill*, 328.

141 *Moorfield Storey:* Quoted in Frederic Cople Jaher, *Doubters and Dissenters: Cataclysmic Thought in America, 1885–1918* (Glencoe: Free Press of Glencoe, 1964), 146.

141 *Ted Jr. thrown out of Wall Street offices:* Hagedorn, *The Roosevelt Family of Sagamore Hill*, 331.

141 *dinners at Tuxedo Park:* Ward, *A First-Class Temperament*, 526.

141 *"We stand equally against..."*: TR to Sir Edward Grey, 15 November 1913, in *Works*, Memorial Edition, 23:146, quoted in Arthur M. Schlesinger Jr., *The Vital Center*, 22.

141 *Hofstadter on TR:* Richard Hofstadter, *The American Political Tradition and the Men Who Made It* (New York: Vintage Books, 1948), ch. 9, "Theodore Roosevelt: The Conservative as Progressive."

142 *William Allen White on TR:* White, *Autobiography*, 259, 157, 175, 253.

142 *"I firmly believe..."*: TR to Benjamin Lindsey, 16 November 1912, in *Letters*, ed. Morison, 7:650.

142 *"You know, it's a funny thing..."*: Perkins, *The Roosevelt I Knew*, 34.

143 *"It is interesting..."*: Ward, *A First-Class Temperament*, 200.

143 *FDR's new duties:* Davis, *FDR: The Beckoning of Destiny*, 314–15.

143 *FDR on absence of Daniels:* Ibid., 321.

143 *FDR's view of Daniels:* Ward, *A First-Class Temperament*, 223; see also Edward J. Marolda, ed., *FDR and the U.S. Navy* (New York: St. Martin's Press, 1998).

143 *house on N Street:* Elliott Roosevelt and James Brough, *An Untold Story: The Roosevelts of Hyde Park* (New York: G. P. Putnam's Sons, 1973), 17.

143 *upper-class attitudes:* Ward, *A First-Class Temperament*, 204, 214; see also Elliott Roosevelt and James Brough, *Mother R.: Eleanor Roosevelt's Untold Story* (New York: G. P. Putnam's Sons, 1977), 79.

143 *"darkies":* Joseph P. Lash, *Eleanor and Franklin* (New York: W. W. Norton & Co., 1971), 239.

143 *FDR as seen by Harvard classmates:* Ward, *A First-Class Temperament*, 262.

144 *Daniels on FDR:* Quoted in Ward, *A First-Class Temperament*, 234.

144 *"His distinguished cousin T.R...."*: Josephus Daniels, *The Wilson Era* (Chapel Hill, N.C.: University of North Carolina Press, 1944), 55.

145 *Wilson's appeal to Americans:* Quoted in Davis, *FDR: The Beckoning of Destiny*, 383.

145 *FDR on the war:* See Ward, *A First-Class Temperament*, 299.

145 *Nobody "seemed the least bit excited..."*: FDR to ER, 2 August 1914, in *FDR: His Personal Letters, 1905–1928*, ed. Elliott Roosevelt (New York: Duell, Sloan & Pearce, 1947–1950), 237–40. Cited hereafter in this chapter as *FDR Letters*.

145 *"running the real work":* FDR to ER, 5 August 1914, in *FDR Letters, 1905–1928*, ed. Elliott Roosevelt, 1:243.

146 *TR on Wilson's war policy:* Quoted in Burns, *The Workshop of Democracy*, 416.

146 *"abject creature":* TR to Archibald Roosevelt, 19 May 1915, in *Letters*, ed. Morison, 8:923.

146 *TR declines invitation to Hyde Park:* Ward, *A First-Class Temperament,* 294, 294n7.

147 *Barnes trial:* Ibid., 197.

147 *"nadir of cowardly infamy":* TR to Arthur Hamilton Lee, 17 June 1915, in *Letters,* ed. Morison, 8:938.

147 *"screaming and shrieking . . .":* Ibid., 8:937.

147 *"pacifist frame of mind":* TR to William Cameron Forbes, 23 May 1916, in *Letters,* ed. Morison, 8:1045.

147 *"grand and noble":* quoted in Brands, *T.R.: The Last Romantic,* 752.

147 *"the multimillionaire and the son of the immigrant . . .":* Quoted in Harbaugh, *The Life and Times of Theodore Roosevelt,* rev. ed., 451.

147 *"preparedness"; TR did nothing to counteract . . . :* Ibid., 454.

147 *"I just know I shall do some awful . . .":* FDR to ER, undated letter, 1915, in *FDR Letters,* 266.

148 *"Lord, how I would like . . .":* TR to John Callan O'Laughlin, 6 May 1915, in *Letters,* ed. Morison, 8:921.

148 *"Don't imagine . . .":* TR, quoted in Harbaugh, *The Life and Times of Theodore Roosevelt,* rev. ed., 456.

148 *"cropper":* TR to Charles Bonaparte, 7 November 1914, quoted in Gable, *The Bull Moose Years,* 223.

148 *"a rap for social justice":* TR to William Allen White, 7 November 1914, in *Letters,* ed. Morison, 8:836.

148 *Thomas Edison:* See TR, *Letters,* ed. Morison, 8:1041n.

148 *"The standpat Republicans . . .":* Corinne Roosevelt Robinson, *My Brother Theodore Roosevelt,* 298.

148 *"Well, the country wasn't . . .":* TR to Anna Roosevelt Cowles, 16 June 1916, in *Letters,* ed. Morison, 8:1063.

149 *Chicago Evening Post:* Article by Julian Mason, June 1916, quoted by Corinne Roosevelt Robinson, *My Brother Theodore Roosevelt,* 100–102.

149 *"staunchest fighters":* TR, quoted in Harbaugh, *The Life and Times of Theodore Roosevelt,* rev. ed., 461.

149 *tearing up Roosevelt's picture; "I had tears in my eyes":* William Allen White, quoted in Gable, *The Bull Moose Years,* 248.

149 *Pinchot on TR's betrayal:* Amos Pinchot, quoted in Harbaugh, *The Life and Times of Theodore Roosevelt,* rev. ed., 462.

149 *"incapable leadership; . . . if we elect Mr. Wilson . . .":* TR, "The Soul of the Nation," Speech of 3 November 1916, in *The Works of Theodore Roosevelt,* ed. Hagedorn, 18:442, 452.

150 *Wilson on declaration of war:* Quoted in Davis, *FDR: The Beckoning of Destiny,* 456.

150 *"I had lost a good deal . . .":* ER, *This Is My Story,* 103.

151 *"I loved it"; "my emancipation and education":* ER, quoted in Joseph P. Lash, *Love Eleanor: Eleanor Roosevelt and Her Friends* (Garden City, N.Y.: Doubleday & Co., 1982), 67.

151 *"Making the ten servants help . . .":* *New York Times* article, 17 July 1917, quoted in *FDR: Letters, 1905–1928,* 350n.

151 *"I am proud to be . . .":* FDR to ER, 18 July 1917, in *FDR Letters, 1905–1928,* 349–50.

151 *"Jew party . . .":* Cook, *Eleanor Roosevelt,* 1:390.

151 *Baruch's great-grandmother danced with Lafayette:* E. Digby Balzell, *The Protestant Establishment: Aristocracy and Caste in America* (New York: Random House, 1964), 32.

151 *"an interesting little man . . .":* Cook, *Eleanor Roosevelt,* 2:317.

151 *wartime activities: The Autobiography of Eleanor Roosevelt* (New York: Harper & Brothers, 1961), pp. 91–95.

151 *"You must resign . . .":* Quoted in Davis, *FDR: The Beckoning of Destiny,* 459.

151 *TR on leading a division:* TR to Newton Diehl Baker, 19 March 1917, in *Letters,* ed. Morison, 8:1164.

152 *"If I am allowed to go . . .":* TR, quoted in Corinne Roosevelt Robinson, *My Brother Theodore Roosevelt,* 330.

152 *"I could do this country most good . . .":* TR to William Allen White, 17 February 1917, in *Letters,* ed. Morison, 8:1153.

152 *TR asks Wilson for permission to fight:* Davis, *FDR: The Beckoning of Destiny,* 459.

152 *"I was charmed . . .":* Wilson, quoted in Harbaugh, *The Life and Times of Theodore Roosevelt,* rev. ed., 471.

152 *cause célèbre; Joffre:* Harbaugh, *The Life and Times of Theodore Roosevelt,* rev. ed., 472; see also TR to Arthur Spring-Rice, 16 April 1917, in *Letters,* ed. Morison, 8:1175n8.

152 *Clemenceau's open letter:* Harbaugh, *The Life and Times of Theodore Roosevelt,* rev. ed., 472.

152 *"I really think the best way . . .":* Ibid., 474.

152 *ER on Wilson's refusal of TR:* Davis, *FDR: The Beckoning of Destiny,* 460.

152 *"utterly pointless and fussy activities":* TR, quoted in Corinne Roosevelt Robinson, *My Brother Theodore Roosevelt,* 332.

152 *"They are keenly desirous . . .":* TR to John Joseph Pershing, 20 May 1917, in *Letters,* ed. Morison, 8:1193.

153 *"You have the fighting tradition! . . .":* TR to Theodore Roosevelt Jr., 9 August 1917, in *Letters,* ed. Morison, 8:1222.

153 *"the pride and the anxiety . . .":* TR to Richard Derby, 1 July 1918, in *Letters,* ed. Morison, 8:1344.

153 *Wilson to Daniels about FDR:* Quoted in Davis, *FDR: The Beckoning of Destiny,* 460.

153 *Wilson's prescient warning:* Harbaugh, *The Life and Times of Theodore Roosevelt,* rev. ed., 466.

153 *"punishment" for Germany:* TR, "War Aims and Peace Proposals" in TR, *Works,* ed. Hagedorn (New York: Charles Scribner's Sons, 1926), 19:379.

153 *"Once lead the people into war . . .":* Quoted in Alexander L. George and Juliette L. George, *Woodrow Wilson and Colonel House* (John Day Co., 1956), 175.

153 *Wilson on force:* Quoted in Davis, *FDR: The Beckoning of Destiny,* 461.

153 *FDR denies that war was a people's movement:* Ibid., 497–98.

154 *Wilson's sedition amendment:* Burns, *The Workship of Democracy,* 441.

154 *"To fight you must be brutal and ruthless":* Quoted in Burns, *The Workshop of Democracy,* 441.

154 *TR's attack on sedition bill:* Harbaugh, *The Life and Times of Theodore Roosevelt,* rev. ed., 477.

154 *lambasting it as unconstitutional:* TR, "Lincoln and Free Speech," in TR, *Works,* ed. Hagedorn, 19:298ff.

154 *FDR's trip to Europe:* Burns, *The Lion and the Fox,* 65; Davis, *FDR: The Beckoning of Destiny,* 517–29.

154 *FDR and Foch:* FDR, Address to the Graduating Class at West Point, 12 June 1935, *Public Papers and Addresses of Franklin D. Roosevelt,* ed. Samuel I. Rosenman (New York: Macmillan Co., 1941), 1935, 250–51.

155 *FDR's return to New York:* Davis, *FDR: The Beckoning of Destiny,* 529.

155 *Discovery of the Mercer letters:* Joseph P. Lash, *Eleanor and Franklin* (New York: W. W. Norton & Co., 1971), 226.

155 *"I don't think you read my letter . . .":* ER to FDR, 24 July 1917, FDR Library.

155 *"inquired if you had told me . . .":* ER to FDR, undated letter, Box 15, FDR Library.

156 *FDR admits and Sara lays down the law:* Lash, *Eleanor and Franklin,* 226.

156 *navy scandal:* Ted Morgan, *FDR: A Biography* (New York: Simon & Schuster, 1985), 257–69; see also Ward, *A First-Class Temperament,* 437–43, 466–69, 487–90.

158 *William Allen White visits TR:* Ward, *A First-Class Temperament,* 421.

158 *"I have only one fight left . . .":* TR, quoted in Corinne Roosevelt Robinson, *My Brother Theodore Roosevelt,* 346.

158 *"we cannot afford . . .":* TR, Speech of 28 March 1918, in *Newer Roosevelt Messages,* ed. William Griffith (New York: Current Literature Publishing Co., 1919), 3:919.

158 *"political democracy with industrial autocracy"; "common good":* TR, "Industrial Justice," in *The Foes of Our Own Household* [1917], in TR, *Works,* ed. Hagedorn, 19:74, 78.

158 *"foolish"; "master of the corporation":* TR, Speech of 28 March 1918, in *Newer Roosevelt Messages,* ed. Griffith 3:927–28.

158 *taxes on excess profits:* Harbaugh, *The Life and Times of Theodore Roosevelt,* rev. ed., 478.

158 *waterpower; soldiers' bill of rights; higher education:* TR, "The Men Who Pay" [1918] in TR, *Works,* ed. Hagedorn, 19:257–58.

158 *active governmental control; "partners in enterprise"; permanency of employment, insurance, leisure:*

TR, "Industrial Justice" [1917], in TR, *Works*, ed. Hagedorn 19:73, 80, 76; and TR, "Washington and Lincoln," 19:60.

158   "*day nurseries* . . .": TR, "Socialism Versus Social Reform," in TR, *Works*, ed. Hagedorn, 19:110.

158   "*up to date*": TR to William Allen White, 4 April 1918, in *Letters*, ed. Morison, 8:1307.

159   "*schemes" like the League of Nations:* TR, "The League of Nations," in TR, *Works*, ed. Hagedorn, 19:405.

159   *Archie's physical and mental wounds:* Edward J. Renehan Jr., *The Lion's Pride: Theodore Roosevelt and His Family in Peace and War* (New York: Oxford University Press, 1998), 212–13.

159   "*talky-talky*": TR to Bob Ferguson, in Ward, *A First-Class Temperament*, 420.

159   *description of funeral and casket:* Senator Foley, in Proceedings in the Senate, 8 January 1919, in *State of New York: A Memorial to Theodore Roosevelt* (Authorized by the Legislature, 21 February 1919), 29–30.

159   "*fun of him*": Ward, *A First-Class Temperament*, 423.

159   "*Our Allies and our enemies* . . .": TR, "President Wilson and the Peace Conference," 26 November 1918, written after the 1918 congressional elections, editorial in the *Kansas City Star*, in *Roosevelt in The Kansas City Star*, ed. Ralph Stout (Boston: Houghton Mifflin Co., 1921), 274.

159   *Wilson's League efforts:* See Burns, *The Workshop of Democracy*, 452.

161   "*the nominee of* this *convention* . . .": FDR seconding Al Smith, 1920, in Davis, *FDR: The Beckoning of Destiny*, 612.

161   *Wilson on Democratic slate and ensuing conversation:* Burns, *The Workshop of Democracy*, 474.

162   *TR Jr. on FDR:* Ward, *A First-Class Temperament*, 532.

162   *ER's reading:* Cook, *Eleanor Roosevelt*, 1:282.

162   "*Oh, dear! I wish I could see you* . . .": Ward, *A First-Class Temperament*, 533 (from Roosevelt Family Papers donated by the children).

162   "*I saw a great deal* . . .": Eleanor Roosevelt, *This Is My Story*, 318.

163   "*This was the first time* . . .": Ibid.

163   *FDR's performance:* Ward, *A First-Class Temperament*, 537; see also Cook, *Eleanor Roosevelt*, 1:279–81.

164   "*idealized* . . .*"; "million-vote smile* . . .": Ward, *A First-Class Temperament*, 534.

164   "*F. made 2 speeches* . . .": ER to Sara Delano Roosevelt, 11 April 1920, Lash, *Eleanor and Franklin*, 249–58; and Lela Stiles, *The Man Behind Roosevelt: The Story of Louis McHenry Howe* (World Publishing Co., 1954), 67–74.

164   "*I never before* . . .": ER, *This Is My Story*, 315.

164   "*I had never had any contacts* . . .": Ibid., 314–15.

165   "*As the newspapermen and I* . . .": Ibid., 318.

165   "*Louis proved to be* . . .": Ibid., 319.

166   "*I would be unfaithful to all* . . ." *and following:* See TR *Letters* generally.

166   "*The ear of the leader* . . .": Quoted in Burns, *The Workshop of Democracy*, 364.

167   *FDR as "realist":* Davis, *FDR: The Beckoning of Destiny*, 513.

167   *Drexel Institute speech:* Quoted in ibid., 514.

167   *Henry Adams to FDR:* Davis, *FDR: The Beckoning of Destiny*, 308.

168   *ER gives FDR a copy of Adams's book:* Ibid., 549.

Four: Rehearsal for the Presidency

170   *FDR lining up a job:* Frank Freidel, *Franklin D. Roosevelt: A Rendezvous with Destiny* (Boston: Little, Brown & Co., 1990), 40.

170   *yachting world:* Richard Hofstadter, "Franklin D. Roosevelt: The Patrician as Opportunist," in *The American Political Tradition and the Men Who Made It* (New York: Vintage Books, 1948), 322.

171   "*Oh, that's all right* . . .": Geoffrey C. Ward, *A First-Class Temperament* (New York: Harper & Row, 1989), 563.

171   *ER on her grandmother's death:* Eleanor Roosevelt, *This Is My Story* (New York: Harper & Brothers, 1937), 299–301.

171   *ER alone on her birthday:* Blanche Wiesen Cook, *Eleanor Roosevelt* (New York: Viking, 1992), 1:257.

171 *"I did not look forward to . . .*": ER, *This Is My Story*, 323.

171 *ER learning to cook:* ER, *This Is My Story*, 323.

172 *"to remove the mystery . . .*": Cook, *Eleanor Roosevelt*, 1:288.

172 *"a very able woman lawyer"; humble and very inadequate:* ER, *This Is My Story*, 324.

172 *"New Women":* See Cook, *Eleanor Roosevelt*, 1:293–96.

172 *"intensive education . . .*": ER, *This Is My Story*, 325.

173 *Nathan Miller; Catt; Coolidge attacks women's colleges:* See Cook, *Eleanor Roosevelt*, 1:291, 290, 303.

173 *"no personal contact with actual work"; "I had begun to realize . . .*": ER, *This Is My Story*, 326.

173 *Monday Sewing Class:* See Joseph P. Lash, *Love, Eleanor: Eleanor Roosevelt and Her Friends* (Garden City, N.Y.: Doubleday & Co., 1982), 79; see also ER, *This Is My Story*, 325.

173 *ER's two worlds:* Cook, *Eleanor Roosevelt*, 1:301.

173 *children granted too many privileges:* Eleanor Roosevelt, *This I Remember* (New York: Harper & Brothers, 1949), 11.

174 *Cornell:* Ward, *A First-Class Temperament*, 748.

174 *prejudice against women with college degrees:* ER, "Women Must Learn to Play the Game as Men Do," *Redbook Magazine*, April 1928, reprinted in *What I Hope to Leave Behind: The Essential Essays of Eleanor Roosevelt*, ed. Allida M. Black (New York: Carlson Publishing, 1995), 200.

174 *"lady":* See Jean Bethke Elshtain, "Eleanor Roosevelt as Activist and Thinker: The Lady, the Life of Duty," in *Halcyon* 8 (1986), 97.

174 *duty of the aristocrat:* James MacGregor Burns, *Roosevelt: The Lion and the Fox* (New York: Harcourt, Brace & Co., 1956), 77.

174 *"perhaps, dear Franklin . . .*": Ibid.

175 *machine that wielded its own power and influence:* See Burns, *Roosevelt: The Lion and the Fox*, 78.

175 *"Erroneously reported dead":* FDR, quoted in Ward, *A First-Class Temperament*, 557.

175 *Daniels finds report "libelous":* Ward, *A First-Class Temperament*, 570; documents in "Newport Matter" file, Roosevelt Family Papers (Business and Personal), FDR Library.

176 *"an utter lack of moral perspective":* Ted Morgan, *FDR: A Biography* (New York: Simon & Schuster, 1985); *The New York Times*, 23 July 1921.

176 New York Times *headline:* Quoted in Ward, *A First-Class Temperament*, 573; see also Freidel, *Franklin D. Roosevelt*, 2:96; documents in "Newport Matter" file, Roosevelt Family Papers (Business and Personal), FDR Library.

176 *"Tell Louis I expect . . .*": FDR to ER, 21 July 1921, in *FDR: His Personal Letters, 1905–1928*, ed. Elliott Roosevelt (New York: Duell, Sloan & Pearce, 1947–1950), 516–18. Cited hereafter in this chapter as *FDR Letters*.

177 *"I'd never felt anything so cold . . .*": Quoted in Earle Looker, *This Man Roosevelt* (New York: Brewer, Warren & Putnam, 1932), 111.

177 *Black party leaves:* Alfred B. Rollins Jr., *Roosevelt and Howe* (New York: Alfred A. Knopf, 1962), 179; Grace Howe to Mary Howe, letter of 7 August 1921, Howe Papers, Group 36, FDR Library.

177 *Didn't feel the usual glow:* Looker, *This Man Roosevelt*, 111.

177 *Dr. Keen:* Quoted in Kenneth S. Davis, *FDR: The Beckoning of Destiny, 1882–1928* (New York: G. P. Putnam's Sons, 1971), 654; see also Ward, *A First-Class Temperament*, 586; *FDR Letters, 1905–1928*, and letter from ER to Rosy Roosevelt, 14 August 1921, 523–25.

178 *"He grinned at us . . .*": Quoted in Ward, *A First-Class Temperament*, 599.

178 *"out of his head":* Ibid., 587.

178 *The ordeal of ER and FDR:* See Richard Thayer Goldberg, *The Making of Franklin D. Roosevelt: Triumph Over Disability* (Cambridge, Mass.: Abt Books, 1981), esp. 37.

178 *polio a dreaded illness:* Goldberg, *The Making of Franklin D. Roosevelt*, 30–31.

178 *"their glorious example . . .*": Quoted in Davis, *FDR: The Beckoning of Destiny*, 660–61; see also Freidel, *Franklin D. Roosevelt*, 100; SDR to Frederic Delano, 2 September 1921, FDR Library.

179 *Draper and FDR in hospital:* See Goldberg, *The Making of Franklin D. Roosevelt*, ch. 4.

179 *Draper's lack of optimism:* Ibid., 52.

179 *"He has such courage . . .*": Quoted in Burns, *Roosevelt: The Lion and the Fox*, 88; and Goldberg, *The Making of Franklin D. Roosevelt*, 45; see also Davis, *FDR: The Beckoning of Destiny*, 665;

and Draper to Lovett, 24 September 1921, originally published in John Gunther, *Roosevelt in Retrospect* (Harper & Brothers, 1950), 226.

179 *"I have always had a very bad tendency . . .":* ER, *This Is My Story*, 338.

179 *"the most trying winter of my entire life":* Ibid., 336.

180 *"He did not bemoan his fate . . .":* Quoted in Goldberg, *The Making of Franklin D. Roosevelt*, 54–55.

180 *"He was the most charming man . . .":* Ibid., 50.

181 *"I am still on crutches . . .":* Rollins, *Roosevelt and Howe*, 187; FDR to John Adriance, 15 December 1923, Group XIV, FDR Letters, FDR Library.

182 *FDR's business speculations:* Davis, *FDR: The Beckoning of Destiny*, 698.

182 *the most remarkable of times:* Described in James MacGregor Burns, *The Workshop of Democracy* (New York: Vintage Books, 1985), 508.

183 *Howe sends congratulatory letters:* Burns, *Roosevelt: The Lion and the Fox*, 91.

184 *"I tried fishing but had no skill . . .":* ER, *This Is My Story*, 345–46.

184 *"I had dropped out of what is known as society . . .":* Ibid., 346–47.

185 *"Have something to say . . .":* Quoted in Joseph P. Lash, *Eleanor and Franklin* (New York: W. W. Norton & Co., 1971), 278.

185 *"Never admit you're licked":* Cook, *Eleanor Roosevelt*, 2:351.

185 *"hard work and unselfish public service . . .":* ER, *This Is My Story*, 344.

185 *"You need not be proud of me . . .":* Quoted in Cook, *Eleanor Roosevelt*, 1:346; ER to FDR, 6 February 1924, FDR Letters, FDR Library.

185 *"It began to dawn upon me . . .":* ER, *This Is My Story*, 342.

185 *FDR still among the most prominent Democrats:* Burns, *Roosevelt: The Lion and the Fox*, 91.

186 *Smith-Roosevelt alliance:* Ibid., 91–92.

186 *education for both:* Burns, *Roosevelt: The Lion and the Fox*, 93.

187 *"To many women, and I am one of them . . .":* ER, *New York Times*, 15 April 1924, quoted in Cook, *Eleanor Roosevelt*, 1:348.

187 *"There's one thing I'm thankful for . . .":* ER to FDR, 9 April 1924, FDR Letters, FDR Library.

187 *women from upstate New York:* ER, *This Is My Story*, 354.

187 *"This was to be a new step in my education . . .":* Ibid.

187 *ER locked out of all-male Resolutions Committee:* Cook, *Eleanor Roosevelt*, 1:350.

187 *"I took my politics so seriously . . .":* ER, *This Is My Story*, 356.

188 *"Women must get into the political game . . .":* ER, interview in *New York Times*, 20 April 1924, in Cook, *Eleanor Roosevelt*, 1:352.

188 *Newspapers called on her:* Lash, *Eleanor and Franklin*, 287.

188 *"It always amuses me . . .":* ER, *This Is My Story*, 362.

188 *Ku Klux Klan:* Davis, *FDR: The Beckoning of Destiny*, 754.

188 *"You equally who come from the great cities . . .":* Joseph D. Proskauer, *A Segment of My Times* (New York: Farrar, Straus & Young, 1950), 50–51.

189 *"a moving and distinguished thing . . .":* Quoted in Rollins, *Roosevelt and Howe*, 216; Walter Lippmann to FDR, 27 June 1924, Group XVI, FDR Letters, FDR Library.

189 *Mark Sullivan, Herald Tribune, and World on FDR:* Quoted in Davis, *FDR: The Beckoning of Destiny*, 756–57; Earle Looker's column "Looker On," 1 July 1924, *Herald Tribune*, and *World*, quoted in *FDR Letters, 1905–1928*, 562.

189 *"In 1920 . . . I did not think . . .":* FDR to Irving Washburn, 24 July 1924, FDR Letters, Group XVI, FDR Library.

189 *"an extraordinary flair for government":* ER, *This I Remember*, 50.

190 *Ted Jr. following his father:* Elliott Roosevelt and James Brough, *An Untold Story: The Roosevelts of Hyde Park* (New York: G. P. Putnam's Sons, 1973), 211.

190 *"willing to do the bidding . . .":* Cook, *Eleanor Roosevelt*, 1:352.

190 *"rough stunt":* ER, *This I Remember*, 31–32.

190 *ER's visit to Omaha Beach cemetery:* ER, "My Day," 1 September 1956, in *Eleanor Roosevelt's My Day*, ed. David Emblidge (New York: Pharos Books, 1991), 3:107.

190 *"The water put me where I am . . .":* Nathan Miller, *FDR: An Intimate History* (Doubleday & Co., 1983), 191.

191 *"almost as well as if I had nothing the matter . . .":* FDR to George Foster Peabody, 14 October 1924, quoted in Davis, *FDR: The Beckoning of Destiny,* 767.

191 *nineteen-year-old principal:* FDR, Remarks to State Superintendents of Education at the White House, 11 December 1935, *PPA,* 1935, 499.

192 *FDR and building of Val-Kill:* Cook, *Eleanor Roosevelt,* 1:325.

192 *ER and Rose Schneiderman:* Lash, *Love Eleanor,* 89; Cook, *Eleanor Roosevelt,* 1:335.

192 *Caroline O'Day; "paid in experience"; "the one thing . . .":* Cook, *Eleanor Roosevelt,* 1:324, 398–99.

193 *"Private Interlude":* ER, *This I Remember,* ch. 3.

194 *Al Smith and FDR:* See Davis, *FDR: The Beckoning of Destiny,* 824–51.

194 *telegrams:* See Freidel, *Franklin D. Roosevelt: A Rendezvous with Destiny,* 53–54.

194 *Al Smith's wisecrack:* Burns, *Roosevelt: The Lion and the Fox,* 101.

195 *FDR wins 1929 election as governor:* Joan Hoff, *Encyclopedia of the American Presidency* (New York: Simon & Schuster, 1994), 2:498.

196 *"God bless you . . .":* Kenneth S. Davis, *FDR: The New York Years, 1928–1933* (New York: Random House, 1979), 63; *New York Times,* 1 January 1929.

196 *"I have had all I can stand of it":* Davis, *FDR: The New York Years,* 53; *New York Times,* 8 November 1928.

197 *ER's reflections on Al Smith:* ER, *This I Remember,* 49–50.

197 *"I've got to be governor . . .":* Frances Perkins, *The Roosevelt I Knew* (New York: Viking Press, 1946), 52–53.

198 *"I want to see something done . . .":* *Public Papers of Franklin D. Roosevelt, 48th Governor of the State of New York,* 1929 (Albany: J. B. Lyon, 1937), 157.

198 *"very brave step . . .":* Quoted in Frank Freidel, *Franklin D. Roosevelt: The Triumph* (Boston: Little, Brown & Co., 1956), 45; he cites *New York Times,* 15 March 1929.

198 *"stopped to change horses . . .":* Freidel, *Franklin D. Roosevelt: The Triumph,* 45.

198 *"sneering and superior tone":* Ibid., 107.

199 *agricultural policy:* Bernard Bellush, *Franklin D. Roosevelt as Governor of New York* (New York: Columbia University Press, 1955), ch. 4.

199 *"must keep them to herself":* ER, "Wives of Great Men," *Liberty,* 1 October 1932, reprinted in *What I Hope to Leave Behind,* ed. Black, 200.

199 Women's Democratic News: Cook, *Eleanor Roosevelt,* 1:383–84.

199 *"guard against the emptiness . . ."; "If anyone were to ask me . . .":* ER, "What I Want Most Out of Life," *Success Magazine,* May 1927, quoted in Cook, *Eleanor Roosevelt,* 1:381–82.

200 *Earl Miller:* On Earl Miller, see Cook, *Eleanor Roosevelt,* 1:429–42.

200 Redbook *article:* ER, "Women Must Learn to Play the Game as Men Do," *Redbook Magazine,* April 1928, reprinted in *What I Hope to Leave Behind,* ed. Black 195–200.

200 *ignorant of the most basic principles:* ER, "Wives of Great Men," reprinted in *What I Hope to Leave Behind,* ed. Black, 216.

200 *"there is no reason why . . .":* *New York Times,* 16 November 1930, quoted in Cook, *Eleanor Roosevelt,* 1:420.

200 *"Can't a woman think . . .":* Quoted in Cook, *Eleanor Roosevelt,* 2:187.

200 *"nerves of iron . . .":* Cook, *Eleanor Roosevelt,* 1:388.

200 *"visceral hatred":* Robert A. Caro, *The Power Broker: Robert Moses and the Fall of New York* (New York: Alfred A. Knopf, 1974), 357, 293.

200 *"accustomed to running and planning everything":* Davis, *FDR: The New York Years,* 61.

201 *Roosevelt's support for Moses:* Caro, *The Power Broker,* 314–19.

201 *ER counsels FDR to hire Perkins:* Cook, *Eleanor Roosevelt,* 1:393.

201 *"unspeakable conditions in crowded tenement districts . . .":* FDR, "Women's Field in Politics," Women's City Club *Quarterly,* 1928, quoted in Cook, *Eleanor Roosevelt,* 1:393.

201 *Todhunter School:* Cook, *Eleanor Roosevelt,* 1:402–6.

201 *"The spirit of the school", "very unlike ourselves"*: ER's comments, made in 1929, quoted in Cook, *Eleanor Roosevelt*, 2:316.
201 *trip to Europe in summer 1929*: ER, *This I Remember*, 58–60.
201 *trip not a success*: Cook, *Eleanor Roosevelt*, 1:412–15.
202 *"recent little Flurry . . ."*: FDR to Howe, 1 December 1929, in *FDR Letters, 1928–1945*, 92.
202 *description of the canal trip*: Taken from Burns, *Roosevelt: The Lion and the Fox*, 118.
202 *"We have got to deinstitutionalize . . ."*: Quoted in Burns, ibid.
202 *not exactly like the navy days . . .*: FDR to Edward McCauley Jr., 21 March 1929, in *FDR Letters, 1928–1945*, 42–43.
203 *"common stock should be planted . . ."*: FDR to Henry Morgenthau Jr., 29 May 1929, in *FDR Letters, 1928–1945*, 60.

Five: People: Pride and Fall

208 *Real income of workers, 1923–28*: Irving Bernstein, *The Lean Years* (New York: Riverside Press, 1960), 65.
208 *"Big business in America . . ."*: Steffens to Jo Davidson, 18 February 1929, in Ella Winter and Granville Hicks, eds., *The Letters of Lincoln Steffens* (New York: Harcourt, Brace & Co., 1938), 2:829–30.
208 *cornucopia of goods and services*: Winifred D. Wandersee, *Women's Work and Family Values* (Cambridge, Mass.: Harvard University Press, 1981), 17.
208 *employment and unemployment*: James T. Patterson, *America's Struggle Against Poverty, 1900–1980* (Cambridge, Mass.: Harvard University Press, 1981), 17–18; see also Wandersee, *Women's Work and Family Values*, 27–28.
209 *pre-1929 middle-class and working-class attitudes*: Robert S. Lynd and Helen Merrell Lynd, *Middletown in Transition* (New York: Harcourt Brace & Co., 1937), ch. 12. See, more generally, Oscar Handlin, *The American People in the Twentieth Century* (Cambridge, Mass.: Harvard University Press, 1954), and Michael E. Parrish, *Anxious Decades: America in Prosperity and Depression, 1920–1940* (New York: W. W. Norton & Co., 1992).
209 *"One of the oldest . . ."*: Ray Liman Wilbur and Arthur Mastick Hyde, *The Hoover Policies* (New York: Charles Scribner's Sons, 1937), 2–3.
209 *"I am convinced we have passed the worst . . ."*: Quoted in David Burner, *Herbert Hoover: A Public Life* (New York: Alfred A. Knopf, 1979), 250; *Public Papers of the Presidents of the United States—Herbert Hoover: 1930*, Address to the Chamber of Commerce, 1 May 1930 (Washington, D.C.: U.S. Government Printing Office, 1976), 171.
209 *"used the word 'depression'"*: Burner, *Herbert Hoover*, 248.
209 *Hoover attends World Series game*: Ibid.
210 *"sing a song . . ."*: Robert S. McElvaine, *The Great Depression: America, 1929–1941* (New York: Times Books, 1984), 19.
210 *"Pack up your troubles . . ."*: Personal memory of James MacGregor Burns.
210 *wage, investment, GNP statistics*: Parrish, *Anxious Decades*, 249–50.
210 *Hoover on voluntary help*: Dixon Wecter, *The Age of the Great Depression, 1929–1941* (New York: Macmillan Co., 1948), 46.
212 *Hoover as a Theodore Roosevelt progressive*: Burner, *Herbert Hoover*, 7off.
212 *FDR joins in claiming economy is "sound"*: Quoted in Kenneth S. Davis, *FDR: The New York Years, 1928–1933* (New York: Random House, 1979), 157; see also Frank Freidel, *Franklin D. Roosevelt: The Triumph* (Boston: Little, Brown & Co., 1956), 86.
212 *Perkins statement contradicts Hoover*: Frances Perkins, *The Roosevelt I Knew* (New York: Viking Press, 1946), 95–96.
212 *"Bully for you . . ."*: Davis, *FDR: The New York Years*, 156.
213 *FDR and unemployment insurance*: Freidel, *FDR: The Triumph*, 218–20.
213 *"acting through its government . . ."*: Ibid. 219; Public Papers and Addresses of Franklin D. Roosevelt, 1928–1932, ed., Samuel I. Rosenman (New York: Random House, 1941) 1931, 173. Cited hereafter in this chapter as PPA.

213 *rise in suicides:* McElvaine, *The Great Depression,* 18.

214 *"The unemployment demonstration . . .":* Quoted in Frances Fox Piven and Richard A. Cloward, *Poor People's Movements: Why They Succeed, How They Fail* (New York: Pantheon Books, 1977), 51; *New York Times,* 7 March 1930.

214 *Fish's resolution to investigate Communist activities:* Bernstein, *The Lean Years,* 427–28; *New York Times,* 23 May 1930, 1.

214 *demonstrations in Chicago and Detroit:* Piven and Cloward, *Poor People's Movements,* 59.

215 *"all Unemployed Leagues that we know of . . .":* Ibid., 73–75.

215 *licked:* Louis Adamic, *My America* (New York: Harper & Brothers, 1938), 298.

215 *"breaking down of the moral fiber . . .":* Quoted in Bernstein, *The Lean Years,* 435.

215 *"we are less worried about revolution . . .":* "Talk of the Town," *New Yorker,* 25 June 1932, 7.

216 *"there was nothing you or your boss . . .":* Cabell Phillips, *From the Crash to the Blitz: 1929–1939* (New York: Macmillan Co., 1969), 2.

216 *"Mellon pulled the whistle . . .":* Piven and Cloward, *Poor People's Movements,* 52.

216 *"have one thing in common—a curious melancholy . . .":* Quoted in Bernstein, *The Lean Years,* 439.

217 *FDR's reaction to routing of bonus army:* Davis, *FDR: The New York Years,* 351.

217 *FDR offers fares to veterans:* Freidel, *FDR: The Triumph,* 327.

217 *"the end of this country as we know it . . .":* Thomas L. Stokes, *Chip Off My Shoulder* (Princeton, N.J.: Princeton University Press, 1940), 303.

Six: The Pragmatists: Making It Work

219 *"Do you know, by God . . .":* Clark Howell to FDR, 2 December 1931, in *FDR: His Personal Letters, 1928–1945,* ed. Elliott Roosevelt (New York: Duell, Sloan & Pearce, 1947–1950), 229–32. Cited hereafter in this chapter as *FDR Letters.*

219 *"in any shape, manner, or form":* FDR to Archibald McNeil, 9 May 1930, *FDR Letters, 1928–1945,* 117.

219 *"no personal desire to run . . .":* FDR to Burton K. Wheeler, 3 June 1930, *FDR Letters, 1928–1945,* 129.

219 *"no hankering, secret or otherwise . . .":* FDR to Mrs. Casper Whitney, 9 December 1930, *FDR Letters, 1928–1945,* 162.

219 *"taking absolutely no part in any movement":* FDR to Jouett Shouse, 9 December 1931, *FDR Letters, 1928–1945,* 216.

219 *doing "the br'er rabbit":* FDR to Henry Morgenthau Sr., 23 June 1931, *FDR Letters, 1928–1945,* 197.

220 *"established powers and precedents":* FDR to Alfred E. Smith, 8 February 1931, *FDR Letters, 1928–1945,* 179; see also FDR to LaRue Brown, 22 December 1931, *FDR Letters, 1928–1945,* 246.

220 *intellectuals attacking the two major parties:* James MacGregor Burns, *The Workshop of Democracy* (New York: Alfred A. Knopf, 1985), 557.

220 *pronouncements of business leaders:* Ibid.

220 *"We cannot squander ourselves . . .":* Ibid.

221 *Eleanor was speaking out:* Blanche Weisen Cook, *Eleanor Roosevelt, 1884–1933* (New York: Viking, 1992), 1:421–24.

221 *"Brother, Can You Spare a Dime?" Songs of the Depression,* Book-of-the-Month Records, 1980.

221 *"The greatest, gaudiest spree in history":* Quoted in Arthur M. Schlesinger Jr., *The Crisis of the Old Order* (Boston: Houghton Mifflin Co., 1957), 145.

221 *"sacred creed of rugged individualism":* Charles A. Beard, "The Myth of Rugged American Individualism," *Harper's Magazine,* December 1931, 13.

221 *businessmen demanded governmental interference:* Howard Zinn, *New Deal Thought* (Indianapolis: Bobbs-Merrill Co., 1966), 2–10.

222 *Veblen on capitalism and "conspicuous consumption":* Max Lerner, ed., *The Portable Veblen* (New York: Viking Press, 1948).

222 *Niebuhr's philosophy:* Reinhold Niebuhr, *Moral Man and Immoral Society* (New York: Charles Scribner's Sons, 1941).

222 *FDR and Lippmann:* Ronald Steel, *Walter Lippmann and the American Century* (Boston: Little, Brown & Co., 1980), 432.

222 *"Lippmann scares me this morning":* James Thurber, *Men, Women, and Dogs* (New York: Harcourt, Brace & Co., 1943); cartoon printed in *The New Yorker,* 1942.

223 *FDR "just doesn't happen to have . . .":* Lippmann to Baker, 24 November 1931; Oral History Collection, "The Reminiscences of Walter Lippmann," in the Yale Lippmann Collection, cited in Steel, *Walter Lippmann and the American Century,* 291.

223 *"a highly impressionable person . . .":* "Today and Tomorrow," *New York Herald Tribune,* 8 January 1932, cited in Steel, *Walter Lippmann and the American Century,* 291–92.

223 *despite Lippmann's "brilliance, it is very clear . . .":* FDR to Morris Llewellyn Cooke, 18 January 1932, in *FDR Letters, 1928–1945,* 254.

223 *favorite hymn; ER asks if he really believes:* Geoffrey C. Ward, *Before the Trumpet: Young Franklin Roosevelt, 1882–1905* (New York: Harper & Row, 1985), 156–57.

224 *shapelessness of FDR's policy:* James MacGregor Burns, *The Crosswinds of Freedom* (New York: Alfred A. Knopf, 1989), 125.

225 *"visionary policies of meddling . . .":* William Randolph Hearst on NBC Network, 2 January 1932; *New York Times,* 3 January 1932, 3; W. A. Swanberg, *Citizen Hearst* (New York: Charles Scribner's Sons, 1961), cites *New York American,* 3 January 1932.

225 *Roosevelt wooing anti-League progressives:* Marion C. McKenna, *Borah* (Ann Arbor, Mich.: University of Michigan Press, 1961).

225 *Baker deserts League, Farley's visit to Hearst, Hearst's reaction: Chicago Herald-Examiner,* 17 January 1932, cited in Kenneth S. Davis, *FDR: The New York Years, 1928–1933* (New York: Random House, 1979), 258–59; see also, *Chicago Herald and American,* 31 January 1932, cited in Frank Freidel, *Franklin D. Roosevelt: The Triumph* (Boston: Little, Brown & Co., 1956), 250 (a slight variation in the quotes).

226 *FDR states position on League: New York Times,* 3 February 1932, 1.

226 *reactions to FDR's statement:* Joseph P. Lash, *Eleanor and Franklin* (New York: W. W. Norton & Co., 1971), 347.

226 *Outraged complaints streamed in:* Davis, *FDR: The New York Years,* 258–60; Lash, *Eleanor and Franklin,* 347.

227 *omission of FDR's statements on League:* Address Before the New York State Grange [excerpts], 2 February 1932, *Public Papers and Addresses of Franklin D. Roosevelt, 1928–1932,* ed. Samuel I. Rosenman (New York: Random House, 1941), 155–57. Cited hereafter in this chapter as *PPA.*

227 *FDR response to Wise and Holmes:* Davis, *FDR: The New York Years,* 263–64.

227 *FDR policy advisers:* See Beatrice Bishop Berle and Travis Beal Jacobs, eds., *Navigating the Rapids, 1918–1971: From the Papers of Adolf A. Berle* (New York: Harcourt Brace Jovanovich, 1973).

228 *who could challenge FDR's ideas:* See Rexford G. Tugwell, *In Search of Roosevelt* (Cambridge, Mass.: Harvard University Press, 1972).

228 *Tugwell and FDR:* Rexford G. Tugwell, *The Brains Trust* (New York: Viking Press, 1968), 19–29; see also Bernard Sternsher, *Rexford Tugwell and the New Deal* (New Brunswick, N.J.: Rutgers University Press, 1964).

230 *"No nation can long endure . . .":* FDR, "Forgotten Man" Speech, 7 April 1932, *PPA* 1928–1932, 624–26.

230 *Smith reaction to "Forgotten Man" speech: New York Times,* 14 April 1932, 6.

230 *FDR Jefferson Day address:* FDR, Address at Jefferson Day Dinner, 18 April 1932, *PPA* 1928–1932, 627–39.

231 *"was weak on relations . . .":* Tugwell, *In Search of Roosevelt,* 128.

231 *FDR's Oglethorpe address:* FDR, Address at Oglethorpe University, 22 May 1932, *PPA* 1928–1932, 639–47.

232 *"The country needs . . .": PPA* 1928–1932, 664.

232 *FDR baits Lindley to write speech:* Samuel I. Rosenman, *Working with Roosevelt* (New York: Harper & Brothers, 1952), 65.

232 *"a larger measure of social planning":* PPA 1928–1932, 642.

233 *length of original speech; subsequent cuts:* Tugwell, *In Search of Roosevelt*, 219–20.

233 *FDR nomination acceptance speech:* The Governor Accepts the Nomination for the Presidency, 2 July 1932, PPA 1928–1932, 647–59.

233 *Rosenman fears speech will land in wastebasket:* Rosenman, *Working with Roosevelt*, 67.

234 *description of the convention:* Chicago Daily News, 1 July 1932, 1 and 3.

234 *Hearst and Garner:* See Ferdinand Lundberg, *Imperial Hearst: A Social Biography* (New York: Equinox Cooperative Press, 1936), and Oliver Carlson and Ernest Sutherland Bates, *Hearst, Lord of San Simeon* (Westport, Conn.: Greenwood Press, 1936, 1970).

235 *Democratic convention deadlock:* Freidel, *Franklin D. Roosevelt: The Triumph*, 307–11; see also Davis, *The New York Years*, 312–28, and Schlesinger, *The Crisis of the Old Order*, 295–314; on key leaders we have used James F. Byrnes Papers, Robert Muldrow Cooper Library, Clemson University.

235 *Politics is "funny":* Quoted in James MacGregor Burns, *Roosevelt: The Lion and the Fox* (New York: Harcourt, Brace & Co., 1956), 138; *New York Times*, 2 July 1932, 1.

235 *"California came here to nominate a President":* Quoted in Burns, *Roosevelt: The Lion and the Fox*, 137; Official Report of the Proceedings of the Democratic National Convention, 1932, 325.

235 *"the forty-four votes of California ...":* Freidel, *Franklin D. Roosevelt: The Triumph*, 311.

235 *ER's letter to Nancy Cook:* Blanche Wiesen Cook, *Eleanor Roosevelt* (New York: Viking, 1992), 1:446.

236 *"That woman is unhappy ...":* Lorena A. Hickok, *Eleanor Roosevelt: Reluctant First Lady* (New York: Dodd, Mead & Co., 1962), 31–33.

236 *a "major role in the crowning ...":* Raymond Moley, *After Seven Years* (New York: Harper & Brothers, 1939), 29.

236 *"You have nominated me ...":* The Governor Accepts the Nomination for the Presidency, 2 July 1932, PPA 1928–1932, 648.

237 *draft:* Davis, *FDR: The New York Years*, 334; Samuel I. Rosenman, *Working with Roosevelt*, 76.

237 *FDR acceptance speech:* The Governor Accepts the Nomination for the Presidency, 2 July 1932, PPA 1928–1932, 647–59.

238 *"I pledge you ...":* Davis points out later italics, in Davis, *FDR: The New York Years*, 335.

239 *Walker's trial; FDR the star:* Herbert Mitgang, *Once Upon a Time in New York: Jimmy Walker, Franklin Roosevelt, and the Last Great Battle of the Jazz Age* (New York: Free Press, 1999), 183ff, 190. See also Herbert Mitgang, *The Man Who Rode the Tiger* (New York: W. W. Norton & Co., 1979), passim.

239 *"hell of a reprimand":* FDR, quoted in Mitgang, *Once Upon a Time in New York*, 202.

239 *Edith Roosevelt at Madison Square Garden:* Cook, *Eleanor Roosevelt*, 1:469–70.

239 *"a little out of date ...":* Quoted in David Burner, *Herbert Hoover* (New York: Alfred A. Knopf, 1979), 311. See also, Donald J. Lisio, *The President and Protest: Hoover, Conspiracy, and the Bonus Riot* (Columbia, Mo.: University of Missouri Press, 1974).

239 *never before "in modern history ...":* FDR, The Governor Accepts the Nomination for the Presidency, 2 July 1932, PPA 1928–1932, 658.

239 *"we had not fully realized ...":* Tugwell, *In Search of Roosevelt*, xxi.

241 *conversation between Huey Long and FDR:* Ibid., 430–32.

241 *"The second most dangerous man ...":* Quoted in Tugwell, *In Search of Roosevelt*, 433.

241 *"so few fanatics ...":* H. L. Mencken, *Making a President* (New York: Alfred A. Knopf, 1932), 105.

242 *"My Dutch is up":* James A. Farley, *Behind the Ballots* (New York: Harcourt, Brace & Co., 1938), 164.

242 *campaigning:* The description of the campaign is drawn largely from Burns, *Roosevelt: The Lion and the Fox*, 143–44.

243 *Pittsburgh speech:* FDR, Campaign Address on the Federal Budget at Pittsburgh, Pa., 19 October 1932, PPA 1928–1932, 797, 810.

Seven: The Policy Makers: Stormy Passage

245 *"preeminently a place of moral leadership"*: James MacGregor Burns, *Roosevelt: The Lion and the Fox* (New York: Harcourt, Brace & Co., 1956), 151.

245 *"Luckily for him . . ."*: Walter Lippmann, "The New Deal—What It Means to Us," *Literary Digest* 19 November 1932, 7.

246 *business and unemployment statistics:* Frank Freidel, *Franklin D. Roosevelt: Launching the New Deal* (Boston: Little, Brown & Co., 1973), 11.

247 *"Tony, keep quiet . . ."*: "How Roosevelt Saw It," *New York Times*, 17 February 1933, 1.

247 *"I do not hate Mr. Roosevelt personally . . ."*: Quoted in Freidel, *FDR: Launching the New Deal*, 173.

247 *"break down the initiative . . ."*: *The State Papers and Other Public Writings of Herbert Hoover*, ed. William Starr Myers (New York: Doubleday, Doran & Co., 1934), 1:526–27.

248 *Frederic Delano gives FDR copy of TR report:* Walter L. Creese, *TVA's Public Planning: The Vision, the Reality* (Knoxville, Tenn.: University of Tennessee Press, 1990), chs. 1–2. Creese cites FDR Letters, F. A. Delano Papers, Box 4, FDR Library.

248 *"My friends, I am determined . . ."*: Informal Extemporaneous Remarks at Montgomery, Alabama, on Muscle Shoals Inspection Trip, 21 January 1933, *PPA* 1933, 888–89.

250 *"someone straight from the ranks . . ."*: Frances Perkins to FDR, 1 February 1933, in *FDR Letters, 1928–1945*, 316.

250 *FDR insists on Frances Perkins:* Freidel, *FDR: Launching the New Deal*, 156.

250 *Stone endorses Hoover to Frankfurter:* Curt Gentry, *J. Edgar Hoover: The Man and the Secrets* (New York: W. W. Norton & Co., 1991), 157.

250 *"it is all right . . ."*: FDR Memorandum to Frankfurter, 22 April 1933, in Max Freedman, ed., *Roosevelt and Frankfurter: Their Correspondence, 1928–1945* (Boston: Little, Brown & Co., 1967), 129.

251 *Berle and FDR:* Berle to Roosevelt, 24 May 1934 and 15 March 1934; Roosevelt to Berle, 24 May 1934, in FDR Letters, President's Personal File 1306, FDR Library.

252 *"abandonment of 90 percent . . ."*: Hoover to Senator David A. Reed, 20 February 1933, in William Starr Myers and Walter H. Newton, *The Hoover Administration* (New York: Charles Scribner's Sons, 1936), 341. For a general description of Hoover's attitude toward Roosevelt at that time, see also David Burner, *Herbert Hoover: A Public Life* (New York: Alfred A. Knopf, 1979), 322.

252 *people watching ceremony:* James MacGregor Burns, *The Crosswinds of Freedom* (New York: Alfred A. Knopf, 1989), 22.

252 *"This is a day . . ." and following:* FDR, Inaugural Address, 4 March 1933, in *Public Papers and Addresses of Franklin D. Roosevelt*, ed. Samuel I. Rosenman (New York: Random House, 1938), 1933, 11–16.

254 *"It was very, very solemn . . ."*: *New York Times*, 5 March 1933, 7.

254 *FDR expresses fear to son:* James Roosevelt with Bill Libby, *My Parents: A Differing View* (Chicago: Playboy Press Books, 1976), 141–42; James Roosevelt and Sidney Schalett, *Affectionately, FDR: A Son's Story of a Lonely Man* (New York: Harcourt, Brace & Co., 1959), 232.

255 *"We were just a bunch of men . . ."*: Raymond Moley, *After Seven Years* (New York: Harper & Brothers, 1939), 148.

255 *"swift and staccato action . . . stressing of conventional . . ."*: Moley, *After Seven Years*, 151; see also Freidel, *FDR: Launching the New Deal*, 220.

255 *ER's bill at Mayflower Hotel:* Eleanor Roosevelt, *This I Remember* (Garden City, N.Y.: Dolphin Books, 1949), 86–87.

255 *"I want to talk for a few minutes . . ."*: The First "Fireside Chat," 12 March 1933, *PPA* 1933, 61–65.

256 *fireside chats:* See Robert J. Brown, *Manipulating the Ether: The Power of Broadcast Radio in the Thirties* (Jefferson, N.C.: McFarland & Co, 1998).

256 *Emergency Banking Relief Act:* See Jeffrey B. Morris and Richard B. Morris, eds. *Encyclopedia of American History* (New York: HarperCollins, 1996), 380–81; see also Frank Freidel, *Franklin D. Roosevelt: A Rendezvous with Destiny* (Boston: Little, Brown & Co., 1990), 94–95.

257 *limited financial impact of Economy Act:* Richard B. Morris, ed., *Encyclopedia of American History* (New York: Harper & Brothers, 1953), 342.

258 *Congressional changes of FDR bills:* James E. Sargent, *Roosevelt and the Hundred Days: Struggle for the Early New Deal* (New York: Garland Publishing, 1981), 224.

259 *"the way to disarm . . .":* FDR, "The Congress Is Informed of the President's Appeal to the Nations of the World," 16 May 1933, *PPA* 1933, 192.

260 *"You can't scold me . . ." and following:* Freidel, *FDR: A Rendezvous with Destiny*, 117.

260 *Opposition to CCC, esp. from Norman Thomas:* Quote is from Freidel, *FDR: Launching the New Deal*, 261, citing *New York Times*, of 15 and 24 March 1933. See also John A. Salmond, *The Civilian Conservation Corps, 1933–42: A New Deal Case Study* (Durham, N.C.: Duke University Press, 1967), 14; and "Job Bill 'Fascism' Alleged By Green," testimony before Congress reported in *New York Times*, 25 March 1933, 4.

261 *"utter rubbish. . . . The camps will be run . . .":* Quoted in Freidel, *Launching the New Deal*, 261.

261 *Extension of planning to a "wider field":* FDR, "A Suggestion for Legislation to Create the TVA," 10 April 1933, *PPA* 1933, 122.

261 *"What are you going to say . . . ?":* Eric F. Goldman, *Rendezvous with Destiny* (New York: Alfred A. Knopf, 1952), 339. Goldman cites his interview with George W. Norris.

262 *"revolution in the countryside":* Arthur M. Schlesinger Jr., *The Coming of the New Deal* (Boston: Houghton Mifflin Co., 1958), 27; Senate Agricultural and Forestry Commission, Agricultural Adjustment Relief Plan: Hearings, 72nd Congress, 2nd Session (1933), 15.

263 *Tugwell on NIRA:* Rexford G. Tugwell, *The Industrial Discipline and the Governmental Arts* (New York: Columbia University Press, 1933).

264 *"There have to be hours adapted to . . .":* Frances Perkins, *The Roosevelt I Knew* (New York: Viking Press, 1946), 194.

264 *Wagner stands ground on 7(a):* J. Joseph Huthmacher, *Senator Robert F. Wagner and the Rise of Urban Liberalism* (New York: Atheneum Publishers, 1968), 147.

265 *fireside chat excerpts:* The Second "Fireside Chat," 7 May 1933, *PPA* 1933, 165.

265 *"a great cooperative movement . . .":* Recommendation to Enact NIRA, 17 May 1933, *PPA* 1933, 202.

265 *"The latter part of this session . . .":* Quoted in Freidel, *FDR: Launching the New Deal*, 452; he cites Hiram Johnson to his sons, 16 June 1933, Johnson mss.

265 *"As I saw it . . .":* Eleanor Roosevelt, *This I Remember* (New York: Harper & Brothers, 1949), 74–75.

265 *the mail was Missy's department:* Ibid., 76.

265 *"My zest in life . . .":* Doris Kearns Goodwin, *No Ordinary Time: Franklin and Eleanor Roosevelt: The Home Front in World War II* (New York: Simon & Schuster, 1994), 90.

266 *New Deal geared toward men:* Suzanne Mettler, *Dividing Citizens: Gender and Federalism in New Deal Public Policy* (Ithaca, N.Y.: Cornell University Press, 1998), 19.

266 *women's division of CWA:* Joseph P. Lash, *Eleanor and Franklin* (New York: W. W. Norton & Co., 1971), 389.

266 *slaughtering of piglets:* Ibid., 383.

266 *over 300,000 pieces of mail:* ER, *This I Remember*, 99.

266 *"we can't spear any money . . .":* Letter from Joseph Blin Jr. to Eleanor Roosevelt, 23 December 1933, in FDR Letters, FDR Library.

266 *"Oh Mrs. Roosevelt we do not want charity . . .":* Letter from Bertie Baugher to Eleanor Roosevelt, 3 January 1934, in FDR Letters, FDR Library.

266 *"Your the first president's wife . . .":* Letter from Joseph Blin Jr. to Eleanor Roosevelt, 23 December 1933, in FDR Letters, FDR Library.

267 *"There are certain persons . . .":* Secretary to Mrs. Roosevelt to Joseph Blin Jr., 8 January 1934, in FDR Letters, FDR Library.

267 *In three days . . . five o'clock tea:* Lash, *Eleanor and Franklin*, 360; Bess Furman, *White House Profile* (Indianapolis: Bobbs-Merrill Co., 1951), 320.

267 *the boys were frequent visitors:* See Furman, *White House Profile*.

268 *"[I]t can be done . . .":* *New York Times*, 14 May 1933.

268 *"I simply will not have it!":* Kenneth S. Davis, *FDR: The New Deal Years, 1933–1937* (New York: Random House, 1986), 173.

268 *"No maid, no secretary . . .":* Will Rogers, quoted by Lash, *Eleanor and Franklin*, 368.

268 *"7-cent luncheons":* Lash, *Eleanor and Franklin*, 362.

268 *"I always thought when people . . .":* Martha Strayer, quoted in ibid., 364.

269 *These "Gridiron Widows" parties . . . :* Furman, *White House Profile*, 322; see also Lash, *Eleanor and Franklin*, 364, and ER, *This I Remember*, 93–94.

269 *press conferences for women:* See Lorena A. Hickok, *Eleanor Roosevelt: Reluctant First Lady* (Dodd, Mead & Co., 1981).

269 *"I really beat Franklin . . . !":* Quoted in Blanche Wiesen Cook, *Eleanor Roosevelt: 1933–1938* (New York: Viking, 1999), 2:41.

269 *"subsistence homesteads, work camps . . .":* Furman, *White House Profile*, 320.

269 *George VI of England:* Lorena A. Hickok, *Reluctant First Lady* (New York: Dodd, Mead & Co., 1962), 109–10.

270 *Howe talked daily . . . :* See Alfred B. Rollins Jr., *Roosevelt and Howe* (New York: Alfred A. Knopf, 1962).

270 *"I served many sandwiches . . .":* *New York Times*, 17 May 1933, 10; ER, *This I Remember*, 111–13.

271 *"Hoover sent the army . . .":* Friedel, *FDR: Launching the New Deal*, 265.

271 *"It is such fine things . . .":* Lash, *Eleanor and Franklin*, 366–67. He cites letter to ER from Josephus Daniels, 26 May 1933.

271 *"Eleanor, if you want to be president . . .":* Malvina Thompson Schneider, in interview with Joseph P. Lash, quoted in Lash, *Eleanor and Franklin*, 390.

271 *mining jobs down by almost 150,000:* Price V. Fishback, *Soft Coal, Hard Choices: The Economic Welfare of Bituminous Coal Miners, 1890–1930* (Oxford: Oxford University Press, 1992), 20.

272 *degradation of human beings:* William E. Brooks, "Arthurdale—A New Chance," *Atlantic Monthly*, February 1935, 199; Pickett, *For More Than Bread: An Autobiographical Account of Twenty-two Years' Work with the American Friends Service Committee* (Boston: Little, Brown & Co., 1953), 23–24.

272 *"I really would like . . .":* FDR to George Norris, 17 April 1933, in FDR Letters, FDR Library.

272 *"This is no way for people . . .":* M. L. Wilson, "The Place of Subsistence Homesteads in Our National Economy," address, Philadelphia, 27 December 1933 (Department of Agriculture release), 5–6; cited in Arthur M. Schlesinger Jr., *The Coming of the New Deal*, 363.

272 *in nearby factories:* *New York Times*, 11 February 1934, 3.

273 *better life for their citizens:* See Tamara K. Hareven, *Eleanor Roosevelt: An American Conscience* (New York: Da Capo Press, 1975), 91, 92.

273 *taking detailed notes:* *New York Times*, 19 August 1933, 2; Pickett, *For More Than Bread*, 45, 48.

273 *"The conditions I saw . . .":* *The Autobiography of Eleanor Roosevelt* (New York: Harper & Row, 1958), 177–78.

273 *Eleanor told one story:* ER, *This I Remember*, 126–27.

274 *dinner in their new homes:* *New York Times*, 23 November 1933, 7.

275 *thereby weakening the union:* Pickett, *For More Than Bread*, 62–63.

275 *"completely cleared, stocked, and electrified farms":* *New York Times*, 4 February 1934, 6.

275 *high costs of Arthurdale:* Wesley Stout, "The New Homesteaders," *Saturday Evening Post*, 4 August 1934.

275 *"Never in this country . . .":* From "Is Reedsville Communistic? Mrs. Roosevelt says, 'No,'" *Literary Digest*, 21 April 1934, 45.

275 *planted their first crops:* Brooks, "Arthurdale—A New Chance," 197.

275 *Tugwell's attitude:* See Bernard Sternsher, *Rexford Tugwell and the New Deal* (New Brunswick, N.J.: Rutgers University Press, 1964), 266–67.

276 *"Only a few . . .":* ER, *This I Remember*, 128.

276 *FDR's trip along the Maine coast:* FDR to Edward M. House, 12 June 1933, in *FDR: His Personal Letters, 1928–1945*, ed. Elliott Roosevelt (New York: Duell, Sloan & Pearce, 1947–1950), 350–51. Cited hereafter in this chapter as *FDR Letters*.

276 *"Square-jawed, thick-necked, red-faced . . .":* Schlesinger, *The Coming of the New Deal*, 105.

277 *scholars on TR and Croly:* Arthur M. Schlesinger Jr., *The Vital Center: The Politics of Freedom* (Boston: Houghton Mifflin Co., 1949), 178–80.

278 *"Heavens what a girl!"*: FDR to James A. Farley, 17 August 1933, in *FDR Letters, 1928–1945*, 358.

278 *"through representatives of their own choosing"*: Schlesinger, *The Coming of the New Deal*, 137.

278 "LABOR MUST ORGANIZE . . . ": Quoted in ibid., 139.

279 *longshoremen's strike:* George Martin, *Madam Secretary Frances Perkins* (Boston: Houghton Mifflin Co., 1976), 313–22.

280 *labor statistics:* Irving Bernstein, *A Caring Society: The New Deal, the Worker, and the Great Depression* (Boston: Houghton Mifflin Co., 1985), 92–93.

280 *to calm him down:* Frances Perkins, *The Roosevelt I Knew*, 202–3.

281 *"Do you not know this?":* Letter from California woman to FDR, 9 October 1934, FDR Letters, President's Personal File, Container 5, Box R, FDRL.

281 *"By 1934, we really began to suffer . . .":* *The Autobiography of Malcolm X*, as told by Alex Haley (New York: Ballantine Books, 1964), 13.

282 *"The Lord must have practiced . . .", "Expunge the brains trust":* FDR Letters, Container 4, Folder H, and Container 5, Box R, FDRL.

282 *"All the big guns have started shooting . . .":* FDR to William C. Bullitt, 29 August 1934, in *FDR Letters, 1928–1945*, ed. Elliott Roosevelt, 417.

282 *"During June and the summer . . .":* FDR to Edward M. House, 7 May 1934, in *FDR Letters*, 401.

282 *Kennedy and SEC:* Davis, *FDR: The New Deal Years*, 369.

283 *Keynes's open letter: New York Times*, 31 December 1933, 2.

284 *"You can tell the professor . . .":* FDR to Felix Frankfurter, 22 December 1933, in Freedman, ed., *Roosevelt and Frankfurter: Their Correspondence*, 183–84.

284 *"No two or two hundred . . .":* FDR to Berle, 6 November 1935, in FDR Letters, PPF, Box 1306, FDRL.

Eight: The Populace: Armageddon

286 *"Throughout the world":* FDR, Annual Message to Congress, 4 January 1935, in *Public Papers and Addresses of Franklin D. Roosevelt*, ed. Samuel I. Rosenman (New York: Random House, 1938), 1935, 15, 16. Cited hereafter in this chapter as *PPA.*

287 *comprehensive social insurance programs:* George Martin, *Madam Secretary Frances Perkins* (Boston: Houghton Mifflin Co., 1976), 347–48.

287 *vulnerable Americans:* James MacGregor Burns, *The Crosswinds of Freedom* (New York: Alfred A. Knopf, 1989), 66.

288 *FDR's judgments and how he learned:* Ibid., 28.

289 *"discouraged and bitter":* Arthur M. Schlesinger Jr., *The Age of Roosevelt: The Politics of Upheaval* (Boston: Houghton Mifflin Co., 1960), 3:213; see also Michael Vincent Namorato, ed., *The Diary of Rexford G. Tugwell* (New York: Greenwood Press, 1992), entry of 24 February 1935, 224–25.

289 *FDR and the World Court:* Michael Dunne, *The United States and the World Court, 1920–1935* (New York: St. Martin's Press, 1988).

289 *"I am inclined to think that . . .":* FDR to Joseph T. Robinson, 30 January 1935, in *FDR: His Personal Letters, 1928–1945*, ed. Elliott Roosevelt (Duell, Sloan & Pearce, 1947–1950), 450. Cited hereafter in this chapter as *FDR Letters.*

289 *"the unemployment problem is solved no more here . . .":* Quoted in Schlesinger, *The Age of Roosevelt: The Politics of Upheaval*, 2.

289 *"Things ain't too good . . .":* FDR Letters, Herbert Bayard Swope to James A. Farley, 12 March 1935, Democratic National Committee Records, OF 300, FDRL.

290 *FDR and American Liberty League:* Arthur M. Schlesinger Jr., *The Age of Roosevelt: The Coming of the New Deal* (Boston: Houghton Mifflin Co., 1958), 2:486–87.

290 *"right-thinking" people:* George Wolfskill and John A. Hudson, *All but the People: Franklin D. Roosevelt and His Critics, 1933–1939* (Toronto: Macmillan Co., 1969), 160.

290 *FDR joking with the press:* See Frederick Rudolph, "The American Liberty League, 1934–1940," in *American Historical Review* 56:1 (October 1950), 23.

290   *FDR's unmailed letter:* James MacGregor Burns, *Roosevelt: The Lion and the Fox* (New York: Harcourt, Brace & Co., 1956), 206.

290   *FDR angered by attacks on New Deal:* William E. Leuchtenburg, *Franklin D. Roosevelt and the New Deal, 1932–1940* (New York: Harper & Row, 1963), 146.

290   *"If we continue to stand":* Quoted in Wolfskill and Hudson, *All but the People,* 143.

291   *old gentleman's silk hat:* FDR, Address Delivered at Democratic State Convention, Syracuse, N.Y., 29 September 1936, *PPA* 1936, 385.

291   *Hofstadter on betrayal of FDR:* Richard Hofstadter, *The American Political Tradition and the Men Who Made It* (New York: Alfred A. Knopf, 1948), 330.

291   *"The surest prescription...":* Schlesinger, *The Age of Roosevelt: The Coming of the New Deal,* 2:475.

291   *"I am convinced that the heart of their hatred...":* Eric F. Goldman, *Rendezvous with Destiny,* quoted in Wolfskill and Hudson, *All but the People,* 316.

291   *psychological security:* Schlesinger, *The Age of Roosevelt: The Coming of the New Deal,* 2:472.

292   *Lippmann on fall of business leaders:* Mark H. Leff, *The Limits of Symbolic Reform: The New Deal and Taxation, 1933–1939* (Cambridge: Cambridge University Press, 1984), 158.

292   *"Five negroes...":* Schlesinger, *The Age of Roosevelt: The Coming of the New Deal,* 2:485.

292   *"Well, let's hope somebody shoots him":* Frederick Lewis Allen, *Since Yesterday: The Nineteen Thirties in America* (New York: Harper & Brothers, 1940), 233.

292   *"change is the order of the day":* FDR, Annual Message to the Congress, 4 January 1935, *PPA* 1935, 15.

292   *"the most serious threat...":* FDR, Opening of the 1936 Presidential Campaign, 29 September 1936, *PPA* 1936, 389.

292   *"individual self-interest...":* FDR, First "Fireside Chat" of 1935, 28 April 1935, *PPA* 1935, 133.

292   *U.S. Chamber of Commerce meeting and FDR's response:* *Newsweek* 5:19 (11 May 1935), 5–6; FDR, 201st Press Conference, 3 May 1935, *PPA* 1935, 162–63.

292   *"one hundred percent record...":* Quoted in Arthur M. Schlesinger Jr., *The Age of Roosevelt: The Politics of Upheaval* (Boston: Houghton Mifflin Co., Sentry Edition, 1966), 273.

292   *"sterile":* Frederick Lewis Allen, *Since Yesterday: The Nineteen Thirties in America,* 234.

293   *conservatives who preferred "the leaders of the past":* Al Smith, December 1933, quoted in Wolfskill and Hudson, *All but the People,* 164.

293   *conservative women's organizations:* See ibid., 168–69.

293   *accusations made by Liberty League:* See Wolfskill and Hudson, *All but the People,* 161–62; see also Albert Fried, *FDR and His Enemies* (New York: St. Martin's Press, 1999).

293   *Liberty League scorned equality:* Rudolph, "The American Liberty League," 33.

293   *"Long Island safe for polo players":* William Leuchtenburg, *The FDR Years: On Roosevelt and His Legacy* (New York: Columbia University Press, 1995), 124.

293   *Oval Office meeting of FDR and Long:* Glen Jeansonne, *Messiah of the Masses: Huey P. Long and the Great Depression* (New York: HarperCollins, 1993), 150.

294   *Long compares FDR to a "scrootch owl":* Quoted in Alan Brinkley, *Voices of Protest: Huey Long, Father Coughlin, and the Great Depression* (New York: Alfred A. Knopf, 1982), 64; see also Harnett T. Kane, *Louisiana Hayride: The American Rehearsal for Dictatorship, 1928–1940* (William Morrow & Co., 1941), 101.

294   *"The New Deal is Christ's deal...":* Quoted in Brinkley, *Voices of Protest,* 108–10; see also Schlesinger, *The Age of Roosevelt: The Politics of Upheaval,* 23.

294   *Upton Sinclair situation:* Burns, *Roosevelt: The Lion and the Fox,* 200–1.

295   *"sick chicken case":* Freidel, *Franklin D. Roosevelt: A Rendezvous with Destiny* (Boston: Little, Brown & Co., 1990), 160–61.

295   *"I raise my hand in reverence...":* Quoted in Schlesinger, *The Age of Roosevelt: The Politics of Upheaval,* 3:284; *New York Times,* 2 June 1935, 28.

296   *"horse-and-buggy" days:* FDR, 209th Press Conference, 31 May 1935, *PPA* 1935, 209.

296   *the legislative struggle:* Freidel, *FDR: A Rendezvous with Destiny,* 152.

296   *Roosevelt at work:* This paragraph is adapted from Burns, *Roosevelt: The Lion and the Fox,* 223.

296 *NLRA assures "right of collective bargaining":* FDR, Presidential Statement upon Signing NLR Act, 5 July 1935, *PPA* 1935, 294.

297 *"at least some protection":* FDR, Presidential Statement upon Signing the Social Security Act, 14 August 1935, *PPA* 1935, 324.

297 *"knock-down and drag-out fight . . .":* Marriner S. Eccles, *Beckoning Frontiers: Public and Personal Reminiscences* (New York: Alfred A. Knopf, 1951), 175.

298 *Long's ghostwritten book:* See Edward F. Haas, "My First Days in the White House: The Presidential Fantasy of Huey Pierce Long, in *Huey at 100: Centennial Essays on Huey P. Long,* Glen Jeansonne, ed. (Ruston, La.: McGinty Publications, 1995), 49–61; see also Glen Jeansonne, *Messiah of the Masses,* 165.

298 *Long's election plans for 1936 and 1940:* Jeansonne, *Messiah of the Masses,* 168.

298 *Long's filibusters:* Ibid., 154–55.

298 *"beaten, ignorant . . .":* Sherwood Anderson to Laura Lou Copenhaver, March 1935, in Howard Mumford Jones, ed., *Letters of Sherwood Anderson* (Little, Brown & Co., 1953), 310.

299 *All the King's Men:* See Alan Brinkley, "Robert Penn Warren, T. Harry Williams, and Huey P. Long: Mass Politics in the Literary and Historical Imaginations," in *Huey at 100,* ed. Jeansonne, 17–32.

299 *voting statistics:* Brinkley, *Voices of Protest: Huey Long, Father Coughlin, and the Great Depression,* 207–8.

299 *Long and share the wealth:* See Glen Jeansonne, Introduction, in Jeansonne, ed., *Huey at 100.*

299 *"Ev'ry man a king. . .":* Quoted in Schlesinger, *The Age of Roosevelt: The Politics of Upheaval,* 3:66.

299 *"I believe in him . . .":* Ibid., 3:25.

300 *populists getting together:* See Brinkley, *Voices of Protest,* 211–12; Kane, *Louisiana Hayride,* 197; and Glen Jeansonne, *Gerald L. K. Smith, Minister of Hate* (New Haven, Conn.: Yale University Press, 1988), 48–63.

300 *While Roosevelt was dueling:* See Brinkley, *Voices of Protest.*

300 *people listening to Coughlin and Long:* Conklin to Louis M. Howe, 26 February 1935, in FDR Letters, President's Personal File 200, Container 2, Folder A, FDRL. Hereafter cited as PPF.

301 *Coughlin and local Share Our Wealth chapters:* Brinkley, *Voices of Protest,* 187.

301 *Townsendite meeting in Chicago:* Donald R. McCoy, *Angry Voices* (Lawrence, Kans.: University Press of Kansas, 1958), 138.

301 *"You name the mill town . . .":* Frances Fox Piven and Richard A. Cloward, *Poor People's Movements: Why They Succeed, How They Fail* (New York: Pantheon Books, 1977), 115.

301 *"to get their share . . .":* McCoy, *Angry Voices,* 63.

301 *student "strike":* Schlesinger, *The Age of Roosevelt: The Politics of Upheaval,* 3:199; see also Richard A. Reiman, *The New Deal and American Youth: Ideas and Ideals in a Depression Decade* (Athens, Ga.: University of Georgia Press, 1992), 187.

302 *"permanent nonpartisan federation":* Piven and Cloward, *Poor People's Movements,* 75.

303 *social security:* Freidel, *FDR: A Rendezvous with Destiny,* 145.

303 *1939 amendments to federal act:* Suzanne Mettler, *Dividing Citizens: Gender and Federalism in New Deal Public Policy* (Ithaca, N.Y.: Cornell University Press, 1998), 97ff.

303 *"Our revenue laws have operated . . .":* FDR, A Message to the Congress on Tax Revision, 19 June 1935, *PPA* 1935, 271.

303 *new taxes with Revenue Act of 1935:* Irving Bernstein, *A Caring Society* (Boston: Houghton Mifflin Co., 1985), passim.

303 *employment statistics, August 1935–February 1936:* Ibid., 151.

304 *"the construction of highways . . .":* Quoted in Ibid., 150; see also Donald S. Howard, *The WPA and Federal Relief Policy* (New York: Russell Sage Foundation, 1943), 126.

305 *"Roosevelt is essentially a broker":* Quoted in William E. Leuchtenburg, *Franklin D. Roosevelt and the New Deal,* 89. See also John Franklin Carter, *The New Dealers,* by unofficial observer (New York: Simon & Schuster, 1934), 25; and Ronald Steel, *Walter Lippmann and the American Century* (Boston: Little, Brown & Co., 1980).

305   *"Can the presidential system . . .":* Quoted in Leuchtenburg, *Franklin D. Roosevelt and the New Deal*, 87–88. He cites *American Political Science Review* 38 (1934), 866, 2nd session of the 73rd Congress.

305   *"Interest-group democracy . . .":* Leuchtenburg, *Franklin D. Roosevelt and the New Deal*, 87.

306   *"bureaucratic minuets":* Piven and Cloward, *Poor People's Movements*, 82.

306   *LIPA and New Deal:* McCoy, *Angry Voices*, ch. 2.

307   *"failure can be expected . . .":* Quoted in ibid., 44.

307   *"Experimental method is not just . . .":* John Dewey, *Liberalism and Social Action* (New York: G. P. Putnam's Sons, 1935).

307   *"a coherent body of ideas . . .":* Schlesinger, *The Age of Roosevelt: The Politics of Upheaval*, 3:155.

308   *Animosity between Roosevelt and business:* Letter from Roy W. Howard to FDR, 6 September 1935, *PPA 1935*, 352–53.

308   *break between Roosevelt and business:* Business Week, 20 July 1935, 32.

308   *"disturbing effects . . .";* *"static";* *"no creative enterprise";* no benefits to society; *"wider distribution of wealth":* FDR, Message to the Congress on Tax Revision, 19 June 1935, *PPA 1935*, 272–73.

308   *"sterile":* FDR, An Exchange of Letters, Letter to Mr. Roy W. Howard, *PPA 1935*, 355.

308   *"Mammon" had once ruled:* FDR, Address at Atlanta, Georgia, 29 November 1935, *PPA 1935*, 471.

308   *TR Jr.'s Lincoln Day speech:* Wolfskill and Hudson, *All but the People*, 237.

308   *William Allen White:* Schlesinger, *The Age of Roosevelt: The Coming of the New Deal*, 2:489.

309   *WASP establishment's fear:* E. Digby Baltzell, *The Protestant Establishment: Aristocracy and Caste in America* (New York: Random House, 1964), 248.

309   *"If you destroy the leisure class . . .":* Quoted in Schlesinger, *The Age of Roosevelt: The Coming of the New Deal*, 2:479.

309   *Vanderbilt recalled:* Cornelius Vanderbilt, *Farewell to Fifth Avenue*, (New York: Simon & Schuster, 1935), 246.

309   *"Regardless of party . . .":* *Time* 27:17 (27 April 1936), 9.

309   *"shattered":* Adolf Berle, quoted in David Kennedy, *Freedom from Fear: The American People in Depression and War, 1929–1945* (New York: Oxford University Press, 1999), 284.

309   *Roosevelt despised:* Marquis W. Childs, "They Hate Roosevelt," *Harper's Monthly Magazine* 172 (May 1936), 634–42; on FDR as traitor to his class, see also Allen, *Since Yesterday*, 230ff.

310   *FDR had exploded one of the most popular myths:* Burns, *Roosevelt: The Lion and the Fox*, 240.

310   *"autocracy and aggression"; "economic autocracy":* FDR, Annual Message to the Congress, 3 January 1936, *PPA 1936*, 10, 16.

310   *"naked class appeal":* William Leuchtenburg, *The FDR Years*, 299.

310   *upper class encourages class antagonism:* FDR, Campaign Address, Wichita, Kansas, 13 October 1936, *PPA 1936*, 462; FDR, Campaign Address at Madison Square Garden, 31 October 1936, *PPA 1936*, 569.

310   *Hester Street and Park Avenue:* FDR, Address at Thomas Jefferson Dinner, 25 April 1936, *PPA 1936*, 178.

310   *"palace of privilege . . .":* FDR, Acceptance of the Renomination for the Presidency, 27 June 1936, *PPA 1936*, 235.

310   *"The underlying issue . . .":* FDR, Campaign Address at Cleveland, Ohio, 16 October 1936, *PPA 1936*, 506.

311   *FDR's code of honor and reaction of businessmen:* Rexford G. Tugwell, *In Search of Roosevelt* (Cambridge, Mass.: Harvard University Press, 1972), 143–47.

311   *"Knight of the* Nourmahal":* Burns, *Roosevelt: The Lion and the Fox*, 211.

311   *"I wish you could have heard . . .":* Wolfskill and Hudson, *All but the People*, 308.

311   *"invited battle"; "earned the hatred . . .":* FDR, Annual Message to Congress, 3 January 1936, *PPA 1936*, 13, italics added.

311   *"Grand":* William Leuchtenburg, *The FDR Years*, 299.

311   *film about Pasteur:* FDR, Address at Rollins College, 23 March 1936, *PPA 1936*, 147.

311   *Elliott's radio stations:* Peter Collier with David Horowitz, *The Roosevelts: An American Saga* (New York: Simon & Schuster, 1994), 376–77.

312 *"The church was beautiful . . ."*: Quoted in Blanche Wiesen Cook, *Eleanor Roosevelt: 1933–1938* (New York: Viking, 1999), 2:457.

312 *John becomes a Republican; Tuxedo Park:* Doris Kearns Goodwin, *No Ordinary Time: Franklin and Eleanor Roosevelt: The Home Front in World War II* (New York: Simon & Schuster, 1994), 635; Geoffrey C. Ward, *A First-Class Temperament: The Emergence of Franklin Roosevelt* (New York: Harper & Row, 1989), 526.

312 *"gentlemen in well-warmed . . ."; "human necessity":* FDR, Address at Atlanta, Georgia, 29 November 1935, *PPA* 1935, 474.

312 *"I am not for a return . . ."*: Quoted in Schlesinger, *The Age of Roosevelt: The Coming of the New Deal,* 497.

312 *patricians and multimillionaires:* Vanderbilt, *Farewell to Fifth Avenue,* 239ff.

313 *Hearst assault against Roosevelt; Mencken on Roosevelt and New Deal; "silver spoon" . . . vacationing; "You cannot take men . . .":* Wolfskill and Hudson, *All but the People,* 191, 174, 194, 19–20. See also David Nasaw, *The Chief: The Life of William Randolph Hearst* (Boston: Houghton Mifflin Co., 2000).

314 *anti-Semites' hatred of FDR:* Wolfskill and Hudson, *All but the People,* especially ch. 3, "The Jew Deal."

314 *"the rich richer . . .":* FDR Letters, PPF 200, container 1, FDRL.

314 *"You have not kept the faith":* FDR Letters, PPF 200, container 2, FDRL.

314 *"Dear Dictator Delano":* Ibid.

314 *Lippmann's visit to Hyde Park:* Steel, *Walter Lippmann,* 316–17.

314 *"I was so tired . . .":* Quoted in Freidel, *FDR: A Rendezvous with Destiny,* 185. He cites Morgenthau's Diaries, 2 December 1935.

314 *Gallup poll rating at 50 percent:* Kenneth S. Davis, *FDR: The New Deal Years, 1933–1937* (New York: Random House, 1986), 571; Raymond Moley, *After Seven Years* (New York: Harper & Brothers, 1939), 318.

316 *"in every way that human effort . . .":* FDR, Address on the Accomplishments and Future Aims for Agriculture, 28 September 1935, *PPA* 1935, 380.

316 *Boulder Dam dedication speech:* FDR, Address at the Dedication of the Boulder Dam, 30 September 1935, *PPA* 1935, 397–402.

316 *democracy "is not a static thing . . .":* FDR, Address at Los Angeles, Calif., 1 October 1935, *PPA* 1935, 405.

316 *"summon our intelligence":* FDR, Address at San Diego Exposition, 2 October 1935, *PPA* 1935, 410.

317 *Like TR, FDR could capitalize on fear:* Freidel, *FDR: A Rendezvous with Destiny,* 146.

317 *public opinion polling:* Hadley Cantril, ed., *Public Opinion, 1935–46* (Princeton, N.J.: Princeton University Press, 1951), 541ff. Cantril served privately as an in-depth pollster for Roosevelt.

317 *maximum radio audience:* FDR, Annual Message to Congress, 3 January 1936, *PPA* 1936, 8–18.

318 *"largest collection of millionaires . . .":* Wolfskill and Hudson, *All but the People,* 165.

319 *Smith speech to Liberty League:* Quoted in Davis, *FDR: The New Deal Years,* 607. He cites the *New York Times,* 6 January 1936.

319 *"President Roosevelt has become . . .":* Herbert Mitgang, *Once upon a Time in New York: Jimmy Walker, Franklin Roosevelt, and the Last Great Battle of the Jazz Age* (New York: Free Press, 1999), 227.

319 *"rapidly becoming the most despised . . .":* Jeansonne, *Gerald L. K. Smith, Minister of Hate,* 47. See also, Nadine Block, ed., *Current Biography, 1943* (New York: H. W. Wilson Company, 1943), 708.

320 Georgia Woman's World: Jeansonne, *Gerald L. K. Smith, Minister of Hate,* 47; see also Schlesinger, *The Age of Roosevelt: The Politics of Upheaval,* 3:522.

320 *FDR's tribute to TR:* FDR, Dedication of the Theodore Roosevelt Memorial, 19 January 1936, *PPA* 1936, 61–65.

320 *FDR invokes TR's name:* FDR, Address at the Dedication of the New Department of Interior Building, 26 April 1936, *PPA* 1936, 167–68; FDR, Informal Extemporaneous Remarks at a Luncheon in Dallas, 12 June 1936, *PPA* 1936, 214–15; FDR, Campaign Address at Chicago, 14 October 1936, *PPA* 1936, 482.

320 *FDR rising above interest-group politics:* *PPA* 1936, 5.

321 *"There's one issue in this campaign . . .":* Quoted in Burns, *Roosevelt: The Lion and the Fox,* 271.

321 *Good Neighbor League:* Some of this paragraph is taken substantially from Burns, *Roosevelt: The Lion and the Fox,* 270.

323 *politics of paranoia, xenophobia, and anti-Semitism:* See Richard Hofstadter, *The Paranoid Style in American Politics, and Other Essays* (New York: Alfred A. Knopf, 1965), passim. See also Richard Hofstadter, *Anti-Intellectualism in Amerian Life* (New York: Alfred A. Knopf, 1963).

323 *"Roosevelt administration, on one hand . . .":* Quoted in Charles J. Tull, *Father Coughlin and the New Deal* (Syracuse, N.Y.: Syracuse University Press, 1965), 122.

323 *description of Landon:* Burns, *Roosevelt: The Lion and the Fox,* 270.

324 *FDR urges Governor Lehman to run again:* FDR to Herbert Lehman, 29 June 1936, in *FDR Letters, 1928–1945,* 596; Address at the Thomas Jefferson Day Dinner, 25 April 1936, *PPA 1936,* 177; Letter to Lehman to Become a Candidate for Reelection, 29 June 1936, *PPA 1936,* 236–37.

324 *"rid our land of kidnappers . . .":* Leuchtenburg, *The FDR Years,* 126.

324 *FDR and Moley quarrel:* Davis, *FDR: The New Deal Years,* 635. See also Samuel I. Rosenman, *Working with Roosevelt* (New York: Harper & Brothers, 1952).

325 *FDR's fall at the convention:* Michael F. Reilly and William J. Slocum, *Reilly of the White House* (New York: Simon & Schuster, 1947).

325 *FDR's speech at Democratic National Convention:* Burns, *Roosevelt: The Lion and the Fox,* 273–74; FDR, Acceptance of the Renomination for the Presidency, 27 June 1936, *PPA 1936,* 230–36. See also *New York Times,* 28 June 1936.

326 *FDR's departure from convention:* Burns, *Roosevelt: The Lion and the Fox,* 275. See also *New York Times,* 28 June 1936.

326 *"slimy group" of New Dealers:* G. L. K. Smith, quoted in Jeansonne, *Gerald L. K. Smith, Minister of Hate,* 55; Herbert Harris, "That Third Party," *Current History,* October 1936, 85.

326 *"I have seen war . . .":* FDR, Address at Chautauqua, N.Y., 14 August 1936, *PPA 1936,* 289.

326 *300th anniversary speech:* FDR, Address Delivered at the Harvard University Tercentenary Celebration, 18 September 1936, *PPA 1936,* 362–63.

326 *"The President smiles and sails and fishes . . .":* Entry of 18 July 1936, *The Secret Diary of Harold L. Ickes: The First Thousand Days, 1933–1936* (New York: Simon & Schuster, 1953), 639.

326 *ER's memo to Farley:* Schlesinger, *The Politics of Upheaval,* 588.

327 *"For the good of the country . . .":* Joseph P. Lash, *Eleanor and Franklin* (New York: W. W. Norton & Co., 1971), 443.

327 *"to offset a Press. . .":* FDR to Edward M. House, 25 August 1936, in *FDR Letters, 1928–1945,* 610.

327 *"Reform if you would preserve":* Burns, *Roosevelt: The Lion and the Fox,* 280; FDR, The Opening of the 1936 Presidential Campaign, 29 September 1936, *PPA 1936,* 383–90.

327 *"the stink of money . . .":* Leuchtenburg, *The FDR Years,* 112.

327 *FDR and William Allen White in Emporia:* Burns, *Roosevelt: The Lion and the Fox,* 280–81; FDR, Rear-Platform Extemporaneous Remarks at Emporia, Kansas, 13 October 1936, *PPA 1936,* 465.

328 *Landon's criticism:* Kenneth S. Davis, *FDR: The New Deal Years,* 643.

328 *"Free lunch to hoboes . . .":* Leuchtenburg, *The FDR Years,* 112.

328 *Mrs. Landon; crowds want Eleanor:* Lash, *Eleanor and Franklin,* 447.

328 *northeast campaign swing:* Ickes Diary, 695.

328 *Bridgeport and Pittsburgh:* Leuchtenburg, *The FDR Years,* 141, 143.

328 *"For twelve years, this nation . . .":* FDR, Campaign Address at Madison Square Garden, 31 October 1936, *PPA 1936,* 566–73. See Burns, *Roosevelt: The Lion and the Fox,* 282–83. Quotes are taken from a recording of the speech at the FDR Library.

Nine: Checkmate?

334 *election results:* See Richard B. Morris, ed., *Encyclopedia of American History* (Harper & Brothers, 1953), passim.

334 *"drawn a class line . . .";* *"the rich were for Landon . . .";* *No longer could people credibly deny:* Wil-

liam E. Leuchtenburg, *The FDR Years: On Roosevelt and His Legacy* (New York: Columbia University Press, 1995), 154, 300.

334 *"closest that America had come to class warfare"*: Donald McCoy, quoted in Leuchtenburg, *The FDR Years*, 300.

334 *trains leaving Grand Central:* Leuchtenburg, *The FDR Years*, 300.

334 *"We've grown class conscious"; voting in Pittsburgh, Chicago, among Jews:* Ibid., 301, 155, 156.

335 *"Just keep it and I'll call on you . . ."*: Frank Freidel, *Franklin D. Roosevelt: A Rendezvous with Destiny* (Boston: Little, Brown & Co., 1990), 203; William E. Leuchtenburg, "Election of 1936," in Arthur M. Schlesinger Jr., ed., *History of American Presidential Elections, 1789–1968* (New York: Chelsea House Publishers, 1971), 3:2833.

336 *"The Pollywogs were given . . ."*: FDR to ER, 26 November 1936, in *FDR, His Personal Letters, 1928–1945*, ed. Elliott Roosevelt (New York: Duell, Sloan & Pearce, 1947–1950), 632, cited hereafter in this chapter as *FDR Letters*.

336 *"You have been given . . ."*: FDR to ER, 30 November 1936, in *FDR Letters, 1928–1945*, 634.

336 *"There was real enthusiasm . . ."*: FDR to ER, 30 November 1936, in Ibid., 634–35.

337 *FDR takes oath of office:* James MacGregor Burns, *Roosevelt: The Lion and the Fox* (New York: Harcourt, Brace & Co., 1956), 291; Samuel I. Rosenman, *Working with Roosevelt* (New York: Harper & Brothers, 1952), 144.

337 *Inaugural speech:* FDR, The Second Inaugural Address, 20 January 1937, in *Public Papers and Addresses of Franklin D. Roosevelt*, ed. Samuel I. Rosenman (New York: Macmillan Co., 1941), 1937, 4–5. Cited hereafter in chapter as *PPA*.

338 *"Very confidentially, I may give you . . ."*: FDR to Frankfurter, 15 January 1937, in Max Freedman, ed., *Roosevelt and Frankfurter: Their Correspondence, 1928–1945* (Boston: Little, Brown & Co., 1967), 377.

338 *FDR message to Congress on Supreme Court:* FDR, The President Presents a Plan for the Reorganization of the Judicial Branch of the Government, 5 February 1937, *PPA* 1937, 56.

339 *"And now you have blown me off the top . . ."*: Frankfurter to FDR, 7 February 1937, in Freedman, ed., *Roosevelt and Frankfurter*, 380–81.

339 *"We are celebrating the 1936 victory . . ."*: FDR, Speech at Democratic Victory Dinner, 4 March 1937, *PPA* 1937, 113ff.

340 *Decline of support for "court-packing" bill:* Kenneth S. Davis, *FDR: The New Deal Years, 1933–1937* (New York: Random House, 1986), 706; see also Kenneth S. Davis, *FDR: Into the Storm, 1937–1940* (New York: Random House, 1993), 75, 79.

340 *Chief Justice Hughes and the court bill:* See David Joseph Danelski and Joseph S. Tulchin, eds., *The Autobiographical Notes of Charles Evans Hughes* (Cambridge, Mass.: Harvard University Press, 1973), passim.

341 *"A switch in time saves nine . . ."*: Quoted in Davis, *FDR: Into the Storm*, 81.

341 *"Today is a very, very happy day . . ."*: FDR, 360th Press Conference, 13 April 1937, *PPA* 1937, 153–54. See also *New York Times*, 14 April 1937.

343 *previously proposed amendments:* FDR to Charles C. Burlingham, 23 February 1937, in *FDR Letters, 1928–1945*, 661.

343 *"howling their heads off"*: Ibid.

343 *"Give me ten million dollars . . ."*: Burns, *Roosevelt: The Lion and the Fox*, 295.

344 *"no hard feelings"*: Harold L. Ickes, *The Secret Diary of Harold L. Ickes: The First Thousand Days, 1933–1936* (New York: Simon & Schuster, 1953), 704.

344 *"We are kindred spirits! . . ."*: FDR to Claude G. Bowers, 15 January 1937, in *FDR Letters, 1928–1945*, 651.

345 *"in accord with the views . . ."*: Davis, *Into the Storm*, 80, 96–99.

345 *Roberts's role:* Charles A. Leonard, *A Search for a Judicial Philosophy: Mr. Justice Roberts and the Constitutional Revolution of 1937* (Port Washington, N.Y.: Kennikat Press, 1971), passim. See also Freedman, ed., *Roosevelt and Frankfurter: Their Correspondence*, 392–97.

346 *"team" of "three well-matched horses":* FDR, Address at the Democratic Victory Dinner, March 4, 1937, *PPA* 1937, 116. See also FDR to Jerome D. Green, 24 March 1937, *FDR Letters, 1928–1945*, 669.

346 *"There was a lot of feeling . . .":* FDR, Press Conference, July 1937, *PPA* 1937, 310–11.
347 *American isolationist sentiment:* Manfred Jonas, *Isolationism in America, 1935–1941* (Ithaca, N.Y.: Cornell University Press, 1966), 1.
347 *Gallup Poll:* George Gallup and Claude Robinson, "American Institute of Public Opinion— Surveys, 1935–1938," *Public Opinion Quarterly* 3 (July 1938), 388.
348 *if "our American ideals are to survive . . .":* Quoted in Jonas, *Isolationism in America*, 94; Nancy Schoonmaker and Doris Fielding Reid, eds., *We Testify* (New York: Smith & Durrell, 1941), 81.
349 *Perkins gets membership in ILO passed:* Burns, *Roosevelt: The Lion and the Fox,* 251; see also Frances Perkins, *The Roosevelt I Knew* (New York: Viking Press, 1946).
349 *FDR keeps in touch with world politics:* Burns, *Roosevelt: The Lion and the Fox,* 248.
350 *FDR's friend in Lima discloses information:* Letters of Fred Morris Dearing to FDR, 23 October and 2 December 1935, in Edgar Nixon, ed., *Franklin D. Roosevelt and Foreign Affairs* (Cambridge, Mass.: Belknap Press of Harvard University Press, 1969), 3:30–34, 104.
350 *"I tell you, Steve . . .":* Letter of Senator Key Pittman to Stephen T. Early, 19 August 1935, in Nixon, ed., *Franklin D. Roosevelt and Foreign Affairs,* 2:608.
350 *Mussolini:* Letter from Alexander C. Kirk to Cordell Hull, 19 August 1935, in ibid., 2:611–12.
351 *revolt in Spain:* Letter from Claude G. Bowers to FDR, 26 August 1936, in ibid., 3:395–97.
352 *"We shun political commitments . . .":* Quoted in ibid., 3:380; FDR, Address at Chautauqua, N.Y., 14 August 1936, *PPA* 1936, 285–92.
352 *"What an unfortunate and terrible catastrophe . . .":* FDR to Claude G. Bowers, 16 September 1936, *FDR Letters,* 3:614–15.
353 *"vast uncharted area . . .":* Speech by Roosevelt at Chautauqua, N.Y., 14 August 1936, in Nixon, ed., *Franklin D. Roosevelt and Foreign Affairs,* 3:380; Address at Chautauqua, N.Y., 14 August 1936, *PPA* 1936, 291.
354 *"there is no prospect of a peace agreement . . .":* Letter of William E. Dodd to R. Walton Moore, 31 August 1936, ibid., 3:406.
354 *"Hitler and Mussolini . . .":* William E. Dodd to FDR, 19 October 1936, ibid., 3:455.
354 *Hitler "simply waiting . . .":* William E. Dodd to FDR, 7 December 1936, ibid., 3:528.
354 *"give up the human system . . .":* William E. Dodd to R. Walton Moore, 31 August 1936, ibid., 3:408.
354 *"democratic countries can save . . .":* William E. Dodd to FDR, 19 October 1936, ibid., 3:455.
354 *"The outstanding menace to peace . . .":* John Cudahy to FDR, 7 January 1937, ibid., 3:573.
356 *dramatic speech in Chicago:* FDR, Address at Chicago, 5 October 1937, *PPA* 1937, 406–11; see also *Chicago Tribune,* 6 October 1937.
357 *"How did it go?" and following:* Burns, *Roosevelt: The Lion and the Fox,* 318–19; see also James A. Farley, *Behind the Ballots* (New York: Harcourt, Brace & Co., 1938).
357 *"It is a terrible thing . . .":* Burns, *Roosevelt: The Lion and the Fox,* 318–19; William E. Leuchtenburg, *Franklin D. Roosevelt and the New Deal, 1932–1940* (New York: Harper & Row, 1963), 226–27.
358 *revealing press conference:* FDR, 400th Press Conference, 6 October 1937, *PPA* 1937, 414–25.

Ten: The Twilight of the New Deal

361 *"Dear Felix . . .":* FDR to Felix Frankfurter, in Max Freedman, *Roosevelt and Frankfurter: Their Correspondence, 1928–1945* (Boston: Little, Brown & Co., 1967), 442.
361 *"Those anxious and confiding Republican . . .";* *"Always more law . . .":* Freedman, *Roosevelt and Frankfurter: Their Correspondence,* 441.
361 *"When will he give . . .":* Ibid., 442.
361 *"one of those old-fashioned . . .":* Ibid., 440.
362 *Black and KKK:* Kenneth S. Davis, *FDR: Into the Storm, 1937–1940* (New York: Random House, 1993), 108–112.
363 *"Nourmahal Gang":* Joseph P. Lash, *Eleanor and Franklin: The Story of Their Relationship* (New York: W. W. Norton & Co., 1971), 506.

363 *FDR joke on Kennedy:* James Roosevelt with Bill Libby, *My Parents: A Differing View* (Chicago: Playboy Press, 1976), 209; see also Davis, *Into the Storm,* 153.

364 *Marshall's Christmas Day sermon:* Davis, *Into the Storm,* 162; *New York Times,* 26 December 1937.

365 *"a final responsibility . . .":* FDR, Annual Message to the Congress, 3 January 1938, in *Public Papers and Addresses of Franklin D. Roosevelt,* ed. Samuel I. Rosenman (New York: Macmillan Co., 1941), 1938, 14. Cited hereafter in this chapter as *PPA.*

366 *"Bert, as they used to say . . .":* James MacGregor Burns, *Roosevelt: The Lion and the Fox* (New York: Harcourt, Brace & Co., 1956), 324.

366 *Jackson Day speech:* FDR, Address at the Jackson Day Dinner, 8 January 1938, in *PPA* 1938, 37–48; Burns, *Roosevelt: The Lion and the Fox,* 324; *Time,* 10 January 1938, 12.

367 *FDR and business:* Burns, *Roosevelt: The Lion and the Fox,* 324; FDR to Fred I. Kent, 11 February 1938, in *FDR, His Personal Letters, 1928–1945,* ed. Elliott Roosevelt (New York: Duell, Sloan & Pearce, 1947–1950), 758–59. Cited hereafter in this chapter as *FDR Letters.*

367 *April 1938 message to Congress:* FDR, Recommendations to the Congress to Curb Monopolies and the Concentration of Economic Power, 29 April 1938, *PPA* 1938, 305–32.

367 *demonstrations in Detroit and Washington:* Burns, *Roosevelt: The Lion and the Fox,* 326.

368 *letter from Keynes:* Quoted in Burns, *Roosevelt: The Lion and the Fox,* 332–33. Letter and Morgenthau's response also quoted in John M. Blum, *From the Morgenthau Diaries: Years of Crisis* (Boston: Houghton Mifflin Co., 1959), 402–4.

368 *"that firm and confident leadership":* Burns, *Roosevelt: The Lion and the Fox,* 327.

368 *speech in northern Georgia:* FDR, Address at Gainesville, Georgia, 23 March 1938, *PPA* 1938, 164–69; also quoted in Burns, *Roosevelt: The Lion and the Fox,* 328.

369 *FDR's meeting with Morgenthau:* Blum, *From the Morgenthau Diaries,* 420.

369 *Morgenthau threatens to resign:* Ibid., 423–42.

370 *FDR's first unsigned bill to become law:* FDR, Address at Arthurdale, West Virginia, 27 May 1938, *PPA* 1938, 364–65.

372 *"efficient basis":* Frank Friedel, *Franklin D. Roosevelt: A Rendezvous with Destiny* (Boston: Little, Brown & Co., 1990), 274.

373 *"I have no inclination to be a dictator . . .":* FDR, The President Refutes Dictatorship Charges Connected with the Pending Reorganization Bill, 29 March 1938, *PPA* 1938; quoted in Burns, *Roosevelt: The Lion and the Fox,* 345–46.

373 *Wagner's defection:* J. Joseph Huthmacher, *Senator Robert F. Wagner and the Rise of Urban Liberalism* (New York: Atheneum Publishers, 1968), 243–45.

373 *"Mr. President, if I were you . . .":* Harold L. Ickes, *The Secret Diary of Harold L. Ickes* (New York: Simon & Schuster, 1954), 2:358–59; see also Burns, *Roosevelt: The Lion and the Fox,* 344–45.

374 *"the sense of serenity . . .":* Frankfurter to FDR, 18 May 1939, in Freedman, *Roosevelt and Frankfurter: Their Correspondence,* 457.

374 *"I know the old health . . .":* FDR to William Allen White, 14 June 1938, in *FDR Letters, 1928–1945,* 791.

374 *defeat of reorganization bill:* Richard Polenberg, *Reorganizing Roosevelt's Government* (Cambridge: Harvard University Press, 1966), 4–6.

374 *FDR's visit to TR in 1905:* FDR, Remarks at a Luncheon in Dallas, Texas, 12 June 1936, *PPA* 1936, 215.

376 *fireside chat before attempted purge:* FDR, Fireside Chat, 24 June 1938, *PPA* 1938, 391–400.

377 *speech in Marietta, Ohio:* Davis, *Into the Storm,* 261; FDR, Address at Marietta, Ohio, 8 July 1938, *PPA* 1938, 427–31.

377 *talk in Covington, Kentucky:* Burns, *Roosevelt: The Lion and the Fox,* 361; Davis, *Into the Storm,* 261; FDR, Address at Covington, Kentucky, 8 July 1938, *PPA* 1938, 437–38.

379 *"the South presents right now . . .":* FDR, Message to the Conference on Economic Conditions of the South, 4 July 1938, *PPA* 1938, 421–22.

379 *exorbitantly high electicity rates; they must elect . . . ; FDR on Senator George:* FDR, Address at Barnesville, Georgia, 11 August 1938, *PPA* 1938, 463, 466–67, 469.

380 *"Mr. President, I want you to know..."*: Davis, *Into the Storm*, 280; James T. Patterson, *Congressional Conservatism and the New Deal: The Growth of the Conservate Coalition in Congress, 1933–1939* (Lexington, Ky.: University of Kentucky Press, 1967), 280.

380 *"I don't believe any family..."*: Davis, *Into the Storm*, 281. FDR, Informal Extemporaneous Remarks at Greenville, S.C., 11 August 1938, *PPA* 1938, 477.

380 *Tydings had run "with the Roosevelt prestige..."*: FDR, 476th Press Conference, 16 August 1938, *PPA* 1938, 489.

380 *speech for Lewis:* FDR, Address at Denton, Maryland, 5 September 1938, *PPA* 1938, 512–520.

381 *"It's a bust":* Burns, *Roosevelt: The Lion and the Fox*, 363; James Aloysius Farley, *Jim Farley's Story: The Roosevelt Years* (New York: Whittlesey House, 1948), 144.

381 *"It takes a long, long time..."*: Burns, *Roosevelt: The Lion and the Fox*, 364; Farley, *Jim Farley's Story*, 144.

382 *idea of Republican convention choosing conservative Democrat for vice president; "I am unable to see much difference..."; Vandenberg to Landon; "we would not whip Mr. Roosevelt...":* Patterson, *Congressional Conservatism and the New Deal*, 255, 256, 258, 259.

382 *formation of National Progressives of America:* Ronald L. Feinman, *Twilight of Progressivism: The Western Republican Senators and the New Deal* (Baltimore: Johns Hopkins University Press, 1981), 149–52.

383 *"good for people's figures!":* FDR to William Phillips, 18 May 1938, in *FDR Letters, 1928–1945*, 785.

383 *state of New Deal in fall 1938:* Burns, *Roosevelt: The Lion and the Fox*, 365.

384 *"Besides cleaning out some bad local situations..."*: FDR to Josephus Daniels, 14 November 1938, in *FDR, His Personal Letters, 1928–1945*, 827.

385 *"Will you not encounter coalition opposition?":* Burns, *Roosevelt: The Lion and the Fox*, 366.

385 *"They say that the Democratic Party..."*: David E. Lilienthal, *The Journals of David E. Lilienthal* (New York: Harper & Row, 1964), 1:64.

386 *The conference's report:* "Report on Economic Conditions of the South," prepared for the President by the National Emergency Council, 25 July 1938, *PPA* 1938, 421.

386 *Maury Maverick on the report:* Bruce J. Schulman, *From Cotton Belt to Sunbelt* (Oxford: Oxford University Press, 1991), 51; see also *New Republic* 96:61 (24 August 1938), 64–75; *Virginia Quarterly Review* 14 (Autumn 1938), 482–482; *Saturday Evening Post* 211, 8 October 1938, 86–91; *Manufacturers Record* 107, August 1938, 13–15.

387 *"The South may not be..."*: Schulman, *From Cotton Belt to Sunbelt*, 122; V. O. Key Jr., *Southern Politics* (New York: Alfred A. Knopf, 1949), 3.

387 *FDR "smoldering against..."*: Patterson, *Congressional Conservatism and the New Deal*, 262; Farley, *Jim Farley's Story*, 95.

388 FDR *"took no pains to hide..."*: Ibid., 261–62; George Creel, *Rebel at Large: Recollections of Fifty Crowded Years* (New York: G. P. Putnam's Sons, 1947), 295.

388 *"high school girl revenge":* Patterson, *Congressional Conservatism and the New Deal*, 262.

388 *story of man in prison and ER's response; "Revolutions do not start...", "'do-gooders' to dinner"; "I was talking with a man..."*: Lash, *Eleanor and Franklin*, 384–85, 467, 453.

389 *"It was essential to restore..."*: Eleanor Roosevelt, *This I Remember* (New York: Harper & Brothers, 1949), 199.

389 *ER's off-the-record conversations with FDR:* Grace Tully, *FDR: My Boss* (New York: Charles Scribner's Sons, 1949), 110.

390 Washington Post *headline:* Blanche Wiesen Cook, *Eleanor Roosevelt: 1933–1938* (New York: Viking, 1999), 2:29.

390 *"She travels—and how she travels..."*: Mary Marshall, "Columnists on Parade: Eleanor Roosevelt," *Nation*, 2 April 1938, 386–87.

391 *"Are you free if you cannot vote...?":* ER, "My Day," 8 December 1938.

391 *"We still do tolerate slavery..."*: *New York Times*, 11 February 1938, 16.

391 *"Anyone in a minority group..."*: *New York Times*, 22 April 1938, 7.

391 *ER reacting to unjust situations:* Lash, *Eleanor and Franklin*, 454–56.

391 *ER asks Tully to help woman:* Tully, *FDR: My Boss*, 106–7.

391 *ER supports and protects women:* Lash, *Eleanor and Franklin,* 463.

391 *striking farmworkers in Arkansas; milk for needy children; peanut vendor:* Ibid., 460, 458, 455.

392 *"horrible sense of obligation . . .":* Ibid., 457.

392 *St. Francis prayer:* Ibid., 454.

392 *meeting of African-American leaders in White House:* Clarence Pickett, *For More than Bread* (Boston: Little, Brown & Co., 1953), 49.

392 *ER ahead of FDR on civil rights issues:* Joanna Schneider Zangrando and Robert L. Zangrando, "ER and Black Civil Rights," in Joan Hoff-Wilson and Marjorie Lightman, eds., *Without Precedent: The Life and Career of Eleanor Roosevelt* (Bloomington, Ind.: Indiana University Press, 1984), 92.

393 *another lynching:* Walter White, *A Man Called White* (New York: Viking Press, 1948), 140; see also his chapter 19 for 1933 lynching statistics.

393 *Costigan-Wagner Anti-Lynching Bill and its difficulties:* White, *A Man Called White,* 166–73.

393 *Senator Theodore Bilbo:* Wolfskill and Hudson, *All but the People: Franklin D. Roosevelt and His Critics, 1933–1939* (Toronto: Macmillan Co., 1969), 43.

393 *ER arranges meeting between FDR and White:* White, *A Man Called White,* 168–70.

393 *"If I come out for the anti-lynching bill . . .":* Ibid., 179–80.

394 *"dynamite":* Lash, *Eleanor and Franklin,* 516–17.

394 *"You can say anything . . .":* Freidel, *Franklin D. Roosevelt: A Rendezvous with Destiny,* 246.

394 *"if I were colored . . .":* Lash, *Eleanor and Franklin,* 518–19.

394 *meeting of conference in Birmingham:* Lash, *Eleanor and Franklin,* 525–26; Cook, *Eleanor Roosevelt,* 2:564–65.

394 *"If the people of the South do not grasp . . .":* Cook, *Eleanor Roosevelt,* 2:565.

395 *National Conference of Negro Youth thank ER:* Lash, *Eleanor and Franklin,* 526.

395 *"we must have courage . . .":* ER, Address of 14 March 1940, in *What I Hope to Leave Behind: The Essential Essays of Eleanor Roosevelt,* ed. Allida M. Black (Brooklyn, N.Y.: Carlson Publishing, 1995), 154.

395 *Early excludes black journalists:* Cook, *Eleanor Roosevelt,* 2:293.

395 *praise from the African-American press:* Lash, *Eleanor and Franklin,* 446.

395 *"the Negro race as a whole . . .":* ER, "The Negro and Social Change," Address of 12 December 1935, in *What I Hope to Leave Behind,* ed. Black, 146.

395 *"The economic situation is the reason . . .":* ER, "Intolerance," *Cosmopolitan,* February 1940, in *What I Hope to Leave Behind,* ed. Black, 158.

395 *ER and Bunche:* Allida M. Black, *Casting Her Own Shadow: Eleanor Roosevelt and the Shaping of Postwar Liberalism* (New York: Columbia University Press, 1996), 88.

396 *"They have taken an action . . .":* ER, "My Day," 27 February 1939, in Lash, *Eleanor and Franklin,* 526.

396 *Endicott Peabody on DAR:* Lash, *Eleanor and Franklin,* 526.

396 *great-aunt Gracie; "I quite understand . . .":* Ibid., 522.

396 *"term of affection"; "eating with someone . . .":* Cook, *Eleanor Roosevelt,* 2:439–40.

396 *"there are in every race certain gifts":* ER, Address of 11 May 1934, in *What I Hope to Leave Behind,* ed. Black, 142.

397 *"Some of My Best Friends . . .":* ER, article in *Ebony* 9 (February 1953), in *What I Hope to Leave Behind,* ed. Black, 171.

397 *"Sometimes it is better . . ."; "I have moments of real terror . . ."; "pretty poor":* Lash, *Eleanor and Franklin,* 524, 536, 538.

398 *ER and NYA:* ER, *This I Remember,* 163.

398 *"bought ourselves time . . ."; "every shade of thought . . .":* Lash, *Eleanor and Franklin,* 469, 544.

398 *ER meets Lash:* Cook, *Eleanor Roosevelt,* 2:504.

398 *AYC begins to support New Deal:* Winifred D. Wandersee, "ER and American Youth: Politics and Personality in a Bureaucratic Age," in Hoff-Wilson and Lightman, eds., *Without Precedent: The Life and Career of Eleanor Roosevelt,* 63–87.

399 *"no doubt that there are many Communists":* Cook, *Eleanor Roosevelt,* 2:522.

399 *"She didn't go around talking down to us . . .":* Ibid.

624 NOTES

399 *House Un-American Activities Committee:* Lash, *Eleanor and Franklin,* 461.
400 *Pinchot as link between TR and FDR:* Walter L. Creese, *TVA's Public Planning: The Vision, the Reality* (Knoxville, Tenn.: University of Tennessee Press, 1990), 35.
400 *Lewis Mumford:* Donald L. Miller, *Lewis Mumford: A Life* (New York: Weidenfeld & Nicholson, 1989), 363–66.
401 *TVA "touches and gives life . . .":* FDR, A Suggestion for Legislation to Create the TVA, 10 April 1933, *PPA* 1933, 122.
401 *"chronic passive-dependency syndrome":* Quoted in Creese, *TVA's Public Planning,* 93. See also Richard A. Ball, "A Poverty Case: The Analgesic Subculture of the Southern Appalachians," in Scott Greer and Ann Lennarson Greer, eds., *Neighborhood and Ghetto: The Local Area in Large Scale Society* (New York: Basic Books, 1974), 126–27.
403 *not primarily "a dam-building program . . .":* Leuchtenburg, *Franklin D. Roosevelt and the New Deal, 1932–1940* (New York: Harper & Row, 1963), 164.
403 *"No other agency did so much . . .":* Ibid., 165.

Eleven: The Nightmare Begins

406 *FDR to Ickes on Spain:* James MacGregor Burns, *Roosevelt: The Lion and the Fox* (New York: Harcourt, Brace & Co., 1956), 356; see also letter to Harold Ickes, 12 May 1938, in *The Secret Diary of Harold L. Ickes: The Inside Struggle, 1936–1939* (New York: Simon & Schuster, 1953), 390.
406 *Martha Gellhorn's reports from Spain:* Joseph P. Lash, *Eleanor and Franklin* (New York: W. W. Norton & Co., 1971), 567.
407 *"I wish that I were not in the White House . . .":* Señora de los Rios to ER, 2 April 1938, in Lash, *Eleanor and Franklin,* 569.
407 *"I gather that even our own State Department . . .":* ER to Martha Gellhorn, 29 June 1938, in ibid.
407 *"simply trying to salve his own conscience . . .":* Eleanor Roosevelt, *This I Remember* (New York: Harper & Brothers, 1949), 161–62.
407 *ER to Leon Henderson at White House dinner:* Story and quote in Kenneth S. Davis, *FDR: Into the Storm, 1937–1940* (New York: Random House, 1993), 399; and John Gunther, *Roosevelt in Retrospect* (New York: Harper & Brothers, 1950), 191; also quoted in Peter Wyden, *The Passionate War: The Narrative History of the Spanish Civil War* (New York: Simon & Schuster, 1983), 472–73.
407 *Hitler's actions and the response to them:* Frank Freidel, *Franklin D. Roosevelt: A Rendezvous with Destiny* (Boston: Little, Brown & Co., 1990), 299; Davis, *FDR: Into the Storm,* 313; Arnold A. Offner, *American Appeasement: United States Foreign Policy and Germany, 1933–1938* (Cambridge, Mass.: Harvard University Press, 1969), 250; Gerhard L. Weinberg, *The Foreign Policy of Hitler's Germany: Starting World War II, 1937–39* (Chicago: University of Chicago Press, 1980), 369–71. See also *The United States in World Affairs: An Account of American Foreign Relations, 1939* (New York: Council on Foreign Relations/Harper & Brothers, 1940), passim.
409 *"I want you to know . . .":* FDR to Williams Phillips, 17 October 1938, in *FDR: His Personal Letters, 1928–1945,* ed. Elliott Roosevelt (Duell, Sloan & Pearce, 1947–1950), 818. Cited hereafter in this chapter as *FDR Letters.*
409 *varying press views of Munich pact:* Charles Callan Tansill, *Back Door to War: The Roosevelt Foreign Policy, 1933–1941* (Chicago: Henry Regnery Co., 1952), 428–30.
409 *"We have sustained . . .":* Churchill, "A Total and Unmitigated Defeat," 5 October 1938, House of Commons, in *Winston S. Churchill: His Complete Speeches, 1897–1963,* ed. Robert Rhodes James (New York: Chelsea House, 1974), 6:6004–13. See also William Manchester, *The Last Lion: Winston Spencer Churchill—Alone 1932–1940* (Boston: Little, Brown & Co., 1988), 368–71.
410 *"Chamberlain's visit to Hitler today . . .":* FDR to William Phillips, 14 September 1938, in *FDR Letters, 1928–1945,* 810.
410 *a new crisis if Hitler fails to follow promises:* FDR to Mackenzie King, 11 October 1938, in ibid., 816.

410 Hitler and Mussolini "are still on the warpath": FDR to Lincoln MacVeagh, 24 March 1939, in ibid., 865.

410 navy appropriations cut: John C. Walter, "Franklin D. Roosevelt and Naval Rearmament, 1932–1938," in Herbert D. Rosenbaum and Elizabeth Bartelme, eds., *Franklin D. Roosevelt: The Man, the Myth, the Era* (New York: Greenwood Press, 1987), 203–18.

411 "President was sure then . . .": Quoted in Davis, *FDR: Into the Storm*, 327; see also Robert E. Sherwood, *Roosevelt and Hopkins: An Intimate History* (New York: Harper & Brothers, 1950), 100.

411 "may have been Jews . . .": George Wolfskill and John A. Hudson, *All but the People: Franklin D. Roosevelt and His Critics* (Toronto: Macmillan Co., 1969), 67.

411 FDR and Dodd: Sheldon Neuringer, "Franklin D. Roosevelt and Refuge for Victims of Nazism, 1933–1941," in Rosenbaum and Bartelme, eds., *Franklin D. Roosevelt: The Man, the Myth, the Era*, 87.

412 Coughlin shut down: Albert Fried, *FDR and His Enemies* (New York: St. Martin's Press, 1999), 211.

412 Gunnar Myrdal; lower echelons of State Department: Quoted in Arthur Schlesinger Jr., "Did FDR Betray the Jews? Or Did He Do More Than Anyone Else to Save Them?" in Verne W. Newton, ed., *FDR and the Holocaust* (New York: St. Martin's Press, 1996), 160.

412 refugee statistics in 1935 and 1936; few Jewish spokesmen: Neuringer, "Franklin D. Roosevelt and Refuge for Victims of Nazism," 87–88.

413 "warm fields of altruism": Ibid., 90.

413 nations squabbled: Freidel, *FDR: A Rendezvous with Destiny*, 296–97.

413 "we have the quota system": FDR, 500th Press Conference, November 15, 1938, *Public Papers and Addresses of Franklin D. Roosevelt*, ed. Samuel I. Rosenman (New York: Macmillan Co., 1941), 1938, 596–601; see esp. 598. Cited hereafter in this chapter as *PPA*.

414 "Unfortunately, in my present position . . ."; "My dear Miss Youngbar . . ."; columns about Spain; "if they perish . . ."; ER aids individual Jews; "This German-Jewish business . . ."; loosening restrictions on immigration quotas: Cook, *Eleanor Roosevelt*, 2:305, 329, 338, 401, 571–73, 497, 557, 562.

414 agitator: Doris Kearns Goodwin, *No Ordinary Time: Franklin and Eleanor Roosevelt: The Home Front in World War II* (New York: Simon & Schuster, 1994), 104.

414 Mussolini changes anticommunist pact: Tansill, *Back Door to War*, 444; entry of 1 January 1939 in *The Ciano Diaries, 1939–1943*, ed. Hugh Gibson (New York: Doubleday & Co., 1946), 3.

414 Munich agreement broken: See Barbara Farnham, *Roosevelt and the Munich Crisis: A Study of Political Decision-Making* (Princeton, N.J.: Princeton University Press, 1997).

415 ER and attempt to aid refugee Jewish children: Blanche Weisen Cook, "Turn Toward Peace: ER and Foreign Affairs," in *Without Precedent: The Life and Career of Eleanor Roosevelt*, ed. Joan Hoff-Wilson and Marjorie Lightman (Bloomington, Ind.: Indiana University Press, 1984), 115.

415 "It is all right for you to support . . .": Neuringer, "Franklin D. Roosevelt and Refuge for Victims of Nazism," 91.

415 resettlement plans: Ibid., 92–95; see also Cook, *Eleanor Roosevelt*, 2:561.

416 "put every obstacle in the way": Goodwin, *No Ordinary Time*, 173.

416 Long quota statistics: Neuringer, "Franklin D. Roosevelt and Refuge for Victims of Nazism," 95–96, 98.

416 no compelling moral leadership: James MacGregor Burns, *The Crosswinds of Freedom* (New York: Vintage Books, 1990), 219.

416 roundups of Italian Jews: Washington Post, National Weekly Edition, 3 July 2000, 14.

416 had to deal with reality; Dawidowicz: Schlesinger, "Did FDR Betray the Jews?" 161.

416 FDR's discussion with Senate Military Affairs Committee: Davis, *FDR: Into the Storm*, 404–8.

417 FDR's meeting with senators regarding neutrality: Ibid., 456–58. Other accounts of this meeting include Joseph Alsop and Robert Kintner, *American White Paper* (New York: Simon & Schuster, 1940), 44–46; Cordell Hull, *The Memoirs of Cordell Hull* (New York: Macmillan Co., 1948), 1:649–51; Alben W. Barkley, *That Reminds Me* (Garden City, N.Y.: Doubleday & Co., 1954), 260–61.

417 *"his tendency to make the executive . . .":* FDR to Sara Delano Roosevelt, 26 October 1902, in *FDR Letters, Early Years,* 481.

417 *"how far do you think I can go . . .":* FDR to Frank Murphy, 1 July 1939, *FDR Letters, 1928–1945,* 899–900.

418 *public letter to Hitler and Mussolini:* FDR, A Message to Chancellor Adolf Hitler and Premier Benito Mussolini, 14 April 1939, *PPA* 1939, 201–5. See also Davis, *FDR: Into the Storm,* 433–40; Robert Dallek, *Franklin D. Roosevelt and American Foreign Policy, 1932–1945* (New York: Oxford University Press, 1979), 186; and Hull, *The Memoirs of Cordell Hull,* 1:622–23.

418 *a house where someone was dying:* Beatrice Bishop Berle and Travis Beal Jacobs, eds., *Navigating the Rapids, 1918–1971: From the Papers of Adolf A. Berle* (New York: Harcourt Brace Jovanovich, 1973), 244.

418 *like old Navy Department days; "the end of everything":* Quoted in Dallek, *FDR and American Foreign Policy,* 198.

419 *"unknown and unknowable destiny yawned . . .":* Memo attached to Charles Edison to FDR, 2 September 1939, *FDR Letters, 1928–1945,* 915–17.

419 *FDR's "Lincolnian calm":* Felix Frankfurter to FDR, 13 September 1939, in Max Freedman, ed., *Roosevelt and Frankfurter: Their Correspondence, 1928–1945* (Boston: Little, Brown & Co., 1967), 499.

419 *FDR on war:* FDR, Fireside Chat on the War in Europe, 3 September 1939, *PPA* 1939, 460–64; for FDR on neutrality, see FDR to Robert E. Wood, 12 October 1939, in *FDR Letters, 1928–1945,* 937–38; and Russell D. Buhite and David W. Levy, *FDR's Fireside Chats* (Norman, Okla.: University of Oklahoma Press, 1992).

421 *letter to Mack:* FDR to John E. Mack, 23 October 1939, in *FDR Letters, 1928–1945,* 945–46.

421 *FDR's reaction to attack on Finland:* FDR, Statement on the Conflict Between Russia and Finland, 1 December 1939, *PPA* 1939, 587–88; FDR to Lincoln MacVeagh, 1 December 1939, *FDR Letters, 1928–1945,* 961.

422 *"Do not seek or expect . . ." and following:* FDR, Address to the Delegates of the American Youth Congress, 10 February 1940, *PPA* 1940, 85–94.

423 *"We shall go on to the end . . .":* Churchill: His Complete Speeches, ed. James, 4 June 1940, 6:6231. See also Joseph P. Lash, *Roosevelt and Churchill, 1939–1941: The Partnership That Saved the West* (New York: W. W. Norton & Co., 1976), 149.

424 *"no more fortified . . .":* Quoted in Freidel, *FDR: Rendezvous with Destiny,* 335–36; also quoted in James R. Leutze, *Bargaining for Supremacy: Anglo-American Naval Collaboration, 1937–1941* (Chapel Hill, N.C.: University of North Carolina Press, 1977), 83.

424 *"our own defense needs and requirements":* Francis Loewenheim, Harold D. Langley, and Manfred Jonas, eds., *Roosevelt and Churchill: Their Secret Wartime Correspondence* (New York: E. P. Dutton & Co., 1975), 96; see also Warren F. Kimball, *Forged in War: Roosevelt, Churchill, and the Second World War* (New York: William Morrow & Co., 1997).

425 *FDR on third term:* ER, *The Autobiography of Eleanor Roosevelt* (New York: Harper & Brothers, 1960), 214.

426 *Democratic platform:* Samuel I. Rosenman, *Working with Roosevelt* (New York: Harper & Brothers, 1952), 211–12. See also Davis, *FDR: Into the Storm,* 598.

426 *FDR's speechwriting team:* Berle and Jacobs, eds., *Navigating the Rapids,* 345; Freedman, ed., *Roosevelt and Frankfurter: Their Correspondence,* passim.

427 *Churchill's secret plea and ensuing "horse trade":* Quoted in Davis, *FDR: Into the Storm,* 606; Loewenheim, Langley, and Jonas, eds., *Roosevelt and Churchill,* 107–9.

427 *"It is for peace that I have labored . . .":* FDR, Address at Philadelphia, Pa., 23 October 1940, *PPA* 1940, 495.

428 *"simply and very honestly . . .":* FDR, Campaign Address at Boston, Mass., 30 October 1940, *PPA* 1940, 517.

428 *Willkie reaction:* Quoted in Freidel, *FDR: Rendezvous with Destiny,* 354–55; also quoted in Ellsworth Barnard, *Wendell Willkie, Fighter for Freedom* (Marquette, Mich.: Northern Michigan University Press, 1966), 258.

428 *historians on Roosevelt's private and public positions:* John T. Flynn, *The Roosevelt Myth* (New York: Devin-Adair Co., 1948), passim; Charles A. Beard, *President Roosevelt and the Coming of the War, 1941* (New Haven, Conn.: Yale University Press, 1948), passim.

428 *opinion poll on the war; "If Hitler defeats England . . .":* Quoted in Manfred Jonas, *Isolationism in America, 1935–1941* (Ithaca, N.Y.: Cornell University Press, 1948), 212–14, 217.

430 *rousing address:* FDR, Address at Jackson Day Dinner, 7 January 1939, *PPA* 1939, 60–68 (italics added).

431 *proposed national health act:* FDR, A Request for Consideration of the Recommendations of the Interdepartmental Committee to Coordinate Health Activities, 23 January 1939, *PPA* 1939, 97–99.

431 *Frankfurter appointed to Supreme Court:* Freedman, ed., *Roosevelt and Frankfurter: Their Correspondence,* 481–82.

Twelve: The Grand Strategists' War

435 *"we may fall by the way":* Francis Loewenheim, Harold D. Langley, and Manfred Jonas, eds., *Roosevelt and Churchill: Their Secret Wartime Correspondence* (New York: E. P. Dutton & Co., 1975), 125.

435 *"We do not need the gallant armies . . .":* Quoted in Frank Freidel, *Franklin D. Roosevelt: A Rendezvous with Destiny* (Boston: Little, Brown & Co., 1990), 361, and in Robert Dallek, *Franklin D. Roosevelt and American Foreign Policy, 1932–1945* (New York: Oxford University Press, 1981), 259; also quoted in Joseph P. Lash, *Roosevelt and Churchill, 1939–1941: The Partnership That Saved the West* (New York: W. W. Norton & Co., 1976), 284. See speech of 9 February 1941, in *Winston S. Churchill, His Complete Speeches, 1897–1963,* ed. Robert Rhodes James (New York: Chelsea House/R. R. Bowker Co., 1974), 6:6348–50.

435 *"Well, boys, Britain's broke . . .":* Loewenheim, Langley, and Jonas, eds., *Roosevelt and Churchill,* 125; J. R. M. Butler, *Lord Lothian, Philip Kerr* (New York: Macmillan Co., 1960), 307.

435 *"he suddenly came out with it . . .":* Quoted in Freidel, *FDR: Rendezvous with Destiny,* 359; Butler, *Lord Lothian,* 224.

436 *"Now, what I am trying to do . . .":* FDR, 702nd Press Conference, 17 December 1940, in *Public Papers and Addresses of Franklin D. Roosevelt,* ed. Samuel I. Rosenman (New York: Macmillan Co., 1941), 1940, 607. Cited hereafter in this chapter as *PPA.*

436 *"seriously threatened . . ." and following:* FDR, Annual Message to the Congress, 6 January 1941, *PPA* 1941, 663ff.

437 *"Surely all of us . . .":* ER, "My Day," 7 January 1941.

437 *"exchange, lease, lend":* Congressional Record, H.R. 1776.

437 *Reactions to Bill 1776:* Freidel, *FDR: Rendezvous with Destiny,* 362.

438 *"Quote me on that":* FDR, 710th Press Conference, 14 January 1941, *PPA* 1940, 711–12.

438 *"There are men . . .":* FDR, Third Inaugural Address, 20 January 1941, *PPA* 1941, 3–6.

438 *inaugural parade:* Based on James MacGregor Burns, *Roosevelt: The Soldier of Freedom* (New York: Harcourt Brace Jovanovich, 1970), 35.

438 *"the most unsordid act":* Quoted in Freidel, *FDR: Rendezvous with Destiny,* 362, and in Warren F. Kimball, *The Most Unsordid Act: Lend-Lease, 1939–1941* (Baltimore: Johns Hopkins Press, 1969), 236; see also Martin Gilbert, *Winston S. Churchill: Finest Hour* (Boston: Houghton Mifflin Co., 1983), 6:569.

439 *"I would like to get them hooked . . .":* Quoted in David Reynolds, *The Creation of the Anglo-American Alliance, 1937–1941* (Chapel Hill, N.C.: University of North Carolina Press, 1982), 168; also quoted in Gilbert, *Winston S. Churchill,* 6:1040.

439 *Lindbergh compared to a "Copperhead":* FDR, 738th Press Conference, 25 April 1941, *PPA* 1941, 138.

440 *polls against war and increased aid to Britain:* Dallek, *Franklin D. Roosevelt and American Foreign Policy,* 267.

440 *the "blunt truth":* FDR, A Radio Address Announcing the Proclamation of an Unlimited National Emergency, 27 May 1941, *PPA* 1941, 181–94.

440   *U.S. knowledge of German plan to attack Russia:* Beatrice Bishop Berle and Travis Beal Jacobs, eds., *Navigating the Rapids, 1918–1971: From the Papers of Adolf A. Berle* (New York: Harcourt Brace Jovanovich, 1973), 362.

440   *no global strategy yet for FDR:* Berle and Jacobs, eds., *Navigating the Rapids,* 363.

441   *Americans strongly favor action against Japanese:* Dallek, *Franklin D. Roosevelt and American Foreign Policy,* 272.

442   *"It is all in the laps . . .":* Quoted in Burns, *Roosevelt: The Soldier of Freedom,* 159; John Morton Blum, *From the Morgenthau Diaries: Years of Urgency, 1938–1941* (Boston: Houghton Mifflin Co., 1965), 391.

442   *news of Pearl Harbor; Knox and FDR reactions:* Burns, *Roosevelt: The Soldier of Freedom,* 162.

442   *Churchill's reaction to news of Pearl Harbor:* Burns, *Roosevelt: The Soldier of Freedom,* 163; Winston S. Churchill, *The Second World War: The Grand Alliance* (Boston: Houghton Mifflin Co., 1950), 3:605; see also telegram of 8 December 1941 in Loewenheim, Langley, and Jonas, eds., *Roosevelt and Churchill,* 169; and James, *Winston S. Churchill, His Complete Speeches,* 6:6523–26.

442   *"on the ground, by God . . .":* Quoted in Burns, *Roosevelt: The Soldier of Freedom,* 165, and in Alexander Kendrick, *Prime Time: The Life of Edward R. Murrow* (Boston: Little, Brown & Co., 1969), 240.

442   *the Pearl Harbor attack:* Burns, *Roosevelt: The Soldier of Freedom,* 453–54; Samuel Eliot Morison, *History of the United States Naval Operations in World War II: The Rising Sun in the Pacific* (Boston: Little, Brown and Co., 1957), vol. 3, ch. 5.

443   *"a date which will live in infamy . . .":* FDR, Address to the Congress Asking That a State of War Be Declared, 8 December 1941, *PPA* 1941, 514–15.

443   *Hitler's Reichstag speech:* William L. Shirer, *The Rise and Fall of the Third Reich: A History of Nazi Germany* (New York: Simon & Schuster, 1960), 1173ff. See also Adolf Hitler, Discorso al Reichstag sulla dichiarazione di guerra agli Stati Uniti, 11 dicembre 1941 (Roma: "Novissima," 1942); Norman H. Baynes, ed., *The Speeches of Adolf Hitler* (New York: Oxford University Press, 1942).

444   *"The English-speaking peoples will . . .":* ER, "My Day," 1 January 1942.

445   *military production goals 1942–43:* FDR, Address to the Congress on the State of the Union, 6 January 1942, *PPA* 1942, 37.

445   *automobile factories slow; other factories quickly convert to war production:* Burns, *Roosevelt: The Soldier of Freedom,* 182; Richard Polenberg, *War and Society: The United States, 1941–1945* (Philadelphia: J. B. Lippincott Co., 1972), 10–12; William Manchester, *The Glory and the Dream: A Narrative History of America, 1932–1972* (Boston: Little, Brown & Co., 1974), 293–94; John R. Craf, *A Survey of the American Economy, 1940–1946* (New York: North River Press, 1947), 33–34.

445   *increased production in 1943; small towns boom again; civilian migration; Nelson needs men to "deal with industry . . .":* Burns, *Roosevelt: The Soldier of Freedom,* 183, 182, 470, 185.

447   *anti-inflation proposals:* Burns, *Roosevelt: The Soldier of Freedom,* 256; FDR, The President Offers a 7-Point Economic Stabilization Program, 27 April 1942, *PPA* 1942, 216–24.

447   *FDR on keeping incomes below $25,000:* Burns, *Roosevelt: The Soldier of Freedom,* 256–57; FDR to Sam Rayburn, 6 September 1942, in *FDR: His Personal Letters, 1928–1945,* ed. Elliott Roosevelt (New York: Duell, Sloan & Pearce, 1947–1950), 1346. Cited elsewhere in this chapter as *FDR Letters.*

447   *"wide discrepancies . . .":* FDR, Seven-Point Economic Stabilization Program, 27 April 1942, *PPA* 1942, 221.

448   *"cooperation and restraint . . .":* FDR, Address on the Ninth Anniversary of the New Deal Farm Program, 9 March 1942, *PPA* 1942, 145.

448   *"I have never been able to bring myself . . .":* FDR, Seven-Point Economic Stabilization Program, *PPA* 1942, 224.

448   *"Here at home . . .":* FDR, Fireside Chat, 28 April 1942, *PPA* 1942, 230.

448   *Frankfurter to FDR:* Burns, *Roosevelt: The Soldier of Freedom,* 257; Max Freedman, ed., *Roosevelt and Frankfurter: Their Correspondence, 1928–1945* (Boston: Little, Brown & Co., 1967), 657.

448   *FDR's ultimatum to Congress:* Burns, *Roosevelt: The Soldier of Freedom,* 260–62; FDR, Message to Congress Asking for Quick Action to Stabilize the Economy, 7 September 1942, *PPA* 1942, 364.

448 *Congressional action after FDR's stabilization speech:* Burns, *Roosevelt: The Soldier of Freedom*, 262.

448 *"total war on taxes":* Quoted in ibid., 261–62; Blum, *From the Morgenthau Diaries*, 51.

449 *cutback of merchant ships:* Freidel, *FDR: Rendezvous with Destiny*, 420.

449 *"I think Mrs. R. . . .":* Malvina Thompson to Esther Lape, 16 December 1941, in Joseph P. Lash, *A World of Love: Eleanor Roosevelt and Her Friends, 1943–1962* (Garden City, N.Y.: Doubleday & Co., 1984), xx–xxi.

449 *ER and Mayris Chaney:* Freidel, *FDR: Rendezvous with Destiny*, 426; more on ER and her appointments to the Office of Civilian Defense, including Chaney, in Joseph P. Lash, *Eleanor and Franklin* (New York: W. W. Norton & Co., 1971), 649–50; *New York Times*, 13 February 1942.

449 *FDR's typical disingenuousness:* Freidel, *FDR: Rendezvous with Destiny*, 426.

449 *"There is a great change . . .":* Malvina Thompson to Esther Lape, no date, 1942, in Lash, *A World of Love*, xxiii.

450 *Nazi violations of "Jefferson's inalienable rights":* FDR, Radio Address Commemorating the 150th Anniversary of the Ratification of the Bill of Rights, 15 December 1941, *PPA* 1941, 554–57.

450 *FBI inquiries and ER's objections:* Curt Gentry, *J. Edgar Hoover: The Man and the Secrets* (New York: W. W. Norton & Co., 1991), 212–22, passim; see also Richard Gid Powers, *Secrecy and Power: The Life of J. Edgar Hoover* (New York: Free Press, 1987), and William W. Keller, *The Liberals and J. Edgar Hoover: Rise and Fall of a Domestic Intelligence State* (Princeton, N.J.: Princeton University Press, 1989).

451 *Hoover investigates Wallace:* Gentry, *J. Edgar Hoover*, 307; see also Powers, *Secrecy and Power*, and Keller, *The Liberals and J. Edgar Hoover*.

451 *Hoover persuades FDR on wiretapping:* Gentry, *J. Edgar Hoover*, 231; see also Powers, *Secrecy and Power*, and Keller, *The Liberals and J. Edgar Hoover*.

451 *FDR "rewards" Hoover:* Gentry, *J. Edgar Hoover*, 226.

451 *internment of Japanese on West Coast:* Dallek, *Franklin D. Roosevelt and American Foreign Policy, 1932–1945*, 334–36. See also D. S. Thomas, R. S. Nishimoto, and others, *Japanese American Evacuation and Resettlement: The Spoilage* (Berkeley, Calif.: University of California Press, 1946–54), vol. 1; Morton Grodzins, *Americans Betrayed: Politics and the Japanese Evacuation* (Chicago: University of Chicago Press, 1949); Stetson Conn, "The Decision to Evacuate," in Kent Roberts Greenfield, ed., *Command Decisions* (New York: Harcourt, Brace & Co., 1959).

452 *"Herd 'em up, pack 'em off . . .":* Quoted in Burns, *Roosevelt: The Soldier of Freedom*, 215.

452 *contentious subject:* Allida Black, interview, 20 July 2000.

452 *"This great lady . . .":* Francis X. Clines, "Memorial Will Honor Japanese-Americans," *New York Times*, 21 October 1999, A14.

453 *"knew so little . . .":* ER to Joseph Lash, 22 April 1943, quoted in Allida M. Black, *Casting Her Own Shadow: Eleanor Roosevelt and the Shaping of Postwar Liberalism* (New York: Columbia University Press, 1996), 145.

453 *ER proposes closing camps; ER visits camp:* Ibid., 145–47.

454 *FDR on congressional "pettiness" and lack of "fighting leadership":* FDR to James M. Cox, 10 April 1943, *FDR Letters, 1928–1945*, 1421.

454 *FDR's dislike of Luce:* W. A. Swanberg, *Luce and His Empire* (New York: Charles Scribner's Sons, 1972), 295–96.

454 *the atomic bomb:* Burns, *Roosevelt: The Soldier of Freedom*, 249–52; Robert Jungk, *Brighter Than a Thousand Suns* (New York: Harcourt, Brace & Co., 1958), 109–11.

455 *"Three months' delay might be fatal":* Quoted in Burns, *Roosevelt: The Soldier of Freedom*, 252; James Phinney Baxter 3, *Scientists Against Time* (Boston: Little, Brown & Co., 1946), 434.

Thirteen: The People's War

457 *Hopkins on FDR and trip to Casablanca:* Robert E. Sherwood, *Roosevelt and Hopkins: An Intimate History* (New York: Harper & Brothers, 1950), 669–73.

458 *"not to hurry or try to force . . .":* Quoted in Robert Dallek, *Franklin D. Roosevelt and American Foreign Policy, 1932–1945* (New York: Oxford University Press, 1981), 371; Bryant, *Turner of the Tide*, 443–45.

458 *Hopkins disagreement with Italy as top priority:* Sherwood, *Roosevelt and Hopkins,* 669–75.

459 *FDR and Churchill on unconditional surrender:* Dallek, *Franklin D. Roosevelt and American Foreign Policy,* 373–75.

459 *FDR letter to Hull on stalled "marriage" between Giraud and de Gaulle:* Quoted in Frank Friedel, *Franklin D. Roosevelt: Rendezvous with Destiny* (Boston: Little, Brown & Co., 1990), 460; Robert Murphy, *Diplomat Among Warriors* (Garden City, N.Y.: Doubleday & Co., 1964), 171–72; Milton Viorst, *Hostile Allies: FDR and Charles de Gaulle* (New York: Macmillan & Co., 1965), ch. 7.

459 *shaking hands for the camera:* Friedel, *FDR: Rendezvous with Destiny,* 463; Sherwood, *Roosevelt and Hopkins,* 693.

460 *King Hassan's support of U.S.:* Speech made by His Majesty King Hassan II on occasion of the 50th anniversary of the ANFA Conference, Fez, Morocco, 12 January 1993.

460 *Stalin wants second front in 1942:* James MacGregor Burns, *Roosevelt: The Soldier of Freedom* (New York: Harcourt Brace Jovanovich, 1970), 233.

460 *Molotov's mission:* Burns, *Roosevelt: The Soldier of Freedom,* 231–37.

461 *FDR's shuffling of war agencies; controlling lives:* FDR to Harold Smith, 3 July 1943, *FDR: His Personal Letters, 1928–1945,* ed. Elliott Roosevelt (New York: Duell, Sloan & Pearce, 1947–1950), 1433–34. Cited hereafter in this chapter as *FDR Letters.* See also Freidel, *FDR: Rendezvous with Destiny,* 435–37.

461 *incomes and after-tax profits:* William L. O'Neill, *A Democracy at War: America's Fight at Home and Abroad in World War II* (New York: Free Press, 1993), 208.

462 *compromise of "maintenance of voluntarily established membership":* Burns, *Roosevelt: The Soldier of Freedom,* 263–64.

462 *number of walkouts increases from 1942 to 1944:* O'Neill, *A Democracy at War,* 212.

462 *"John Lewis, damn your coal-black soul":* Quoted in Burns, *Roosevelt: The Soldier of Freedom,* 337; also in O'Neill, *A Democracy at War,* 210.

462 *"FDR walked with consummate skill . . .":* O'Neill, *A Democracy at War,* 212.

462 *women's pay in 1930s:* Irving Bernstein, *A Caring Society: The New Deal, the Worker, and the Great Depression* (Houghton Mifflin Co., 1985), 291.

462 *union fear of filling veterans' jobs with women:* O'Neill, *A Democracy at War,* 244.

462 *scant equal pay for women:* Ibid.

463 *lack of day care:* See Doris Kearns Goodwin, *No Ordinary Time: Franklin and Eleanor Roosevelt: The Home Front in World War II* (New York: Simon & Schuster, 1994), 417–18; see also Margaret O'Brien Steinfels, *Who's Minding the Children? The History and Politics of Day Care in America* (New York: Simon & Shuster, 1973).

463 *child labor during war:* O'Neill, *A Democracy at War,* 249.

463 *theatened march by blacks on Washington and FDR's response:* Burns, *Roosevelt: The Soldier of Freedom,* 123ff; see also John M. Blum, *V Was for Victory: Politics and American Culture During World War II* (New York: Harcourt Brace Jovanovich, 1976), 182–88.

463 *FDR and "Negro rights":* See Burns, *Roosevelt: The Soldier of Freedom,* 123ff.

464 *difficulties faced by Fair Employment Practices Commission:* Blum, *V Was for Victory,* 196–99.

465 *"Bull" Connor's view of FEPC:* Ibid., 194.

465 *civilian efforts at home:* O'Neill, *A Democracy at War,* 130–37.

466 *"We ask that every schoolhouse . . .":* Quoted in Burns, *Roosevelt: The Soldier of Freedom.*

466 *education losses during war years:* Vannevar Bush, *Science—The Endless Frontier* (National Science Foundation, 1945), 7.

466 *war propaganda efforts:* Blum, *V Was for Victory,* ch. 4.

467 *ER and Sojourner Truth housing project:* Doris Kearns Goodwin, *No Ordinary Time,* 326–28.

468 *chances of survival in different branches of military; unequal rewards for courage; WACs face slander, praised by MacArthur; treatment of African-Americans and homosexuals:* O'Neill, *A Democracy at War,* 322, 327–28, 330–32, 235–238, 328–30; Allan Berube, *Coming Out Under Fire* (New York: Free Press, 1990).

469 *"inconceivable—it would, indeed, be sacrilegious":* FDR, Address to the Congress on the State of the Union, 7 January 1943, in *Public Papers and Addresses of Franklin D. Roosevelt,* ed. Samuel

I. Rosenman (New York: Harper & Brothers, 1950), 1943, 30. Cited hereafter in this chapter as *PPA*.

470 *caution of FDR toward UN:* Dallek, *Franklin D. Roosevelt and American Foreign Policy,* 419; Burns, *Roosevelt: The Soldier of Freedom,* 427. See also Townsend Hoopes and Douglas Brinkley, *FDR and the Creation of the U.N.* (New Haven, Conn.: Yale University Press, 1997).

470 *on 1942 "Declaration":* See Burns, *The Crosswinds of Freedom* (New York: Vintage Books, 1990), 178; see also Hoopes and Brinkley, *FDR and the Creation of the U.N.*

470 *questions reminiscent of death of League of Nations:* Burns, *Roosevelt: The Soldier of Freedom,* 427.

471 *"haunted by the fear . . .":* Joseph P. Lash, *Eleanor and Franklin* (New York: W. W. Norton & Co., 1971), 638.

471 *ER visits England, disagrees with Churchill:* Eleanor Roosevelt, *This I Remember* (New York: Harper & Brothers, 1949), ch. 16; Lash, *Eleanor and Franklin,* 658–68.

471 *U.S. must join with other "liberated people":* ER, "My Day," 1 January 1942.

471 *FDR and ER as Soldiers of the Faith, FDR's moral credo:* Burns, *Roosevelt: The Soldier of Freedom,* 549.

473 *FDR discusses Lincoln with youth leaders:* Kenneth S. Davis, *FDR: Into the Storm, 1937–1940* (New York: Random House, 1993), 563–65.

474 *FDR's evolving view of the UN:* Freidel, *FDR: Rendezvous with Destiny,* 466.

474 *nations "will learn to work together":* Quoted in Burns, *Roosevelt: The Soldier of Freedom,* 429. See FDR, Address of the President on the Signing of the Agreement Establishing the United Nations Relief and Rehabilitation Administration, 9 November 1943, *PPA* 1943, 503.

474 *Churchill on Teheran conference:* Burns, *Roosevelt: The Soldier of Freedom,* 407.

474 *arms buildup in England:* Ibid., 473.

474 *Hitler's fortifications in France:* Stephen E. Ambrose, *D-Day: The Climactic Battle of World War II* (New York: Simon & Schuster, 1994), 36–37.

476 *"we shall return again and again":* FDR, President's D-Day Prayer on the Invasion of Normandy, 6 June 1944, *PPA* 1944–45, 152.

477 *FDR questioned about calling off election:* Quoted in Burns, *Roosevelt: The Soldier of Freedom,* 497.

479 *"I dread another campaign":* ER to Lorena Hickok, in Joseph P. Lash, *A World of Love: Eleanor Roosevelt and Her Friends, 1943–1962* (Garden City, N.Y.: Doubleday & Co., 1984), 129.

479 *"not a tax bill but a tax relief bill":* FDR, The President Vetoes a Revenue Bill, 22 February 1944, *PPA* 1944–45, 80; quoted in Burns, *Roosevelt: The Soldier of Freedom,* 434.

479 *a "calculated and deliberate assault":* Barkley, quoted in Burns, *Roosevelt: The Soldier of Freedom,* 434–36.

480 *FDR chooses a new VP:* Burns, *Roosevelt: The Soldier of Freedom,* 503–5.

480 *FDR's acceptance of Democratic nomination:* FDR, Address Broadcast from a Naval Base . . . to the Democratic National Convention in Chicago, 20 July 1944, *PPA* 1944–45, 202.

480 *"The Dewey-Bricker ticket . . .":* ER to Joseph Lash, 9 July 1944, in Lash, *A World of Love,* 131.

481 *Dewey as TR look-alike:* Richard Norton Smith, *Thomas E. Dewey and His Times* (New York: Simon & Schuster, 1982), 217, 63–65.

481 *Dewey discovers breaking of Japanese codes:* Freidel, *FDR: Rendezvous with Destiny,* 559; Forrest C. Pogue, *George C. Marshall: Organizer of Victory* (New York: Viking Press, 1973), 3:470–73. Smith, *Thomas E. Dewey and His Times,* 425–20.

481 *Dewey calls FDR dupe of radicals:* Quoted in Burns, *Roosevelt: The Soldier of Freedom,* 529; Freidel, *FDR: Rendezvous with Destiny,* 559, 560–62.

481 *"Well, here we are together again . . .":* FDR, Address at Dinner of International Brotherhood of Teamsters, 23 September 1944, *PPA* 1944–45, 284–92; quoted in Burns, *Roosevelt: The Soldier of Freedom,* 521–24.

482 *1944 election:* Smith, *Thomas E. Dewey and His Times,* ch. 12; Steve Fraser, "Election, Presidential, 1944," in *Encyclopedia of the American Presidency* (New York: Simon & Schuster, 1994), 2:509–11.

483 *FDR refutes idea that he is abandoning the New Deal:* FDR, 929th Press Conference, 28 December 1943, *PPA* 1943, 569–75.

483 *"I could not help feeling . . .":* ER, *This I Remember,* 239.

484 *FDR's "second Bill of Rights":* Message to the Congress on the State of the Union, 11 January 1944, *PPA* 1944–45, 40–42. (We quote speech as spoken by FDR over the radio. Written text departs slightly from that given in *PPA.)*

484 *expansion of individual rights:* For an opposing perspective, see Alan Brinkley, *The End of Reform: New Deal Liberalism in Recession and War* (New York: Alfred A. Knopf, 1995), 144.

485 *"Jobs. It's a good old Anglo-Saxon word.":* FDR, 966th Press Conference, 29 August 1944, *PPA* 1944–45, 246.

485 *FDR's plans for creating equality of opportunity:* See, in *PPA* 1944–45: FDR, Statement of the President on Signing the Public Health Service Act, July 1944, 191–92; FDR, Remarks to the Conference on Rural Education, 4 October 1944, 312–17; FDR, Statement by the President on Signing a Bill to Extend Rural Electrification, 22 September 1944, 279–80; FDR, The President Vetoes a Revenue Bill, 22 February 1944, 32–42; FDR, Message to the Congress on the State of the Union, 11 January 1944, 80–83.

486 *"a stronger, a happier, and a more prosperous America":* FDR, Statement by the President on Signing a Bill to Extend Rural Electrification, 22 September 1944, *PPA* 1944–45, 280.

486 *FDR and Willkie plan to realign parties:* Burns, *Roosevelt: The Soldier of Freedom,* 511–13.

486 *no superior officer, only the people:* FDR, The President Announces He Will Accept a Nomination for a Fourth Term, 11 July 1944, *PPA* 1944–45, 197–98.

487 *military achievements by January 1945; those present at Yalta; Poland compromise formula:* Burns, *Roosevelt: The Soldier of Freedom,* 565, 572.

488 *FDR's failure to challenge Churchill on India; "Under no circumstances . . .":* Dallek, *Franklin D. Roosevelt and American Foreign Policy,* 359–60, 511.

489 *"ought to spell the end . . ."; "Twenty-five years ago . . .":* FDR, Address to the Congress Reporting on the Yalta Conference, 1 March 1945, *PPA* 1944–45, 586. (Our text is taken from the radio address and differs slightly from *PPA* text.) Also quoted in Burns, *Roosevelt: The Soldier of Freedom,* 582.

489 *FDR preparing for death?:* Beatrice Bishop Berle and Travis Beal Jacobs, eds., *Navigating the Rapids, 1918–1971: From the Papers of Adolf A. Berle* (New York: Harcourt Brace Jovanovich, 1973), 527; ER, *This I Remember,* 339.

489 *growth of presidency:* See Matthew J. Dickinson, *Bitter Harvest: FDR, Presidential Power, and the Growth of the Presidential Branch* (Cambridge: Cambridge University Press, 1997).

490 *medical checkups; poor health after Yalta:* Freidel, *FDR: Rendezvous with Destiny,* 512–13; Hugh Gallagher, *FDR's Splendid Deception* (Arlington, Va.: Vandamere Press, 1994), 179.

493 *Stalin suspicious, FDR sends telegram:* Burns, *Roosevelt: The Soldier of Freedom,* 585–87.

494 *"I've seen so much now of the Near East . . ."; "Does that sound tired to you?":* Lash, *Eleanor and Franklin,* 718–19.

495 *meetings with Lucy Mercer:* Goodwin, *No Ordinary Time,* 434–35, 499–500.

495 *"The work, my friends, is peace . . .":* FDR, Undelivered Address Prepared for Jefferson Day, 13 April 1945, *PPA* 1944–45, 613–16.

Fourteen: The Entire World Her Family

500 *"My husband and I . . .":* Eleanor Roosevelt, *On My Own* (New York: Harper & Brothers, 1958), 1.

500 *"I find that mentally . . .":* Joseph P. Lash, *A World of Love: Eleanor Roosevelt and Her Friends, 1943–1962* (Garden City, N.Y.: Doubleday & Co., 1984), 188; also Doris Kearns Goodwin, *No Ordinary Time: Franklin and Eleanor Roosevelt: The Home Front in World War II* (New York: Simon & Schuster, 1994), 619.

500 *"I think we had . . .":* quoted in Lash, *A World of Love,* 190.

500 *"certain definite decisions . . . a big vacuum . . .":* Eleanor Roosevelt, *On My Own,* 1–3.

501 *as the country grew stronger, he grew weaker:* Interview with James Roosevelt in Goodwin, *No Ordinary Time,* 631.

501 *"It cannot be the work of one man . . .":* quoted in Joseph P. Lash, *Eleanor: The Years Alone* (New York: W. W. Norton & Co., 1972), 19.
501 *Shumatov's portrait of FDR:* Ibid., 24.
502 *Fala:* Eleanor Roosevelt, *On My Own,* 9–10.
502 *"You would be unbeatable":* Lash, *Eleanor: The Years Alone,* 28.
502 *theatrical producer [John Golden]:* Eleanor Roosevelt, *On My Own,* 6–7.
502 *"Father never told me . . .":* Elliott Roosevelt and James Brough, *Mother R: Eleanor Roosevelt's Untold Story* (New York: G. P. Putnam's Sons, 1977), 85.
502 *"a fifth grader can read me . . .":* ER to her daughter, 27 August 1945, in Bernard Asbell, ed., *Mother and Daughter: The Letters of Eleanor and Anna Roosevelt* (New York: Fromm International Publishing, 1988), 197.
503 *Truman confesses difficulties with Churchill:* Harry Truman to ER, 10 May 1945, ER Papers, FDR Library.
503 *advice to develop personal relationship with Churchill:* ER to Harry S. Truman, 18 May 1945, ibid.
503 *Truman responds in longhand:* Blanche Wiesen Cook, "Eleanor Roosevelt and Human Rights: The Battle for Peace and Planetary Decency," in *Women and American Foreign Policy: Lobbyists, Critics, and Insiders,* ed. Edward P. Crapol (Wilmington, Del.: SR Books, 1992), 103.
503 *discrimination against Japanese-Americans:* Harry S. Truman to Eleanor Roosevelt, 21 December 1945; Harry S. Truman to Tom Clark, 2 December 1945; Truman, Memo for the Attorney General, 17 January 1945; all in HST Manuscript Collection, Official File, quoted in Alonzo L. Hamby, *Beyond the New Deal: Harry S. Truman and American Liberalism* (New York: Columbia University Press, 1973), 65.
503 *Truman needs ER's support:* Allida M. Black, *Casting Her Own Shadow: Eleanor Roosevelt and the Shaping of Postwar Liberalism* (New York: Columbia University Press, 1996), 66.
503 *courteous, slightly aloof defenses:* See ER-HST Correspondence File, FDR Library.
503 *ER urges Murray-Wagner bill; action on wages and prices:* Black, *Casting Her Own Shadow,* 61, 70–75.
503 *"I hope that now you will not insist . . .":* Ibid., 76.
504 *"part of your laughter . . .":* ER, "My Day," 14 April 1953.
504 *ER's friends:* Telephone interview with Curtis Roosevelt, 29 September 1999.
504 *"bloodless revolution":* ER, "My Day," 15 July 1954.
504 *"The history of New York . . .":* ER, "My Day," 8 January 1954.
504 *empathy deepened:* ER, *The Autobiography of Eleanor Roosevelt* (New York: Harper & Brothers, 1960), 413.
504 *Truman's offer and ER's reaction:* Eleanor Roosevelt, *On My Own,* 39.
505 *"You have to do it":* Lash, *Eleanor: The Years Alone,* 36.
505 *plenty of people to help:* Elliott Roosevelt and James Brough, *Mother R,* 69.
505 *"the one hope. . .";* *"fear and trembling":* Eleanor Roosevelt, *On My Own,* 39.
505 *front page headline:* New York Times, 20 December 1945, 1.
505 *Senator Bilbo:* New York Times, 21 December 1945, 1.
505 *departure of delegates:* New York Times, 31 December 1945, 1.
506 *"heavyhearted":* Eleanor Roosevelt, *On My Own,* 40.
506 *dull reading:* Ibid.
506 *"millions of your fellow citizens . . .":* Archibald MacLeish to Eleanor Roosevelt, 27 December 1945, FDR Library.
506 *"We, O Lord, have determined . . .":* New York Times, 31 December 1945, 1.
506 *liberal attitudes toward Soviet Union:* Alonzo L. Hamby, *Beyond the New Deal,* 97–98.
507 *"If we learn to trust them . . .":* ER quoted in New York Times, 3 October 1945, 10.
507 *Brynes in Moscow:* Hamby, *Beyond the New Deal,* 97–98; Randall B. Woods and Howard Jones, *Dawning of the Cold War: The United States' Quest for Order* (Athens, Ga.: University of Georgia Press, 1991).
507 *"Great Britain is always anxious . . .":* ER to Harry S. Truman, 20 November 1945, FDR Library.

508 *Vandenberg asks ER to serve on Committee 3:* Eleanor Roosevelt, *On My Own,* 41–42.

508 *"this proved to be true":* Ibid., 43–44.

509 *bath towels:* ER, "My Day," 22 January 1946.

509 *welcome note from Queen:* ER to Anna, 7 January 1946, in *Mother and Daughter,* ed. Asbell, 206.

509 *opening session of General Assembly:* Lash, *Eleanor: The Years Alone,* 44.

509 *Spaak's acceptance speech:* Ibid., 45.

509 *people applaud ER:* *New York Times,* 14 January 1946, 16.

509 *ER on BBC; at parties; loses voice:* Lash, *Eleanor: The Years Alone,* 47.

509 *"walked on eggs":* Eleanor Roosevelt, *On My Own,* 47.

510 *"very insignificant":* ER to Anna, 11 January 1946, in *Mother and Daughter,* ed. Asbell, 208.

510 *ER meets with women delegates:* Eleanor Roosevelt, *On My Own,* 47; Lash, *Eleanor: The Years Alone,* 49; see also "Meeting of the Women Delegates and Advisers to the General Assembly Called by Mrs. Eleanor Roosevelt, Tuesday, January 15, 1946," Box 4562, FDR Library.

510 *ER noncommittal toward commission on women; "preferred to do her politics with the men":* Lash, *Eleanor: The Years Alone,* 49–50.

510 *"lagged behind":* Eleanor Roosevelt, *On My Own,* 48–49.

510 *"made all the difference...":* ER, Campaign Address for Stevenson, October 1956, in Allida M. Black, ed., *Courage in a Dangerous World: The Political Writings of Eleanor Roosevelt* (New York: Columbia University Press, 1999), 274.

510 *"boys":* ER, quoted in Cook, "Eleanor Roosevelt and Human Rights," 109.

510 *"rude and arrogant" or overly cordial:* Ibid., 107–8.

510 *other countries "would be reassured...":* ER to Anna, 16 January 1946, in *Mother and Daughter,* ed. Asbell, 209.

510 *Byrnes leaving ER out:* Cook, "Eleanor Roosevelt and Human Rights," 108.

511 *Displaced Persons; Dulles asks ER to speak; Vishinsky's wit and ridicule:* Eleanor Roosevelt, *On My Own,* 49–51.

511 *Dulles:* Quoted in *New York Times,* 3 March 1946, 5.

512 *ER's speech:* Lash, *Eleanor: The Years Alone,* 54; Eleanor Roosevelt, *On My Own,* 51.

512 *General Assembly adopts resolution:* *New York Times,* 13 February 1946, 1.

512 *Praise from Dulles:* Quoted in Lash, *Eleanor: The Years Alone,* 54.

512 *"So—against odds...":* ER, quoted in Cook, "Eleanor Roosevelt and Human Rights," 111.

512 *ER "doing a splendid job":* Arthur H. Vandenberg Jr., ed., *The Private Papers of Senator Vandenberg* (Boston: Houghton Mifflin Co., 1952), 240.

512 *"I realize quite well...":* Quoted in Cook, "Turn Toward Peace: Eleanor Roosevelt and Foreign Affairs," in *Without Precedent: The Life and Career of Eleanor Roosevelt,* Joan Hoff-Wilson and Marjorie Lightman, eds. (Bloomington, Ind.: Indiana University Press, 1984), 115.

513 *"An old woman knelt...":* ER, "My Day," 16 February 1946.

513 *children who had wandered in:* Eleanor Roosevelt, *On My Own,* 55–56.

513 *"They made us into soap":* ER, "My Day," 16 February 1946.

513 *"It was everybody's fault":* Lash, *Eleanor: The Years Alone,* 116.

513 *"we never knew...";* *"there were no Nazis...":* ER, "My Day," 1 November 1961.

513 *"weight of human misery":* Lash, *Eleanor: The Years Alone,* 116.

513 *"intimately and shockingly aware...":* Anne Frank, *The Diary of a Young Girl,* trans. B. M. Mooyaart, with an Introduction by Eleanor Roosevelt (Garden City, N.Y.: Doubleday & Co., 1952), 7–8.

513 *"miserable, tortured, terrorized Jews...";* *"while we sit comfortably":* ER, "My Day," 7 November 1945.

513 *"It seems to me urgent...":* Ibid.

513 *"I knew for the first time...":* Elliott Roosevelt and James Brough, *Mother R,* 80.

513 *"I do not happen...":* Quoted in Lash, *Eleanor: The Years Alone,* 115.

514 *ER's feelings toward a Jewish state:* ER to Joseph P. Lash, 18 May 1944, quoted in Lash, *Eleanor: The Years Alone,* 110; ER, "My Day," 12 May 1943, quoted in Lash, 108.

514 *Palestine must "be made a Jewish state":* TR, Address in Carnegie Hall, 28 October 1918, in *Newer Roosevelt Messages,* ed. William Griffith (New York: Current Literature Publishing Co., 1919), 3:1004.

514 *quarantined ship:* New York Times, 17 January 1946, 11.

514 *British White Paper:* Tad Szulc, *The Secret Alliance: The Extraordinary Story of the Rescue of the Jews Since World War II* (New York: Farrar, Straus & Giroux, 1991), 6; Bernard Wasserstein, *Britain and the Jews of Europe, 1939–1945* (London: Institute of Jewish Affairs, 1970), 348–49.

514 *immigration policy in Great Britain and U.S.:* Wasserstein, *Britain and the Jews of Europe,* 115; Szulc, *The Secret Alliance,* 10.

515 *flight to Palestine and its dangers:* Szulc, *The Secret Alliance,* 11–12; see Ze'ev V. Hadari and Ze'ev Tsahoe, *Voyage to Freedom: An Episode in the Illegal Immigration to Palestine* (London: Valentine Mitchell & Co., 1985), 11–12.

515 *"I am very much distressed . . .":* quoted in Lash, *Eleanor: The Years Alone,* 115.

515 *Truman and immigration to Palestine:* Hamby, *Beyond the Cold War,* 92; Lash, *Eleanor: The Years Alone,* 115; Szulc, *The Secret Alliance,* 39; see also Bartley C. Crum, *Behind the Silken Curtain: A Personal Account of Anglo-American Diplomacy in Palestine and the Middle East* (New York: Simon and Schuster, 1947).

515 *"scum of all Europe":* Representative E. E. Cox, Democrat of Georgia, quoted in ER, "My Day," 12 June 1948.

516 *Ernest Bevin backtracks:* Lash, *Eleanor: The Years Alone,* 116.

516 *"We sit safely . . .":* ER, "My Day," 19 August 1946.

516 *"I cannot bear . . .";* *Labor-Socialist government; right of Jewish people to a homeland; "unctuous words"; Anglo-American interest in oil:* Lash, *Eleanor: The Years Alone,* 118–21.

516 *"justice, not oil":* Quoted in David McCullough, *Truman* (New York: Simon & Schuster, 1992), 597.

516 *"obligated" to see it through:* ER, "My Day," 14 May 1947, quoted in Lash, *Eleanor: The Years Alone,* 120.

516 *"The thought of what it must mean . . .":* ER, "My Day" 12 September 1947, quoted in ibid., 121–22.

517 *"She impressed me . . .":* Lash, *Eleanor: The Years Alone,* 122.

517 *"It seems to me . . .":* ER to Miss Binn, 24 October 1947, in Lash, *Eleanor: The Years Alone,* 124.

517 *"accommodate themselves . . .":* ER, "My Day," 16 March 1956; see also "My Day," 23 March 1956.

517 *White House and State Department at war; "A land of milk . . ."; "one of the worst messes . . .":* David McCullough, *Truman,* 601, 609, 612.

518 *"cog in the wheels":* ER to President Truman, 22 March 1948, quoted in Lash, *Eleanor: The Years Alone,* 130.

518 *Truman and ER:* McCullough, *Truman,* 601; Hamby, *Beyond the New Deal,* 220; Lash, *Eleanor: The Years Alone,* 131–32.

518 *"follow instead of lead.":* ER to Marshall, 11 May 1948, in Lash, *Eleanor: The Years Alone,* 132.

518 *stormy White House meetings:* David McCullough, *Truman,* 613–16.

518 *"A new country asking . . .";* *American delegation bypassed:* Ibid., 618.

519 *"Several of the representatives . . . leadership within the United Nations":* ER to Secretary of State Marshall, 16 May 1948, quoted in Lash, *Eleanor: The Years Alone,* 133–34.

519 *"If a wave of hysteria hits us . . .":* ER, "My Day," 27 March 1947.

520 *"a sabotage front . . .":* James MacGregor Burns, *The Crosswinds of Freedom* (New York: Vintage Press, 1990), 235. See also John C. Culver and John Hyde, *American Dreamer: A Life of Henry A. Wallace* (New York: W. W. Norton & Co., 2000).

520 *working within the Democratic party:* James MacGregor Burns, *The Crosswinds of Freedom,* 235; see also Zachary Karabell, *The Last Campaign: How Harry Truman Won the 1948 Election* (New York: Alfred A. Knopf, 2000).

520 *"As a leader . . .":* ER, "My Day," 31 December 1947.

520 *failure to attract women:* Elliott Roosevelt and James Brough, *Mother R,* 100.

520   *ER to Frances Perkins:* McCullough, *Truman,* 702; see also Elliott Roosevelt and James Brough, *Mother R,* 134.

520   *"The Democrats will lose . . .":* ER to Joseph Lash, 23 July 1948, in Lash, *A World of Love,* 273.

521   *ER's enthusiasm about Margaret Chase Smith:* ER, "My Day," 24 June 1948.

521   *ER's endorsements:* ER, "My Day," 11 September 1948.

521   *Truman and James Roosevelt:* Elliott Roosevelt and James Brough, *Mother R,* 136.

521   *ER endorses Truman:* Elliott Roosevelt and James Brough, *Mother R,* 139, 141; McCullough, *Truman,* 702.

521   *"dragged kicking and screaming . . .":* Truman, quoted in Black, *Casting Her Own Shadow,* 83.

521   *ER takes subway to Bronx:* Elliott Roosevelt and James Brough, *Mother R,* 90; Lash, *Eleanor: The Years Alone,* 55.

521   *"We loved your husband":* ER, "My Day," 10 September 1945.

521   *one of their greatest assets:* John P. Humphrey, *Human Rights and the United Nations: A Great Adventure* (Dobbs Ferry, N.Y.: Transnational Publishers, 1984), 5.

522   *"first real test":* Ibid., 4.

522   *tea in Mrs. Roosevelt's apartment:* Ibid., 29.

522   *"promote" full employment:* Lash, *Eleanor: The Years Alone,* 64.

523   *"legal personality":* Humphrey, *Human Rights and the United Nations,* 40.

523   *Madam Mehta:* Eleanor Roosevelt, *On My Own,* 78–79.

523   *"If human rights did not mean . . .":* Humphrey, *Human Rights and the United Nations,* 41.

523   *"There must be a great deal . . .":* *The Autobiography of Eleanor Roosevelt* (New York: Harper & Brothers, 1960), 428; see also Elliott Roosevelt and James Brough, *Mother R,* 91.

523   *"His words rolled out. . .":* "My Day," 6 September 1947; *The Autobiography of Eleanor Roosevelt,* 320.

523   *"We are here . . .":* Humphrey, *Human Rights and the United Nations,* 85–86.

523   *"naïveté and cunning":* Lash, *Eleanor: The Years Alone,* 69.

523   *quasi-amateur style:* Interview with Curtis Roosevelt, 29 September 1999.

524   *shingles:* Elliott Roosevelt and James Brough, *Mother R,* 91.

524   *"I used to think . . .":* Ibid., 146.

524   *roles reversed:* James MacGregor Burns and Stewart Burns, *A People's Charter: The Pursuit of Rights in America* (New York: Alfred A. Knopf, 1991), 421.

524   *"every step forward . . .";* *"slowed up by circumstances . . .":* ER, "The United Nations and You," 13 April 1946, in *What I Hope to Leave Behind: The Essential Essays of Eleanor Roosevelt,* ed. Allida M. Black (Brooklyn, N.Y.: Carlson Publishing, 1995), 539–40.

524   *"business of give-and-take":* Elliott Roosevelt and James Brough, *Mother R,* 142.

524   *"My interest or sympathy . . .";* *human needs:* The Autobiography of Eleanor Roosevelt, 413, 414.

525   *"People glanced at him . . .":* ER, "My Day," 15 May 1948.

525   *"best selves":* ER to Anna Roosevelt, 12 June 1961, in Lash, *A World of Love,* 537.

525   *"I like to have people . . .":* ER to David Gurewitsch, 18 December 1947, in Lash, *A World of Love,* 246.

525   *Christmas Eve with the Lashes:* ER to David Gurewitsch, 20 December 1947, in Lash, *A World of Love,* 247.

525   *Roosevelt family traditions:* Elliott Roosevelt and James Brough, *Mother R,* 85–87.

525   *Wiltwyck School:* ER to David Gurewitsch, 22 December 1947, in Lash, *A World of Love,* 247.

525   *clear and cold:* Ibid., 247.

525   *"I was only trying to indoctrinate . . .":* Ibid., 549.

526   *"I have often differed . . .":* Elliott Roosevelt and James Brough, *Mother R,* 103.

526   *Elliott's new book:* Lash, *Eleanor: The Years Alone,* 90.

526   *"Where was the guidance . . .":* Peter Collier with David Horowitz, *The Roosevelts: An American Saga* (New York: Simon & Schuster, 1994), 453.

526   *"figure of tragedy . . .":* Elliott Roosevelt and James Brough, *Mother R,* 258.

526   *John and Elliott fight;* *"My children would be . . .":* Lash, *A World of Love,* 387.

526   *Elliott and Hall:* Ibid., 553.

526 *ER's TV shows:* Maurine H. Beasley, *Eleanor Roosevelt and the Media* (Urbana, Ill.: University of Illinois Press, 1987), 172ff.

526 *postwar careers of the children:* Collier, *The Roosevelts,* 450–59.

526 *John and Anne:* Lash, *A World of Love,* 486.

527 *"rude":* Interview with Curtis Roosevelt, 16 January 1999, Williamstown, Mass.

527 *no more "reunions":* ER to Anna Roosevelt, 12 June 1961, in Lash, *A World of Love,* 537.

527 *ER and Lorena Hickok:* Cook, *Eleanor Roosevelt,* vol. 2, passim.

527 *"David, my dearest"; "I'm not stupid . . .":* ER to David Gurewitsch, 8 February 1956 and March 1956, in Lash, *A World of Love,* 439–40.

527 *"If you can find it . . .":* ER to David Gurewitsch, undated letter, in Lash, *A World of Love,* 461.

527 *"I need you both . . .":* ER to Edna Gurewitsch, 24 February 1958, in ibid., 481.

528 *National Negro Congress and NAACP petition the UN:* Lash, *Eleanor: The Years Alone,* 66–67; Container 4587, ER Papers, FDR Library.

528 *segregated beaches:* ER, "My Day," 20 March 1953.

528 *"know where I stand":* ER, quoted in Black, *Casting Her Own Shadow,* 100.

528 *"The United Nations Commission . . . family of nations":* ER, "My Day," 13 January 1947.

528 *Frank Holman's opposition:* New York Times, 14 September 1948, 18 November 1948, and 1 February 1949, quoted in Natalie Hevener Kaufman, *Human Rights Treaties and the Senate: A History of Opposition* (Chapel Hill, N.C.: University of North Carolina Press, 1990), 71.

528 *John Bricker:* Kaufman, *Human Rights Treaties and the Senate,* 71.

529 *"What is going on . . .":* ER, "My Day," 17 March 1947, 1 April 1947, 16 April 1947, 5 July 1947, 29 October 1947.

529 *"the French language":* ER, "My Day," 1 October 1948.

529 *"the Russians attack . . .":* ER to Trude Lash, 25 October 1948, in Lash, *A World of Love,* 287.

530 *"nondominant" groups:* Humphrey, *Human Rights and the UN,* 20.

530 *three most important rights:* ER, "The Promise of Human Rights, April 1948, in *What I Hope to Leave Behind,* Black, ed., 556.

530 *separate documents:* Howard Tolley Jr., *The UN Commission on Human Rights* (Boulder, Col.: Westview Press, 1987), 21.

531 *ER's heart not in debate; disappointed:* Humphrey, *Human Rights and the UN,* 86.

532 *"All of us feel . . .":* ER, "My Day," 20 December 1950.

532 *"no legal value":* Lash, *Eleanor: The Years Alone,* 79.

532 *military intervention:* New York Times, 21 September 1999, A1.

532 *Kofi Annan:* Quoted in New York Times, 21 September 1999, A1.

Fifteen: Facing the Future

534 *how could Ike top his role?:* James MacGregor Burns, *The Crosswinds of Freedom* (New York: Vintage Books, 1990), 247.

534 *Nixon against Douglas and ER:* Allida M. Black, *Casting Her Own Shadow: Eleanor Roosevelt and the Shaping of Postwar Liberalism* (New York: Columbia University Press, 1996), 163.

534 *"who would do anything to get elected":* ER, quoted in Black, *Casting Her Own Shadow,* 164.

534 *"very, very serious times . . .":* Elliott Roosevelt and James Brough, *Mother R: Eleanor Roosevelt's Untold Story* (New York: G. P. Putnam's Sons, 1977), 200.

534 *"I regard Mr. Nixon . . .":* Eleanor Roosevelt, *On My Own* (New York: Harper & Brothers, 1958), 167.

534 *"Will the delegates please . . .":* Joseph P. Lash, *Eleanor: The Years Alone* (New York: W. W. Norton & Co., 1972), 210.

534 *"I'm sure the Democratic party . . .":* ER to Lorena Hickok, 7 December 1951, in Rodger Streitmatter, ed., *Empty Without You: The Intimate Letters of Eleanor Roosevelt and Lorena Hickok* (New York: Free Press, 1998), 280.

535 *Ike considered unbeatable:* Elliott Roosevelt and James Brough, *Mother R,* 199.

535 *black delegates walk:* Burns, *The Crosswinds of Freedom,* 350.

535 *Ike refuses to debate:* Elliott Roosevelt and James Brough, *Mother R,* 199; ER, "My Day," 4 September 1952.

535 *"go to Korea"; Stevenson caught in the middle:* Burns, *The Crosswinds of Freedom,* 250.

535 *"far more acute":* John Kenneth Galbraith, *Name-Dropping: From F.D.R. On* (Boston: Houghton Mifflin Co., 1999), 51.

535 *Democrats lack galvanizing message:* Burns, *The Crosswinds of Freedom,* 287.

535 *"national hero"; "those":* Alden Whitman and The New York Times, *Portrait: Adlai E. Stevenson: Politician, Diplomat, Friend* (New York: Harper & Row, 1960), 191, 96, 71, 116.

535 *Eisenhower and human rights:* James MacGregor Burns and Stewart Burns, *A People's Charter* (New York: Vintage, 1993), 423–24.

535 *"The General has a thorough distrust...":* Lash, *A World of Love: Eleanor Roosevelt and Her Friends, 1943–1962* (Garden City, N.Y.: Doubleday & Co., 1984), 385.

536 *Dulles announces end of support for rights declaration:* Lash, *Eleanor: The Years Alone,* 222.

536 *"We have sold out...":* ER, "My Day," 9 April 1953.

536 *ER's last speech at UN:* Elliott Roosevelt and James Brough, *Mother R,* 207.

536 *1984 UN publication:* UN #E.84.1.6, mentioned in Blanche Wiesen Cook, "Eleanor Roosevelt and Human Rights: The Battle for Peace and Planetary Decency;" in *Women and American Foreign Policy: Lobbyists, Critics, and Insiders,* ed. Edward P. Crapol (Wilmington, Del.: SR Books, 1992), 117n.

536 *AAUN:* ER, "My Day," 5 January 1955; Lash, *Eleanor: The Years Alone,* 221.

536 *article by Rosenthal:* New York Times Magazine, 18 January 1953, 10.

537 *"I'll be walking on eggs...":* ER to Anna Roosevelt, 7 February 1952, in Lash, *A World of Love,* 377.

537 *"staggering":* ER to Anna Roosevelt, 25 February 1952, in Lash, *A World of Love,* 379.

537 *father Elliott's footsteps in India:* Geoffrey C. Ward, *Before the Trumpet: Young Franklin Roosevelt, 1882–1905* (New York: Harper & Row, 1985), 287–88, n. 8.

537 *"below anything...":* ER to Anna Roosevelt, 6 March 1952, in Lash, *A World of Love,* 380.

537 *Eleanor in India:* New York Times, 22 July 1953, 25.

537 *Eleanor visits Japan:* Lash, *Eleanor: The Years Alone,* 225; ER to John Golden, 12 June 1953, FDR Library.

538 *weekend with Tito:* New York Times, 18 July 1953, 2.

538 *"What happens in America...":* New York Times, 21 July 1953, 5.

538 *"Instead of having used...":* New York Times Magazine, 18 January 1953, 30.

538 *"police state"... "chicken-hearted":* ER, "My Day," 29 October 1947, in Allida M. Black, ed., *Courage in a Dangerous World: The Political Writings of Eleanor Roosevelt* (New York: Columbia University Press, 1999), 243–44.

539 *"afraid to be themselves... contamination by association":* ER, Address to Americans for Democratic Action, 1 April 1950, in Allida Black, ed., *Courage in a Dangerous World,* 260, 262. On ER and Americans for Democratic Action, see Black, *Casting Her Own Shadow,* 165 and 246, n. 105, 106.

539 *ER as honorary chairman of ADA:* Black, *Casting Her Own Shadow,* 169.

539 *"Actually some of the gentlemen... glad to do so":* ER, 8 July 1953, quoted in Lash, *Eleanor: The Years Alone,* 235.

540 *"very bad man to cross...":* New York Times, 18 January 1953, 4.

540 *"able to obtain..."; students shunning political involvement:* Black, *Casting Her Own Shadow,* 166.

540 *"There are moments...":* ER, "My Day," 3 May 1952.

540 *Bunche:* ER, 12 June 1953, quoted in Lash, *Eleanor: The Years Alone,* 236.

540 *"My devotion to my country... in our free country":* ER, "My Day," 29 August 1952, in Black, ed., *Courage in a Dangerous World,* 266.

540 *"greatest menace to freedom...":* Black, *Casting Her Own Shadow,* 167–68.

541 *"McCarthy's methods...":* New York Times, 21 July 1953.

541 *Eisenhower and book burning:* Black, *Casting Her Own Shadow,* 167.

541 *"serve as leaders"*: ER, "If You Ask Me," *McCall's*, June 1953, quoted in Black, *Casting Her Own Shadow*, 168.

541 *JFK evaded question:* Eleanor Roosevelt, *On My Own*, 164.

541 *Humphrey, Kennedy, et al.:* Black, *Casting Her Own Shadow*, 169–70.

541 *"stand up and be counted"*: Eleanor Roosevelt, *On My Own*, 164n.

541 *"Human blood is all alike . . ."*: ER, "My Day," 2 November 1950.

542 *"centered more around visions . . . of individuals"*: Alan Brinkley, *The End of Reform: New Deal Liberalism in Recession and War* (New York: Alfred A. Knopf, 1995), 267, 170.

542 *ER helps black Americans, compares racism and fascism; FBI file; "Negro" blood; "I do not believe I have interviewed . . ."*: Black, *Casting Her Own Shadow*, 92–93, 90, 87, 89.

542 *"redefinition of Negro's status . . ."*: Gunnar Myrdal, *An American Dilemma: The Negro Problem and Modern Democracy* (New York: Harper & Brothers, 1944), 797.

542 *ER on board of NAACP and on Legal Affairs committee; Walter White and ER:* Black, *Casting Her Own Shadow*, 99, 107, 108.

543 *ER on Tex and Jinx show:* ER, "My Day," 20 May 1954.

543 *integrated civil rights and housing; "Discrimination in housing must be wiped out . . ."*: Black, *Casting Her Own Shadow*, 104, 106, 107.

543 *intermarriage the real concern:* ER, "My Day," 20 May 1954.

543 *"Marriage is purely . . ."*: ER, "My Day," 5 May 1956.

543 *"a red herring"*: Eleanor Roosevelt, *Tomorrow Is Now* (New York: Harper & Row, 1963), excerpt in *What I Hope to Leave Behind: The Essential Essays of Eleanor Roosevelt*, ed. Allida M. Black (Brooklyn, N.Y.: Carlson Publishing, 1995), 189.

543 *treatment of Indian ambassador:* ER, "My Day," 2 September 1955.

544 *"A few days ago . . ."*: ER, "My Day," 4 May 1956.

544 *"I felt that I was not being treated right . . ."*: Rosa Parks, quoted in Howell Raines, *My Soul Is Rested: Movement Days in the Deep South Remembered* (New York: G. P. Putnam's Sons, 1977), 44; also quoted in Stewart Burns, *Social Movements of the 1960s* (Boston: Twayne Publishers, 1990), 4; Rosa Parks radio interview by Sidney Roger, Montgomery, Ala., 1956 (cassette recording from Pacifica Radio Archive, Los Angeles).

544 *"Gandhi's theory . . ."*: ER, "My Day," 12 March 1956.

544 *ER's meeting with Rosa Parks:* Letter from Myles Horton to Martin Luther King Jr., 24 May 1956, Martin Luther King Papers, Boston University, Box 14A.

544 *"I suppose we must realize . . . not continue to bear injustice"*: ER, "My Day," 14 May 1956.

545 *ER and Parks in Madison Square Garden:* Martin Luther King Jr. to A. Philip Randolph, 5 October 1956, Martin Luther King Papers, Boston University, Box 62.

545 *ER's wire to Martin Luther King Jr.:* Martin Luther King Papers, Boston University, Box 56-1017-001.

545 *King-ER correspondence:* Letters in Martin Luther King Papers, Boston University.

545 *"I think if I were a member . . . area of discrimination"*: ER to Richard Bolling, 20 January 1956, quoted in Lash, *Eleanor: The Years Alone*, 248.

546 *"Mrs. Truman is the last lady"*: *New York Times*, 13 October 1945, 17.

546 *Washington's theaters all segregated:* ER, "My Day," 15 October 1945.

546 *silent about Till lynching:* Black, *Casting Her Own Shadow*, 110–11; see also John B. Martin, *Adlai Stevenson and the World* (Garden City, N.Y.: Doubleday & Co., 1977), 258.

546 *"the South has been invited . . ."*: Stevenson, quoted in Martin, *Adlai Stevenson and the World*, 122.

546 *"My goodness . . ."*: Ibid., 131.

547 *Stevenson's speechwriters; "I cannot foretell . . ."*: Ibid., 248.

547 *"a stroke of the pen"*: Lash, *Eleanor: The Years Alone*, 249.

547 *make progress "gradually"*: Black, *Casting Her Own Shadow*, 110.

547 *"To Negro Americans . . ."*: Letter from Roy Wilkins to Adlai Stevenson, 9 February 1956, quoted in Lash, *Eleanor: The Years Alone*, 249.

547 *"stand on civil rights . . ."*: ER to Roy Wilkins, 15 February 1956, quoted in Lash, *Eleanor: The Years Alone*, 249.

547   *ER submits and withdraws resignation:* Lash, *Eleanor: The Years Alone,* 250–51.
547   *Lehman and Stevenson; moderate southerners; "Punitive action . . .", "almost grudging . . .":* Whitman, *Portrait: Adlai E. Stevenson,* 264–69.
548   *minimizing the differences; "unwitting":* Black, *Casting Her Own Shadow,* 111, 110.
548   *no "cleavage"; "Yet the papers . . .":* Lash, *Eleanor: The Years Alone,* 249–50.
548   *"inheritor" of FDR:* Elliott Roosevelt and James Brough, *Mother R,* 232.
548   *"I don't look forward to it":* ER to Adlai Stevenson, 13 June 1956, FDR Library.
548   *King and Wallace:* Black, *Casting Her Own Shadow,* 114.
548   *plank rejects enforcement pledge:* Martin, *Adlai Stevenson and the World,* 349; see also Black, *Casting Her Own Shadow,* 113.
548   *five southern members vote no anyway:* Black, *Casting Her Own Shadow,* 114.
549   *"Pretty good wording . . .":* ER to Trude W. and Joseph P. Lash, 22 July 1956, in Lash, *Eleanor: The Years Alone,* 252.
549   *"had to face more reporters . . .": The Autobiography of Eleanor Roosevelt* (New York: Harper & Brothers, 1960), 355.
549   *"we must have a candidate . . .":* Whitman, *Portrait: Adlai E. Stevenson,* 146.
549   *"I visited a number . . .":* ER, "My Day," 15 August 1956.
549   *ER's convention speech:* ER speech file, 13 August 1956, FDR Library.
550   *"I may have been very wrong . . .":* ER to David Gurewitsch, 17 August 1956, in Lash, *Eleanor: The Years Alone,* 258.
550   *letdown; "the old Stevenson"; "ordeal":* Whitman, *Portrait: Adlai E. Stevenson,* 352, 354.
550   *"If you can speak . . .":* ER to Adlai Stevenson, 10 October 1956, FDR Library.
551   *"I felt that we could take time . . .": Christian Register,* June 1948, in Black, *Courage in a Dangerous World,* 248.
551   *"We must use patience . . .":* ER, Stevenson Campaign Address, October 1956, in Black, *Courage in a Dangerous World,* 275.
551   *"They would like to see . . .":* ER to Adlai Stevenson, 13 June 1956, FDR Library.
552   *"How could we have had worse leadership . . . ?":* ER, "My Day," 2 November 1956.
552   *Eisenhower's new burden:* Burns, *The Crosswinds of Freedom,* 256.
552   *"one of the weakest . . .":* Elliott Roosevelt and James Brough, *Mother R,* 236.
552   *"No one could have done more . . .":* Whitman, *Portrait: Adlai E. Stevenson,* 392.
552   *ER as power broker:* Black, *Casting Her Own Shadow,* 115.
552   *"helped to convince a number . . .":* Joanna Schneider Zangrando and Robert L. Zangrando, "ER and Black Civil Rights," in Joan Hoff-Wilson and Marjorie Lightman, eds., *Without Precedent: The Life and Career of Eleanor Roosevelt* (Bloomington, Ind.: Indiana University Press, 1984), 103.
553   *"not my duty . . .":* ER, *Autobiography,* 412.
553   *"looked at everything . . .":* Eleanor Roosevelt, *This Is My Story,* 173.
553   *"none of us know . . .":* ER, "My Day," 5 December 1956.
553   *Christmas Eve column:* ER, "My Day," 24 December 1956.
553   *civil rights bill of 1957: Encyclopedia of American History,* eds. Richard B. Morris and Jeffrey B. Morris (New York: HarperCollins, 1996), 507.
553   *"The whole point . . .":* ER, "My Day," 6 August 1957, in Black, ed., *Courage in a Dangerous World,* 281.
554   *Section III:* Black, *Casting Her Own Shadow,* 124.
554   *first bill passed since Reconstruction: Encyclopedia of American History,* eds. Richard B. Morris and Jeffrey B. Morris 1996 edition, 507.
554   *not "satisfied with crumbs . . .":* ER, "My Day," 9 August 1957, in Black, ed., *Courage in a Dangerous World,* 280–81; see also Black, *Casting Her Own Shadow,* 124–25.
554   *"costly victory . . . white and colored people alike":* Ibid.
554   *"I understand . . .":* ER to Lyndon Johnson, 17 August 1957, in Black, ed. *Courage in a Dangerous World,* 281.
554   *attack on Eastland:* ER, "My Day," 20 April 1957.

554   *Scripps-Howard chain drops column:* Black, *Casting Her Own Shadow,* 117.
554   *others start printing it:* Elliott Roosevelt and James Brough, *Mother R,* 241.
554   *violence in North Carolina and Texas:* Black, *Casting Her Own Shadow,* 117–18.
554   *"it seems to me that I cannot afford . . .":* ER, *Autobiography,* 416.
554   *Faubus and Eisenhower:* Black, *Casting Her Own Shadow,* 118.
555   *"Human beings have a break point . . .":* ER, "My Day," 24 May 1957.
555   *ER's support of SCEF denounced by Eastland, too controversial for NAACP; black boys' case a cause célèbre; no politician helpful:* Black, *Casting Her Own Shadow,* 118–24.
555   Meet the Press *interview:* 20 October 1957, in Allida M. Black, ed., *What I Hope to Leave Behind: The Essential Essays of Eleanor Roosevelt* (Brooklyn, N.Y.: Carlson Publishing, 1995), 447–55.
556   *"The Negroes are going . . .":* ER to Lyndon Johnson, 29 January 1960, quoted in Black, *Casting Her Own Shadow,* 125.
556   *civil disobedience:* Joseph L. Rauh Jr. to ER, 18 May 1959, in ibid., 126.
556   *"I had the most wonderful dream . . .":* ER, quoted in ibid., 127.
556   *ER on apartheid:* ER, "My Day," 26 March 1960; see Black, *Casting Her Own Shadow,* 234n., 105.
556   *evening vote calls:* Black, *Casting Her Own Shadow,* 125.
556   *Civil Rights Act of 1960:* Encyclopedia of American History, ed. Morris and Morris, 509.
556   *Mike Wallace interview:* 23 November 1957, in *What I Hope to Leave Behind,* ed. Black, 457–64.
557   *Stevenson "remote":* Whitman, *Portrait: Adlai E. Stevenson,* 213.
557   *"better campaigner in 1952 . . .":* ER, "My Day," 12 July 1960.
557   *Johnson at FDR memorial:* Elliott Roosevelt and James Brough, *Mother R,* 253; Lash, *Eleanor: The Years Alone,* 279.
557   *Johnson, Symington, Humphrey:* Elliott Roosevelt and James Brough, *Mother R,* 252–56.
557   *"radically against" supporting JFK:* Galbraith, *Name-Dropping,* 52.
557   *Joe Kennedy and McCarthy:* Black, *Casting Her Own Shadow,* 172.
557   *a Catholic might be more loyal to pope:* Elliott Roosevelt and James Brough, *Mother R,* 160.
557   *Lash on ER's anti-Catholicism:* Lash, *Eleanor: The Years Alone,* 282.
557   *ER endorses JFK in 1952:* ER, "My Day," 27 September 1952.
558   *ER and JFK's 1956 hotel meeting:* Black, *Casting Her Own Shadow,* 176.
558   *"I do not see how . . .":* Elliott Roosevelt and James Brough, *Mother R,* 234.
558   *television show:* Lash, *Eleanor: The Years Alone,* 306, 304.
558   *ER and JFK on TV:* Galbraith, *Name-Dropping,* 52.
558   *ER doubts JFK's "independence":* Lash, *Eleanor: The Years Alone,* 280.
558   *"It is obvious to me . . .":* ER, "My Day," 30 June 1960.
558   *Stevenson advisers come out for JFK:* Black, *Casting Her Own Shadow,* 184; Lash, *Eleanor: The Years Alone,* 288.
558   *ER's wishful scenario:* ER, "My Day," 12 July 1960, in Black, ed., *Courage in a Dangerous World,* 295; Lash, *Eleanor: The Years Alone,* 288–89.
559   *"It would not only be . . .":* ER, "My Day," 7 July 1960.
559   *"serve country and party . . .":* Lash, *Eleanor: The Years Alone,* 290.
559   *Stevenson's indecisiveness:* Ibid., 295–97.
559   *ER on JFK's Negro support:* Ibid., 293.
559   *eleven state caucuses:* Ibid., 295.
559   *"I could have murdered him":* Quoted in Black, *Casting Her Own Shadow,* 185.
559   *"almost in tears":* David Lilienthal, quoted in Lash, *Eleanor: The Years Alone,* 295.
559   *ER tells JFK to speak to her through Franklin:* Elliott Roosevelt and James Brough, *Mother R,* 259; Lash, *Eleanor: The Years Alone,* 296.
559   *ER criticizes Democratic convention and bossism:* ER, *Autobiography,* 425ff; ER, "Are Political Conventions Obsolete?" unpublished article, in Black, ed., *Courage in a Dangerous World,* 471.
560   *Democratic fund-raiser and* Times *headline:* Black, *Casting Her Own Shadow,* 287.
560   *ER wants JFK to find position for Stevenson:* Elliott Roosevelt and James Brough, *Mother R,* 260.

560   *JFK goes to Hyde Park:* Lash, *Eleanor: The Years Alone,* 297.

560   *ER's advice to him:* Black, *Casting Her Own Shadow,* 189–91.

560   *ER finds JFK likable:* ER, "My Day," 17 August 1960, in Black, ed., *Courage in a Dangerous World,* 296.

560   *ER endorses JFK:* Ibid., 295.

560   *"Whether I will take any trips . . .":* Black, *Casting Her Own Shadow,* 191; Lash, *Eleanor: The Years Alone,* 298.

561   *"did not give either side . . .":* ER, "My Day," 12 October 1960.

561   *"bad language":* ER, "My Day," 12 October 1960.

561   *"all the youth and energy . . .":* ER, "My Day," 11 November 1960, in Black, ed., *Courage in a Dangerous World,* 297.

561   *ER refuses seat in presidential box:* Elliott Roosevelt and James Brough, *Mother R,* 264.

561   *ER sits in bleachers:* Black, *Casting Her Own Shadow,* 192; Lash, *Eleanor: The Years Alone,* 300.

561   *"cold & beautiful . . .":* ER to Lorena Hickok, 23 January 1961, in Rodger Streitmatter, ed., *Empty Without You: The Intimate Letters of Eleanor Roosevelt and Lorena Hickok,* 287.

561   *JFK can't "bear being in the same room":* Lash, *A World of Love,* 541.

562   *"The commission will try . . .":* ER, "My Day," 16 February 1962.

562   *JFK's press conference and voice; "I wish you could get someone . . .":* ER to JFK, 22 July 1961; JFK to ER, 28 July 1961, FDR Library; Lash, *Eleanor: The Years Alone,* 318.

562   *"give way to apprehension . . .":* ER, "My Day," 29 May 1962; Lash, *Eleanor: The Years Alone,* 320–21.

562   *ER and women appointees:* Lash, *Eleanor: The Years Alone,* 317.

562   *King asks ER to pressure JFK:* 15 February and 24 March 1961, in Black, *Casting Her Own Shadow,* 194.

562   *ER asks RFK to intercede for King:* Black, *Casting Her Own Shadow,* 193; Lash, *Eleanor: The Years Alone,* 320.

562   *ER lobbies RFK on public housing:* Black, *Casting Her Own Shadow,* 193.

562   *"When you cease . . .":* ER to Mr. Horne, 19 February 1960; in Lash, *Eleanor: The Years Alone,* 302.

563   *ER commutes to Brandeis:* Lash, *Eleanor: The Years Alone,* 303–4; Elliott Roosevelt and James Brough, *Mother R,* 249–50.

563   *article in Harper's:* "Where I Get My Energy?" *Harper's Magazine,* January 1959, 218; reprinted in Black, ed., *What I Hope to Leave Behind,* 43–47.

563   *"I think I have a good deal . . .":* Lash, interview with ER, 11 October 1961, in Lash, *Eleanor: The Years Alone,* 303.

563   *Wiltwyck boys, "colored" ladies, Bernstein et al. at Val-Kill; ordered to leave neighbor's land:* Lash, *Eleanor: The Years Alone,* 307, 311–12.

563   *"Everything was grist . . .":* ER, *Autobiography,* 410.

563   *margarine commercial:* ER, *Autobiography,* 417; Burns, *The Crosswinds of Freedom,* 433.

564   *ER's 1962 trips:* Lash, *Eleanor: The Years Alone,* 322.

564   *ER selfless:* Aubrey Immelman and Jennifer Jo Hagel, "A Comparison of the Personalities of Eleanor Roosevelt and Hillary Rodham Clinton," unpublished paper, International Society of Political Psychology, Montreal, 1998.

564   *ER chairs Committee of Inquiry:* Black, *Casting Her Own Shadow,* 128–29.

564   *"one of the most difficult experiences"; heartbreaking cases:* Eleanor Roosevelt, *Tomorrow Is Now,* excerpt in Black, ed., *What I Hope to Leave Behind,* 183–92.

564   *social revolution; "democratic living . . .":* Ibid., 184, 188–89.

565   *"Etiquette is not just . . .":* ER, "Modern Children and Old-Fashioned Manners," in Black, ed., *What I Hope to Leave Behind,* 337.

565   *"I can't work . . .":* Lash, *Eleanor: The Years Alone,* 324.

565   *trip made against doctor's advice:* Ibid., 325.

565   *Dirksen and Eastland "evil men":* ER, "My Day," 6 August 1962.

566   *ER goes to campaign rally:* Elliott Roosevelt and James Brough, *Mother R,* 271.

566 *ER helps Robert Morgenthau:* Lash, *Eleanor: The Years Alone,* 312.

566 *John helps Rockefeller:* Lash, *A World of Love,* 566.

566 *"old people running":* Lash, *Eleanor: The Years Alone,* 327; Lash, *A World of Love,* 557.

566 *fourteen for breakfast:* Lash, *A World of Love,* 556.

566 *"let her go":* Lash, *Eleanor: The Years Alone,* 326.

566 *"It'll never come together . . .":* Elliott Roosevelt and James Brough, *Mother R,* 273.

566 *pine boughs:* William Turner Levy and Cynthia Eagle Russett, *The Extraordinary Mrs. R: A Friend Remembers Eleanor Roosevelt* (New York: John Wiley & Sons, 1999), 245.

Epilogue: A Century of Reform

569 *TR "cold and priggish":* Edmund Morris, *The Rise of Theodore Roosevelt* (New York: Coward, McCann & Geoghegan, 1979), 77.

572 *"Dear Mr. Roosevelt . . .":* Eva S. Conners to FDR, 4 January 1935, in PPF 200B, Container 20, FDR Library.

572 *Lowi, Milkis, and Sandel:* For an able analysis of criticism by post–New Deal scholars, see Bruce Miroff, "The Anti–New Deal Turn in Political Science and James MacGregor Burns's FDR," paper delivered at the annual meeting of the American Political Science Association, Washington, D.C., 31 August 2000.

573 *"The revolution in our social thinking . . . a chance of fulfillment":* Eleanor Roosevelt, *Tomorrow Is Now,* excerpt in Allida M. Black, ed., *What I Hope to Leave Behind: The Essential Essays of Eleanor Roosevelt* (Brooklyn, N.Y.: Carlson Publishing, 1995), 192.

ACKNOWLEDGMENTS

Discussions some years ago with Eleanor Roosevelt and later with her daughter, Anna, about their White House years provided a starting point for this book. Recently we had long conversations with Anna's son Curtis Roosevelt—the "Buzzie" in the Roosevelt White House.

We wish to thank Deborah Burns (who at a young age met the former First Lady) for extensive research on the Roosevelts. Joan S. Burns brought her editorial and writing experience to bear on the manuscript. Milton Djuric made important contributions to our coverage of the Progressive era.

We appreciate the great helpfulness of the professional staff at the Franklin D. Roosevelt Library in Hyde Park, New York. We are also indebted to Alison O'Grady and Walter Komorowski of the Williams College Library, Donna Chenail and her colleagues in the Faculty Secretarial Office at Williams College, and our student Lisa Chadderdon. Our editor, Brendan Cahill, provided skillful assistance, and our friend and agent, Fifi Oscard, cheered us on. We have borrowed some deathless prose from earlier works by J. M. Burns based on research at the FDR Library.

We owe a special debt to John Gable, the Director of the Theodore Roosevelt Association, for introducing us to Sagamore Hill and for generously sharing with us his extensive knowledge of all three Roosevelts.

INDEX

Aaron, Daniel, 101
Abernathy, Ralph, 544
Acheson, Dean, 520, 538–39
Adams, Alva, 378
Adams, Brooks, 21, 127, 131
Adams, Charles F., Jr., 21, 35
Adams, Henry, 21, 39, 49, 70, 167–68
Addams, Jane, 117, 133
African-Americans, 9, 34, 195, 402, 552
  in the armed forces, 466, 468–69, 542
  ER and, 320, 381, 388, 390, 392–97, 463,
    464, 467, 502, 504, 575
  civil rights, 392, 541–56, 562, 564–65, 574
  FDR and, 143, 381, 392, 393–94, 411,
    463–65, 485, 551
  lynchings of, 392–94, 543, 546, 551, 555
  migration during World War II, 446, 466
  New Deal programs and, 261, 305, 385, 392
  progressive movement and, 66
  racial discrimination, *see* racial
    discrimination
  TR and, 38, 61–62, 105, 134–35
  Wilson and, 135
  see also names of individuals
Afro-American, 394–95
Agricultural Adjustment Act (AAA), 260,
  262, 266, 287, 301, 371
agriculture, *see* farmers
Albania, 415, 439
Aldrich, Nelson, 98, 126
Allenswood School, 88–89, 171

All the King's Men (Warren), 298–99
Alsop, Joseph, 114, 115
America First Committee, 437, 439
American Association for the United
  Nations, 536, 538
American Bar Association, 128, 528
American Business Man, 361
American Construction Council, 263
American Dilemma, An (Myrdal), 395
American Federation of Labor, 64, 215,
  241, 301
American Friends Service Committee, 390
American Historical Society, 85
American Indians, 62, 502
American Individualism (Hoover), 239
American Legion, 163
American Liberty League, *see* Liberty
  League
American Medical Association, 431
American Railway Union, 64, 73
Americans for Democratic Action, 539,
  548, 556, 560
American Tobacco Company, 71
American Youth Congress, 301–2, 312, 398,
  399
  FDR talks with, 421–23, 473
Anderson, Marian, 395–96, 566
Anderson, Sherwood, 215, 298
Anglo-American Committee of Inquiry
  on Jewish refugees, 515
Annan, Kofi, 532

Anti-Comintern Pact, 415
anti-Semitism, 107, 412–13, 432, 478, 517
    Father Coughlin and, 299–300, 323
    among isolationists, 348, 412
    Jewish refugees of World War II, *see*
        Jews, refugees of World War II
    Nazi Germany and, 45, 259, 362, 406–7,
        408, 412, 413, 414, 428, 454, 514
    patricians and, 18, 21, 98, 143, 151, 200,
        313, 411
    ER's class views, 143, 151, 200, 201,
        504, 512, 513
"Appalachian Report," 248
Army, U.S., 438
    Rough Riders, 49–50, 51, 79, 159
    Specialized Education Program, 466
    veteran "bonus army" and, 216–17
    women in, 465–66, 468, 541
Arthur, Chester A., 34, 63
Arthurdale, 271, 274–75, 276
As He Saw It (Roosevelt), 526
Associated Press, 265, 267, 273
Astor, John Jacob, 23
Astor, Mrs. John Jacob, 17
Astor, Vincent, 311, 363
Atlanta Constitution, 409
Atlantic Monthly, 26
atomic weapons, 502, 507–8, 552
    development of, 454–55
Australia, 413, 531
Austria, 407–8
Autobiography (Roosevelt), 1, 20, 25, 37, 68–
    69, 76

Babson, Roger, 220
Badlands of South Dakota, 27, 35
Baer, George F., 72, 73–74
Baker, George Pierce, 83
Baker, Newton D., 225–26, 235, 249
balanced budget, FDR's commitment to,
    229, 243, 257, 262, 264, 284, 290, 365,
    367
    end of, 297

balance-of-power theories of foreign
    policy, 77, 473
Balfour Declaration, 514
Bancroft, George, 2
Bankhead, William B., 373
banks and banking:
    Banking Act of 1935, 297
    Emergency Banking Relief Act, 256–57
    national banking holiday, 255, 256
    run on the, 251
Barkley, Alben W., 297, 377, 378, 479, 480
Barnes, William, Jr., 120, 146–47
Baruch, Bernard, 151, 249, 348, 411
Battle of Britain, 426
Battle of the Bulge, 487, 489
Beard, Charles A., 221, 348
beer and wine, legalization of, 257, 258, 262
Belafonte, Harry, 563
Belgium, 423
Bellamy, Edward, 64, 67
Belmont, August, Jr., 70
Bennett, Dr. E. H., 177
Benton, Thomas Hart, 39
Berle, Adolf A., Jr., 228, 243, 250, 251, 284,
    309, 418, 426
Berlin, post-war, 529
Bernstein, Irving, 280, 304, 462
Bernstein, Leonard, 563
Bethune, Mary McLeod, 394, 395, 504, 540
Beveridge, Sir William, 213
Bevin, Ernest, 516
Biddle, Francis, 312, 449, 452
Bilbo, Theodore, 393, 505
Bismarck, Otto von, 439
Black, Allida, 452, 541, 552, 557
Black, Frank, 50, 51
Black, Hugo L., 263, 362
Black, Van Lear, 176–77, 181
blacks, *see* African-Americans
Blaine, James G., 35, 50
Blin, Joseph, Jr., 266–67
Bloom, Sol, 505
Blum, John, 39
Boettinger, John, 526

Bohlen, Charles E., 491
Bohr, Niels, 454
Bok, Edward, 65
Bolling, Richard, 545
Bonaparte, Charles, 71
Bookbinder, Hyman, 560
Borah, William, 225, 281, 323, 347, 349, 382, 417
Boston Brahmins, 14, 17, 18, 21
Boston Watchman, 72
Boulder Dam, 281, 316
Bowers, Claude G., 224, 344, 351, 352
Bowles, Chester, 503, 521
Brady, Diamond Jim, 87
Brady, Governor of Alaska, 21
Brandeis, Louis, 134, 228, 251, 296
    FDR's "court reform" and, 338, 340–41, 345
Brandeis University, 563
Bretton Woods agreement, 492
Brichah, 515
Bricker, John, 384, 480, 528
Bridges, Henry, 279
Brinkley, Alan, 541–42
Britain, 246, 415, 531
    Canada and, 45
    Central America and, 77
    colonialism, 471, 488, 507
    Jewish refugees and, 514–15
    labor in, 215, 349
    Lend-Lease and, 435–36, 438–39
    Palestine and, 514–17
    Spanish Civil War and, 352, 353, 406, 471
    Suez Canal and, 552
    World War I and, 145, 146
    in World War II, 419, 423, 444, 458, 477
        Battle of Britain, 426
        Churchill's appeals for U.S. destroyers, 423, 424, 427
        events leading to, 407–10, 414–19
        see also Churchill, Winston
Brooklyn Daily Eagle, 24
Brooks, Williams, 272
Browder, Earl, 324
Brown, John, 124

Brown, Lathrop, 79, 82
Brownsville, Texas regiment, 105
Brown v. Board of Education of Topeka, Kansas, 543, 545, 546–47, 548, 553
Bruenn, Dr. Howard, 490
Bryan, Charles W., 189
Bryan, William Jennings, 45–46, 58–59, 63, 138, 146, 472
Bryant, William Cullen, 2
budget balancing, *see* balanced budget, FDR's commitment to
budget deficit, 369, 447
Bulgaria, 507
Bulkley, Robert, 377
Bullitt, William C., 282, 312, 418, 419
"Bull Moose Party," *see* National Progressive Party ("Bull Moose Party")
Bulloch, Irvine, 1
Bulloch, James, 1
Bulloch, Martha, *see* Roosevelt, Martha Bulloch
Bunche, Dr. Ralph, 395, 505, 540, 542
Burner, David, 209
Bush, Vannevar, 424, 466
business:
    New Deal programs and legislation, 263–65, 277–79, 289, 295–96
    1936 presidential election and, 321
    plutocrats, *see* plutocrats and plutocracy
    regulation of, 53, 62, 66, 69, 92, 94, 132, 133, 221
    taxation of, *see* taxation, of business
    TR and, 53–54, 57, 62, 103–4, 133–34
        collusion of politics and business, 33, 42, 52–53
        regulation of, 53, 62, 69, 71, 92, 94, 132, 133
        taxation of, 53
        trusts, *see* trusts, TR and
    trusts, *see* trusts
    during World War II, 444–47, 449, 461–62

Business Advisory Council, 321
Business Week, 308
Butler, Paul, 548
Byrnes, James F., 348, 505, 507, 510, 520

Camp, Lawrence, 380
campaign finance reform, TR and, 135
Campobello estate, 80, 111, 113, 138, 144,
    145, 155, 175, 176, 276, 526, 565
Canada, 45
Cannon, "Uncle Joe," 99
capitalism, 220, 222, 577
    laissez-faire, *see* laissez-faire
    economics
Cardozo, Justice Benjamin N., 254, 296
Carnegie, Andrew, 18, 69
Caro, Robert, 200
Carow, Edith, *see* Roosevelt, Edith (née
    Carow)
Carter, Boake, 348
Carter, Jimmy, 577
Carter, Ledyard & Milburn, 109
Casablanca conference, 457–61
Cassin, René, 522, 529
Catholics, 156, 195, 557
    FDR and, 143, 406, 411
    patricians and, 196–97, 557
    Spanish Civil War and, 351, 352, 406,
        407
Catt, Carrie Chapman, 173, 506
Celler, Emanuel, 566
Cermak, Anton J., 247
Chamberlain, Neville, 408–9, 410, 415,
    419, 423
Chandler, Albert B. "Happy," 377
Chaney, Mayris, 449
Chang, Dr. Pen-chun, 522
Chanler, Lewis, 115
Channing, Edward, 83
Chapman, Carrie, 320
Chase, Stuart, 228, 306, 348
checks and balances, *see* Constitution,
    U.S., checks and balances

Chiang Kai-shek, 441, 493
Chiang Kai-shek, Madame, 471
Chicago Evening Post, 149
Chicago Press, 30
Chicago Times, 409
Chicago Tribune, 130, 344, 348, 356, 454
Chicago Workers Committee, 215
child labor, 172, 291, 463
    laws, 54, 64, 125, 135, 136, 149, 186, 372
    NRA and, 277, 279, 296
Childs, Marquis, 556
China, 349, 487, 490, 493
    communists and civil war in, 493,
        522
    Japanese aggression in, 354–56, 364,
        441–42
    Open Door policy, 355
Choate, Joseph H., 29, 32
Churchill, Mrs. Winston, 492, 509
Churchill, Winston S., 423–24, 440, 442,
    478, 503, 507, 509
    appeasement at Munich and, 409–10
    atomic bomb development and, 455
    Casablanca conference, 457–61
    ER and, 471
    Lend-Lease program and, 435–36, 438–
        39
    pleas for U.S. destroyers, 423–24,
        427
    Teheran conference, 474
    United Nations and, 470, 506
    Yalta conference, 487–89
Cigarmakers' Union, 31
Civil Aeronautics Authority, 375
Civilian Conservation Corps (CCC),
    260–61, 270, 271, 301–2, 321, 375, 397,
    438, 462
civil rights, 520, 531, 535, 541–56, 564–65
    ER and, 392, 541–46, 548–53, 555–56,
        562, 564–65, 574
    Stevenson and, 546–47, 548, 575
    see also human rights
Civil Rights Act of 1957, 553–54
Civil Rights Act of 1960, 556, 557

Civil Service Commission, U.S., 38–40, 372
Civil War, 1, 38, 124
Civil Works Administration, 266
Clark, Beauchamp "Champ," 138
Clark, Bennett, 384
class warfare, 37, 46, 54, 66, 129, 230, 319, 334–35, 366, 571
Clemenceau, Georges, 152, 154
Cleveland, Grover, 32, 35, 38, 39, 63, 69, 70, 73, 74, 75, 170
Clifford, Clark, 518
Coast Guard, U.S., 469
Cohen, Benjamin, 251, 340, 364, 411, 415
Cohen, Lizabeth, 334–35
Cohn, Roy, 541
Cold War, 506, 507, 519, 520, 528, 529
Collier's, 103
colonialism, 471, 488, 507, 537
Columbia Law School:
  FDR at, 80, 108–9
  TR at, 14–15, 24, 28
Colvin, Dr. D. Leigh, 324
Commission for the Relief of Belgium, 211–12
Commission on Fair Employment Practices, 464–65
Commission on the Status of Women, 562
Committee of Inquiry into the Freedom Struggle in the South, 564
Common Sense, 307
Communism and communists, 577
  American Youth League and, 422
  during the Depression, 214, 215, 301–2, 306, 399
  McCarthyism and post-war anticommunism, 519, 528–29, 535, 538–41, 558
  New Deal criticized as communistic, 319, 327, 431
  red-baiting, 182, 319, 481, 534
Communist Control Act of 1954, 541
Communist party, 214, 215, 220, 324, 334, 542

Compton, Karl, 424
Conant, James B., 424, 455
Congress, U.S., 70, 157, 159, 216, 245, 449, 515
  civil rights legislation and, 553–54
  Constitutional checks and balances and, 75, 108, 346, 375
  elections:
    1934, 286
    1936, 335
    1938, 375–81, 383–84, 386, 430, 575
    1946, 519
    1950, 539
    1956, 552
  FDR's presidency and, 243, 275, 280, 286–87, 289, 362, 369–70, 372–74, 404, 414, 447, 448, 478, 479, 483, 485, 490, 571
  "court reform," 338–42, 378, 387
  European refugees and, 413
  first hundred days, 255, 258–65
  Four Freedoms speech to, 436–37
  isolationists, 260, 281, 289, 315, 347–49, 350, 357, 406, 415–16, 420, 421, 427, 430, 438
  Lend-Lease program and, 437–38
  repeal of arms embargo, 420
  Second Hundred Days, 296–98
  stalemate, 430–31, 432
  U.S. involvement in World War II and, 443
  FDR's Senate race, 144–45
  House Un-American Activities Committee, 214, 312, 370, 383, 399, 502, 529, 538, 539
  League of Nations, Senate battle for, 160
  Southern Democrats, *see* Southern Democrats
  TR and, 99, 103–4, 105, 108
Congressional Medal of Honor, 50, 57
Connally, Tom, 378, 505
Conners, Eva S., 572
Connor, Eugene "Bull," 465

conservation movement, 107–8
  TR and, 12, 107–8, 123–24, 125, 132
Constitution, U.S., 99–100
  amending the, 343
  checks and balances in, 75, 108, 167, 346,
    375, 417
  commerce clause, 295, 396
  Eighteenth Amendment, repeal of, 233,
    238
  Nineteenth Amendment, 183
  presidential foreign policy powers
    and, 347
  Sixteenth Amendment, 96
Cook, Blanche Wiesen, 156, 172, 414
Cook, Nancy, 183, 192, 193, 201, 236
Cooke, Morris L., 400
Coolidge, Calvin, 170, 173, 175, 189, 216,
  247, 287
Corcoran, Tom, 251, 340, 372, 374
Cornell University, 174
Corr, Maureen, 556
Cosmopolitan, 65
Costigan, Edward, 393
Costigan-Wagner Anti-Lynching Bill,
  393–94, 551
Coughlin, Father Charles, 293, 294, 295,
  299–300, 301, 314, 317, 322–23, 326, 327,
  334, 335, 348, 373, 412, 571
Council of National Defense, 424
Covenant on Civil and Political Rights,
  536
Cox, James M., 161, 225, 240, 251
Coxey, Jacob, 63
Crane, Stephen, 65
Creel, George, 388
Crimson, The, 82, 84, 85
Croly, Herbert, 13, 95, 125, 128, 277
Crucible, The, 538
Cuba, 27, 336
  Spain and, 45, 47–50, 77
Cudahy, John, 354
Cummings, Homer, 279, 338, 363
Curie, Marie, 454

Curtis, George William, 22
Czechoslovakia, 408, 409, 414, 415, 429,
  511

Daladier, Edouard, 409
Daley, Richard, 559
Daniels, Josephus, 137, 143, 144, 145–46,
  147, 154, 157, 167, 175, 176, 251, 271, 384
Danilevsky, Nadia, 273
Daughters of the American Revolution,
  320, 396, 546
Davidson, John Wells, 134
Davis, Alice, 273
Davis, Elmer, 467
Davis, John W., 189, 249
Davis, Kenneth, 83
Davis, Norman, 249, 251
Davis, William H., 461
Dawes, Charles, 189
Dawidowicz, Lucy, 416
Debs, Eugene, 154
  as socialist candidate, 78, 133, 139, 162
  as union leader, 64, 69, 73
de Gaulle, Charles, 423, 459
de Kooning, Willem, 304
Delano, Frederic A., 178, 248
Delano, Laura, 494
Delano, Sara, *see* Roosevelt, Sara (née
  Delano)
Delano family, 14, 80
de los Rios, Señora, 407
Democratic National Committee, 220,
  249, 322
Democratic National Convention:
  1912, 137–38
  1920, 161
  1924, 186, 187, 188–89
  1928, 195
  1932, 232–33, 234–38
  1936, 324–26
  1940, 426
  1944, 480

1952, 534
1956, 548–50, 552
1960, 558–60 •
Democratic party:
in cities, *see individual cities*
FDR's desire to change, by uniting
liberals of both parties, 430, 486,
551, 556, 571
lack of solutions for Depression
problems, 211, 220–21
Southern Democrats, *see* Southern
Democrats
see also presidential elections;
individual Democrats
Democratic State Committee of New
York, 183
Denmark, 423
Denver Republican, 125–26
Department of Commerce and Labor,
569
creation of, 100
Depression, Great, 203, 212–17, 229, 241,
246, 576–77
Hoover presidency and, 209–11, 212,
216–17, 219–21, 251–52
New Deal programs to alleviate, *see*
New Deal; *specific programs*
De Priest, Oscar, 261
Dern, George, 312
Dewey, George, 48
Dewey, John, 240, 306, 307
Dewey, Thomas E., 384, 480–81, 520
Diary of a Young Girl, The (Frank), 513
Dickerman, Marion, 183, 192, 193, 201, 235
Dies, Martin, 370
direct election of senators, 132, 136
direct primary, 117, 136, 137
Dirksen, Everett, 565
Displaced Persons (DPs), 511–16
Displaced Persons Act of 1948, 515
Dodd, William E., 354, 411–12
Dominican Republic, 76
Dos Passos, John, 240

Douglas, Helen Gahagan, 521, 534
Douglas, Lewis, 257, 264, 276, 284, 290, 298
Douglas, Paul, 228, 306, 521
Douglas, Justice William O., 431, 480
Downey, Sheridan, 378, 383
Draper, Dr. George, 179
Dred Scott decision, 127
Drexel Institute, 167
DuBois, W. E. B., 306, 542
Dulles, John Foster, 505, 511, 512, 536, 552
Dunn, Admiral Herbert O., 157
Dunne, Finley Peter, 65
Du Pont, 71, 197
du Pont, Ethel, 312, 364, 526
du Pont family, 312, 571

Earhart, Amelia, 270
Earle, George, 384
Early, Stephen, 164, 311, 338, 350, 364, 393–
94, 395, 463
Eastland, James, 554, 555, 565
Eaton, Charles, 505
Eccles, Marriner, 367, 369
Economy Act, 258
Eden, Anthony, 487
Edison, Thomas, 148
Education of Henry Adams, The, 168
Egypt, 439, 552
Einstein, Albert, 454, 455
Eisenhower, Dwight D., 217, 502, 521, 566
as commander of U.S. forces in the
European Theater, 471, 476
presidency, 535–36, 541, 552, 554, 555, 575
as presidential candidate, 534, 535, 547,
548, 552
elections:
Congressional, *see* Congress, U.S.,
elections
presidential, *see* presidential elections
Eliot, Charles W., 9, 13, 24, 45, 67, 83, 576
Elizabeth II, Queen of England, 471, 509
Elkins Act, 567

Emergency Banking Relief Act, 256–57
Emergency Maternal and Infant Care
    program, 463
Emerson, Faye, 489, 526
Employers' Liability Act of 1906, 99, 103–4
Emporia Gazette, 409
England, *see* Britain
Enterprise, 281
environmental movement, 108
    see also conservation movement
Erie Canal, 50
Espionage Act of 1917, 154
Ethiopia, 315, 350–51, 356
Ethridge, Mark, 464–65
Everybody's, 65
executive reorganization bill of 1938,
    372–74

Fair Employment Practices Commission,
    485
Fala (dog), 438, 481, 482, 502
Farley, James, 226, 234, 240, 242, 249, 277,
    289, 299, 324, 335, 346, 363, 372, 381, 566
Farm Bureau Federation, 262
Farmer-Labor Political Federation, 306
farmers, 163, 182, 241, 289, 314, 391, 461
    programs to aid:
        FDR and, 140, 199, 233, 238, 242, 262,
            280, 287, 301, 302, 321
        TR and, 132
    sharecroppers and tenant farmers, 287,
        305, 394, 541
Farm Moratorium Act, 341
fascism, 220, 494, 542, 577
    in Italy, *see* Mussolini, Benito, and
        fascist Italy
    Nazi Germany, *see* Nazi Germany
    in Spain, *see* Spain, civil war in
Faubus, Orval, 554
Fay, Elton, 236
Fayerweather, Margaret, 494
FDR: A Career in Progressive Democracy
    (Lindley), 232

Fechner, Robert, 261
Federal Bureau of Investigation (FBI),
    450–51, 542, 554
federalism, TR and, 124
Federal Reserve Act of 1913, 97
Federal Reserve Board, 280, 297
Federal Reserve System, 367
Fermi, Enrico, 454, 455
Fidelity and Deposit, 170, 176, 181
Finland, 421, 422, 423
Fish, Hamilton (father), 116, 117
Fish, Hamilton (son), 214, 347, 427
Fitzgerald, F. Scott, 221
Flanagan, Hallie, 304
Flynn, John T., 429
Foch, Marshal Ferdinand, 154–55
Food, Drugs and Cosmetic Act of 1938, 370
Ford, Henry, 220, 247, 278, 400
Forest Service, U.S., 107
Fortune, 428, 429
Four Freedoms, 471, 472, 524, 572
    FDR's speech, 436–37
Fox, Dixon Ryan, 22
France, 154, 215, 246, 349
    colonialism and, 488
    Spanish Civil War and, 352, 353, 406
    Suez Canal and, 552
    Vichy government, 423
    World War II and, 419, 423, 429, 487
        Allied cross-channel invasion, 458,
            460, 474–75, 476–77, 481
        events leading to, 353–54, 407–10,
            415
        the resistance, 423, 459
Franco, General Francisco, 353, 356, 406–
    7, 407, 415
Frank, Anne, 513
Frankfurter, Felix, 128, 151, 228, 250, 251,
    284, 361, 364, 374, 401, 411, 427, 448
    FDR's "court reform" and, 338, 339, 340
    as Supreme Court justice, 431–32
Fraser, Peter, 511
Freedom Riders, 564
Freidel, Frank, 317, 474

French Indochina, 441, 488
Frick, Henry Clay, 98
Fulbright, J. William, 470
Furman, Bess, 267, 269

Gable, John, 134
Galbraith, John Kenneth, 535, 557, 558
Gallup polls, 314–15, 340
Gannett, Frank, 373
Garfield, James, 34
Garner, James Nance, 225, 234–35, 265, 338, 340, 378, 417, 425, 438
Gaulle, Charles de, *see* de Gaulle, Charles
Gellhorn, Martha, 406–7
General Electric, 197, 198, 240
General Federation of Women's Clubs, 462
George, Henry, 36–38, 64
George, Walter F., 379, 380, 381
George V, King of England, 154
George VI, King of England, 269
Georgia:
    racial discrimination in, 528
    Warm Springs, 190–92, 363, 368, 491, 494–95, 500
Gerard, James W., 144–45
Germany, 45, 76, 215
    under Hitler, *see* Nazi Germany
    post-war refugees camps, 512–13
    in World War I, 145, 146, 149–50
GI Bill of Rights, 492
Gifford, Walter F., 211
Giraud, General Henri, 459
Glass, Carter, 297, 381, 386
Godkin, E. L., 24, 67
Goldberg, Richard Thayer, 180
Gompers, Samuel, 64, 99
Good Neighbor Policy, 336
Goodwin, Doris Kearns, 414
Göring, Hermann, 349
Gould, Jay, 31
Gould, Lewis, 66, 131
Gould family, 18

government, role of, 13
    FDR's vision of, 484
    laissez-faire capitalists and, 67
    TR and, 76, 125, 129
Gracie, Annie Bulloch, 396
Grant, Ulysses S., 34
Greece, 439
Greeley, Horace, 34
Gridiron Club Dinner, 269, 492–93
Gromyko, Andrei, 516
Groton School, 163, 171, 184, 276
    FDR at, 56, 81–82, 569, 570
    TR's address to, 55–56, 85, 569
Guam, 49
Guffey, Joseph F., 328
Gurewitsch, David, 504, 525, 527, 550, 562–63, 566
Gurewitsch, Edna, 527

Hagedorn, Hermann, 135, 141
Hague Conference of 1907, 106
Hahn, Otto, 454
Haiti, 336
Hall, Anna, *see* Roosevelt, Anna (née Hall) (ER's mother)
Hall, Edith ("Pussie"), 87
Hall, Edward, 87
Hall, Mary (née Ludlow), 150, 171
    raising of ER, 86, 87, 88, 164
Hall, Maude, 87
Hall, Valentine, 87
Hamby, Alonzo, 506–7
Hamilton, Alexander, 135, 224
Hamilton, John D. M., 382
Hanna, Mark, 46, 52, 58, 59, 61, 69, 74, 98
Harbaugh, William, 95, 97, 102, 128, 147
Harding, Warren G., 161, 162, 170, 175
Harper's, 563
Harper's Weekly, 31, 52, 63–64
Harriman, Averill, 312, 546, 549
Harriman family, 18
Harrison, Benjamin, 38, 39–40, 63
Harrison, George, 322

Harrison, Pat, 377, 385
Harvard University, 313, 326
    FDR at, 80, 82–85, 113, 570
    Natural History Society, 12
    Porcellian Club, 9–10, 12, 62, 82, 91
    TR at, 8–10, 11–13
Hassan II, King of Morocco, 460
Hay, John, 46, 61, 106, 107
Hayes, Rutherford B., 34, 73
Haymarket Massacre, 73
health care program, national, 172, 287,
    431, 492, 502
Hearst, William Randolph, 48, 160, 225,
    234, 235, 243, 327, 344, 348
    newspapers, 313, 348
Helm, Edith B., 267, 450
Hemingway, Ernest, 407
Henderson, Leon, 407
Hepburn Act, 92, 569
Herring, Pendleton, 305
Hess, Jake, 27, 28
Hewitt, Abram S., 36, 37
Hickok, Lorena, 236, 265, 269, 273, 312, 399,
    414, 479, 504, 527, 534, 561
Higgins, Andrew, 475
Higginson, Henry Lee, 18
Hillman, Sidney, 463
Hindenburg, Paul von, 245
Hiroshima, 454, 537
Hiss, Alger, 505, 539
History of New York (Irving), 15
Hitler, Adolf, 245, 259, 315, 349, 353–54,
    421, 433, 439, 441
    declares war on the U.S., 443–44
    events leading to World War II, 407–
        10, 414–19
    FDR's 1939 message to, 418
    as military leader, 475–76
    Nuremberg speech, 411
    Spanish Civil War and, 353
    see also Nazi Germany
Hobart, Garret, 58
Hofstadter, Richard, 23, 100–101, 103, 141,
    291, 569, 570

Holman, Frank, 528
Holmes, Oliver Wendell, Jr., 100, 288, 431,
    576
Holmes, Reverend, John Haynes, 227
home mortgage legislation, 258
Home Owners Loan Corporation, 321
homosexuals in the armed forces, 469
Hook, Sidney, 240
Hoover, Herbert, 194, 195, 199, 230, 252,
    277, 338, 348, 481–82
    1932 presidential election and, 239, 243
    presidency of, 209–10, 212, 216–17, 219–
        21, 245–47, 251–52
    during World War I, 211–12
Hoover, J. Edgar, 250, 450–51, 535, 542
Hopkins, Harry, 266, 273, 276, 287, 290, 312,
    315, 316, 364, 369, 372, 391, 397, 411, 426,
    435–36, 442, 487, 493
    at Casablanca conference, 457, 458
    as chief of staff, 431
    death of, 501
    as secretary of commerce, 431
    White House quarters, 267, 424
    WPA and, 302, 303, 304, 367
Hopkins, Robert, 458
House, Colonel Edward, 241, 251, 276, 282,
    327
House of Morgan, 97, 147
housing, integration of, 543, 562
Houston, 363, 377, 378
Houston, Sam, 320
Howard, Roy, 307–8
Howe, Louis, 177, 184, 186, 202, 223, 233,
    240, 267
    death of, 364, 493
    ER and, 164–65, 171, 183, 185, 226, 235,
        268, 269, 270, 271, 364, 501, 504
    FDR's polio and, 178, 179, 193
    FDR's political career and, 138, 143, 156,
        180, 183, 185, 193, 194, 227
    New York State senate seat, 138, 140
    1932 presidential election, 233, 234,
        236, 237
    U.S. Senate race, 144

FDR's presidency and, 254, 270, 289, 321
health problems, 274, 315
subsistence homesteads and, 274
How the Other Half Lives (Riis), 42, 103
Hughes, Charles Evans, 116, 117, 148, 149, 160, 197, 225, 337, 340, 341, 345
Hull, Cordell, 186, 249, 259, 279, 336, 350, 354, 356, 357, 363, 425, 441, 459, 470, 474, 480, 492
human rights, 472, 573, 574, 575, 577
Universal Declaration of Human Rights, 521–25, 527, 536, 574, 575
see also civil rights
Humphrey, Hubert, 521, 541, 557
Humphrey, John, 522, 523, 524, 529
Hungary, 415, 552
Hunting Big Game in the Eighties (Roosevelt), 87
Hyde Park, 79, 108, 113, 114
FDR's New York State senate seat representing, 114, 115–18

Ibn Saud of Saudi Arabia, 514
Ickes, Harold L., 250, 264, 272, 276, 289, 315, 316, 321, 326, 352, 363, 417, 440, 453, 492, 502
African-Americans and, 396, 397
executive reorganization bill and, 372, 373–74
PWA and, 280–81, 302, 367
Spanish Civil War and, 406, 407
If Christ Came to Chicago (Stead), 65
immigrants and immigration, 3, 18, 24, 41, 80, 98–99, 114, 139, 241, 348
disenfranchisement of, 23–24
European refugees of World War II, 514–15
ER and, 413–14, 415
FDR and, 408, 411–13, 415–16, 421
quotas, 412–13, 414, 416
progressive movement and, 66

income tax, 59, 303
corporate, 297, 303
Sixteenth Amendment and, 96
state, 213
TR and, 95, 96, 125
India, 537
India and the Awakening East (Roosevelt), 537
individualism, 13, 40, 95, 102, 221, 232, 263, 291, 311
materialism and, 70
Industrial Discipline, The (Tugwell), 263
Industrial Relations Board, 184
inflation, 447, 448, 479
Influence of Sea Power Upon History, The (Mahan), 46
inheritance tax, 59, 297
passage of, 96
TR and, 54, 95, 96, 125
Inland Waterways Commission, 107
integration, *see* civil rights
Inter-American Conference for the Maintenance of Peace, 335–36
"interest-group democracy," 305, 320–21
Intergovernmental Committee on Refugees, 413
International Bank for Reconstruction and Development, 492
internationalism, 225–26, 347, 349
International Labor Organization, 349
International Ladies' Garment Workers Unions, 182
International Monetary Fund, 492
International Workers of the World (IWW), 163
Interstate Commerce Act of 1887, 64, 92, 569
Interstate Commerce Commission, 64, 104, 134
interventionism, 348, 429, 440
FDR's interventionist nonintervention, 356–59, 362, 407–11, 415–16, 418–19

Irving, Washington, 15
isolationism, 66, 147, 225
    after outbreak of World War II, 427,
        429
    prior to World War II, 260, 281, 289,
        315, 347–49, 350, 355, 356, 398, 406,
        410, 412, 417
    FDR's interventionist
        nonintervention, 356–59, 362,
        407–11, 415–16, 418–19
    FDR's 1936 campaign and, 315, 351–
        52, 353
Israel, 537
    recognition of, 518–19
    Suez Canal and, 552
    see also Palestine
Italy:
    anti-Semitism in, 416
    under Mussolini, *see* Mussolini, Benito,
        and fascist Italy
Ivens, Joris, 407
Iwo Jima, 493

Jackson, Robert, 451
James, Henry, 45
James, William, 12, 83
Japan, 347
    Axis power pact, 362, 414, 415
    China and, 354–56, 364, 441–42
    peace treaty with Russia, 106–7,
        355
    seizure of South Manchuria, 245–46,
        349, 355
    women's movement in, 537
    in World War II, 441–42, 487, 488, 490,
        493
    Pearl Harbor, 442–43, 481
Japanese-Americans, 503
    internment of, 451–53
Jeansonne, Glen, 320
Jefferson, Thomas, 46, 135–36, 224, 230,
    231, 320, 349, 472, 485
Jefferson and Hamilton (Bowers), 224

Jews, 9, 62, 504
    anti-Semitism, *see* anti-Semitism
    homeland for, *see* Palestine
    1936 presidential election and, 335
    refugees of World War II, 511–16
        ER and, 413–14, 415, 511–14, 516–17
        FDR and, 408, 411–13, 415–16, 421
    TR and, 44, 99, 107, 413
    see also names of individuals
Joffre, Marshal Joseph, 152, 154
Johnson, Hiram, 127, 132, 265, 347, 349, 382
Johnson, General Hugh, 276–78, 279, 280,
    281, 321
Johnson, Lady Bird, 557
Johnson, Lyndon B., 378, 554, 556, 557,
    566, 572, 577
Johnson, Mordecai, 392
Jones, Jesse, 494
Jordan, 537
Josephson, Matthew, 240
judiciary:
    FDR's battle for "court reform," 128–
        29, 336–47, 354, 362, 378, 387, 577
    Supreme Court, *see* Supreme Court, U.S.
    TR and, 32, 99–100, 124, 125, 139, 431
    plebiscites on judicial decisions, 32,
        127–28, 343, 346
Jungle, The (Sinclair), 65, 92–93, 114, 294
Justice Department, U.S., 503, 542, 553

Kaiser, Henry, 480
Kansas City Star, 153, 158
Keen, Dr. William, 177, 178
Kefauver, Estes, 546
Kelley, Florence, 117
Kellogg-Briand Pact, 409
Kennedy, Jacqueline, 561, 562, 566
Kennedy, John F., 2, 76, 541, 557–62, 564,
    566, 572, 575, 577
Kennedy, Joseph P., 235, 241, 427–28, 557,
    561, 575
    as ambassador, 363, 418–19
    as SEC chairman, 282

Kennedy, Robert, 541, 562, 566
Kent, Samuel N., 157
Key, V. O., 387
Keynes, John Maynard, 283–84, 368
Keynesian economics, 229, 283–84, 368
King, Mackenzie, 410
King, Dr. Martin Luther, Jr., 544, 545, 548, 553, 562, 565
Kissinger, Henry, 77
Kittredge, George Lyman, 83
Knickerbocker Club, 87, 113
"Knickerbocker" families, 15–16, 17, 18, 21, 26
Knickerbocker Trust Company, 97
Knox, Frank, 324, 420, 425, 442, 466, 476
Knox, Philander, 70, 71
Korea, 355
Korean War, 535
Koretsky, Vladimir, 523
Kreisler, Fritz, 154
Kristallnacht, 413, 428
Krock, Arthur, 502
Ku Klux Klan, 182, 188, 362, 465, 543

labor and unions, 63–64, 135, 139, 215, 241
  in Britain, 215
  child labor, *see* child labor
  in 1920s, 182
  1936 presidential election and, 321
  New Deal and, 263–64, 278–79, 296, 301, 314, 372
    Section 7(a), 264, 278, 296, 301
  progressive movement and, 66, 132
  social legislation benefiting, 31–32, 54, 64, 94, 100, 372, 374
  strikes, *see* strikes
  TR and, 31–32, 33, 53–54, 62, 69, 94, 99, 103, 124, 125, 132, 158, 320
    coal strike of 1902, 71–76
  during World War II, 461–62
Labor Party, 36, 38
Ladies' Home Journal, 65
La Follette, Philip, 382, 383, 384, 429

La Follette, Robert, 63, 66, 126, 127, 130, 133, 147, 382
La Follette, Robert, Jr., 240, 258, 264, 295
LaGuardia, Fiorello, 383, 449, 464
Lahey, Dr. Frank, 490
laissez-faire economics, 13, 40, 65, 67, 76, 134, 221, 258, 263, 291
Landon, Alf M., 323–24, 327, 328, 334, 381, 382
Landon, Mrs. Alf M., 328
Lanham Act, 463
Lape, Esther, 184, 185, 449, 506
Larooco, 190
Lash, Joseph, 156, 392, 398, 453, 471, 480, 500, 504, 510, 514, 517, 520, 525, 549
Lash, Trude, 504, 525, 549, 566
Lasker, Mary, 560
Latin America, 105, 347
  FDR trip to, 335–36
  Monroe Doctrine, 76–77
Lawrence, John L., 190
Lawson, Thomas W., 65
Lazarus, Rabbi, 322
LCVP (Landing Craft, Vehicle and Personnel), 475
League for Independent Political Action, 306–7
League of Nations, 162, 172, 186, 350, 353, 355, 357, 470, 514
  FDR and, 161, 225–27, 289, 290, 487
  Japan and, 246, 247
  Spanish Civil War and, 407
  TR and, 153, 158
  Wilson and, 159–60, 240
League of Women Voters of New York State, 172, 183
Leahy, William, 487
Lebanon, 537
Lee, Alice, *see* Roosevelt, Alice (née Lee)
Lee, Arthur Hamilton, 129, 147
Lee, Robert E., 320
Lee family, 14, 35
LeHand, Marguerite "Missy," 170–71, 176, 184, 190, 265, 315, 324, 364, 374, 493, 501

Lehman, Herbert, 324, 374, 383, 384, 480, 547, 566

Lemke, William, 322, 334, 335, 341

Lend-Lease program, 435–36, 437–39, 460

Leopold, King of Belgium, 423

lesbians in the armed forces, 469

Leuchtenburg, William, 290, 305, 334, 403

Lewis, David, 380

Lewis, John L., 278–79, 303, 335, 377, 383, 425, 462

Liberty League, 290, 291, 293, 312, 318–19, 571

Lilienthal, David, 385, 400–401, 402–3

Lincoln, Abraham, 1–3, 34, 102, 129, 131, 170, 189, 231, 316, 320, 374, 376, 473, 576

Lindbergh, Anne Morrow, 438

Lindbergh, Charles A., 348, 412, 414, 439

Lindley, Ernest K., 232, 359

Lipchitz, Jacques, 304

Lippmann, Walter, 189, 222–23, 245, 284, 292, 305, 314, 452, 502, 576

Livingston, Mrs. John Henry, 563

Lloyd, Henry Demarest, 64, 68

Lodge, Henry Cabot, 26, 35, 38–39, 40, 44, 46, 50, 58, 61, 68, 100, 123, 125, 128, 146, 147, 149, 152, 167

　　League of Nations and, 160, 240

Lodge, Henry Cabot, Jr., 557

Loeb family, 18

London Economic Conference of 1933, 259, 349

London *Morning Post,* 106

Long, Breckinridge, 380, 416

Long, Huey P., 234, 240–41, 293–94, 295, 298–99, 300, 301, 303, 311, 314, 571, 577

　　assassination of, 314, 319

Long, John D., 46, 48, 58, 61

Longworth, Alice (née Roosevelt) (TR's daughter), 33, 57, 88, 155

　　wedding of, 91

Longworth, Nicholas, 91

Look, 547

Looking Backward (Bellamy), 67

Los Angeles Times, 409

Lovett, Dr. Robert W., 178

Low, Seth, 72

Lowell, A. Lawrence, 83

Lowenstein, Allard, 563

Lowi, Theodore, 572

Luce, Henry, 454

Luce Clare Boothe, 521

Ludlow, Mrs. E. Livingston, 79

Lusitania, 146

Luxembourg, 423

lynchings, 392–94, 543, 546, 551, 555

McAdoo, William Gibbs, 188, 189, 235, 378, 383

McAllister, Ward, 17

MacArthur, General Douglas, 217, 241, 468, 476, 481, 487

McCall's, 541, 563

McCarran, Pat, 378

McCarthy, Joseph, and McCarthyism, 519, 528–29, 535, 538–41, 558, 575

McClure's, 65

McCormack, John, 479

McCormick, Robert, 344, 348, 356, 454

McCoy, Donald, 301

McCullough, David, 10, 56

McFarland, Gerald, 22

McIntyre Marvin, 364, 463

Mack, John, 421

McKim, Charles F., 109

McKinley, William, 45, 46, 48, 58, 62, 63, 69, 78

　　assassination of, 2, 59, 61

MacLeish, Archibald, 427, 438, 506

Maggie: A Girl of the Streets (Crane), 65

Mahan, Alfred Thayer, 46, 167

Maine, U.S battleship, 48

Malcolm X, 281

Malik, Charles, 522

Manchukuo, 355

Manhattan Project, *see* atomic weapons, development of

Markham, Edwin, 325

Marshall, General George, 458, 476, 481, 487
  as secretary of state, 517, 518, 519, 529, 531
Marshall, Chief Justice John, 53
Marshall, Reverend Mr. Peter, 364
Marshall, Justice Thurgood, 542
Marshall Plan, 518, 520, 539–40
Martin, Agnes, 559
Martin, John, 546
Martin, Mr. and Mrs. Bradley, 43
Maverick, Maury, 347, 378, 386
Meat Inspection Act, 94, 100, 569
meatpacking industry, 92–94, 370
Meet the Press, 555
Mehta, Madam Hansa, 523
Mellon, Andrew, 337
Mencken, Henry L., 241, 313
Menuhin, Yehudi, 467
Mercer, Lucy, 501
  FDR's affair with, 155–56, 157, 162, 171
  FDR's renewed friendship with, 495
  hiring of, 144
Merriam, Frank F., 294
Meyer, Dillon, 453
Meyer, George von Lengerke, 62
Milkis, Sidney, 572
Miller, Arthur, 538
Miller, Earl, 200, 236, 504
Miller, Nathan, 172
Mills, Ogden, estate of, 421
miners, 132, 182, 462
  coal strike of 1902, 71–76
  subsistence homesteads for, 271–76, 389
  minimum wage, 135, 341
  TR and, 33, 54, 132
Miroff, Bruce, 27
Mitchell, John, 72, 73
Mohammed V, King of Morocco, 460
Moley, Raymond, 227, 230, 236, 250, 251, 255, 259, 315, 321, 324
Molotov, Vyacheslav, 460, 487
Monroe, James, 349, 472
Monroe Doctrine, 76–77, 349

Montgomery, Alabama, bus boycott in, 544–45, 553
Moody, William, 71
Moore, Ronnie, 564
Moral Man and Immoral Society (Niebuhr), 222, 433
Morgan, Arthur E., 400, 402–3
Morgan, Harcourt A., 400
Morgan, J. P., 29, 32, 68, 97, 309, 569
  coal strike of 1902 and, 74–75
  financial bailout of U.S. government, 70
  Northern Securities Company and, 69–71
  Panic of 1907 and, 97
Morgan family, 18
Morgantown, West Virginia, 273–74, 389
Morgenthau, Elinor, 192, 500, 504
Morgenthau, Henry, Jr., 192, 199, 203, 250, 287, 312, 314, 363–64, 365, 367, 368, 369, 391, 411, 447, 448, 466–67
Morgenthau, Henry, Sr., 219
Morgenthau, Robert, 558, 566
Morris, Edmund, 569
Morris, Gouverneur, 38, 39
Morrison, Herbert, 514–15
Morse, Wayne, 461
Morton Hall, 25, 27–29, 29, 35
Moses, Robert, 200–201
Moskowitz, Belle, 200
Moton, Robert, 392
Mountaineer Crafts Cooperative, 274
Mowry, George, 127, 131–32
muckrakers, 65, 92, 101, 102, 103, 114, 240, 370
Mugwumps, 22–24, 26, 35, 52, 65, 98, 99
  clean government and, 22–24, 28, 99
Muir, John, 108
Mumford, Lewis, 400, 403
Munich pact, 409, 410, 414, 429
Murphy, Charles F., 120, 121, 137, 144, 146, 161, 186
Murphy, Frank, 383, 384
Murray, Joe, 28, 29–30

Murray, Pauli, 504
Murray-Wagner Full Employment Act, 502, 503
Murrow, Edward R., 442, 549
Muscle Shoals, 247–49, 400
Mussolini, Benito, and fascist Italy, 347, 349, 354, 361, 362, 408, 410, 414, 415, 421, 439
   Allied war strategy and, 458
   FDR's 1939 message to, 418
   invasion of Ethiopia, 315, 350–51, 356
   Spanish Civil War and, 352
   surrender of, 493
   in World War II, 423
"My Day," 390, 444, 471, 483–84, 501, 502, 513, 514, 516, 517, 520, 525, 529, 536, 538, 540, 541, 543, 544, 546, 551–52, 553, 557, 558, 560, 562, 563, 565
Myrdal, Gunnar, 395, 412, 542

Namibia, 532
Nation, The, 24, 228, 264, 383, 390
National Association of Colored People (NAACP), 392, 393, 397, 528, 542, 545, 547, 548, 555
   Legal Defense and Education Fund, 542
National Biscuit Company, 69
National Citizens' Political Action Committee, 502
National Conference of Negro Youth, 395
National Conference on Fundamental Problems in the Education of Negroes, 396
National Conservation Commission, 107
National Credit Corporation, 210
National Defense Research Committee, 424
national economic planning, 229
National Education Association, 398
National Industrial Recovery Act, 263–65, 272, 276
National Labor Relations Act, 296, 301, 341
National Labor Relations Board, 312, 431

National League of Women Voters, 172–73
National Monuments Act, 107
National Negro Congress, 528
National Negro Council, 463
national parks, TR and, 107
National Progressive Party ("Bull Moose Party"), 142, 571–72
   presidential election of 1912, 131–36, 138–39, 140, 142, 166, 316, 323–24, 346
   presidential election of 1916, 148–49
National Progressives of America, 382–83
National Recovery Administration (NRA), 264, 276–79, 280, 281, 282, 289, 305, 312, 367, 462
   Supreme Court decision affecting, 295–96
National Social and Political Conference of 1899, 64
National Training School for Delinquent Girls, 395
National Union for Social Justice, 323, 326
National War Labor Board, 461–62
National Youth Administration (NYA), 304, 321, 397–99, 438, 540
   ER and, 269
Naval Expansion Act of 1938, 370
Naval War of 1812, The (Roosevelt), 12, 24, 46
Navy, U.S., 438, 469
   FDR as assistant secretary of, 80, 142–44, 145–48, 151, 153–55, 276, 347
   in 1938, 410
   Pearl Harbor, 442–43, 481
   TR as assistant secretary of, 46–49
   V-12 education program, 466
Navy League, 146
Nazi Germany, 245, 259, 347, 353–54, 513, 514
   Anschluss, 407–8, 412, 414
   anti-Semitism, *see* anti-Semitism, Nazi Germany and
   concentration camps, 414, 511
   events leading to World War II, 407–10, 414–19

FDR's response to events leading to
World War II and, 353, 354, 362,
408–11, 416–18
invasion of Poland, 418, 429
Kristallnacht, 413, 414, 428
rearmament of, 353
World War II and, 423, 426, 427, 439–
41, 443–44, 489–90
Allied cross-channel invasion, 458,
460, 468, 474–75, 476–77, 481
see also Hitler, Adolf
Nelson, Donald, 447
Netherlands, 423
Neuringer, Sheldon, 412
Neutrality Act, 352, 356, 417
New Deal, 329, 362, 363, 392, 431, 438, 462,
473, 494, 534, 571
accused of being communistic, 319, 327,
431
bureaucracy created by, 304, 372
experimental nature of, 258
FDR's 1932 acceptance speech and,
236–38
Keynes's advice for, 282–84, 368
1936 presidential politics and, 321
in 1938, 365–72, 384–85
1944 domestic agenda, 483–87, 494
One Hundred Days, 252–65, 370, 568
programs called socialist, 260, 261, 306,
402
results of, 280–82, 313–14
Second Hundred Days, 296–98, 302–5, 307
Supreme Court and, 295–96, 313, 339,
341, 344, 375, 571
TR's reformist agenda and, 142, 277
during World War II, 467
see also specific legislation and programs
New Democracy (Weyl), 13
New Haven Railroad, 71
New Nationalism, *see* Roosevelt,
Theodore, New Nationalism
New Orleans Times-Picayune, 409
Newport, Rhode Island, 68, 173
naval scandal, 156–57, 175–76

New Republic, The, 228, 383, 429
Newsboys' Lodging House, 20, 25, 87
Newsland Act, 569
New York Advertiser, 42, 44
New York American, 226
New York American and Journal, 72
New York Churchman, 72
New York City, 114
Board of Police Commissioners, 41–
44, 62
Four Hundred, 17, 18, 68, 79, 81
Health Board, 42
leisure class of, 15–18, 20–21, 68, 85, 98–
99
mayoralty race of 1886, 36–38, 170
plutocrats of, 18–19
reform movement in, 22–24
Tammany Hall, *see* Tammany Hall
TR's entry into politics of, 25, 27–29,
36–38
New York City Police Academy, 44
New York Daily News, 409
New Yorker, The, 215, 222, 311
New York Evening Post, 32, 93–94, 361
New York Evening Sun, 41
New York Evening World, 189
New York Globe, 119
New York Herald, 44, 86, 125
New York Herald Tribune, 189, 222–23, 232,
341, 381, 448
New York Journal, 42, 44, 48
New York Junior League, 266
New York Post, 194, 554
New York State:
governor, 324, 480
FDR as, 80, 194–203, 212–13, 217
TR as, 50–57, 62, 70
legislature, 566
FDR and, 80, 115–22, 136–38, 140
TR and, 28–33, 70, 565
office-holding qualifications, 22
Tammany machine, *see* Tammany
Hall
New York State Council for Parks, 201

New York State Fisheries Commission, 108

New York Sun, 31, 44, 63, 78

New York Times, The, 23, 29, 62–63, 119, 128, 139, 176, 187, 200, 214, 268, 403, 409, 505, 518, 537, 540, 560

New York Times Magazine, The, 536–37

New York Tribune, 62, 134

New York World, 41, 42, 43, 44, 361

New York Yacht Club, 113

Nichols, Louis, 535

Niebuhr, Reinhold, 222, 306, 433

Nimitz, Admiral Chester, 476, 481, 487

Nixon, E. D., 544

Nixon, Richard, 77, 519, 554, 561
  ER and, 534

Norfolk Virginian-Pilot, 409

Norris, Frank, 65, 198

Norris, George, 132, 240, 247, 248, 258, 261, 262, 272, 295, 321, 335, 382, 383, 451

North Africa, World War II fighting in, 444, 458

Northern Securities Company, 69–71

Norton, Charles Eliot, 21

Norway, 423

Nourmahal, 311, 363

Nye, Gerald P., 347, 352

O'Connor, D. Basil "Doc," 170, 227

O'Connor, John J., 381

Octopus, The (Norris), 65

O'Day, Caroline, 192

Odum, Howard, 400

Office of Civilian Defense, 449

Office of Production Management, 463

Office of War Information, 467

Oglethorpe University, FDR speech at, 231–32, 233

O'Gorman, James, 120

O'Neal, Edward A., 262

Our World (Willkie), 470

Outlook, 43

Oxford Pledge, 302

Oyster Bay:
  FDR at, 56
  TR and, 11, 56–57, 59, 88, 106, 140–41, 159
  see also Roosevelt family, Oyster Bay

Pahlevi, Shah Mohammed Reza, 492

Painter, Nell, 125, 132

Pakistan, 537

Palestine, 513–19
  ER and, 513–14
  partition of, 518
  TR and, 514
  see also Israel

Panama Canal project, 105

Panic of 1907, 97, 104

Parini, Jay, 71–72

Parker, Alton B., 78

Parkman, Francis, 22, 23, 64

Parks, Rosa, 544–45

Pasvolsky, Leo, 505

Patman, Wright, 216

patricians, 14–19, 504, 563, 573–74
  anti-Semitism and, *see* anti-Semitism, patricians and
  attitude toward the governing class and politics, 25, 32–33, 114, 118, 576
  Catholics and, 196–97, 557
  clubs and, 25, 28, 98, 113, 175
  as dying class, 21, 141
  ER as, *see* Roosevelt, Eleanor, as patrician
  FDR and, *see* Roosevelt, Franklin Delano, the patricians and
  Mugwumps, *see* Mugwumps
  New York, *see* New York, leisure class of
  TR and, *see* Roosevelt, Theodore, the patricians and

patronage, 22, 24, 31, 52, 143, 388

Patton, George S., Jr., 217

Pavlov, Alexei P., 524

Peabody, Endicott, 55, 79, 81, 310, 396

Peabody, George Foster, 190, 191, 322
Peace Corps, 562
Pearl Harbor, 442–43, 481
Pearson, Drew, 506
Pell, Herbert, 141
Pepper, George Wharton, 18
Perkins, Frances, 89, 103, 114, 122, 183, 184, 213, 432, 520, 566
  as New York State government, 201, 212
  as secretary of labor, 250, 260, 264, 269, 279, 280, 287, 349, 363, 391, 397, 449
Perkins, George, 127
Pershing, General John J., 152
Pétain, Marshal Philippe, 423
Philadelphia and Reading Coal and Iron Company, 72
Philadelphia Inquirer, The, 409
Philadelphia patrician families, 17, 18
philanthropy, 18, 89
  FDR and, 113, 170, 174, 310–11
  of Theodore, Sr., 20–21, 28
Philippines, 49, 59, 77, 355, 487, 490
Philipps, Cabell, 216
Phillips, David Graham, 65
Phillips, William, 250, 383, 409, 410
Pickett, Clarence, 272, 392
Pinchot, Gifford, 108, 149, 400
Pirenne, Henri, 68
Pittman, Key, 350
Pittsburgh Post Gazette, 362
Platt, Tom, 46, 50–51, 52, 53, 57, 58
Platt Amendment, 336
plutocrats and plutocracy, 23, 72
  fashionable society and, 18–19
  FDR's relationship with, 290–93, 296, 297, 303, 307–13, 318–19, 329, 344, 366, 368–69, 571, 573
  Mugwumps and, 22, 23
  TR's attacks on, 3, 68–69, 71, 98, 104, 125, 129, 141, 303
Poland, 354, 415, 418, 419, 423, 429, 488, 493, 511, 512
Polier, Judge Justine Wise, 415

Politics as Duty, and as a Career (Storey), 22
Pollock, Jackson, 304
poll taxes, 478
populists, 294–95, 298–300, 571, 577
  see also names of individuals
Porcellian Club, 9–10, 12, 62, 82, 91
Post Office, U.S., 39
Powell, Adam Clayton, 545–46
Powell, Thomas Reed, 341
Presbyterian Hospital, New York City, 179, 183
presidency, executive power of the, 224
  FDR and, 347, 490, 572
  TR and, 75, 94, 100, 103, 108, 417
  Wilson and, 154
presidential elections:
  1884, 34–35
  1888, 38
  1892, 38
  1896, 45–46
  1900, 58–59, 78
  1904, 77–78, 97–98
  1912, 123–36, 137–39, 140, 141, 142, 316, 323–24, 346
  1916, 148–49
  1920, 161–64, 170, 175, 316
  1924, 186, 188–89, 193
  1928, 193–94, 195, 209
  1932, 219–20, 225–26, 232–43, 576
  1936, 315–16, 320–39, 334–35, 345–46, 351–52, 353, 576
  1940, 425–28, 435, 576
  1944, 477–83, 492, 576
  1948, 519, 520–21, 576
  1956, 546–52, 576
  1960, 556–61, 576
Princeton University, 9
Profiles in Courage (Kennedy), 558
Progress and Poverty (George), 36
Progressive, The, 429
progressive reform and progressive movement, 3, 63–67, 98, 117, 183, 212, 295, 335, 577
  FDR and, 136, 140, 321, 382–83

progressive reform and progressive
  movement (*continued*)
  TR and, 66–67, 102, 103, 123–25, 126–36,
    141–42, 158–59, 240, 281, 571–72
  Wilson and, 137
Prohibition, 66, 148, 186, 188, 195, 220
  repeal of, 233, 238
Prohibition party, 324, 334
Promise of American Life, The (Croly), 13,
  95
Proskauer, Joseph M., 183, 188
"Prospects of Mankind," 558
Public Duty of Educated Men, The (Curtis),
  22
Public Utility Holding Company Act,
  297
public works, 503
  during Hoover administration, 211
  New Deal and, 238, 257, 264, 280, 284,
    288, 302, 303–5, 321, 367, 368
Public Works Administration (PWA),
  280–81, 302, 367, 375, 385
Puerto Rico, 49, 77
Pullman strike, 63, 73
Pure Food and Drug Act, 94, 100, 132, 370,
  569

Quay, M. S., 74
Queen Elizabeth, 505–6, 508

racial discrimination, 52–28, 182, 195, 305,
  463, 490, 575
  in the armed forces, 466
  civil rights, *see* civil rights
  ER and, *see* African-Americans, ER
    and
  FDR and, *see* African-Americans, FDR
    and
  Japanese-Americans, internment of,
    451–53
  lynchings, 392–94, 543, 546, 555

progressive movement and, 66
segregation, 394, 395, 463–64, 466, 468–
  69, 502, 527–28, 542
soldiers'-vote act and, 478
in the South, *see* South, the, racism in
TR's opposition to, 40, 61–62
railroads, 69, 73, 92, 100
Randolph, A. Philip, 463, 464, 545
Rankin, John, 478
Rauh, Joseph, 556, 564
Rayburn, Sam, 235, 297, 373, 374, 479
Read, Elizabeth, 172
Reagan administration, 577
Reconstruction Finance Corporation, 211,
  370
Redbook Magazine, 200
Red Cross, 151, 165, 210, 465, 541
Reed, T. B., Speaker of the House, 46
Reed, Stanley, 338
Reilly, Mike, 428
Reno, Milo, 262, 300
Republican National Convention:
  1884, 33–35
  1912, 130
  1916, 148–49
  1936, 323, 324
  1940, 426, 480
  1944, 480
  1952, 534
Republican party:
  of Lincoln, 1, 34, 131
  Mugwumps and, *see* Mugwumps
  New York, 25, 27–29, 30, 50–51, 53, 58
  reformers, 34
  Regulars or Old Guard, 33, 34, 92, 94,
    95, 97–98, 105, 123, 126, 127, 131, 482,
    572
  see also presidential elections;
    individual Republicans
Resettlement Administration, 275
Revenue Act of 1935, 297, 303
Reynolds, James, 93
Reynolds, Robert, 348

Rhineland, Germany's reoccupation of, 353, 356

Richmond Times-Dispatch, 409

Riis, Jacob, 42, 44, 102, 103

Rivington Street Settlement House, 89, 171

Robert E. Peary, 445

Roberts, Justice Owen D., 341, 344, 345

Robeson, Paul, 542

Robinson, Douglas, 69

Robinson, Jo Ann, 544

Robinson, Joseph T., 195, 289, 341–42

Robinson, Teddy, 114, 115

Rockefeller, John D., 65, 69, 96–97, 569

Rockefeller, Nelson, 566

Rockefeller family, 18

Rogers, Edith Nourse, 465–66

Rogers, Will, 210, 268

Romania, 107, 413, 439, 507

Rommel, Marshal Erwin, 475, 477

Roosevelt, Alice (née Lee) (TR's first wife), 10, 14, 15, 31, 57
  death of, 33, 36
  marriage to TR, 14

Roosevelt, Alice (TR's daughter), *see* Longworth, Alice (née Roosevelt) (TR's daughter)

Roosevelt, Anna (FDR's daughter), 111, 120, 171, 173, 184, 194, 199, 248, 267, 364, 494, 502, 510, 525–27, 537
  education of, 173–74
  ER's relationship with, 179, 495

Roosevelt, Anna (née Hall) (ER's mother), 85–86

Roosevelt, Anna (TR's sister) (Bamie, Bysie), 9, 14, 33, 56, 143, 144

Roosevelt, Anne (John's wife), 526

Roosevelt, Archie (TR's son), 57, 152, 154

Roosevelt, Corinne (TR's sister), 8, 126, 148, 158, 159

Roosevelt, Cornelius Van Schaack, 1, 19

Roosevelt, Edith (née Carow) (TR's second wife), 16, 57, 88, 139, 159, 239
  marriage, 35–36, 37

Roosevelt, Eleanor, 82, 115, 138, 144, 168, 223, 289, 294, 312, 363, 432, 433, 489, 500–566, 573–76
  African-Americans and, *see* African-Americans, ER and
  American Association for the United Nations and, 536, 538
  childhood of, 85–88
  children's issues and, 390, 391, 397–99, 421, 463
  civil rights and, 392, 541–46, 548–53, 555–56, 564–65, 574
  columns, 266, 390, 391, 437, 444, 453, 471, 483–84, 501, 502, 513, 514, 516, 517, 520, 525, 529, 536, 538, 540, 541, 543, 544, 546, 551–52, 553, 554, 557, 558, 560, 562, 563, 565
  death of, 2, 566
  depression, 156, 162
  education of, 85, 88–89, 171
  engagement to FDR, 78–79, 90–91
  FDR's campaigns and:
    for governor, 202, 576
    for New York State senate, 116
    for president, 326–27, 328, 427, 479, 480, 482, 576
    for vice presidency, 162–65, 170
  FDR's death and funeral and, 495, 500–501
  on FDR's law studies, 109
  FDR's polio and, 177–82
  FDR's political career and, 156, 170–71, 194, 199, 200, 425, 576
  as first lady, *see this entry under* as first lady
  FDR's positions and policies and, 266, 267, 271, 314, 317, 389, 393–94, 397, 403, 467, 471, 483–84, 494, 541–42
  internment of Japanese-Americans, 452–53
  the League of Nations, 226
  Shadow New Deal, 389–90, 399
  Spanish Civil War, 406–7

Roosevelt, Eleanor (*continued*)
  fears, overcoming, 111, 185, 270
  as first lady, 254, 255, 265–76, 284, 295,
      315, 385, 388–99
    African-Americans and, *see* African-
        Americans, ER and
    as conscience of the White House,
        406–7, 414, 452, 524, 551
    FDR's policies and, *see this entry
        under* FDR's positions and
        policies and
    fears about becoming, 235–36, 265
    White House duties, 268, 390, 494
  as grandmother, 199, 527, 550, 560
  health, 138, 494, 524
  last years, 562–63, 564, 565–66
  Howe and, 164–65, 171, 183, 185, 226, 235,
      268, 269, 270, 271, 364, 501, 504
  human rights and, *see* human rights
  intellectual awakening, 173, 174
  lectures, 266
  Lincoln and, 2–3
  McCarthyism and, 538–41
  mail, 265, 266–67, 268
  marriage of, 2, 79
  Lucy Mercer and, 144, 155–56, 157, 162,
      171, 495, 501
  as mother, 111, 116, 156, 163, 171, 173–74,
      175, 179, 185, 201, 259–60, 364, 495,
      525–27
  New York City apartment, 172, 500
  at Office of Civilian Defense, 449
  partnership with FDR, 184, 201, 470–71,
      471, 487, 493–94, 500, 524
  as patrician, 3, 87–89, 143, 151, 173, 174,
      175, 196–97, 392, 504, 513, 570
    departure from life of, 150–51, 171–72,
        184, 188, 565, 573
  politics and, 183–85, 186–90, 195, 199–
      200, 236, 326–27, 480, 510, 534–35,
      575, 576
    ignorance as young woman, 122
  1948 election, 519, 520–21, 576
  1956 election, 546–53, 576

  1960 election, 556–61, 576
    urged to run for office, 502, 520–21
  women's issues, *see this entry under*
      women's issues and
  press conferences for women
      reporters, 269, 395, 471
  Sara Roosevelt and, 90, 111, 156, 173, 192
  self-assurance, 88, 89
  self-discipline, 87
  sense of duty, 87–88
  Shadow New Deal, 389–90, 399
  Spanish Civil War and, 406–7, 414, 471
  subsistence homesteads and, 269, 271–
      76, 389, 392
  as teacher, 192–93, 200, 201, 236, 563
  TR and, *see* Roosevelt, Theodore, ER
      and
  Truman and, *see* Truman, Harry, ER
      and
  Tugwell and, 228
  United Nations and, *see* United
      Nations, ER and
  Val-Kill and, *see* Val-Kill
  volunteer work before becoming first
      lady, 89, 151, 165, 171
  Warm Springs and, 191
  wedding of, 79
  women's issues and, 163, 172–73, 183, 186,
      187, 195, 200, 201, 221, 266, 269, 390,
      391, 462, 484, 510, 536, 537, 562, 575,
      see this entry under women's issues
  as world leader, 574–75
  during World War I, 150–51, 165, 171, 270
Roosevelt, Elliott (ER's brother), 87
Roosevelt, Elliott (FDR's son), 171, 184,
    267–68, 311–12, 364, 495, 502, 524, 525–
    27, 557, 561
  1932 campaign and, 241, 242
  in World War II, 457, 525
Roosevelt, Elliott (TR's brother, ER's
    father), 88, 537
  alcoholism, 14, 86, 87
  childhood of, 1–2
  death of, 79

ER and, 86–87
lifestyle of, 20, 68
Roosevelt, Emlen, 29
Roosevelt, Ethel (TR's daughter), 57
Roosevelt, Franklin, Jr. (FDR's son), 111,
    144, 201, 260, 267–68, 276, 362, 495,
    505, 525–27
marriage of, 312, 364
in World War II, 457–58, 525
Roosevelt, Franklin Delano, 78–91, 151, 202
assassination attempt on, 247
as assistant secretary of the navy, 80,
    142–44, 145–48, 151, 153–55, 166, 167,
    276, 347, 570
scandal involving, 156–57, 175–76
atomic weapon development and, 455
birth of, 14
brain trust, 227–28, 233, 234, 237, 242,
    243, 250–51, 319, 426–27
bully pulpit, 259, 308
as campaigner, 115–17, 118, 168, 315–16, 576
for governor, 194, 202, 576
1932 presidential election, 239–43
1936 presidential election, 321–22,
    327–29, 335
1940 presidential election, 427–28
1944 presidential election, 481–82
for vice president, 161–62, 163–64
childhood of, 56, 80, 85
Christian views, 432, 433, 471–72
conservation and, 136
death of, 2, 495, 501
education of:
    at Columbia Law School, 80, 108–9
    at Groton, 56, 81–82, 567, 570
    at Harvard, 80, 82–85, 113, 570
engagement to ER, 78–79, 90–91
ER and, *see* Roosevelt, Eleanor
finances, 109, 156, 157, 182
fireside chats, 202, 255–56, 258, 264–65,
    326, 339, 340, 375–76
during World War II, 419–20, 448
foreign policy, *see* World War II;
    specific countries and issues

funeral, 500–501
hatred of, 290–93, 308, 329, 571, 573
health, 157, 361
    fourth term and, 479–80, 482, 489,
        490–92
    pneumonia, 155
    polio, *see this entry under* polio
    typhoid fever, 138
isolationists and, *see* isolationism
law practice, 109–10, 113, 170
Library at Hyde Park, 492
Lincoln and, 2–3, 316
Lippmann and, 222–23
marriage of, 2
Lucy Mercer and, 155–56, 157, 162, 171,
    495
as military leader, 476, 493
New Deal, *see* New Deal
as New York State governor, 80, 194–
    203, 212–13, 217
in New York State legislature, 80, 115–
    22, 136–38, 140
the patricians and, 96, 113, 114, 143, 174–75
    heritage, 3, 80, 82, 174, 311, 313, 570
    hostility between, 290–93, 296, 297,
        307–13, 318–19, 329, 366, 368–69,
        571, 573
personality of, 168, 175, 202–3, 288
    college years, 84
    frivolousness, 110, 156
    polio's effect on, 182
philosophical beliefs, 223
physical appearance, 119, 163–64, 181,
    229
polio, 177–82, 184, 188, 189, 193, 194, 220,
    361, 363, 491–92
    Warm Springs and, 190–92
political ambition, 113, 114, 140, 195–96,
    199, 202
Hoover administration, the
    Depression, and, 211–13, 217,
    219–20
League of Nations position and,
    225–27

Roosevelt, Franklin Delano (*continued*)
  political beliefs, 223–24, 239
  as political manipulator, 246, 294, 425–
    26, 472
  Porcellian Club, rejection from, 82, 91
  pragmatism, 3, 227, 233, 240, 243, 245,
    300, 359, 414, 484, 524, 551
  presidency, 245–496, 570–73
    balanced budget and, *see* balanced
      budget, FDR's commitment to
    cabinets, 249–51, 254, 363–64, 425–26
    Congressional elections of 1938 and,
      375–81, 383–84, 386, 430, 575
    as experimenter, 258, 288
    foreign policy, *see* World War II;
      specific countries and issues
    last hundred days, 489–96
    move to the left in late 1935, 316–18
    1932 transition from Hoover
      presidency, 245–52
    New Deal, *see* New Deal
    One Hundred Days, 252–65, 287, 370,
      570
    "second Bill of Rights," 484–86, 572
    Second Hundred Days, 296–98, 302–
      5, 307
    World War II and, *see* World War II
  presidential elections:
    1932, 211–13, 217, 219–20, 225–27, 230–43
    1936, 315–16, 320–29, 334–35, 345–46,
      351–52, 353
    1940, 425–28, 435
    1944, 477–83, 492
  press conferences and press
    management, 258–59, 358–59, 437–
    48, 439, 477
  as realist and idealist, 472–74
  refugees of World War II and, 408,
    411–13, 415–16, 421
  Senate race, 144–45, 170
  speeches, 251, 354, 366
    annual messages to Congress, 286,
      317–18, 365–66, 436–37
    Bill of Rights tribute, 450

  at Chautauqua, 1936, 351–52, 353
  Chicago foreign policy address,
    summer 1937, 356–59
  Democratic Victory Dinner, 1937,
    339, 347
  fireside chats, *see this entry under*
    fireside chats
  Four Freedoms, 436–37
  inaugural speech, 1933, 252–54, 287, 432
  inaugural speech, 1941, 437–48
  at Jackson Day Dinner 1939, 430
  at Madison Square Garden, 1936,
    328–29, 334, 344
  1932 election and, 226, 227, 229–33,
    236–38, 239, 242
  at 1936 Democratic convention, 325–26
  nominating Al Smith, 186, 188–89, 193
  at Oglethorpe University, 231–32
  after Pearl Harbor, 443
  at People's Forum in Troy, 136–37
  seconding Al Smith nomination, 161
  State of the Union, 1943, 469–70
  State of the Union, 1944, 484
  Teamsters Union dinner, 1944, 481–82
  undelivered, 495–96
  Supreme Court and:
    appointments, 341–42, 362, 431–32
    "court reform," 128–29, 336–47, 354,
      362, 378, 387, 577
  TR and, 56, 78, 142, 146, 157, 231, 240,
    247, 258, 265, 310, 316, 374, 448, 481
    admiration and emulation of, 80, 85,
      91, 108, 110, 113, 114, 119, 136, 137,
      144, 165–66, 193, 570
    coal strike settlement, 75
    dedication of Theodore Roosevelt
      Memorial, 320
    Roosevelt name as aid in
      campaigning, 116
    testimony at libel trial, 146–47
    transformational leadership, 403, 404,
      483–87, 489
  United Nations and, *see* United
    Nations, FDR and

as vice-presidential candidate, 80, 160–64, 170, 175

Wilson and, 137–38, 140, 142–43, 145, 149, 153, 161, 165, 166–67, 231, 240, 316, 324, 570

World War II and, *see* World War II

Roosevelt, George, 102

Roosevelt, Hall (ER's brother), 86, 90, 150

Roosevelt, Helen, 80

Roosevelt, James (FDR's father), 56, 81, 82, 115

  death of, 84

  marriage of, 14

Roosevelt, James (FDR's son), 111, 163, 171, 178, 184, 187, 188, 254, 267–68, 276, 362, 363, 521, 525–27, 557

  1932 campaign and, 241, 242

  as presidential assistant, 364, 369

Roosevelt, James "Rosy" (FDR's half brother), 80, 85

Roosevelt, James "Taddy," 80

Roosevelt, John (FDR's son), 201, 241, 242, 276, 312, 362, 495, 525–27, 534, 560

Roosevelt, Kermit (TR's son), 57, 106, 146, 147, 152, 154

Roosevelt, Martha Bulloch (TR's mother), 1, 8, 10–11, 14, 19, 552

  TR's political career and, 29

Roosevelt, Quentin (TR's son), 57, 152–53, 154, 158, 159, 190, 201

Roosevelt, Robert B., 107–8

Roosevelt, Sara (née Delano), 56, 75, 80, 109, 114, 115, 146, 155, 164, 173, 393, 561, 573–74

  as dominating mother, 84, 90, 108

  ER and, 90, 111, 156, 173, 192

  FDR's financial dependence on, 109, 156, 157

  FDR's polio and, 178–79

  FDR's political career and, 118, 140, 174, 183

  as grandmother, 111, 163

  marriage of, 14

Roosevelt, Theodore, 8–78, 122–36, 212, 222, 225, 563

  African safari and European tour, 113, 122

  as assistant secretary of the navy, 46–49, 125

  attempted assassination of, 138–39

  as author, 12, 38, 39, 85, 101, 153, 158

    Autobiography, 1, 20, 25, 37, 68–69, 76

    The Naval War of 1812, 12, 24, 46

  Badlands and, 27, 35

  big business and, *see* business, TR and

  "Bull Moose Party" and, 131–36, 138–39, 140, 142, 148–49, 166, 316, 323–24, 346, 571–72

  "bully pulpit," 100, 103

  childhood of, 1–2, 10–11

  on Civil Service Commission, 38–40

  clean government and, 55, 62, 99

  as conservationist and naturalist, 12, 107–8, 123–24, 132

  cruel edge to, 11, 41, 105

  death of, 157–59, 224

  education of, 8

    at Columbia Law School, 14–15, 24, 28

    at Harvard, 8–10, 11–13

  ER and, 78–79, 88, 90–91, 122, 129, 140, 152, 494

  FDR and, *see* Roosevelt, Franklin Delano, TR and

  health:

    asthma, 9, 10, 11

  jingoism, 45, 47, 105

  judiciary and, *see* judiciary, TR and

  labor and, *see* labor and unions, TR and

  libel trial, 146–47

  Lincoln and, 1–3, 102, 129

  magnetism of, 47, 52

  marriage to Alice Lee, 14

  marriage to Edith Carow, 35–36, 37

  moral leadership of, 27, 31, 41, 55, 95, 99–100, 104–5, 113, 123, 130, 166, 569

  foreign policy and, 77

Roosevelt, Theodore (*continued*)
  as nationalist, 45, 47, 95
  New Nationalism, 125, 133, 263, 277
  New York City Board of Police
    Commissioners, presidency of,
    41–44, 62
  New York City mayoralty race of 1886,
    36–38, 170
  New York State Assembly seat, 28–33,
    70, 565
  as New York State governor, 50–57,
    62, 70
  Nobel Peace Prize, 105, 107, 355
  party loyalty and, 35, 36, 39
  the patricians and, 32–33, 43, 104, 113,
    125–26, 129, 565
    disdain for, 20, 21, 25–26, 27, 67–68,
      95–96, 98, 297, 569
    hatred of TR, 98–99, 125, 126, 129,
      140–41, 148, 297
  heritage and youth, 3, 8–10, 18, 19, 20
  physical appearance, 9, 30
  political life, initial interest in, 24, 25–29
  poverty, attitudes toward, 31–32, 40, 42
  presidency, 247–48, 336, 347, 355, 370,
    374, 431, 569–70, 576
    coal strike of 1902, 71–76
    election of 1904, 77–78
    election of 1912, 123–36, 138–39, 140,
      142, 316, 324
    election of 1916, 148–49
    executive power and, 75, 94, 100, 103,
      108
    first term, 2, 61–78
    Monroe Doctrine and, 76–77
    second term, 91–108
    trusts and, 69–71, 94, 100, 133, 569
  progressive reform and, *see* progressive
    reform and progressive
    movement, TR and
  public reputation, building of, 42–43,
    44, 47, 50, 113
  Rough Riders and, 49–50, 51, 79, 159
  Russo-Japanese peace treaty and, 106–7

  as speaker, 9, 131–32
  verbal rage against adversaries, 41,
    59, 104–5, 166
  sports and, 11
  Square Deal, 125
  transformational leadership, 569
  as vice president, 58–59, 70
  World War I and, 146, 147, 151–53
Roosevelt, Theodore, Jr. (TR's son), 57,
  141, 152–53, 154, 162, 190, 308
  death in World War II, 57
Roosevelt, Theodore, Sr., 1, 11, 17, 18, 23,
  25, 56, 576
  death of, 10
  ethical and moral standards set by, 10,
    20–21
  mansion built by, 19–20
  as philanthropist, 20–21, 28
Roosevelt Enterprises, 526
Roosevelt family, 8, 15, 19, 84–85, 504
  Oyster Bay, 80, 88, 91
  split with Hyde Park Roosevelts,
    140, 162, 190
Root, Elihu, 29, 61, 70, 74–75, 98, 106, 126,
  130, 133
Rosenman, Sam, 221, 227, 236, 324, 338, 357,
  364, 411, 426
Rosenthal, A. M., 536, 538
Rothko, Mark, 304
Rough Riders, 49–50, 51, 79, 159
Royce, Josiah, 83
rural electrification, 485, 492
Rural Electrification Administration, 375,
  379, 400
Rusk, Dean, 518
Russell, Richard, 554
Russia:
  -Japanese peace treaty, 106–7, 355
  pogroms in, 107, 413
  see also Soviet Union
Rutherford, Ernest, 454
Rutherford, Lewis, 18
Rutherfurd, Lucy Mercer, *see* Mercer, Lucy
Rutherfurd, Winthrop, 157, 495

Sabalo, 176–77
Sacco-Vanzetti trial, 432
Sachs, Dr. Alexander, 455
Sagamore Hill (Oyster Bay home), 57, 88, 141
St. Andrew's Boys Club of Boston, 113
Saltonstall, Dick, 10, 12
Saltonstall, Leverett, 384
Saltonstall, Rose, 10
Sandel, Michael, 572
Sandifer, Durward, 510, 517
Santayana, George, 83
"Sarah Knisley's Arm," 103
Saturday Evening Post, 275, 291, 388
Saudi Arabia, 514, 529
Schecter v. United States, 295–96
Schine, David, 541
Schlesinger, Arthur, Jr., 276–77, 547, 549, 558
Schlesinger, Arthur, Sr., 18
Schlosser, John F., 115–16, 118
Schneiderman, Rose, 183, 192
Schofield, Major General J. M., 74
Schurz, Carl, 22, 32, 33, 35, 52
Scott, Hazel, 546
Scripps-Howard newspapers, 554
Second World Youth Congress, 398–99
Secret Service, 268, 271
Securities and Exchange Commission, 282, 431
securities regulation, 257, 282
sedition law during World War I, 154
segregation, *see* racial discrimination, segregation
Seligman, Jesse, 32
Seligman family, 18
settlement houses, 64, 89, 117, 132, 165
Sheehan, William F. "Blue-eyed Billy," 119–20
Sheldon, Charles, 64
Shepard, Edward, 119–20
Sherman Antitrust Act of 1890, 64, 69, 71, 73, 134
Sherwood, Robert, 426–27
Shouse, Jouett, 219, 290

Shumatov, Madame Elizabeth, 501
Sinclair, Upton, 65, 92–93, 101, 114, 294, 370
Sklar, Martin, 125
Smith, Al, 121, 122, 136, 161, 183–84, 189–90, 193–97, 420
   break with FDR and New Deal, 314, 318–19, 323, 327, 571
   1932 election and, 219, 230, 234, 235, 238–39, 241
   as presidential candidate, 186, 188–89, 193–94, 195, 557
Smith, Ellison D. "Cotton," 380, 381
Smith, Gerald L. K., 319–20, 322–23, 326, 327, 335, 348, 491
Smith, James R., Jr., 137
Smith, Margaret Chase, 521
Smith, Moses, 203
Smoot-Hawley tariff, 225, 230
Snell, Bertrand H., 366
social Darwinism, 40
Social Gospel movement, 64
socialism and socialists, 101, 102, 154, 198, 200, 571
   during the Depression, 215, 220, 301–2, 306
   New Deal programs and, 260, 261, 306, 402, 571
Socialist party, 38, 142
   Debs as candidate for, 78, 133, 139, 162
   Norman Thomas and, *see* Thomas, Norman
Social Justice, 323, 412
Social Security Act, 297, 298, 299, 303, 341
   drafting of, 287
social security insurance, TR and, 132, 135
Social Security program, 312, 317, 321, 328
soldiers'-vote act of 1944, 478, 483, 486
Sorensen, Theodore, 560
South, the:
   civil rights movement and, *see* civil rights
   desegregation of, 543, 544–45, 548, 551, 553
   Powell rider on school construction bill, 545–46, 547, 548
   economy of, 385–87, 388, 394, 401–4, 575

South, the (*continued*)
racism in, 387, 388, 392–95, 397, 465, 478, 527–28, 531, 543–44, 547, 553–54, 575
South Africa, 529, 532, 556
Southern Christian Leadership Conference, 544
Southern Conference Education Fund, 555
Southern Conference for Human Welfare, 394
Southern Democrats, 339, 370, 379–82, 384, 386, 387–88, 486, 494, 531, 551, 556, 571
1956 Democratic Convention and, 548, 550
Southern States Industrial Council, 386
Souvestre, Marie, 88–89, 171, 193
Soviet Union, 349, 422, 508, 517–20, 529, 536–37
Eastern Europe and, 506–7, 511, 529, 552
events leading to World War II and, 415, 418
Soviet-Nazi nonaggression pact, 418, 421
human rights and, 523, 524, 529, 531
Palestine and, 516, 518
U.S. recognition of, 349
in World War II, 419, 421, 422–23, 444, 460, 468, 476, 487, 488, 489–90
casualties, 469
Nazi assault on, 440
see also Stalin, Joseph
Spain:
civil war in, 351–53, 354, 356, 364, 406–7, 410, 414, 415, 471
Cuba and, 45, 47–50, 77
Spanish-American War, 48–50, 59, 77
Spanish Earth, The, 407
Sparkman, John, 535
Spellman, Cardinal Francis Joseph, 557
Spencer, Herbert, 40, 319
"spheres of influence," 77, 473, 474, 493
Springwood (Roosevelt estate), 56, 146, 175, 199, 203, 421, 566

Stalin, Joseph, 460, 493
Soviet-Nazi nonaggression pact, 418
Teheran conference, 474
United Nations and, 470, 506
Yalta conference, 487–89
see also Soviet Union
Standard Oil, 65, 69, 71, 96–97
Stars and Stripes, 462
State Department, U.S., 349–50, 412, 470, 494, 517–19
events leading to World War II and, 409
Jewish refugees and, 515, 517
McCarthyism and, 538–39
Spanish Civil War and, 407
United Nations and, 508
states' rights, 387, 402
Stead, W. T., 65
Steffens, Lincoln, 42, 44, 65, 208, 240
Stettinius, Edward, 505
Stevenson, Adlai E., 58, 541, 558–59, 560, 566
as presidential candidate, 521, 535, 546–48, 550, 551, 552, 556–57, 575
United Nations and, 505, 510, 561
Stimson, Henry L., 117, 225, 246, 355, 425, 440, 466, 476
stock market, 182, 290, 368
"Black Tuesday" of October 1937, 365
crash, 201–2, 212
in 1930, 209
Stokes, Thomas L., 217
Stone, Justice Harlan Fiske, 250
Storer, Mrs. Bellamy, 46
Storey, Moorfield, 22, 141
Straight, Willard, 576
Strassman, Fritz, 454
Straus, Jesse, 241
Straus, Oscar, 98
Stravinsky, Igor, 304
strikes, 73, 279, 391
coal strike of 1902, 71–76
court injunctions to prevent, 104
in 1920s, 182
Pullman strike, 63, 73

of steel industry, 76
during Truman administration, 503–4
during World War II, 461–62
Strong, Josiah, 68
subsistence homesteads, 305, 392
ER and, 269, 271–76, 389
Suckley, Margaret, 494, 501
Suez Canal, 552
Sullivan, "Big Tim," 119
Sullivan, Mark, 189
Sulzberger, Arthur Hays, 432
Summer Birds of the Adirondacks, The
(Roosevelt), 12
Sumners, Hatton, 338
Supreme Court, U.S., 71, 99–100, 104, 127–
28, 451, 461
appointments, 134, 362, 431–32
Brown v. Board of Education of Topeka,
Kansas, 543, 545, 546–47, 548, 553
FDR's "court reform" and, 128–29, 336–
47, 354, 362, 378, 387, 577
Knight case, 69
New Deal legislation and, 295–96, 313,
339, 341, 344, 375, 571
see also individual justices
sweatshops, 279
Triangle Shirtwaist fire, 122, 136
Swope, Herbert Bayard, 289
Symington, Stuart, 557
Syria, 537
Szilard, Leo, 454, 455

Taft, Robert A., 348, 384, 426, 438, 452,
478, 480, 534
Taft, William Howard, 46, 108, 117, 123,
126, 127, 159, 160
election of 1912, 130–31, 133, 139
Talmadge, Eugene, 319, 380
Tammany Hall, 31, 32, 36, 38, 42, 62,
119–21, 144, 160, 186, 227, 239, 241,
243, 570
Taney, Chief Justice Roger, 128
Tarbell, Ida, 65

tariffs, 38, 182, 225, 230, 242
taxation, 64, 283, 485
of business, 53, 221, 297, 303, 308, 370
of estates and gifts, 297
income tax, *see* income tax
of inheritance, *see* inheritance tax
during World War II, 447, 448, 488, 492
1944 tax bill, 479
Taylorism, 143–44
Teapot Dome scandal, 190
Teheran conference, 474, 492
tenements, 42, 80
working conditions in, 31–32, 54, 127
Tennessee Coal and Iron Company, 97
Tennessee Valley Authority (TVA),
247–49, 251, 260, 261, 302, 305, 317,
385–87, 399–404
Tex and Jinx, 543
Thomas, Elmer, 378
Thomas, Norman, 198, 240, 243, 282, 306,
324, 334, 335, 348, 383
Thompson, Malvina "Tommy," 267, 268,
449, 501, 504, 505
Thurber, James, 222
Thurmond, Strom, 553
Tilden, Samuel J., 23, 34
Tilden Commission, 23
Till, Emmett, 543, 546, 555
Time, 309, 310, 454
Tito, Yosep Broz, 537–38
Todhunter School for Girls, 192–93, 200
Tomorrow Is Now (Roosevelt), 543, 564,
573
Toscanini, Arturo, 304
Townsend, Dr. Francis E., 294–95, 300,
301, 303, 317, 322, 326, 335, 571
Townsend, John, Jr., 505
transformational leadership, 576
of FDR, 403, 404, 483–87, 489
of TR, 569
Triangle Shirtwaist fire, 122, 136
Trimble, William, 28
TR's entry into politics of, 5, 27–29, 36–38
Truman, Bess, 546

Truman, Harry S., 549, 561, 572
  becomes president, 495
  ER and, 495, 502, 503–5, 513, 515, 520–21,
    529, 549, 566, 575
  presidency, 503–4, 507, 515, 517–19, 519–
    21, 531, 546, 575
  as vice president, 480, 492
Truman, Margaret, 518
trusts, 64, 367, 431
  TR and, 69–71, 94, 100, 133, 569
Tugwell, Rexford Guy, 227–30, 231, 232,
  239–40, 243, 250, 251, 263, 275, 289,
  311, 370
Tully, Grace, 315, 357, 364, 391, 493, 495
Turner, Frederick Jackson, 83
Tuttle, Charles H., 203
Tuxedo Park, New York, 141, 312
Tweed, Boss William, 22, 23
Tydings, Millard, 380, 381, 384

unemployment, 63
  during FDR administrations, 263, 280,
    289, 302, 313, 365, 368, 385, 397
  during Hoover administration, 203,
    210, 211, 212, 214, 215, 246, 251
  during Truman administration, 503
unemployment insurance:
  FDR program for New York State, 213
  Social Security Act and, 303
Union Pacific Railroad, 21
Union party, 322
unions, *see* labor and unions; *individual
  unions*
United Feature Syndicate, 390
United Mine Workers, 72, 275, 278, 335
United Nations, 522
  ER and, 470–71, 472, 494, 502, 504–12,
    518, 534, 535, 536, 562
  Universal Declaration of Human
    Rights, 521–25, 527, 529–31, 536,
    574, 575
  FDR and, 470, 472, 474, 485, 487–88,
    490, 494, 506

General Assembly, 522, 529, 536
  organizational meeting of, 504–12
  partition of Palestine, 517
  Special Committee on Palestine
    (UNSCOP), 516, 517, 518
  Stevenson and, 505, 510, 561
  Yalta conference and, 487–89, 490
United Nations and Human Rights, The, 536
United Nations Relief and Rehabilitation
  Administration, 474
U.S. Chamber of Commerce, 292, 293
United States Housing Authority, 375
United States Steel Corporation, 69, 97
Universal Declaration of Human Rights,
  521–25, 527, 529–32, 536, 574, 575
utilities, 64, 242
  public, 136, 197–99, 247–49
  Public Utility Holding Company Act, 297
  taxation of, 53

Val-Kill, 192, 500, 501, 522, 525, 526, 563
Val-Kill Furniture Factory, 192, 200, 267
Vallee, Rudy, 210
Van Buren, Martin, 118–19
Vandenberg, Arthur, 382, 474, 505, 508, 512
Vanderbilt, Cornelius, 114, 309
Vanderbilt, Mrs. Cornelius, 81
Vanderbilt, Mrs. Frederick, 79
Vanderbilt, Mrs. William, 18
Vanderbilt, William, 18
Vanderbilt estate, 421
Vanderlip, Narcissa, 172
Van Devanter, Justice Willis, 341, 345, 362
Van Rosenvelt, Claes Martensen, 80, 411
Veblen, Thorstein, 16, 18, 222
Venezuela, 76
veterans, 241, 365
  "bonus army," 216–17, 270–71
  Economy Act and, 257
Villard, Oswald Garrison, 306, 348
Vireo, 177
Vishinsky, Andrei, 487, 511–12
von Schaeffer-Bernstein, Carola, 512

wages-and-hours bill of 1938, 372, 374

Wagner, Robert, 121, 122, 136, 258, 264, 296, 341, 373, 383, 384, 393, 426, 431, 566

Jewish refugees and, 415

Wald, Lillian, 228, 322

Walker, Frank, 505

Walker, Jimmy, 214, 238, 239, 319

Wallace, George, 548

Wallace, Henry, 250, 264, 363, 368, 418, 451, 479, 480, 494, 507

as third-party candidate, 520

as vice president, 426

Wallace, Mike, 556–57

Ward, Geoffrey, 147

War Department, U.S., 48, 50

Warm Springs, 190–92, 363, 368, 491, 494–95, 500

War Production Board, 447

Warren, Robert Penn, 298–99

Washington, Booker T., 61–62, 105

Washington, George, 348–49, 425, 472

Washington Post, 94, 157, 390, 409

Washington Star, 216

Watson, General Edwin, 455

Watson, Edwin ("Pa"), 493

Wave of the Future, The (Lindbergh), 438

Wealth Against Commonwealth (Lloyd), 68

Weber, Max, 16, 25

Weld, Minot, 10

Wells, H. G., 18

Westbrook, Judge T. R., 31

Weyl, Walter E., 13

Weyler, General Valeriano, 47

Wharton, Edith, 15, 16, 18, 20, 43

Wheeler, Burton K., 240, 295, 297, 340–41, 437

White, Walter, 392, 393–94, 395, 463, 504, 506, 542–43

White, William Allen, 47, 66–67, 123, 135, 141, 142, 148, 149, 152, 158, 308, 327–28, 374, 409

White Citizens Councils, 543, 554

White House:

ER and African-Americans at the, 392, 395

living quarters, 267–68

White House Conference on Natural Resources of 1908, 247–48

Wilhelmina, Queen of the Netherlands, 423

Wilkins, Roy, 547

Williams, Aubrey, 287, 397, 398, 464, 545

Willkie, Wendell L., 426, 427, 428, 470, 480, 482, 486

Wilson, Edmund, 220, 240

Wilson, M. L., 272

Wilson, Woodrow, 25, 73, 223

FDR and, 137–38, 140, 142–43, 149, 153, 161, 165, 166–67, 231, 316, 324, 570

as governor, 117, 137

New Freedom, 133

presidency of, 134, 145–47, 152, 153, 158, 161, 247, 574

League of Nations, 159–60, 240

World War I leadership, 150, 153

presidential election of 1912, 133, 135, 137–38, 139, 324

presidential election of 1916, 149

Wiltwyck Training School, 525, 563

Winant, John Gilbert, 312, 480

Winchell, Walter, 478

Winning of the West, The (Roosevelt), 39

Wise, Rabbi Stephen, 227

women, 490

in the armed forces, 465–66, 468, 541

ER and women's issues, *see* Roosevelt, Eleanor, women's issues and

in the labor force, 385, 461

equal pay for, 186

limiting work week for, 122, 136, 186

minimum wage for, 135

during World War II, 446, 462–63

political conventions and, 134, 186, 187

suffrage for, *see* women's suffrage

TR and:

employment opportunities, 44

suffrage, 54–55, 62, 132, 134

working conditions, 53–54, 125, 134

United Nations and, 510

Women's Ambulance and Defense corps of America, 465, 466

Women's Army Auxiliary Corps
(WAACs), 466, 468, 541
Women's Army Corps (WAC), 468
Women's Democratic News, 192, 199
Women's Political Council, 544
women's suffrage, 117, 137
ER and, 121–22
FDR and, 121–22, 136
Nineteenth Amendment, 183
TR and, 54–55, 62, 132, 134
Women's Trade Union League, 183, 462
Wood, Colonel Leonard, 49
Wood, General Robert E., 437
Woodin, William, 249, 250, 255, 364
Woodring, Harry, 424
Workers' Alliance of America, 306
workmen's compensation, 132, 137
FDR and, 136
TR and, 94, 100, 125
Works Progress Administration (WPA),
269, 297, 302, 303–5, 317, 321, 367, 375, 385
World Court, 185, 226, 289, 349
World's Week, The, 94
World War I, 145–47, 149–50, 150–55, 158,
270, 348, 417, 459
war debt issue, 246
World War II:
atomic weapon development, 454–55
Axis power pact, 362, 414
Battle of Britain, 426
Battle of the Bulge, 487, 489
bond drives, 466–67
Casablanca conference, 457–61
cash-and-carry program, 424
casualties, 467, 469
events leading to, 407–10, 414–19
FDR's inaction and, 407–11, 415, 416–
18
FDR's policy between Nazi invasion of
Poland and Pearl Harbor, 419–42
Lend-Lease, 435–36, 437–39
waiting on "events," 440, 442

German invasion of Poland, 418–19
industrial mobilization of U.S., 444–
47, 449, 461–62
isolationism and, *see* isolationism, prior
to World War II
Lend-Lease program, 435–36, 437–39,
460
Normandy invasion, 474–75, 476–77,
481
planning, 458, 460, 468
in the Pacific, *see* Japan, in World
War II
Pearl Harbor, 442–43, 481
propaganda, 466–67
rearmament in U.S., 10, 411, 421, 424,
436
refugees of:
ER and, 413–14, 415, 511–14, 516–17
FDR and, 408, 411–13, 415–16, 421
Teheran conference, 474, 492
unconditional surrender as Allied
issue, 459, 493
V-E Day, 501
Yalta conference, 490, 491, 492, 494
Wright, Richard, 542

Yale University, 9, 10
Yalta conference, 487–89, 490, 491, 492,
494
Yorktown, 281
Young, Owen D., 198, 240
Young Communist League, 301–2,
398
Young People's Socialist League, 301–2
Yugoslavia, 439, 511, 512, 537–38

Zangara, Joe, 247
Zangrando, Joanna Schneider,
552–53
Zangrando, Robert L., 552–53